TWELFTH EDITION

Human GEOGRAPHY

LANDSCAPES OF HUMAN ACTIVITIES

JEROME D. FELLMANN

University of Illinois, Urbana-Champaign

MARK D. BJELLAND

Gustavus Adolphus College

DANIEL R. MONTELLO

University of California-Santa Barbara

ARTHUR GETIS

San Diego State University

JUDITH GETIS

Connect
Learn
Succeed™

HUMAN GEOGRAPHY: LANDSCAPES OF HUMAN ACTIVITIES, TWELFTH EDITION

Published by McGraw-Hill, a business unit of The McGraw-Hill Companies, Inc., 1221 Avenue of the Americas, New York, NY 10020.

1 2 3 4 5 6 7 8 9 0 DOW/DOW 1 0 9 8 7 6 5 4 3

ISBN 978–0–07–131859–4
MHID 0–07–131859–3

www.mhhe.com

Brief Contents

Contents

Contents   v

Thirteen

HUMAN IMPACTS ON THE ENVIRONMENT 425

List of Boxes

Chapter 12

Chapter 13

Preface

This twelfth edition of *Human Geography* retains the organization and structure of its earlier versions. Like them, it seeks to introduce its users to the scope and excitement of geography and its relevance to their daily lives and roles as informed citizens. We recognize that for many students, human geography may be their first or only work in geography and this, their first or only textbook in the discipline. For these students particularly, we seek to convey the richness and breadth of human geography and to give insight into the nature and intellectual challenges of the field of geography itself. Our goals are to be inclusive in content, current in data, and relevant in interpretations. These goals are elusive. Because of the time lapse between world events and the publication of a book, events inevitably outpace analysis. We therefore depend on a continuing partnership with classroom instructors to incorporate and interpret current events and emerging geographic patterns.

Organization

The text can easily be read in a one-semester course. The emphasis is on key concepts and theories in human geography, which can then be applied to understanding patterns of human activities and current events. Chapter 1 sets the stage by briefly introducing students to the scope, methods, and background basics of geography as a discipline and to the tools—especially maps—that all geographers employ. It is supplemented by Appendix A, which gives a more detailed treatment of map projections than is appropriate in a general introductory chapter. Both are designed to be helpful, with content supportive of, not essential to, the later chapters of the text.

The arrangement of those chapters reflects our own sense of logic and teaching experiences. Chapters 2 through 4 introduce major themes and fundamental concepts in human geography. Chapter 2 examines the basis of culture, culture change, and cultural regionalism. Chapter 3 offers a comprehensive review of concepts of spatial interaction and spatial behavior. Chapter 4 considers population structures, patterns, and change. Chapters 5 through 7 discuss the foundations for different social and cultural identities: language and religion (Chapter 5), ethnicity (Chapter 6), and folk and popular culture (Chapter 7). Chapter 7 also examines the landscape expressions of cultural distinction. Chapters 8, 9, and 10 focus on economic geography, beginning with activities connected to the Earth and natural resources (Chapter 8), then exploring the changing geographies of manufacturing and service industries (Chapter 9), and concluding with an examination of inequality and issues in economic development (Chapter 10). Chapter 11 examines the organization of urban systems and urban space, while Chapter 12 explores the political organization of territory. Chapter 13 draws together in sharper focus selected aspects of the human impact on the environment, demonstrating the relevance of human geographic concepts and patterns to matters of current national and global environmental concern.

Among those concepts is the centrality of gender issues that underlie all facets of human geographic inquiry. Because they are so pervasive and significant, we felt it unwise to relegate their consideration to a single separate chapter, thus artificially isolating women and women's concerns from all the topics of human geography for which gender distinctions and interests are relevant. Instead, we have incorporated significant gender/female issues within the several chapters where those issues apply—either within the running text of the chapter or, very often, highlighted in boxed discussions.

We hope by means of this structure to convey to students the logical integration that we recognize in the broad field of human geography. We realize that our sense of organization and continuity is not necessarily that of instructors using this text and have designed each chapter to be reasonably self-contained, able to be assigned in any sequence that satisfies the arrangement preferred by the instructor.

New to This Edition

We are pleased to welcome Daniel Montello to the author team, beginning with the twelfth edition. Dr. Montello brings research experience in spatial cognition, environmental perception, behavioral geography, and geographic information science to enrich these important topics in human geography. For a complete biography, see page xix.

Although the text's established framework has been retained in this twelfth edition, Chapters 7, 10, and 13 have been substantially reorganized, each chapter has been revised to improve readability, and every chapter contains at least brief text additions or modifications to reflect current data. All chapters contain new or revised illustrations, maps, and photos.

The twelfth edition contains many new and updated topics, including the following:

New Maps

Many existing maps have been updated for the twelfth edition of *Human Geography*. In addition, new maps introduced in this edition include:

- A set of maps showing the effect of scale on area and detail
- Mean center of population for the United States, 1790–2010
- A 3-D space-time path for a day in the life of a college student
- World transportation patterns
- Major international migration flows
- A dot distribution map of racial and ethnic groups in Chicago
- A reproduction of 1860 map of the slave population in the American South
- A choropleth map of Native Americans in the United States based on the 2010 Census
- Major international stock exchanges and trading hours
- Internet users around the world
- Prevalence of diarrheal diseases, malaria, and HIV/AIDS
- Population change in the 100 largest metropolitan areas in the United States, 2000–2010
- Concentration of homeless shelters in Vancouver, British Columbia

New Boxes

Many of the boxed elements in the text have been updated, and the following new boxes have been introduced:

- "Vancouver, Canada: Chinatown Versus Ethnoburb," in Chapter 6
- "Eating Locally on the College Campus," in Chapter 8
- "Where Do Your Clothes Come From?" In Chapter 9
- "What is Poverty?" In Chapter 10
- "Millennium Development Goals," in Chapter 10
- "Sustainable Cities," in Chapter 11
- "From Kyoto to Durban: Global Climate Change Treaties," in Chapter 13

New/Revised Topics

New and revised topics in this book include the following:

- An expanded discussion of region types to include administrative regions
- Sample population pyramids for university towns, retirement communities, Indian reservations, and a community struggling with deindustrialization
- Additional material on Thomas Robert Malthus, neo-Malthusian perspectives on population, and critiques of neo-Malthusian arguments

- An expanded discussion of religious change, diversity, and non-Christian religions in North America
- New material on transnationalism, ethnoburbs, and North American Chinatowns
- New discussion of tourism in ethnic towns and ethnic neighborhoods
- Updated data for ethnic groups in the United States from the 2010 Census
- Moved material on survey systems and settlement patterns from Chapter 6 to Chapter 7
- New and revised material on cultural landscapes, including principles of landscape interpretation, heritage landscapes, and landscapes of consumption
- New discussion about and illustrative photos of contemporary building styles
- New material on sustainable agriculture
- New use of the von Thünen model to explain the historical geography of U.S. agricultural development
- New background information on fossil fuels and peak oil theory, and new material on newly exploited resources in North America, such as the Marcellus Shale
- Expanded discussion of the services industry and distinguishing characteristics of consumer services and producer services
- New material on the tourism industry
- New material on the new international division of labor, *maquiladoras,* the rise of China, and commodity chains
- Expanded coverage of explanations for underdevelopment, including critiques of modernization theory
- Updated information on progress toward meeting the United Nations Millennium Development Goals (MDGs)
- A new table presenting data on the size of the informal economy
- New material on the flow of remittances between developed and developing countries
- Additional background information on foreign debt and the role of the International Monetary Fund (IMF) and World Bank
- Expanded discussion of the effect of the automobile on urban forms
- A new postmodern city model
- A revised discussion of human impacts on the environment
- A new discussion of transboundary water resources and water conflict
- An expanded discussion of environmental justice and conflicts over unwanted facilities
- A new table on per capita carbon dioxide emissions

The Art of Human Geography

Many of the world maps have been put on a Robinson projection, which permits some exaggeration of size in the high latitudes in order to improve the shapes of landmasses. Size and shape are most accurate in the temperature and tropical zones. The color palette for the maps was specifically chosen to accommodate most colorblind readers.

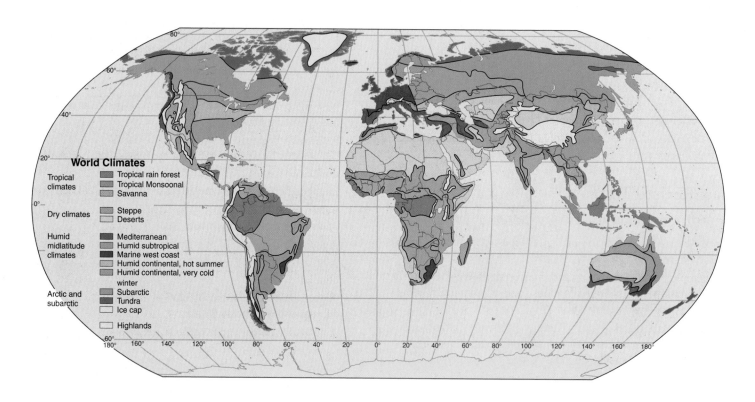

Features

- The "Key Concepts" alert students to the main themes of the chapter.

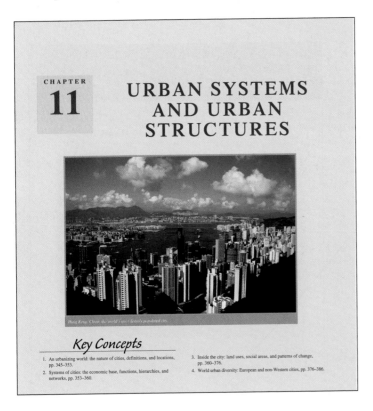

- Chapter introductions take the form of interest-arousing vignettes to focus student attention on the subject matter that follows.

- The boxed inserts that are part of each chapter expand on ideas included within the text or introduce related examples of chapter concepts and conclusions, often in gender-related contexts.

- Almost every chapter contains at least one special-purpose box labeled "Geography and Citizenship." These boxes introduce a discussion of a topic of current national or international interest and conclude with a set of questions designed to induce thought and class discussion of the topic using human geographic insights students have mastered.

- Each chapter also includes other pedagogical aids. The "Summary" iterates the main points of the chapter and provides a bridge to the chapter that follows.

- New terms and special usages of common words and phrases are identified in boldface or italic type. The boldface terms are included in the "Key Words" list at the end of each chapter and are defined in an inclusive cross-referenced glossary at the end of the text.
- "For Review" contains questions that direct student attention to important concepts developed within the chapter.
- The "Key Concept Review" section in the end-of-chapter material summarizes the main points of the chapter and conveys additional information and explanation as integral parts of the text.

- Appendix B is a modified version of the Population Reference Bureau's 2011 World Population Data Sheet, which contains economic and demographic data and projections for countries, regions, and continents. These provide a wealth of useful comparative statistics for student projects and study of world patterns.

- Appendix C, a single-page "United States, Canada, and Mexico Reference Map," provides name identification of all U.S. states, Mexican states, and Canadian provinces and shows the location of principal cities.

Teaching and Learning Supplements

McGraw-Hill offers various tools and technology products to support *Human Geography*. Instructors can obtain teaching aids by calling the Customer Service Department at 800–338–3987, visiting the McGraw-Hill website at www.mhhe.com, or contacting their local McGraw-Hill sales representative.

Teaching Supplements for Instructors

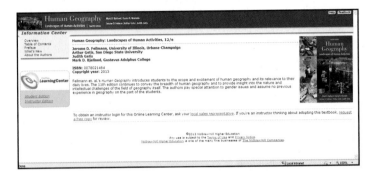

Human Geography Website at http://www.mhhe.com/fellmann12e

The *Human Geography* **Website** offers a wealth of teaching and learning aids for instructors. In addition to all of the student assets available, instructors will appreciate the following:

- A password-protected Instructor's Manual
- Access to the online **Presentation Center** including all of the illustrations, photographs, and tables from the text in convenient JPEG and PowerPoint format
- Microsoft PowerPoint lecture outlines
- Test bank files in Microsoft Word format

Presentation Center (found at www.mhhe.com/fellmann12e)

Build instructional materials wherever, whenever, and however you want!

Accessed through the website, the **Presentation Center** is an online digital library containing assets such as art, photos, tables, PowerPoints, and other media types that can be used to create customized lectures, visually enhanced tests and quizzes, compelling course websites, or attractive printed support materials.

Access to your book, access to all books!

The **Presentation Center library** includes thousands of assets from many McGraw-Hill titles. This ever-growing resource gives instructors the power to utilize assets specific to an adopted textbook as well as content from all other books in the library.

Nothing could be easier!

Presentation Center's dynamic search engine allows you to explore by discipline, course, textbook chapter, asset type, or keyword. Simply browse, select, and download the files you need to build engaging course materials. All assets are copyrighted by McGraw-Hill Higher Education but can be used by instructors for classroom purposes.

Instructors will find the following digital assets for *Human Geography* at OLC Presentation Center:

- **Color Art** Full-color digital files of all illustrations in the text can be readily incorporated into lecture presentations, exams, or custom-made classroom materials.
- **Photos** Digital files of photographs from the text can be reproduced for multiple classroom uses.
- **Tables** Every table that appears in the text is provided in electronic format.
- **PowerPoint Lecture Outlines** Ready-made presentations that combine art and photos and lecture notes are provided for each of the 13 chapters of the text. These outlines can be used as they are or tailored to reflect your preferred lecture topics and sequences.
- **PowerPoint Slides** For instructors who prefer to create their lectures from scratch, all illustrations, photos, and tables are pre-inserted by chapter into blank PowerPoint slides for convenience.

Learning Supplements for Students

Human Geography Website at http://www.mhhe.com/fellmann12e

The website for *Human Geography* is a great place to review chapter material and enhance your study routine. Visit this site for access to the following online study tools:

- Chapter quizzing
- Critical thinking questions
- Interactive maps
- Case studies

Additional Teaching/Learning Tools

The **ANNUAL EDITIONS** series is designed to provide students with convenient, inexpensive access to current, carefully selected articles from the public press. They are updated on a regular basis through a continuous monitoring of over 300 periodicals. Each volume presents articles written for a general audience by experts and authorities in their fields. Organizational features include: an annotated listing of selected World Wide Web sites; an annotated table of contents; a topic guide; a general introduction; brief overviews for each section; and an online instructor's resource guide with testing materials. *Using Annual Editions in the Classroom* is offered as a practical guide.

- *Annual Editions: Developing World 13/14 by Griffiths* (ISBN 978-0078135910; MHID 0078135915)
- *Annual Editions: Geography, 23/e by Pitzl* (ISBN 978-0-07-351551-9; MHID 0-07-351551-5)
- *Annual Editions: Global Issues 12/13 by Jackson* (ISBN 9780078051180; MHID 0078051185)
- *Annual Editions: World Politics 12/13 edition by Weiner and* ISBN 9780078051258; MHID 0078051258

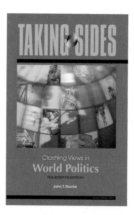

The **TAKING SIDES** volumes present current issues in a debate-style format designed to stimulate student interest and develop critical thinking skills. Each issue is thoughtfully framed with an issue summary, an issue introduction, and a postscript or challenge questions. The pro and con essays—selected for their liveliness and substance—represent the arguments of leading scholars and commentators in their fields. **Taking Sides** readers feature annotated listings of selected World Wide Web sites. An online instructor's resource guide with testing materials is available for each volume. *Using Taking Sides in the Classroom* is an excellent resource for practical suggestions on incorporating this effective approach in your classroom.

- *Taking Sides: Clashing Views on African Issues,* 4/e by Moseley (ISBN 9780078050084; MHID 0078050081)
- *Taking Sides: Clashing Views on Global Issues,* 7/e Harf/Lombardi (ISBN 9780078050442; MHID 0078050448)
- *Taking Sides: Clashing Views on Latin American Issues* by DeGrave et al. (ISBN 978-0-07-351504-5; MHID 0-07-351504-3)
- *Taking Sides: Clashing Views in World Politics,* 15/e by Rourke (ISBN 9780078050176; MHID 0078050170)

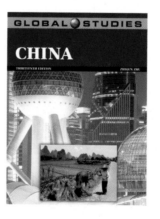

GLOBAL STUDIES is a unique series designed to provide comprehensive background information and selected world press articles on the regions and countries of the world. Each **Global Studies** volume includes an annotated listing of World Wide Web sites. An online instructor's resource guide with testing materials is now available for many of the **Global Studies** volumes.

- *Global Studies: Africa,* 14/e by Krabacher et al. (ISBN 9780078026232; MHID 0078026237)
- *Global Studies: China,* 14/e by Zhu (ISBN 9780078026195; MHID 0078026199)

- *Global Studies: Europe,* 10/e by Frankland (ISBN 978-0-07-337976-0; MHID 0-07-337976-X)
- *Global Studies: India and South Asia,* 10/e by Norton (ISBN 9780078026171; MHID 0078026172)
- *Global Studies: Japan and the Pacific Rim,* 11/e by Collinwood (ISBN 9780078026249; MHID 0078026245)
- *Global Studies: Latin America,* 15/e by Goodwin (ISBN 9780078026263; MHID 0078026261)
- *Global Studies: The Middle East,* 13/e by Layachi (ISBN 9780073527758; MHID 0073527750)
- *Global Studies: Russia, the Eurasian Republics, and Central/ Eastern Europe,* 12/e by Ioffe (ISBN 9780073401478; MHID 0073401471)

The STUDENT ATLAS series combines full-color maps and data sets to introduce students to the importance of the connections between geography and other areas of study such as world politics, environmental issues, and economic development. These thematic atlases will give students a clear picture of the recent agricultural, industrial, demographic, environmental, economic, and political changes in every world region.

- *Student Atlas of World Geography,* 7/e by Allen (ISBN 978-0073527628; MHID 0073527629)
- *Student Atlas of World Politics,* 10/e by Allen (ISBN 978-0078026201; MHID 0078026202)

Electronic Textbooks

CourseSmart

CourseSmart is a new way for faculty to find and review eTextbooks. It's also a great option for students who are interested in accessing their course materials digitally and saving money. CourseSmart offers thousands of the most commonly adopted textbooks across hundreds of courses from a wide variety of higher education publishers. It is the only place for faculty to review and compare the full text of a textbook online, providing immediate access without the environmental impact of requesting a print exam copy. At CourseSmart, students can save money, reduce their impact on the environment, and gain access to powerful web tools for learning, including full text search, notes and highlighting, and email tools for sharing notes between classmates. **www.CourseSmart.com**

Tegrity

Tegrity Campus is a service that makes class time available all the time by automatically capturing every lecture in a searchable format for students to review when they study and complete assignments. With a simple one-click, start-and-stop process, you can capture all computer screens and corresponding audio. Students replay any part of any class with easy-to-use browser-based viewing on a PC or Mac.

Educators know that the more students can see, hear, and experience class resources, the better they learn. With Tegrity Campus, students quickly recall key moments by using the Tegrity Campus's unique search feature. This search helps students efficiently find what they need, when they need it, across an entire semester of class recordings. Help turn all your students' study time into learning moments immediately supported by your lecture.

To learn more about Tegrity, watch a two-minute Flash demo at http://tegritycampus.mhhe.com.

Customizable Textbooks: Create™

create Create what you've only imagined. Introducing McGraw-Hill Create—a new, self-service website that allows you to create custom course materials—print and eBooks—by drawing upon McGraw-Hill's comprehensive, cross-disciplinary content. Add your own content quickly and easily. Tap into other rights-secured third-party sources as well. Then, arrange the content in a way that makes the most sense for your course. You can even personalize your book with your course name and information. Choose the best format for your course: color print, black-and-white print, or eBook. The eBook is now viewable on an iPad, too. And when you are finished customizing, you will receive a free PDF review copy in just minutes! Visit McGraw-Hill Create–**www.mcgrawhillcreate.com**—today and begin building your perfect book.

Acknowledgments

It is with great pleasure that we again acknowledge our debts of gratitude to both departmental colleagues—at the University of Illinois, Urbana-Champaign; at Gustavus Adolphus College; and at both San Diego State University and the University of California, Santa Barbara—and all others who have given generously of their time and knowledge in response to our requests. These have been identified in earlier editions, and although their names are not repeated here, they know of our continuing appreciation.

We specifically, however, wish to recognize with gratitude the advice, suggestions, corrections, and general assistance in matters of content and emphasis provided by the following reviewers of the manuscript for this edition:

Paula J. Barancyk, *Indiana University North West*

Mark Bonta, *Delta State University*

Wayne Brew, *Montgomery County Community College*

Scott Brown, *Francis Marion University*

Scott Carlin, *Long Island University, C. W. Post Campus*

Meera Chatterjee, *University of Akron*

Carolyn Coulter, *Atlantic Cape Community College*

Tracy Edwards, *Frostburg State University*

Susan Hartley, *University of Minnesota—Duluth*

Linda Murphy, *Blinn College*

Kerry Pataki, *Portland Community College*

Darren Purcell, *University of Oklahoma*

Jeffrey Richetto, *University of Alabama*

Stacey Roush, *Montgomery County Community College*

Roger Seyla, *University of Cincinnati*

Ingrid Weinbauer, *University of Utah*

Killian Ying, *California State University, Los Angeles*

Robert C. Ziegenfus, *Kutztown University of Pennsylvania*

We appreciate their invaluable help, as well as that of the many other previous reviewers recognized in earlier editions of this book. No one, except the authors, of course, is responsible for final decisions on content, or for errors of fact or interpretation that the reader may detect.

A final note of thanks is reserved for the publisher's "book team" members separately named on the copyright page. It is a privilege to emphasize here their professional competence, unflagging interest, and always courteous helpfulness:

Jerome D. Fellmann
Mark D. Bjelland
Daniel R. Montello
Arthur Getis
Judith Getis

Meet the Authors

Jerome D. Fellmann

Jerome Fellmann received his B.S., M.S., and Ph.D. degrees from the University of Chicago. Except for visiting professorships at Wayne State University, the University of British Columbia, and California State University/Northridge, his professional career has been spent at the University of Illinois at Urbana-Champaign. His teaching and research interests have been concentrated in the areas of human geography in general and urban and economic geography in particular, in geographic bibliography, the geography of Russia and the CIS, and geographic education. His varied interests have been reflected in articles published in the *Annals of the Association of American Geographers, Professional Geographer, Journal of Geography,* the *Geographical Review,* and elsewhere. He is the coauthor of McGraw-Hill's *Introduction to Geography.* In addition to teaching and research, he has held administrative appointments at the University of Illinois and served as a consultant to private corporations on matters of economic and community development.

Mark D. Bjelland

Mark Bjelland received his B.S. and M.S. degrees from the University of Minnesota and University of Washington, respectively. He worked for six years as a consultant on transportation systems in Minneapolis–Saint Paul, water management for communities in Washington State, environmental cleanups on First Nations reservations in British Columbia, Canada, and major urban redevelopments in Vancouver, British Columbia. Intrigued by the geographical questions he encountered in his work, he left engineering consulting to earn a Ph.D. in geography from the University of Minnesota. He wrote his dissertation comparing deindustrialization, environmental justice, and brownfields redevelopment in the United States and Canada. He is professor and chair of geography at Gustavus Adolphus College, where he has taught for 15 years. He has been a visiting scholar in the geography department at the University of British Columbia, received a Fulbright Foundation German Studies award to study urban planning in post-reunification Germany, and was awarded a U.S.-U.K. Fulbright Scholar Award to spend a year at Cardiff University in Wales researching the redevelopment of derelict industrial land and the creation of eco-communities. He loves to take geography students into the field, and in addition to local field trips to farms, small towns, and cities, he has led field courses to the Pacific Northwest and Europe. His research interests include urban and economic geography, environmental justice, urban sustainability, and religious diversity. His interests have been reflected in book chapters and articles published in *The Professional Geographer, The Encyclopedia of Geography, Research Journal of the Water Pollution Control Federation, Urban Geography,* and elsewhere. He is a co-author of McGraw-Hill's *Introduction to Geography.*

Daniel R. Montello

Daniel R. Montello received his B.A. degree from the Johns Hopkins University and his M.A. and Ph.D. degrees in environmental psychology from Arizona State University. He was also a postdoctoral fellow at the University of Minnesota and a visiting professor at North Dakota State University. He is currently professor of geography and affiliated professor of psychology at the University of California, Santa Barbara (UCSB), where he has been on the faculty since 1992. Dan teaches graduate and undergraduate courses in human geography, behavioral geography, cognitive science, statistics, research methods, cognitive issues in cartography and GIS, and environmental perception and cognition. His research is in the areas of spatial, environmental, and geographic perception, cognition, affect, and behavior. Specific research topics he and his colleagues have investigated include how people navigate in built and natural environments, how people find and lose their way, how children and adults develop an understanding of space and place (including how they acquire and use distance and direction knowledge), how people perceive and reason with maps and other visualizations, how people express their experience of place and space in language, how individuals and groups of people are similar and different in spatial thinking, how spatial relations interrelate with social relations, how people and information systems conceptualize geographic reality, and how human psychology relates to aspects of Earth science (including climate science and geology). Dan has co-authored or edited three books, including 2006's *An Introduction to Scientific Research Methods in Geography* by SAGE Publications, with Paul C. Sutton. He and his co-authors have also published around 80 articles and book chapters. Dan is currently co-editor of the academic journal *Spatial Cognition and Computation* and sits on the editorial boards of *Environment and Behavior* and the *Journal of Environmental Psychology.* He has served as a reviewer for several funding agencies around the world and over 50 academic journals in the fields of geography, cartography, geographic information science, psychology, education, cognitive science, computer science, anthropology, communication, economics, and planning. He is a member of the Association of American Geographers, the Psychonomic Society, and the Sigma Xi Scientific Honor Society.

Arthur Getis

Arthur Getis received his B.S. and M.S. degrees from Pennsylvania State University and his Ph.D. from the University of Washington. He is the coauthor of several geography textbooks, as well as two books dealing with map pattern analysis. He has also published widely in the areas of urban geography, spatial analysis, and geographical information systems. He is co-editor of *Journal of Geographical Systems* and for many years served on the editorial boards of *Geographical Analysis* and *Papers in Regional Science*. He has held administrative appointments at Rutgers University, the University of Illinois, and San Diego State University (SDSU) and currently holds the Birch Chair of Geographical Studies at SDSU. In 2002 he received the Association of American Geographers Distinguished Scholarship Award. Professor Getis is a member of many professional organizations and has served as an officer in, among others, the Western Regional Science Association and the University Consortium for Geographic Information Science.

Judith Getis

Judith Getis earned her B.A. and a teaching credential from the University of Michigan and her M.A. from Michigan State University. She has coauthored several geography textbooks and written the environmental handbook *You Can Make a Difference*. In addition to numerous articles in the fields of urban geography and geography education, she has written technical reports on topics such as solar power and coal gasification. She and her husband, Arthur Getis, were among the original unit authors of the High School Geography Project, sponsored by the National Science Foundation and the Association of American Geographers. In addition, Mrs. Getis was employed by the Urban Studies Center at Rutgers University; taught at Rutgers; was a social science examiner at Educational Testing Service, Princeton, New Jersey; developed educational materials for Edcom Systems, Princeton, New Jersey; and was a professional associate in the Office of Energy Research, University of Illinois.

In Memory Of

Judith M. Getis
Jerome D. Fellmann

INTRODUCTION:
Some Background Basics

The imprint of human activity created by this windfarm dominates this California landscape.

Key Concepts

Getting Started

The fundamental question asked by geographers is "What difference does it make where things are located?" For example, it matters a great deal that languages of a certain kind are spoken in certain places. But knowledge of the location of a specific language group is not of itself particularly significant. Geographic study of a language requires that we try to answer questions about why and how the language shows different characteristics in different locations and how the present distribution of its speakers came about. In the course of our study, we would logically discuss such concepts as migration, acculturation, the diffusion of innovation, the effect of physical barriers on communication, and the relationship of language to other aspects of culture. As geographers, we are interested in how things are interrelated in different regions and give evidence of the existence of "spatial systems."

What Is Geography?

Many people associate the word *geography* simply with describing *where* things are and the characteristics of things at particular locations; where are countries such as Myanmar and Uruguay, what are the populations of cities such as Timbuktu or Almaty, or where are large deposits of natural resources such as petroleum or iron ore? Some people pride themselves on knowing which are the longest rivers, the tallest mountains, and the largest deserts. Such factual knowledge about the world has value, permitting us to place current events in their proper spatial setting. When we hear of an earthquake in Turkey or an assault in Timor-Leste, we at least can visualize where they occurred. Knowing *why* they occurred in those places, however, is considerably more important.

Geography is much more than place names and locations. It is the study of spatial variation, of how and why things differ from place to place on the surface of the Earth. It is, further, the study of how observable spatial patterns evolved through time. Just as knowing the names and locations of organs in the human body does not equip one to perform open-heart surgery, and just as memorizing the periodic table does not enable one to formulate new medications, so knowing where things are located geographically is only the first step toward understanding why things are where they are, and what events and processes determine or change their distribution. Why is Chechnya but not Tasmania wracked by insurgency, and why do you find a concentration of French speakers in Quebec but not in other parts of Canada? Why are famines so frequent and severe in East Africa and why, among all the continents, has African food production and distribution failed to keep pace with population growth over the past half century?

In answering questions such as these, geographers focus on the interaction of people and social groups with their environment—planet earth—and with each other; they seek to understand how and why physical and cultural spatial patterns evolved through time and continue to change. Because geographers study both the physical environment and the human use of that environment, they are sensitive to the variety of forces affecting a place and to the interactions among them. To explain why Brazilians burn a significant portion of the tropical rain forest each year, for example, geographers draw on their knowledge of the climate and soils of the Amazon Basin; population pressures, landlessness, and the need for more agricultural area in rural Brazil; the country's foreign debt status; midlatitude markets for lumber, beef, and soy beans; and economic development objectives. Understanding the environmental consequences of the burning requires knowledge of, among other things, the oxygen and carbon balance of the Earth; the contribution of the fires to the greenhouse effect, acid rain, and depletion of the ozone layer; and the relationship between deforestation, soil erosion, and floods. Thus, one might say that geography is the "study of the Earth as the home of humanity."

Geography, therefore, is about geographic space and its content. We think of and respond to places from the standpoint not only of where they are but, rather more importantly, of what they contain or what we think they contain. Reference to a place or an area usually calls up images about its physical nature or what people do there and often suggests, without conscious thought, how those physical objects and human activities are related."Colorado," "mountains," and "skiing" might be a simple example. The content of area, that is, has both physical and cultural aspects, and geography is always concerned with understanding both (Figure 1.1).

Although space is central to geography, time is important, too. How do places change over time, how do structures and processes change location over time, and how do patterns of interaction change over time? Buffalo, New York, was one of the ten largest cities in the United States around 1900. Its location at the western terminus of the Erie Canal, and then along rail lines for transporting the manufacturing and agricultural products of the Midwest, attracted job seekers and investors. Now it is around the 65th largest city in the United States and continuing to shrink in population (in both absolute terms and relative to fast-growing cities such as Houston and Phoenix). Manufacturing in the United States decreased dramatically at the end of the 20th century, and agricultural products have found other routes to move. In other words, geography is about both static and dynamic aspects of space and place.

Evolution of the Discipline

The fundamental inspiration for geographical thought probably originated with the recognition of "areal differentiation"—that one place is different than another. Climate varies, plants vary, people vary. This insight surely occurred in prehistoric times. Early developments in the study of geography took place in ancient Egypt, China, Mesopotamia, the Arab world, Greece, and Rome. This early work was motivated by practical problems in astronomy, land surveying and agriculture, trade, and military activity. From the beginning, geographic thought was characterized by three scholarly traditions: a literary tradition, including travel logs written about foreign places; a cartographic tradition, in which places were mapped; and a mathematical tradition, which involved measuring and calculating spatial and nonspatial information about places. Although their relative importance to geographic scholarship has varied over time, all three traditions are still active parts of the study of geography.

Geography, the "mother of sciences," initiated in antiquity lines of inquiry that led to the development of separate disciplines such as anthropology, demography, geology, ecology,

Figure 1.1 The ski development at Whistler Mountain, British Columbia, Canada, site of 2010 Winter Olympic events, clearly shows the interaction of physical environment and human activity. Climate and terrain have made specialized human use attractive and possible. Human exploitation has placed a cultural landscape on the natural environment, thereby altering it.

and economics. Geography's combination of interests was apparent even in the work of the early Greek geographers who first gave structure to the discipline. Geography's name was coined by the Greek scientist Eratosthenes over 2,200 years ago from the words *geo,* "the Earth," and *graphein,* "to write." From the beginning, that writing focused both on the physical structure of the Earth and on the nature and activities of the people who inhabited the different lands of the known world. To Strabo (*ca.* 64 B.C.–A.D. 20), the task of geography was to "describe the several parts of the inhabited world . . . to write the assessment of the countries of the world [and] to treat the differences between countries." Even earlier, Herodotus (*ca.* 484–425 B.C.) had found it necessary to devote much of his book to the lands, peoples, economies, and customs of the various parts of the Persian Empire as necessary background to an understanding of the causes and course of the Persian wars.

Greek (and, later, Roman) geographers measured the Earth, devised the global grid of parallels and meridians (marking latitudes and longitudes—see page 20), and drew upon that grid surprisingly sophisticated maps of their known world (Figure 1.2). They explored the apparent latitudinal variations in climate and described in numerous works the familiar Mediterranean basin and the more remote, partly rumored lands of northern Europe, Asia, and equatorial Africa. Employing nearly modern concepts, they described river systems, explored causes of erosion and patterns of deposition, cited the dangers of deforestation, described areal variations in the natural landscape, and noted the consequences of environmental abuse. Against that physical backdrop, they focused their attention on what humans did in home and distant areas—how they lived; what their distinctive similarities

and differences were in language, religion, and custom; and how they used, altered, and perhaps destroyed the lands they inhabited. Strabo, indeed, cautioned against the assumption that the nature and actions of humans were determined solely by the physical environment they inhabited. He observed that humans were active elements in a human—environmental partnership.

These are enduring and universal interests. The ancient Chinese, for example, were as involved in geography as an explanatory viewpoint as were Westerners, though there was no exchange between them. Further, as Christian Europe entered its Middle Ages between A.D. 500 and 1400 and lost its knowledge of Greek and Roman geographical work, Muslim scholars—who retained that knowledge—undertook to describe and analyze their known world in its physical, cultural, and regional variation (see "Roger's Book").

Modern geography had its origins in the surge of scholarly inquiry that, beginning in the 17th century, gave rise to many of the traditional academic disciplines we know today. In its European rebirth, geography from the outset was recognized—as it always had been—as a broadly based integrative study. Patterns and processes of the physical landscape were early interests, as was concern with humans as part of the Earth's variation from place to place. The rapid development of geology, botany, zoology, and other natural sciences by the end of the 18th century strengthened regional geographic investigation and increased scholarly and popular awareness of the intricate interconnections of items in space and between places. By that same time, accurate determination of latitude and longitude and scientific mapping of the Earth made assignment of place information more reliable and comprehensive.

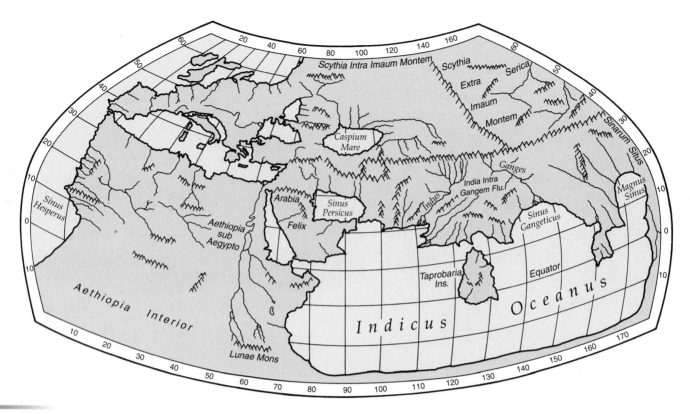

Figure 1.2 World map of the 2nd-century A.D. Greco–Egyptian geographer–astronomer Ptolemy. Ptolemy (Claudius Ptolemaeus) adopted a previously developed map grid of latitude and longitude based on the division of the circle into 360°, permitting a precise mathematical location for every recorded place. Unfortunately, errors of assumption and measurement rendered both the map and its accompanying six-volume gazetteer inaccurate. Ptolemy's map, accepted in Europe as authoritative for nearly 1,500 years, was published in many variants in the 15th and 16th centuries. The version shown here summarizes the extent and content of the original. Its underestimation of the Earth's size convinced Columbus that a short westward voyage would carry him to Asia.

During the 19th century, national censuses, trade statistics, and ethnographic studies gave firmer foundation to human geographic investigation. By the end of the 19th century, geography had become a distinctive and respected discipline in universities throughout Europe and in other regions of the world where European academic examples were followed. The proliferation of professional geographers and geography programs resulted in the development of a whole series of increasingly specialized disciplinary subdivisions.

Geography and Human Geography

Geography's specialized subfields are not entirely distinct but are interrelated. Geography in all its subdivisions is characterized by three dominating interests. The first is in the areal variation of physical and human phenomena on the surface of the Earth. Geography examines relationships between human societies and the natural environments that they occupy and modify. The second is a focus on the spatial systems[1] that link physical phenomena and human activities in one area of the Earth with other areas.

Together, these interests lead to a third enduring theme, that of regional analysis: geography studies human-environment—"ecological"—relationships and spatial systems in specific locational settings. This areal orientation pursued by some geographers is called *regional geography* (see also page 15). Similar to many of the articles in *National Geographic magazine*, regional geography typically focuses on a comprehensive understanding of physical and human characteristics of particular regions. For some, the regions of interest may be large: Southeast Asia or Latin America, for example; others may focus on smaller areas differently defined, such as Alpine France or the Corn belt in the United States.

Other geographers choose to identify particular classes of things, rather than segments of the Earth's surface, for specialized study. These *systematic geographers* may focus their attention on one or a few related aspects of the physical environment or of human populations and societies. In each case, the topic selected for study is examined in its interrelationships with other spatial systems and areal patterns. *Physical geographers* practice systematic geography by directing their attention to the natural environmental side of the human-environment structure. Their concerns are with landforms and their distribution, with atmospheric conditions and climatic patterns, with soils or vegetation associations, and the like. The other systematic branch of geography—and the subject of this book—is *human geography.*

---

[1] A "system" is simply a group of elements organized in a way that every element is to some degree directly or indirectly interdependent with every other element. For geographers, the systems of interest are those that distinguish or characterize different regions or areas of the Earth.

The Arab geographer Idrisi, or Edrisi (*ca.* A.D. 1099–1154), a descendant of the Prophet Mohammed, was directed by Roger II, the Christian king of Sicily in whose court he served, to collect all known geographical information and assemble it in a truly accurate representation of the world. An academy of geographers and other scholars was gathered to assist Idrisi in the project. Books and maps of classical and Islamic origins were consulted, mariners and travelers interviewed, and scientific expeditions dispatched to foreign lands to observe and record. Data collection took 15 years before the final world map was fabricated on a silver disc some 200 centimeters (80 inches) in diameter and weighing over

135 kilograms (300 pounds). Lost to looters in 1160, the map is survived by "Roger's Book," containing the information amassed by Idrisi's academy and including a world map, 71 part maps, and 70 sectional itinerary maps.

Idrisi's "inhabited earth" is divided into the seven "climates" of Greek geographers, beginning at the equator and stretching northward to the limit at which, it was supposed, the Earth was too cold to be inhabited. Each climate was then subdivided by perpendicular lines into 11 equal parts beginning with the west coast of Africa on the west and ending with the east coast of Asia. Each of the resulting 77 square compartments was then discussed in sequence in "Roger's Book."

Though Idrisi worked in one of the most prestigious courts of Europe, there is little evidence that his work had any impact on European geographic thought. He was strongly influenced by Ptolemy's work and misconceptions and shared the then common Muslim fear of the unknown western ocean. Yet Idrisi's clear understanding of such scientific truths as the roundness of the Earth, his grasp of the scholarly writings of his Greek and Muslim predecessors, and the faithful recording of information on little-known portions of Europe, the Near East, and North Africa set his work far above the mediocre standards of contemporary Christian geography.

Human Geography

Human geography deals with the world as it is and with the world as it might be made to be. Its emphasis is on people: where they are, what they are like, how they interact over space, and what kinds of landscapes of human use they erect on the natural landscapes they occupy. It encompasses all those interests and topics of geography that are not directly concerned with the physical environment or, like cartography, are concerned with geographic techniques that apply to all domains of geography. Its content provides integration for all of the social sciences, for it gives to those sciences the necessary spatial and systems viewpoint that they might otherwise lack. For example, economists are often concerned with trends and patterns over time but do not fully appreciate that many of their interests concern patterns over space, too. Similarly, psychologists have long been interested in mind and behavior but have often failed to recognize the spatial context of this mind and behavior. At the same time, human geography draws on other social sciences in the analyses identified with its subfields, such as *behavioral, political, economic,* and *social geography* (Figure 1.3). As Figure 1.3 suggests, human geographers also carry out work in areas traditionally recognized as part of the humanities, including history, philosophy, languages, and literature.

Human geography admirably serves the objectives of a liberal education. It helps us to understand the world we occupy and to appreciate the circumstances affecting peoples and countries other than our own. It clarifies the contrasts and similarities in societies and cultures and in the human landscapes they have created in different regions of the Earth. Its models and explanations of how things are interrelated in particular places and regions give us a clearer understanding of the economic, social, and political systems within which we live and operate. Its analyses of those spatial systems make us more aware of the realities and prospects of our own society in an increasingly connected and competitive

world. Our study of human geography, therefore, can help make us better-informed citizens, more able to understand the important issues facing our communities and our countries and better prepared to contribute to their solutions. Importantly, it can also help open the way to wonderfully rewarding and diverse careers as professional geographers (see "Careers in Geography").

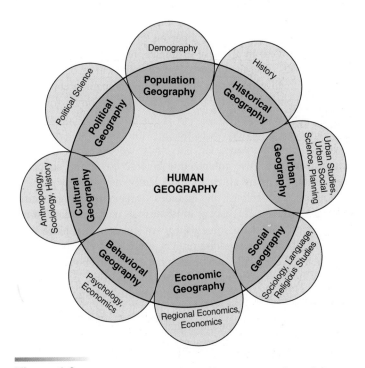

Figure 1.3 Some of the subdivisions of human geography and the allied fields to which they are related. Geography retains its ties to them and shares their insights and data, reinforcing its role as an essential synthesizer of data, concepts, and models that have integrative regional and spatial implications.

Core Geographic Concepts

The topics included in human geography are diverse, but that very diversity emphasizes the reality that all geographers—whatever their particular topical or regional specialties—are united by the similar questions they ask and the common set of basic concepts they employ to consider their answers. Of either a physical or cultural phenomenon they will inquire: What is it? Where is it? How did it come to be what and where it is? Where is it in relation to other things that affect it or are affected by it? How is it changing? How is it part of a functioning whole? How do people affect it? How does its location affect people's lives and the content of the area in which it is found? These and similar questions are rooted in geography's central concern with **space** and **place** and in the special meanings geographers attach to those terms.

For geographers, *space* implies areal extent and may be understood in both an absolute and a relative sense. *Absolute space* is about fixed coordinate systems, like latitude and longitude, and measurement units, like miles or kilometers. Such absolute space remains the same in all contexts. In contrast, *relative space* is comparative and varies with context. As such, it is more flexible in recognizing that different ways of "measuring" space are more relevant for particular domains of human activity. For instance, different cultures think of space differently depending on their livelihood and travel habits. Economically, spaces vary depending on how much money it costs to get from one place to another. In other cases, relative spaces are mental or subjective, as when a route seems longer because a person thinks that it goes through a dangerous area. In all these examples, relative space measures space in terms other than those of a fixed physical layout.

For human geographers, *place* is the companion concept to *space*. In common understanding, *place* is a synonym for *location*. In human geography, however, *place* refers to the attributes and values we individually associate with a location. Our home town and neighborhood, the university we attend or the high school from which we graduated, a favorite downtown shopping area, and the like are all examples. Clearly, our *sense of place*—the impressions, feelings, and attitudes we have regarding specific locations and their complex of attributes—is unique to each of us, though we often share some aspects of our sense of place with other members of our culture or subculture. And clearly, too, we can even have a well-developed sense of place about locations we may never have personally experienced: Rome or Mecca or Jerusalem, for example, or—closer to home—Mount Rushmore or the Washington Mall. Of course, our sense of place may largely reflect a **place stereotype** rather than reality.

Our individual or group sense of place and attachments can, of course, set us off from others. Our home neighborhood that we find familiar and view favorably may equally be seen as alien and, perhaps, dangerous by others. The attributes and culture of places shape the lives and outlooks of those who inhabit them in ways basic to the socioeconomic patterning of the world. The viewpoints, normative behavior, religious and cultural beliefs, and ways of life absorbed and expressed by a middle-class, suburban American are undoubtedly vastly different from the understandings, cultural convictions, and life expectations of, for example, a young, unemployed male resident of Baghdad or the slums of Cairo. The implicit, ingrained, place-induced differences between the two help us understand the resistance to the globalization of Western social and economic values by those of different cultural backgrounds and place identification.

The sense of place is reinforced by recognized local and regional distinctiveness. It may be diminished or lost and replaced by a feeling of **placelessness** as the uniformity of brand-name fast-food outlets, national retail store chains, uniform shopping malls, repetitive highway billboards, and the like spread nationally and even internationally, reducing or eliminating the uniqueness of formerly separated locales and cultures. We'll examine some aspects of the sense of place and placelessness as we look at folk and popular cultures in Chapter 7.

Geographers use the word *spatial* as an essential modifier in framing their questions and forming their concepts. Geography, they say, is a *spatial* science. It is concerned with *spatial behavior* of people, with the *spatial relationships* that are observed between places on the Earth's surface, and with the *spatial processes* that create or maintain those behaviors and relationships. The word *spatial* comes, of course, from *space*, and to geographers, it always carries the idea of the way items are distributed, the way movements occur, and the way processes operate over the whole or a part of the surface of the Earth. The geographer's space, then, is Earth space, the surface area occupied or available to be occupied by humans. Spatial phenomena have locations on that surface, and spatial interactions occur between places, things, and people within the Earth area available to them. The need to understand those relationships, interactions, and processes helps frame the questions that geographers ask.

Additionally, those questions have their starting point in basic observations about the location and nature of places and about how places are similar to or different from one another. Such observations, though simply stated, are profoundly important to our comprehension of the world we occupy.

- Places have location, direction, and distance with respect to other places.
- A place has size; it may be large or small. Scale is important.
- A place has both physical structure and cultural content.
- The attributes of places develop and change over time.
- The elements of places interrelate with other places.
- The content of places is structured and explainable.
- Places may be generalized into regions of similarities and differences.

These are basic notions understandable to everyone. They also are the means by which geographers express fundamental observations about the Earth spaces they examine and put those observations into a common framework of reference. Each of the concepts is worth further discussion, for they are not quite as simple as they at first seem.

Geographic Features

Of course, space and (especially) place are not empty. **Geographic features** include natural features such as mountains, rivers, forests, oceans, and atmospheric fronts. They also include cultural features such as buildings, roads, cornfields, cities, and countries. Although all geographic features, like all material entities of any kind, are in reality three-dimensional, we often think of them or depict them on a map as if their dimensionality were less. So zero-dimensional features are thought of as points; an example might be a water well or a mountain peak. One-dimensional features are like lines, whether curved or straight; an example might be a river or a highway. Two-dimensional features are like areas or polygons; an example might be a forest or a neighborhood. Finally, some features are best thought of as being fully three-dimensional or volumetric. An oil deposit and a cloud are examples of this. It is important to recognize that the most appropriate way to think about a feature's dimensionality can depend greatly on the scale with which you examine it. A city may be a point when looking at a map of an entire country, but it becomes much more like an area when you zoom in to it.

Our discussion of feature dimensionality suggests something else about the way we conceptualize geographic features. They are typically thought of as being like discrete objects or like continuous fields. **Objects** are discrete entities that we think of as having sharp boundaries and being separated by space that may be conceived of as empty. Features like mountain peaks or roads are objects. **Fields** are continuously varying surfaces on the Earth that we think of as completely covering the space of the landscape they occupy without overlapping other fields. Features like average precipitation and landform elevations are fields. The distinction between objects and fields is admittedly abstract, and there are features like water bodies that can readily be thought of in either way, or as a combination of the two. Human population is another intriguing example. At one scale, people are discrete objects; but at another scale, we can treat populations as a density field that may be said to have a nonzero value anywhere that is inhabited. However, it usually seems to make more sense to treat features and properties as more like objects or more like fields, even if we accept that this is sometimes imperfect. And if the distinction seems esoteric, we discuss below how it is quite important for the practical issue of how best to represent and model the world in computerized geographic information systems.

Location, Direction, and Distance

Location, direction, and *distance* are everyday ways of assessing the space around us and identifying our position in relation to other items and places of interest. They are also essential in understanding the processes of spatial interaction that figure so importantly in the study of human geography.

Location

The location of places and objects is the starting point of all geographic study, as well as all our personal movements and spatial actions in everyday life. We think of and refer to location in at least two different senses, *absolute* and *relative*.

Absolute location is the identification of place by some precise and accepted system of coordinates; it therefore is sometimes called *mathematical location*. We have several such accepted systems of pinpointing positions. One of them is the global grid of parallels and meridians (discussed later, beginning on page 18). With it, the absolute location of any point on the Earth can be accurately described by reference to its degrees, minutes, and seconds of **latitude** and **longitude** (Figure 1.4).

Other coordinate systems are also in use. Survey systems such as the township, range, and section description of property in much of the United States give mathematical locations on a regional level, while street address precisely defines a building according to the reference system of an individual town. For convenience or special purposes, locational grid references may be superimposed on the basic global grid. The Universal Transverse Mercator (UTM) system, for example, based on a set of 60 longitude zones, is widely used in geographic information system (GIS) applications and, with different notations, as a military grid reference system. Absolute location is unique to each described place, is independent of any other characteristic or observation about that place, and has obvious value in the legal or scientific description of places, in measuring the distance separating places, or in finding directions between places on the Earth's surface.

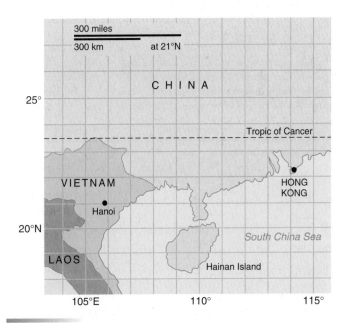

Figure 1.4 The latitude and longitude of Hong Kong is 22° 15′ N, 114° 10′ E (read as 22 degrees, 15 minutes north; 114 degrees, 10 minutes east). The circumference of the Earth measures 360 degrees; each degree contains 60 minutes, and each minute has 60 seconds of latitude or longitude. What are the coordinates of Hanoi?

The study of geography is an essential part of a liberal arts education and helps students become better citizens as they come to understand local, national, and global issues.

Can it, as well, be a pathway to employment for those who wish to specialize in the discipline? The answer is "Yes," in a number of different types of jobs. One broad cluster is concerned with supporting the field itself through teaching and research. Teaching opportunities exist at all levels, from elementary to university postgraduate. Teachers with some training in geography are increasingly in demand in elementary and high schools throughout the United States, reflecting geography's inclusion as a core subject in the federally adopted *Educate America Act* (Public Law 103-227) and the national determination to create a geographically literate society. At the college level, specialized teaching and research in all branches of geography have long been established, and geographically trained scholars are prominently associated with urban, community, and environmental studies, regional science, locational economics, and other interdisciplinary programs.

Because of the breadth and diversity of the field, training in geography involves the acquisition of techniques and approaches applicable to a wide variety of jobs outside the academic world. Modern geography is both a physical and social science and fosters a wealth of technical skills. The employment possibilities it presents are as many and varied as are the agencies and enterprises dealing with the natural environment and human activities, and with the acquisition and analysis of spatial data.

Many professional geographers work in government, either at the state or local level, or in a variety of federal agencies and international organizations. Although many positions do not carry a geography title, physical geographers serve as water, mineral, and other natural resource analysts; weather and climate experts; soil scientists; and the like. An area of recent high demand is for environmental managers and technicians. Geographers who have specialized in environmental studies find jobs in both public and private agencies. Their work may include assessing the environmental impact of proposed development projects on such things as air and water quality and endangered species, as well as preparing the environmental impact statements required before construction can begin.

Human geographers work in many different roles in the public sector. Jobs include data acquisition and analysis in health care, transportation, population studies, economic development, and international economics. Many geography graduates find positions as planners in local and state governmental agencies concerned with housing and community development, park and recreation planning, and urban and regional planning. They map and analyze land use plans and transportation systems, monitor urban land development, make informed recommendations about the location of public facilities, and engage in basic social science research.

Most of these same specializations are also found in the private sector. Geographic training is ideal for such tasks as business planning and market analysis; factory, store, and shopping-center site selection; community and economic development programs for banks, public utilities, and railroads; and similar applications. Publishers of maps, atlases, news and travel magazines, and the like employ geographers as writers, editors, and mapmakers.

The combination of a traditional, broadly based liberal arts perspective with the technical skills required in geographic research and analysis gives geography graduates a competitive edge in the labor market. These field-based skills include familiarity with geographic information systems (GISs), cartography and computer mapping, remote sensing and photogrammetry, and competence in data analysis and problem solving. In particular, students with expertise in GIS, who are knowledgeable about data sources, hardware, and software, are finding that they have ready access to employment opportunities. The following table, based on the booklet "Careers in Geography,"* summarizes some of the professional opportunities open to students who have specialized in one (or more) of the various subfields of geography. Also, be sure to read the informative discussions under the "Careers in Geography" option on the home page of the Association of American Geographers at **www.aag.org/.** Additional links on the topic of geography careers can be found in the Online Learning Center for this text. That connection may be found at the end of this chapter.

Geographic Field of Concentration	Employment Opportunities
Geographic technology	Cartographer for federal government (agencies such as Defense Mapping Agency, U.S. Geological Survey, or Environmental Protection Agency) or private sector (e.g., Environmental Systems Research Institute, ERDAS, Intergraph, or Bentley Systems); map librarian; GIS specialist for planners, land developers, real estate agencies, utility companies, local government; remote-sensing analyst; surveyor
Physical geography	Weather forecaster; outdoor guide; coastal zone manager; hydrologist; soil conservation/agricultural extension agent
Environmental geography	Environmental manager; forestry technician; park ranger; hazardous waste planner
Cultural geography	Community developer; Peace Corps volunteer; map librarian
Economic geography	Site selection analyst for business and industry; market researcher; traffic/route delivery manager; real estate agent/broker/appraiser; economic development researcher
Urban and regional planning	Urban and community planner; transportation planner; housing, park, and recreation planner; health services planner
Regional geography	Area specialist for federal government; international business representative; travel agent; travel writer
Geographic education or general geography	Elementary/secondary school teacher; college professor; overseas teacher

*"Careers in Geography," by Richard G. Boehm. Washington, D.C.: National Geographic Society, 1996. Previously published by Peterson's Guides, Inc.

Figure 1.5 The reality of *relative location* on the globe may be strikingly different from the impressions we form from maps with conventional projections like the Mercator. The position of Russia with respect to North America when viewed from a polar perspective emphasizes a closer relative location than many people realize.

Figure 1.6 The *site* of New Orleans is hardly ideal for building a city. The city was built by the French on the most suitable high ground they could find near the mouth of the Mississippi River. The site extends north from the "high ground" along the Mississippi River to former swamp and marshland near Lake Pontchartrain. Much of the city and its suburbs are located below sea level on sinking soils composed of soft sediments deposited by past river floods.

When geographers—or real estate agents—remark that "location matters," their reference is usually not to absolute but to **relative location**—the position of a place in relation to that of other places or activities (Figure 1.5). Relative location expresses spatial interconnection and interdependence and may carry social (neighborhood character) and economic (assessed valuations of vacant land) implications. On an immediate and personal level, we think of the location of the school library not in terms of its street address or room number but where it is relative to our classrooms, or the cafeteria, or some other reference point. On the larger scene, relative location tells us that people, things, and places exist not in a spatial vacuum but in a world of physical and cultural characteristics that differ from place to place.

New York City, for example, may in absolute terms be described as located at (approximately) latitude 40° 43′ N and longitude 73° 58′ W. We have a better understanding of the *meaning* of its location, however, when reference is made to its spatial relationships: to the continental interior through the Hudson–Mohawk lowland corridor or to its position on the eastern seaboard of the United States. Within the city, we gain understanding of the locational significance of Central Park or the Lower East Side not solely by reference to the street addresses or city blocks they occupy, but by their spatial and functional relationships to the total land use, activity, and population patterns of New York City.

In view of these different ways of looking at location, geographers make a distinction between the *site* and the *situation* of a place. **Site,** an absolute location concept, refers to the physical and cultural characteristics and attributes of the place itself. It is more than mathematical location, for it tells us something about the internal features of that place. The site of New Orleans, for example,

extends from the natural levee on the Mississippi River to Lake Pontchartrain, much of which lies below sea level (Figure 1.6). **Situation,** on the other hand, refers to the external relations of a locale. It is an expression of relative location with particular reference to items of significance to the place in question. The situation of New Orleans might be described as being as close as possible to the mouth of the Mississippi River, which drains 41% of the land area of the continental United States, taking in much of the area from the Appalachian Mountains to the Rocky Mountains. Waterways on the Upper Mississippi, Missouri, Arkansas-Red-White, Ohio, and Tennessee River systems drain through the Lower Mississippi, connecting New Orleans to many of the country's important agricultural and manufacturing regions (Figure 1.7). While the flood-prone site makes it a challenging place to build a city, the incredible advantages offered by its situation have inspired generations of residents to make it their home.

Direction

Direction is a second universal spatial concept. Like location, it has more than one meaning and can be expressed in absolute or relative terms. **Absolute direction** is based on global or macroscopic features such as the cardinal points of north, south, east, and west, or on the directions to prominent stars. These appear uniformly and independently in all cultures, derived from the obvious "givens" of nature: the rising and setting of the sun for east and west, the sky location of the noontime sun and of certain fixed stars for north and south, or the direction toward or away from the center of an island.

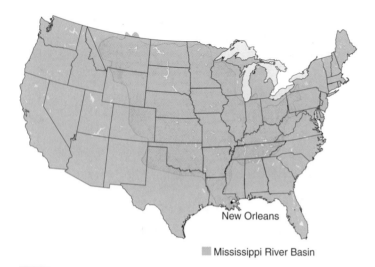

Figure 1.7 The *situation* of New Orleans is ideal for building a city. As the port at the mouth of the Mississippi River, New Orleans receives imports from Europe, Latin America, Asia, and Africa and exports grain, other food products, and petroleum from the United States. New Orleans is connected to 14,500 miles of waterways as the Mississippi River drains a basin that stretches from the Rocky Mountains to the Appalachian Mountains.

We also commonly use **relative** or *relational* **directions.** In the United States, we worry about conflict in the "Near East" or economic competition from the "Far Eastern countries." These directional references are culturally based and locationally variable, despite their reference to cardinal compass points. The Near and the Far East locate parts of Asia from the European perspective; they are retained in the Americas by custom and usage, even though one would normally travel westward across the Pacific, for example, to reach the "Far East" from California, British Columbia, or Chile. Another important example of relative directional terms include body-centered terms like "left," "right," "in front of," and "behind."

Distance

Distance joins location and direction as a commonly understood term that has dual meanings for geographers. Like its two companion spatial concepts, distance may be viewed in both an absolute and a relative sense.

Absolute distance refers to the physical separation between two points on the Earth's surface measured by some accepted standard unit such as miles or kilometers for widely separated locales, feet or meters for more closely spaced points. **Relative distance** transforms those linear measurements into other units that could be more meaningful for the spatial relationship in question.

To know that two competing malls are about equidistant in miles from your residence is perhaps less important in planning your shopping trip than is knowing that because of street conditions or traffic congestion, one is 5 minutes and the other 15 minutes away (Figure 1.8). Many people, in fact, think of time distance rather than physical distance in their daily activities; downtown is 20 minutes by bus, the library is a 5-minute walk. In some instances, money rather than time may be the distance transformation. An

Figure 1.8 **Lines of equal travel time** (*isochrones:* from Greek, *isos,* equal, and *chronos,* time) mark off the different linear distances accessible within given spans of time from a starting point. The fingerlike outlines of isochrone boundaries reflect variations in road conditions, terrain, traffic congestion, and other aids or impediments to movement. On this map, the areas within 5–30 minutes' travel time from downtown San Diego are recorded for the year 2002. Note the effect of freeways on travel time.

urban destination might be estimated to be a $10 cab ride away, information that may affect either the decision to make the trip at all or the choice of travel mode to get there. As a college student, you already know that rooms and apartments are less expensive at a greater distance from campus. And a walk uphill may well seem longer than one that slopes gently downhill; in some situations, effort is an expression of relative distance between places.

A *psychological* transformation of distance is also frequent. The solitary late-night walk back to the car through an unfamiliar or dangerous neighborhood may seem far longer than a daytime stroll of the same distance through familiar and friendly territory. A first-time trip to a new destination frequently seems much longer than the return trip over the same path. Distance relationships, their measurement, and their meaning for human spatial interaction are fundamental to our understanding of human geography. They are a subject of Chapter 3, and reference to them recurs throughout this book.

Size and Scale

When we say that a place may be large or small, we speak both of the nature of the place itself and of the generalizations that can be made about it. In either instance, geographers are concerned with **scale.** Although scale is always about relative size (whether spatial or temporal), we use the term in different ways. We can, for example, study a problem—say, population or agriculture—at the local scale, the regional scale, or on a global scale. Here the reference is purely to the size of unit studied. In this sense, "large-scale" means large units or areas studied, and "small-scale" means small units or areas studied. In a technical, cartographic sense, scale tells us the ratio between the length of physical distance on a map and the actual length of the mapped distance on the surface of the Earth (see page 18). Whatever the scale of a map, it is a feature of every map and important to recognizing the areal meaning of what is shown on that map.

In both senses of the word, *scale* implies something about the degree of generalization involved (Figure 1.9). Generalization is averaging over details, so that a large-scale unit of study (and a small-scale map) generalizes more than a small-scale unit of study (and large-scale map). Geographic inquiry may be broad or narrow; it occurs at many different size scales. Climate may be an object of study, but research and generalization focused on climates of the world will differ in degree and kind from study of the microclimates of a city. Awareness of scale is very important. In geographic work, concepts, relationships, and understandings that have meaning at one scale may not apply at another.

As another example, the study of world agricultural patterns may refer to global climatic regimes, cultural food preferences, levels of economic development, and patterns of world trade. These large-scale relationships are of little concern to the study of crop patterns within single counties of the United States, where topography, soil and drainage conditions, farm size, ownership, and capitalization, or even personal management preferences, may be of greater explanatory significance.

Physical and Cultural Attributes

All places have physical and cultural attributes that distinguish them from other places and give them character, potential, and meaning. Geographers are concerned with identifying and analyzing the details of those attributes and, particularly, with recognizing the interrelationship between the physical and cultural components of area: the human—environmental interface.

Physical characteristics refer to such natural aspects of a locale as its climate and soil, the presence or absence of water supplies and mineral resources, its terrain features, and the like. These **natural landscape** attributes provide the setting within which human action occurs. They help shape—but do not dictate—how people live. The resource base, for example, is physically

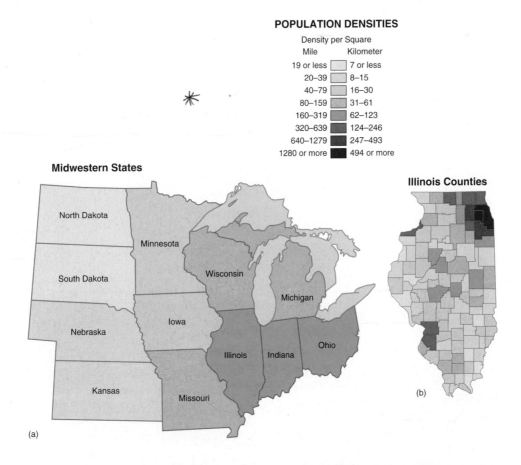

Figure 1.9 Population density and map scale. "Truth" depends on one's scale of inquiry. Map (*a*) reveals that the maximum year 2010 population density of Midwestern states was no more than 123 people per square kilometer (319 per sq mi). From map (*b*), however, we see that population densities in three Illinois counties exceeded 494 people per square kilometer (1,280 per sq mi) in 2010. If we were to reduce our scale of inquiry even further, examining individual city blocks in Chicago, we would find densities reaching 2,500 or more people per square kilometer (10,000 per sq mi). Scale matters!

determined, though how resources are perceived and utilized is, to some extent, culturally conditioned.

Environmental circumstances directly affect agricultural potential and reliability; indirectly they may influence such matters as employment patterns, trade flows, population distributions, and national diets. The physical environment simultaneously presents advantages and drawbacks with which humans must deal. Thus, the danger of typhoons in central China or monsoonal floods in Bangladesh must be balanced against the agricultural bounty derived from the regions' favorable terrain, soil, and moisture conditions.

At the same time, by occupying a given place, people modify its environmental conditions. The existence of the U.S. Environmental Protection Agency (EPA; and its counterparts elsewhere) is a reminder that humans are the active and frequently harmful agents in the continuing interplay between the cultural and physical worlds (Figure 1.10). Virtually every human activity leaves its imprint on an area's soils, water, vegetation, animal life, and other resources and on the atmosphere common to all Earth space. The impact of humans has been so universal and so long exerted that essentially no purely "natural landscape" any longer exists. One can even find human-made debris in the middle of the ocean and air pollution in the Arctic.

The visible expression of that human activity is the **cultural landscape.** It, too, exists at different scales and different levels of visibility. Differences in agricultural practices and land use between Mexico and southern California are evident in Figure 1.11, while the signs, structures, and people of, for instance, Los Angeles's Chinatown leave a smaller, more confined imprint within the larger cultural landscape of the metropolitan area itself.

Although the focus of this book is on the human characteristics of places, geographers are ever aware that the physical content of an area is also important in understanding the activity patterns of people and the interconnections between people and the environments they occupy and modify. Those interconnections and modifications are not static or permanent, however, but are subject to continual change. For example, marshes and wetlands, when drained, may be transformed into productive, densely settled farmland, while the threat or occurrence of eruption of a long-dormant volcano may quickly and drastically alter established patterns of farming, housing, and transportation on or near its flanks.

The Changing Attributes of Place

The physical environment surrounding us seems eternal and unchanging but, of course, it is not. In the framework of geologic time, change is both continuous and pronounced. Islands form and disappear; mountains rise and are worn low to swampy plains; vast continental glaciers form, move, and melt away, and sea levels fall and rise in response. Geologic time is long, but the forces that give shape to the land are timeless and relentless.

Even within the short period of time since the most recent retreat of continental glaciers—some 11,000 or 12,000 years ago—the environments occupied by humans have been subject to change. Glacial retreat itself marked a period of climatic alteration, extending the area habitable by humans to include vast reaches of northern Eurasia and North America formerly covered by thousands of feet of ice. With moderating climatic conditions came associated changes in vegetation and fauna. On the global scale, these were natural environmental changes; humans were as yet too few in numbers and too limited in technology to alter materially the course of physical events. On the regional scale, however, even early human societies exerted an impact on the environments they occupied. Fire was used to clear forest undergrowth, to maintain

Figure 1.10 Sites such as this landfill are all-too-frequent reminders of the adverse environmental impacts of humans and their waste products. Here, bulldozers compact solid waste and spread a daily cover at a "sanitary" landfill.

Figure 1.11 This NASA image reveals contrasting cultural landscapes along the Mexico-California border. Move your eyes from the Salton Sea (the dark patch at the top of the image) southward to the agricultural land extending to the edge of the image. Notice how the regularity of the fields and the bright colors (representing growing vegetation) give way to a marked break, where irregularly shaped fields and less prosperous agriculture are evident. Above the break is the Imperial Valley of California; below the border is Mexico.

© NASA

or extend grassland for grazing animals and to drive them in the hunt, and later to clear openings for rudimentary agriculture.

With the dawn of civilizations and the invention and spread of agricultural technologies, humans accelerated their management and alteration of the now no longer "natural" environment. Even the classical Greeks noted how the landscape they occupied differed—for the worse—from its former condition. With growing numbers of people and particularly with industrialization and the spread of European exploitative technologies throughout the world, the pace of change in the content of area accelerated. The built landscape—the product of human effort—increasingly replaced the natural landscape. Each new settlement or city, each agricultural assault on forests, each new mine, dam, or factory changed the content of regions and altered the temporarily established spatial interconnections between humans and the environment.

Characteristics of places today are the result of constantly changing past conditions. They are, as well, the forerunners of differing human-environmental balances yet to be struck. Geographers are concerned with places at given moments of time. But to understand fully the nature and development of places, to appreciate the significance of their relative locations, and to comprehend the interplay of their physical and cultural characteristics, geographers must view places as the present result of the past operation of distinctive physical and cultural processes (Figure 1.12).

You will recall that one of the questions geographers ask about a place or thing is "How did it come to be what and where

it is?" This is an inquiry about process and about becoming. The forces and events shaping the physical and cultural environment of places today are an important focus of geography. They are, particularly in their human context, the subjects of most of the separate chapters of this book. To understand them is to appreciate more fully the changing human spatial order of our world.

Interrelations Between Places

The concepts of relative location and distance that we earlier introduced lead directly to a fundamental spatial reality: Places interact with other places in structured and comprehensible ways. In describing the processes and patterns of that **spatial interaction,** geographers add *accessibility* and *connectivity* to the ideas of location and distance.

Tobler's First Law of Geography tells us that in a spatial sense, everything is related to everything else, but that relationships are stronger when items are near one another. Our observation, therefore, is that interaction between places tends to diminish in intensity and frequency as distance between them increases—a statement of the idea of *distance decay,* which we explore in Chapter 3. Think about it—are you more likely to go to a fast-food outlet next door or to a nearly identical restaurant across town? Human decision making is unpredictable in many ways and decisions are frequently made for obscure reasons, but in this case you can see how you will probably frequent the nearer place more often.

(a)

(b)

Figure 1.12 **The process of change in a cultural landscape.** (*a*) In 1913, Miami, Florida, was just a small settlement on the banks of the Miami River amidst woodlands and wetlands. (*b*) By the end of the 20th century, it had grown from a few thousand inhabitants to some 350,000, with buildings, streets, and highways completely transforming its natural landscape.

Sources: (a) Historical Museum of Southern Florida; (b) South Florida Water Management District.

Consideration of distance implies assessment of **accessibility.** How easy or difficult is it to overcome the "friction of distance"? That is, how easy or difficult is it to surmount the barrier of the time and space separating places? Distance isolated North America from Europe until the development of ships (and aircraft) that reduced the effective distance between the continents. All parts of the ancient and medieval city were accessible by walking; they were "pedestrian cities," a status lost as cities expanded in area and population with industrialization. Accessibility between city districts could be maintained only by the development of public transit systems whose fixed lines of travel increased ease of movement between connected points and reduced it between areas not on the transit lines themselves. Later, the invention and widespread adoption of the automobile had its own profound effects on urban form and activity patterns.

Accessibility, therefore, suggests the idea of **connectivity,** a broader concept implying all the tangible and intangible ways in which places are linked: by physical telephone lines, street and road systems, pipelines and sewers; by unrestrained walking across open countryside; by radio and TV broadcasts beamed outward from a central source. Where routes are fixed and flow is channelized, *networks*—the patterns of routes connecting sets of places—determine the efficiency of movement and the connectedness of points. Very rapid and uniform accessibility and connectivity are expected in today's advanced societies. Technologies and devices to achieve it proliferate, as our own lifestyles show. Cell phones, e-mail, broadband wireless Internet access, instant messaging, and more have considerably reduced time and distance barriers to communication that formerly separated and isolated individuals and groups, especially in the developed world, and have reduced our dependence on physical movement and on networks fixed in the landscape. The realities of accessibility and connectivity, that is, clearly change over time (Figure 1.13).

There is, inevitably, interchange between connected places. **Spatial diffusion** is the process of dispersion of an idea or an item from a center of origin to more distant points with which it is directly or indirectly connected. The rate and extent of that diffusion are affected by the distance separating the originating center of, say, a new idea or technology and other places where it is eventually adopted. Diffusion rates are also affected by population densities, means of communication, obvious advantages of the innovation, and importance or prestige of the originating *node.* These ideas of diffusion are further explored in Chapter 2.

Geographers study the dynamics of spatial relationships. Movement, connection, and interaction are part of the social and economic processes that give character to places and regions. Geography's study of those relationships recognizes that spatial interaction is not just an awkward necessity but a fundamental organizing principle of human life on Earth. That recognition has become universal, repeatedly expressed in the term *globalization.* **Globalization** implies the increasing interconnection of peoples and societies in all parts of the world as the full range of social, cultural, political, economic, and environmental processes becomes international in scale and effect. Promoted by continuing advances in worldwide accessibility and connectivity related in part to developments in the technologies of transportation and communication, globalization encompasses other core geographic concepts of spatial interaction, accessibility, connectivity, and diffusion. More detailed implications of globalization will be touched on in later chapters of this text.

The Structured Content of Place

A starting point for geographic inquiry is how objects are distributed in area—for example, the placement of churches or supermarkets within a town. That interest distinguishes geography from

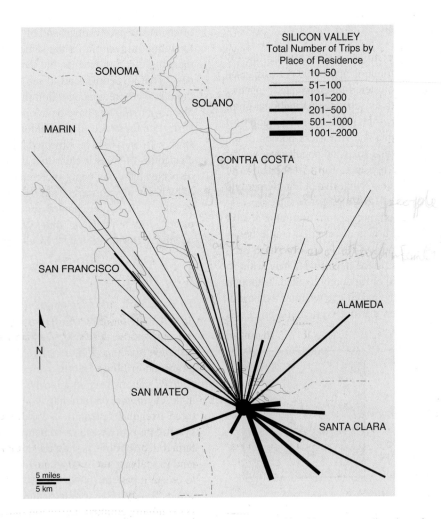

Figure 1.13 An indication of one form of spatial interaction and *connectivity* is suggested by this map recording the volume of daily work trips within the San Francisco Bay area to the Silicon Valley employment node (geographers sometimes refer to these displays as *spider diagrams,* for obvious reasons). The ends of the lines define the outer reaches of a physical interaction region defined by the network of connecting roads and routes. The region changed in size and shape over time as the network was enlarged and improved, the Valley employment base expanded, and the commuting range of workers increased. The map, of course, gives no indication of the global reach of the Valley's *accessibility* and interaction through other means of communication and interchange.

Source: Redrawn with permission from Robert Cervero, Suburban Gridlock. © 1986 Center for Urban Policy Research, Rutgers, the State University of New Jersey.

other sciences, physical or social, and underlies many of the questions geographers ask: Where is a thing located? How is that location related to other items? How did the location we observe come to exist? Such questions carry the conviction that the contents of an area are comprehensibly arranged or structured. The arrangement of items on the Earth's surface is called **spatial distribution** and may be analyzed by the elements common to all spatial distributions: *density, dispersion,* and *pattern.* In addition, pairs or larger sets of distributions often show *spatial association.*

Density

Density is usually thought of as a measure of the number or quantity of a specific feature within a defined unit of area. In fact, density does not apply only to areas. Thus, one can speak of the density of point (zero-dimensional) features, like gas stations, within a unit of a linear (one-dimensional) feature, like a highway, or within a unit of an areal (two-dimensional) feature, like a

county. Similarly, one can speak of the density of linear features, like highways, within a unit of an areal feature, like a county. It is therefore not simply a count of items but of items in relation to the space in which they are found. When the relationship is absolute, as in population per square kilometer, for example, or dwelling units per acre, we are defining *arithmetic density* (see Figure 1.9). Sometimes it is more meaningful to relate item numbers to a specific kind of space. *Physiological density,* for example, is a measure of the number of persons per unit area of arable land. Density defined in population terms is discussed in Chapter 4.

A density figure is a statement of fact, but not necessarily one useful in itself. Densities are normally employed comparatively, relative to one another. High or low density implies a comparison with a known standard, with an average, or with a different area. Ohio, with 107 persons per square kilometer (277 per sq mi) in 2000, might be thought to have a high density compared with neighboring Michigan at 68 per square kilometer (175 per sq mi), and a low one in relation to New Jersey at 438 (1134 per sq mi).

Dispersion *Sự phân tán*

Dispersion (or its opposite, **concentration**) is a statement of the extent to which features within a distribution are spread out (dispersed or scattered) from each other, or clustered (agglomerated) together (Figure 1.14). Dispersion is an entirely separate distributional property from density. Figure 1.15 shows the population distributions of San Bernardino County in California and an eastern portion of the state of Iowa. Both have similar spatial areas and populations, so that they both have similar arithmetic densities. But the population in eastern Iowa is rather evenly spread out, while that of San Bernardino is quite concentrated (near the city of Los Angeles to the west).

The phenomenon of dispersion or concentration must always be judged against the standard of how a distribution would be arranged if it were generated randomly—if it were not based on a systematic cause. For example, a police department may want to know whether crimes are clustered or randomly located. Although it is sometimes easy to see with the naked eye whether a distribution is dispersed or clustered, often it is not. Systematic processes often act against a background of "noise," so they are not so evident to simple inspection. At the same time, people are good at seeing meaningful arrangements, but they are not good at seeing randomness. That is, people tend to see clusters, for instance, even when there is no more concentration than would be expected by chance alone. Geographers have developed formal statistical tests to try to verify the existence of nonrandom dispersion or clustering that is stronger than would be expected by chance alone. A comparison to chance also makes it clear that distributions can be nonrandomly dispersed either by being more clustered than expected by chance, or by being *less clustered* (more dispersed) than would be expected by chance. In a later chapter, for example, we will see that central place theory predicts that cities of a given size will be spread more widely across a region than would be expected by chance alone.

Pattern

The geometric arrangement of feature in space is called **pattern.** Like dispersion, pattern refers to distribution, but in a way, that emphasizes the design or shape of feature locations rather than just their spacing (Figure 1.16). The distribution of towns along a railroad or houses along a street may be seen as *linear*. A *centralized* pattern may involve items concentrated around a single node. A *random* pattern may be the best description of an unstructured irregular distribution. Like dispersion, patterns created by systematic processes are sometimes easy to confuse with unpatterned distributions created by random processes. That is, people tend to see patterns even when no systematic process has operated to create a pattern (for instance, have you ever seen a face in the clouds?). Again, geographers have statistical tests to try to verify the existence of nonrandom patterns that are stronger than would be expected by chance alone.

An example of a patterned distribution includes that resulting from the rectangular system of land survey adopted in much of the United States under the Ordinance of 1785, which created a checkerboard rural pattern of "sections" and "quarter-sections" of farmland (see Figure 6.26 in Chapter 6). As a result, in most American cities, streets display a *grid* or *rectilinear* pattern. The same is true of cities in Canada, Australia, New Zealand, and South Africa, which adopted similar geometric survey systems. The *hexagonal* pattern of service areas of farm towns is a mainstay of central place theory discussed in Chapter 11. These references to the geometry of distribution patterns help us visualize and describe the

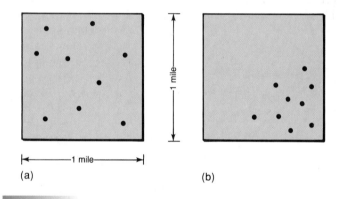

Figure 1.14 Density and dispersion each tell us something different about how items are distributed in an area. *Density* is simply the number of items or observations within a defined area; it remains the same no matter how the items are distributed. The density of houses per square mile, for example, is the same in both (*a*) and (*b*). *Dispersion* is a statement about nearness or separation. The houses in (*a*) are more *dispersed* than those shown *clustered* in (*b*).

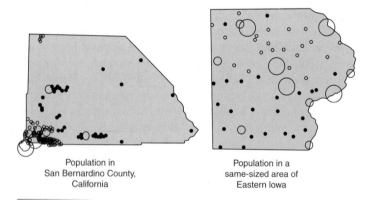

Population in San Bernardino County, California

Population in a same-sized area of Eastern Iowa

Figure 1.15 Density and dispersion are separate properties of spatial distributions. The population distribution of San Bernardino County, California, on the left is highly concentrated, while that of eastern Iowa on the right is highly dispersed, even though both regions have about equal area and population, and thus equal arithmetic density.

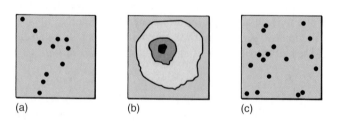

Figure 1.16 *Pattern* describes spatial arrangement and design. The *linear* pattern of towns in (*a*) perhaps traces the route of a road or railroad or the course of a river. The urban land use in (*b*) with its categories of residential and commercial activities represents a circular pattern, while the dots in (*c*) are *randomly* distributed.

structured arrangement of items in space. They help us make informed comparisons between areas and use the patterns we discern to ask further questions about the interrelationship of things.

Spatial Association

Two distributions of features often spatially correspond with each other. That is, places where one feature is found are more likely (or less likely) than chance to be the places where a different type of feature is found. This is **spatial association** or covariation. For example, counties in Texas where consuming alcoholic beverages is allowed by law tend to be the same counties that have a majority of Catholic residents, while so-called dry counties are more likely to have a majority of Protestant residents (Figure 1.17). Spatial association is very similar to looking for spatial pattern, except that it is a spatial pattern involving two or more distributions simultaneously. Like pattern, geographers attempt to identify associations that are clearly stronger than would be expected by chance alone.

Place Similarity and Regions

The distinctive characteristics of places in content and structure immediately suggest two geographically important ideas. The first is that no two places on the surface of the Earth can be *exactly* the same. Not only do they have different absolute locations, but—as in the features of the human face—the precise mix of physical and cultural characteristics of a place is never exactly duplicated.

Because geography is a spatial science, the inevitable uniqueness of place would seem to impose impossible problems of generalizing spatial information. That this is not the case results from the second important idea: The physical and cultural content of an area and the dynamic interconnections of people and places show patterns of spatial similarity. For example, a geographer doing fieldwork in France might find that all farmers in one area use a similar specialized technique to build fences around their fields. Often, such similarities are striking enough for us to conclude that spatial regularities exist. They permit us to recognize and define **regions**—Earth areas that display significant elements of internal uniformity and external difference from surrounding territories. Places are, therefore, both unlike and like other places, creating patterns of areal differences and of coherent spatial similarity.

The problem of the historian and the geographer is similar. Each must generalize about items of study that are essentially unique. The historian creates arbitrary but meaningful and useful historical periods for reference and study. The "Roaring Twenties" and the "Victorian Era" are shorthand summary names for specific time spans, internally quite complex and varied but significantly distinct from what went before or followed after. The region is the geographer's equivalent of the historian's era. It is a device of areal generalization that segregates into component parts the complex reality of the Earth's surface. In both the time and the space needed for generalization, attention is focused on key unifying elements or similarities of the era or area selected for study. In both the historical and geographical cases, the names assigned

Data for 1971

Status in 1972

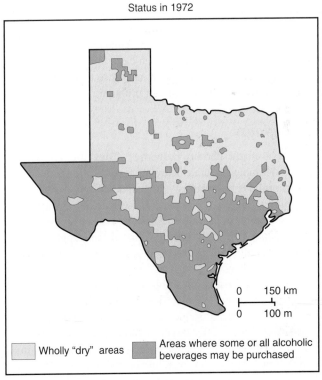

☐ Dominantly Baptist and Methodist areas ☐ Dominantly Catholic and Lutheran areas

☐ Wholly "dry" areas ☐ Areas where some or all alcoholic beverages may be purchased

0   150 km
0   100 m

Figure 1.17 The distributions of religion and alcohol sales in Texas show a spatial correlation. Catholic and Lutheran areas generally choose to be "wet," and Baptist-Methodist areas retain prohibition. Both the Baptist and Methodist churches have traditionally taken a stand again beverages. (From 38th Annual Report of the Texas Alcoholic Beverage Commission, Austin, 1972, p. 49; and Churches and Church Me United States: 1971, National Council of the Churches of Christ in the U.S.A., 1974.)

to those times and places serve to identify the time span or region and to convey between speaker and listener a complex set of interrelated attributes.

All of us have a general idea of the meaning of region, and all of us refer to regions in everyday speech and action. We visit "the old neighborhood" or "go downtown"; we plan to vacation or retire in the "Sunbelt"; or we speculate about the effects of weather conditions in the "Corn Belt" on next year's food prices. In each instance, we have mental images of the areas mentioned, and in each, we have engaged in an informal place classification to pass along quite complex spatial, organizational, or content ideas. We have applied the **regional concept** to bring order to the immense diversity of the Earth's surface. In the end, we can see that there is nothing particularly exotic or peculiar about using similarities to group unique entities into similarity classes. All people in all cultures and time periods (including all of us!) do it constantly when they recognize that two unique objects they can sit on are both "chairs" or two unique woody plants are both "trees." In other words, regionalizing is spatial *categorization,* and categorization appears to be culturally and historically universal to all people.

Regions are not just "given" in nature, any more than "eras" are entirely given in the course of human events. Regions are, in part, devised; they are spatial summaries designed to bring order to the infinite diversity of the Earth's surface. At their root, they are based on the recognition and mapping of *spatial distributions*—the territorial occurrence of environmental, human, or organizational features selected for study. For example, the location of Welsh speakers in Britain is a distribution that can be identified and mapped. As many spatial distributions exist as there are imaginable physical, cultural, or connectivity elements of area to examine. Since regions are partially mental constructs, different observers employing different criteria may bestow the same regional identity on differently bounded areal units. In each case, however, the key characteristics that are selected for study are those that contribute to the understanding of a specific topic or problem.

Types of Regions

Thus, all regions share certain properties. They are all two-dimensional geographic features. They all have location and size (area). All regions have boundaries, which divide places inside the region from places outside the region. These boundaries vary in their degree of sharpness or vagueness, however, as we discuss below. Regions also vary in the permeability of their boundaries. That is, boundaries allow material, energy, people, and information to move across them more or less easily (with more or less effort, time, and cost), and permeability in one direction may be different than in the other. We also observe that regions are often *hierarchically organized.* Regions at one scale of size or importance are often contained by larger or more important regions in one direction, and contain smaller or less important regions in the other direction. The simplest example of region hierarchies is probably the relationship of larger and smaller political regions: states or provinces are within countries, while entities like counties and cities are within states or provinces.

Regions may be *administrative, thematic, functional,* or *perceptual.* An **administrative region** is created by law, treaty, or ʳulation. It includes political regions such as countries and states,

bureaucratic regions such as school and voting districts, and cadastral (real estate) regions. Even the end zone on a football field is an administrative region. The boundaries of administrative regions are different than the boundaries of the other three types of regions, in that they are as sharp as measurement precision allows, or at least potentially (as soon as someone cares about the location of administrative boundaries, they can be made very precise by diplomats, lawyers, and surveyors). Given these precise boundaries, administrative regions have *uniform membership functions*—every place within the region is fully and equally representative of the region. Interestingly, this is an exception to the rule stated above that "no two places are identical," insofar as all places within the boundaries of an administrative region are generally treated identically with respect to administrative rules and procedures.

Thematic regions (sometimes called formal or uniform regions in other texts) are based on one or more objectively measurable themes or properties (Figure 1.18a). Examples are soil regions, where one type of soil predominates, or dialect regions, where most people speak a certain language using a given dialect. Unlike administrative regions, thematic regions typically have boundaries varying in vagueness—they are "fuzzy" rather than sharp. The transition between the deciduous forest and the grasslands is not sharp but gradual, as fewer and smaller trees give way to larger grassy areas without trees. Of course, maps usually show boundaries like these as being sharp, but that sharpness is largely a handy fiction that makes it easier to display and think about the regions. As a corollary to these fuzzy or vague boundaries, thematic regions have non-uniform membership functions. At particular places within a given dialect region, for example, virtually 100 percent of the residents speak the dialect, while in other places, only a slight majority do. In such a case, which is quite common, one can say that certain places within the region are more strongly or clearly representative of the region.

Functional regions emerge from patterns of interaction over space and time that connect places (Figure 1.18b). Examples include the region in which most people shop at a particular shopping center or listen to a particular radio station. In physical geography, the movement of air and water currents defines functional regions; a watershed is an important example. Often, functional regions have a pointlike core from which interaction originates, and thus they are sometimes called *nodal regions,* but they need not originate from a point. Certain famous wind patterns form functional regions when they originate from a linear feature rather than a point. Of course, like thematic regions, functional regions general have vague boundaries and non-uniform membership functions; you can literally hear the "fuzziness" of functional regions defined by radio stations as you drive further from the transmission tower.

Finally, **perceptual regions** (also called *cognitive regions*) are the informal subjective regions defined by people's beliefs, feelings, and images. They reflect the universal tendency for humans to regionalize parts of the Earth's surface, even though the particular regions identified certainly vary across cultures and historical times. Again, like thematic and functional regions, perceptual regions typically have vague boundaries and non-uniform membership functions. Two places may both be thought of as "downtown," for example, but one is seen to represent downtown more clearly than the other. In addition, perceptual regions like downtown are often culturally shared. In this case, perceptual

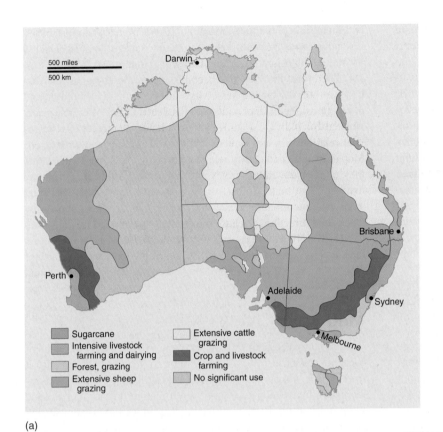

(a)

Figure 1.18 (a) **This generalized land use map of Australia** is composed of thematic *regions* whose internal physical and cultural characteristics show essential similarities, setting them off from adjacent territories of different conditions of use.

Legend:
- Sugarcane
- Intensive livestock farming and dairying
- Forest, grazing
- Extensive sheep grazing
- Extensive cattle grazing
- Crop and livestock farming
- No significant use

(b)

Figure 1.18 (b) The functional (or nodal) regions shown on this map were based on linkages between large banks of major central cities and the "correspondent" banks they served in smaller towns in the 1970s, before the advent of electronic banking and bank consolidation.

Source: (b) Redrawn by permission from Annals of the Association of American Geographers, John R. Borchert, vol. 62, p. 358, Association of American Geographers, 1972.

regions may be called *vernacular regions*. Vernacular regions are real in the minds of cultural group members and are often reflected in regionally based names employed by businesses, by sports teams, or in advertising slogans. The frequency of references to "Dixie" in the southeastern United States represents that kind of regional consensus and awareness. Geographer Wilbur Zelinsky created his map of the perceptual regions of North America by counting the frequency that regional terms were used in the names of businesses (Figure 1.19). At a different scale, such urban ethnic enclaves (see Chapter 6) as "Little Italy" or "Chinatown" have comparable regional identities in the minds of their inhabitants. However, perceptual regions are not always culturally shared; they may be idiosyncratic to just one person or a couple of people. For example, a child growing up in a rural community may have a special place where he or she goes to hang out and daydream. What perceptual regions do you have clearly in mind?

Maps

Maps are pictorial models of portions of the Earth's surface and the distributions of features on that surface. The spatial distributions, patterns, and relations of interest to geographers usually cannot easily be observed or interpreted in the landscape itself. Many, such as landform or agricultural regions or major cities, are so extensive spatially that they cannot be seen or studied in their totality from one or a few vantage points. Others, such as regions of language usage or religious belief, are spatial phenomena, but are not tangible or readily visible to someone walking around in the environment. Various interactions, flows, and exchanges imparting the dynamic quality to spatial interaction may not be directly observable at all. And even if all matters of geographic interest could be seen and measured through field examination, the infinite variety of tangible and intangible content of area would make it nearly impossible to isolate for study and interpretation the few items of interest selected for special investigation in any particular situation.

Therefore, the map has become one of the essential and distinctive tools of geographers. Maps allow spatial distributions and interactions of whatever nature to be reduced to an observable scale, isolated for individual study, and combined or recombined to reveal relationships not directly measurable in the landscape itself. Maps highlight and clarify relevant properties, but at the same time, they omit or downplay irrelevant properties. For instance, subway maps in most major cities focus on showing connections between stops but intentionally leave out accurate information about distances and directions because most riders do not need this information (Fig. 1.20). But maps can serve their purpose only if their users have a clear idea of their strengths and limitations, the diversity of map styles, and the conventions observed in their preparation and interpretation.

Map Scale

We have already seen that scale (page 10) is a vital element of every map. Because it is a much reduced version of the reality it summarizes, a map generalizes the data it displays. *Scale*—the relationship between size or length of a feature on the map and the same item on the Earth's surface—determines the amount of that generalization. The smaller the scale of the map, the larger is the area it covers and the more generalized are the data it portrays. The larger the scale, the smaller is the depicted area and the more accurately can its content be represented (Figure 1.21). It may seem backward, but large-scale maps show small areas, and small-scale maps show large areas.

Map scale is selected according to the amount of generalization of data that is acceptable and the size of area that must be

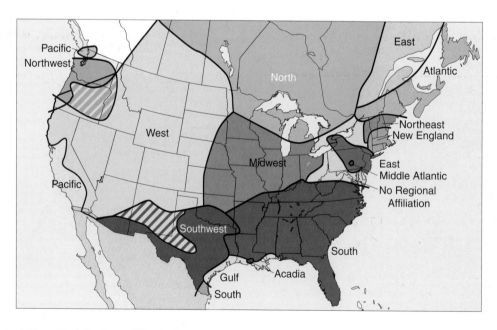

Figure 1.19 **Perceptual (Cognitive) Regions of North America.**

Redrawn by permission from Annals of the Association of American Geographers, Wilbur Zelinsky, "North America's Vernacular Regions, Vol. 70, No. 1, p. 14, 1980.

Figure 1. 20 Schematic network maps. A traveler viewing a shematic map of the Washington, DC, Metro system. It clearly shows train lines and connections at stations, essential for using the Metro system, but omits quantitative information about distances and directions along the system lines that are of little use to most riders.

depicted. The user must consider map scale in evaluating the reliability of the spatial data that are presented. Regional boundary lines drawn on the world maps in this and other books or atlases would cover many kilometers or miles on the Earth's surface. They obviously distort the reality they are meant to define, and on small-scale maps major distortion is inevitable. In fact, a general rule of thumb is that the larger the Earth area depicted on a map, the greater is the distortion built into the map.

This is so not only because geographic features must be generalized more on smaller-scale maps, but because a map has to depict the curved surface of the three-dimensional earth on a two-dimensional sheet of paper. The term **projection** designates the method chosen to represent the Earth's curved surface as a flat map—to **develop** the Earth's surface. Since absolutely accurate representation is impossible, all projections inevitably distort. To start with, all maps break a continuous Earth surface at some arbitrarily chosen juncture (the places shown on the right and left sides of most maps are next to each other in reality). If that weren't enough, projections also distort one or more of the four main spatial properties of maps—area, shape, distance, or direction.[2] Specific projections may be selected, however, to

[2] A more detailed discussion of map projections, including examples of their different types and purposes, may be found in Appendix A, beginning on page 453.

Figure 1.21 The effect of scale on area and detail. The larger the scale, the greater the number and kinds of features that can be included. Notice how individual buildings are visible in the large-scale map (upper left), while the city of Boston is a mere point symbol in the smallest scale map (lower left). Scale may be reported to the map user in one (or more) of three ways. A *verbal* scale is given in words ("1 centimeter to 1 kilometer" or "1 inch to 1 mile"). A *representative fraction* (such as that placed at the left, below each of the four maps shown here) is a numerical expression of how many linear units on the Earth's surface are represented by one unit on the map. In the upper-left map, for example, one map inch represents 25,000 inches on the ground. A *graphic scale* (such as that placed at the right and below each of these maps) is a line or bar marked off in map units but labeled in ground units.

minimize distortion of a particular spatial property or compromise the amount of distortion in one property by increasing distortion in another.

The Globe Grid

As we have seen, geography is about the planet Earth and the natural and human structures and processes found there. The Earth is the third planet from the sun in our solar system. It revolves around the sun about once every 365 days, and it rotates once approximately every 24 hours around an axis that stretches from one pole to the other. The equator is the imaginary circle around the middle that separates the Earth into Northern and Southern hemispheres. The Earth is sometimes called the "water planet" because its surface is about 71 percent water and only 29 percent land. The shape of the Earth is close to a ball, but it is not perfectly spherical; instead, it is a *bumpy oblate spheroid.* We say "bumpy" because of the topographic features like mountains and canyons. We say "oblate" because the physics of spinning objects causes the Earth to bulge slightly around its equator. That is, while the Earth's circumference is about 25,000 miles around, and its diameter is about 8,000 miles, the Earth is approximately 27 miles wider at the equator than it is from pole to pole. So the Earth is not a perfect sphere but a flattened "spheroid." That said, the Earth is very nearly a perfectly smooth ball; if it were shrunk to the size of a billiard ball, it would be as round and about as smooth!

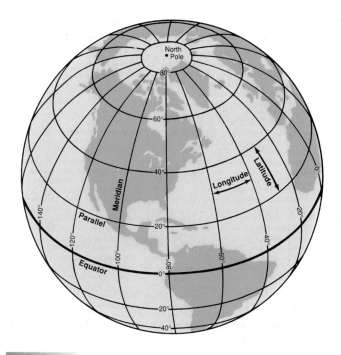

Figure 1.22 The grid system of parallels of latitude and meridians of longitude. Since the meridians converge at the poles, parallels become increasingly shorter away from the equator. On the globe, the 60th parallel (60°) is only one-half as long as the equator, and a degree of longitude along it measures only about 55 1/2 kilometers (about 34 1/2 miles) compared with about 111 kilometers (about 69 miles) at the equator (0°).

In order to represent and communicate information about the Earth, we construct models of it. Since the Earth is three-dimensional and nearly spherical, it makes sense to construct a three-dimensional spherical model to understand it. This is called a **globe.** In order to identify locations on the Earth surface in a precise and standardized way, a grid of lines is laid over the globe, called the **graticule.** The graticule identifies two dimensions of Earth-surface location with lines running horizontally, in the direction of the equator, and lines running vertically, from pole to pole (Figure 1.22). The horizontal lines are called **parallels,** and they encode latitude, which refers to locations north or south of the equator. Since the Earth is a spherical shape, the locations of latitude lines are expressed in angular terms as degrees north or south (°N or °S). Intermediate latitude lines are expressed in terms of angular minutes and seconds, or tenths and hundredths of degrees. The equator is 0° (neither north nor south), the North Pole is 90°N, and the South Pole is 90°S. The vertical lines are called **meridians** and they encode longitude. Meridians express location east or west, but there is no natural vertical line equivalent to the equator to use as an origin line. Instead, an international treaty from over a century ago established an origin line passing through the Greenwich Observatory outside London; this longitude line is called the **prime meridian.** Like latitude, the locations of longitude lines are expressed in angular terms as degrees, either east or west of the prime meridian (°E or °W). The prime meridian is 0° (neither east nor west), the city of Beijing in China is about 116°E, and the city of Vancouver in Canada is about 123°W. On the opposite side of the Earth from the prime meridian, running vertically through the Pacific Ocean, is the 180° meridian line (also neither east nor west). Incidentally, many people confuse the 180° meridian line with the International Date Line (where the date of the day of the year changes forward or back, depending on your direction of travel), but the two are different and coincide only in some places.

Maps are geographers' primary tools of spatial analysis. All spatial analysis starts with locations, and all locations are related to the global grid of latitude and longitude. Since these lines of reference are drawn on the spherical Earth, their projection onto a map distorts their grid relationships. The extent of variance between the globe grid and a map grid helps tell us the kind and degree of distortion that the map will contain.

Only the globe grid itself retains all of these characteristics. To project it onto a surface that can be laid flat is to distort some or all of these properties and consequently to distort the reality the map attempts to portray.

How Maps Show Data

The properties of the globe grid and of various projections are the concern of the cartographer; **cartography** is the art and science of maps and map-making. Geographers are more interested in the depiction of spatial data and in the analysis of the patterns and interrelationships those data present. Out of the myriad items comprising the content of an area, the geographer must, first, select those that are of concern to the problem at hand and, second, decide on how best to display them for study or demonstration. In that effort, geographers can choose among different types of maps and different systems of symbolization. These symbols use properties like shape, color, and size to represent geographic meaning, in somewhat the same way that words represent meaning in language.

Maps can first be classified as either reference maps or thematic maps. **Reference maps** are *general-purpose*. Their purpose is simply to show without analysis or interpretation a variety of natural or human-made features of an area or of the world as a whole, including showing the locations of features accurately. Reference maps answer the question "What is there?". Familiar examples are highway maps, city street maps, topographic maps (Figure 1.23), atlas maps, and the like. Until about the middle of the 18th century, the general-purpose or reference map was the only type of map, for the function of the mapmaker (and the explorer who supplied the new data) was to "fill in" the world's unknown areas with reliable locational information. With the passage of time, scholars saw the possibility of using the accumulation of locational information to display and study the spatial patterns of social and physical data. The maps they made of climate, vegetation, soil, population, and other distributions introduced the thematic map, the second major class of maps.

Thematic maps are specific-purpose maps—they present a specific spatial distribution or a single category of data—that is, presents a graphic theme. Thematic maps could be called *statistical* or *graph maps*; they answer the question "What is the pattern of this variable?" The way the information is shown on such a map may vary according to the type of information to be conveyed, the level of generalization that is desired, and the symbolization selected. Thematic maps may be either *qualitative* or *quantitative*. The principal purpose of the qualitative map is to show the distribution of a particular class of information. The world location of producing oil fields, the distribution of U.S. national parks, or the pattern of areas of agricultural specialization within a state or country are examples. The interest is in where things are in an approximate way, and nothing is reported about—in the examples cited—barrels of oil extracted or in reserve, number of park visitors, or value or volume of crops or livestock produced.

In contrast, quantitative thematic maps show the spatial characteristic of numerical data. Usually, a single variable such as population, average rainfall, median income, annual wheat production, or average land value is chosen, and the map displays differences from place to place in that variable. Important types of quantitative thematic maps include graduated circle, dot, isoline, and choropleth maps (Figure 1.24).

Graduated circle maps use circles of different size to show the magnitude of a variable of interest in different places; the larger the circle, the greater the magnitude of the variable. They are examples of the more general class of thematic symbols called *proportional area symbols* that include shapes other than circles. On *dot maps*, a single or specified number of occurrences of the item studied is recorded by a single dot. An *isoline map* features lines that connect points registering equal values of the item mapped (*iso* means "equal"). For example, *isotherms* shown on daily weather maps connect points recording the same temperature at the same moment of time or the same average temperature during the day. Identical elevations above sea level may be shown by a form of isoline called a *contour line*.

A *choropleth map* presents average value of the data studied per preexisting areal unit—dwelling unit rents or assessed values by city block, for example, or (in the United States) population densities by individual townships within counties. Each unit area on the map is then shaded or colored to suggest the magnitude of the event or item found within its borders. Where the choropleth map is based on the absolute number of items within the unit area, as it is in Figure 1.24d, rather than on areal averaging (total numbers, for example, instead of numbers per square kilometer), a misleading statement about density may be conveyed. That is, if the same magnitude is shown with the same shading or color, large areal units will dominate the visual field, even though they actually represent a much less dense concentration of the feature in question.

A *statistical map* records the actual numbers or occurrences of the mapped item per established unit area or location. The actual count of each state's colleges and universities shown on an outline map of the United States or the number of traffic accidents at each street intersection within a city are examples of statistical

Figure 1.23 **A portion of the Santa Barbara, California, topographic quadrangle** of the U.S. Geological Survey 1:24,000 series. Topographic maps portray landscape features of relatively small areas. Elevations and shapes of landforms, streams and other water bodies, vegetation, and coastal features are recorded, often with great accuracy. Because cultural items that people have added to the physical landscape, such as roads, railroads, buildings, political boundaries, and the like, are also frequently depicted on them, topographic maps are classed as general purpose or reference maps by the International Cartographic Association. The scale of the original map no longer applies to this photographic reduction.

Source: U.S. Geological Survey.

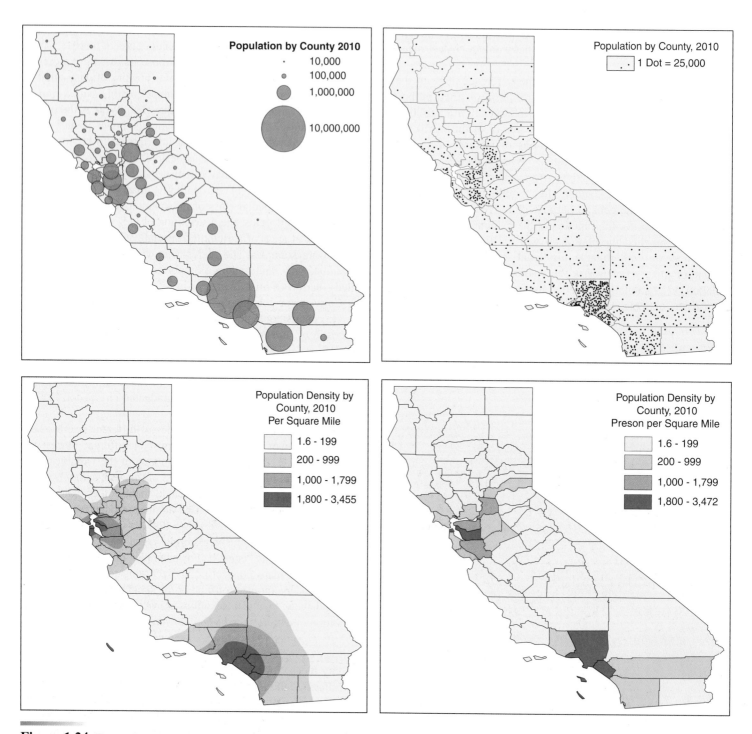

Figure 1.24 Types of thematic maps. Although population is the theme of each, these different California maps present their information in strikingly different ways. (*a*) In the graduated circle map, the area of the circle is approximately proportional to the absolute number of people within each county. (*b*) In a dot-distribution map where large numbers of items are involved, the value of each dot is identical and stated in the map legend. The placement of dots on this map does not indicate precise locations of people within the county, but simply their total number. (*c*) Population density is recorded by the isopleth map, while the choropleth map (*d*) may show absolute values, as here, or, more usually, ratio values such as population per square kilometer.

maps. A *cartogram* uses such statistical data to transform space so that the largest areal unit on the map is the one showing the greatest statistical value (Figure 1.25).

Maps communicate information but, as in all forms of communication, the message conveyed by a map reflects the intent and, perhaps, the biases of its author. Maps are persuasive because of the implied precision of their lines, scales, color and symbol placement, and information content. But maps, as communication devices, can subtly or blatantly manipulate the message they impart or contain intentionally false information (Figure 1.26).

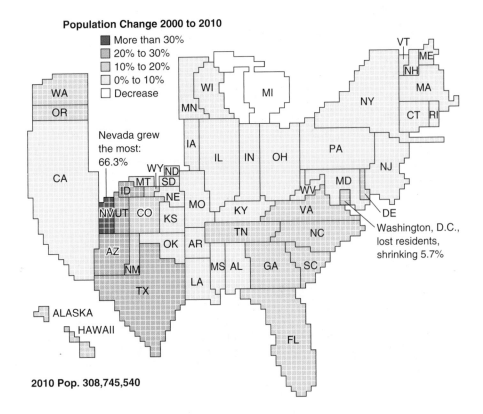

Population Change 2000 to 2010

- More than 30%
- 20% to 30%
- 10% to 20%
- 0% to 10%
- Decrease

Nevada grew the most: 66.3%

Washington, D.C., lost residents, shrinking 5.7%

2010 Pop. 308,745,540

Figure 1.25 A cartogram in which each state is sized according to its number of residents in the year 2010 as reported by the U.S. Bureau of the Census. The cartogram also shows the percent change in population between 2000 and 2010.

Source: U.S. Bureau of the Census.

In fact, maps cannot help but be selective in the information they present and simplify this information by using cartographic symbols. Maps always show features at a different scale than they exist in reality, and the necessity to use projections to show the Earth's surface as flat always introduces some spatial distortion, as we discussed above. Maps, then, can distort and lie as readily as they can convey verifiable spatial data or scientifically valid analyses. The more that map users are aware of those possibilities, and the more understanding of map projections, symbolization, and common forms of thematic and reference mapping standards they possess, the more likely they are to reasonably question and clearly understand the messages maps communicate.

Contemporary Geospatial Technologies

The growth and advancement of three interrelated geospatial technologies—global positioning systems, remote sensing, and geographic information systems—has revolutionized geography and increased the geographer's ability to collect, analyze, and visually represent some forms of geographic data. Global positioning systems (GPSs) rely upon a system of 24 orbiting satellites, Earth-bound tracking stations that control the satellites, and portable receivers that determine exact geographic locations based on the time delay in signals received from three or more satellites

(technically, they determine location from an inference based on the time required for several signals to travel from the satellite to the Earth and back). Remote sensing allows the collection of vast amounts of geographic data, while geographic information systems (GISs) can integrate GPS, remote sensing, and other forms of spatial data. Google Earth and interactive mapping and navigation websites such as MapQuest are everyday uses of contemporary geographic research technologies.

Remote Sensing

Remote sensing is a relatively new term, but the process that it describes—detecting the nature of an object and the content of an area from a distance—is more than 150 years old. Soon after the development of the camera, photographs were being taken from balloons and kites. In the early 20th century, fixed-wing aircraft provided a platform for the camera and photographer, and by the 1930s, aerial photography from planned positions and routes permitted reliable data gathering for large and small area mapping purposes. Even today, high- and low-altitude aerial photography with returned film remains a widely used remote sensing technique. Standard photographic film detects reflected energy within the visible portion of the electromagnetic spectrum. It can be supplemented by special sensitized infrared film that has proved particularly useful for the recording of vegetation and hydrographic features and by nonphotographic imaging techniques, including thermal scanning (widely used for studying various aspects of water features

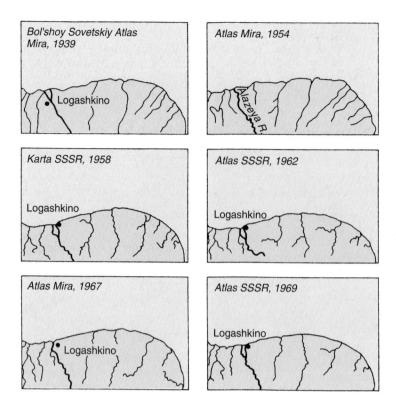

Figure 1.26 **The wandering town of Logashkino,** as traced in various Soviet atlases by Mark Monmonier. Deliberate, extensive cartographic "disinformation" and locational falsification, he reports, became a Cold War tactic of the Soviet Union. We usually use—and trust—maps to tell us exactly where things are located. On the maps shown, however, Logashkino migrates from west of the river away from the coast to east of the river on the coast, while the river itself gains and loses a distributary and, in 1954, the town itself disappears. The changing misinformation, Monmonier suggests, was intended to obscure from potential enemies the precise location of possible military targets.

Source: Mark Monmonier, How to Lie with Maps, *2nd Ed. © 1996. Reprinted by permission of the University of Chicago Press.*

such as ocean currents and water pollution and, because it can be employed during nighttime hours, for military surveillance and energy budget observations) and radar mapping (also operative night and day and useful for penetrating clouds and haze).

For more than 30 years, spacecraft (with or without crews) have supplemented the airplane as the vehicle for imaging Earth features. Among the advantages of satellites are the speed of coverage and the fact that views of large regions can be obtained. In addition, they are equipped to record and report back to Earth digitized information from multiple parts of the electromagnetic spectrum, including some that are outside the range of human eyesight. Satellites enable us to map the invisible, including atmospheric and weather conditions, in addition to providing images with applications in agriculture and forest inventory, land use classification, identification of geologic structures and mineral deposits, and more. The different sensors of the American Landsat satellites, first launched in 1972 (Landsat 7 was put aloft in 1999), are capable of resolving objects between 15 and 60 meters (50 and 200 ft) in size. Even sharper images are yielded by the French SPOT satellite (launched in 1986); its sensors can show objects that are larger than 10 meters (33 ft). Satellite imagery is relayed by electronic signals to receiving stations, where computers convert them into photolike images for use in scientific research and in mapping programs.

Geographic Information Systems (GISs)

Increasingly, digital computers, mapping software, and computer-based display units and printers are employed in the design and production of maps and in the development of databases used in map production. In computer-assisted cartography, the content of standard maps—reference and thematic—is digitized and stored in computers. The use of computers and printers in map production permits increases in the speed, flexibility, and accuracy of many steps in the mapmaking process but in no way reduces the obligation of the mapmaker to employ sound judgment in the design of the map or the communication of its content.

Geographic information systems (GISs) extend the use of digitized data and computer manipulation to investigate and display spatial information of all types. A GIS is both an integrated software package for handling, processing, and analyzing geographical data and a computer database in which every item of information is tied to a precise geographic location. In the section above that introduced geographic features, we discussed the fact that some features are better conceived of as objects and others as fields. As we mentioned there, this has implications for how we represent geographic information in the GIS. In the *vector approach,* reminiscent of object conceptualization, the precise location of each object—point, line, or area—in a distribution is described. In the *raster approach,* reminiscent of the field conceptualization, the study area is divided into a set of small (usually) square cells, with the content of each cell described or quantified (the rasters are analogous to pixels on a computer screen). The vector approach is more often suitable for human or cultural data, such as roads or cities, while the raster approach is more often suitable for natural geographic data, like elevations or rainfall. In either approach, a vast amount of different spatial information can be stored, accessed, compared, processed, analyzed, and displayed.

A GIS database, then, can be envisioned as a set of discrete informational overlays linked by reference to a basic locational grid of latitude and longitude (Figure 1.27) or some other coordinate system. The system then permits the separate display of the spatial information contained in the database. It allows the user to overlay maps of different themes, analyze the relations revealed, and compute spatial relationships. It shows aspects of spatial associations otherwise difficult to display on conventional maps, such as flows, interactions, and three-dimensional characteristics. In short, a GIS database, as a structured set of spatial information, has become a powerful tool for performing geographical analysis and synthesis.

A GIS data set may contain a great amount of place-specific information collected and published by the U.S. Census Bureau, including population distribution, race, ethnicity, income,

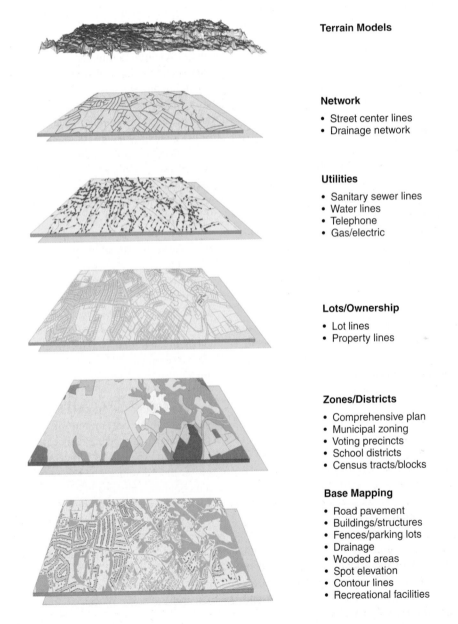

Terrain Models

Network
- Street center lines
- Drainage network

Utilities
- Sanitary sewer lines
- Water lines
- Telephone
- Gas/electric

Lots/Ownership
- Lot lines
- Property lines

Zones/Districts
- Comprehensive plan
- Municipal zoning
- Voting precincts
- School districts
- Census tracts/blocks

Base Mapping
- Road pavement
- Buildings/structures
- Fences/parking lots
- Drainage
- Wooded areas
- Spot elevation
- Contour lines
- Recreational facilities

Figure 1.27 A model of a GIS. A GIS incorporates three primary components: data storage capability, computer graphics programs, and statistical packages. In this example, the different layers of information are to be used in different combinations for city planning purposes. Different data sets, all selected for applicability to the questions asked, may be developed and used in urban geography, economic geography, transportation planning, industrial location work, and similar applications.

Source: Reprinted by permission of Shaoli Huang.

housing, employment, industry, farming, and so on. It may also hold environmental information downloaded from satellite imagery or taken from Geological Survey maps and other governmental and private sources. In human geography, the vast and growing array of spatial data has encouraged the use of GIS to explore models of regional economic and social structure; to examine transportation systems and urban growth patterns; and to study patterns of voting behavior, disease incidence, accessibility of public services, and a vast array of other topics. GISs are essential tools in the process of voter redistricting. For physical geographers, the analytic and modeling capabilities of GIS are fundamental to the understanding of processes and interrelations in the natural environment.

Because of the growing importance of GIS in all manner of public and private spatial inquiries, demand in the job market is high and growing for those skilled in its techniques. Most university courses in GIS are taught in Geography departments, and "GIS/remote sensing" is a primary occupational specialty for which many geography undergraduate and graduate majors seek preparation.

Mental Maps

Maps that shape our understanding of distributions and locations or influence our perception of the world around us are not always drawn on paper. We carry with us *mental maps* that in some ways are more accurate in reflecting our view of spatial reality than the formal maps created by geographers or cartographers. **Mental maps** are internal models or representations of an area or an environment developed by an individual on the basis of information or impressions received, interpreted, and stored. Sometimes, they leave out what are believed to be unnecessary details, and only important elements are incorporated. We use this information— this mental map—in organizing our daily activities: selecting our destinations and the sequence in which they will be visited, deciding on our routes of travel, recognizing where we are in relation to where we wish to be. A mental route map may also include reference points to be encountered on the chosen path of connection or on alternate lines of travel.

Such mental maps are every bit as real to their creators (and we all have them) as are the street maps or highway maps commercially available, and they are a great deal more immediate in their impact on our spatial decisions. We may choose routes or avoid neighborhoods not on objective grounds but on emotional or perceptual ones. In those choices, characteristics of people such as age or gender play an important role. For instance, the mental maps of women may contain danger zones where fear of sexual assault, harassment, or encounter with persons or conditions felt to be threatening is a determinant in routes chosen or times of journey. Whole sections of a community may be voids on our mental maps, as unknown as the interiors of Africa and South America were to Western Europeans two centuries ago. Our areas of awareness generally increase with the increasing mobility that comes with age, affluence, and education and may be enlarged or restricted for different social groups within the city (Figure 1.28).

Systems, Maps, and Models

The contents of areas are interrelated and constitute a **spatial system** that, in common with all systems, functions as a unit because its component parts are interdependent. Only rarely do individual elements of area operate in isolation, and to treat them as if they do is to lose touch with spatial reality. The systems of geographic concern are those in which the functionally important variables are spatial: location, distance, direction, density, connectivity, and the other basic concepts that we have reviewed. The systems that they define are not the same as regions, though spatial systems may be the basis for regional identification.

Systems have components, and the analysis of the role of components helps reveal the operation of the system as a whole. To conduct that analysis, individual system elements must be isolated for separate identification and, perhaps, manipulated to see their function within the structure of the system or subsystem. Maps and models are devices that geographers use to achieve that isolation and separate study.

Maps, as we have seen, are effective to the degree that they can segregate at an appropriate level of generalization those system elements selected for examination. By compressing, simplifying, and abstracting reality, maps record in manageable dimension the real-world conditions of interest. A model is a simplified abstraction of reality, designed to clarify relationships between its elements. Maps are a type of **model**, representing reality in an idealized form to make certain aspects more clear.

The complexities of spatial systems analysis—and the opportunities for quantitative analysis of systems made possible by computers and sophisticated statistical techniques—have led geographers to use other kinds of models in their work. Model building is the technique scientists use to simplify complex situations, to eliminate (as does the map) unimportant details, and to isolate for special study and analysis the role of one or more interacting elements in a total system. Models also allow geographers to conduct experiments on a simulation of a portion of reality instead of the reality itself, which is often very difficult, unethical, or impossible to do.

An interaction model discussed in Chapter 3, for instance, suggests that the amount of exchange expected between two places depends on the distance separating them and on their population size. The model indicates that the larger the places and the closer their distance, the greater is the amount of interaction. Such a model helps us to isolate the important components of the spatial system, to manipulate them separately, and to reach conclusions concerning their relative importance. When a model satisfactorily predicts the volume of intercity interaction in the majority of cases, the lack of agreement in a particular case leads to an examination of the circumstances contributing to the disparity. The quality of connecting roads, political barriers, or other variables may affect the specific places examined, and these causative elements may be isolated for further study.

Indeed, the steady pursuit of more refined and definitive analysis of human geographic questions—the "further study" that continues to add to our understanding of how people occupy and utilize the Earth, interact with each other, and organize and alter

NORTHRIDGE

BOYLE HEIGHTS

WESTWOOD

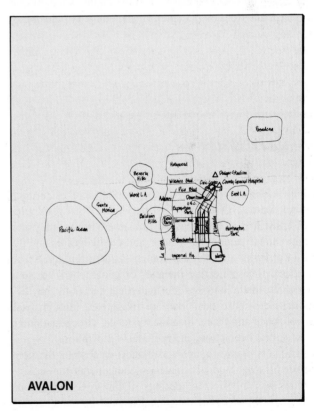

AVALON

Figure 1.28 Four mental maps of Los Angeles. The upper-middle-income residents of the Northridge and Westwood communities have expansive views of the metropolis, reflecting their mobility and area of travel. Inner-city residents of the Avalon community display a more restricted view of the city because of their lower incomes, social isolation, and reliance on public transportation. Even more limited is the mental map of Hispanic residents of the Boyle Heights community, which reflects their spatial and linguistic isolation within the metropolitan area.

Source: From Department of City Planning, City of Los Angeles, The Visual Environment of Los Angeles, 1971. *Reprinted by permission.*

Earth space—has led to the remarkably diversified, fascinating, and interesting yet coherent field of modern human geography. With the content of this introductory chapter as background to the nature, traditions, and tools of geography, we are ready to begin its exploration.

The Structure of This Book

By way of getting started, it is useful for you to know how the organization and topics of this text have been structured to help you reach the kinds of understandings we seek.

We begin in Chapters 2–4 with introductory material on cultural processes and spatial interactions among an unevenly distributed and expanding world population. Chapter 2 introduces the components and structure of culture, culture change, diffusion, and divergence. Chapter 3 presents characteristics of spatial interaction and spatial behavior that are common to all peoples and cultures. Chapter 4 examines population geography and the factors driving patterns of population movement, growth, and distribution.

While the book's first four chapters focus on geographic themes common to all peoples and cultures, Chapters 5–7 turn to the features that distinguish societies and culture realms and create patterns of unity and diversity in the cultural landscape. While there are innumerable ways in which human populations differ, we focus on spatial patterns of three major points of contrast: language and religion (Chapter 5), and ethnicity (Chapter 6).

Further, we examine the diversity of cultural identities and the expressions of those cultures in the landscape (Chapter 7). We pay particular attention to folk cultures—the material and nonmaterial aspects of daily life among groups insulated from outside influences through spatial isolation or cultural barriers (Chapter 7). Patterns of cultural diversity are in constant tension with unifying forces as the world experiences greater spatial interaction. Thus, we also examine ways in which folk cultures are undergoing erosion under the influence of globalized popular cultures.

Our focus shifts in Chapters 8–10 to the dynamic patterns of the global economy, examining spatial patterns of food and raw material production (Chapter 8), manufacturing and services (Chapter 9), and finally measures, spatial patterns, and models of economic development (Chapter 10). Economic development is generally accompanied by more formal systems of organizing society, resources, and territory. Thus, in Chapters 11–12, we examine systems of functional organization within systems of cities and inside individual cities (Chapter 11), as well as systems of political control of geographic space that range from the local to the international scale (Chapter 12). Human impact on the environment is an integral part of each chapter and is the topic of the concluding chapter of the book (Chapter 13). In concluding with human impacts, we return to the underlying concern of all geographic study: the relationship between human geographic patterns and processes and both the present conditions and future prospects of the physical and cultural landscapes we inhabit.

Summary

Geography is the study of the Earth's surface and its physical and cultural content. Throughout its long history, geography has remained consistent in its focus on human-environmental interactions, the interrelatedness of places, and the likenesses and differences in physical and cultural content of area that exist from place to place. The collective interests of geographers are summarized by the spatial and systems analytical questions they ask. The responses to those questions are interpreted through basic concepts of space and place, location, distance, direction, content evolution, spatial interaction, and regional organization.

Geographers employ maps and models to abstract the complex reality of space and to isolate its components for separate study. Maps are imperfect renderings of the three-dimensional Earth and its parts on a two-dimensional surface. In that rendering, some or all of the characteristics of the globe grid are distorted, but convenience and data manageability are gained. Spatial information may be depicted visually in a number of ways, each designed to simplify and to clarify the infinite complexity of spatial content. Geographers also use verbal and mathematical models for the same purpose, to abstract and analyze.

In their study of the Earth's surface as the occupied and altered space within which humans operate, some geographers concentrate on the integration of physical and cultural phenomena in a specific Earth area (regional geography). Other geographers may, instead, emphasize systematic geography through study of the Earth's physical systems of spatial and human concern or, as here, devote primary attention to people. This is a text in *human geography*. Its focus is on human interactions both with the physical environments people occupy and alter and with the cultural environments they have created. We are concerned with the ways people perceive the landscapes and regions they occupy, act within and between them, make choices about them, and organize them according to the varying cultural, political, and economic interests of human societies. This is a text clearly within the social sciences, but like all geography, its background is the physical Earth as the home of humans. As human geographers, our concern is with how that physical Earth has nurtured particular cultural choices and patterns, while at the same time that physical Earth has been altered by societies and cultures. In the next chapter, we begin with an inquiry about the roots and nature of culture.

KEY WORDS

absolute direction 9
absolute distance 10
absolute location 7
accessibility 14
administrative region 18
cartography 22
concentration 16
connectivity 14
cultural landscape 12
density 15
dispersion 16
develop 21
field 7
functional region 18
geographic feature 7
geographic information system (GIS) 26
globalization 14
globe 22

graticule 22
latitude 7
longitude 7
mental map 28
meridian 22
model 28
natural landscape 11
object 7
parallel 22
pattern 16
perceptual region 18
place 6
place stereotype 6
placelessness 6
prime meridian 22
projection 21
reference map 23
region 17

regional concept 18
relative direction 10
relative distance 10
relative location 9
remote sensing 25
scale 11
site 9
situation 9
space 6
spatial association 17
spatial diffusion 14
spatial distribution 15
spatial interaction 13
spatial system 28
thematic map 23
thematic region 18

FOR REVIEW

1. In what two meanings and for what different purposes do we refer to *location?*

2. Describe the *site* and the *situation* of the town where you live, work, or go to school.

3. What kinds of distance transformations are suggested by the term *relative distance?* How is the concept of *psychological distance* related to relative distance?

4. What are the common elements of *spatial distribution?* What different aspects of the spatial arrangement of things do they address?

5. What are the common characteristics of *regions?* How are *thematic* and *functional* regions different in concept and definition? What is a *perceptual region?*

6. List at least four properties of the globe grid (graticule). Why are globe grid properties distorted on maps?

7. What does *prime meridian* mean? What happens to the length of a degree of longitude as one approaches the poles?

8. What different ways of displaying statistical data on maps can you name and describe?

KEY CONCEPTS REVIEW

1. **What is the nature of geography and the role of human geography?** pp. 2–5.
   Geography is a *spatial* science concerned with how the content of Earth areas differs from place to place. It is the study of spatial variation in the world's physical and cultural (human) features. The emphasis of human geography is on the spatial variations in characteristics of peoples and cultures, on the way humans interact over space, and the ways they utilize and alter the natural landscapes they occupy, even as those landscapes influence culture.

2. **What are the fundamental geographic observations and their underlying concepts?** pp. 5–15.
   Basic geographic observations all concern the characteristics, content, and interactions of places. Their underlying concepts involve such place specifics as location, direction, distance, size, scale, physical and cultural attributes, interrelationships, and regional similarities and differences.

3. **What are the regional concept and the generalized characteristics of regions?** pp. 15–18.
   The regional concept tells us that physical and cultural features of the Earth's surface are rationally arranged by understandable processes. All recognized regions are characterized

by location, spatial extent, defined boundaries, and position within a hierarchy of regions. Regions may be "thematic" or "functional" in nature.

4. **Why do geographers use maps, and how do maps show spatial information?** pp. 18–25.

Maps are tools that geographers use to perform spatial analyses such as identifying regions and analyzing their content. They permit the study of areas and areal features too extensive to be completely viewed or understood on the Earth's surface itself. Thematic (statistical) maps may be either qualitative or quantitative. Their data may be shown in graduated circle, dot distribution, isoline, choropleth, or cartogram form.

5. **In what ways in addition to maps may spatial data be visualized or analyzed?** pp. 25–27.

Informally, we all create "mental maps" reflecting highly personalized but culturally overlapping impressions and information about the spatial arrangement of things (for example, buildings, streets, landscape features). More formally, geographers recognize the content of areas as forming a spatial system to which techniques of spatial systems analysis and model building are applicable.

ROOTS AND MEANING OF CULTURE:
INTRODUCTION

South African San hunter-gatherers are modern-day followers of the world's oldest, most enduring livelihood system.

Key Concepts

They buried him there in the cave where they were work-ing, less than 6 kilometers (4 miles) from the edge of the ice sheet. Outside stretched the tundra, summer feeding grounds for the mammoths whose ivory they had come so far to col-lect. Inside, near where they dug his grave, were stacked the tusks that they had gathered and were cutting and shaping. They prepared the body carefully and dusted it with red ocher, then buried it in an elaborate grave with tundra flowers and offerings of food, a brace-let on its arm, a pendant about its throat, and 40 to 50 polished rods of ivory by its side. It rested there, in modern Wales, undisturbed for some 18,000 years until discovered early in the 19th century. The 25-year-old hunter had died far from the group's home, some 650 kilometers (400 miles) away, near present-day Paris, France. He had been part of a routine annual summer expedition overland from the forested south across the as-yet-unflooded English Chan-nel to the mammoths' grazing grounds at the edge of the glacier.

As always, they were well prepared for the trip. Their boots were carefully made. Their sewn-skin leggings and tunics served well for travel and work; heavier fur parkas warded off the evening chill. They carried emergency food, fire-making equipment, and braided cord that they could fashion into nets, fishing lines, ropes, or thread. They traveled by reference to sun and stars, recogniz-ing landmarks from past journeys and occasionally consulting a crude map etched on bone.

Although the hunters returned bearing the sad news of their companion's death, they also brought the ivory to be carved and traded among the scattered peoples of Europe, from the Atlantic Ocean to the Ural Mountains.

As shown by their tools and equipment, their behaviors and be-liefs, these Stone Age travelers displayed highly developed and distinctive characteristics, primitive only from the vantage point of our own different technologies and customs. They represented the culmination of a long history of development of skills, of in-vention of tools, and of creation of lifestyles that set them apart from peoples elsewhere in Europe, Asia, and Africa, who pos-sessed still different cultural heritages.

To writers in newspapers and the popular press, the word *culture* means the arts (literature, painting, music, and the like). To a social scientist, however, **culture** is the specialized behav-ioral patterns, understandings, adaptations, and social systems that summarize a group of people's learned way of life. In this broader sense, culture is an ever-present part of the regional differences that are the essence of human geography. The visible and invisible evidences of culture—buildings and farming patterns, language, political organization, and ways of earning a living, for example—are all parts of the spatial diversity that human geographers study. Cultural differences over time may present contrasts as great as those between the Stone Age ivory hunters and modern urban Americans. Cultural differences in space result in human land-scapes with variations as subtle as the differing "feel" of urban Paris, Moscow, or New York, or as obvious as the sharp contrasts of rural Zimbabwe and the U.S. Midwest (Figure 2.1).

Because such tangible and intangible cultural differences exist and have existed in various forms for thousands of years, human geography attempts first to describe the pattern of cultural practices (traits) across the Earth's surface. Then it addresses the question

(a)

(b)

Figure 2.1 Culture is reflected in agricultural practices and in the look of the landscape. Compare (*a*) farmers using oxen to plow fields for planting in Bhutan and (*b*) the extensive fields and mechanized farming of the U.S. Midwest.

of why? Why, since humankind constitutes a single species, are cultures so varied? What and where were the origins of the differ-ent culture traits we now observe? How, from whatever limited areas individual culture traits developed, were they diffused over a wider portion of the globe? How did people who had roughly similar origins come to display significant areal differences in technology, social structure, ideology, and the innumerable other expressions of human cultural diversity? In what ways and why are there distinctive cultural variations even in presumed "melting pot" societies, such as the United States and Canada, or in the histori-cally homogeneous, long-established countries of Europe? How is knowledge about cultural differences important to us today? Some of the answers to these questions are to be found in the way that separate human groups developed techniques to solve regionally varied problems such as securing food, clothing, and shelter, and in the process, created a really distinctive customs and ways of life.

Components of Culture

Culture is transmitted within a society to succeeding generations by imitation, instruction, suggestion, and example. In short, while the capacity for culture is biological, culture itself is learned. As members of a social group, individuals acquire integrated sets of behavioral patterns, environmental and social perceptions, and knowledge of existing technologies. Of necessity, each of us learns the culture in which we are born and reared. But we need not—indeed, cannot—learn its totality. Age, sex, status, or occupation may dictate aspects of the cultural whole to which an individual is more or less likely to be exposed, and which it is more or less appropriate for an individual to internalize.

A culture, that is, despite overall generalized and identifying characteristics and even an outward appearance of uniformity, displays a social structure—a framework of roles and interrelationships of individuals and established groups. Each individual learns and is expected to adhere to the rules and conventions not only of the culture as a whole, but also of those specific to the subculture to which he or she belongs. And that subgroup may have its own recognized social structure (Figure 2.2). Think back to the different subgroups and aspects of your own national culture that you became part of (and left) as you progressed from childhood through high school and on to college-age adulthood and, perhaps, to first employment.

Many different cultures, then, can coexist within a given area, each with its own influence on the thoughts and behaviors of their separate members. Subcultures are groups that can be distinguished from the wider society by their cultural patterns. Within the United States, for example, we can readily recognize a variety of subcultures within the larger "American" culture: white, black, Hispanic, Asian American, or other ethnic groups; gay and straight; urban and rural; and many others. Human geography increasingly recognizes the pluralism of cultures within regions. In addition to examining the separate content and influence of those subcultures, it attempts to record and analyze the varieties of contested cultural interactions between them, including those of a political and economic nature.

Culture is a complexly interlocked web of behaviors, attitudes, and material artifacts. Realistically, its full and diverse content cannot be appreciated, and in fact may be wholly misunderstood, if we concentrate our attention only on limited, obvious traits. Distinctive eating utensils, the use of gestures, or the ritual of religious ceremony may summarize and characterize a culture for the casual observer. These are, however, individually insignificant parts of a much more complex structure that can be appreciated only when the whole is experienced.

Out of the richness and intricacy of human life, we seek to isolate for special study those more fundamental cultural variables that give structure and spatial order to societies. We begin with *culture traits*, the smallest distinctive units of culture. **Culture traits** range from the language spoken to the tools used or the games played. A trait may be an object (a fishhook, for example), a technique (weaving and knotting of a fishnet), or a belief (in the spirits resident in water bodies). Traits are the most elementary expression of culture, the building blocks of the complex behavioral patterns of distinctive groups of peoples. Of course, the same

Figure 2.2 Both the traditional rice farmer of rural Japan and the Tokyo commuter are part of a common Japanese culture. They occupy, however, vastly different positions in its social structure.

trait—the Christian religion, perhaps, or the Spanish language—may be part of more than one culture. Similarly, traits are sometimes clearly distinct, as in two completely different rules about the appropriateness of marrying first cousins, or somewhat overlapping, as in preferences for one or the other of two styles of rap music that share many common aspects.

But our discussion should not imply that culture traits exist in isolation—they are always interrelated. Individual cultural traits that are functionally interrelated comprise a **culture complex.** The existence of such complexes is universal. Keeping cattle was a *culture trait* of the Masai of Kenya and Tanzania. Related traits included the measurement of personal wealth by the number of cattle owned, a diet containing milk and the blood of cattle, and disdain for labor unrelated to herding. The assemblage of these

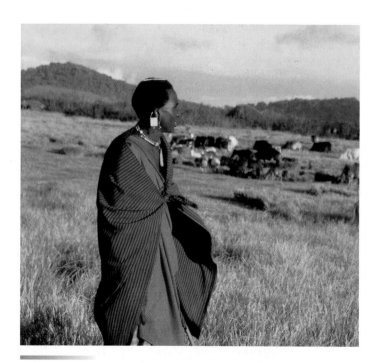

Figure 2.3 The formerly migratory Masai of Kenya are now largely sedentary, partially urbanized, and frequently owners of fenced farms. Cattle formed the traditional basis of Masai culture and were evidence of wealth and social status.

and other related traits yielded a culture complex descriptive of one aspect of Masai society (Figure 2.3). In exactly the same way, religious complexes, business behavior complexes, sports complexes, and others can easily be recognized in any society.

In the United States, for example, some environmentalists would like to wean Americans from their automobiles. However, a study of American culture reveals the difficulty in making such a change because automobiles are part of an interrelated cultural complex. Automobile brands and models speak of a person's status in U.S. society. Movies, video games, and sports often give automobiles a central role; movies such as *The Fast and the Furious* series, video games such as *Grand Theft Auto,* and NASCAR are familiar examples. Entire suburban landscapes have been built around the needs of the automobile. Even rites of passage often focus on the automobile: driver's education, passing the driver's exam, getting one's first automobile, picking up a date in one's automobile, and the practice of decorating the newlywed couple's automobile at the end of the wedding ceremony.

A **cultural system** is a broader generalization than a culture complex and refers to the collection of interacting culture traits and complexes that are shared by a group within a particular territory. Multiethnic societies, perhaps further subdivided by linguistic differences, varied food preferences, and a host of other internal differentiations, may nonetheless share enough joint characteristics to be recognizably distinctive cultural systems to themselves and others. Certainly, citizens of the "melting pot" United States would identify themselves as *Americans,* together constituting a unique culture system on the world scene.

Culture traits, complexes, and systems have a real extent. When they are plotted on maps, the regional character of the components

of culture is revealed. Although human geographers are interested in the spatial distribution of these individual elements of culture, their usual concern is with the **culture region,** a portion of the Earth's surface occupied by populations sharing recognizable and distinctive cultural characteristics. Examples include the political organizations societies devise, the religions they espouse, the form of economy they pursue, and even the type of clothing they wear, eating utensils they use, or kind of housing they occupy. There are as many such conceptual culture regions as there are culture traits and complexes recognized for population groups. Their recognition will be particularly important in the discussions of ethnic, folk, and popular culture that will occur in later chapters of this book. In those later reviews, as within the present chapter, we must keep in mind that within any single recognized culture region, groups united by the specific mapped characteristics may be competing and distinctive in other important culture traits.

Finally, a set of culture regions showing related culture complexes and landscapes may be grouped to form a **culture realm.** The term recognizes a large segment of the Earth's surface having an assumed fundamental uniformity in its cultural characteristics and showing a significant difference in them from adjacent realms. Culture realms are, in a sense, culture regions at the broadest scale of recognition. In fact, the scale is so broad and the diversity within the recognized realms so great that the very concept of realm may mislead more than it informs.

Indeed, the current validity of distinctive culture realms has been questioned in light of an assumed globalization of all aspects of human society and economy. The result of that globalization, it has been suggested, is a homogenization of cultures as economies are integrated and uniform consumer demands are satisfied by standardized commodities produced by international corporations. Certainly, the increasing mobility of people, goods, and information has reduced the rigidly compartmentalized ethnicities, languages, and religions of earlier periods. Cultural flows and exchanges have increased over the recent decades, and with them has come a growing worldwide intermixture of peoples and customs. Despite that growing globalism in all facets of life and economy, however, the world is far from homogenized. Although an increased sameness of commodities and experiences is encountered in distant places, even common and standardized items of everyday life—branded soft drinks, for example, or American fast-food franchises—take on unique regional meanings and roles, conditioned by the total cultural mix they enter. Those multiple regional cultural mixes are often defiantly distinctive and separatist as recurring incidents of ethnic conflict, civil war, and strident regionalism attest. Rather than successfully leveling and removing all regional contrasts, as frequently predicted, globalization continues to be countered by powerful forces of regionalism, place identity, and ethnicity.

If a global culture can be discerned, it may best be seen as a combination of multiple territorial cultures rather than a standardized uniformity. It is those territorially different cultural mixtures that are recognized by the culture realms suggested on Figure 2.4, which is only one of many such possible divisions. The spatial pattern and characteristics of these generalized realms will help us place the discussions and examples of human geography of later chapters in their regional contexts.

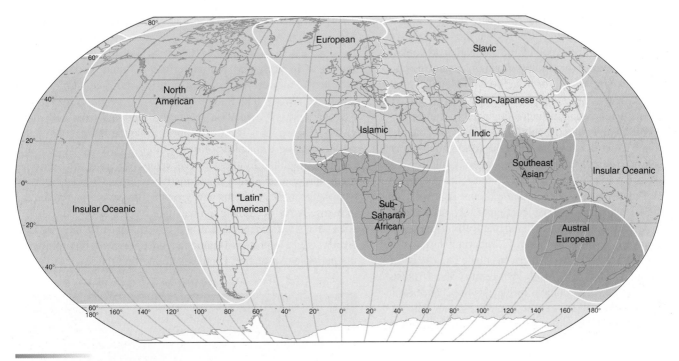

Figure 2.4 **Culture realms of the modern world.** This is just one of many possible subdivisions of the world into multifactor cultural regions.

Interaction of People and Environment

Culture develops in a physical environment that, in its way, contributes to differences among people. In premodern subsistence societies, the acquisition of food, shelter, and clothing, all parts of culture, depends on the utilization of the natural resources at hand. The interrelations of people to the environment of a given area, their perceptions and utilization of it, and their impact on it are interwoven themes of **cultural ecology**—the study of the relationship between a culture group and the natural environment that it occupies.

Cultural ecologists see evidence that subsistence pastoralists, hunter-gatherers, and gardeners adapted their productive activities—and, by extension, their social organizations and relationships—to the specific physical limitations of their different local habitats. Presumably, similar natural environmental conditions influenced the development of similar adaptive responses and cultural outcomes in separate, unconnected locales. That initial influence, of course, does not predetermine the details of the subsequent culture.

Environments as Controls

Geographers have long focused on the role of the physical environment in shaping human culture. However, most geographers today dismiss as intellectually limiting and demonstrably invalid extreme versions of **environmental determinism,** the belief that the physical environment exclusively shapes humans and their cultures. Environmental factors alone cannot account for the cultural variations that occur around the world. Levels of technology, systems of organization, and ideas about what is true and right are not dictated by environmental circumstances.

The environment does place certain limitations on the human use of territory. Such limitations, however, must be seen not as absolute, enduring restrictions but as relative to technologies, cost considerations, national aspirations, and linkages with the larger world. Human choices in the use of landscapes are affected by group perception of the feasibility and desirability of their settlement and exploitation. These are not circumstances inherent in the land. Mines, factories, and cities have been created in the formerly nearly unpopulated tundra and forests of Siberia as a reflection of Russian developmental programs, not in response to recent environmental improvement.

Possibilism is the viewpoint promoted by late-19th- and early-20th-century French geographer Paul Vidal de la Blache. He argued that the natural environment constrains or limits culture, making some cultural variants more or less possible than others, but it does not strictly determine culture. The needs, traditions, and level of technology of a culture affect how that culture assesses the possibilities of an area and shape what choices the culture makes regarding them. Each society uses natural resources in accordance with its circumstances. Changes in a group's technical abilities or objectives bring about changes in its perceptions of the usefulness of the land. Possibilism is thus a form of environment-culture interactionism.

Unlike some social scientists, however, geographers generally do not accept the extreme opposite of environmental determinism—**cultural autonomy**—that cultures are equally likely to develop any particular set of cultural traits no matter what the environmental circumstances. For example, evidence suggests the nature of some environmental limitations on the use of land area. The vast majority of the world's population is differentially concentrated on less than one-half of the Earth's land surface, as Figure 4.21 indicates. Areas with relatively mild climates and flat topographies that offer a supply of fresh water, fertile soil, and abundant mineral resources are densely settled, reflecting in part the different potentials of the land under earlier technologies to support population. Even today, the polar regions, high and rugged mountains, deserts, and some hot and humid lowland areas contain very few people. If resources for feeding, clothing, or housing ourselves within an area are lacking, or if we do not recognize them there, there is no inducement for people to occupy a territory.

Environments that do contain such recognized resources provide the framework within which a culture operates. Coal, oil, and natural gas have been in their present locations throughout human history, but they were rarely of use to preindustrial cultures and did not impart any understood advantage to their sites of occurrence. Not until the Industrial Revolution did coal deposits gain importance and come to influence the location of such great industrial complexes as the Midlands in England, the Ruhr in Germany, and the steel-making districts formerly so important in parts of northeastern United States. Native Americans made one use of the environment around Pittsburgh, while 19th-century industrialists made quite another. The environment influences the chances that a thriving steel industry will develop in one place rather than another, but only when the technological and economic conditions in the culture support steel-making as an activity.

Human Impacts

People are also able to modify their environment, and this is the other half of the human-environment relationship of geographic concern. Geography, including cultural geography, examines both the reactions of people to the physical environment and their impact on that environment. By using our environment, we modify it—in part, through the material objects we place on the landscape: cities, farms, roads, and so on (Figure 2.5). The form these take is the product of the kind of culture group in which we live. The **cultural landscape,** the Earth's surface as modified by human action, is the tangible physical record of a given culture. House types, transportation networks, parks and cemeteries, and the size and distribution of settlements are among the indicators of the use that humans have made of the land.

Human actions, both deliberate and inadvertent, have modified or even destroyed the environment for perhaps as long as humankind has existed. People have used, altered, and replaced the vegetation in wide areas of the tropics and midlatitudes. They have hunted to extinction vast herds and whole species of animals. They have, through overuse and abuse of the Earth and its

resources, rendered sterile and unpopulated formerly productive and attractive regions.

Fire has been called the first great tool of humans, and the impact of its early and continuing use is found on nearly every continent. Poleward of the great rain forests of equatorial South America, Africa, and South Asia lies the *tropical savanna* of extensive grassy vegetation separating scattered trees and forest groves (Figure 2.6). The trees appear to be the remnants of naturally occurring tropical dry forests, thorn forests, and scrub now largely obliterated by the use, over many millennia, of fire to remove the unwanted and unproductive trees and to clear off old grasses for more nutritious new growth. The grasses supported the immense herds of grazing animals that were the basis of hunting societies. After independence, the government of Kenya in East Africa sought to protect its national game preserves by prohibiting the periodic use of fire. It quickly found that the immense herds

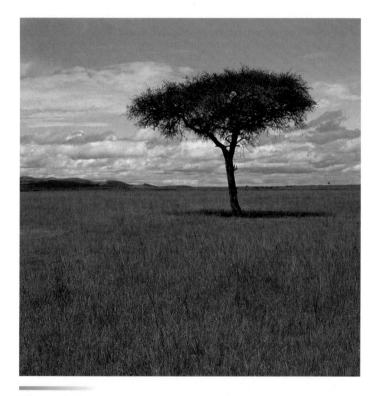

Figure 2.6 The parklike landscape of grasses and trees characteristic of the tropical savanna is seen in this view from Kenya, in Africa.

Figure 2.5 The physical and cultural landscapes of Cape Town, South Africa, in juxtaposition. Advanced societies are capable of so altering the circumstances of nature that the cultural landscapes that they create become the main controlling environment.

of gazelles, zebras, antelope, and other grazers (and the lions and other predators that fed on them) that tourists came to see were being replaced by less-appealing browsing species—rhinos, hippos, and elephants. With fire prohibited, the forests began to reclaim their natural habitat and the grassland fauna was replaced.

The same form of vegetation replacement occurred in midlatitudes. The grasslands of North America were greatly extended by Native Americans who burned the forest margin to extend grazing areas and to drive animals in the hunt. The control of fire in modern times has resulted in the advance of the forest once again in formerly grassy areas of Colorado, northern Arizona, and other parts of the U.S. West.

Examples of adverse human impact abound. The *Pleistocene overkill*—the Stone Age loss of whole species of large animals on all inhabited continents—is often ascribed to the unrestricted hunting to extinction carried on by societies familiar with fire who drove animals and used hafted weapons (with handles) to slaughter them. With these methods, according to one estimate, about 40 percent of African large-animal genera passed to extinction. The majority of large mammal, reptile, and flightless bird species had disappeared from Australia around 46,000 years ago; in North America, some two-thirds of original large mammals had succumbed by 11,000 years ago under pressure from the hunters migrating to and spreading across the continent. Although some have suggested that climatic changes or pathogens carried by dogs, rats, and other camp followers were at least partially responsible, human action is the more generally accepted explanation for the abrupt faunal changes. No uncertainty exists in the record of faunal destruction by the Maori of New Zealand or of Polynesians who had exterminated some 80 percent to 90 percent of South Pacific bird species—as many as 2,000 in all—by the time Captain James Cook arrived in the 18th century. Similar destruction of key marine species—Caribbean sea turtles, sea cows off the coast of Australia, sea otters near Alaska, and others elsewhere—as early as 10,000 years ago resulted in environmental damage whose effects continue to the present.

Chaco Canyon Desolation

It is not certain when they first came, but by A.D. 1000, the Anasazi people were building a flourishing civilization in present-day Arizona and New Mexico. They were corn farmers, thriving during the 300 years or so of the medieval warm period, beginning about A.D. 900 in the American Southwest. In the Chaco Canyon alone, they erected as many as 75 towns, all centered around pueblos, huge stone-and-adobe apartment buildings as tall as five stories and with as many as 800 rooms. These were the largest and tallest buildings of North America prior to the construction of iron-framed "cloudscrapers" in major cities at the end of the 19th century. An elaborate network of roads and irrigation canals connected and supported the pueblos. About A.D. 1200, the settlements were abruptly abandoned. The Anasazi, advanced in their skills of agriculture and communal dwelling, were— according to some scholars— forced to move on by the ecological disaster their pressures had brought to a fragile environment.

They needed forests for fuel and for the hundreds of thousands of logs used as beams and bulwarks in their dwellings. The pinyon-juniper woodland of the canyon was quickly depleted. For larger timbers needed for construction, the Anasazi first harvested stands of ponderosa pine found some 40 kilometers (25 miles) away. As early as A.D. 1030 these, too, were exhausted, and the community switched to spruce and Douglas fir from mountaintops surrounding the canyon.

When they were gone by 1200, the Anasazi fate was sealed—not only by the loss of forest but by the irreversible ecological changes deforestation and agriculture had occasioned. With forest loss came erosion that destroyed the topsoil. The surface water channels that had been built for irrigation were deepened by accelerated erosion, converting them into enlarging arroyos useless for agriculture.

The material roots of their culture destroyed, the Anasazi turned upon themselves; warfare convulsed the region and, compelling evidence suggests, cannibalism was practiced. Smaller groups sought refuge elsewhere, re-creating on reduced scale their pueblo way of life but now in nearly inaccessible, highly defensible mesa and cliff locations. The destruction they had wrought destroyed the Anasazi in turn.

Figure 2.7 Now treeless, Easter Island once was lushly forested. The statues (some weighing up to 85 tons) dotting the island were rolled to their locations and lifted into place with logs.

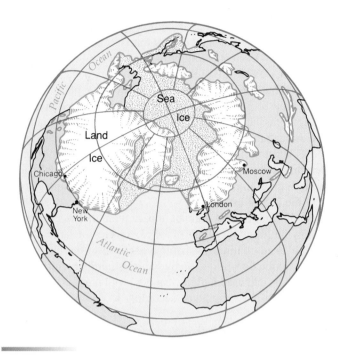

Figure 2.8 **Maximum extent of glaciation.** In their fullest development, glaciers of the most recent Ice Age covered large parts of Eurasia and North America. Even areas not covered by ice were affected as ocean levels dropped and rose and climate and vegetation regions changed with glacial advance and retreat.

Not only the destruction of animals but of the life-supporting environment itself has been a frequent consequence of human misuse of areas (see the feature "Chaco Canyon Desolation"). North Africa, the "granary of Rome" during the empire, became wasted and sterile in part because of mismanagement. Roman roads standing high above the surrounding barren wastes give testimony to the erosive power of wind and water when natural vegetation is unwisely removed and farming techniques are inappropriate. Easter Island in the South Pacific was covered lushly with palms and other trees when Polynesians settled there about A.D. 400. By the beginning of the 18th century, Easter Island had become the barren wasteland that it remains today. Deforestation increased soil erosion, removed the supply of timbers needed for the vital dugout fishing canoes, and made it impossible to move the massive stone statues that were significant in the islanders' religion (Figure 2.7). With the loss of livelihood resources and the collapse of religion, warfare broke out and the population was decimated. A similar tragic sequence is occurring on Madagascar in the Indian Ocean today. Despite current romantic notions, early societies did not necessarily live in harmony with their environment.

However, economic and technological developments in culture allow much greater impacts on the natural environment, and in general, the more technologically advanced and complex the culture, the more apparent is its impact on the natural landscape. In sprawling urban-industrial societies, the cultural landscape has come to outweigh the natural physical environment in its impact on most people's daily lives. It interposes itself between "nature" and humans, and residents of the cities of such societies—living and working in climate-controlled buildings, driving to enclosed shopping malls—can go through life with much less contact with or concern about the physical environment.

Roots of Culture

Earlier humans found the physical environment more immediate and controlling than we do today. Some 11,000 years ago, the massive glaciers—moving ice sheets of great depth—that had covered much

of the land and water of the Northern Hemisphere (Figure 2.8) began to retreat. Animal, plant, and human populations that had been spatially confined by both the ice margin and the harsh climates of middle-latitude regions began to spread, colonizing newly opened territories. The end of the *Paleolithic* (Old Stone Age) is the period near the end of glaciation during which small and scattered groups like the ivory hunters at this chapter's start began to develop regional variations in their ways of life and livelihood.

All were **hunter-gatherers,** preagricultural people dependent on the year-round availability of plant and animal foodstuffs that they could secure with the rudimentary stone tools and weapons at their disposal. Even during the height of the Ice Age, the unglaciated sections of western, central, and northeastern Europe, which today are home to productive farms, forests and cities, were then covered with tundra vegetation, the mosses, lichens, and low shrubs typical of areas too cold to support forests. Southeastern Europe and southern Russia had forest, tundra, and steppe (grasslands), and the Mediterranean areas, which today have shrub and scrub-oak vegetation, had forest cover (Figure 2.9). Gigantic herds of herbivores—reindeer, bison, mammoth, and horses—browsed, bred, and migrated throughout the tundra and the grasslands. Abundant animal life filled the forests.

Human migration northward into present-day Sweden, Finland, and Russia demanded a much more elaborate set of tools and provision for shelter and clothing than had previously been required. It necessitated the crossing of a number of ecological barriers and the occupation of previously avoided difficult environments. By the end of the Paleolithic period, humans had spread to all the continents but Antarctica, carrying with them their adaptive hunting-gathering cultures and social organizations.

Figure 2.9 Late Paleolithic environments of Europe. During the late Paleolithic period, new food-gathering, shelter, and clothing strategies were developed to cope with harsh and changing environments, so different from those in Europe today.

The settlement of the lands bordering the Pacific Ocean is suggested in Figure 2.10. As they occupied different regions, hunter-gatherers focused on a diversity of foodstuffs. Some specialized in marine or river resources, while others were wholly dependent on land plants and animals. In all cases, their material culture reflected the different climate and vegetation regions they occupied, the tools they developed to exploit the resources on which they depended, and the housing and clothing solutions they differently adopted. Even today, African Bushmen have few cultural similarities with Inuit (Eskimo) hunting-fishing societies, though both culture groups are spoken of as "hunter-gatherers."

While spreading, the total population also increased. But hunting and foraging bands require considerable territory to support a relatively small number of individuals. There were contacts between groups and, apparently, even planned gatherings for trade, socializing, and selecting mates from outside the home group. Nevertheless, the bands tended to live in isolation. Estimates place the Paleolithic population of the entire island of Great Britain, which was on the northern margin of habitation, at only some 400–500 persons living in widely separated families of 20–40 people. Total world population at about 9000 B.C. probably ranged from 5 to 10 million. Variations in the types of tools characteristic of different population groups steadily increased as people migrated and encountered new environmental problems.

Improved tool technology greatly extended the range of possibilities in the use of locally available materials. The result was more efficient and extensive exploitation of the physical environment than had been possible earlier. At the same time, regional contrasts in plant and animal life and in environmental conditions accelerated the differentiation of culture between isolated groups who under earlier, less varied conditions had shared common characteristics.

Figure 2.10 Settlement of the Americas and the Pacific basin. Genetic studies suggest humans spread around the globe from their Old World origins beginning some 100,000 years ago. Their time of arrival in the Western Hemisphere, however, is uncertain. The older view claimed that earliest migrants to the Americas, the ancestors of modern Amerindian groups, crossed the Bering land bridge in three different waves beginning 11,500 years ago. Recent evidence suggests that those North Asian land migrants encountered (and conquered or absorbed) earlier occupants who had arrived from Europe, Polynesia, and coastal East Asia by boat traveling along frozen or open shorelines. Although genetic and linguistic research yields mixed conclusions, physical evidence considered solid by some investigators indicates that the first Asian arrivals came at least 22,000 years and more likely 30,000 or more years ago. Eastern United States artifacts that have been assigned dates of 17,000 to 30,000 years ago hint at European arrivals as early as those of coastal Asians; a South Carolina site found in 2004 has been dated at 50,000 years ago. Many researchers, however, caution that any New World population dates earlier than 18,000 years ago are questionable, and that the first migrants from that period probably were most closely related to prehistoric Jomon and later Ainu groups of Japan who crossed over the Bering land bridge.

Within many environments, even harsh ones, the hunting and foraging process was not particularly demanding of either time or energy. Recent studies of South African San people (Bushmen), for example, indicate that such bands survive well on the equivalent of a 2½-day workweek. Time was available for developing skills in working flint and bone for tools, in developing regionally distinctive art and sculpture, and in making decorative beads and shells for personal adornment and trade. By the end of the Ice Age (about 11,000 to 12,000 years ago), language, religion, long-distance trade, permanent settlements, and social stratification within groups appear to have been well developed in many culture areas.

What was learned and created was transmitted within the cultural group. The increasing variety of adaptive strategies and technologies and the diversity of noneconomic creations in art, religion, language, and custom meant an inevitable cultural variation of humankind. That diversification began to replace the rough social uniformity among hunting and gathering people that had been based on their similar livelihood challenges, informal leadership structures, small-band kinship groups, and the like (Figure 2.11).

Seeds of Change

The retreat of the last glaciers marked the end of the Paleolithic era and the beginning of successive periods of cultural evolution, leading from basic hunting and gathering economies at the outset through the development of agriculture and animal husbandry to, ultimately, the urbanization and industrialization of modern societies and economies. Since not all cultures passed through all stages at the same time, or even at all, **cultural divergence** between human groups became evident.

Glacial recession brought new ecological conditions to which people had to adapt. The weather became warmer and forests began to appear on the open plains and tundras of Europe and northern China. In the Middle East, where much plant and animal domestication would later occur, savanna (grassland) vegetation replaced more arid landscapes. Populations grew and, through hunting, depleted the large herds of grazing animals already retiring northward with the retreating glacial front.

Further population growth demanded new food bases and production techniques, for the **carrying capacity**—the number of persons supportable within a given area by the technologies at their disposal—of the Earth for hunter-gatherers is low. The *Mesolithic* (Middle Stone Age) period, from about 11,000 to 5000 B.C. in Europe, marked the transition from the collection of food to its production. These stages of the Stone Age—occurring during different time spans in different world areas—mark distinctive changes in tools, tasks, and social complexities of the cultures that experienced the transition from "Old" to "Middle" to "New" Stone Age.

Figure 2.11 Hunter-gatherers practiced the most enduring lifestyle in human history, trading it for the sometimes more arduous life of farmers due to the necessity to provide larger quantities of less diversified foodstuffs for a growing population. For hunter-gatherers (unlike their settled farmer rivals and successors), age and sex differences, not caste or economic status, were and are the primary basis for the division of labor and of interpersonal relations. Here, a San (Bushman) hunter of Botswana, Africa, stalks his prey. Men also help collect the gathered food that constitutes 80 percent of the San diet.

Agricultural Origins and Spread

The population of hunter-gatherers rose slowly at the end of the glacial period. As rapid climatic fluctuation adversely affected their established plant and animal food sources, people independently, in more than one world area, experimented with the *domestication* of plants and animals. There is no agreement on whether the domestication of animals preceded or followed that of plants. The sequence may well have been different in different areas. What appears certain is that animal domestication—the successful breeding of species to serve human needs—began during the Mesolithic, not as a conscious economic effort by humans but as outgrowths of the keeping of small or young wild animals as pets and the attraction of scavenger animals to the refuse of human settlements. The assignment of religious significance to certain animals and the docility of others to herding by hunters all strengthened the human-animal connections that ultimately led to full domestication. Eventually, nearly everyone in the world would come to obtain their food via agriculture rather than hunting and gathering (see discussion of Innovation below). This had such dramatic effects on the way humans spent their daily lives, as well as the way they interrelated with the natural environment, that it is often referred to as the *Agricultural Revolution*.

Radiocarbon dates suggest the occurrence of the domestication of pigs in southeastern Turkey and of goats in the Near East as early as 8000–8400 B.C., of sheep in Turkey by about 7500 B.C., and of cattle and pigs in both Greece and the Near East about 7000 B.C. North Africa, India, and southeastern Asia were other Old World domestication sources, as were—less successfully—Mesoamerica and the Andean Uplands. Although there is evidence that the concept of animal domestication diffused from limited source regions, once its advantages were learned, numerous additional domestications were accomplished elsewhere. The widespread natural occurrence of species able to be domesticated made that certain. Cattle of different varieties, for example, were domesticated in India, north-central Eurasia, Southeast Asia, and Africa. Pigs and various domestic fowl are other examples.

The domestication of plants, like that of animals, appears to have occurred independently in more than one world region over a time span of between 10,000 and perhaps as long as 20,000 years ago. A strong case can be made that most widespread Eurasian food crops were first cultivated in the Near East beginning some 12,000 years ago, and dispersed rapidly from there across the mid-latitudes of the Old World. However, clear evidence also exists that African peoples were raising crops of wheat, barley, dates, lentils, and chickpeas on the floodplains of the Nile River as early as 18,500 years ago. In other world regions, farming began more recently; the first true farmers in the Americas appeared in Mexico no more than 5,000 years ago.

Familiarity with plants of desirable characteristics is universal among hunter-gatherers. In those societies, females were assigned the primary food-gathering role and thus developed the greatest familiarity with nutritive plants. Their fundamental role in initiating crop production to replace less reliable food gathering seems certain. Indeed, women's major contributions as innovators of technology—in food preparation and clothing production, for example—or as inventors of such useful and important items as baskets and other containers, baby slings, yokes for carrying burdens, and the like are unquestioned.

Agriculture itself, however, may not have been an "invention" as such, but the logical extension to food species of plant selection and nurturing habits developed for nonfood varieties. Plant poisons applied to hunting arrows or spread on lakes or streams to

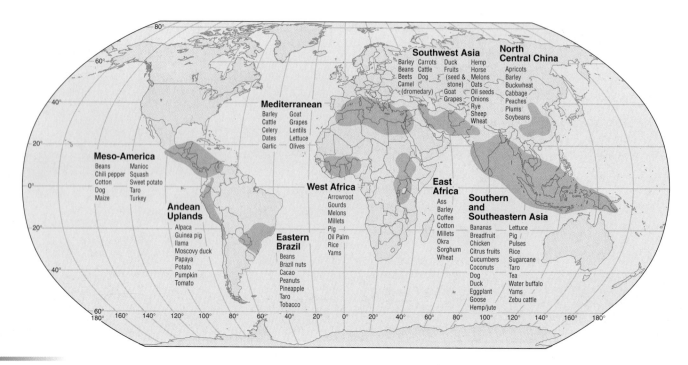

Figure 2.12 **Chief centers of plant and animal domestication.** The Southern and Southeastern Asia center was characterized by the domestication of plants such as taro, which are propagated by the division and replanting of existing plants (vegetative reproduction). Reproduction by the planting of seeds (e.g., maize and wheat) was more characteristic of Mesoamerica and Southwest Asia. The African and Andean areas developed crops reproduced by both methods. The lists of crops and livestock are selective, not exhaustive.

stun fish made food gathering easier and more certain. Plant dyes and pigments were universally collected or prepared for personal adornment or article decoration. Medicinal and mood-altering plants and derivatives were known, gathered, protected, and cultivated by all early cultures. Indeed, persuasive evidence exists to suggest that early gathering and cultivation of grains was not for grinding and baking as bread but for brewing as beer, a beverage that became so important in some cultures (for religious and nutritional reasons) that it may well have been a first and continuing reason for sedentary agricultural activities.

Nevertheless, full-scale domestication of food plants, like that of animals, can be traced to a limited number of origin areas identified by geographer Carl Sauer and other scientists (Figure 2.12). Although there were several source regions, certain uniformities united them. In each, domestication focused on plant species selected apparently for their capability of providing large quantities of storable calories or protein. In each, there was a population that was already well fed and able to devote time to the selection, propagation, and improvement of plants available from a diversified vegetation. Agricultural innovation would likely have occurred in relatively fertile and productive areas like river valleys and coastal plains. Some speculate, however, that grain domestication in the Near East may have been a forced inventive response, starting some 13,000 years ago, to food shortages reflecting abrupt increases in summertime temperatures and aridity in the Jordan Valley. That environmental stress—reducing summer food supplies and destroying habitats of wild game—favored the selection and cultivation of short-season annual grains and legumes whose seeds could be stored and planted during cooler, wetter winter growing seasons.

In the tropics and humid subtropics, selected plants were apt to be those that reproduced vegetatively—from roots, tubers, or cuttings. Outside of those regions, wild plants reproducing from seeds were more common and the objects of domestication. Although there was some duplication, each of the origin areas developed crop complexes characteristic of itself alone, as Figure 2.12 summarizes. From each, there was dispersion of crop plants to other areas, slowly at first under primitive systems of population movement and communication (Figure 2.13), more rapidly and extensively with the onset of more modern transportation and communication technologies.

While adapting wild plant stock to agricultural purposes, the human cultivators, too, adapted. They assumed sedentary residence to protect the planted areas from animal, insect, and human predators. They developed labor specializations and created more formalized and expansive religious structures in which fertility and harvest rites became important elements. The regional contrasts between hunter-gatherer and sedentary agricultural societies increased. Where the two groups came in contact, farmers were the victors and hunter-gatherers the losers in the competition for territorial control. The contest continued into modern times. During the past 500 years, European expansion totally dominated the hunting and gathering cultures it encountered in large parts of the world such as North America and Australia (See the feature "Is Geography Destiny?"). Even today, in the rain forests of central Africa, Bantu farmers put continuing pressure on hunting and gathering Pygmies, and in southern Africa, Hottentot herders and Bantu farmers constantly advance on the territories of the San (Bushmen) hunter-gatherer bands. The contrast and conflict between the hunter-gatherers and agriculturalists provide dramatic evidence of cultural divergence.

(a)

(b)

Figure 2.13 The migration of the first farmers out of the Middle East into Europe starting about 10,000 years ago is presumably traced by blood and gene markers. If the gene evidence interpretation is valid, the migrants spread at a rate of about 1 kilometer (five-eighths of a mile) per year, gradually interbreeding with and replacing the indigenous European hunter-gatherers throughout that continent.

Source: Adapted from L. Luca Cavalli-Sforza, Paolo Menozzi, and Alberto Piazza. The History and Geography of Human Genes. *Princeton, N.J.: Princeton University Press (1994).*

Figure 2.14 (*a*) The Mediterranean scratch plow, the earliest form of this basic agricultural tool, was essentially an enlarged digging stick dragged by an ass, an ox, or—as here in the mountains of Peru—by a pair of oxen. The scratch plow represented a significant technological breakthrough in human use of tools and animal power in food production. (*b*) Its earliest evidence is found in Egyptian tomb drawings and in art preserved from the ancient Middle East, but it was elsewhere either independently invented or introduced by those familiar with its use. (See also Figure 2.17a.)

Neolithic Innovations

The domestication of plants and animals began during the Mesolithic period, but in its refined form it marked the onset of the *Neolithic* (New Stone Age). Like other Stone Age levels, the Neolithic was more a stage of cultural development than a specific span of time. The term implies the creation of an advanced set of tools and technologies to deal with the conditions and needs encountered by an expanding, sedentary population whose economy was based on the agricultural management of the environment (Figure 2.14).

Not all peoples in all areas of the Earth made the same cultural transition at the same time. In the Near East, from which most of our knowledge of this late prehistoric period comes, the Neolithic lasted from approximately 8000 to 3500 B.C. There, as elsewhere, it brought complex and revolutionary changes in human life. Culture began to alter at an accelerating pace, and change itself became a way of life. In an interconnected adaptive web, technological and social innovations came with a speed and genius surpassing all previous periods.

In his 1997 Pulitzer Prize–winning book *Guns, Germs, and Steel: The Fates of Human Societies,* Jared Diamond argues that "history followed different courses for different peoples because of differences among peoples' environments, not because of biological differences among peoples themselves." The environmental differences that counted—and that led to world dominance by Eurasians—were the availability in Eurasia of an abundance of plants and animals suitable for domestication on a landmass whose east-west orientation made easy the long-distance transfer of animals, food crops, and technologies. No other continent had either of those advantages, according to Diamond.

Food production was the key. Although agriculture was independently developed in several world areas after the end of the Ice Age, the inhabitants of the Middle East were fortunate in having an abundance of plants suitable for domestication. These included six of the eight most important food grasses, among them ancestral wheat, plants that adapted easily to cultivation, grew rapidly, and had high nutritive value and high population-supporting potential. Eurasia also

had an abundance of large animals that could be domesticated, including the cow, goat, pig, sheep, and horse, giving a further spur to population growth. In addition, by living in close proximity to animals, Eurasians contracted and developed immunities to the epidemic diseases that would later devastate the inhabitants of other continents when the diseases were brought to their shores by Eurasian explorers and colonizers.

The food-producing technologies developed in such hearth regions as the Middle East were easily diffused along the immense east-west axis of Eurasia, where roughly similar climates suited to the same crop and livestock mix were encountered from China to Spain. In addition, Eurasia's great size meant a great number of different people, each capable of developing new technologies that in turn could be diffused over long distances. Population growth, agricultural productivity, and inventive minds led to civilizations—central governments, cities, labor specializations, textiles, pottery, writing, mathematics, long-distance trade, metal working, and eventually, the guns that conquering Eurasians carried to other continents.

No other world region enjoyed Eurasia's environmental and subsequent population and technological advantages. The few food crops developed in Africa or the Americas could not effectively diffuse across the climatic and ecological barriers in those north-south aligned continents. Because of accidents of nature or massive predation of large animals by early inhabitants, sub-Saharan Africa and Australia yielded no domesticated animals, and the Americas had only the localized llama. Without the food bases and easy latitudinal movement of Eurasia, populations elsewhere remained smaller, more isolated, and collectively less inventive. When the voyages of discovery and colonization began in the 15th century, Eurasian advantages proved overwhelming. Decimated by diseases against which they had no resistance, without the horses, armor, firearms, or organization of their conquerors, inhabitants of other continents found themselves quickly subdued and dominated—not, in Diamond's opinion, because of innate inferiority, but because of geographical disadvantages that limited or delayed their developmental prospects.

Humans learned the arts of spinning and weaving plant and animal fibers. They learned to use the potter's wheel and to fire clay and make utensils. They developed techniques of brick making, mortaring, and construction, and they discovered the skills of mining, smelting, and casting metals. On the foundation of such technical advancements, a more complex exploitative culture appeared and a more formal economy emerged. A stratified society based on labor and role specialization replaced the rough equality of adults in hunting and gathering economies (various forms of sex-role division of labor largely continued, however). Special local advantages in resources or products promoted the development of long-distance trading connections, which the invention of the sailboat helped to maintain.

By the end of the Neolithic period, certain spatially restricted groups, having created a food-producing rather than a foraging society, undertook the purposeful restructuring of their environment. They began to modify plant and animal species; to manage soil, terrain, water, and mineral resources; and to use animal energy to supplement that of humans. They used metal to make refined tools and superior weapons—first pure copper, and later the alloy of tin and copper that produced the harder, more durable bronze. Humans had moved from adopting and shaping to the art of creating.

As people gathered together in larger communities, new and more formalized rules of conduct and control emerged, especially important where the use of land was involved. We see the beginnings of governments to enforce laws and specify punishments for wrongdoers. The protection of private property, so much greater in amount and variety than that carried by the nomad, demanded more complex legal codes, as did the enforcement of the rules of societies increasingly stratified by social privileges and economic status.

Religions became more formalized. For the hunter, religion could be individualistic, and his worship was concerned with personal health and safety. The collective concerns of farmers were based on the calendar: the cycle of rainfall, the seasons of planting and harvesting, the rise and fall of waters to irrigate the crops, and so on. Religions responsive to those concerns developed rituals appropriate to seasons of planting, irrigation, harvesting, and thanksgiving. An established priesthood was required, one that stood not only as an intermediary between people and the forces of nature, but also as an authenticator of the timing and structure of the needed rituals. In daily life, occupations became increasingly specialized. Metal-workers, potters, sailors, priests, merchants, scribes, and in some areas, warriors complemented the work of farmers and hunters.

Culture Hearths

The social and technical revolutions that began in and characterized the Neolithic period were initially spatially confined. The new technologies, the new ways of life, and the new social structures diffused from those points of origin and were selectively adopted by people who were not a party to their creation. The term **culture hearth** is used to describe such centers of innovation and invention, from which clusters of key culture traits and elements moved to exert an influence on surrounding regions.

The hearth may be viewed as the "cradle" of any culture group whose developed systems of livelihood and life created a distinctive cultural landscape. Most of the thousands of hearths that evolved across the world remained at low levels of social and technical development. Only a few developed the trappings of *civilizations*. The definition of that term is not precise, but indicators of its achievement are commonly assumed to be writing, metallurgy, long-distance trade connections, astronomy and mathematics, social stratification and labor specialization, formalized governmental systems, and a structured urban culture.

Several major culture hearths emerged in the Neolithic period. Prominent centers of early creativity were found in Egypt, Crete, Mesopotamia, the Indus Valley of the Indian subcontinent, northern China, southeastern Asia, several locations in sub-Saharan Africa, in the Americas, and elsewhere (Figure 2.15). They arose in widely separated areas of the world, at different times, and under differing ecological circumstances. Each displayed its own unique mix of culture traits.

All major culture hearths were centered around relatively urbanized landscapes, the indisputable mark of civilization first encountered in the Near East 5,500–6,000 years ago, but the urbanization of each was somewhat differently arrived at and expressed

(Figure 2.16). In some hearth areas, such as Mesopotamia and Egypt, the transition from settled agricultural village to urban form was gradual and prolonged. In Minoan Crete, urban life was less explicitly developed than in the Indus Valley, where early trade contacts with the Near East suggest the importance of exchange in fostering urban growth (see the feature "Social Collapse"). Trade seems particularly important in the development of West African culture hearths, such as Ghana and Kanem. Coming later (from the 8th to the 10th centuries) than the Nile or Mesopotamian centers, their numerous stone-built towns seem to have been supported both by an extensive agriculture whose origins were probably as early as those of the Middle East and, particularly, by long-distance trade across the Sahara. The Shang kingdom on the middle course of the Huang He (Yellow River) on the North China Plain had walled cities containing wattle-and-daub buildings but no monumental architecture.

Each culture hearth showed a rigorous organization of agriculture resulting in local productivity sufficient to enable a significant number of people to engage in nonfarm activities. Therefore, each hearth region saw the creation of a stratified society that included artisans, warriors, merchants, scholars, priests, and administrators. Each also developed or adopted astronomy, mathematics, and the all-essential calendar. Each, while advancing in cultural diversity and complexity, exported technologies, skills, and learned behaviors far beyond its own boundaries.

Writing appeared first in Mesopotamia and Egypt at least 5,000 years ago, as cuneiform in the former and as hieroglyphics in the latter. The separate forms of writing have suggested to some that they arose independently, in separate hearths. Others maintain that the idea of writing originated in Mesopotamia and spread outward to Egypt, to the Indus Valley, to Crete, and perhaps even to China, though independent development of Chinese ideographic writing is

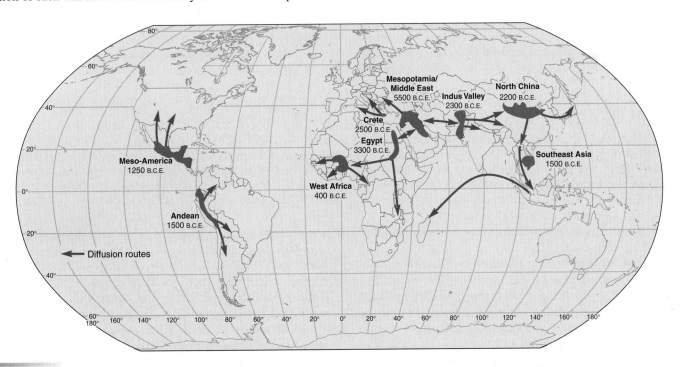

Figure 2.15 Early culture hearths of the Old World and the Americas. The B.C.E. (Before the Common Era, equivalent to B.C.) dates approximate times when the hearths developed complex social, intellectual, and technological bases and served as cultural diffusion centers.

Figure 2.16 Urbanization was invariably a characteristic of culture hearths of both the Old and the New Worlds. Pictured is the Pyramid of the Sun and Avenue of the Dead at Teotihuacán, a city that at its height between A.D. 300 and 700 spread over nearly 18 square kilometers (7 square miles). Located some 50 kilometers (30 miles) northeast of Mexico City in the Valley of Mexico, the planned city of Teotihuacán featured broad, straight avenues and an enormous pyramid complex. The Avenue of the Dead, bordered with low stone-faced buildings, was some 3 kilometers (nearly 2 miles) in length.

 Social Collapse

Sustainable development requires a long-term balance between human actions and environmental conditions. When either poor management of resources by an exploiting culture or natural environmental alteration unrelated to human actions destroys that balance, a society's use of a region is no longer "sustainable" in the form previously established. Recent research shows that over 4,000 years ago an unmanageable natural disaster spelled the death of half a dozen ancient civilizations from the Mediterranean Sea to the Indus Valley.

That disaster took the form of an intense, 300-year drought that destroyed the rain-based agriculture on which many of the early civilizations were dependent. Although they prospered through trade, urban societies were sustained by the efforts of farmers. When, about 2200 B.C., fields dried and crops failed through lack of rain, urban and rural inhabitants alike were forced to flee the dust storms and famine of intolerable environmental deterioration.

Evidence of the killer drought that destroyed so many Bronze Age cultures—for example, those of Mesopotamia, early Minoan Crete, and the Old Kingdom in Egypt—includes cities abandoned in 2200 B.C. and not reoccupied for over 300 years; deep accumulations (20–25 cm, or 8–10 in.) of windblown sand over farmlands during the same three centuries; abrupt declines in lake water levels; and thick lake-bed and seabed deposits of windblown debris.

Similar, but differently timed drought periods—such as the catastrophic aridity between A.D. 800 and 1000 that destroyed Mayan culture in Mesoamerica—have been blamed for the collapse of advanced societies in the New World as well. Not even the most thriving of early urban cultures were immune to restrictions imposed by nature.

usually assumed. The systems of record keeping developed in New World hearths were not related to those of the Old, but once created, they spread widely in areas under the influence of Andean and Mesoamerican hearths. In Mesoamerica, distinctive Zapotec, Olmec, and Maya writing systems apparently emerged between 2,600 and 2,300 years ago. Skill in working iron, so important in Near Eastern kingdoms, was an export of sub-Saharan African hearths.

The anthropologist Julian Steward proposed the concept of **multilinear evolution** to explain the common characteristics of widely separated cultures developed under similar ecological circumstances. He suggested that each major environmental zone—arid, high-altitude, midlatitude steppe, tropical forest, and so on—tends to induce common adaptive traits in the cultures of those who exploit it. Those traits were, at base, founded on the development of agriculture and the emergence of similar cultural and administrative structures in the several culture hearths. But *similar* does not imply *identical*. Steward simply suggested that since comparable sequences of developmental events cannot always or even often be explained on the basis of borrowing or exporting of ideas and techniques (because of time and space differences in the cultures sharing them), they must be regarded as evidence of parallel creations based on similar ecologies. From similar origins, but through separate adaptations and independent innovations, distinctive cultures emerged.

In contrast, spatially separated cultures also show similarities because of the spatial spread (diffusion) of cultural traits from common origin sites. In some cases, cultural innovations are passed on along trade routes and through group contact rather than being the result of separate and independent creation. Although the extreme form of this idea, that cultures show similarities primarily—perhaps even solely—because of diffusion from one or only a very few common origin sites (a view known as *diffusionism*) is long out of favor, recent archaeological discoveries apparently document some very long-distance transfer of ideas, technologies, and language by migrating peoples.

In any event, the common characteristics deriving from multilinear evolution and the spread of specific culture traits and complexes contained the roots of **cultural convergence.** That term describes the sharing of technologies, organizational structures, and even cultural traits and artifacts that is so evident among widely separated societies in a modern world united by rapid communication and efficient transportation. Convergence in those worldwide traits is, for many observers, proof of the pervasive globalization of culture.

The Structure of Culture

Understanding a culture fully is, perhaps, impossible for one who is not part of it (and it is difficult for those inside it, as well). For analytical purposes, however, the traits and complexes of culture—its building blocks and expressions—may be grouped and examined as subsets of the whole. The anthropologist Leslie White suggested that for analytical purposes, a culture could be viewed as a three-part structure composed of subsystems that he termed *ideological, technological,* and *sociological.* Specific traits within each subsystem of culture can be labeled *mentifacts, artifacts,* or *sociofacts.* Together, according to these interpretations, the subsystems—identified by their separate components—comprise the system of culture as a whole. But we emphasize that this subdivision is for analytic purposes only; in reality, they are integrated, with each acting on the others and, in turn, affected by them. The **ideological subsystem** consists of ideas, beliefs, and knowledge of a culture and of the ways in which these things are expressed in speech or other forms of communication. Mythologies and theologies, legend, language, literature, philosophy, ethical systems, and folk wisdom make up this category. Passed on from generation to generation, these abstract belief systems, or **mentifacts,** tell us what we ought to believe, what we should value, and how we ought to act. Two basic strands of the ideological subsystem—language and religion—are the subject of Chapter 5.

The **technological subsystem** is composed of the material objects, together with the techniques of their use, by means of which people live. The objects are the tools and other instruments that enable us to feed, clothe, house, defend, transport, and amuse ourselves. We must have food, we must be protected from the elements, and we must be able to defend ourselves. The material objects that we use to fill these needs are **artifacts** (Figure 2.17). In Chapter 10, we will examine the relationship between technological subsystems and regional patterns of economic development.

(a)

(b)

Figure 2.17 **Artifacts are an important component of culture.** (*a*) This Chinese farmer plowing with an ox uses artifacts (tools) typical of the lower technological levels of subsistence agriculture. (*b*) Cultures with advanced technological subsystems use complex machinery to harness inanimate energy for productive use.

Culture Change

The recurring theme of cultural geography is change. No culture is, or has been, characterized by a permanently fixed set of material objects, systems of organization, or even ideologies. Admittedly, all of these may be long-enduring within a stable, isolated society at equilibrium with its resource base. Such isolation and stability have always been rare. On the whole, while cultures are essentially conservative, they are always in a state of flux. Some changes are major and pervasive. The transition from hunter-gatherer to sedentary farmer, as we have seen, affected markedly every facet of the cultures experiencing that change and the experiences of the people living in those cultures. Profound, too, was the impact of the Industrial Revolution and its associated urbanization on all the societies that it has touched.

Not all change is so extensive as that following the introduction of agriculture or mechanized manufacturing. Many changes are so slight individually as to go almost unnoticed at their inception, though cumulatively they may substantially alter the affected culture. Think of how the culture of the United States differs today from what you know it to have been in 1940—not in essentials, perhaps, but in the innumerable electrical, electronic, and transportational devices that have been introduced and in the social, behavioral, and recreational changes they and other technological changes have wrought. Among these latter have been shifts in employment patterns to include greater participation by women in the waged workforce and associated adjustments in attitudes toward the role of women in the society at large. Such cumulative changes occur because the cultural traits of any group are not independent; they are clustered in a coherent and integrated pattern. Change on a small scale can have wide repercussions as associated traits accommodate to the adopted adjustment. Change, both major and minor, within cultures is induced by *innovation, diffusion,* and *acculturation.*

Innovation

Innovation implies changes to a culture that result from ideas created within the social group itself and adopted by the culture. The novelty may be an invented improvement in material technology, like the bow and arrow or the jet engine. It may involve the development of nonmaterial forms of social structure and interaction: feudalism, for example, or Christianity. It may be a new form of popular music or a new way of styling hair.

Many innovations are of little consequence by themselves, but sometimes the widespread adoption of seemingly inconsequential innovations may bring about large changes when viewed over a period of time. A new musical style such as hip-hop "adopted" by a few people may spread to others and bring with it changes to vernacular speech, clothing styles, dance styles, graffiti art, and other forms of entertainment, which, in turn, which may affect retailers' advertising campaigns and consumers' spending. Eventually, a new cultural form will be identified that may have an important impact on the thinking processes of the adopters and on those who come into contact with the adopters. Notice that a broad definition of innovation is used, but notice also that what is important is whether or not innovations are accepted and adopted.

Premodern and traditional societies characteristically are not innovative. In societies at equilibrium with their environment and with no unmet needs, change has no obvious or immediate adaptive value and little reason to occur. Indeed, all societies have an innate resistance to change since innovation inevitably creates tensions between the new reality and other established socioeconomic conditions. Those tensions can be resolved only by adaptive changes elsewhere in the total system. The gap that may develop between, for example, a newly adopted technology and other, slower-paced social traits has been called *cultural lag.* Complaints about youthful fads or the glorification of times past are familiar examples of reluctance to accept or adjust to change.

Innovation and invention—frequently under stressful conditions—have marked the history of humankind. As we have seen, growing populations at the end of the Ice Age necessitated an expanded food base. In response, domestication of plants and animals appears to have occurred independently in more than one world area. Indeed, a most striking fact about early agriculture is the near universality of its development or adoption within a very short span of human history. In 10,000 B.C., the world population of no more than 10 million was exclusively hunter-gatherers. By A.D. 1500, only 1 percent of the world's 350 million people still followed that way of life. Today, much less than 1 percent of the world's 7 billion people do. The revolution in food production represented by the advent of agriculture affected every facet of the threefold subsystems of culture of every society accepting it. All innovation has a radiating impact on the web of culture; the more basic the innovation, the more pervasive its consequences.

In most modern societies, innovative change has become common, expected, and inevitable. The rate of invention, at least as measured by the number of patents granted, has steadily increased, and the period between idea conception and product

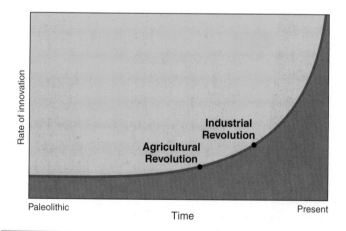

Figure 2.20 The trend of innovation through human history. Hunter-gatherers, living in equilibrium with their environment and their resource base during the Paleolithic period had little need for innovation and no necessity for cultural change. The Agricultural Revolution accelerated the diffusion of the ideas and techniques of domestication, urbanization, and trade. With the Industrial Revolution, dramatic increases in all aspects of socioeconomic innovation began to alter cultures throughout the world.

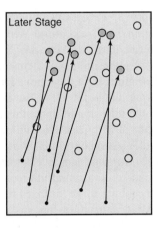

Initial Stage

Later Stage

(a) RELOCATION DIFFUSION

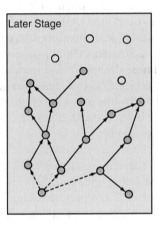

Initial Stage

Later Stage

(b) EXPANSION DIFFUSION

○ Non-Adopter
◉ Adopter of innovation

Figure 2.21 Processes of diffusion. (*a*) In *relocation diffusion,* innovations or ideas are transported to new areas by carriers who permanently leave the home locale (see Figure 6.24). (*b*) In *expansion diffusion,* a phenomenon spreads from one place to another, but in the process remains and is often intensified in the place of origin (see Figure 5.28).

Source: Redrawn by permission from Spatial Diffusion, *by Peter R. Gould, Resource Paper no. 4, page 4, Association of American Geographers, 1969.*

availability has been decreasing. A general axiom is that the more ideas available and the more minds able to exploit and combine them, the greater the rate of innovation. The spatial implication is that larger urban centers of advanced technologies tend to be centers of innovation. This is not just because of their size but because of the opportunities they provide for the exchange of ideas. Indeed, ideas not only stimulate new thoughts and viewpoints but also create circumstances in which societies come to develop new solutions increasingly as a cultural practice in itself (Figure 2.20).

Diffusion

Diffusion is the process by which an idea or innovation is transmitted from one individual or group to another across space. Diffusion may assume a variety of forms, each different in its impact on social groups. Basically, however, two processes are involved:

(1) People move, for any of a number of reasons, to a new area and take their culture with them. For example, immigrants to the American colonies brought with them crops and farming techniques, building styles, and concepts of government that were alien to their new home. (2) Information about an innovation (e.g., hybrid corn or compact discs) may spread throughout a society, perhaps aided by local or mass media advertising; or new adopters of an ideology or way of life—for example, a new religious creed—may be inspired or recruited by immigrant or native converts. The former is known as *relocation diffusion,* the latter as *expansion diffusion* (Figure 2.21).

Expansion diffusion involves the spread of a culture trait from one place to others when people who did not formerly practice the trait adopt it after direct or indirect contact with those who do practice the trait. In the process, the thing diffused also remains—and is frequently intensified—in the origin area. Islam, for example, expanded from its Arabian Peninsula origin locale across much of Asia and North Africa. At the same time, it strengthened its hold over its Near Eastern birthplace by displacing practitioners of tribal, Christian, and Jewish religions. The term *expansion* refers to the fact that this process of diffusion necessarily involves an increase in the number of people or societies practicing the trait. Furthermore, as potential adopters become adopters and serve to pass on the innovation to others, the number of contacts of adopters with potential adopters will compound. Consequently, the innovation will spread slowly at first and then more and more rapidly until saturation occurs or a barrier is reached. The incidence of adoption under expansion diffusion is represented by the S-shaped curve in Figure 2.22.

When adoption of an innovation spreads from an area where it is practiced to a neighboring area, reflecting *distance decay* (Chapter 3), it is termed **contagious diffusion.** This pattern of diffusion reflects the importance of direct contact between those who developed or have adopted the innovation and those who newly encounter it, and is reminiscent of the course of infectious diseases (Figure 2.23). Contagious diffusion results in the continuous spread of innovations, like "waves." In some instances, however, geographic distance is less important in the transfer of ideas than is communication between major centers or important people. News of new clothing styles, for example, quickly

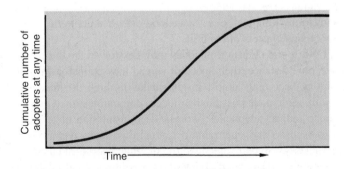

Figure 2.22 The diffusion of innovations over time. The number of adopters of an innovation rises at an increasing rate until the point at which about one-half of the total who ultimately decide to adopt the innovation have made the decision. At that point, the number of adopters increases at a decreasing rate.

Figure 2.23 The pattern of *contagious diffusion* is sensitive to both time and distance, as suggested by the diffusion pathways of the European influenza pandemic of 1781. The pattern there was a wavelike radiation from a Russian origin area.

Source: Based on Gerald F. Pyle and K. David Patterson, Ecology of Disease 2, *no. 3 (1984): 179.*

spreads internationally between major cities and only later filters down irregularly to smaller towns and rural areas. The pattern of transferring ideas first between larger places or prominent people and only later to smaller or less important points or people is known as **hierarchical diffusion.** The Christian faith in Europe, for example, spread from Rome as the principal center to provincial capitals and thence to smaller Roman settlements in largely pagan-occupied territories (see Figure 5.22). Today, new discoveries are shared among scientists at leading universities before they appear in textbooks or become general knowledge through the public press. The hierarchical pattern takes place because, in many cases, distance is largely overcome by communication networks; this implies contact through indirect means, such as the Internet or mass media. Big cities or leading scientists, connected by strong information flows, are "closer" than their simple distance separation suggests. Hierarchical diffusion results in patterns of innovation "jumping" over space, and often results in the formation of new clusters of the trait.

While the diffusion of ideas may be slowed by the need to overcome distance, their speed of spread may be increased to the point of becoming almost instantaneous through the *space-time compression* made possible by modern communication. Given access to radios; telephones; worldwide transmission of television news, sports, and entertainment programs; and—perhaps most importantly—to computers and the Internet, people and areas distantly separated can rapidly share in a common fund of thought and innovation. Modern communication technology, that is, has encouraged and facilitated the globalization of culture.

In contrast to expansion diffusion, **relocation diffusion** occurs when the innovation is carried to new areas by migrating individuals or populations that possess it (Figure 2.21a); in

Chapter 3, we learn that migration is also known by geographers as *residential relocation*. Mentifacts, sociofacts, or artifacts are therefore introduced into new locales by new settlers who become part of populations not themselves associated or in contact with the origin area of the innovation. The spread of religions by settlers or conquerors is a clear example of relocation diffusion, as was the diffusion of agriculture to Europe from the Middle East (Figure 2.13). Christian Europeans brought their faiths to areas of colonization or economic penetration throughout the world. At the world scale, massive relocation diffusion resulted from the European colonization and economic penetration that began in the 16th century. More localized relocation diffusion continues today as Asian refugees or foreign "guest workers" bring their cultural traits to their new areas of settlement in Europe or North America. Like expansion diffusion, relocation diffusion spreads cultural traits across the landscape, but unlike it, relocation diffusion does not entail an increase in the number of people or societies practicing the trait. Also, because migration often reflects patterns of distance decay, wherein people move over short distances, or it reflects patterns of long-distance relocation over transportation networks like highways or airline routes, relocation diffusion can also be characterized as reflecting patterns of contagious or hierarchical diffusion.

For either expansion or relocation diffusion, innovations may be relatively readily diffused to, and accepted by, cultures that have basic similarities and compatibilities. Continental Europe and North America, for example, could easily and quickly adopt the innovations of the Industrial Revolution diffused from England with which they shared a common ethnic, economic, and technological background. Industrialization was not quickly accepted in Asian and African societies of totally different cultural conditioning. On the ideological level, too, successful diffusion depends on acceptability of the innovations. The attempt by Mohammed Reza Pahlavi, the shah of Iran, at rapid westernization of traditional Iranian Islamic culture after World War II provoked a traditionalist backlash and revolution that deposed him and reestablished clerical control of the state in 1979.

The conclusion must be, therefore, that diffusion cannot be viewed solely as the outcome of contact and knowledge dispersal. The acceptance of new traits, artifacts, or ways of doing or thinking by a potential receiving population depends not just on information flow to that population but also upon its entire cultural and economic structure. Innovation may be rejected not because of lack of knowledge but because the new trait violates the established cultural norms of the culture to which it is introduced. For example, cash crop specialization recommended to a peasant agricultural society may be rejected not because it is not understood, but because it unacceptably disrupts the knowledge base and culture complex devoted to assured food security in a subsistence farming economy. Similarly, less disruptive new production ideas—chemical fertilizers, deep-well irrigation, hybrid seeds, and the like—may be rejected simply because, though understood, they are not affordable. Culture is a complex organized system and culture change involves alteration of the system's established structure in ways that may be rejected even after knowledge of an innovation is received and understood.

Documenting Diffusion

The places of origin of many ideas, items, and technologies important in contemporary cultures are only dimly known or supposed, and their routes of diffusion are speculative at best. Gunpowder and printing are presumed to be the products of Chinese inventiveness; the lateen sail has been traced to the Near Eastern culture world. The moldboard plow is ascribed to 6th-century Slavs of northeastern Europe. The sequence and routes of the diffusion of these innovations has not been documented.

In other cases, such documentation exists, and the process of diffusion is open to analysis. Clearly marked is the diffusion path of the custom of smoking tobacco, a practice that originated among Amerindians. Sir Walter Raleigh's Virginia colonists, returning home in 1586, introduced smoking to English court circles, and the habit very quickly spread among the general populace. England became the source region of the new custom for northern Europe; smoking was introduced to Holland by English medical students in 1590. The Dutch and English together spread the habit by sea to the Baltic and Scandinavian areas and overland through Germany to Russia. The innovation continued its eastward diffusion, and within a hundred years, tobacco had spread across Siberia and was, in the 1740s, reintroduced to the American continent at Alaska by Russian fur traders.

Wal-Mart Diffusion to 1990

Source: Map based on data from Thomas O. Graff and Dub Ashton, "Spatial Diffusion of Wal-Mart: Contagious and Reverse Hierarchical Elements." Professional Geographer *46, 1 (1994): 19–29.*

A second route of diffusion for tobacco smoking can be traced from Spain, where the custom was introduced in 1558, and from which it spread more slowly through the Mediterranean area into Africa, the Near East, and Southeast Asia.

In more recent times, hybrid corn was first adopted by imaginative farmers of northern Illinois and eastern Iowa in the mid-1930s. By the late 1930s and early 1940s, the new seeds were being planted as far east as Ohio and north to Minnesota, Wisconsin, and northern Michigan. By the late 1940s, all commercial corn-growing districts of the United States and southern Canada were cultivating hybrid corn varieties.

A similar pattern of diffusion marked the expansion of the Wal-Mart store chain. From its origin in northwest Arkansas in 1962, the discount chain had spread throughout the United States by the 1990s to become the country's largest retailer in sales volume. In its expansion, Wal-Mart displayed a "reverse hierarchical" diffusion, initially spreading by being price-competitive with small-town merchants before opening its first stores in larger cities and metropolitan areas (see map).

It is not always possible, of course, to determine the precise point of origin or the routes of diffusion of innovations now widely adopted (see the feature "Documenting Diffusion"). Nor is it always certain whether the existence of a cultural trait in two different areas is the result of diffusion or of **independent** (or *parallel*) **invention.** Cultural similarities do not necessarily prove that diffusion has occurred. The pyramids of Egypt and of the Central American Maya civilization most likely were separately conceived and are not necessarily evidence, as some have proposed, of pre-Columbian voyages from the Mediterranean to the Americas (or of visits by aliens from outer space, as has also been suggested). A Neolithic monument-building culture, after all, has only a limited number of shapes from which to choose.

Historical examples of independent, parallel invention are numerous: logarithms by John Napier (1614) and Jost Bürgi (1620), the calculus by Sir Isaac Newton (1672) and Gottfried Leibniz (1675), and the telephone by Elisha Gray and Alexander Graham Bell (1876) are commonly cited. It appears beyond doubt that agriculture was independently developed not only in both the New

World and the Old, but also in more than one culture hearth in each of the hemispheres.

Acculturation and Cultural Modification

A culture group may undergo major modifications in its own identifying traits by adopting some or all of the characteristics of another, dominant culture group. Such is the case in **acculturation**—discussed at greater length in Chapter 6 (p. 176–189)—as immigrant populations take on the values, attitudes, customs, and speech of the receiving society, which itself undergoes change from absorption of the arriving group. A different form of contact and subsequent cultural alteration may occur in a conquered or colonized region where the subordinate or subject population is either forced to adopt the culture of the new ruling group, introduced through relocation diffusion, or does so voluntarily, overwhelmed by the superiority in numbers or t he technical level of the conqueror. Tribal Europeans in areas of Roman conquest, native populations in the wake of Slavic

Figure 2.24 Baseball, an import from America, is one of the most popular sports in Japan, attracting millions of spectators annually.

occupation of Siberia, and Native Americans stripped of their lands following European settlement of North America experienced this kind of cultural modification or adoption.

In extreme cases, of course, small and, particularly, primitive indigenous groups brought into contact with conquering or absorbing societies may simply cease to exist as separate cultural entities. Although presumably such cultural loss has been part of all of human history, its increasing occurrence has been noted over the past 500 years. By one informed estimate, at least one-third of the world's inventory of human cultures has totally disappeared since A.D. 1500, along with their languages, traditions, ways of life, and, indeed, their very identity and memory of their existence.

In many instances, close contact between two different groups may involve adjustments of the original cultural patterns of both rather than disappearance of either. For example, changes in Japanese political organization and philosophy were imposed by occupying Americans after World War II, and the Japanese voluntarily adopted some of the more frivolous aspects of American life (Figure 2.24). In turn, American society was enriched by the selective importation of Japanese cuisine, architecture, and philosophy, demonstrating the two-way nature of cultural diffusion. Where that two-way flow reflects a more equal exchange of cultural outlooks and ways of life, a process of *transculturation* has occurred. That process is observable within the United States as massive South and Central American immigration begins to intertwine formerly contrasting cultures, altering both.

Contact Between Regions

Virtually all cultures are amalgams of innumerable innovations spread spatially from their points of origin and integrated into the structure of the receiving societies. It has been estimated that no more than 10 percent of the cultural items of any society are traceable to innovations created by its members and that the other 90 percent come to the society through diffusion (see the feature "A Homemade Culture"). Since, as we have seen, the pace of innovation is affected strongly by the mixing of ideas among alert, responsive people and is increased by exposure to a variety of cultures, the most active and innovative historical hearths of culture were those at crossroad locations and those deeply involved in distant trade and colonization. Ancient Mesopotamia and classical Greece and Rome had such locations and involvements, as did the West African culture hearth after the 5th century and, much later, England during the Industrial Revolution and the spread of the British Empire.

Recent changes in technology permit us to travel farther than ever before, with greater safety and speed, and to communicate

A Homemade Culture

Reflecting on an average morning in the life of a "100% American," Ralph Linton noted:

> Our solid American citizen awakens in a bed built on a pattern which originated in the Near East but which was modified in Northern Europe before it was transmitted to America. He throws back covers made from cotton, domesticated in India, or linen, domesticated in the Near East, or wool from sheep, also domesticated in the Near East, or silk, the use of which was discovered in China. All of these materials have been spun and woven by processes invented in the Near East. . . . He takes off his pajamas, a garment invented in India, and washes with soap invented by the ancient Gauls. . . .
>
> Returning to the bedroom, . . . he puts on garments whose form originally derived from the skin clothing of the nomads of the Asiatic steppes [and] puts on shoes made from skins tanned by a process invented in ancient Egypt and cut to a pattern derived from the classical civilizations of the Mediterranean. . . . Before going out for breakfast he glances through the window, made of glass invented in Egypt, and if it is raining puts on overshoes made of rubber discovered by the Central American Indians and takes an umbrella invented in southeastern Asia. . . .
>
> [At breakfast] a whole new series of borrowed elements confronts him. His plate is made of a form of pottery invented in China. His knife is of steel, an alloy first made in southern India, his fork a medieval Italian invention, and his spoon a derivative of a Roman original. He begins breakfast with an orange, from the eastern Mediterranean, a cantaloupe from Persia, or perhaps a piece of African watermelon. With this he has coffee, an Abyssinian plant. . . . [H]e may have the egg of a species of bird domesticated in Indo-China, or thin strips of flesh of an animal domesticated in Eastern Asia which have been salted and smoked by a process developed in northern Europe.
>
> When our friend has finished eating . . . he reads the news of the day, imprinted in characters invented by the ancient Semites upon a material invented in China by a process invented in Germany. As he absorbs the accounts of foreign troubles he will, if he is a good conservative citizen, thank a Hebrew deity in an Indo-European language that he is 100% American.

Source: Ralph Linton, The Study of Man: An Introduction. © 1936, renewed 1964, pp. 326–327. Reprinted by permission of Prentice Hall, Inc., Upper Saddle River, N.J.

without physical contact more easily and completely than was previously possible. This intensification of contact has resulted in an acceleration of innovation and in the rapid spread of goods and ideas. Several millennia ago, innovations such as smelting of metals took hundreds of years to diffuse. Today, worldwide diffusion—through Internet interest groups, for example—may be almost instantaneous.

Obstacles do exist, of course. *Diffusion barriers* are any conditions that hinder either the flow of information or the movement of people and thus retard or prevent the acceptance of an innovation. Because of the *friction of distance,* generally the farther two areas are from each other, the less likely is interaction to occur, an observation earlier (p. 53) summarized by the term *distance decay.* Distance and barriers as factors in spatial interaction are further explored in Chapter 3. For now, it is sufficient to note that distance may be an *absorbing barrier,* halting the spread of an innovation.

Political restrictions, religious taboos, and other social customs are cultural barriers to diffusion. The French Canadians, although close geographically to many Anglo-Canadian centers of diffusion such as Ottawa and Toronto, strive to be only minimally influenced by them. Both their language and culture complex govern their selective acceptance of Anglo influences, and restrictive French-only language regulations are enforced to preserve the integrity of their distinctive French culture. In a more extreme fashion, the Afghan Taliban and other Mideast fundamentalist groups adamantly or violently reject Western sociocultural values, seeking to preserve their religious and cultural purity through isolation from secular, non-Islamic influences. Traditional groups, perhaps controlled by firm religious conviction, may largely reject culture traits and technologies of the larger society in whose midst they live (see Figure 7.2 in Chapter 7).

Adopting cultures do not usually accept items intact that originate outside the receiving society. Diffused ideas and artifacts commonly undergo some alteration of meaning or form that makes them acceptable to a borrowing group. The process of the fusion of the old and new is called **syncretism** and is a major feature of culture change. It can be seen in alterations to religious ritual and dogma made by convert societies seeking acceptable conformity between old and new beliefs. For example, slaves brought voodoo from West Africa to the Americas where it thrived in Haiti and Louisiana. Over the years, it absorbed influences from French and Spanish Catholicism, American Indian spiritual practices, and even Masonic tradition. Despite those adaptive mixings, many believers consider themselves to be Catholics and see no contradiction between Christianity and their faith in protective spirits and other tenets of voodoo. On a more familiar level, syncretism is reflected in subtle or blatant alterations of imported cuisines to make them conform to the demands of the American palate and fast-food franchises (Figure 2.25).

Figure 2.25 Foreign foods modified for American tastes represent syncretism in action.

Summary

The web of culture is composed of many strands. Together, culture traits and complexes in their spatial patterns create human landscapes, define culture regions, and distinguish culture groups. Those landscapes, regions, and group characteristics change through time as human societies interact with their environments, develop for themselves new solutions to collective needs, or are altered through innovations adopted from outside the group itself. The cultural similarity of a preagricultural world composed solely of hunter-gatherers was lost as domestication of plants and animals in many world areas led to the emergence of culture hearths of wide-ranging innovation and to a cultural divergence between farmers and gatherers. Innovations spread outward from their origin points, carried by migrants through relocation diffusion or adopted by others through a variety of expansion diffusion and acculturation processes. Although diffusion barriers exist, most successful or advantageous innovations find adopters, and both cultural modification and cultural convergence of different

societies result. The details of the technological, sociological, and ideological subsystems of culture define the differences that still exist between world areas.

The ivory hunters who opened our chapter showed how varied and complex the culture of even a primitive group can be. Their artifacts of clothing, fire making, hunting, and fishing displayed diversity and ingenuity. They were part of a structured kinship system and engaged in organized production and trade. Their artistic efforts and ritual burial customs speak of a sophisticated set of abstract beliefs and philosophies. Their culture complex did not develop in isolation; it reflected at least in part their contacts with other groups, even those far distant from their Paris Basin homeland. As have culture groups always and everywhere, the hunters continued their own pursuits and interacted with others in spatial settings. They exhibited and benefited from structured *spatial behavior,* the topic to which we next turn our attention.

KEY WORDS

acculturation 55
artifact 49
carrying capacity 42
contagious diffusion 53

cultural autonomy 37
cultural convergence 49
cultural divergence 42
cultural ecology 37

cultural integration 50
cultural landscape 38
cultural system 36
culture 34

FOR REVIEW

1. What is included in the concept of *culture?* How is culture transmitted? What personal characteristics affect the aspects of culture that any single individual acquires or fully masters?

2. What do we mean by *domestication?* When and where did the domestication of plants and animals occur? What impact on culture and population numbers did plant domestication have?

3. What is a *culture hearth?* What new traits of culture characterized the early hearths? Identify and locate some of the major culture hearths that emerged at the close of the Neolithic period.

4. What do we mean by *innovation?* By *diffusion?* What different processes and patterns of diffusion can you describe? Discuss the role played by innovation and diffusion in altering the cultural structure in which you are

a participant from that experienced by your great-grandparents.

5. Differentiate between *culture traits* and *culture complexes,* and between *environmental determinism* and *possibilism.*

6. What are the components or subsystems of the three-part system of culture? What characteristics are included in each of the subsystems?

KEY CONCEPTS REVIEW

1. **What are the components of culture and nature of culture–environment interactions?** pp. 34–40.
   Culture traits and complexes may be grouped into culture regions and realms. Differing developmental levels color human perceptions of environmental opportunities. In general, as the active agents in the relationship, humans exert adverse impacts on the natural environment.

2. **How did cultures develop and diverge** (pp. 40–42)**, and where did cultural advances originate?** pp. 42–49.
   From Paleolithic hunting and gathering to Neolithic farming and then to city civilizations, different groups made differently timed cultural transitions. All early cultural advances had their origins in a few areally distinct "hearths."

3. **What are the structures of culture and forms of culture change?** pp. 49–58.
   All cultures contain ideological, technological, and sociological components that work together to create cultural integration. Cultures change through innovations that they themselves invent or that diffuse from other areas and are accepted or adapted.

SPATIAL INTERACTION AND SPATIAL BEHAVIOR

The blurred lights of traffic on the Avenue des Champs Elysees in Paris, France, typify spatial interaction in contemporary society.

Key Concepts

1. The three bases for spatial interaction, pp. 61–63.

2. Measuring the likelihood of spatial interaction, pp. 63–66.

3. The forms and nature of human spatial behavior, pp. 66–72.

4. Information and cognition in human spatial behavior, pp. 72–77

5. Migration patterns, types, and controls, pp. 78–90.

*E*arly in January of 1849 we first thought of migrating to California. It was a period of National hard times . . . and we longed to go to the new El Dorado and "pick up" gold enough with which to return and pay off our debts.

Our discontent and restlessness were enhanced by the fact that my health was not good. . . . The physician advised an entire change of climate thus to avoid the intense cold of Iowa, and recommended a sea voyage, but finally approved of our contemplated trip across the plains in a "prairie schooner."

Full of the energy and enthusiasm of youth, the prospects of so hazardous an undertaking had no terror for us, indeed, as we had been married but a few months, it appealed to us as a romantic wedding tour.[1]

So begins Catherine Haun's account of their nine-month journey from Iowa to California, just two of the quarter-million people who traveled across the continent on the Overland Trail in one of the world's great migrations. The migrants faced months of grueling struggle over badly marked routes that crossed swollen rivers, deserts, and mountains. The weather was often foul, with hailstorms, drenching rains, and burning summer temperatures. Graves along the route were a silent testimony to the lives claimed by buffalo stampedes, Indian skirmishes, cholera epidemics, and other disasters.

What inducements were so great as to make emigrants leave behind all that was familiar and risk their lives on an uncertain venture? Catherine Haun alludes to economic hard times gripping the country and to their hope for riches to be found in California. Like other migrants, the Hauns were attracted by the climate in the West, which was said to be always sunny and free of disease. Finally, like most who undertook the perilous journey west, the Hauns were young, moved by restlessness, a sense of adventure, and a belief that greater opportunities awaited in a new land. They, like their predecessors back to the beginnings of humankind, were acting in space and across space on the basis of acquired information and anticipation of opportunity—prepared to pay the price in time, money, and hardship costs of overcoming distance.

A fundamental question in human geography is: What considerations influence how individual human beings use space and act within it? Related queries include: Are there discernible controls on human spatial behavior? How does distance affect human interaction? How do our beliefs about places influence our spatial activities? How do we overcome the consequences of distance in the exchange of commodities and information? How are movement and migration decisions (like that of the Hauns) reached? How have new technologies enabled increased spatial interaction across great distances and contributed to globalization? These questions address geography's concern with understanding spatial interaction.

Spatial interaction is contact between places, and in human geography, means the movement of people, ideas, and commodities (goods bought and sold) from place to place. The Hauns were engaging in spatial interaction (Figure 3.1). International trade, the movement of semitrailers on the expressways, radio broadcasts, and business or personal telephone calls are other familiar examples. Such movements and exchanges are designed to achieve

Figure 3.1 A public bus negotiates a washed-out section of highway on one of the major routes connecting the capital city of Kathmandu with southern Nepal and India. Movement in Nepal is more difficult than in developed countries because of the limited road network, narrow, winding mountain roads, and frequent landslides. A ride on a public bus in Nepal can be an adventure in sharing space with people, agricultural produce, and livestock.

effective integration between different points of human activity. Movement and contact of whatever nature between places serve to smooth out the spatially differing availability of required resources, commodities, information, or opportunities. Whatever the particular purpose of a movement, there is inevitably some manner of trade-off balancing the benefit of the interaction with the costs that are incurred in overcoming spatial separation. Because commodity movements represent simple demonstrations of the principles underlying all spatial interactions, let us turn to them first.

Bases for Interaction

Neither the world's resources nor products are uniformly distributed. Commodity flows are responses to these differences; they are links between points of supply and locales of demand. Such response may not be immediate, or even direct. Factors such as the awareness of supplies or markets, the presence or absence of transportation connections, costs of movement, and the ability to pay for things wanted and needed—all that and more affect the structure of commodity exchange. Underlying these, however, is a basic set of controlling principles governing spatial interaction.

A Summarizing Model

Geographer Edward Ullman (1912–1976) speculated on the essential conditions affecting such interactions and proposed an explanatory model. He observed that spatial interaction is effectively controlled by three flow-determining factors that he called *complementarity, transferability,* and *intervening opportunity.* Although Ullman's model deals with commodity flows, it has—as we shall see—applicability to information transfers and human movements as well.

Complementarity

For two places to interact, one place must have what another place wants and can secure. That is, one place must have a supply of an

---

[1]From Catherine Haun, "A Woman's Trip Across the Plains in 1849," in Lillian Schlissel, *Women's Diaries of the Westward Journey* (New York: Schocken Books, 1982).

item for which there is an effective demand in the other, as evidenced by desire for the item, purchasing power to acquire it, and means to transport it. The word describing this circumstance is **complementarity.** Effective supply and demand are important considerations; mere differences from place to place in commodity surplus or deficit are not enough to initiate exchange. For example, Greenland and the Amazon basin are notably unlike in their natural resources and economies, but their amount of interaction is minimal. Supply and market must come together, as they do in the flow of seasonal fruits and vegetables from California's Imperial Valley to the urban markets of the American Midwest and East or in the movement of manganese from Ukraine to the steel mills of Western Europe. The massive movement of crude and refined petroleum clearly demonstrates complementarity in international trade (Figure 3.2). More generalized patterns of complementarity underlie the exchanges of the raw materials and agricultural goods of less developed countries for the money or industrial commodities of the developed states.

Transferability

Even when complementarity exists, spatial interaction occurs only when conditions of **transferability**—acceptable costs of an exchange—are met. Spatial movement responds not just to availability and demand but to considerations of time and cost. Transferability is an expression of the mobility of a commodity and is a function of three interrelated conditions: (1) the characteristics and value of the product; (2) the distance, measured in time and money penalties, over which it must be moved; and (3) the ability of the commodity to bear the costs of movement. If the time and money costs of traversing a distance are too great, exchange

does not occur. That is, mobility is not just a physical matter but an economic one as well. If a given commodity is not affordable upon delivery to an otherwise willing buyer, it will not move in trade, and the potential buyer must seek a substitute or go without.

Transferability is not a constant condition. It differs between places over time, depending upon what is being transferred and how it is to be moved. In the 1820s, the newly opened Erie Canal cut shipping costs from Buffalo to New York City by 90 percent. However, the growth of railroads and highways across New York State provided quicker alternatives and caused great declines in commercial canal traffic during the 20th century. More recently, containerized shipping has had a similar effect on the global shipments of goods. An increasing scarcity of high-quality ores will enhance the transferability of lower-quality mine outputs by increasing their value. Low-cost bulk commodities not economically moved by air may be fully transferable by rail or water. Poorly developed and costly transportation may inhibit exchanges even at short distance between otherwise willing traders. In short, transferability expresses the changing relationships between the costs of transportation and the value of the product to be shipped.

Intervening Opportunity

Complementarity can be effective only in the absence of more attractive alternative sources of supply or demand closer at hand or cheaper. **Intervening opportunities** serve to reduce supply/demand interactions that otherwise might develop between distant complementary areas. A supply of Saharan sand is not enough to assure its flow to sand-deficient Manhattan because supplies of sand are more easily and cheaply available within the

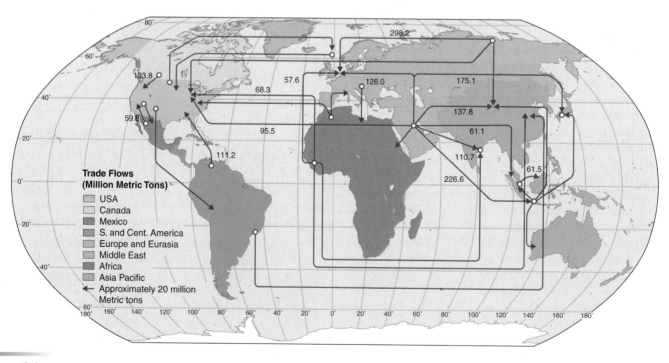

Figure 3.2 **Major international crude oil and other product exports flow, 2007.** Complementarity is so basic in initiating interaction that even relatively low-value bulk commodities such as coal, fertilizer, and grain move in trade over long distances. For many years, despite fluctuating prices, petroleum has been the most important commodity in international trade, moving long distances in response to effective supply and demand considerations.

Source: Adapted from The BP Amoco Statistical Review of World Energy, 2008.

New York metropolitan region. For reasons of cost and convenience, a purchaser is unlikely to buy identical commodities at a distance when a suitable nearby supply is available. When it is, the intervening opportunity demonstrates complementarity at a shorter distance.

Similarly, markets and destinations are sought, if possible, close at hand. Growing metropolitan demand in California reduces the importance of Midwestern markets for western fruit growers. The intervening opportunities offered by Chicago or Philadelphia reduce the number of job seekers from Iowa searching for employment in New York City. People from New England are more likely to take winter vacations in Florida, which is relatively near and accessible, than in Southern California, which is not. That is, opportunities that are discerned closer at hand reduce the pull of opportunities offered by a distant destination (Figure 3.3). Patterns of spatial interaction are dynamic, reflecting the changeable structure of apparent opportunity.

Measuring Interaction

Complementarity, transferability, and intervening opportunity—the controlling conditions of commodity movement—help us understand all forms of spatial interaction, including choosing a restaurant, where to go to college, or where to buy a house—even the once-in-a-lifetime transcontinental adventure of the Hauns. The study of unique spatial interactions, such as the discovery of an Inuit carving in a Miami gift shop, is interesting but does not establish general patterns. In this chapter, we focus on general principles that govern the frequency and intensity of interaction both to validate the three preconditions of spatial exchange and to establish the probability that any given potential interaction will actually occur. Our interest is similar to that of the physical scientist investigating, for example, the response of a gas to variations in temperature and pressure. The concern there is with all of the gas molecules and the probability of their collective reactions; the action of any particular molecule is of little interest. Similarly, we are mostly concerned here with the probability of aggregate, not individual (disaggregate), behavior.

Figure 3.3 (*a*) The volume of expected customers for a shopping mall based solely on their complementarity and distance apart, may be (*b*) reduced if a new mall opens as an intervening opportunity nearer to the customers.

That concern with aggregate behavior c[...] a great deal of spatial interaction of vital import[...] real world and in human geography. Most theoret[...] vational studies of spatial interaction have focused on [...] normative spatial behavior of fully physically and eco[...] capable Western-culture adults. That standard does not [...] the individual or collective spatial problems and actions of [...] others as children, the poor, the elderly, the disabled, or socia[...] disadvantaged individuals or groups, nor does it recognize the[...] very real, though often subtle, differences between male and female spatial action responses and decisions. Our orientation to the North American culture realm means also that the aggregate spatial behavioral norms that we discern there fail to recognize the many and varied sociocultural, economic, legal, and similar constraints on spatial behavior operative in other culture areas of the world. Nevertheless, observational evidence suggests that the same basic influences on personal spatial behavior that we recognize here have universal applicability, despite their inevitable modification in different contexts.

Distance Decay

In all manner of ways, the lives and activities of people everywhere are influenced by the **friction of distance.** That phrase reminds us that distance has a retarding effect on human interaction because there are increasing penalties in time and cost associated with longer-distance, more expensive interchanges. We visit nearby friends more often than distant friends; we go more frequently to the neighborhood convenience store cluster than to the farther regional shopping center. Telephone calls or mail deliveries between nearby towns are greater in volume than those to more distant locations. An informal study showed that college students living in dormitories near the cafeteria are more likely to use the cafeteria; students living farther away do not visit the cafeteria as often (we assume that students who dislike cafeteria food do not choose to live in more distant dormitories!).

Our common experience, clearly supported by maps and statistical data tracking all kinds of flows, is that most interactions occur over short distances. That is, interaction decreases as distance increases, a reflection of the fact that transferability costs increase with distance. More generally stated, **distance decay** describes the decline of an activity or function with increasing distance from its point of origin. Because of distance decay, closer places interact more and tend to be more similar in a variety of ways. This is a very general trend that is seen so often in geographic phenomena (including those of physical geography such as weather patterns) that it is widely known as the **First Law of Geography,** so named by geographer Waldo Tobler (1930–): "Everything is related to everything else, but near things are more related than distant things." As the examples in Figure 3.4 demonstrate, for instance, near destinations have a disproportionate pull over more distant points in commodity movements. However, it is also evident that the rate of distance decay varies with the type of activity. It usually declines nonlinearly at a decelerating rate so that the reduction is fastest at close distances, reducing more and more slowly as one gets farther and farther away. Thus, the amount of interaction between two points 80 kilometers (50 miles) apart would usually be

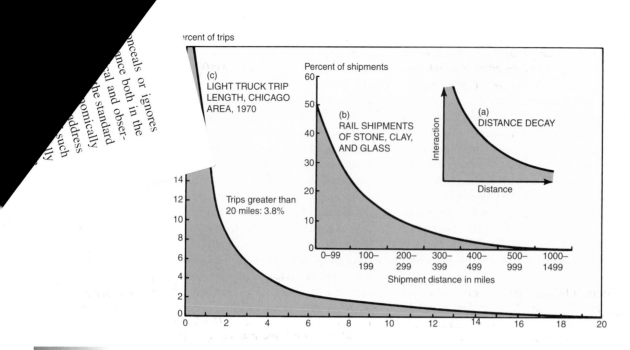

rcent of trips

(c)
LIGHT TRUCK TRIP
LENGTH, CHICAGO
AREA, 1970

Trips greater than
20 miles: 3.8%

Percent of shipments

(b)
RAIL SHIPMENTS
OF STONE, CLAY,
AND GLASS

(a)
DISTANCE DECAY

Interaction

Distance

Shipment distance in miles

Figure 3.4 **The shape of distance decay.** The geographer Waldo Tobler summarized the concept of distance decay in proposing his First Law of Geography: "Everything is related to everything else, but near things are more related than distant things." Distance decay curves vary with the type of flow. (*a*) is a generalized statement of distance decay, (*b*) summarizes U.S. data for a single year, and (*c*) suggests the primary use of light trucks as short-haul pickup and delivery vehicles.

Source: (c) Data from Chicago Area Transportation Study, A Summary of Travel Characteristics, *1977.*

less than half that between points 40 kilometers (25 miles) apart, rather than exactly one half. It is also interesting to note that while distance decay in human geography occurs primarily because of the extra "cost" caused by the friction of distance, just as in other areas of geography, other factors can contribute to declining interaction in economic or social contexts, such as declining familiarity and interest with increasing distance.

When the friction of distance is reduced by lowered costs or increased ease of flow, the slope of the distance decay curve is flattened and more total area is effectively united than when those costs are high. This, of course, is the phenomenon of **space-time compression** that we introduced in Chapter 2. When automobiles and expressways became widely available in the second half of the 20th century, U.S. cities underwent massive geographic expansion as the friction of distance was sharply reduced and large areas of rural land were brought within a reasonable commute time from the city. Figure 3.4 shows that distance decay is evident for both truck and rail shipments, but that the more expensive mode (trucking) is typically used for shorter distances.

The Gravity Concept

Interaction decisions are not based on distance or distance/cost considerations alone. The large regional shopping center attracts customers from a wide radius because of the variety of shops and goods its very size promises. We go to distant big cities "to seek our fortune," rather than to the nearer small town. That is, we are attracted by the expectation of opportunity that we associate with larger rather than smaller places. That expectation is summarized by another model of spatial interaction, the **gravity model,** also drawn from the physical sciences.

In the 1850s, Henry C. Carey (1793–1879), in his Principles of Social Science, observed that the physical laws of gravity and motion developed by Sir Isaac Newton (1642–1727) were applicable to the aggregate actions of humans. Newton's law of universal gravitation states that the gravitational pull between any two objects is proportional to the product of their masses and inversely proportional to the square of the distance between them. More simply put, Newton's law tells us that big things have a stronger attraction force (greater gravitational pull) than do small objects, and that things close to each other have stronger mutual attraction than do objects at greater distance—and that the attraction decreases very rapidly with even small increases in separation. Here is Newton's law of physical gravity:

$$F_{ij} = g \frac{M_i M_j}{d_{ij}^2}.$$

This equation states that the amount of gravitational force between two bodies *i* and *j* equals the product of their masses, divided by the square of the distance between them, and multiplied by the gravitational constant. By analogy, Carey's law of social gravity is

$$I_{ij} = k \frac{P_i P_j}{D_{ij}^B}.$$

This equation states that the amount of interaction (frequency or rate) between two places *i* and *j* equals the product of their "interaction masses," divided by the distance between them raised to some exponent, and multiplied by the interaction constant. Notice some differences between the physical and social laws. Unlike the physical law, the mass of a place in the social law is expressed in terms of some measure of how attractive the place is to interaction; population is often used, as suggested by the letter *P*, but many other measures are possible, such as size, social status, the diversity of commodities offered, and so on (for instance, one might prefer to go to a shopping center with more different stores). Importantly, distance may not be straight-line physical distance but some other measure of physical separation, such as distance along the roads connecting places (*route distance*). Alternatively, it is often more relevant to express distance in non-spatial terms, such as travel time, cost, or effort (for most of us, walking downhill is more alluring than walking uphill). Unlike in physical gravity, where the force of attraction declines as the square of distance (the *inverse-square law*), in social gravity, the force of interaction attraction declines at somewhat different rates depending on the domain of interaction (visiting a friend versus visiting a relative, for instance, or shopping for bread versus shopping for caviar). In many domains, the distance exponent is a fractional number (but almost always greater than 1). Finally, social gravity requires multiplication by a constant at the end just like physical gravity does. However, this social "constant" is actually variable across interaction domains, and unlike the *g* in physical gravity that represents something profound about the nature of the physical world, the *k* in social gravity is probably best thought of as just a mathematical way to get the interaction numbers to work out properly as the output of the equation.

Carey's second observation—that large cities have greater drawing power for individuals than do small ones—was subsequently addressed by the **law of retail gravitation,** proposed by William J. Reilly (1899–1970) in 1931. Using the population and distance inputs of the gravity model, Reilly determined the breaking-point (BP) location between two towns where one would expect to find the boundary separating the market areas of the two towns. The market areas are functional regions for each town that enclose the area where each town exerts controlling influence over retail trade; beyond that boundary, the other town dominates. Residents within a town's market area will likely travel to that town to shop. **Reilly's Breaking-Point Law** is:

$$BP_{(from\ i)} = \frac{D_{ij}}{1 + \sqrt{\dfrac{P_j}{P_i}}}.$$

This equation states that the BP location (the market area boundary) between two towns *i* and *j*—expressed as distance from town *i*, equals the distance between the two towns divided by 1, plus the square root of the population of town *j* divided by the population of town *i*. As with all social gravity models, distance may be measured as various forms of physical or nonphysical separation. Because the breaking point between cities of unequal size will lie farther from the larger of the two, its spatially greater drawing power is captured (Figure 3.5).

Later studies in location theory, city systems, trade area analysis, and other social topics all suggest that the gravity model can be used to account for a wide variety of interaction flow patterns

Figure 3.5 The *law of retail gravitation* provides a quick determination of the trade boundary (or breaking point) between two cities. In the diagram, cities 1 and 2 are 201 kilometers (125 miles) apart. Reilly's law tells us that the breaking point between them lies 81.6 kilometers (50.7 miles) distant from City 1. A potential customer located at *M*, midway (100.5 km or 62.5 mi) between the cities, would lie well within the trade zone of City 2. A series of such calculations would define the "trade area" of any single city.

in human geography, including population migration, commodity flows, journeys to work or to shop, telephone call volumes, and the like. Each such flow pattern suggests that size as well as distance influences spatial interaction. Carey's observation, made some 150 years ago, initiated a type of analysis that in modified form is used today for a variety of practical studies that help us better understand the "friction of distance."

Interaction Potential

The spatial interaction models of distance decay and gravitational pull we have considered thus far deal with only two places at a time. The world of reality is rather more complex. All cities, not just city pairs, within a regional system of cities have the possibility of interacting with each other. Indeed, the more specialized the goods produced in each separate center—that is, the greater their collective complementarity—the more likely it is that such multiple interactions will occur. Similarly, shoppers often have more than two stores or shopping centers to choose from on any given shopping trip.

A **potential model,** also based on the principles of social gravity, provides an estimate of the interaction opportunities available to a center in such a multicentered network. It tells us the relative interaction pull of each point in relation to all other places within a region. It does so by summing the interaction attractiveness and distance relationships between all points of potential interaction within an area. The concept of potential is applicable whenever the measurement of the intensity of spatial interaction is of concern—as it is in studies of retail behavior, marketing, land values, broadcasting, commuting patterns, and the like.

Movement Biases

Distance decay and the gravity models help us understand the bases for interaction in an idealized area without natural or cultural barriers to movement or restrictions on routes followed, and in which only rational interaction decisions are made. Even under those model conditions, the pattern of spatial interaction that develops for whatever reason inevitably affects the conditions under which future interactions will occur. An initial structure of centers and connecting flows will tend to freeze into the landscape a mutually reinforcing continuation of that same pattern. The predictable flows of shoppers to existing shopping centers make those centers attractive to other merchants. New store openings increase customer flow; increased flow strengthens the developed pattern of spatial interaction. And increased road traffic calls for the highway improvement that encourages additional traffic volume.

Such an aggregate regularity of flow is called a **movement bias.** We have already noted a distance bias that favors short movements over long ones. There is also direction bias, in which of all possible directions of movement, actual flows are restricted to only one or a few. Direction bias is simply a statement that from a given origin, flows are not random (Figure 3.6); rather, certain places have a greater attraction than do others. The movement patterns from an isolated farmstead are likely oriented to a favored shopping town. On a larger scale, in North America or Siberia, long-distance freight movements are directionally biased in favor of east-west flows. Direction bias is reflected in not just the orientation but also the intensity of flow. Movements from a single point—from Novosibirsk in Siberia, for example, or from Winnipeg, Canada, or Kansas City in the United States—may occur in all directions; they are in reality more intense along the east-west axis, in part because of the primary landmass orientations of these large countries.

Such directional biases are in part a reflection of network bias, a shorthand way of saying that the presence or absence of connecting channels strongly affects the likelihood that spatial interaction, including transportation and communication, will occur. A set of routes and the places that they connect are collectively called a **network;** in abstract terms, the places are called **nodes** and the connecting routes are called **links.** Networks facilitate spatial interaction along their links and between nodes they directly connect. Flows cannot occur between all nodes if not all nodes are linked, at least indirectly. In Figure 3.6a, the interchange between *A* and *X,* though not necessarily impossible, is unlikely because the route between them is indirect and circuitous. In information flows, a worker on the assembly line is less likely to know of company production plans than is a secretary in the executive offices; these two workers are tied into quite different information networks.

In Chapter 2, where we focused on cultural diffusion, we were reminded that there are obstacles to interaction in particular directions besides just distance. **Barriers** impede spatial interaction, either by blocking it totally, slowing it down, or redirecting it. Barriers to human interaction may be physical, as in mountains, oceans, or freeways (when you try to go *across* them rather than *along* them); sociocultural, as in groups of people speaking different languages or zoning laws that disallow certain land-use activities; and even psychological, as in areas people don't know about or are afraid of.

Human Spatial Behavior

Humans are not commodities and individually do not necessarily respond predictably to the impersonal dictates of spatial interaction constraints. Yet, to survive, people must be mobile and collectively do react to distance, time, and cost considerations of movement in space and to the implications of complementarity, transferability, and intervening opportunity. Indeed, an exciting line of geographic inquiry involves how individuals make spatial behavioral decisions and how those separate decisions may be summarized by models and generalizations to explain collective actions. These geographers approach geographic problems of human spatial **behavior** at the individual or *disaggregate* level. Geographers taking this **behavioral approach** believe they can improve models of spatial behavior such as those based on social gravity or economic rationality (see Chapter X) by learning more about the way people actually make decisions about where and how to travel and perform other geographic acts. They also recognize that problems involving the psychology of place, space, and environment are geographic problems in their own right because geographers study all aspects of space, place, and environment. As such, behavioral geographers appreciate that the spatial behaviors of individual people depend, in part, on what people believe to be true about themselves and the world, and how people actually

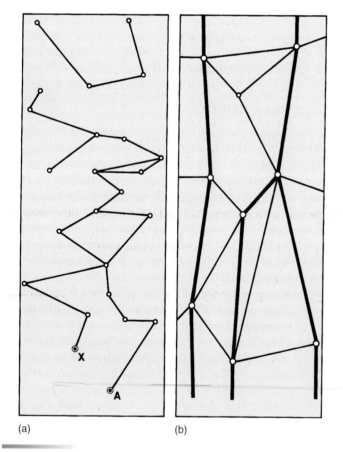

(a)   (b)

Figure 3.6 Direction bias. (*a*) When direction bias is absent, movements tend to be almost random, occurring in all possible directions, but less likely between points, such as *A* and *X,* that are not directly connected. (*b*) Direction bias indicating predominantly north-south movements, likely as a result of transportation routes and/or major destinations being aligned north to south.

remember and reason about properties of themselves and the world—their **cognition.** They further appreciate that humans do not make decisions only rationally or consciously; many decisions result from nonconscious mental activities and are influenced by emotions and **attitudes.** Finally, an individual analysis of human geography reminds us that no two people are exactly the same; whether based on age, culture, gender, genetic heritage, social class, training, or some other aspect of personal background or experience, people may differ somewhat in their geographic behavior. Models that treat all people as identical are oversimplifications, according to this approach.

Mobility is the general term applied to all types of human movement through space and time. Two aspects of that mobility behavior concern us. The first is the daily or temporary use of space—the journeys to stores, to work, or to school, or for longer periods on vacation or visiting friends and relatives. These types of mobility are often designated as **temporary travel** and have no suggestion of relocation of residence (Figure 3.7); people intend to return home after such trips, if not the same day, then relatively soon thereafter. The second type of mobility is the longer-term commitment related to decisions to leave the home territory permanently and find residence in a new location (residential relocation). This second form of spatial behavior is termed **migration.** The distinction between temporary travel and migration is important to a geographic analysis of spatial mobility and is usually fairly clear, but there are ambiguous cases. College students "migrate" to their campus housing from home but may return to that home every summer and after they graduate. Seasonal farm workers may be away from their home for much of the year, following the ripening fruits and vegetables, only to return home at the end of the harvest season. Refugees forced out of their home may intend to return when political, economic, or environmental conditions (see below) permit, but for many of these forced migrants, that time never comes. And of course, nomadic people permanently live in temporary housing that moves with them in a never-ending cycle of residential mobility.

Both aspects of temporary and permanent mobility imply a time dimension. Humans' spatial actions are not instantaneous, even

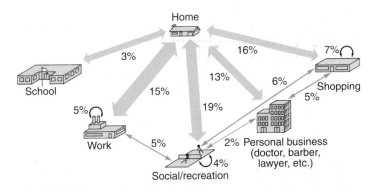

Figure 3.7 Seven County Minneapolis–St. Paul Metropolitan Area travel patterns. The numbers are the percentage of all urban trips taken on a typical weekday. In recent decades, the relative importance of work and school trips has decreased, while other types of trips have risen in importance.

Source: Data from Metropolitan Council: The 2000 Travel Behavior Inventory.

with improvements to transportation technologies. They operate over time, frequently imparting a rhythm to individual and group activity patterns and imposing choices among time-consuming behaviors. Elements of both aspects of human spatial behavior are also embodied in how individuals conceive of space and act within it, and how they respond to information affecting their space-behavioral decisions. The nature of those cognitions and responses affect us all in our daily movements. The more permanent movement embodied in migration involves additional and less common decisions and behaviors, as we shall see later in this chapter.

Individual Activity Space

One of the realities of life is that groups and countries draw boundaries around themselves and divide space into territories that are, if necessary, defended. Some see the concept of **territoriality**—the emotional attachment to and the defense of home ground—as a root explanation of much of human action and response. It is true that some individual and collective activity appears to be governed by territorial defense responses: the conflict between street groups in claiming and protecting their "turf" (and their fear for their lives when venturing beyond it) and the sometimes violent rejection by an ethnic urban neighborhood of any different advancing population group that it considers threatening. On a more individualized basis, each of us claims as **personal space** the zone of privacy and separation from others that our culture or our physical circumstances require or permit. Anglo Americans strive for greater face-to-face separation in conversations than do Latin Americans. Personal space on a crowded beach or in a department store is acceptably more limited than it is in our homes or when we are studying in a library (Figure 3.8).

For most of us, our personal sense of territoriality is a tempered one. We regard our homes and property as defensible private domains but open them to innocent visitors, known and unknown, or to those on private or official business. Nor do we confine our activities so exclusively within controlled home territories as street-gang members do within theirs. Rather, we have a more or less extended home range, an **activity space** or area within which we typically move freely on our rounds of regular activity, sharing that space with others who are also about their daily affairs. Figure 3.9 depicts activity spaces for a suburban family of five for an average weekday. Note that the activity space is different for each individual.

The types of trips that individuals make, and thus the extent of their activity space, depend on at least three interrelated variables: their stage in life course; the means of mobility at their command; and the demands or opportunities implicit in their daily activities. The first variable, stage in life, refers to membership in specific age groups. School-age children usually travel short distances to lower schools and longer distances to upper-level schools. After-school activities tend to be limited to walking or to bicycle trips to nearby locations. Greater mobility is characteristic of high-school students. Adults responsible for household duties make shopping trips and trips related to child care, as well as journeys away from home for social, cultural, or recreational purposes. Wage-earning adults usually travel farther from home

(a)

(b)

Figure 3.8 Our demanded *personal space* is not necessarily uniform in shape or constant in size. We tolerate strangers closer to our sides than directly in front of us; we accept more crowding in an elevator than in a store. We accept the press of the crowd on a popular beach (*a*)—as do these students on spring break in the Florida Keys (*b*), but tend to distance ourselves from others in a public square.

To recreational activity

Shopping center

Elementary school

Middle school

Friend

YMCA

Home

— Husband
— Wife
— Oldest child
— Middle child
— Youngest child

— Car
- - Bicycle
··· Walk

1/2 mile

1/2 km

To work

Park

Figure 3.9 Activity space for each member of a family of five for a typical weekday. Routes of regular movement and areas recurrently visited help to foster a sense of territoriality and to affect one's cognitions of space.

than other family members. Elderly people may, through infirmity or interests, have less extensive activity spaces.

The second variable that affects the extent of activity space is mobility, or the ability to travel. An informal consideration of the cost and effort required to overcome the friction of distance is implicit. Where incomes are high, automobiles are available, and the cost of fuel is reckoned as minor in the family budget, mobility may be great and individual activity space large. In societies or neighborhoods where cars are not a standard means of conveyance, the daily non-emergency activity space may be limited to walking, bicycling, or taking infrequent trips on public transportation. Wealthy suburbanites are far more mobile than are residents of inner-city slums, a circumstance that affects ability to learn about, seek, or retain work and to have access to medical care, educational facilities, and social services.

A third factor limiting activity space is the individual assessment of the existence of possible activities or opportunities. In subsistence economies where the needs of daily life are satisfied at home, the impetus for journeys away from home is minimal. If there are no stores, schools, factories, or even roads, expectations and opportunities are limited. Not only are activities spatially restricted, but **awareness space**—knowledge of opportunity locations beyond normal activity space—is minimal, distorted, or absent. In low-income neighborhoods of modern cities in any country, poverty and isolation limit the inducements, opportunities, destinations, and necessity of travel (Figure 1.25). Opportunities plus mobility conditioned by life stage bear heavily on the amount of spatial interaction in which individuals engage.

The Tyranny of Time

Whatever their activity, people are always located somewhere. Furthermore, they are always located somewhere at some time of the day or night, and they spend various periods of time at each location before moving through space and time to new locations. The study of the temporal characteristics of activities in conjunction with their spatial characteristics is known as **time geography.** We can depict this by drawing a graph that shows activity locations and movements around the landscape plotted against time on the vertical axis. This graph of a person's activity locations at certain times is a **space-time path.** Figure 3.10 shows a daily space-time path, but weekly, yearly, or even lifetime paths are possible. Whatever the temporal scale, space-time paths are notable for their tendency to show cyclic, nonrandom patterns of recurring activity locations at particular times, such as daily or seasonal patterns.

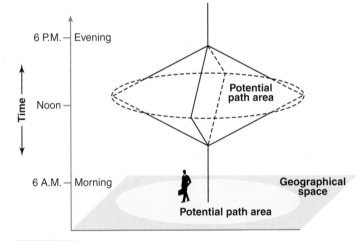

Figure 3.10 **The space-time prism.** An individual's daily prism has both geographical limits and totally surrounding space-time walls. The *time* (vertical axis) involved in movement affects the space that is accessible, along with the time and space available for other than travel purposes. (*a*) When collecting firewood for household use may take an entire day, as it does in some deforested developing countries, no time or space is left for other activities, and the gatherer's space-time prism may be represented by almost a straight line. (*b*) Walking to and from work or school and spending the required number of hours there leave little time to broaden one's area of activity. (*c*) The automobile permits an extension of the geographical boundaries of the driver's space-time prism; the range of activity possibilities and locations is expanded for the highly mobile.

The activities of humans—eating, sleeping, traveling between home and destination, working, or attending classes—all consume time and involve space. An individual's spatial reach is restricted because one cannot be in two different places at the same moment or engage simultaneously in activities that are spatially separate. Further, since there is a finite amount of time within a day and each of us is biologically bound to a daily rhythm of day and night, sleeping and eating, time tyrannically limits the spatial choices we can make and the activity space that we can command.

The daily space-time constraints of our time geography may be represented by a **space-time prism,** the volume of space and length of time within which our activities must be confined. Its size and shape are determined by our mobility and our locational responsibilities; its boundaries define what we can or cannot accomplish spatially and temporally (Figure 3.11). If our circumstances demand that we walk to work or school (Figure 3.11), the sides of our prism are steep and the space available for our activities is narrow; steep diagonals mean slow travel and indicate that we cannot go as far in a given time period. We cannot use time spent in transit for most other activities, and the area reasonably accessible to the pedestrian is limited. The space-time prism for the driver (Figure 3.10) has more shallow-angled sides and the individual's spatial range is wide; shallow diagonals mean

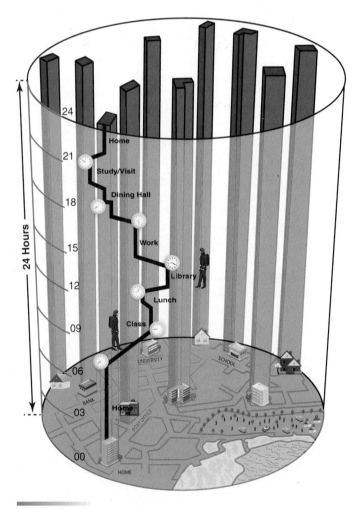

Figure 3.11 The school-day space-time path for a hypothetical college student.

Space, Time, and Women

From a time-geography perspective, it is apparent that many of the limitations that women face in their choices of employment or other activities outside the home reflect the restrictions that women's time budgets and travel paths place on their individual daily activities.

Consider the case* of the unmarried working woman with one or more pre-school-age children. The location and operating hours of available child-care facilities may have more of an influence on her choice of job than do her labor skills or the relative merits of alternative employment opportunities. For example, the woman may not be able to leave her home before a given hour because the only full-day child-care service available to her is not open earlier. She must return at a specified time to pick up her child and arrive home to prepare food at a reasonable (for the child) dinner time. Her travel mode and speed determine the outer limits of her daily space-time prism.

Suppose both of two solid job offers have the same working hours and fall within her possible activity space. She cannot accept the preferred, better-paying job because drop-off time at the child-care center would make her late for work, and work hours would make her miss the center's closing time. On the other hand, although the other job is acceptable from a child-care standpoint, it leaves no time (or store options) for shopping or errands except during the lunch break. Job choice and shopping opportunities are thus determined not by the woman's labor skills or awareness of store price comparisons, but by her time-geography constraints. Other women in other job skill, parenthood, locational, or mobility circumstances experience different but comparable space-path restrictions.

Mobility is a key to activity mix, time-budget, and activity space configurations. Again, research indicates that women are frequently disadvantaged. Because of their multiple work, child-care, and home maintenance tasks, women on average make more—though shorter—trips than men, leaving less time for alternate activities.

The lower income level of many single women with or without children limits their ability to own cars and leads them to use public transit disproportionately to their numbers—to the detriment of both their money and time-space budgets. They are, it has been observed, "transportation deprived and transit dependent."

Geographer Mei-Po Kwan used geographic information system (GIS) and travel diaries to create three-dimensional diagrams of the time-geography patterns of a sample of men and women who all had driver's licenses and access to automobiles. Despite their relative affluence, Kwan found that women experience more time-geography constraints than men because of their child-care, school drop-off, or other responsibilities. Women with other adults in the household to share domestic responsibilities experienced fewer constraints, and women with the most time-geography constraints were more likely to have to accept part-time work.

*Suggested by Risa Palm and Allan Pred, "A Time-Geographic Perspective on Problems of Inequality for Women," Institute of Urban and Regional Development, Working Paper No. 236, University of California, Berkeley, 1974.

Source: Mei-Po Kwan, 1999. "Gender, the home-work link, and space-time patterns of non-employment Activities, Economic Geography, 75(4): 370–394 (1999).

rapid travel and indicate that we can go farther in a given time period. The area of the prism determines what spatially defined activities are possible, for no activity can exceed the bounds of the prism (see the feature "Space, Time, and Women"). That is, space-time paths are constrained to fit within space-time prisms. Since most activities have their own time constraints, the choices of things you can do and the places in which you can do them are strictly limited. Scheduled class hours, travel time from residence to campus, and dining hall location and opening and closing hours, for example, may be the constraints on your space-time path (Figure 3.11). If you also need part-time work, your choice of jobs is restricted by their respective locations and work hours, for the job, too, must fit within your daily space-time prism. Parenting responsibilities, particularly for single parents, place major constraints on the spatial range of individuals. In households where one partner (typically the woman) bears greater responsibilities for childcare and household chores, their job choices may be limited by their narrow time-geographic constraints, and they may be forced to accept lower pay and/or a less prestigious job. In other words, all people have *space-time budgets* that dictate how far they can travel in a given time period. Geographers apply the study of these space-time budgets and other aspects of time geography to problems such as traffic control, mass transit, and highway and parking structure design.

Distance and Human Interaction

People make many more short-distance trips than long ones, a statement in human behavioral terms of the concept of distance decay. If we drew a boundary line around our activity space, it would be evident that trips to the boundary are taken much less often than short-distance trips around the home. The tendency is for the frequency of trips to fall off very rapidly beyond an individual's **critical distance**—the distance beyond which cost, effort, and means strongly influence our willingness to travel. Figure 3.12 illustrates the point with regard to journeys from the homesite.

Regular movements defining our individual activity space are undertaken for different purposes and are differently influenced by time and distance considerations. The kinds of activities that individuals engage in can be classified according to type of trip: journeys to work, to school, to shop, for recreation, and so on. People in nearly all parts of the world make these same types of journeys, though the spatially variable requirements of culture, economy, and personal circumstance dictate their frequency, duration, and significance to an individual (Figure 3.13). A small child, for example, will make many trips up and down the block but is inhibited by parental admonitions from crossing the street. Different but equally effective distance constraints control adult behavior.

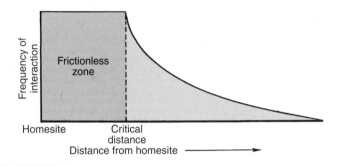

Figure 3.12 Critical distance. This general diagram indicates how most people observe distance. For each activity, there is a distance beyond which the intensity of contact declines. This is called the *critical distance*. The distance up to the critical distance is identified as a *frictionless zone*, in which time or distance considerations do not effectively figure in the decision to take the trip.

The journey to work plays a decisive role in defining the activity space of most adults. Formerly restricted by walking distance or by the routes and schedules of mass transit systems, the critical distances of work trips have steadily increased in European and Anglo American cities as the private automobile figures more importantly in the movement of workers (Figure 3.14). Daily or weekly shopping may be within the critical distance of an individual, and little thought may be given to the cost or the effort involved. That same individual, however, may relegate shopping for special goods to infrequent trips and carefully consider their cost and effort. The majority of our social contacts tend to be at short distance within our own neighborhoods or with friends who live relatively close at hand; longer social trips to visit relatives are less frequent. In all such trips, however, the distance decay function is clearly at work (Figure 3.15).

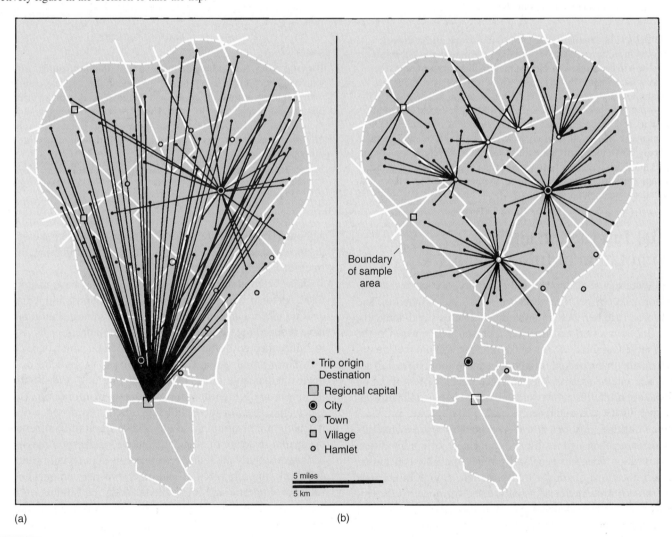

(a)   (b)

Figure 3.13 Travel patterns for purchases of clothing and yard goods of (*a*) rural cash-economy Canadians and (*b*) Canadians of the Old Order Mennonite sect. These strikingly different travel behaviors mapped many years ago in central Canada demonstrate the great differences that may exist in the action spaces of different culture groups occupying the same territory. At that time, "modern" rural Canadians, owning cars and wishing to take advantage of the variety of goods offered in the more distant regional capital, were willing and able to travel longer distances than were neighboring people of a traditionalist culture who had different mobility and whose different demands in clothing and other consumer goods were, by preference or necessity, satisfied in nearby small settlements. Unpublished studies suggest that similar contrasts in mobility and purchase travel patterns currently exist between buggy-using Old Order Amish (see Figure 7.2 in Chapter 7) and their car-driving neighbors.

Source: Robert A. Murdie, "Cultural differences in consumer travel," Economic Geography *41(3) (Worcester, Mass.: Clark University, 1965). Redrawn by permission.*

Figure 3.14 The frequency distribution of work and nonwork trip lengths in minutes in the seven-county Minneapolis–St. Paul metropolitan area. Studies in various metropolitan areas support the conclusions documented by this graph: work trips are usually longer than other recurring journeys. In the United States in the early 1990s, the average work trip covered 17.1 kilometers (10.6 miles), and half of all trips to work took under 22 minutes; for suburbanites commuting to the central business district, the journey to work involved between 30 and 45 minutes. By 2000, increasing sprawl had lengthened average commuting distances and, also because of growing traffic congestion, had increased the average work trip commuting time to 25 minutes; many workers had commutes of more than 45 minutes.

Source: Metropolitan Council: The 2000 Travel Behavior Inventory.

Spatial Interaction and the Accumulation of Information

Critical distances, even for the same activity, are somewhat different for each person. The variables of life stage, mobility, and opportunity, together with an individual's interests and demands, help define how often and how far a person will travel. On the basis of these variables, we can make inferences about the amount of information that a person is likely to acquire about his or her activity space and the area beyond. The accumulation of information about the opportunities and rewards of spatial interaction helps increase and justify movement decisions.

For information flows, however, space has a somewhat different meaning than it does for the movement of commodities. Communication does not necessarily imply the time-consuming physical relocations of freight transportation, though in the case of letters and print media, it usually does. In modern telecommunications, the process of information flow may be very quick regardless of distance. The result is extensive space-time compression. A Bell System report tells us that in 1920, putting through a transcontinental telephone call took 14 minutes and eight operators and cost more than $15 for a 3-minute call. By 1940, the call completion time was reduced to less than 1½ minutes, and the cost fell to $4. In the 1960s, direct distance dialing allowed a transcontinental connection in less than 30 seconds, and electronic switching has now reduced the completion time to little more than that involved in dialing a number and answering

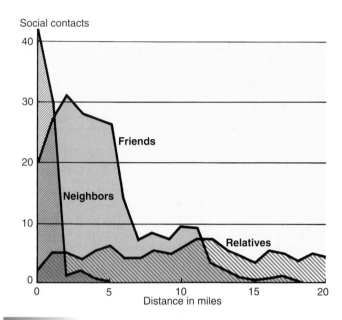

Figure 3.15 **Social interaction as a function of distance.** Visits with neighbors on the same street are frequent; they are less common with neighbors around the corner and diminish quickly to the vanishing point after a residential relocation. Friends exert a greater spatial pull, though the distance decay factor is clearly evident. Visits with relatives offer the greatest incentive for longer distance (though relatively infrequent) journeys.

Source: Frederick P. Stutz, "Distance and network effects on urban social travel fields," Economic Geography 49(2) (Worcester, Mass.: Clark University, 1973), p. 139. Redrawn by permission.

a phone. The extra price of long-distance conversation essentially disappeared with the advent of voice communication over the Internet early in this century.

The Internet and communication satellites have made worldwide personal and mass communication almost immediate and data transfers a matter of moments. The same technologies that have reduced the time separation of communications have tended to reduce their cost separation. Domestic mail, which once charged a distance-based postage, is now carried nationwide or across town for the same price. In the modern world, transferability is no longer a very significant consideration in information flows. A speculative view of the future suggests that as distance ceases to be much of a determinant of the cost or speed of communication, the spatial structure of economic and social decision making may be fundamentally altered. Determinations about where people live and work, the role of cities and other existing command centers, flows of domestic and international trade, constraints on human mobility, and even the concepts and impacts of national boundaries may fundamentally change with new and unanticipated consequences for patterns of spatial interaction.

Information Flows

Spatially significant information flows are of two types: individual (person-to-person) exchanges and mass (source-to-area) communication. A further subdivision into formal and informal interchange recognizes, in the former, the need for an interposed channel (radio, press, postal service, or telephone, for example) to convey messages. Informal communication requires no such institutionalized message carrier.

Short-range informal individual communication is as old as humankind itself. Contacts and exchanges between individuals and within small groups tend to increase as the complexity of social organization increases, as the size and importance of the population center grow, and as the range of interests and associations of the communicating person expands. Each individual develops a **personal communication field,** the informational counterpart of that person's activity space. Its size and shape are defined by the individual's contacts in work, recreation, shopping, school, or other regular activities. Those activities, as we have seen, are functions of the age, sex, education, employment, income, and so on of each person. An idealized personal communication field is suggested in Figure 3.16.

Each interpersonal exchange constitutes a link in the individual's personal communication field. Each person, in turn, is a node in the communication field of those with whom he or she makes or maintains contact. The total number of such separate informal networks essentially equals the total count of people alive. Despite the number of those networks, all people, in theory, are interconnected by multiple shared nodes (Figure 3.17). One debated claim suggested that through such interconnections, no person in the United States is more than six links removed from any other person, no matter where located or how unlikely the association.

Mass communication is the formal, structured transmission of information in essentially a one-way flow between single points of origin and broad areas of reception. There are few transmitters and many receivers. The mass media are by nature "space filling." From single origin points, they address their messages by print, radio, or television to potential receivers within a defined area. The number and location of disseminating points, therefore, are related to their spatial coverage characteristics, to the minimum size of area and population necessary for their support, and to the capability of the potential audiences to receive their message. The coverage area is determined both by the nature of the medium and by the corporate intent of the agency.

There are no inherent spatial restrictions on the dissemination of printed materials, though of course limitations and restrictions may be imposed by obscenity laws, religious prohibitions, restrictions in some countries on certain forms of political speech, and the like. And not everyone has access to bookstores or libraries or funds to buy printed material, and not everyone can read. Unlike the distance limitations on the transmission of AM or FM radio waves, however, these restrictions are independent of the area over which printed material could be physically distributed and made available.

In the United States, much book and national magazine publishing is localized in metropolitan New York City, as have the services supplying news and features for sale to the print media located there and elsewhere in the country. Paris, Buenos Aires, Moscow, London—indeed, the major metropolises and/or capital cities of other countries—show the same spatial concentration. Regional journals emanate from regional capitals, and major metropolitan newspapers, though serving primarily their home markets, are distributed over (or produce special editions for distribution within) tributary areas whose size and shape depend on the intensity of competition from other metropolises. A spatial information hierarchy has thus emerged.

Hierarchies are also reflected in the market-size requirements for different levels of media offerings. National and international organizations are required to expedite information flows (and, perhaps, to control their content), but market demand is heavily weighted in favor of regional and local coverage. In the electronic media, the result has been national networks with local affiliates acting as the gatekeepers of network offerings and adding to them locally originating programs and news content. A similar market subdivision is represented by the regional editions of national newspapers and magazines.

The technological ability to fill space with messages from different mass media is useless if receiving audiences do not exist. In illiterate societies, publications cannot inform or influence. Unless the appropriate receivers are widely available, television and radio broadcasts are a waste of resources. Perhaps no invention in history has done more to weld isolated individuals and purely person-to-person communicators into national societies exposed to centralized information flows than has the low-cost transistor radio. Its battery-powered transportability converts the remotest village and the most isolated individual into a receiving node of entertainment, information, and political messages. The direct satellite broadcast of television programs to community antennae or communal sets brings that mass medium to remote areas of Arctic Canada, India, Indonesia, and other world areas able to invest in the technology but as yet unserved by ground stations.

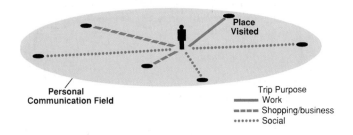

Figure 3.16 A personal communication field is determined by individual spatial patterns of communication related to work, shopping, business trips, social visits, and so on.

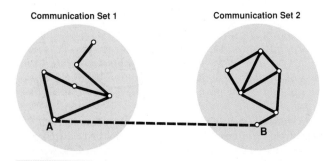

Figure 3.17 Separate population sets (groups) are interconnected by the links between individuals. If link A–B exists, everyone in the two sets is linked.

Information and Cognition

Human spatial interaction, as we have seen, is conditioned by a number of factors. Complementarity, transferability, and intervening opportunities help pattern the movement of commodities and peoples. Flows between points and over area are influenced by distance decay and partially explained by gravity and potential models. Individuals in their daily affairs operate in activity spaces that are partly determined by stage in life, mobility, and a variety of socioeconomic characteristics. In every instance of spatial interaction, however, decisions are based on people's beliefs about the opportunity or feasibility of movement, exchange, and the satisfaction of needs and desires, not the objective truth about these things.

More precisely, our actions and decisions are based on our cognition—the awareness that we have, as individuals, of home and distant places, and the beliefs that we hold about their properties. Geographers often refer to such cognitions about Earth locations with the term **place perception,** which is our beliefs, impressions, and feelings—rational or irrational, consciously realized or not—about the natural and cultural characteristics of an area and about its opportunity structure. (Used in this way, geographers are treating the term *perception* as synonymous with cognition.) Whether our views accord with those of others or accurately reflect the "real" world seen in objective terms is not all that matters. Our cognitions are important because the decisions that we make about how to spend our time or about what actions to take in space are not based directly on reality but on our assumptions and impressions of reality.

maximum interaction potential, people commonly set psychological barriers around themselves so that only a limited number of those possible interactions and information exchanges actually occur. We raise barriers against information overload and to preserve a sense of privacy that permits the filtering out of information that does not directly affect us. There are obvious barriers to long-distance information flows as well, such as time and money costs, mountains, oceans, rivers, and differing religions, languages, ideologies, and political systems.

Barriers to information flow give rise to what we earlier (p. 66) called *direction bias.* In the present usage, this implies a tendency to have greater knowledge of places in some directions than in others. Not having friends or relatives in one part of a country may represent a barrier to individuals, so interest in and knowledge of the area beyond the "unknown" region are low. In the United States, both northerners and southerners tend to be less well informed about each other's areas than about the western part of the country. Traditional communication lines in the United States follow an east-west rather than a north-south direction, the result of early migration patterns, business connections, and the pattern of the development of major cities. In Russia, directional bias favors a north-south information flow within the European part of the country and less familiarity with areas far to the east. Within Siberia, however, east-west flows dominate.

When information about a place is sketchy, blurred pictures develop. These influence the impressions that we have of places and cannot be discounted. Many important decisions are made on the basis of incomplete information or biased reports, such as decisions to visit or not, to migrate or not, to hate or not, even

Cognition of Environment

Psychologists and geographers are interested in determining how we arrive at our cognitions of place and environment both within and beyond our normal activity space. The images we form firsthand of our home territory have been in part reviewed in the discussion of mental maps in Chapter 1. The cognitions we have about more distant places are less directly derived (Figure 3.18). In technologically advanced societies, television and radio, magazines and newspapers, books and lectures, travel brochures and hearsay all combine to help us develop a mental picture of unfamiliar places and of the interaction opportunities that they may contain. Again, however, the most effectively transmitted information seems to come from word-of-mouth reports. These may be in the form of letters or visits from relatives, friends, and associates who supply information that helps us develop ideas about relatively unknown areas.

There are, of course, barriers to the flow of information, including that of distance decay. Our knowledge of close places is greater than our knowledge of distant points; our contacts with nearby persons theoretically yield more information than we receive from afar. Yet in crowded areas with

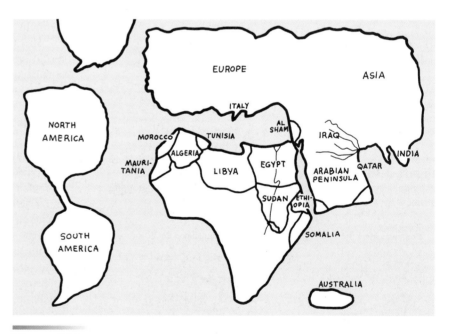

Figure 3.18 A Palestinian student's view of the world. This map was drawn by a Palestinian high-school student from Gaza, and it reflects the instruction and classroom impressions that the student has received. The Gaza curriculum conforms to the Egyptian national standards and thus is influenced by the importance of the Nile River and pan-Arabism. Al Sham is the old, but still used, name for the area that includes Syria, Lebanon, and Palestine. The map might be quite different in emphasis if the Gaza school curriculum were designed by Palestinians or if it had been drawn by an Israeli student.

to make war or not. Awareness of places is usually accompanied by opinions about them, but there is no necessary relationship between the depth of knowledge and the beliefs held (see the discussion of mental maps and place stereotypes in Chapter 1). In general, the more familiar we are with a locale, the more sound the factual basis of our mental image of it will be. But individuals form firm impressions of places totally unknown to them personally, and these may color interaction decisions.

One way to determine how individuals envisage home or distant places is to ask them what they think of different locales. For instance, they may be asked to rate places according to desirability—perhaps residential desirability—or to make a list of the 10 best and the 10 worst cities in their country of residence. Certain regularities appear in such inquiries. Figure 3.19 presents some residential desirability data elicited from college students in three provinces of Canada. These and comparable preference maps derived from studies conducted by researchers in many countries suggest that people generally like the place where they are from but also like some places far away that are widely popular in their culture For example, students from colleges around the United States tend to rate West Coast states such as California highly, but unless they are from states in the Southeast or the Plains Region, they tend to rate those states poorly. Individuals tend to be indifferent to unfamiliar places and areas and to dislike those that have competing interests (such as distasteful political and military activities or conflicting economic concerns) or a physical environment believed to be unpleasant.

On the other hand, places believed to have superior climates or landscape amenities are rated highly in preference map studies and favored in tourism and migration decisions. Holiday tours to Spain, the south of France, and the Mediterranean islands are heavily booked by the British seeking to escape their damp, cloudy climate. A U.S. Census Bureau study indicates that "climate" is, after work and family proximity, the most often reported reason for interstate moves by adults of all ages. International studies reveal a similar migration motivation based not only on climate, but also on concepts of natural beauty and amenities.

Perception of Natural Hazards

Less certain is the negative impact on spatial interaction or relocation decisions of assessments of *natural hazards*. Natural hazards are elements, processes, or events in the environment that can

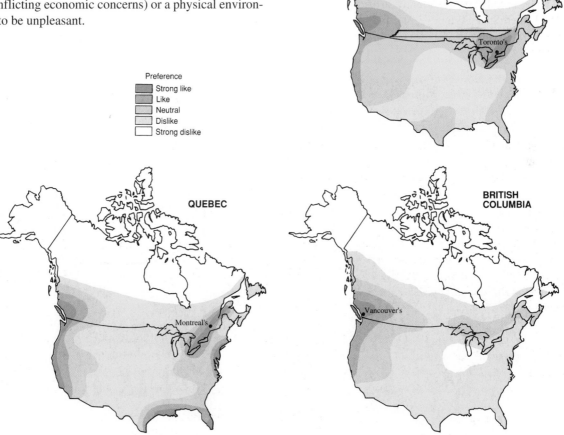

Figure 3.19 **Residential preferences of Canadians.** These maps show the residential preference of a sampled group of Canadians from the provinces of British Columbia, Ontario, and Quebec, respectively. Note that each group of respondents prefers its own area, but all like the Canadian and U.S. west coasts.

Source: Herbert A. Whitney, "Preferred locations in North America: Canadians, clues, and conjectures," Journal of Geography *83(5), p. 222. (Indiana, Pa.: National Council for Geographic Education, 1984). Redrawn by permission.*

cause harm to humans. While the term implies that these hazards are "natural," human adaptation and location decisions always play a major role in determining how disastrous the results are. For example, where we decide to build homes and businesses, and how we construct them, has a major impact on how much destruction is caused by an earthquake.

Mental images of home areas do not generally include an acknowledgment of potential natural dangers as an overriding concern. The cyclone that struck the delta area of Bangladesh on November 12, 1970, left at least 500,000 people dead, yet after the disaster, the movement of people into the area swelled the population above precyclone levels—a resettlement repeated after other, more recent cyclones. The July 28, 1976, earthquake in the Tangshan area of China devastated a major urban industrial complex, with casualties estimated at about a quarter-million, and between 50,000 and 100,000 city dwellers and villagers reportedly perished during and after the January 2001 quake in Gujarat state of western India. In both cases, rebuilding began almost immediately, as it usually does following earthquake damage (Figure 3.20) or after the devastation of earthquake-induced tsunamis like the December 2004 inundation of the Indonesian, Thai, and Indian coasts. The human response to even such major and exceptional natural hazards is duplicated by a general tendency to discount dangers from more common hazard occurrences. Johnstown, Pennsylvania, has suffered recurrent floods, and yet its residents rebuild; violent storms like Hurricane Katrina recurrently strike the Gulf and East coasts of the United States (Figure 3.21), and people remain

or return. Californians contemplating a move to Kansas may be concerned about tornadoes there but be unconcerned about earthquake dangers at home.

Why do people choose to settle in areas of high-consequence hazards in spite of the potential threat to their lives and property? Why do hundreds of thousands of people live along the San Andreas Fault in California, build houses in Pacific coastal areas known to experience severe erosion during storms, return to flood-prone river valleys in Europe or Asia, or avalanche-threatened Andean valleys? What is it that makes the risk worth taking? Ignorance of natural hazard danger is not necessarily a consideration. People in seismically active regions of the United States and Europe, at least, do believe that damaging earthquakes are a possibility in their districts but, research indicates, are reluctant to do anything about the risk. Similar awareness and reticence accompanies other low-incidence/high-consequence natural dangers. Less than one-tenth of 1 percent of respondents to a federal survey gave "natural disaster" as the reason for their interstate residential move. Geographers have long wondered about these residential decisions by people in the face of repeated hazards. Are they paradoxical, foolish, or, in some way, rational? There are many reasons why natural hazard risk does not deter settlement or adversely affect space-behavioral decisions. Of importance, of course, is the persistent belief that the likelihood of an earthquake or a flood or other natural calamity is sufficiently remote so that it is not reasonable or pressing to modify behavior because of it. People are influenced by their natural optimism (which some might call

Figure 3.20 Destruction from the San Francisco earthquake and fire. The first shock struck San Francisco early on the morning of April 18, 1906, damaging the city's water system. Fire broke out and raged for three days. It was finally stopped by dynamiting buildings in its path. When it was over, some 700 people were dead or missing, and 25,000 buildings had been destroyed. Locally, the event is usually referred to as the Great Fire of 1906, suggesting a denial of the natural hazard in favor of assigning blame to correctable human error. Post-destruction reconstruction began at once. Rebuilding following earthquake damage is the general rule.

Figure 3.21 People waiting to be rescued from a New Orleans rooftop following Hurricane Katrina's assault in late August of 2005. More than 1,600 died, hundreds of thousands were left homeless, and tens of billions of dollars of damage were incurred from the storm, which was immediately followed by government and private efforts at recovery and rebuilding.

Table 3.1	
Common Responses to the Uncertainty of Natural Hazards	
Eliminate the Hazard	
Deny or Denigrate Its Existence	**Deny or Denigrate Its Recurrence**
"We have no floods here, only high water."	"Lightning never strikes twice in the same place."
"It can't happen here."	"It's a freak of nature."
Eliminate the Uncertainty	
Make It Determinate and Knowable	**Transfer Uncertainty to a Higher Power**
"Seven years of great plenty.... After them seven years of famine."	"It's in the hands of God."
"Floods come every five years."	"The government is taking care of it."

Source: Burton and Kates , "The perception of natural hazards in resource management," 3 *Natural Resources Journal* 435 (1964). Used by permission of the University of New Mexico School of Law, Albuquerque, N.M.

willful ignoring of real risks) and the predictive uncertainty about timing or severity of a rare but calamitous event. Past experiences in high-hazard areas might be relevant. If people have not suffered much damage in the past, they may be optimistic about the future. If, on the other hand, past damage has been great, they may think that the probability of repetition in the future is low, which often represents fallacious thinking (Table 3.1). Lightning may well be *more* likely to strike in the same place, because the first strike we hear about is evidence that the place is attractive to lightning (think of a metal tower on a hill).

Perception of place as attractive or desirable may be quite divorced from any understanding of its hazard potential. Attachment to locale or region may be an expression of emotion and economic or cultural attraction, not just a rational assessment of risk. The culture hearths of antiquity discussed in Chapter 2 and shown on Figure 2.15 were for the most part sited in flood-prone river valleys; their enduring attraction was undiminished by that potential danger. The home area, whatever disadvantages an outside observer may discern, exerts a force of attachment to place and identification with place that is not easily dismissed or ignored.

Indeed, high-hazard areas are often sought out because they possess desirable topography or scenic views, as do, for instance, coastal areas subject to storm damage. Once people have purchased property in a known hazard area, they may be unable to sell it for a reasonable price even if they so desire. They think that they have no choice but to remain and protect their investment. The cultural hazard—loss of livelihood and investment—appears more serious than whatever natural hazards there may be. Carried further, it has been observed that spatial adjustment to perceived natural hazards is a luxury not affordable to impoverished people in general or to the urban and rural poor of Third World countries in particular. Forced by population growth and economic necessity to exert ever-greater pressures upon fragile environments or to occupy

at higher densities hazardous hillside and floodplain slums, their margin of safety in the face of both chronic and low-probability hazards is minimal to nonexistent (Figure 3.22). In sum, these considerations suggest that there are great economic, cultural, and ideological benefits to living in hazardous places, which when taken together, apparently outweigh the risks to most people.

Figure 3.22 Many of the poor of Rio de Janeiro, Brazil, occupy steep hillside locations above the reach of sewer, water, and power lines that keep the more affluent at lower elevations. Frequent heavy rains cause mudflows from the saturated hillsides that wipe away the shacks and shelters that insecurely cling to them, and deposit the homes and hopes of the poor in the richer neighborhoods below.

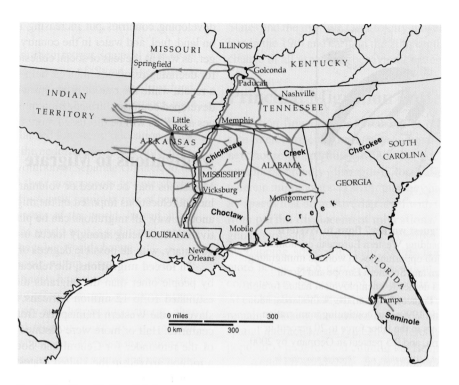

Figure 3.25 **Forced migrations: The Five Civilized Tribes.** Between 1825 and 1840, some 100,000 southeastern Native Americans were removed from their homelands and transferred by the Army across the Mississippi River to "Indian Territory" in present-day Oklahoma. By far, the largest number consisted of members of the "Five Civilized Tribes" of the South: Cherokees, Choctaws, Chickasaws, Creeks, and Seminoles. Settled, Christianized, literate small-farmers, their forced eviction and arduous journey—particularly along what the Cherokees named their "Trail of Tears" in the harsh winter of 1837–1838—resulted in much suffering and death.

Less than fully voluntary migration—**reluctant relocation**—of some 8 million Indonesians has taken place under an aggressive governmental campaign begun in 1969 to move people from densely settled Java (roughly 775 per square kilometer or 2000 people per square mile) to other islands and territories of the country, in what has been called the "biggest colonization program in history." International refugees from war and political turmoil or repression numbered nearly 13.5 million in 2005, according to the United Nations.

In recent decades, the vast majority of new international migrants has been absorbed by the developed countries. But there has also been an increasing flight from developing countries to other developing regions, and many countries with the largest refugee populations are among the world's poorest. Sub-Saharan Africa alone houses over 3 million refugees (Figure 3.26). Between 2003 and 2007, Iran, Syria, and Jordan became home to millions of Iraqis fleeing persecution, terrorism, and war. Additionally, at the end of 2005, the Internal Displacement Monitoring Centre estimated that there were 25.3 million people in some 40 countries worldwide who were "refugees" in their own countries as a result of conflicts or human rights violations; in a search for security or sustenance, they had left their home area but not crossed an international boundary. The total did not include those additional millions internally displaced by environmental disasters such as the southeast Asian tsunami in 2004 or Hurricane Katrina in 2005.

Poverty is the great motivator. Some 30 percent of the world's population—nearly 2 billion persons—have less than $1 per day

of income. In addition, many are victims of drought, floods, other natural catastrophes, or wars and terrorism. Poverty in developing countries is greatest in the countryside; rural areas are home to around 750 million of the world's poorest people. Of these, some 20 to 30 million move each year to towns and cities, many as "environmental refugees" abandoning land so eroded or exhausted it can no longer support them. In the cities, they join the 40 percent or more of the labor force that is unemployed or underemployed in their home country and seek legal or illegal entry into more promising economies of the developed world. All, rural or urban, respond to the same basic forces—the push of poverty and the pull of perceived or hoped-for opportunity.

Those motivating forces are controlling in much of the international flow of illegal migrants whose economic condition in their homelands, they feel, is so intolerable that to seek employment they risk their lives in flight by unsafe boat and raft or through forbidding natural boundary barriers as involuntary but unforced migrants. Without immigration papers or legal status, subject to arrest and deportation or worse, illegal immigrants able to find work and income satisfy some of their migration objectives by sending money home to ensure their families' survival. Immigrants from poor countries, the World Bank estimated, sent more than 260 billion traceable dollars home in 2006; money sent through informal channels increased that total by as much as 50 percent. The traceable **remittance** amount alone in 2005 was on a par with the total of foreign direct investment in developing countries and twice the value of foreign aid. The estimated

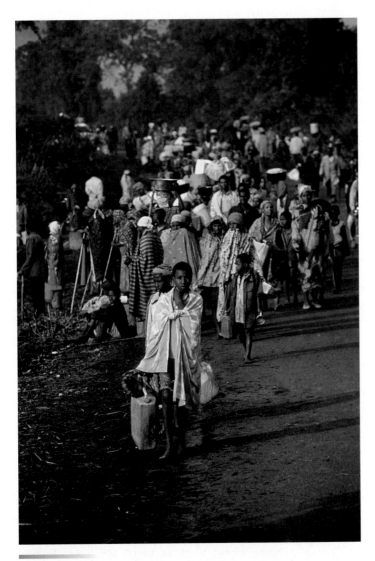

Figure 3.26 Rwandan refugees near the border of Rwanda and Tanzania. More than 1 million Rwandans fled into neighboring Zaire (now, the Democratic Republic of the Congo), Tanzania, Uganda, and Burundi in 1994 to escape an interethnic civil war in their home country and the genocide that killed at least 750,000 people. Early in the 21st century, more than 14 million Africans remained uprooted (that is, internally displaced and refugees combined). Fleeing war, repression, and famine, millions of people in developing nations have become reluctant migrants from their homelands.

17 million Latin American immigrants (again, not all illegal) in the United States sent an estimated $45 billion a year in legal and illegal remittances to their home countries in 2006 ($19 billion to Mexico alone). For some Latin American countries, those remittances account for about 20 percent of the money circulating in their economies.

The great majority of migratory movements, however, are **voluntary migrations** (volitional), representing individual response to the factors influencing all spatial interaction decisions. At root, migrations take place because the migrants believe that their opportunities and life circumstances will be better at their destination than they are at their present location.

Controls on Migration

Economic considerations crystallize most migration decisions, though nomads fleeing the famine and spreading deserts of the Sahel obviously are impelled by different economic imperatives than is the executive considering a job transfer to Montreal or the resident of Appalachia seeking factory employment in the city. Among the aging, affluent populations of highly developed countries, retirement amenities figure importantly in beliefs about the residential attractiveness of areas. Educational opportunities, major life events such as getting married, moving closer to family members, and environmental attractions or repulsions are but a few other possible migration motivations. Migration theorists attribute international economic migrations to a series of often overlapping mechanisms. Differentials in wages and job opportunities between home and destination countries are perhaps the major driving force in such individual migration decisions. Those differentials are in part rooted in a built-in demand for workers at the bottom of the labor hierarchy in more prosperous developed countries whose own workers disdain low-income, menial jobs. Migrants are available to fill those jobs, some argue, because advanced economies make industrial investment in developing or colonial economies to take advantage of lower labor costs there. New factories inevitably disturb existing economies, employ primarily short-term female workers, and leave a residue of unemployed males available and prone to migrate in search of opportunity. If successful, international economic migrants, male or female, help diversify sources of family income through their remittances from abroad, a form of household security that in itself helps motivate some international economic migration.

Negative home conditions that impel the decision to migrate are called **push factors.** They might include loss of job, lack of professional opportunity, overcrowding or slum clearance, or a variety of other influences, including poverty, war, and famine. The presumed positive attractions of the migration destination are known as **pull factors.** They include all the attractive attributes believed to exist at the new location—safety and food, perhaps, or job opportunities, better climate, lower taxes, quality schools, more room, and so forth. Very often, migration is a result of both push and pull factors. But it is important to recognize that it is the migrant's beliefs about the areal pattern of opportunities and want satisfaction that is important here, whether or not those beliefs are supported by objective reality.

The concept of place utility helps us to understand the decision-making process that potential voluntary migrants undergo. **Place utility** is the measure of an individual's satisfaction with a given residential location. The decision to migrate is a reflection of the appraisal—the perception—by the prospective migrant of the current homesite compared to other sites of which something is known or hoped for. In the evaluation of comparative place utility, the decision maker considers not only the believed value of the present location, but also the expected place utility of potential destinations. Seen in this way, we can understand that all migrations not strictly forced are a combined response to push factors at the current location relative to the pull factors of potential new residential sites.

Those evaluations are matched with the individual's aspiration level, that is, the level of accomplishment or ambition that the person sees for herself or himself. Aspirations tend to be adjusted to what one considers attainable. If one finds present circumstances satisfactory, then **spatial search** behavior—the process by which locational alternatives are evaluated—is not initiated. If, on the other hand, dissatisfaction with the home location is felt, then a utility is assigned to each of the possible migration locations. The utility is based on past or expected future rewards at various sites. Because new places are unfamiliar to the searcher, the information received about them acts as a substitute for the personal experience of the homesite. Decision makers can do no more than sample information about place alternatives and, of course, there may be errors in both information and interpretation. Ultimately, these anticipated utilities depend on beliefs—place perceptions—about the places being considered and on the motivations of potential migrants that prompt them to consider long-distance migration, or even relocation of residence within the local area. In the latter instance, of course, the spatial search usually involves actual site visits in evaluating the potential move (Figure 3.27). Of course, even actual visits cannot generally show people everything important there is to know about a place being considered for a new home (just as one date does not usually tell us whom to marry!).

One goal of the potential migrant is to avoid physically dangerous or economically unprofitable outcomes in the final migration decision. Place utility evaluation, therefore, requires assessments not only of hoped-for pull factors of new sites, but also of the potentially negative economic and social reception the migrant might experience at those sites. An example of that observation can be seen in the case of the large numbers of young Mexicans and Central Americans who have migrated both legally and illegally to the United States (Figure 3.28). Faced with poverty and overpopulation at home, they regard the place utility in Mexico as minimal. With a willingness to work, they learn from friends and relatives of job opportunities north of the border and, hoping for success or even wealth, quickly place high utility on relocation to the United States. Many know that dangerous risks are involved in entering the country illegally, but even legal immigrants face legal restrictions or rejections that are advocated or designed to reduce the pull attractions of the United States (see the feature "Broken Borders").

Another migrant goal is to reduce uncertainty about the move and the new residential destination. That objective may be achieved either through a series of transitional relocation stages or when the migrant follows the example of known predecessors. **Step migration** involves the place transition from, for example, rural to central city residence through a series of less extreme locational changes—from farm to small town to suburb and, finally, to the major central city itself. **Chain migration** assures that the mover is part of an established migrant flow from a common origin to a prepared destination. An advance group of migrants, having established itself in a new home area, is followed by second and subsequent migrations originating in the same home district and frequently united by kinship or friendship ties. Public and private services for legal migrants and informal service networks for undocumented or illegal migrants become established and contribute to the continuation or expansion of the chain migration flow. Ethnic and foreign-born enclaves in major cities and rural areas in a number of countries are the immediate result, as we shall see more fully in Chapter 6.

Sometimes the chain migration is specific to occupational groups. For example, nearly all newspaper vendors in New Delhi, in the north of India, come from one small district in Tamil Nadu, in the south of India. Most construction workers in New Delhi come either from Orissa, in the east of India, or Rajasthan, in the northwest. The diamond trade of Mumbai, India, is dominated by a network of about 250 related families who come from a small town several hundred miles to the north. Many members of particular small towns in Mississippi ended up in the same neighborhood in Chicago as part of the great internal migration of African Americans from the rural South to northern and western cities during the mid-twentieth century.

Certainly, not all immigrants stay permanently at their first destination. Of the some 80 million newcomers to the United States between 1900 and 1980, some 10 million returned to their homelands or moved to another country. Estimates for Canada indicate that perhaps 40 of each 100 immigrants eventually leave, and about 25 percent of newcomers to Australia also depart permanently. Therefore, a corollary of all out-migration flows is **counter** (or **return**) **migration,** the likelihood that as many as 25 percent of all migrants will return to their place of origin.

Figure 3.27 An example of a residential spatial search. The dots represent the house vacancies in the price range of a sample family. Note (1) the relationship of the new house location to the workplaces of the married couple; (2) the relationship of the old house location to the chosen new homesite; and (3) the limited total area of the spatial search. This example from the San Fernando Valley area of Los Angeles is typical of intraurban moves.

Source: Redrawn by permission from J. O. Huff, Annals of the Association of American Geographers, Vol. 76, *217–221. Association of American Geographers, 1986. Reprinted by permission of Blackwell Publishing Ltd.*

(a)

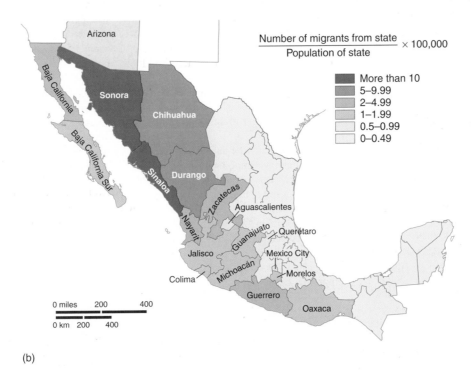

(b)

Figure 3.28 (*a*) Undocumented (illegal) Mexican immigrants running from the U.S. Border Patrol. (*b*) The undocumented migration rate to Arizona. The Arizona region and nearby Mexican states have longstanding ties that reach back to the early 1800s. In many respects, the international border cuts through a cultural region. Note that distance decay is evident in the likelihood a person will migrate to the United States. Over half of the migrants come from three nearby Mexican states: Sonora, Sinaloa, and Chihuahua.

Source: (b) Redrawn from John Harner, "Continuity amidst change," The Professional Geographer 47, No. 4, Figure 2, p. 403. Association of American Geographers, 1995. Reprinted by permission of Blackwell Publishing Ltd.

Geography and Citizenship

Broken Borders

Migrants can enter a country legally—with a passport, visa, working permit, or other authorization—or illegally. Some aliens enter a country legally but on a temporary basis (as a student or tourist, for example), but then remain after their official departure date. Others arrive claiming the right of political asylum but actually seeking economic opportunity. The U.S. Department of Homeland Security estimates that between one-fourth and one-third of the illegal residents in the United States entered the country legally but then overstayed their visas.

Although it is impossible to determine the precise number of people residing illegally in the United States, a number that changes daily, most authorities estimate there are anywhere from 10 to 12 million. About 55 percent have come from Mexico, another 20 to 25 percent from other Latin American countries and the Caribbean, 13 percent from Asia, and the remainder from Canada, Europe, and Africa. The rising tide of emotion against undocumented immigrants is directed mainly against those from Latin America, most of whom are unskilled workers.

Once they are in the United States, Latin American immigrants find work in agricultural fields, animal slaughtering and meat-packing facilities, construction, hotels, and restaurants. Many work in private residences as maids, nannies, and gardeners. While most undocumented workers initially enter California, Arizona, Texas, or Florida, and many remain in those states, they go where they find jobs. Many blend into the large migrant communities not just of Los Angeles, El Paso, and Houston, for example, but also those of Chicago and New York City. Iowa and North Carolina have some of the fastest growing populations of illegal immigrants. The demand for their labor is great enough that nearly all of the males have higher labor force participation rates than native-born men (92 percent versus 83 percent).

Concern over the growing number of illegal aliens has been reflected in a number of actions in recent years. Security fears since the September 11, 2001, assaults on the World Trade Center and Pentagon have led to more stringent visa applicant background checks, greater restrictions on admitting refugees and asylum seekers, stricter enforcement of Immigration and Naturalization Service (INS) rules on alien residency reports and visa time restrictions, and stricter border controls.

Greater efforts are being made to deter illegal crossings along the 3,380-kilometer (2,100-mile) U.S.-Mexico border. To supplement the 120 kilometers (75 miles) of steel fences near a few U.S. cities, the Bush administration in 2007 proposed 1,125 kilometers (700 miles) of new fencing, and Congress approved money for a small portion of it. The administration also increased the number of Border Patrol agents, who use automotive vehicles, helicopters, unmanned aircraft known as *drones,* night-vision cameras, and hidden electronic sensors for surveillance. In parts of Arizona and California, self-appointed Minutemen—groups of volunteer militia—patrol the border "to protect our country from a 40-year long invasion across our southern border with Mexico," as one vigilante put it.

Because the burden of coping with illegal immigration falls mostly on state and local governments, four states (Florida, Texas, Arizona, and California) have sued the federal government—so far unsuccessfully—to win reimbursement for the costs of illegal immigration.

Concerned that large numbers of undocumented immigrants impose a financial burden on taxpayers, pack schools and public health clinics, and result in the reduction of services to legal residents, voters in California approved Proposition 187, which barred illegal immigrants and their families from public schools, social services, and non-emergency health care. The courts struck down Proposition 187, declaring most of the provisions to be unconstitutional, and the measure was never implemented.

In Arizona, a new law targeting employers of undocumented workers took effect on January 1, 2008. Employers are required to check the status of each worker with the federal government. A company found to have knowingly hired an illegal resident has its business license suspended for 10 days for the first offense. A second offense results in the permanent revocation of the business license. Other states are considering similar legislation.

Millions of illegal residents managed to legalize themselves by taking advantage of government amnesties offered between 1984 and 2000. In his State of the Union address in 2005, President George W. Bush called for a temporary-worker program that would legalize the presence of millions of undocumented workers. "We should not be content with laws that punish hard-working people who want only to provide for their families . . . It is time for an immigration policy that permits temporary guest workers to fill jobs that Americans will not take," he declared. Congressional efforts to pass a comprehensive immigration reform bill failed in 2007, however. It called for more border security, a guest-worker program, and a path to citizenship for those already here. The issue of illegal immigration continues to be prominent in political and policy debates in the United States.

Questions to Consider

1. It is estimated that some 800,000 undocumented immigrants enter the United States each year, and most find gainful employment, yet the country issues only

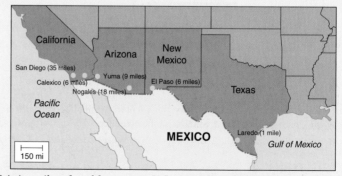

Existing miles of steel fences near U.S. cities along the Mexico border, 2007.

5,000 visas a year for unskilled foreigners seeking year-round work. Should the United States increase the number of visas available?

2. Making illegal crossings more difficult in California has not diminished the number of migrants making the journey north; it has simply pushed *coyotes,* the people who lead migrants across the border, into Arizona. Some people believe resourceful migrants will always find a way to get across the border. As one observer noted, "It's like putting rocks in a river—the water just goes around it." Do you think there is any way to seal the entire U.S./Mexico border, or will immigration continue so long as the income gap between the United States and Latin America remains great? Could the United States reduce immigration pressures by improving the Mexican economy?

3. Why is anti-immigrant sentiment directed chiefly against unauthorized immigrants from Latin America? Will such feelings eventually fade, as did earlier ones about the immigration of Irish Catholics, Chinese, Eastern Europeans, and other groups?

4. With regard to President Bush's proposal for a temporary-worker program,

the libertarian Cato Institute argues that when there is no immigration barrier, *circular migration* occurs, with migrant workers entering and leaving almost at will. It cites Puerto Rico as an example; many who move to the U.S. mainland stay for just a few years, and out-migration from the island is very low. A temporary-worker program, on the other hand, encourages migrants to move north with their entire families, and those who are already in the United States stay for good because border crossings become more expensive and dangerous. If you were a member of Congress, would you be in favor of creating a guest-worker program? Why or why not?

5. It is often said that illegal aliens perform jobs that Americans won't take. Why do you think many immigrants are willing to work for low wages, often under poor working conditions? Would Americans take the jobs if they paid, say, $20 per hour and offered health care and other benefits?

6. What would happen if all states followed Arizona's lead in passing and enforcing laws targeting employers of undocumented workers? One in 10 or 11 workers in Arizona is undocumented,

and opponents of the legislation contend that the state has put its economy in jeopardy. The workers tend to be reliable, they fill necessary jobs, spend their wages in the communities in which they live and work, and most pay taxes because employers in the construction, hotel, restaurant, and other industries withhold taxes from paychecks.

7. Should illegal residents already here be given the opportunity to get worker permits and the possibility of eventual citizenship if they have no criminal record, pay a fine, and demonstrate that they are gainfully employed and have paid taxes?

8. Do you believe the federal government has an obligation to fully or partially reimburse state and local governments for the costs of education, medical care, incarceration, and other legal services for unauthorized immigrants? Why or why not?

9. Should the United States require citizens to have a national identification card and to present it to officials upon demand? If so, would all people who look like they may have been born abroad feel it necessary to carry proof of citizenship at all times?

Within the United States, return migration—defined as moving back to one's state of birth—makes up about 20 percent of all domestic moves. That figure varies dramatically between states. More than a third of recent in-migrants to West Virginia, for example, were returnees—as were over 25 percent of those moving to Pennsylvania, Alabama, Iowa, and a few other states. Such widely different states as New Hampshire, Maryland, California, Florida, Wyoming, and Alaska were among the several that found returnees were fewer than 10 percent of their in-migrants. Interviews suggest that states deemed attractive draw new migrants in large numbers, while those with high proportions of returnees in the migrant stream are not believed to be desirable destinations by other than former residents. The preference maps we looked at above reveal these sorts of place preferences.

Once established, origin and destination pairs of places tend to persist. Areas that dominate a locale's in- and out-migration patterns make up the **migration fields** of the place in question. As we would expect, areas near the point of origin comprise the largest part of the migration field (remember distance decay and

the First Law), though larger cities more distantly located may also be prominent as the ultimate destination of hierarchical step migration (Figure 3.29). As Figure 3.30 shows, some migration fields reveal a distinctly channelized pattern of flow. The channels link areas that are in some way tied to one another by past migrations, by economic trade considerations, or some other affinity. The flow along them is greater than otherwise would be the case (such as predicted by a standard gravity model) but does not necessarily involve individuals with personal or family ties. The former streams of southern blacks and whites to northern cities, of Scandinavians to Minnesota and Wisconsin, and of U.S. retirees to Florida and Arizona or their European counterparts to Spain, Portugal, or the Mediterranean coast are all examples of **channelized migration.**

Voluntary migration is responsive to the other controls that influence all forms of spatial interaction. Push-pull factors may be equated with complementarity; costs (emotional and financial) of a residence relocation are expressions of transferability. Other things being equal, large cities exert a stronger migrant pull than

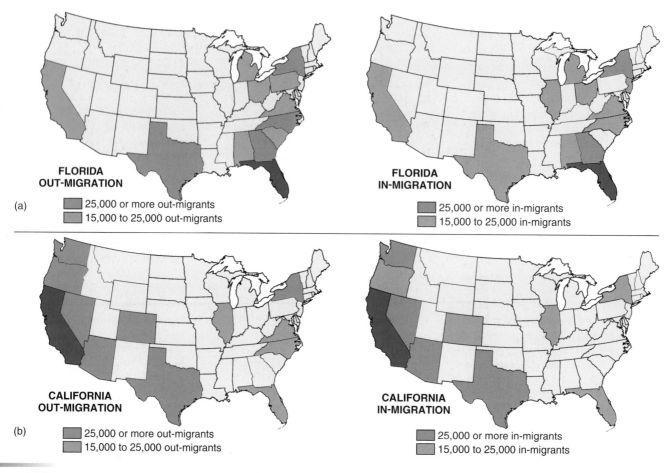

Figure 3.29 **The migration fields of Florida and California in 2005–2010.** (*a*) For Florida, nearby Georgia receives most out-migrants, but in-migrants originate in large numbers from the northeastern United States. (*b*) For California, the nearby western states receive large numbers of out-migrants, and there are fewer in-migrants from those states.

Source: U.S. Census Bureau.

do small towns, a reflection of the impact of the gravity model. We noted the influence of distance decay in migration studies. Movers seek to minimize the friction of distance. In selecting between two potential destinations of equal merit, a migrant tends to choose the nearer as involving less effort and expense. And since information about distant areas may be less complete and less certain than knowledge about nearer localities, short moves are favored over long ones. Research indicates that determined migrants with specific destinations in mind are unlikely to be deterred by distance considerations. However, groups for whom push factors determine the migration decision more than specific destination pulls are likely to limit their migration distance in response to encountered apparent opportunities. For them, intervening opportunities affect locational decisions. The concept of hierarchical migration also helps explain some movement decisions. Individuals in domestic relocations tend to move up the level in the urban hierarchy, from small places to larger ones. Often, levels are skipped on the way up; only in periods of general economic decline is there considerable movement down the hierarchy. Since suburbs of large cities are considered part of the metropolitan area, the movement from a town to a suburb is considered a move up the hierarchy.

Observations such as these were summarized in the 1870s and 1880s as a series of "laws of migration" by E. G. Ravenstein (1834–1913). Among those that remain relevant are the following:

- Most migrants go only a short distance.
- Longer-distance migration favors big-city destinations.
- Most migration proceeds step by step.
- Most migration is rural to urban.
- Each migration flow produces a counterflow.
- Most migrants are adults; families are less likely to make international moves.
- Most international migrants are young males.

The latter two "laws" introduce the role of personal attributes (and attitudes) of migrants: their age, sex, education, and economic status. Migrants do not represent a cross section of the populace from which they come. Selectivity of movers is evident, and the selection shows some regional differences. In most societies, young adults are the most mobile (Figure 3.31). In the United States, mobility peaks among those in their twenties, especially the later twenties, and tends to decline thereafter. Among West

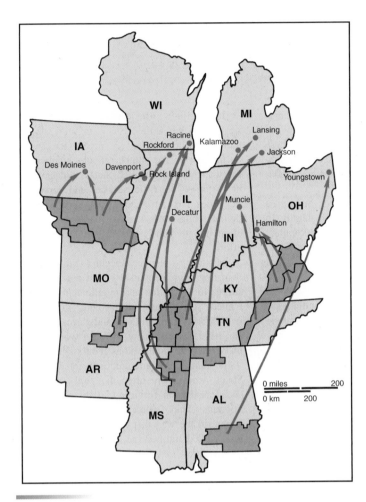

Figure 3.30 In the United States in the late 20th century, channelized migration flows from the rural south to midwestern cities of medium size. Distance is not the only determinant of flow direction. Through family and friendship links, the rural southern areas were tied to particular midwestern destinations.

Source: Redrawn by permission from Proceedings of the Association of American Geographers, *C. C. Roseman, Vol. 3, p. 142. Copyright © Association of American Geographers. Reprinted by permission of Blackwell Publishers.*

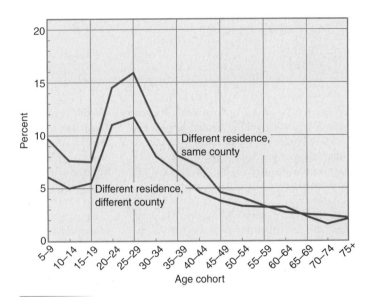

Figure 3.31 **Percentage of 2004 population over 5 years of age with a different residence than in 2003.** Young adults figure most prominently in both short- and long-distance moves in the United States, an age-related pattern of mobility that has remained constant over time. For the sample year shown, 28 percent of people in their 20s moved, whereas fewer than 5 percent of those 65 and older did so. Short-distance moves predominate; 58 percent of the 39 million total U.S. movers between March 2003 and March 2004, relocated within the same county and another 20 percent moved to another county in the same state. Some two-thirds of intracounty (mobility) moves in that year were made for housing-related reasons; long-distance moves (migration) were made for work-related (31 percent) and family (25 percent) reasons.

Source: U.S. Bureau of the Census.

African cross-border migrants, a World Bank study reveals, the age group 15–39 predominated. Young adults have weaker ties to their place of origin than older adults, being less likely to have careers or stable employment, mates, children, houses, and other material possessions. They are also generally healthier with more energy and endurance for the challenges of relocation.

Ravenstein's conclusion that young adult males are dominant in economically pushed international movement is less valid today than when first proposed. In reality, women and girls now comprise 40 to 60 percent of all international migrants worldwide (see the feature "Gender and Migration"). It is true that legal and illegal migrants to the United States from Mexico and Central America are primarily young men, as were first-generation "guest workers" in European cities. But population projections for West European countries suggest that women will shortly make up the largest part of their foreign-born population, and in one-third of the countries of sub-Saharan Africa, including Burkina Faso, Swaziland, and Togo, the female share of foreign-born populations was as large as

the male. Further, among rural to urban migrants in Latin America since the 1960s, women have been in the majority.

Female migrants are motivated primarily by economic pushes and pulls. Surveys of women migrants in Southeast Asia and Latin America indicate that 50 percent to 70 percent moved in search of employment and commonly first moved while in their teens. The proportion of young, single women is particularly high in rural-to-urban migration flows, reflecting their limited opportunities in increasingly overcrowded agricultural areas. To the push and pull factors normally associated with migration decisions are sometimes added family pressures that encourage young women with few employment opportunities to migrate as part of a household's survival strategy. In Latin America, the Philippines, and parts of Asia, emigration of young girls from large, landless families is more common than from smaller families or those with land rights. Their remittances of foreign earnings help maintain their parents and siblings at home.

An eighth internationally relevant observation may be added to those cited in Ravenstein's list: On average, emigrants tend to be relatively well educated. A British government study reveals that three-quarters of Africa's emigrants have higher (beyond high school) education, as do about half of Asia's and South America's. Of the more than 1 million Asian Indians living in the United States, more than three-quarters of those of working age have at least a bachelor's degree. The loss to home countries can be draining; about 30 percent of all highly educated West

Gender and Migration

Gender is involved in migration at every level. In a household or family, women and men are likely to play different roles regarding decisions or responsibilities for activities such as child care. These differences, and the inequalities that underlie them, help determine who decides whether the household moves, which household members migrate, and the destination for the move. Outside the household, societal norms about women's mobility and independence often restrict their ability to migrate.

The economies of sending and receiving areas play a role as well. If jobs are available for women in the receiving area, women have an incentive to migrate, and families are more likely to encourage the migration of women as necessary and beneficial. Thousands of women from East and Southeast Asia have migrated to the oil-rich countries of the Middle East, for example, to take service jobs.

The impact of migration is also likely to be different for women and men. Moving to a new economic or social setting can affect the regular relationships and processes that occur within a household or family. In some cases, women might remain subordinate to the men in their families. A study of Greek-Cypriot immigrant women in London and of Turkish immigrant women in the Netherlands found that although these women were working for wages in their new societies, these new economic roles did not affect their subordinate standing in the family in any fundamental way.

In other situations, however, migration can give women more power in the family. In former Zaire [now the Democratic Republic of the Congo], women in rural areas moved to towns to take advantage of job opportunities there, and gain independence from men in the process.

One of the keys to understanding the role of gender in migration is to disentangle household decision-making processes. Many researchers see migration as a family decision or strategy, but some members will benefit more than others from those decisions.

For many years, men predominated in the migration streams flowing from Mexico to the United States. Women played an important role in this migration stream even when they remained in Mexico. Mexican women influenced the migration decisions of other family members; they married migrants to gain the benefits from and opportunity for migration; and they resisted or accepted the new roles in their families that migration created.

In the 1980s, Mexican women began to migrate to the United States in increasing numbers. Economic crises in Mexico and an increase in the number of jobs available for women in the United States, especially in factories, domestic service, and service industries, have changed the backdrop of individual migration decisions. Now, women often initiate family moves or resettlement efforts.

Mexican women have begun to build their own migration networks, which are key to successful migration and resettlement in the United States. Networks provide migrants with information about jobs and places to live and have enabled many Mexican women to make independent decisions about migrating.

In immigrant communities in the United States, women are often the vital links to social institution services and to other immigrants. Thus, women have been instrumental in the way that Mexican immigrants have settled and become integrated into new communities.

Source: From Nancy E. Riley, "Gender, power, and population change," *Population Bulletin,* 52(1), May 1997, pp. 32–33. Reprinted by permission of Population Reference Bureau.

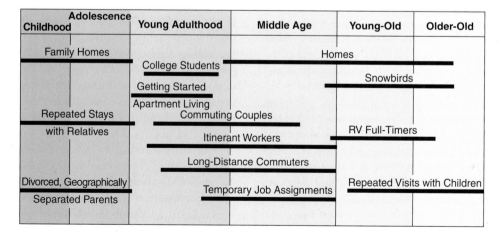

Figure 3.32 Examples of multiple residences by stage in life. Each horizontal line represents a period of time in a possible new residence.

Source: From K. McHugh, T. Hogan, and S. Happel, "Multiple residence and cyclical migration," The Professional Geographer 47(3), Figure 1, p. 253. Association of American Geographers, 1995. Reprinted by permission of Blackwell Publishing Ltd.

African Ghanaians and Sierra Leoneans live abroad. Outward migration of the educated affects developed countries as well as poorer developing states. It is claimed that from 1997 to 2002, between 15 percent and 40 percent of each year's graduating classes from Canadian colleges emigrated to the United States, while in Europe, half the mid-1990s' graduating physics classes at Bucharest University left the country.

For modern Americans, the decisions to migrate are more ordinary, but individually just as compelling. They appear to involve (1) major life events (e.g., getting married, having children, getting a divorce, etc.); (2) changes in the career course (getting a first job or a promotion, receiving a career transfer, seeking work in a new location, retiring, etc.); or (3) changes of residence associated with individual personality (Figure 3.32). Work-related relocations are most important in U.S. long-distance (intercounty) migrations, and in both intra- and interstate relocations, more migrants move down the urban hierarchy—that is, from larger to smaller centers—than vice versa. Some observers suggest that pattern of deconcentration reflects modern transportation and communication technologies, more and younger retirees, the cost of housing, and the attractions of amenity-rich smaller places. Some people, of course, simply seem to move often for no discernible reason, whereas others settle into a community permanently. For other developed countries, a somewhat different set of summary migration factors may be present.

Globalization

We have seen how the cost of communication affects the degree of spatial interaction. Since the 1980s, the Internet and relatively low transportation costs have made it increasingly easy to buy goods from abroad and to travel throughout the world. There has been simultaneously a strong international movement to reduce barriers to trade and to foreign investment and ownership. For example, the creation of the European Union (EU) has dismantled restrictive national borders there, and its monetary unit, the euro, makes possible financial transactions in a single currency over a massive multinational common market.

Integration and interdependence characterize globalization and affect economic, political, and cultural patterns across the world. The unification of Eastern and Western Europe or the creation of regional trade alliances such as the North American Free Trade Agreement (NAFTA) in North America or Mercosur in South America is as much a function of the revolution in communication and computer technology as it is of the will of political or financial leaders. Low-cost, high-speed computers, communication satellites, fiber-optic networks, and the Internet are the main technologies of the revolution, with robotics, microelectronics, e-mail, cell phones, and more making their contributions.

The fact that a consumer in Italy can order a book from Amazon.com or clothes from Land's End, obtain news from CNN, or make an investment through the London Stock Exchange while talking on a cell phone to a colleague in Tokyo is revolutionary and proof that globalization brings about greater world integration and spatial interaction (Figure 3.33). The Web browsers built into even basic mobile phone handsets enable large numbers of people to be fully integrated into the global community. The cell phone's

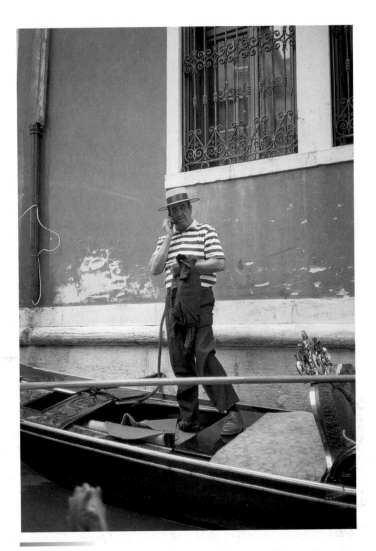

Figure 3.33 The old and the new: a traditional gondolier in Venice, Italy, conducting business on a cell phone.

capacity for immediate voice, instant message, and Internet data transfer has made it an agent of universal globalization in the early 21st century.

International banking is a financial case in point with nearly instantaneous movements across borders of billions of dollars in response to changing foreign exchange values and investment opportunities. Split-second changes in all the interconnected markets are certain. Within minutes of the September 11, 2001, attacks on the World Trade Center, stock markets everywhere went down as investors sensed that the international marketplace was in danger of losing stability. Internationalization of finance is also demonstrated by the immense sums in foreign investments held by citizens of all countries. American ownership of foreign stocks and bonds directly or through mutual funds and pension plans, for example, tie citizens of this country to the economic institutions of distant areas; at the same time, people outside the United States have significant holdings in U.S. companies and in U.S. treasury bonds. The U.S. subprime lending crisis and housing price bubble collapse of 2008 led to financial crises and an economic slowdown around the globe.

Transnational corporations (TNCs), discussed more fully in Chapter 9, are important forces driving the globalization of the world economy. With headquarters in one country and subsidiary companies, factories, warehouses, laboratories, and so on in several others, some 65,000 transnational corporations control several hundred thousand affiliates worldwide and sell their multitude of products on the international market. TNCs, by some estimates controlling about one-third of the world's productive assets, exploit the large differential in wage rates around the world to keep production costs low, not only decentralizing manufacturing and other business activities internationally but also diffusing the infrastructure and technology of modern business and industry to formerly underdeveloped regions, integrating them more fully and competitively into the global economy. At the same time, many employment opportunities decrease for citizens of the developed countries where most of the owners and stockholders of the TNCs reside.

The internationalization of popular culture is more apparent to most of the world's people than is the less visible globalization of commerce and industry. In widely different culture realms, teenagers wear Yankee baseball caps, Gap shirts, Levis, and Reeboks; eat at McDonald's; drink coffee at Starbucks; and listen to pop music on their iPod. The culture they embrace is largely Western in origin and chiefly American. U.S. movies, television shows, video games, software, music, food, and fashion are marketed worldwide. They influence the beliefs, tastes, and aspirations of people in virtually every country, though their effect is most pronounced on young people. Like the globalization of finance, industry, and commerce, this internationalization of popular culture is further evidence of the transformative nature and impact of modern spatial behavior and interaction.

Summary

Spatial interaction is the dynamic evidence of a world marked by large differences between places and of the interdependence between geographic locations. The term refers to the movement of goods, information, people, ideas—indeed, of every facet of economy and society—between one place and another. It includes the daily spatial activities of individuals and the collective patterns of their short- and long-distance behavior in space. The principles and constraints that unite, define, and control spatial behavior in this sense constitute an essential organizing focus for the study of human geographic patterns on the Earth.

We have seen that whatever the type of spatial behavior or flow, a limited number of recurring mechanisms of guidance and control are encountered. Three underlying bases for spatial interaction are complementarity, which encourages flows between areas by balancing supply with demand or satisfying need with opportunity; transferability, which affects movement decisions by introducing cost, effort, and time considerations; and intervening opportunities, which suggests that costs of overcoming distance may be reduced by finding closer alternate points where needs can be satisfied. The flows of commodities, ideas, and people governed by these interaction factors are interdependent and additive. Flows of commodities establish and reinforce traffic patterns, for example, and also channelize the movement of information and people.

Those flows and interactions may further be understood by the application of uniform models to all forms of spatial interaction from interregional commodity exchanges to an individual's daily pattern of movement. Distance decay tells us of the inevitable decline of interaction with increasing distance. The gravity model suggests that major centers of activity can exert interaction pulls that partly compensate for distance decay. Recognition of movement biases explains why spatial interaction in the objective world may deviate from that proposed by abstract models.

Humans in their individual and collective short- and long-distance movements are responsive to these impersonal spatial controls. Their spatial behaviors are also influenced by their separate circumstances. Each has an activity and awareness space reflective of individual socioeconomic and life-stage conditions. Each differs in mobility. Each has unique wants and needs and beliefs about their satisfaction. Human response to distance decay is expressed in a controlling critical distance beyond which the frequency of interaction quickly declines. That decline is partly conditioned by unfamiliarity with distant points outside normal activity space. Beliefs about home and distant territory therefore color interaction flows and space evaluations. In turn, those beliefs, well or poorly based, underlie travel and migration decisions, part of the continuing spatial diffusion and interaction of people. It is to people and their patterns of distribution and regional growth and change that we turn our attention in the following chapter.

KEY WORDS

activity space 67
attitude 67
awareness space 69
barrier 66
behavior 66

behavioral approach 66
chain migration 82
channelized migration 85
cognition 67
complementarity 62

counter migration 82
critical distance 70
distance decay 63
First Law of Geography 63
forced migration 79

FOR REVIEW

1. What is meant by spatial interaction? What are the three fundamental conditions governing all forms of spatial interaction? What is the distinctive impact or importance of each of the conditions?

2. What variations in distance decay curves might you expect if you were to plot shipments of ready-mixed concrete, potato chips, and computer parts? What do these respective curves tell us about transferability?

3. What is activity space? What factors affect the areal extent of an individual's activity space?

4. On a piece of paper, and following the model of Figure 3.11, plot your space-time path for your movements on a typical class day. What alterations in your established movement habits might be necessary (or become possible) if (a) Instead of walking, you rode a bike? (b) Instead of biking, you drove a car? (c) Instead of driving, you had to use the bus?

5. What does the idea that transportation and communication are space-adjusting imply? In what ways has technology affected the "space adjustment" in commodity flows? In information flows?

6. Recall the places that you have visited in the past week. In your movements, were the rules of distance decay and critical distance operative? What variables affect your critical distances?

7. What considerations influence the decision to migrate? How do perceptions of place utility induce or inhibit migration?

8. What is a migration field? Some migration fields show a channelized flow of people. Select a particular channelized migration flow (such as the movement of Scandinavians to Michigan, Wisconsin, and Minnesota, or people from the Great Plains to California, or southern blacks to the North) and speculate why a channelized flow developed.

KEY CONCEPTS REVIEW

1. **What are the three bases for all spatial interaction?** pp. 61–63.
Spatial interaction reflects areal differences and is controlled by three "flow-determining" factors. Complementarity implies a local supply of an item for which effective demand exists elsewhere. Transferability expresses the costs of movement from source of supply to locale of demand. An intervening opportunity serves to reduce flows of goods between two points by presenting nearer or cheaper sources.

2. **How is the likelihood of spatial interaction probability measured?** pp. 63–66.
The probability of aggregate spatial movements and interactions may be assessed by the application of established models. Distance decay is the decline of interaction with increase in separation; the gravity model tells us that distance decay can in part be overcome by the enhanced attraction of larger centers of activity; and movement bias helps explain interaction flows contrary to model predictions.

3. **What are the forms, attributes, and controls of human spatial behavior?** pp. 66–72.
While humans react to distance, time, and cost considerations of spatial movement, their spatial behavior is also affected by separate conditions of activity and awareness space, of individual economic and life-stage circumstances, by degree of mobility, and by unique beliefs of wants and needs.

"*Zero, possibly even negative [population] growth*" *was the 1972 slogan proposed by the prime minister of Singapore, an island country in Southeast Asia. His nation's population, which stood at 1 million at the end of World War II (1945), had doubled by the mid-1960s. To avoid the overpopulation he foresaw, the government decreed "Boy or girl, two is enough" and refused maternity leaves and access to health insurance for third or subsequent births. Abortion and sterilization were legalized, and children born fourth or later in a family were to be discriminated against in school admissions policy. In response, by the mid-1980s birth rates had fallen to below the level necessary to replace the population, and abortions were terminating more than one-third of all pregnancies.*

"At least two. Better three. Four if you can afford it" was the national slogan proposed by that same prime minister in 1986, reflecting fears that the stringencies of the earlier campaign had gone too far. From concern that overpopulation would doom the country to perpetual Third World poverty, Prime Minister Lee Kuan Yew was moved to worry that population limitation would deprive it of the growth potential and national strength implicit in a youthful, educated workforce adequate to replace and support the present aging population. His 1990 national budget provided for sizable long-term tax rebates for second children born to mothers under 28. Not certain that financial inducements alone would suffice to increase population, the Singapore government annually renewed its offer to take 100,000 Hong Kong Chinese who might choose to leave when China took over that territory in 1997.

The policy reversal in Singapore reflects an inflexible fact of population: the structure of the present controls the content of the future. The size, characteristics, growth trends, and migrations of today's populations help shape the well-being of peoples yet unborn but whose numbers and distributions are now being determined. The numbers, age, and sex distribution of people; patterns and trends in their fertility and mortality; and their density of settlement and rate of growth both affect and are affected by the social, political, and economic organization of a society. Through population analysis, we can understand the relationship between population and resources, evaluate national and international population policies, and make reasoned forecasts of what the future may bring.

Population geography provides the background concepts and theories to understand and forecast the size, composition, and distribution of the human population. It differs from **demography,** the statistical study of human population, in its concern with *spatial* analysis—location, density, pattern, and relationship to the physical environment. Regional natural resources, standard of living, food supply, and conditions of health and well-being are basic to geography's population concerns. In addition, they are fundamental expressions of the human–environmental relationships that are one of the core themes of human geography.

Population Growth

Sometime in early 2012, a human birth raised the Earth's population to 7 billion people. In 1999, the count reached 6 billion. That is, in just over 12 years, the world population grew by 1 billion, an average of 77 million people annually, or some 210,000 per day. By contrast, it took from the beginning of human history to about the year 1800 to reach 1 billion, and another 130 years to add the second billion. However, annual increases have been declining from values of 80 to 87 million reported by the U.N. Population Division through the 1980s and early 1990s. Even with the slower pace of estimated increase, the United Nations in 2010 projected that the world would likely contain about 9.3 billion inhabitants in 2050. U.N. projections of world population for the year 2100 ranged from a low of 6.2 billion to a high of 15.8 billion, with a medium value of 10.1 billion.

All demographic forecasts agree, however, that essentially all of any future growth will occur in countries now considered "developing," (Figure 4.1), with especially rapid growth in the 48 least-developed states. The world's 10 most populous countries are mostly found in the developing regions of the world, and that trend will become even more pronounced by 2050 (Table 4.1). We will return to these projections and to the difficulties and disagreements inherent in making them later in this chapter.

Just what is implied by numbers in the millions and billions? With what can we compare the 2011 population of Estonia in Europe (about 1.3 million) or of China (about 1.3 billion)? It is difficult to appreciate a number as vast as 1 million or 1 billion, and the great distinction between them. Here is an example offered by the Population Reference Bureau to help visualize the immensity of these numbers.

- A 2.5-centimeter (1-inch) stack of U.S. paper currency contains 233 bills. If you had a *million* dollars in thousand-dollar bills, the stack would be 11 centimeters (4.3 inches) high. If you had a *billion* dollars in thousand-dollar bills, your pile of money would reach 109 meters (358 feet)—about the length of a football field.

Table 4.1

World's Most Populous Countries, 2008 and 2050

2008		2050	
Country	Population (millions)	Country	Population (millions)
China	1,346	India	1,692
India	1,241	China	1,313
United States	312	Nigeria	433
Indonesia	238	United States	423
Brazil	197	Pakistan	314
Pakistan	177	Indonesia	309
Nigeria	162	Bangladesh	226
Bangladesh	151	Brazil	223
Russia	143	Ethiopia	174
Japan	128	Philippines	150

Source: Population Reference Bureau, 2011.

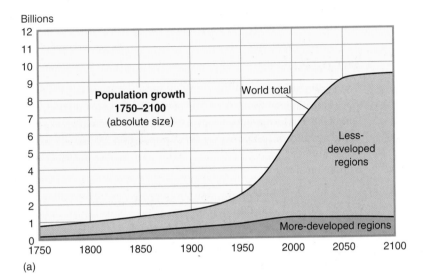

Billions

Population growth 1750–2100 (absolute size)

World total

Less-developed regions

More-developed regions

(a)

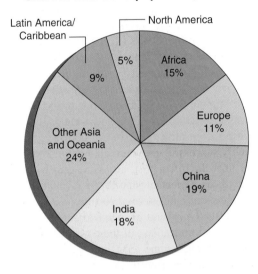

Share of total world population, 2011

Latin America/Caribbean

North America

North America 5%

Africa 15%

Europe 11%

China 19%

India 18%

Other Asia and Oceania 24%

Latin America/Caribbean 9%

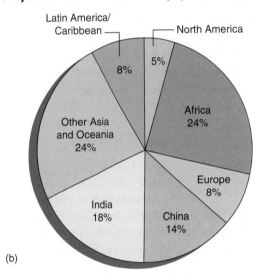

Projected share of total world population, 2050

Latin America/Caribbean

North America

North America 5%

Africa 24%

Europe 8%

China 14%

India 18%

Other Asia and Oceania 24%

Latin America/Caribbean 8%

(b)

Figure 4.1 **World population numbers and projections.** (*a*) After two centuries of slow growth, world population began explosive expansion after World War II (ended in 1945). Numbers in more developed regions at the middle of the century will be the same or lower than at its start, thanks to population stability or decline below present levels. However, higher fertility rates and immigration are projected to increase the U.S. population by more about one-third between 2010 and 2050, and large-volume immigration into Europe could alter its population decline projections. Between 2010 and 2100, nearly all population growth is projected to take place in 58 high-fertility countries. The high-fertility countries are all classified as "less developed," and 39 are located in Africa, 9 in Asia, 6 in Oceania, and 4 in Latin America/Caribbean. (*b*) Africa is forecast to grow faster than the other world regions, increasing its share of the world's population substantially. India, North America, and Latin America/Caribbean are forecast to grow at a pace that maintains their share of world population. China and Europe will decline slightly in total population and see a decline in their share of world population.

Sources: (a) Estimates from Population Reference Bureau and United Nations Population Fund; (b) Based on United Nations and U.S. Bureau of the Census data and projections.

The implications of the present numbers and the potential increases in population are of vital current social, political, and ecological concern. Population numbers were much smaller some 12,000 years ago when continental glaciers began their retreat, people spread to formerly unoccupied portions of the globe, and human experimentation with food sources initiated the Agricultural Revolution. The 5 or 10 million people who then constituted all of humanity obviously had considerable potential to expand their numbers. In retrospect, we see that the natural resource base of the earth had a population—supporting capacity far in excess of the pressures exerted on it by early hunting and gathering groups.

Some observers maintain that despite a large and growing world population, the adaptive and exploitive ingenuity of humans will generate solutions to resource shortages. To them, population growth means more pressure for innovations and a larger pool of human talent to generate those innovations. Others, however, frightened by the resource demands of a growing world population that had already expanded fourfold—from 1.6 billion to 6.1 billion—in the century from 1900 to 2000, compare the Earth to a lifeboat or spaceship with an ever-increasing number of passengers. They point to recurring problems of malnutrition and starvation (though these are realistically more a matter of failures of distribution than of inability to produce enough foodstuffs worldwide). They cite global climate change, air and water pollution, the loss of forest and farmland, rising prices of many minerals and fossil fuels, and other evidences of strains on world resources as signs that the world population has reached the Earth's physical capacity.

On a worldwide basis, populations grow only one way: The number of births in a given period exceeds the number of deaths. Ignoring for the moment regional population changes resulting from migration, we can conclude that humans have been highly successful in overcoming natural controls on their numerical growth. In contrast, current estimates of slowing population growth and eventual stability or decline in world totals clearly indicate that humans by their individual and collective decisions may effectively limit growth and control global population numbers. The implications of these observations will become clearer after we define some terms important in the study of population and explore their significance.

Some Population Definitions

Demographers employ a wide range of measures of population composition and trends, though all their calculations start with a count of events: of individuals in the population, of births, deaths, marriages, and so on. Demographers convert those counts to *rates* to make them more meaningful and useful in population analysis.

Rates simply record the frequency of occurrence of an event during a given time frame for a designated population—for example, the marriage rate as the number of marriages performed per 1000 population in the United States last year. Demographers also place populations into *cohort* groups as they calculate birth rates, death rates, and so on. A **cohort** is a population group unified by a specified temporal characteristic—the age cohort of 0–4 years, perhaps, or the college class of 2015 (Figure 4.2). Basic values and rates useful in the analysis of world population and population trends have been reprinted with the permission of the Population Reference Bureau as Appendix B to this book. Comparing values

Figure 4.2 Whatever their differences may be by race, sex, or ethnicity, these babies will forever be clustered demographically into a single *birth cohort.*

in Appendix B and studying the choropleth maps in this chapter will help illustrate the discussion that follows.

Birth Rates

The **crude birth rate (CBR),** often referred to simply as the *birth rate,* is the annual number of live births per 1000 population. It is "crude" because it relates births to total population without regard to the age or sex composition of that population. A country with a population of 2 million and with 40,000 births a year would have a crude birth rate of 20 per 1000.

$$\frac{40,000}{2,000,000} = \frac{20}{1000} = 20 \text{ per thousand}$$

The birth rate of a country is, of course, strongly influenced by the age and sex structure of its population, the customs and family size expectations of its inhabitants, and its population policies. Because these conditions vary widely, recorded national birth rates vary—as of 2011, from a high of 40 or more in 16 sub-Saharan African states to 10 or fewer per 1,000 in Japan, Singapore, South Korea, Taiwan, and 18 European countries, including Germany. Birth rates of 30 or above per 1,000 are considered *high* and are found in sub-Saharan Africa, Afghanistan, Guatemala, Iraq, Jordan, Laos, the Palestinian Territory, and Timor-Leste. In these countries, poverty is widespread and a high proportion of the female population is young. In many of them, birth rates may be significantly higher than official records indicate. Available data suggest that every year around 50 million births go unregistered and therefore uncounted.

Birth rates of less than 18 per 1,000 are reckoned *low* and are characteristic of industrialized, urbanized countries. All European countries, as well as the United States, Canada, Australia, New Zealand, and the more industrialized countries of Asia have low rates. In recent years, low birth rates have been observed in an increasing number of developing states. Some of these, such as China (see "China's Way—and Others"), have adopted effective family planning programs. In others, changed cultural norms have reduced desired family size. *Transitional* birth rates (between 18 and 30 per 1,000) characterize some, mainly smaller, developing and newly industrializing countries, though giant India entered that group in 1994.

As the recent population histories of Singapore and China indicate, birth rates are subject to change. The transition to low birth rates of European countries and of some of the areas that they colonized is usually ascribed to industrialization, urbanization, and, in recent years, maturing populations. While restrictive family planning policies in China rapidly reduced the birth rate from over 33 per 1,000 in 1970 to 18 per 1,000 in 1986, industrializing Japan experienced a comparable 15-point decline in the decade 1948–1958 with little governmental intervention. Indeed, the stage of economic development appears closely related to variations in birth rates among countries, although rigorous testing of this relationship proves it to be imperfect (Figure 4.3). As a group, the more developed states of the world showed a crude birth rate of 11 per 1,000 in 2011; less developed countries (excluding China) registered about 25 per 1000 (down from 35 in 1990).

Religious and political beliefs can also influence birth rates. In a number of different religions, more devout individuals tend

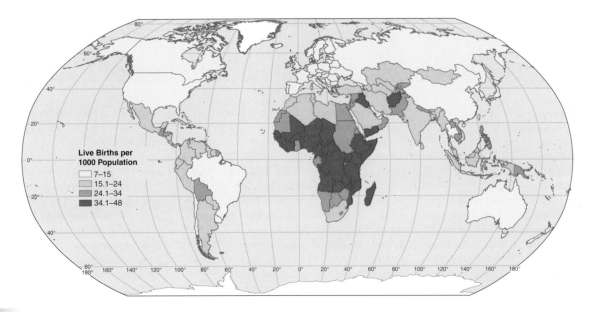

Figure 4.3 **CBRs, 2011.** The map suggests a degree of precision that is misleading in the absence of reliable, universal registration of births. The pattern shown serves, however, as a generally useful summary of comparative reproduction patterns.

Source: Data from Population Reference Bureau, 2011.

to have more children. The convictions of many Roman Catholics and Muslims that their religion forbids the use of artificial birth control techniques often led to high birth rates among believers. However, predominantly Catholic Italy has one of the world's lowest birth rates. Islam itself does not prohibit contraception, and birth rates vary widely across Muslim countries. Regional variations in projected percentage contributions to world population growth are summarized in Figure 4.4.

Fertility Rates

Crude birth rates display such regional variability because of differences in age and sex composition and/or disparities in births among those of reproductive-age. The rate is "crude" because its denominator contains persons who have no chance at all of giving birth—males, young girls, and old women. For example, we would expect a very low crude birth rate in a community with a high percentage of elderly. The **total fertility rate (TFR)** is a more refined and thus more accurate measure for showing the rate and probability of reproduction among fertile females, the only segment of population capable of bearing children.

The TFR (Figure 4.5) tells us the average number of children that would be born to each woman if, during her childbearing years, she bore children at the current year's rate for women that age. Thus, a TFR of 3 means that the average woman in a population would be expected to have three births in her lifetime. The fertility rate is not affected by the share of women in their childbearing years and best summarizes the expected reproductive behavior of women. Thus, it is a more useful and more reliable figure for comparative and predictive purposes than the crude birth rate.

Although a TFR of 2.0 would seem sufficient exactly to replace present population (one baby to replace each parent), in reality replacement levels are reached only with TFRs of 2.1 to 2.3 or more. The fractions over 2.0 are required to compensate for infant

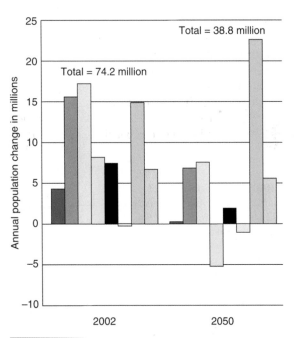

Figure 4.4 **Projected contributions to world population growth by region 2002 and 2050.** The annual increase in the world population is projected to slow in the first half of the 21st century, down from a peak of 87.4 million in 1989–1990. At the beginning of the 21st century, Today, all world regions are growing, except Eastern Europe and the newly independent states of the former Soviet Union. By 2050, sub-Saharan Africa is projected to be the major contributor to world population growth. By then, virtually all population growth will be taking place in the world's developing countries.

Source: U.S. Census Bureau, Global Population Profile: 2002, 2004.

China's Way—and Others

An ever larger population is "a good thing," Chairman Mao announced in 1965 when China's birth rate was 37 per 1000 and population totaled 540 million. At Mao's death in 1976, numbers reached 852 million, though the birth rate then had dropped to 25. During the 1970s, when it became evident that population growth was consuming more than half of the annual increase in the country's gross domestic product, China introduced a well-publicized campaign advocating the "two-child family" and providing services, including abortions, supporting that program. In response, China's birth rate dropped to 19.5 per 1000 by the late 1970s.

"One couple, one child" became the slogan of a new and more vigorous population control drive launched in 1979, backed by both incentives and penalties to assure its success in China's tightly controlled society. Late marriages were encouraged; free contraceptives, cash awards, abortions, and sterilizations were provided to families limited to a single child. Penalties, including steep fines, were levied for second births. At the campaign's height in 1983, the government ordered the sterilization of either husband or wife for couples with more than one child. Infanticide—particularly the abandonment or murder of female babies—was a reported means both of conforming to a one-child limit and of increasing the chances that the one child would be male.

By 1986, China's officially reported crude birth rate had fallen to 18 per 1000, far below the 37 per 1000 then registered among the rest of the world's less developed countries. The one-child policy was relaxed in 1984 to permit two-child limits in rural areas where the majority of the Chinese population still resides, but in 2002, it was partially reinstated as nationwide law following documentation of extensive underreporting of rural births. In contrast, newly prosperous urbanites have voluntarily reduced their fertility to well below replacement levels, with childless couples increasingly common.

Nationally, past and current population controls have been so successful that by 2000 China's population was 300 million less than it otherwise would have been. Indeed, demographers and government officials express serious concerns that population decrease, not increase, is the problem next to be confronted. Projections suggest that by 2042, because of lowered fertility rates, China's population numbers will actually start falling. The country is already beginning to face a pressing social problem: a declining proportion of working-age persons and an absence of an adequate welfare network to care for a rapidly growing number of senior citizens.

Concerned with their own increasing numbers, many developing countries have introduced their own less extreme programs of family planning, stressing access to contraception and sterilization. International agencies have encouraged these programs, buoyed by such presumed success as the 21% fall in fertility rates in Bangladesh from 1970 to 1990 as the proportion of married women of reproductive age using contraceptives rose from 3% to 40% under intensive family planning encouragement and frequent adviser visits.

Research suggests that fertility falls because women decide they want smaller families, not because they have unmet needs for contraceptive advice and devices. Nineteenth-century northern Europeans without the aid of science had lower fertility rates than their counterparts today in middle-income countries. With some convincing evidence, improved women's education has been proposed as a surer way to reduce births than either encouraged contraception or China's coercive efforts. Studies from individual countries indicate that 1 year of female schooling can reduce the fertility rate by between 5% and 10%. Yet the fertility rate of uneducated Thai women is only two-thirds that of Ugandan women with secondary education. Obviously, other cultural factors besides educational levels are at work.

and childhood mortalities. The concept of *replacement level fertility* is useful here. It marks the level of fertility at which each successive generation of women produces exactly enough children to ensure that the same number of women survive to have offspring themselves. In general, then, the higher the level of mortality in a population, the higher the replacement level of fertility will be. For Mozambique early in the 21st century, the replacement level fertility was 3.4 children per woman.

On a worldwide basis, the TFR in 2011 was 2.5, down from 3.6 two decades earlier. The more developed countries recorded a 1.7 TFR in 2011. That decrease has been dwarfed in amount and significance by the rapid changes in reproductive behavior in much of the developing world. Since 1960, the average TFR in the less developed world has fallen by half from the traditional 6.0 or more to 2.6 in 2011. That dramatic decline reflects the fact that women and men in developing countries are marrying later

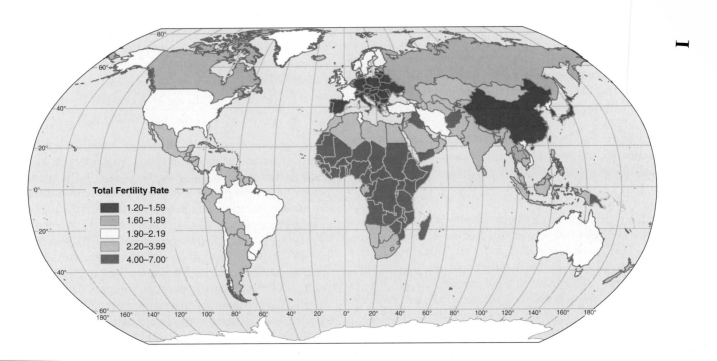

Figure 4.5 **Total fertility rate (TFR)** indicates the average number of children that would be born to each woman if, during her childbearing years, she bore children at the same rate as women of those ages actually did in a given year. Since the TFR accounts for the age distribution of a population, two countries with identical birth rates may have quite different fertility rates and therefore different prospects for growth. Depending on mortality conditions, a TFR of 2.1 to 2.3 or more children per woman is considered the "replacement level," at which a population will eventually stabilize.

Source: Data from Population Reference Bureau, 2011.

and having fewer children, following the pattern earlier set in the developed world. There has been, as well, a great increase in family planning and contraceptive use. By 2001, according to a UN world fertility report, 92% of all national governments supported family planning and distributed contraceptives, either directly or indirectly.

The recent fertility declines in developing states have been more rapid and widespread than anyone expected. The TFRs for so many of them have dropped so dramatically since the early 1960s (Figure 4.6), that the fantastic world population projections issued then are now generally discounted and rejected. Indeed, in 2010, the United Nations estimated that nearly 50 percent of global population lived in countries with fertility rates of 2.1 or less. China's decrease from a TFR of 5.9 births per woman in the period 1960–1965 to officially about 1.5 in 2011 and comparable drops in TFRs of Bangladesh, Brazil, Mozambique, and other states demonstrate that fertility reflects cultural values, not biological imperatives.

In fact, demographers have long assumed that recently observed developing country—and therefore global—fertility rate declines to the replacement level would continue and in the long run lead to stable population numbers. However, nothing in logic or history requires population stability at any level. Indeed, the experience of sub-replacement fertility in most developed countries suggests the real possibility of absolute decline.

World regional and national fertility rates reported in Appendix B and other sources are summaries that conceal significant variations between population groups. India's published TFR of 2.6 is a pooled number that hides the variation between a low value of 1.8 in the state of Kerala and 4.4 in Uttar Pradesh. The

U.S. 2008 national average fertility rate of 2.1 does not reveal that the TFR for Hispanics was 2.9, compared to 2.1 for African Americans, or only 1.8 for non-Hispanic whites.

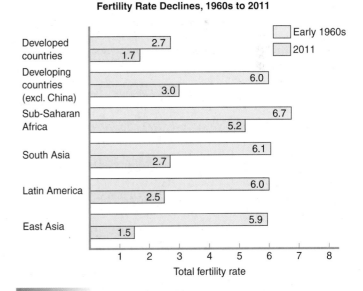

Figure 4.6 **Differential fertility rate declines.** Fertility has declined most rapidly in Latin America and Asia and much more slowly in sub-Saharan Africa. In more than 20 developing countries, the 2011 fertility rate was below the replacement level, as it was for developed countries as a group. Europe and East Asia were far below, with 2011 TFR of 1.6 and 1.5, respectively; the United States, however, with a TFR of 2.0 is just below the replacement point of 2.1.

Sources: Population Reference Bureau and United Nations Population Fund.

ath Rates

The **crude death rate (CDR),** also called the **mortality rate,** is calculated in the same way as the CBR: the annual number of events per 1,000 population. In the past, a valid generalization was that the death rate, like the birth rate, varied with national levels of development. Characteristically, highest rates (over 20 per 1,000) were found in the less-developed countries of Africa, Asia, and Latin America; lowest rates (less than 10) were associated with developed states of Europe and North America. That correlation mostly disappeared as dramatic reductions in death rates occurred in developing countries in the years following World War II. Infant mortality rates and life expectancies improved as antibiotics, vaccinations, and pesticides to treat diseases and control disease carriers were made available in almost all parts of the world and as increased attention was paid to funding improvements in urban and rural sanitary facilities and safe water supplies.

Indeed, by 1994 death rates for less-developed countries as a group actually dropped below those for the more developed states and have remained lower since (Figure 4.7). Notably, that reduction did not extend to maternal mortality rates (see the feature "The Risks of Motherhood"). Like crude birth rates, death rates are affected by a population's age distribution. Countries with a high proportion of elderly people, such as Sweden, have higher death rates than those with a high proportion of young people, such as Iceland, despite relative equality in other national conditions affecting health and longevity. The pronounced youthfulness of populations in developing countries, as much as improvements in sanitary and health conditions, is an important factor in the recently reduced mortality rates of those areas.

To overcome that lack of comparability, death rates can be calculated for specific age groups. The *infant mortality rate,* for example, is the ratio of deaths of infants aged 1 year or under per 1,000 live births:

$$\frac{\text{deaths age 1 year or less}}{1,000 \text{ live births}}$$

Infant mortality rates are significant because it is at these ages that the greatest declines in mortality have occurred, largely as a result of better health services. The drop in infant mortality accounts for a large part of the decline in the general death rate in the last few decades, for mortality during the first year of life is usually greater than in any other year.

Two centuries ago, it was not uncommon for 200–300 infants per 1,000 to die in their first year. Today, rates are in the single digits in developed countries and below 50 for the world as a whole (Figure 4.8). Still, striking world regional and national variations remain. The highest infant mortality rates are in Afghanistan and in war-torn or politically unstable countries in Africa. For all of sub-Saharan Africa, infant mortality rates are near 80 per 1,000. In contrast, infant mortality rates in more developed countries are more uniformly in the 2–7 range. Infant mortality rates are not solely a matter of the economic status of a country. For example, the U.S. infant mortality rate exceeds that of Canada, South Korea, Japan, Singapore, most Northern and Western European countries, and even Cuba. Nor are rates uniform within a country. In the United States, African Americans have an infant mortality rate more than twice that of Asians, whites, or Hispanics.

Modern medicine and sanitation have increased life expectancy and altered age-old relationships between birth and death

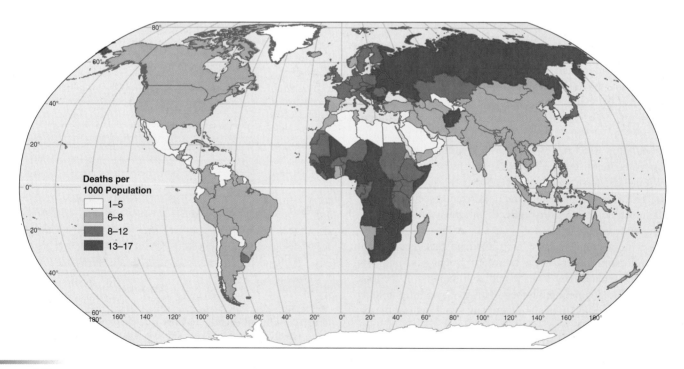

Figure 4.7 **CDRs** show less worldwide variability than do the birth rates displayed in Figure 4.3. The widespread availability of at least minimal health protection measures and a generally youthful population in the developing countries yield death rates frequently lower than those recorded in "old age" Europe. With its youthful population, Mexico has a lower death rate than the United States.

Source: Data from Population Reference Bureau, 2011.

The Risks of Motherhood

The worldwide leveling of CDRs does not apply to pregnancy-related deaths. In fact, the maternal mortality ratio—maternal deaths per 100,000 live births—is the single greatest health disparity between developed and developing countries. According to the World Health Organization (WHO), approximately 1,000 women die each day from preventable causes related to pregnancy and childbirth; Each year, more than a million children are left motherless by maternal deaths. As shown in the chart, the geography of maternal mortality is highly uneven; 99 percent of maternal deaths take place in less-developed states where, as a group, the maternal mortality ratio is some 21 times greater than in the more developed countries. Pregnancy complications, childbirth, and unsafe abortions are the leading slayers of women of reproductive age throughout the developing world, though the incidence of maternal mortality is by no means uniform, as the chart indicates. According to 2008 data, the risk is 1 death in 70 pregnancies in Afghanistan, versus 1 in 50,000 in Greece.

Other countries with extraordinarily high maternal death ratios are found in war-torn or politically unstable areas of Africa, such as Burundi, Chad, Guinea-Bissau, Liberia, Sierra Leone, and Somalia.

The vast majority of maternal deaths in the developing world are preventable. Most result from causes rooted in the social, cultural, and economic barriers confronting females in their home environment throughout their lifetimes: malnutrition, anemia, lack of access to timely basic maternal health care, physical immaturity due to stunted growth, and unavailability of adequate prenatal care or trained medical assistance at birth. Part of the problem is that women are considered expendable in societies in which their status is low, although the correlation between women's status and maternal mortality is not exact. In those cultures, little attention is given to women's health or their nutrition, and pregnancy, although a major cause of death, is simply considered a normal condition warranting no special consideration or management.

Given the immense human suffering associated with preventable maternal deaths, the United Nations included improving maternal health among its eight Millennium Development Goals (MDGs). Specifically, the goal calls for reducing the maternal mortality rate by three-quarters between 1990 and 2015. Substantial progress has been made in all world regions. The most dramatic improvements have been in South Asia, which saw its rate drop from 590 to 280 deaths per 100,000 births. Meanwhile, sub-Saharan Africa has lowered its rate from 870 to 640, yet still has the furthest to go to meet the goal.

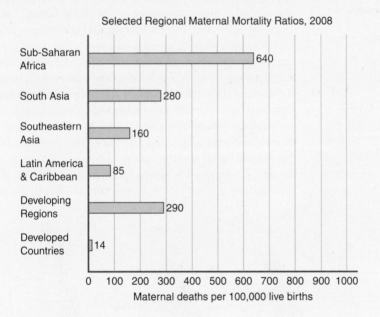

Selected Regional Maternal Mortality Ratios, 2008

Sub-Saharan Africa — 640
South Asia — 280
Southeastern Asia — 160
Latin America & Caribbean — 85
Developing Regions — 290
Developed Countries — 14

Maternal deaths per 100,000 live births

Source: Graph data from Trends in Maternal Mortality: 1990 to 2008. *Geneva, Switzerland: WHO Press, 2010.*

rates. In the early 1950s, only five countries, all in northern Europe, had life expectancies at birth of over 70 years. In the first decade of the 21st century, some 75 countries outside of Europe and North America—though none in sub-Saharan Africa—were on that list. The availability and employment of modern methods of health and sanitation have varied regionally, and the least developed countries have least benefited from them. In such underdeveloped and impoverished areas as much of sub-Saharan Africa, the chief causes of death other than HIV/AIDS are those no longer of immediate concern in more developed lands: diseases such as malaria, and water-borne diseases caused by a lack of sanitation, such as cholera, dysentery, and typhoid.

HIV/AIDS has undermined global improvements in life expectancies and reductions in adult death rates and infant and childhood mortalities. AIDS has become the fourth most common cause of death worldwide and is forecast to surpass the Black Death of the 14th century—which caused an estimated 25 million deaths in Europe and 13 million in China—as history's worst-ever epidemic. According to a report by UNAIDS, AIDS is expected to kill 68 million people between 2000 and 2020 in the 45 most affected countries; about 55 million of those deaths will occur in sub-Saharan Africa. The United Nations estimated nearly 40 million people were HIV positive in 2006. Some 90 percent of those infected live in developing countries, and 65 percent reside in sub-Saharan Africa, where women account for 60 percent of all cases. In that hardest-hit region, as much as one-fourth of the adult population in some countries is HIV positive, and average life expectancy has been cut drastically. In South Africa, the life expectancy of a baby born in the early 21st century should have been 66 years; AIDS has cut that down to 47. In Botswana, it is

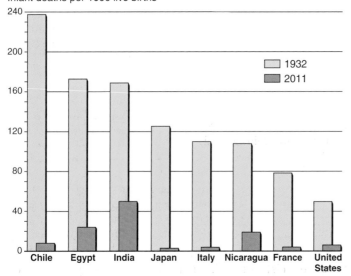

Infant deaths per 1000 live births

Figure 4.8 **Infant mortality rates for selected countries.**
Dramatic declines in the rate have occurred in all countries, a result of international programs of health care delivery aimed at infants and children in developing states. Nevertheless, the decreases have been proportionately greatest in the urbanized, industrialized countries, where sanitation, safe water, and quality health care are widely available.

Sources: Data from U.S. Bureau of the Census and Population Reference Bureau.

34 years instead of 70; in Zimbabwe, the decline has been to 37 years from 69. Overall, AIDS has killed some 17 million Africans since the 1950s when HIV (originally a disease of monkeys) appears to have established itself in Africa as a virulent human epidemic strain. Along with the deep cuts in sub-Saharan

life expectancies, total population by 2015 is now projected to be 60 million less than it would have been in the absence of the disease.

Southern Africa's economies are based on farming, and women do much of the farming as well as managing households. Because AIDS kills more women than men, sub-Saharan food insecurity is rising and food shortages result because many young adults are too feeble to farm. Malnutrition, starvation, and susceptibility to other diseases are thus AIDS costs added to lost economic productivity.

Population Pyramids

A **population pyramid** is a powerful means of visualizing and comparing a population's age and sex composition. The term *pyramid* describes the diagram's shape for many countries in the 1800s, when the display was created: a broad base of younger age groups and a progressive narrowing toward the apex as older populations were thinned by death. Now many different shapes are formed, each reflecting a different population history (Figure 4.9), and some suggest "population profile" is a more appropriate label. By showing the size of different age cohorts, the pyramids highlight the impact of "baby booms," population-reducing wars, birth rate reductions, and external migrations.

A rapidly growing country such as Uganda has most people in the lowest age cohorts; the percentage in older age groups declines successively, yielding a classic pyramid shape with stepped sides. Typically, female life expectancy is reduced in older cohorts of less developed countries, so that for Uganda, the proportion of females in older age groups is lower than in, for example, New Zealand. Female life expectancy and mortality rates may also be affected by cultural rather than economic developmental causes (see the feature "Millions of Women Are Missing"). In New Zealand, a wealthy country with a very slow rate of growth, the population

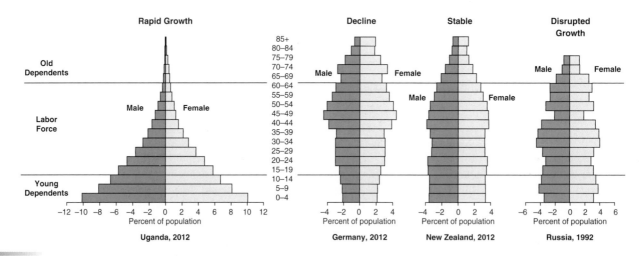

Figure 4.9 **Four patterns of population structure.** These diagrams show that population "pyramids" assume many shapes. The age distribution of populations reflects the past, records the present, and foretells the future. In countries such as Uganda, social costs related to the young are important and economic expansion is vital to provide employment for new entrants in the labor force. Germany's negative growth means a future with fewer workers to support a growing demand for social services for the elderly. The 1992 pyramid for Russia reported the sharp decline in births during World War II as a "pinching" of the 45–49 cohort, and showed in the large deficits of men above age 65 the heavy male mortality of both World Wars and late-Soviet period sharp reductions in Russian male longevity.

Sources: The 2012 pyramids for Uganda, Germany, and New Zealand: U.S. Bureau of the Census, International Data Bases; and for Russia; Carl Haub, "Population Change in the Former Soviet Republics." Population Bulletin 49, No. 4 (1994).

is nearly equally divided among the age groups, giving a "pyramid" with almost vertical sides. Below-replacement fertility rates create a pyramid with smaller cohorts at the bottom, as in the case of Germany. Among older cohorts, as Germany shows, there may be more women than men because of the greater life expectancy of the former. The impacts of war, as Russia's 1992 pyramid vividly demonstrated, were evident in that country's depleted age cohorts and male-female disparities. The sharp contrasts between the pyramids for Germany and Uganda are representative of the differing population concerns of the developing and developed regions of the world. The unique demographics of college towns retirement communities, Indian reservations, and mostly Hispanic border towns are clearly revealed in their population pyramids (Figure 4.10).

The population profile provides a quickly visualized demographic picture of practical and predictive value. For example, the percentage of a country's population in each age group strongly influences demand for goods and services within that national economy. A country with a high proportion of young has a high demand for educational facilities and certain types of health delivery services. In addition, of course, a large portion of the population is too young to be employed (Figures 4.10 and 4.11). On the other hand, a population with a high percentage of elderly people is burdened with high costs for pensions and health care, and these people must be supported by a smaller working-age population. Thus, as the profile of a national population changes, differing demands are placed on a country's social and economic systems (Figure 4.12). The **dependency ratio** is a simple measure of the number of economic dependents, old or young, that each 100 people in the productive years (usually, 15–64) must support. Population pyramids give visual evidence of that ratio.

Population pyramids also foretell future problems resulting from present population policies or practices. The strict family-size rules and widespread preferences for sons in China, for example, skews the pyramid in favor of males. On current evidence, about 1 million excess males a year enter an imbalanced marriage market in China. The 40 million bachelors China is likely to have in 2020, unconnected to society by wives and children, may pose threats to social order and, perhaps, national stability not foreseen or planned when family control programs were put in place, but clearly suggested by population pyramid distortions.

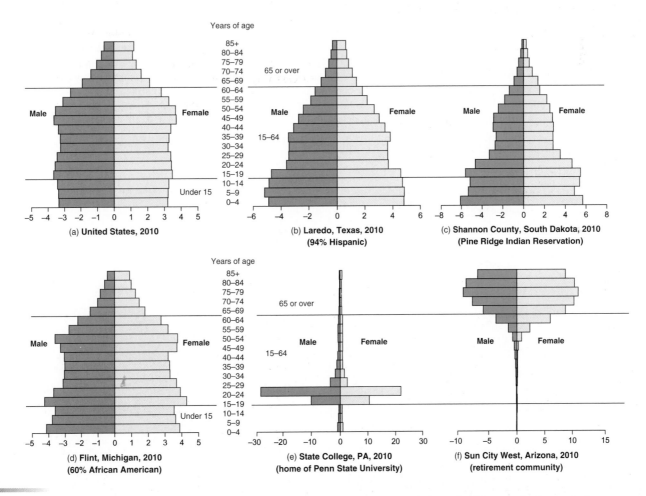

Figure 4.10 **Population pyramids for different communities.** The 2010 pyramids show the dramatic differences in the population structure across the United States. Laredo, Texas, on the U.S.-Mexico border, and Shannon County, South Dakota, on the Pine Ridge Indian Reservation, both display youthful populations with high birth rates. The pyramid for Shannon County also shows missing young adults and middle-aged adults who have moved away to urban areas. Flint, Michigan, is slightly more youthful than the total U.S. population, with fewer elderly due to out migration and lower life expectancies for African Americans. College towns and retirement communities create age-segregated places.

Source: U.S. Bureau of the Census, 2010.

Millions of Women Are Missing

Worldwide, according to one UN estimate, between 113 million and 200 million women are demographically missing, victims of nothing more than their sex. Their absence is the result of sex-selective abortions, female infanticide, abandonment, mistreatment, and violence in countries where boys are favored. If the UN estimate is correct, between 1.5 and 3 million women and girls are lost to gender-based discrimination and violence each year in a regionally variable pattern. The majority of that loss appears due to birth disparities.

The existence of sex-selective abortion is a tragic example of the interrelationship between technology (artifacts), social relationships (sociofacts), and belief systems (mentifacts). In China and India, the combination of a deeply ingrained cultural preference for boys and widespread availability of ultrasound technology has fueled the growth of sex-selective abortions. Traditionally in these societies, a married woman will care for her husband's parents in their old age. This practice has created the widespread perception that having a girl is an economic burden, while the birth of a boy is a blessing. Since higher-income families

have greater access to ultrasound tests, they are more likely to abort a female fetus, even against government directives.

The evidence for the missing women starts with a comparision against a normal **sex ratio:** Between 103 and 106 males are conceived and born for every 100 females. Normally, girls are hardier and more resistant to disease than boys, and in populations where the sexes are treated equally in matters of nutrition and health care, the number of males and females tends to equalize as they age. However, in many Asian countries, the ratio of males to females has been rising since the 1980s. East Asia has the most dramatic imbalances with an overall male-to-female sex ratio of 119 baby boys for every 100 baby girls. China's male-to-female sex ratio at birth has increased from a normal ratio in the early 1980s to 121 boys for every 100 girls during 2000 to 2005. India and Pakistan have the greatest percentage of "missing" women at about 8 percent of their total female population.

Sex ratio deviations are most striking for second and subsequent births. In China, South Korea, Taiwan, and Hong Kong, for example,

the most recent figures for first-child sex ratios are near normal, but rise to 121 boys per 100 girls for a second Chinese child and to 185 per 100 for a third Korean child. On that evidence, the problem of missing females is getting worse.

A 2010 United Nations report on Asia suggests that there is a rising number of missing females, with 43 million missing from both China and India.

But not all poor countries show the same disparities. In sub-Saharan Africa, where poverty and disease are perhaps more prevalent than on any other continent, but where there is no tradition of deadly violence against women, there are 102 females for every 100 males, and in Latin America and the Caribbean, there are equal numbers of males and females. To a lesser extent, the sex ratio disparities due to sex-selective abortions are also found among East Asian and South Asian immigrant communities in North America. Cultural norms and practices, not poverty or underdevelopment, seem to determine the fate and swell the numbers of the world's millions of missing women.

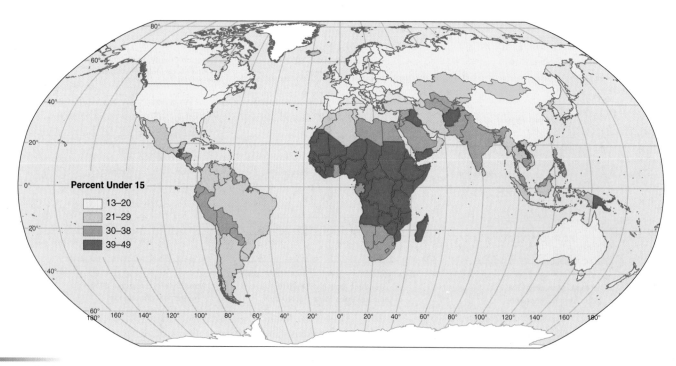

Figure 4.11 **Percentage of population under 15 years of age.** A high proportion of a country's population under 15 increases the dependency ratio of that state and promises future population growth as the youthful cohorts enter childbearing years.

Source: Data from Population Reference Bureau, 2008.

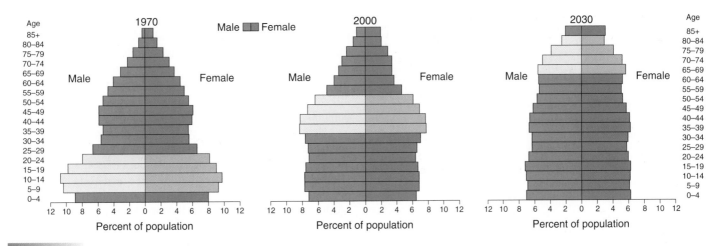

Figure 4.12 **The progression of the "boomers"**—the baby boom cohort born between 1946 and 1964—through the U.S. population pyramid has been associated with changing American lifestyles and expenditure patterns. In 1970, national priorities focused on the needs of children and young adults, such as building schools and expanding universities. At the turn of the 21st century, boomers formed the largest share of the working-age adult population, and their wants and spending patterns shaped the national culture and economy. By 2030, the pyramid foretells, their desires and support needs—now for retirement facilities and old-age care—will again be central concerns.

Source: Redrawn from Christine L. Himes, "Elderly Americans," Population Bulletin 56, no. 4 (December 2001), Fig. 1.

Natural Increase and Doubling Times

Knowledge of a country's sex and age distributions also enables demographers to forecast its future population levels, though the reliability of projections decreases with increasing length of forecast (Figure 4.13). Thus, a country with a high proportion of young people will experience a high rate of natural increase unless there is a very high mortality rate among infants and juveniles or fertility and birth rates change materially. The **rate of natural increase** of a population is derived by subtracting the crude death rate from the crude birth rate. *Natural* means that increases or decreases due to migration are not included. If a country had a birth rate of 22 per 1,000 and a death rate of 12 per 1,000 for a given year, the rate of natural increase would be 10 per 1,000. This rate is usually expressed as a percentage, that is, as a rate per 100 rather than per 1,000. In the example given, the annual increase would be 1 percent.

The rate of increase can be related to the time it takes for a population to double if the present growth rate remains constant—that is, the **doubling time.** Table 4.2 shows that it would take 70 years for a population with a rate of increase of 1 percent (approximately the rate of growth of Thailand or Argentina at the turn of the century) to double. A 2 percent rate of increase—recorded in 2011 by Egypt—means that the population would

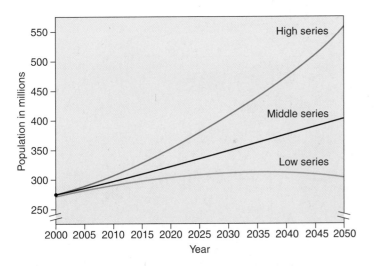

Figure 4.13 **Possible population futures for the United States.** As these population projections to 2050 illustrate, expected future numbers vary greatly because the fertility, birth and death rate, and immigration flow assumptions that they are based on are different. Depending on those assumptions, 2000 Census Bureau projections of the U.S. population in 2050 ranged from 314 million (low series) to 553 million (high series). The middle series estimate of 404 million is the one most often cited. The folly of basing planning decisions on very long range projections is made clear by the Bureau's extension of its trends for a full century. By 2100, it calculates, U.S. population could range from a low series 283 million to a high series 1.2 billion.

Source: U.S. Bureau of the Census.

Table 4.2	
Doubling Time in Years at Different Rates of Increase	
Annual Percentage Increase	**Doubling Time (Years)**
0.5	140
1.0	70
2.0	35
3.0	24
4.0	18
5.0	14
10.0	7

Table 4.3

Population Growth and Approximate Doubling Times Since A.D. 1

Year	Estimated Population	Doubling Time (Years)
1	250 million	
1650	500 million	1650
1804	1 billion	154
1927	2 billion	123
1974	4 billion	47
World population may reach:		
2030	8 billion	56[a]

[a]The final estimate of doubling time reflects assumptions of decreasing and stabilizing fertility rates. No current projections contemplate a further doubling to 16 billion people.

Source: United Nations.

double in only 35 years. (Population doubling time can be roughly estimated by applying the Rule of 70, which works for exponential growth and simply involves dividing 70 by the growth rate.) How could adding only 20 people per 1,000 cause a population to grow so quickly? The principle is the same as that used to compound interest in a bank.

Until recently, for the world as a whole, the rates of increase have risen over the span of human history. Therefore, the doubling time has decreased (Table 4.3). Growth rates vary regionally, and in countries with high rates of increase (Figure 4.14), the doubling time is less than the 60 years projected for the world as a whole at 2011 growth rates. As world fertility rates continue to decline, the population doubling times will increase, as they have since 1990.

Here, then, lies the answer to the earlier question. Even small annual additions accumulate to large total increments because we are dealing with geometric or exponential (1, 2, 4, 8) rather than arithmetic (1, 2, 3, 4) growth. The ever-increasing world base population has reached such a size that each additional doubling results in an astronomical increase in the total. A simple mental exercise suggests the inevitable consequences of such doubling, or **J-curve**, growth. Take a very large sheet of the thinnest paper you can find and fold it in half. Fold it in half again. After 7 or 8 folds, the sheet will have become as thick as a book—too thick for further folding by hand. If you could make 20 folds, the stack would be nearly as high as a football field is long. From then on, the results of further doubling are astounding. At 40 folds, the stack would be well on the way to the moon, and at 70, it would reach twice as far as the distance to the nearest star. Rounding the bend on the J-curve, which Figure 4.15 suggests the world population did around 1900, fostered dire predictions of inevitable unsupportable pressures on the planet's population support capabilities.

Today, rates of natural increase in developed countries, particularly in Europe, are approaching zero or even negative values. But individual country growth is also dependent on patterns of

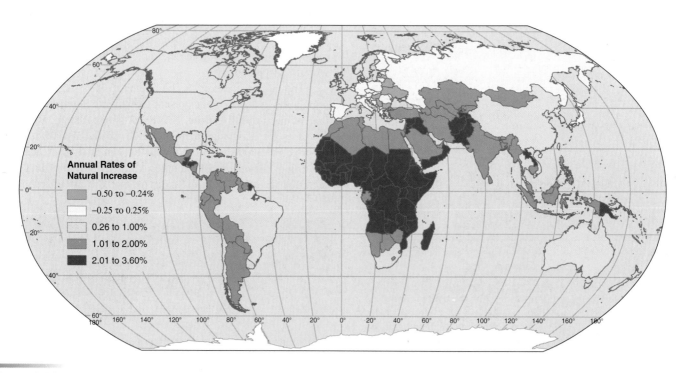

Figure 4.14 **Annual rates of natural increase.** The world's 2011 rate of natural increase (1.2%) would mean a doubling of population in 60 years. Since many demographers now anticipate world population will stabilize at around 9.5 billion (in about A.D. 2100) and perhaps actually decline after that, the "doubling" implication and time frame of current rates of natural increase reflect mathematical, not realistic, projections. Many individual continents and countries, of course, deviate widely from the global average rate of growth and have vastly different potential doubling times. Africa as a whole has the highest rates of increase, followed by Latin America and the Caribbean. Europe as a whole (including Russia) had a natural increase rate of 0.0.

Source: Data from Population Reference Bureau, 2011.

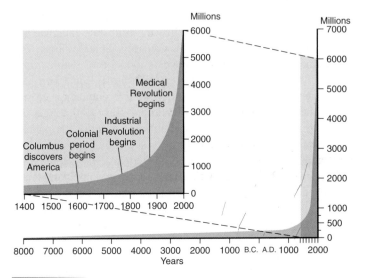

Figure 4.15 World population growth 8000 B.C. to A.D. 2000. Notice that the bend in the J-curve begins in the mid-1700s when industrialization started to provide new means to support the population growth through improvements in agriculture and food supply. Improvements in medical science, sanitation, and nutrition reduced death rates in the late 19th and early 20th centuries in the industrializing countries.

immigration and emigration. For example, Canada has a 0.4% rate of natural increase and a doubling time of 175 years; but with its high rates of immigration, it had, however, an *overall* growth rate of 1 percent with a doubling time of 64 years.

With replacement or below-replacement fertility rates throughout the developed world and declining fertility rates in most of the developing world, doubt is cast on the applicability of long-term doubling time projections. Although the doubling times are easier to understand than growth rates, they can be very misleading because they are based on the dubious assumption that present growth rates will continue indefinitely.

The Demographic Transition Model

Exponential population growth cannot continue indefinitely on a finite planet. Some form of braking mechanism must operate to control population growth. If voluntary population limitation is not undertaken, involuntary controls such as famine, disease, or resource wars may occur.

One attempt to summarize the observed voluntary population control that has accompanied economic development and modernization is the **demographic transition** model. The model traces the changing levels of human fertility and mortality associated with industrialization, health care improvements, urbanization, and changing cultural attitudes regarding childbearing. As societies move through the model's stages, high birth and death rates are replaced by low rates (Figure 4.16). During the intermediate stages of the model, populations grow rapidly before stabilizing in the final stage.

The *first stage* of the demographic transition model is characterized by high birth and high (but fluctuating) death rates. Birth rates and death rates are similar, and population grows slowly. Demographers think that it took from approximately A.D. 1 to A.D. 1500 for the population to increase from 250 million to 500 million, a doubling time of a millennium and a half. Growth was not steady, of course. There were periods of regional expansion that were usually

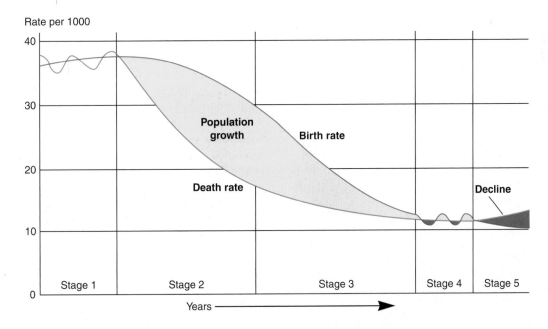

Figure 4.16 Stages in the demographic transition. During the first stage, birth and death rates are both high, and population grows slowly. When the death rate drops and the birth rate remains high, there is a rapid increase in numbers. During the third stage, birth rates decline, and population growth is less rapid. The fourth stage is marked by low birth and death rates and, consequently, by stabilization of the population. The negative growth rates of many European countries and the falling birth rates in other regions suggest that a fifth stage, one of population decline, is regionally—and ultimately worldwide—a logical extension of the transition model.

offset by sometimes catastrophic decline. Wars, epidemics, poor harvests, and natural disasters took heavy tolls. For example, the bubonic plague (the Black Death), which swept across Europe in the 14th century, is estimated to have killed between one-third and one-half of the population of that continent and epidemic diseases brought by Europeans to the Western Hemisphere are believed to have reduced New World native populations by 95 percent within a century or two of first contact. The high birth rates, high death rates, and slow population growth of the first stage describe all of human history until about A.D. 1750, when Western Europe entered stage two of the transition. Over the past 150 years, the decline in death rates that signaled the transition to stage two diffused around the globe. Today, death rates in even the poorest countries are below 20 per 1,000 and no country remains in stage one of the demographic transition.

The *second stage* of the transition model is usually associated with the consequences of Europe's Industrial Revolution and modernization. Rapid population growth during the second demographic stage results as birth rates outstrip death rates. Life expectancies increase dramatically due to advances in medicine, sanitation, agricultural productivity, and food distribution. Urbanization during the second stage provides the stage on which sanitation, medical, and food distribution improvements are concentrated (Figure 4.17). Birth rates do not fall as soon as death rates; ingrained cultural beliefs and social relationships—mentifacts and sociofacts—change more slowly than technologies. In most traditional societies, large families are valued for their social and economic advantages. Children are the focus of activities and rituals by which culture is transmitted, and in low-income families, they contribute economically by starting work at an early age, especially on farms or family businesses, and by supporting their parents in old age.

The *third stage* of the demographic transition occurs when birth rates decline as people begin to control family size. In urbanized, industrialized cultures, raising children is expensive. In fact, such cultures may view children as economic liabilities rather than assets. In addition, declining childhood mortality rates make

Figure 4.17 Liverpool, England, in the late 19th century. A modernizing Europe experienced improved living conditions and declining death rates during that century of progress.

parents feel that they can have fewer children, knowing that most of them are likely to survive. When the birth rate falls and the death rate remains low, the rate of population increase slows.

The classic demographic transition model ends with a *fourth* and final stage characterized by very low, nearly equal birth and death rates. At this point, a condition of zero population growth approaches as natural increase rates drop to zero. With longer life expectancies and fewer births, a significant aging of the population accompanies this stage.

In some countries that have completed the demographic transition, death rates equal or exceed birth rates and populations are actually declining. This extension of the fourth stage into a *fifth* stage of population decrease has so far been largely confined to the rich, industrialized world—notably Europe and Japan—but increasingly promises to affect much of the rest of the world as well. The dramatic decline in fertility that has been recorded in almost all countries since the 1980s means that a majority of the world's population resides in areas where the only significant population growth is from demographic momentum (see the section "Population Prospects," later in this chapter).

The Western Experience

The original transition model was devised to describe the experience of northwest European countries as they transitioned from rural-agrarian societies to urban-industrial ones. It may not accurately predict the course of events for all developing countries. In Europe, church and municipal records, some dating from the 16th century, show that people tended to marry late, if at all. In England before the Industrial Revolution, as many as half of all women in the 15–50 age cohort were unmarried. Infant mortality was high, life expectancy low. With the coming of industrialization in the 18th and 19th centuries, immediate factory wages instead of long apprenticeship programs permitted earlier marriage and more children. Since improvements in sanitation and health came only slowly, death rates remained high. Around 1800, 25 percent of Swedish infants died before their first birthday. Population growth rates remained below 1 percent per year in France throughout the 19th century.

Beginning about 1860, first death rates and then birth rates began their significant, though gradual, decline. This "mortality revolution" came first, as an *epidemiological transition*: formerly fatal epidemic diseases became endemic (that is, essentially continual within a population). As people developed partial immunities, mortality rates declined. Improvements in livestock raising, crop rotation, fertilizer use, and new crops from overseas colonies (the potato was an early example) raised the level of health of the European population in general.

At the same time, sewage systems and sanitary water supplies became common in larger cities, reducing the frequency of water-borne illnesses such as cholera and typhoid (Figure 4.18). Deaths due to infectious, parasitic, and respiratory diseases and to malnutrition declined, while those related to chronic illnesses associated with an aging population increased. Western Europe passed from a first stage, the "Age of Pestilence and Famine," to the "Age of Degenerative and Human-Origin Diseases." However, recent increases in drug- and antibiotic-resistant diseases,

Figure 4.18 Pure piped water replacing individual or neighborhood wells, and sewers and waste treatment plants instead of privies, became increasingly common in urban Europe and North America during the 19th century. Their modern successors, such as the Las Vegas, Nevada, treatment plant shown here, helped complete the *epidemiologic transition* in developed countries.

pesticide resistance of disease-carrying insects, and such new scourges of both the less-developed and more-developed countries as AIDS cast doubt on the stability of that ultimate stage (see the feature "Our Delicate State of Health"). Nevertheless, even the resurgence of old and emergence of new scourges such as malaria, tuberculosis, and AIDS are unlikely to have decisive demographic consequences on the global scale.

In Europe, the striking reduction in death rates was echoed by similar declines in birth rates as societies began to alter their traditional concepts of ideal family size. In cities, child labor laws and mandatory schooling meant that children no longer were important contributors to family economies. As "poor-relief" legislation and other forms of social welfare substituted for family support structures, the value of children as a social safety net declined. Family consumption patterns altered as the Industrial Revolution made widely available consumer goods that once were considered luxuries. For some, children came to be seen as hindrance rather than aid to social mobility, lifestyle improvement, and self-expression. Perhaps most important were changes in the education levels, career opportunities, and social status of women that spread the conviction that control over childbearing was within their power and to their benefit.

A Divided World, A Converging World

The dramatic decline in mortality that had emerged only gradually throughout the European world occurred with startling speed in developing countries after 1950. The increasing availability in developing countries of Western technologies of medicine and public health, including antibiotics, insecticides, sanitation,

immunization, infant and child health care, and the eradication of smallpox, quickly and dramatically increased life expectancies. Such imported technologies and treatments accomplished in a few years what it took Europe 50 to 100 years to experience. Sri Lanka, for example, sprayed extensively with DDT to combat malaria; life expectancy there jumped from 44 years in 1946 to 60 only eight years later. With similar public health programs, India also experienced a steady reduction in its death rate after 1947. Simultaneously, with international sponsorship, food aid cut the death toll of developing states during drought and other disasters. Thus, the second stage of the demographic transition—declining death rates accompanied by continuing high birth rates—diffused worldwide.

Many countries in Africa, Latin America, and southern Asia display the characteristics of this second stage in the population model. Ghana, with a birth rate of 31 and a death rate of 8, and Guatemala, with rates of 30 and 6, are typical. The annual rates of increase for such countries are 2.3 to 2.4 percent, and their populations will double in about 30 years. Such rates, of course, do not mean that the full impact of modernization has been worldwide; they do mean that the underdeveloped societies have been beneficiaries of the life preservation techniques it generated.

Birth rate declines, of course, depend in part on technology, but even more important is social acceptance of the idea of fewer children and smaller families. That acceptance has diffused broadly but unevenly worldwide. The steep declines in birth rates in developing countries indicate that most of them have moved into the third or fourth stages of the demographic transition (Figure 4.19). In 1984, only 18 percent of world population lived in countries with fertility rates at or below replacement levels (that is, countries that had achieved the fourth stage demographic transition).

Our Delicate State of Health

Death rates have plummeted, and the benefits of modern medicines, antibiotics, and sanitary practices have enhanced both the quality and length of life in the developed and developing world. Far from being won, however, the struggle against infectious and parasitic diseases is growing in intensity and is, perhaps, unwinnable. More than a half century after the discovery of antibiotics, the diseases they were to eradicate are on the rise, and both old and new disease-causing microorganisms are emerging and spreading all over the world. Infectious and parasitic diseases kill between 17 and 20 million people each year; they officially account for one-quarter to one-third of global mortality.

The six leading infectious killers are, in order, acute respiratory infections such as pneumonia, diarrheal diseases, AIDS, tuberculosis, malaria, and measles. In addition, AIDS kills 1.8 million yearly, three-quarters of them in sub-Saharan Africa, dramatically altering the population structure in the most affected countries. The incidence of infection, of course, is much greater than the occurrence of deaths. Nearly 30 percent of the world's people, for example, are infected with the bacterium that causes tuberculosis, but only 2 to 3 million are killed by the disease each year. More than 500 million people are infected with such tropical diseases as malaria, sleeping sickness, schistosomiasis, and river blindness, with perhaps 3 million annual deaths. Newer pathogens

are constantly appearing, such as those causing Lassa fever, Rift Valley fever, Ebola fever, hantavirus pulmonary syndrome, West Nile encephalitis, hepatitis C, and severe acute respiratory syndrome (SARS). In fact, at least 30 previously unknown infectious diseases have appeared since the mid-1970s.

The 1918–1919 Spanish Flu pandemic demonstrates how diseases can diffuse globally with devastating effect. Striking as World War I was drawing to an end, the epidemic's spread was likely aided by massive troop movements as it diffused along shipping routes. The influenza virus struck down the young and healthy and killed an estimated 20 to 40 million people. The spread and virulence of infectious diseases are linked to the dramatic changes so rapidly occurring in the earth's physical and social environments. Climate change permits temperature-restricted pathogens to invade new areas and claim new victims. Deforestation, wetland drainage, and other human-induced alterations to the physical environment disturb ecosystems and simultaneously disrupt the natural system of controls that keep infectious diseases in check.

Rapid population growth and explosive urbanization, increasing global tourism, population-dislocating wars and migrations,

Botswana in 2020

and expanding world trade all increase interpersonal disease-transmitting contacts. Some disease-causing microbes, have expanded their range as previously isolated areas are opened up by new roads and air routes.

The most effective weapons in the battle against epidemics battle are already known. They include improved health education; disease prevention and surveillance; research on disease vectors and incidence areas (using GIS and spatial analysis); drug therapy; mosquito control programs; clean water supplies; and distribution of such simple and cheap remedies as childhood immunizations and oral rehydration therapy. All, however, require expanded investment and attention to those spreading infectious diseases—many with newly developed antibiotic-resistant strains—so recently thought to be no longer of concern.

By 2010, however, 42 percent lived in such countries, and it is increasingly difficult to distinguish between developed and developing societies on the basis of their fertility rates. Those rates in many separate Indian states (Kerala and Tamil Nadu, for example) and in such countries as Sri Lanka, Thailand, South Korea, and China are below those of the United States and some European countries. Significant decreases to near the replacement level have also occurred in the space of a single generation in many other Asian and Latin American states with high recent rates of economic growth. Increasingly, it appears, low fertility is becoming a feature of both rich and poor, developed and developing states.

The demographic transition model assumes an inevitable course of events from the high birth and death rates of premodern (nonindustrialized) societies to the low and stable rates of advanced (industrialized) countries. The model fails to anticipate, however, that the European experience would not be matched by all developing countries. Some developing societies remain in the second stage of the model, unable to realize the economic

gains and social changes necessary to progress to the third stage of falling birth rates. Thus, despite a substantial convergence of fertility rates, many observers point to a continuing and growing demographic divide. On one side of the divide are the low-fertility countries that are home to 42 percent of the world's population. The low fertility rates of these mostly wealthy countries guarantee future population decline and rapid aging. On the other side of the divide are a group of high-fertility countries that account for just 18 percent of the world's population but are projected to triple in size and increase their global population share to 42 percent by 2100. Nearly all of the high-fertility countries are included on the United Nation's list of least-developed countries. Most of them are in sub-Saharan Africa, and all suffer from low per capita income, illiteracy, low standards of living, and inadequate health facilities and care.

The established patterns of both high- and low-fertility regions tend to be self-reinforcing. Low growth permits the expansion of personal income and the accumulation of capital to enhance the

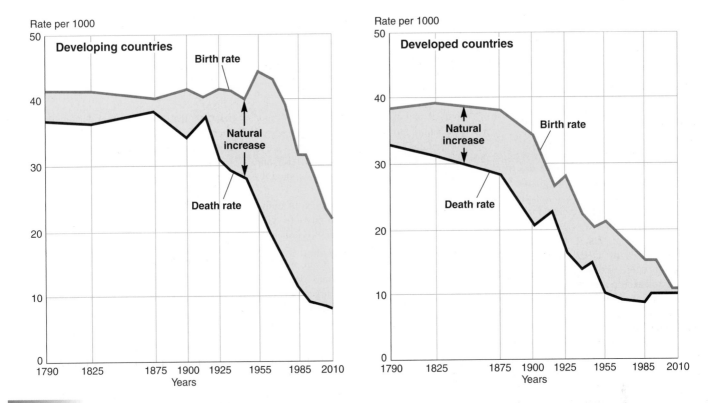

Figure 4.19 **World birth and death rates to 2010.** The "population explosion" after World War II (1939–1945) reflected the effects of drastically reduced death rates in developing countries without simultaneous and compensating reductions in births. Today, however, three interrelated trends appear in many developing countries: (1) fertility has overall dropped further and faster than was predicted; (2) contraceptive acceptance and use has increased markedly; and (3) age at marriage is rising. In consequence, the demographic transition had been compressed from a century to a generation in some developing states.

Source: Revised and redrawn from Elaine M. Murphy, World Population: Toward the Next Century, *revised ed. (Washington, D.C.: Population Reference Bureau, 1989) and Population Reference Bureau, annual* World Population Data Sheet.

quality of life and make large families less attractive or essential. In contrast, in high-fertility regions, population growth requires spending on social services that otherwise might have been invested to promote economic expansion. Growing populations place ever greater demands on limited natural resources. As the environmental base deteriorates, productivity declines, undermining the economic progress on which the demographic transition depends (see "International Population Policies"). The vastly different future prospects for personal and national prosperity between the high-fertility countries and the rest of the world make the demographic divide a matter of continuing international concern.

The Demographic Equation

Change in a region's population stems from three basic life events: people are born, they migrate, and they die. Migration involves the long-distance movement of people from one residence to another. When that relocation occurs across political boundaries, it affects the population structure of both the origin and destination regions. The **demographic equation** summarizes the contribution made to regional population change over time by the combination of *natural change* (births minus deaths) and *net migration* (difference between in-migration and out-migration). **Zero population growth (ZPG)** is the condition for individual countries when births plus

immigration equals deaths plus emigration. On a global scale, of course, all population change is accounted for by natural change. The impact of migration on the demographic equation often increases as the population size of the areal unit decreases.

$$P_f = P_i + \text{Births} + \text{In-Migration} - \text{Deaths} - \text{Out-Migration}$$

where:

P_f = Final Population
P_i = Initial Population

Population Relocation

In the past, emigration proved an important device for relieving the pressures of rapid population growth during the demographic transition for many European countries (Figure 4.20). For example, in one 90-year span, 45 percent of the natural increase in the population of the British Isles emigrated, and between 1846 and 1935, some 60 million Europeans of all nationalities left that continent. Today, the major population relocations connect growing countries going through the second and third stages of the demographic transition with aging societies in the fourth stage. Yet, despite recent massive movements of economic and political refugees across Asian, African, and Latin American boundaries, emigration today provides no comparable relief valve for developing countries. Total

Geography and Citizenship

International Population Policies

After a sometimes rancorous nine-day meeting in Cairo in September 1994, the U.N. International Conference on Population and Development endorsed a strategy for stabilizing the world's population at 7.27 billion by no later than 2015. The 20-year program of action accepted by 179 signatory countries sought to avoid the environmental consequences of excessive population growth. Its proposals were therefore linked to discussions and decisions of the U.N. Conference on Environment and Development held in Rio de Janeiro in June 1992.

The Cairo plan abandoned several decades of top-down governmental programs that promoted "population control" (a phrase avoided by the conference) based on targets and quotas and, instead, embraced for the first time policies giving women greater control over their lives, greater economic equality and opportunity, and a greater voice in reproduction decisions. It recognized that limiting population growth depends on programs that lead women to want fewer children and make them partners in economic development. In that recognition, the Conference accepted the documented link between increased educational access and economic opportunity for women and falling birth rates and smaller families. Earlier population conferences—1974 in Bucharest and 1984 in Mexico City—did not fully address these issues of equality, opportunity, education, and political rights; their adopted goals failed to achieve hoped-for changes in birth rates in large part because women in many traditional societies had no power to enforce contraception and feared their other alternative, sterilization.

The earlier conferences carefully avoided or specifically excluded abortion as an acceptable family planning method. It was the more open discussion of abortion in Cairo that elicited much of the spirited debate that registered religious objections by the Vatican and many Muslim and Latin American states to the inclusion of legal abortion as part of health care, and to language suggesting approval of sexual relations outside of marriage. Although the final text of the conference declaration did not promote any universal right to abortion and excluded it as a means of family planning, some delegations still registered reservations to its wording on both sex and abortion. At conference close, however, the Vatican endorsed the declaration's underlying principles, including the family as "the basic unit of society" and the need to stimulate economic growth, and to promote "gender equality, equity, and the empowerment of women."

A special United Nations "Cairo + 5" session in 1999 recommended some adjustments in the earlier agreements. It urged emphasis on measures ensuring safe and accessible abortion in countries where it is legal, called for school children at all levels to be instructed in sexual and reproductive health issues, and told governments to provide special family planning and health services for sexually active adolescents, with particular stress on reducing their vulnerability to AIDS.

In 2004, the UN reported progress toward reaching the Cairo and Cairo + 5 goals. The consensus was that much remained to be done to broaden programs for the poorest population groups, to invest in rural development and urban planning, to strengthen laws ending discrimination against women, and to encourage donor countries to fully meet their agreed-on contributions to the program. Nevertheless, positive Cairo plan results were also seen in declining fertility rates in many of the world's most populous developing countries. Some demographers and many women's health organizations pointedly claim that those declines have little to do with government planning policies. Rather, they assert, current lower and falling fertility rates are the expected result of women assuming greater control over their economic and reproductive lives. The director of the U.N. Population Division noted: "A woman in a village making a decision to have one or two or at most three children is a small decision in itself. But . . . compounded by millions and millions . . . of women in India and Brazil and Egypt, it has global consequences."

That women are making those decisions, population specialists have observed, reflects important cultural factors emerging since Cairo. Satellite television brings contraceptive information to even remote villages and shows programs of small, apparently happy families that viewers think of emulating. Increasing urbanization reduces some traditional family controls on women and makes contraceptives easier to find, and declining infant mortality makes mothers more confident their babies will survive. Perhaps most important, population experts assert, is the dramatic increase in most developing states in female school attendance and corresponding reductions in the illiteracy rates of girls and young women who will themselves soon be making fertility decisions.

Questions to Consider

1. Do you think it is appropriate or useful for international bodies to promote policies affecting such purely personal or national concerns as reproduction and family planning? Why or why not?

2. Do you think that current international concerns over population growth, development, and the environment are sufficiently valid and pressing to risk the loss of long-enduring cultural norms and religious practices in many of the world's traditional societies? Why or why not?

3. The Cairo plan called for sizeable monetary pledges from developed countries to support enhanced population planning in the developing world. For the most part, those pledges have not been honored. Do you think the financial obligations assigned to donor countries are justified in light of the many other international needs and domestic concerns faced by their governments? Why or why not?

4. Many environmentalists see the world as a finite system unable to support ever-increasing populations; to exceed its limits would cause frightful environmental damage and global misery. Many economists counter that free markets will keep supplies of needed commodities in line with growing demand and that science will, as necessary, supply technological fixes in the form of substitutes or expansion of production. In light of such diametrically opposed views of population growth consequences, is it appropriate or wise to base international programs solely on one of them? Why or why not?

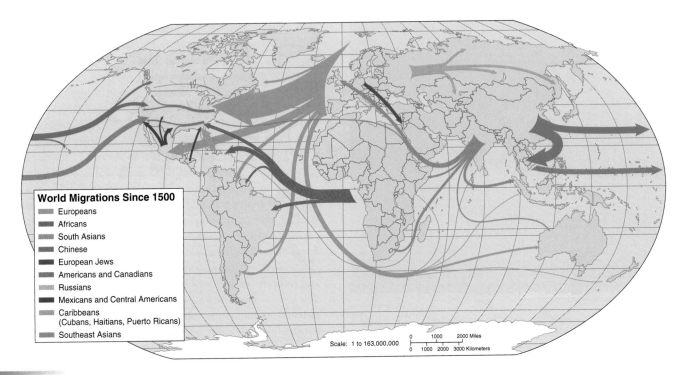

Figure 4.20 Principal migrations since 1500. The arrows show the direction and relative magnitude of the major voluntary and forced international migration since about 1500. More recently, there have been significant population movements into the United Kingdom, France, Belgium, and the Netherlands from their former colonies and from less-prosperous countries within the EU.

Source: Shaded zones after Daniel Noin, Géographie de la Population *(Paris: Masson, 1979), p. 85.*

population numbers are too great to be much affected by migrations of even millions of people. In only a few countries—Afghanistan, Cuba, El Salvador, and Haiti, for example—have as many as 10% of the population emigrated in recent decades.

Net migration, the balance between in-migration and out-migration, is positive for the developed countries as a group, and negative for the less-developed countries. Net migration rates are modest, but the direction of movement reflects the demand for additional workers in high-income countries that have completed the demographic transition and the ample supply of willing workers in rapidly growing, low-income countries. The highest negative (net out-migration) rates are found in Lithuania, small island states in Oceania, and war-torn Somalia. Lithuania joined the European Union (EU) in 2004 and since has been losing large numbers of young workers to other EU countries with stronger economies. The highest positive (net in-migration) rates are found in oil-producing states in the Near East.

Immigration Impacts

Where cross-border movements are massive enough, migration may have a pronounced impact on the demographic equation and result in significant changes in the population structures of both the origin and destination regions. Past European and African migrations, for example, not only altered but substantially created the population structures of new, sparsely inhabited lands of colonization in the Western Hemisphere and Australasia. In some decades of the late 18th and early 19th centuries, 30% to more than 40% of population increase in the United States was accounted for by immigration. Similarly, eastward-moving Slavs colonized under populated Siberia and overwhelmed native peoples.

Migrants are rarely a representative cross section of the population group they leave, and they add an unbalanced age and sex component to the group they join. A recurrent research observation is that emigrant groups are heavily skewed in favor of young singles. Whether males or females dominate the outflow varies with circumstances. Although males traditionally far exceeded females in international flow, in recent years females have accounted for between 40% and 60% of all transborder migrants.

At the least, then, the receiving country will have its population structure altered by an outside increase in its younger age cohorts. The results are both immediate in a modified population pyramid, and potential in future impact on birth rates. The origin area will have lost a portion of its young, active members of child-bearing years. It perhaps will have suffered distortion in its young adult sex ratios, and it certainly will have recorded a statistical aging of its population. The destination society will likely experience increases in births associated with the youthful newcomers and, in general, have its average age reduced.

World Population Distribution

The world's population is not uniformly distributed over the Earth. The most striking feature of the world population distribution map (Figure 4.21) is the very unevenness of the pattern. Some land areas are nearly uninhabited, others are sparsely settled, and still others contain dense agglomerations of people. Until about 2007, rural folk—unevenly concentrated—always outnumbered urban people. After 2007, however, urbanites will remain dominant with cities capturing most of the world's population growth.

as late marriage, or celibacy, nature would enact "destructive" checks on overpopulation:

> The power of population is so superior to the power in the earth to produce subsistence for man that premature death must in some shape or other visit the human race. The vices of mankind are active and able ministers of depopulation . . . But should they fail in the war of extermination, sickly seasons, epidemics, pestilence, and plague, advance in terrific array, and sweep off their thousands and ten thousands. Should success be still incomplete, gigantic inevitable famine stalks in the rear, and with one mighty blow, levels the population with the food of the world. (44)

Allied with the property-owning elite, Malthus was pessimistic about the lower social classes' ability to restrain their reproduction. He argued against charity because alleviating the suffering of the hungry would merely encourage them to increase in number, while discouraging thrift and hard work. Malthus was not alone in drawing pessimistic conclusions about population growth and resources; Hung Liangchi of China wrote in the 19th century that "Within a hundred years or so, the population can increase from fivefold to twentyfold, while the means of subsistence . . . can increase only from three to five times."

Malthus did not have the benefit of witnessing the demographic transition that was just getting underway or more recent advances in contraceptives and food production technology. Yet that did not stop the revival of his ideas after World War II, when many developing countries entered the second stage of the demographic transition. **Neo-Malthusians,** most notably **Paul Ehrlich,** a Stanford University biologist and author of the best-seller *The Population Bomb,* updated Malthus's arguments for the 20th century. As a population biologist, Ehrlich was familiar with animal studies that showed a steep J-curve of population growth followed by dieback when numbers exceeded the carrying capacity of the environment. Sounding the alarm in 1968, Ehrlich wrote:

> The battle to save humanity is over. In the 1970s and 1980s hundreds of millions of people will starve to death despite any crash programs embarked upon now. At this late date, nothing can be done to prevent a substantial increase in the world death rate, although many lives could be saved through dramatic programs to "stretch" the carrying capacity of the earth by increasing food production and providing for more equitable distribution of whatever food is available. But these programs will only provide a stay of execution unless they are accompanied by determined and successful efforts at population control (1968, xi).

Neo-Malthusianism gained popularity among environmentalists and international development specialists who viewed rapid population growth as damaging the environment and diverting scarce resources from capital investment. In order to lift living standards, the existing national efforts to lower mortality rates had to be balanced by governmental programs to reduce birth rates. Thus, neo-Malthusian thinking became the basis for national and international programs of population control. These programs were promoted around the world by the United Nations and non-governmental organizations and were especially influential in Asian countries such as China and India.

Arrayed against the pessimism of Malthus and the neo-Malthusians are a number of competing perspectives, most notably the Marxist critique of Malthus and the economic theories of Esther Boserup and Julian Simon. **Karl Marx** rejected the Malthusian interpretation of poverty, arguing that what appeared to be overpopulation was actually the unemployed surplus labor population needed by the capitalist system. Danish economist Esther Boserup developed the **Boserup thesis,** on the basis of detailed historical and field studies, which argues that past agricultural improvements occurred as a result of population pressure. In order to feed more people, farmers developed new ways to use their land and labor more intensively. In other words, population growth was a stimulus, not a deterrent, to development. American economist **Julian Simon** went further, developing an optimistic cornucopian perspective on population growth. Simon argued that resources do not exist in nature but are created by human ingenuity, which is the world's ultimate resource base. For example, a resource such as oil was just a black gooey substance until humans discovered ways of refining it and capturing its energy content. For cornucopians, more people means more scientists and inventors. Since the time of Malthus, they observed, the world's population had grown from 900 million to 7 billion without the predicted dire consequences—proof that Malthus failed to recognize the importance of technology in raising the carrying capacity of the Earth. Still higher population numbers, they suggest, are sustainable, perhaps even with improved standards of living for all.

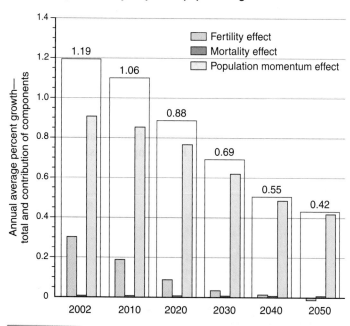

The components of yearly world population growth: 2010–2050

Figure 4.29 **Effects of population momentum, 2010–2050.**
Population momentum represents the lingering effects of past high fertility. Worldwide declines in total fertility rates will not immediately be reflected by equivalent declines in the growth of population. Because of past high fertility, the numbers of women in their childbearing years are increasing both absolutely and relative to the rest of the population. As a result, population momentum will account for a growing share of projected world population increase.

Source: U.S. Bureau of the Census, 2004.

An intermediate view admits that products of human ingenuity, such as the Green Revolution (discussed in Chapter 8), allowed food production to keep pace with rapid population growth but warns that continued gains in food production technology are not guaranteed. Both complacency and inadequate research support have hindered continuing progress in recent years. And even if further advances are made, they observe, not all countries or regions have the social and political will or capacity to take advantage of them. Those that do not will fail to keep pace with the needs of their populace and will sink into varying degrees of poverty and environmental decay, creating national and regional—though not necessarily global—crises.

Drawing upon both nationalistic and Marxist concepts, many less-developed countries rejected the neo-Malthusian population control programs promoted by Western states (See the feature "International Population Policies"). They maintained that remnant colonial era social, economic, and class structures, rather than population increase, hindered their development. Some government leaders recognized a link between population size and power and pursued pronatalist policies that encouraged childbearing, as did Mao's China during the 1950s and early 1960s. Africa and the Middle East have been generally less receptive to neo-Malthusian arguments because of established cultural preferences for large families. Islamic fundamentalist resistance to birth restrictions has had an influence in the Near East and North Africa, although the Muslim theocracy in Iran has endorsed a range of contraceptive options and supports an aggressive family planning program. Predominantly Roman Catholic countries in southern Europe, Central America, and South America have witnessed substantial fertility declines despite the official pronatalist policies of the church.

Population Prospects

Regardless of population philosophies, theories, or cultural norms, the fact remains that many or most developing countries are showing significantly declining population growth rates. Global fertility and birth rates are falling to an extent not anticipated by pessimistic Malthusians and at a pace that suggests a peaking of world population numbers sooner—and at lower totals—than previously projected and possible decline in the developed world. In all world regions, steady and continuous fertility declines have been recorded over the past years, reducing fertility from global 5-children-per-woman levels in the early 1950s to 2.5 per woman by 2011. Most continuing population growth in developed countries is due to momentum from the past, and aging will be an inevitable consequence of the recent changes in fertility patterns.

Population Implosion in the Developed World?

For much of the last half of the 20th century, demographers and economists focused on a "population explosion" and its implied threat of a world with too many people and too few resources of food and minerals to sustain them. By the end of that century, those fears for some observers were being replaced by a new prediction of world regions with too few rather than too many people.

That possibility was suggested by two related trends. The first became apparent by 1970 when it was noted that the total fertility rates (TFRs) of 19 countries, almost all of them in Europe, had fallen below the **replacement level**—the level of fertility at which populations replace themselves—of 2.1. Simultaneously, Europe's population pyramid began to become noticeably distorted, with a smaller proportion of young and a growing share of middle-aged and retirement-age inhabitants. The decrease in native working-age cohorts had already, by 1970, encouraged the influx of non-European "guest workers" whose labor was needed to maintain economic growth and to sustain the generous security provisions guaranteed to what was becoming the oldest population of any continent.

Many countries of Western and Eastern Europe sought to reverse their birth rate declines by adopting pronatalist policies. The communist states of the East rewarded pregnancies and births with generous family allowances, free medical and hospital care, extended maternity leaves, and child care. France, Italy, the Scandinavian countries, and others gave similar bonuses or awards for first, second, and later births. Despite those inducements, however, reproduction rates continued to fall. By 2003, every one of the 43 European countries and territories had fertility rates below replacement levels in widespread response to a host of cultural influences and personal lifestyle decisions. Those decisions were influenced by increased educational levels of women with longer years of schooling and deferred marriage ages, opportunities for women to work in challenging careers, and the increasing cost of rearing children. Cultural expectations about ideal family size have shifted downward, and an increasing number of adults are choosing personal pursuits over family obligations. The effect on national growth prospects has been striking. For example, the populations of Spain and Italy are projected to shrink by a quarter between 2000 and 2050 (and that of Ukraine by 43 percent between 2005 and 2050). Europe as a whole is forecast to shrink by 70 million people by mid-century. "In demographic terms," France's prime minister remarked, "Europe is vanishing."

Europe's experience soon was echoed in other societies of advanced economic development on all continents. By 1995, Canada, Australia, New Zealand, Japan, Taiwan, South Korea, Singapore, and other older and newly industrializing countries (NICs) registered fertility rates below the replacement level. As they have for Europe, simple projections foretold their aging and declining population. Japan's numbers, for example, began to decline in 2006 when 21 percent of its population was age 65 or older; Taiwan forecasts negative growth by 2035.

The second trend indicating to many that world population numbers should stabilize and even decline during the lifetimes of today's college cohort is a simple extension of the first: TFRs are being reduced to or below the replacement levels in countries at all stages of economic development in all parts of the world. Exceptions to the trend are found in Africa, especially Sub-Saharan Africa, and in some areas of South, Central, and West Asia; but even in those regions, fertility rates have been decreasing in recent years. "Powerful globalizing forces [are] at work pushing toward fertility reduction everywhere," was an observation of the French National Institute of Demographic Studies.

Achievement of zero population growth has social and economic consequences not always perceived by its advocates. These inevitably include an increasing proportion of older citizens, fewer young people, a rise in the median age of the population, and a growing old-age dependency ratio with ever-increasing pension and social service costs borne by a shrinking labor force.

Momentum

Reducing fertility levels even to the replacement level of about 2.1 births per woman does not mean an immediate end to population growth. Because of the age composition of many societies, numbers of births will continue to grow even as fertility rates per woman decline. The reason is to be found in **population** (or **demographic**) **momentum,** which is similar to a car continuing to coast for some time after the driver has lifted their foot from the accelerator pedal. The key to that is the age structure of a country's population.

When a high proportion of the population is young, the product of past high fertility rates, larger numbers enter the childbearing age each year; that is the case for major parts of the world today. The populations of developing countries are far younger than those of the established industrially developed regions (see Figure 4.11), with over 40% in Africa below the age of 15. The fertility of these young people has yet to be realized. A population with a greater number of young people tends to grow rapidly regardless of the level of childbearing. The results will continue to be felt until the youthful cohorts mature and work their way through the population pyramid (Figure 4.29).

Inevitably, while this is happening, even the most stringent national policies limiting growth cannot stop it entirely. A country with a large present population base will experience large numerical increases despite declining birth rates. Indeed, the higher fertility was to begin with and the sharper its drop to low levels, the greater will be the role of momentum even after rates drop below replacement. For example, Iran has recently implemented strong population policies that have lowered fertility rates to 1.9, well below replacement values. However, due to momentum, the population is projected to grow from 78 to 100 million by 2050.

Aging

Eventually, of course, young populations grow older, and even the youthful developing countries are beginning to face the consequences of that reality. The problems of a rapidly aging population that already confront the industrialized economies are now being realized in the developing world as well. Throughout human history, young people outnumbered the elderly; sometime between 2015 and 2020, persons 65 years and older will outnumber those under 5 years of age. Europe is the oldest world region and Africa is the youngest. Japan leads the world in the percentage of its population aged 65 and older, at 21.6 percent. Italy and Germany are close behind.

The progression toward older populations is considered irreversible, the result of the now-global demographic transition from high to low levels of fertility and mortality. The youthful majorities of the past are unlikely to occur again. By 2050, the UN projects, one out of five persons worldwide will be 60 years old or older.

In the developing world, older persons are projected to make up 20 percent of the population by 2050 in contrast to the 8 percent over age 60 there in 2000. Since the demographic transition took place more quickly, the pace of aging will be much faster in the developing countries. Thus, they will have less time than the developed world did to adjust to the consequences of that aging. And those consequences will be experienced at lower levels of personal and national income and economic strength.

In both rich and poor states, the working-age populations will face increasing burdens and obligations. The potential support ratio, or PSR (the number of persons aged 15–64 years per one citizen aged 65 or older), has steadily fallen. Between 1950 and 2000, it dropped from 12 to 9 workers for each older person; by mid-century, the PSR is projected to drop to 4. The implications for social security programs, private pension plans, health insurance, government finances, and social support obligations are ominous. Exacerbating the strain on resources, the sharp increase in the oldest population (80 years or older) will require greater expenditures for health and long-term care. We can expect strained government budgets to become normal. The consequences of population aging appear most intractable for the world's poorest developing states that generally lack health, income, housing, and social service support systems adequate to the needs of their older citizens. To the social and economic implications of their present population momentum, therefore, developing countries must add the aging consequences of past patterns and rates of growth (Figure 4.30).

Figure 4.30 These senior residents of a Moroccan nursing home are part of the rapidly aging population of many developing countries. Worldwide, the over-60 cohort will number some 22 percent of total population by 2050 and be larger than the number of children less than 15 years of age. But by 2020, a third of Singapore citizens will be 55 or older, and China will have as large a share of its population over 60—about one in four—as will Europe. Already, the numbers of old people in the world's poorer countries are beginning to dwarf those in the rich world. There are nearly twice as many persons over 60 in developing countries as in the advanced ones, but most are without the old age assistance and welfare programs that developed countries have put in place.

Summary

Birth, death, fertility, and growth rates are important in understanding the size, composition, distribution, and spatial trends of population. Recent "explosive" increases in human numbers and the prospects of continuing population expansion may be traced to sharp reductions in death rates, increases in longevity, and the impact of demographic momentum on a youthful population largely concentrated in the developing world. Control of population growth historically was accomplished through a demographic transition first experienced in European societies that adjusted their fertility rates downward as death rates fell and life expectancies increased. The introduction of advanced technologies of preventive and curative medicine, pesticides, and famine relief have reduced mortality rates in developing countries pushing developing regions into stage two of the demographic transition.

Even with the advent of more widespread fertility declines, the 7 billion human beings present today will still likely grow to perhaps 9.2 billion by the middle of the 21st century. That growth will largely reflect increases unavoidable because of the size and youth of populations in developing countries. Eventually, a new balance between population numbers and carrying capacity of the world will be reached, as it has always been following past periods of rapid population increase.

People are unevenly distributed over the earth. The ecumene, or permanently inhabited portion of the globe, is discontinuous and marked by pronounced differences in population concentrations and numbers. South Asia, East Asia, Europe, and northeastern United States/southeastern Canada represent the world's greatest population clusters, though smaller areas of great density are found in other regions and continents.

As respected geographer Glenn Trewartha once commented, "population is the point of reference from which all other elements [of geography] are observed." Certainly, population geography is the essential starting point of the human component of the human–environment concerns of geography. But human populations are not merely collections of numerical units; nor are they to be understood solely through statistical analysis. Societies are distinguished not just by abstract statistical data, but by experiences, beliefs, and aspirations that collectively constitute what social scientists call *culture*. It is to that fundamental human diversity that we next turn our attention.

KEY WORDS

agricultural density 116
arithmetic density 115
Boserup thesis 120
carrying capacity 117
cohort 96
crude birth rate (CBR) 96
crude death rate (CDR) 100
crude density 115
demographic equation 111
demographic transition 107
demography 94
dependency ratio 103
doubling time 105

ecumene 115
Ehrlich, Paul 120
food security 116
J-curve 106
Malthus, Thomas Robert 119
Marx, Karl 120
mortality rate 100
natural increase 105
neo-Malthusianism 120
nonecumene 115
overpopulation 116
physiological density 116
population (demographic) momentum 122

population density 115
population geography 94
population projection 118
population pyramid 102
rate of natural increase 105
rates 96
replacement level 121
S-curve 119
Simon, Julian 120
sex ratio 104
total fertility rate (TFR) 97
zero population growth
   (ZPG) 111

FOR REVIEW

1. How do the *crude birth rate* and the *fertility rate* differ? Which measure is the more accurate statement of the amount of reproduction occurring in a population?

2. How is the *crude death rate* calculated? What factors account for the worldwide decline in death rates since 1945?

3. How is a *population pyramid* constructed? What shape of "pyramid" reflects the structure of a rapidly growing country? Of a population with a slow rate of growth? What can we tell about future population numbers from those shapes?

4. What variations do we discern in the spatial pattern of the *rate of natural increase* and, consequently, of population growth? What rate of natural increase would double population in 35 years?

5. How are population numbers projected from present conditions? Are projections the same as predictions? If not, in what ways do they differ?

6. Describe the stages in the *demographic transition*. Where has the final stage of the transition been achieved? Why do some analysts doubt the applicability of the demographic transition to all parts of the world?

7. Contrast *crude population density, physiological density,* and *agricultural density*. For what differing purposes might each be useful? How is *carrying capacity* related to the concept of density?

8. What was Malthus's underlying assumption concerning the relationship between population growth and food supply? In what ways do the arguments of *neo-Malthusians*

differ from the original doctrine? What governmental policies are implicit in *neo-Malthusianism?*

9. Why is *population momentum* a matter of interest in population projections? In which world areas are the implications of demographic momentum most serious in calculating population growth, stability, or decline?

KEY CONCEPTS REVIEW

1. **What are some basic terms and measures used by population geographers?** pp. 96–107.

A *cohort* is a population group, usually an age group, treated as a unit. *Rates* record the frequency of occurrence of an event over a given unit of time. Rates are used to trace a wide range of population features and trends: births, deaths, fertility, infant or maternal mortality, natural increase, and others. Those rates tell us both the present circumstances and likely prospects for national, country group, or world population structures. Population pyramids give visual evidence of the current age and sex cohort structure of countries or country groupings.

2. **What are meant and measured by the demographic transition model and the demographic equation?** pp. 107–113.

The *demographic transition* model traces the presumed relationship between population growth and economic development. In Western countries, the transition model historically displayed four stages: (a) high birth and death rates; (b) high birth and declining death rates; (c) declining births and reduced growth rates; and (d) low birth and death rates. A fifth stage of population

decline is observed for some aging societies. The transition model has been observed to be not fully applicable to all developing states. The *demographic equation* attempts to incorporate cross-border population migration into projections of national population trends.

3. **What descriptive generalizations can be made about world population distributions and densities?** pp. 113–118.

World population is primarily concentrated north of the equator, in lower (below 200 meters) elevations, along continental margins. Major world population clusters include *East Asia* with 25% of the total, *South Asia* with over 20%, *Europe* and *northeastern United States/southeastern Canada* with significant but lesser shares of world population. Other smaller but pronounced concentrations are found discontinuously on all continents. Within the permanently inhabited areas—the "ecumene"—population densities vary greatly. Highest densities are found in cities; almost one-half of the world's people are urban residents now and the vast majority of world population growth over the first quarter of the 21st

century will occur in cities of the developing world.

4. **What are population projections, and how are they affected by various controls on population growth?** pp. 118–122.

Population projections are merely calculations of the future size, age, and sex composition of regional, national, or world populations; they are based on current data and manipulated by varying assumptions about the future. As simple calculations, projections cannot be wrong. They may, however, totally misrepresent what actually will occur because of faulty current data or erroneous assumptions used in their calculation. They may also be invalid because of unanticipated self-imposed or external brakes on population growth, such as changing family size desires or limits on areal carrying capacity that slow or halt current growth trends. Even with such growth limitations, however, population prospects are always influenced greatly by *demographic momentum,* the inevitable growth in numbers promised by the high proportion of younger cohorts yet to enter childbearing years in the developing world, and by the consequences of global population aging.

LANGUAGE AND RELIGION:
Mosaics of Culture

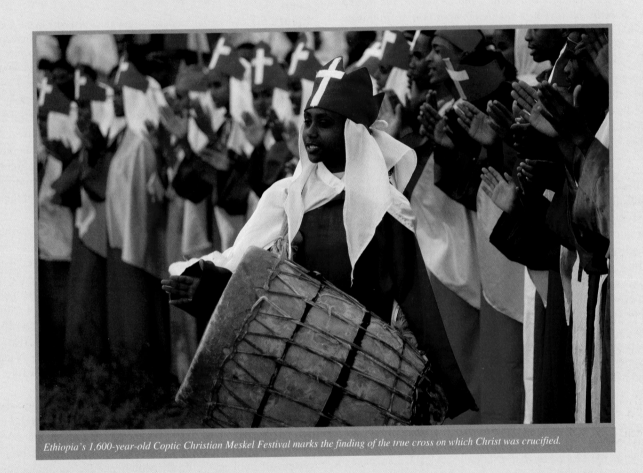

Ethiopia's 1,600-year-old Coptic Christian Meskel Festival marks the finding of the true cross on which Christ was crucified.

Key Concepts

Language

1. The classification, spread, and distribution of the world's languages; the nature of language change, pp. 126–134.

2. Language standards and variants, from dialects to official tongues, pp. 134–142.

3. Language as source of cultural identity and landscape relic, pp. 143–146.

Religion

1. The cultural significance and role of religion, pp. 146–147.

2. How world religions are classified and distributed, pp. 147–150.

3. The origins, nature, and diffusions of principal world religions, pp. 150–164.

*W*hen God saw [humans become arrogant], he thought of something to bring confusion to their heads: he gave the people a very heavy sleep. They slept for a very, very long time. They slept for so long that they forgot the language they had used to speak. When they eventually woke up from their sleep, each man went his own way, speaking his own tongue. None of them could understand the language of the other any more. That is how people dispersed all over the world. Each man would walk his way and speak his own language and another would go his way and speak in his own language. . . .

God has forbidden me to speak Arabic. I asked God, "Why don't I speak Arabic?" and He said, "If you speak Arabic, you will turn into a bad man." I said, "There is something good in Arabic!" And He said, "No, there is nothing good in it! . . ."

Here, I slaughter a bull and I call [the Muslim] to share my meat. I say, "Let us share our meat." But he refuses the meat I slaughter because he says it is not slaughtered in a Muslim way. If he cannot accept the way I slaughter my meat, how can we be relatives? Why does he despise our food? So, let us eat our meat alone. . . . Why, they insult us, they combine contempt for our black skin with pride in their religion. As for us, we have our own ancestors and our own spirits; the spirits of the Rek, the spirits of the Twic, we have not combined our spirits with their spirits. The spirit of the black man is different. Our spirit has not combined with theirs.[1]

In this chapter, we examine two prominent threads in the tapestry of cultural diversity—language and religion. Language and religion are basic components of cultures, the learned ways of life of different human communities. They help identify who and what we are and clearly place us within larger communities of persons with similar characteristics. At the same time, as the words of Chief Makuei suggest, they separate and divide peoples of different tongues and faiths. Language and religion are mentifacts, components of the ideological subsystem of culture that help shape the belief system of a society and transmit it to succeeding generations. Both within and between cultures, language and religion are fundamental strands in the complex web of culture, serving to shape and to distinguish people and groups.

They are ever-changing strands. Languages evolve in place, responding to the dynamics of social and economic change and spatial interaction in a closely integrated world. New artifacts and sociofacts demand new words like "retweet" and "cyberbullying," which entered the *Oxford English Dictionary* in 2011. Languages diffuse in space, carried by streams of migrants, colonizers, and conquerors. They may be rigorously defended and preserved as essential elements of cultural identity, or they may be abandoned in the search for acceptance into a new society. Religions, too, are

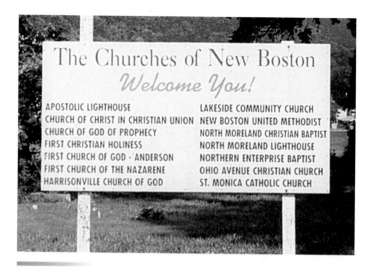

Figure 5.1 Advertised evidence of religious diversity in the United States. The sign details only a few Christian congregations. In reality, the United States has become the most religiously diverse country in the world, with essentially all of the world's faiths represented within its borders.

dynamic, sweeping across national, linguistic, and cultural boundaries by conversion, conviction, and conquest. Their broad spatial patterns—distinctive culture regions in their own right—are also fundamental in defining the culture realms outlined in Figure 2.4, while at a different scale, religious differences may contribute to the cultural diversity and richness within the countries of the world (Figure 5.1).

Classification of Languages

On a clear, dark night, the unaided eye can distinguish between 4,000 and 6,000 stars, a number comparable to some estimates of the probable total number of the world's languages. In reality, no precise figure is possible, for even today in Africa, Latin America, New Guinea, and elsewhere, linguists race to identify and classify the tongues spoken by isolated peoples before some disappear.

In the broadest sense, **language** is any systematic method of communicating ideas, attitudes, or intent through the use of mutually understood signs, sounds, or gestures. For our geographic purposes, we may define language as an organized system of spoken words by which people communicate with each other with mutual comprehension. But such a definition fails to recognize the gradations among languages or to grasp the varying degrees of mutual comprehension between two or more of them. The language commonly called "Chinese," for example, is more properly seen as a group of distinct but related languages—Mandarin, Cantonese, Hakka, and others—that are as different from each other as are such comparably related European languages as Spanish, Italian, French, and Romanian. "Chinese" has uniformity only in the fact that all of the varied Chinese languages are written alike. No matter how it is pronounced, the same symbol for *house* or for *rice*, for example, is

---

[1]The words of Chief Makuei Bilkuei of the Dinka, a Nilotic people of the southern Sudan. His comments are directed at the attempts to unite into a single people the Arabic Muslims of the north of the Republic of the Sudan with his and other black, Luo-speaking animist and Christian people of the country's southern areas. Recorded by Francis Mading Deng, *Africans of Two Worlds: The Dinka in Afro-Arab Sudan.* Copyright © 1978 Yale University Press, New Haven, CT. Reprinted by permission of the author.

The Geography of Language

Forever changing and evolving, language in spoken or written form makes possible the cooperative efforts, the group understandings, and shared behavior patterns that distinguish culture groups. Language is the most important medium by which culture is transmitted. It is what enables parents to teach their children about the world they live in and what they must do to become functioning members of society. Some argue that the language of a society structures the perceptions of its speakers. By the words that it contains and the concepts that it can formulate, language is said to influence the attitudes, understandings, and responses of the society to which it belongs.

If that conclusion be true, one aspect of cultural heterogeneity may be easily understood. The 7 billion people on Earth speak many thousands of different languages. Knowing that more than 1,500 languages and language variants are spoken in sub-Saharan Africa (though 85 percent of Africans speak one or more variants of 15 core languages) gives us a clearer appreciation of the political and social divisions in that continent. Europe alone has some 230 languages and dialects

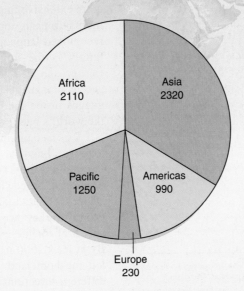

Figure 5.2 **World distribution of living languages, 2009.** Of the perhaps 6,900 languages still spoken today, one-third are found in Asia, 31 percent in Africa, 18 percent in the Pacific area, 14 percent in the Americas, and 3 percent in Europe. Linguists' estimates of the number of languages ever spoken on Earth range from 31,000 to as many as 300,000 or more. Assuming the lower estimate (or even one considerably smaller), dead languages far outnumber the living. One or two additional tongues, most spoken in the forests of Papua New Guinea or in Indonesia are lost each week.

Source: Estimates based on Ethnologue, *16th edition, 2009.*

(Figure 5.2). Language is a hallmark of cultural diversity, an often fiercely defended symbol of cultural identity that helps to distinguish the world's diverse social groups.

recognized by all literate speakers of any Chinese language variant (Figure 5.3). Again, the language known as "Arabic" represents a number of related but distinct tongues, so Arabic spoken in Morocco differs from Palestinian Arabic, roughly as Portuguese differs from Italian.

Languages differ greatly in their relative importance, if "importance" can be taken to mean the number of people using them. More than half of the world's inhabitants are native speakers of just eight of its thousands of tongues, and at least half regularly use or have competence in just four of them. That restricted language dominance reflects the reality that the world's linguistic diversity is rapidly shrinking. Of the at most 6,900 tongues still remaining, over half are no longer being learned by children or used in everyday life and are endangered. One estimate anticipates that no more than 600 of the world's current living languages will still be in existence in A.D. 2100. Table 5.1 lists those languages currently spoken as a primary tongue by 90 million or more people. At the other end of the scale are a number of rapidly declining languages whose speakers number in the hundreds or, at most, the few thousands.

The diversity of languages is simplified when we classify them into families. A **language family** is a group of languages descended from a single, earlier tongue. By varying estimates, from at least 30 to perhaps 100 such families of languages are found worldwide. The families, in turn, may be subdivided into subfamilies, branches, or groups of more closely related tongues. Some 2,000 years ago, Latin was the common language spoken throughout the Roman Empire. The fall of the empire in the 5th century A.D. broke the unity of Europe, and regional variants of Latin began to develop in isolation. In the course of the next several centuries, these Latin derivatives, changing and developing as all languages do, emerged as the individual Romance languages—Italian, Spanish, French, Portuguese, and

HOUSE   **RICE**   **TREE**

Figure 5.3 All literate Chinese, no matter which of the many languages of China they speak, recognize the same ideographs for *house*, *rice*, and *tree*.

Table 5.1

First Languages Spoken by 90 Million or More People as of 2009

Language	Millions of Speakers	Approximate % of World Population
Mandarin[a] (China)	1,213	18
Spanish	329	5
English	328	5
Hindi/Urdu[b] (India, Pakistan)	243	4
Arabic[c]	221	3
Bengali (Bangladesh/India)	181	3
Portuguese	178	3
Russian/Belorussian	144	2
Japanese	122	2
German	90	1

[a]The official dialect of Mandarin is spoken by perhaps 845 million; as many as 1,500 other dialects, many mutually incomprehensible, are also designated as "Mandarin."

[b]Hindi and Urdu are basically the same language: Hindustani. Written in the Devangari script, it is called *Hindi*, the official language of India; in the Arabic script, it is called *Urdu*, the official language of Pakistan.

[c]The figure given includes speakers of the many often mutually unintelligible versions of colloquial Arabic. Classical or literary Arabic, the language of the Koran, is uniform and standardized but restricted to formal usage as a spoken tongue. Because of its religious association, Arabic is a second language for many inhabitants of Muslim countries with other native tongues.

Sources: Based on data from *Ethnologue: Languages of the World*, 19th ed.; Linguisphere 2000; and other sources.

from the Netherlands to western Poland. The classification of languages by origin and historical relationship is called a *genetic classification.*

Further tracing of language roots tells us that the Romance and the Germanic languages are individual branches of an even more extensive family of related languages derived from proto-Indo-European, or simply Indo-European. Of the principal recognized language clusters of the world, the Indo-European family is the largest, embracing most of the languages of Europe and a large part of Asia, and the introduced—not the native—languages of the Americas (Figure 5.4). All told, languages in the Indo-European family are spoken by about half the world's peoples.

By recognizing similar words in most Indo-European tongues, linguists deduce that the Indo-European people—originally hunters and fishers but later switching to agriculture—developed somewhere in eastern Europe or the Ukrainian steppes about 5,000 years ago (though some conclude that central Turkey was the more likely site of origin and that the ancestral tongue existed 8,700 to 10,000 or more years ago). By at least 2500 B.C., their society apparently fragmented; they left the homeland, carrying segments of the parent culture in different directions. Some migrated into Greece, others settled in Italy, still others crossed central and western Europe, ultimately reaching the British Isles. Another group headed into the Russian forest lands, and still another branch crossed Iran and Afghanistan, eventually to reach India. Wherever this remarkable people settled, they appear to have dominated local populations and imposed their language on them. For example, the word for *sheep* is avis in Lithuanian, *ovis* in Latin, *avis* in Sanskrit (the language of ancient India), and *hawi* in the tongue used in Homer's Troy. Modern English retains its version in the word *ewe.* All, linguists infer, derive from an ancestral word, *owis* in Indo-European. Similar relationships and histories can be traced for other protolanguages.

World Pattern of Languages

The present world distribution of major language families (Figure 5.5) records not only the migrations and conquests of our linguistic ancestors but also the continuing dynamic pattern of recent human movement, settlement, and colonizations. Indo-European languages have been carried far beyond their Eurasian homelands from the 16th century onward by western European colonizers in the Americas, Africa, Asia, and Australasia. In the process of linguistic imposition and adoption, innumerable indigenous languages and language groups have been modified or totally lost. Most of the estimated 1,000 to 2,000 Amerindian tongues of the Western Hemisphere disappeared in the face of European conquest and settlement (Figure 5.6).

The Slavic expansion eastward across Siberia beginning in the 16th century obliterated most of the Paleo-Asiatic languages there. Similar loss occurred in Eskimo and Aleut language areas. Large linguistically distinctive areas comprise the northern reaches of both Asia and America (see Figure 5.5). Their sparse

Romanian—of modern Europe and of the world colonized by their speakers. Catalan, Sardinian, Provençal, and a few other spatially restricted tongues are also part of the Romance language group.

Family relationship between languages can be recognized through similarities in their vocabulary and grammar. By tracing regularities of sound changes in different languages back through time, linguists are able to reconstruct earlier forms of words and, eventually, determine a word's original form before it underwent alteration and divergence. Such a reconstructed earlier form is said to belong to a **protolanguage.** In the case of the Romance languages, of course, the well-known ancestral tongue was Latin, which needs no such reconstruction. Its root relationship to the Romance languages is suggested by modern variants of *panis*, the Latin word for "bread": *pane* (Italian), *pain* (French), *pan* (Spanish), *pão* (Portuguese), *pâine* (Romanian). In other language families, similar word relationships are less confidently traced to their protolanguage roots. For example, the Germanic languages, including English, German, Dutch, and the Scandinavian tongues, are related descendants of a less well-known proto-Germanic language spoken by peoples who lived in southern Scandinavia and along the North Sea and Baltic coasts

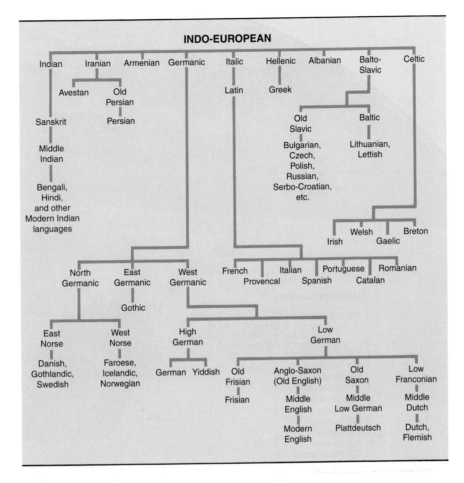

INDO-EUROPEAN

Figure 5.4 The Indo-European linguistic family tree. Euskara (Basque), Estonian, Finnish, Hungarian, Maltese, and Lappish are the only European languages not in the Indo-European family. (See also Figure 5.8.)

populations are losing the mapped languages as the indigenous people adopt the tongues of the majority cultures of which they have been forcibly made a part. In the Southern Hemisphere, the several hundred original Australian languages also loom large spatially on the map but have at most 50,000 speakers, exclusively Australian aborigines. Numerically and effectively, English dominates that continent.

Examples of linguistic conquest by non-Europeans also abound. In Southeast Asia, formerly extensive areas identified with different members of the Austro-Asiatic language family have been reduced through conquest and absorption by Sino-Tibetan (Chinese, Thai, Burmese, and Lao, principally) expansion. Arabic—originally a minor Afro-Asiatic language of the Arabian Peninsula—was dispersed by the explosive spread of Islam through much of North Africa and southwestern Asia, where it largely replaced a host of other locally variant tongues and became the official or the dominant language of more than 20 countries and over 250 million people. The more than 300 Bantu languages found south of the "Bantu line" in sub-Saharan Africa are variants of a proto-Bantu carried by an expanding, culturally advanced population that displaced more primitive predecessors (Figure 5.7).

Language Diffusion

Language diffusion represents the increase or relocation over time in the geographic area within which a language is spoken. The Bantu of Africa or the English-speaking settlers of North America displaced preexisting populations and replaced the languages previously spoken in the areas of penetration. Therefore, we find one explanation of the spread of language families to new areas of occurrence in massive population relocations such as those accompanying the colonization of the Americas or of Australia. That is, languages may spread through migration in a process called *relocation diffusion.*

Latin, however, replaced earlier Celtic languages in western Europe not by force of numbers—Roman legionnaires, administrators, and settlers never represented a majority population—but by the gradual abandonment of their former languages by native populations brought under the influence and control of the Roman Empire and, later, of the Western Christian church. Adoption rather than eviction of language was the rule followed in perhaps the majority of historical and contemporary instances of language spread. Knowledge and use of the language of a dominating culture may be seen as a necessity when that language is the medium of commerce, law, civilization, and personal prestige.

nationhood. Swahili, a pidgin formed from a number of Bantu dialects with major vocabulary additions from Arabic, originated in the coastal areas of East Africa and spread inland first by Arab ivory and slave caravans and later by trade during the period of English and German colonial rules. When Kenya and Tanzania gained independence, they made Swahili the national language of administration and education. Other examples of creolization are Afrikaans (a pidginized form of 17th-century Dutch used in the Republic of South Africa); Haitian Creole (the language of Haiti, derived from the pidginized French used in the slave trade); and Bazaar Malay (a pidginized form of the Malay language, a version of which is the official national language of Indonesia).

Lingua Franca

A **lingua franca** is an established language used habitually for communication by people whose native tongues are mutually incomprehensible. For them, it is a second language, one learned in addition to the native tongue. Lingua franca, literally "Frankish tongue," was named from the dialect of France adopted as their common tongue by the Crusaders assaulting the Muslims of the Holy Land. Later, it endured as a language of trade and travel in the eastern Mediterranean, useful as a single tongue shared in a linguistically diverse region.

Between 300 B.C. and A.D. 500, the Mediterranean world was unified by Common Greek. Later, Latin became a lingua franca, the language of empire and, until replaced by the vernacular European tongues, of the Church, government, scholarship, and the law. Outside the European sphere, Aramaic served the role from the 5th century B.C. to the 4th century A.D. in the Near East and Egypt; Arabic followed Muslim conquest as the unifying language of that international religion after the 7th century. Mandarin Chinese and Hindi in India have a lingua franca role in their linguistically diverse countries. The immense linguistic diversity of Africa has made regional lingua francas such as Swahili necessary (Figure 5.13), and in a world of increased spatial interaction, English increasingly serves as the lingua franca of globalization.

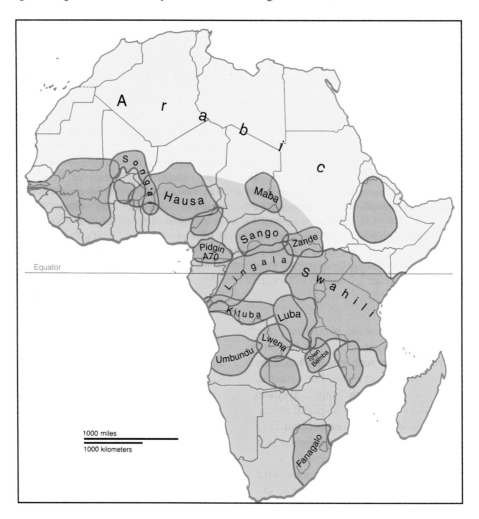

Figure 5.13 Lingua francas of Africa. The importance and extent of competing lingua francas in sub-Saharan Africa change over time, reflecting the spread of populations and the relative economic or political stature of speakers of different languages. In many areas, an individual may employ different lingua francas, depending on activity: dealing with officials, trading in the marketplace, conversing with strangers. Among the elite in all areas, the preferred lingua franca is apt to be a European language. When a European tongue is an official language (Figure 5.14) or the language of school instruction, its use as a lingua franca is more widespread. Throughout northern Africa, Arabic is the usual lingua franca for all purposes.

Source: Adapted from Bernd Heine, Status and Use of African Lingua Francas *(Munich: Weltforum Verlag; and New York: Humanities Press, 1970).*

Militant Fundamentalism

The term *fundamentalism* entered the social science vocabulary in the late 20th century to describe conservative, reactionary religious movements. Originally, it designated an American Christian movement named after a set of volumes—*The Fundamentals: A Testimony of the Truth*—published between 1910 and 1915 and embracing both traditional religious orthodoxy and ethical precepts. More recently, fundamentalism has become a generic description for all religious movements that seek to regain and publicly institutionalize traditional social and cultural values that are usually rooted in the teachings of a sacred text or written dogma.

Springing from rejection of the secularist tendencies of modernity, fundamentalism is now found in every dominant religion wherever a western-style society has developed, including Christianity, Islam, Hinduism, Judaism, Sikhism, Buddhism, Confucianism, and Zoroastrianism. Fundamentalism is, therefore, a reaction to the modern world; it represents an effort to draw upon a "golden age" religious tradition in order to cope with and counteract an already changing society that is denounced as trying to erase the true faith and traditional religious values. The near-universality of fundamentalist movements is seen by some as another expression of a widespread rebellion against the presumed evils of secular globalization.

Fundamentalists always place a high priority on doctrinal conformity and its necessity to achieve salvation. Further, they are convinced of the morally superior and unarguable correctness of their beliefs and the necessity of the unquestioned acceptance of those beliefs by the general society. Since the truth is knowable and indisputable, fundamentalists hold, there is no need to discuss it or argue it in an open forum. To some observers, therefore, fundamentalism is by its nature undemocratic, and states controlled by fundamentalist regimes combining politics and religion, of necessity, stifle debate and punish dissent. In the modern world, that rigidity seems most apparent in Islam where, it is claimed, "all Muslims believe in the absolute inerrancy of the Quran . . ." (*The Islamic Herald,* April 1995) and several countries—for example, the Islamic Republic of Iran and the Islamic Republic of Pakistan—proclaim by official name their administrative commitment to religious control.

In most of the modern world, however, such commitment is not overt or official, and fundamentalists often believe that they and their religious convictions are under mortal threat. They view modern secular society—with its assumption of equality of competing voices and values—as trying to eradicate the true faith and religious verities. Initially, therefore, every fundamentalist movement begins as an intrareligious struggle directed

against its own co-religionists and countrymen in response to a perceived assault by the liberal or secular society that they inhabit. At first, the group may blame its own weakness and irresolution for the oppression they feel and the general social decay they perceive. To restore society to its idealized standards, the aroused group may exhort its followers to ardent prayer, ascetic practices, and physical or military training.

If it is unable peacefully to impose its beliefs on others, some fundamentalist groups—seeing themselves as the savior of society—may justify other more extreme actions against perceived oppressors. Initial protests and nonviolent actions may escalate to attacks on corrupt public figures thwarting their vision and to outright domestic guerrilla warfare. That escalation is advanced and gains willing supporters when inflexible fundamentalism is combined with the unending poverty and political impotence felt in many—particularly Middle Eastern—societies today. When an external culture or power—commonly a demonized United States—is seen as the unquestioned source of the pollution and exploitation frustrating their social vision, some fundamentalists have been able to justify any extreme action and personal sacrifice for their cause. In their struggle it appears an easy progression from domestic dispute and disruption to international terrorism.

most widespread; Buddhism is largely an Asian religion. Hinduism, the largest ethnic faith, is essentially confined to the Indian subcontinent, showing the spatial restriction characteristic of most ethnic and traditional religions even when found outside of their homeland area. Small Hindu emigrant communities in Africa, southeastern Asia, Britain, or the United States, for example, tend to remain isolated even in densely crowded urban areas. Although it is not localized beyond Israel, Judaism is also included among the ethnic religions because of its identification with a particular people and cultural tradition.

Extensive areas of the world are peopled by those who practice tribal or traditional religions, often in concert with the universalizing religions to which they have been outwardly converted. Tribal religions are found principally among peoples who have not yet been fully absorbed into modern cultures and economies or who are on the margins of more populous and advanced societies. Although the areas assigned to tribal religions in Figure 5.19 are

significant, the number of adherents is small and declining. Table 5.2 presents a reasonable ranking of the major religions of the world by estimated number of adherents. The list is not exhaustive; the *World Christian Encyclopedia* tabulates 10,000 distinct religions, including nearly 12,000 Christian denominations.

Frequently, members of a particular religion show areal concentration within a country. Thus, in urban Northern Ireland, Protestants and Catholics reside in separate areas whose boundaries are clearly understood. The "Green Line" in Beirut, Lebanon, marked a guarded border between the Christian East and the Muslim West sides of the city, while within the country as a whole, regional concentrations of adherents of different faiths and sects are clearly recognized.

The world map misses finer-scale detail and the reality of religious diversity in a given location. For example, the map identifies western Canada as mainly Protestant Christian, while a trip to the Vancouver suburb of Richmond, British Columbia, would

Table 5.2

Major Religions Ranked by Estimated Number of Adherents

Religion	Number of Adherents (millions)
Christianity	2,100
Islam	1,500
Secular/Nonreligious/Agnostic/Atheist	1,100
Hinduism	900
Chinese traditional religions	394
Buddhism	376
Tribal/animist religions	300
African traditional religions	100
Sikhism	23
Judaism	14
Baha'ism	7
Jainism	4
Shinto	4
Cao Dai	4
Zoroastrianism	2.6
Tenrikyo	2
Neo-Paganism	1
Unitarian-Universalism	0.8
Rastafarianism	0.6
Scientology	0.5

Source: *Adherents.com.*

complicate that picture. Lined up next to each other on a short stretch of a single street, one finds a Hindu temple, a Sikh temple, a Buddhist temple, a Buddhist monastery, an Islamic mosque, several Protestant Christian Chinese churches, a Muslim high school, and a Christian high school. Further research would reveal that a high percentage of Vancouver residents claim no religious adherence at all. Religious diversity within countries may reflect the degree of toleration that a majority culture affords minority religions. In predominantly Muslim Indonesia (55 percent to 88 percent of the population, depending on the definition), Christian Bataks, Hindu Balinese, and Muslim Javanese for many years lived in peaceful coexistence. By contrast, the fundamentalist Islamic regime in Iran has persecuted and executed those of the Baha'i faith. The world map of religion has other limitations. Data on religious affiliation are imprecise since most nations do not have religious censuses, and religious groups report their membership differently. When communism was supreme in the former Soviet Union and Eastern European countries, official atheism dissuaded many from

openly professing or practicing any religion; in nominally Christian Europe and North America, many who are counted as Christians are not active church members and may have renounced religion altogether.

The Principal Religions

Each of the major religions has its own mix of cultural values and expressions, its own pattern of innovation and spatial diffusion (Figure 5.20), and its unique impact on the cultural landscape. Together, they contribute importantly to the worldwide pattern of human diversity.

Judaism

We begin our review of world religions with **Judaism,** whose belief in a single God laid the foundation for both Christianity and Islam. Unlike its universalizing offspring, Judaism is closely identified with a single ethnic group. It emerged some 3,000 to 4,000 years ago in the Near East, one of the ancient culture hearth regions (see Figure 2.15). Early Near Eastern civilizations, including those of Sumeria, Babylonia, and Assyria, developed writing, codified laws, and formalized polytheistic religions featuring rituals of sacrifice and celebrations of the cycle of seasons.

Judaism was different. The Israelites' conviction that they were a chosen people, bound with God through a covenant of mutual loyalty and guided by complex formal rules of behavior, set them apart from other peoples of the Near East. Theirs became a distinctively *ethnic* religion, the determining factors of which are descent from Israel (the patriarch Jacob), the Torah (law and scripture), and the traditions of the culture and the faith. Early military success gave the Jews a sense of territorial and political identity to supplement their religious self-awareness. Later conquest by a series of empires led to their dispersion (*diaspora*) across much of the Mediterranean world and farther east into Asia by A.D. 500 (Figure 5.21).

Alternately tolerated and persecuted in Christian Europe, occasionally expelled from countries, and usually, as outsiders of different faith and custom, spatially isolated in special residential quarters (ghettos), Jews managed to retain their faith. Two separate branches of Judaism developed in Europe during the Middle Ages. The Sephardim were originally based in the Iberian Peninsula and expelled from there in the late 15th century; with ties to North African and Babylonian Jews, they retained their native Judeo-Spanish language (Ladino) and culture. Between the 13th and 16th centuries, the Ashkenazim, seeking refuge from intolerable persecution in western and central Europe, settled in Poland, Lithuania, and Russia (Figure 5.21). It was from Eastern Europe that many of the Jewish immigrants to the United States came during the later 19th and early 20th centuries, though German-speaking areas of central Europe were also important source regions.

The Holocaust, which resulted in the murder of perhaps one-third of the world's Jewish population, fell most heavily upon the Ashkenazim. The establishment of the state of Israel in 1948

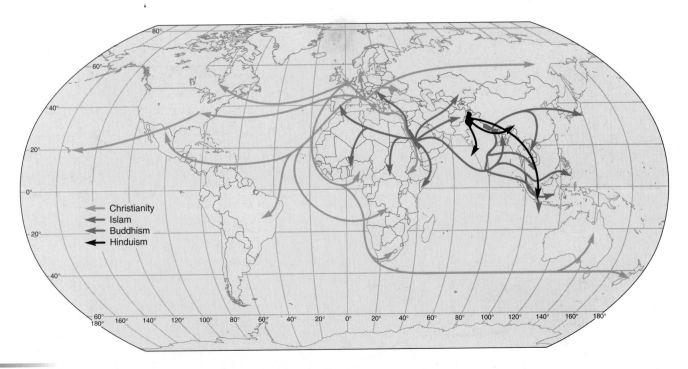

Figure 5.20 **Innovation areas and diffusion routes of major world religions.** The monotheistic (single deity) faiths of Judaism, Christianity, and Islam arose in southwestern Asia, the first two in Palestine in the eastern Mediterranean region and the last in western Arabia near the Red Sea. Hinduism and Buddhism originated within a confined hearth region in the northern part of the Indian subcontinent. Their rates, extent, and directions of diffusions are suggested here and detailed on later maps.

was a fulfillment of the goal of *Zionism*, the belief in the need to create an autonomous Jewish state in Palestine. It represented a determination that Jews not lose their identity by absorption into alien cultures and societies. The new state represented a reversal of the preceding 2,000-year history of dispersal and relocation diffusion. Israel became largely a country of immigrants, an ancient homeland again identified with a distinctive people and an ethnic religion. The Sephardim and Ashkenazim are present in roughly equal numbers In Israel. Of the world's 13 million Jews, about 5 million live in Israel and 6 million live in North America, where they are mostly found in the larger urban areas.

Judaism's imprint on the cultural landscape has been subtle and unobtrusive. The Jewish community reserves space for the practice of communal burial; the spread of the cultivated citron in the Mediterranean area during Roman times has been traced to Jewish ritual needs; and the religious use of grape wine assured the cultivation of the vine in their areas of settlement. The synagogue as place of worship can take on a wide variety of architectural styles. The essential for a religious service is a community of at least 10 adult males, not a specific structure. Orthodox Jews are a subgroup that adheres to a stricter set of beliefs and practices, one of which forbids driving a car on the Sabbath—the day of worship. This simple rule means that Orthodox Jews tend to live close together in cities. Orthodox Jews often construct *eruvin,* simple wire enclosures strung from utility poles or streetlights that define a home territory for purposes of obeying prohibitions against carrying objects outside the home on the Sabbath. Many non-Jews are surprised to discover they live within an *eruv.*

Christianity

Christianity had its origin in the life and teachings of Jesus, a Jewish preacher of the 1st century of the modern era, whom his followers believed was the Christ, the savior promised in the Jewish Scriptures. Christians understand their religion as fulfilling the promises of Judaism and extending them to all humankind rather than to just a chosen people.

As a universal religion, Christianity spread quickly among the underclasses of both the eastern and western parts of the Roman Empire, carried by missionaries to major cities and ports along the excellent system of Roman roads and sea lanes (Figure 5.22). *Expansion diffusion* followed the establishment of missions and colonies of converts in locations distant from the hearth region. Important among them were the urban areas that became administrative seats of the new religion. For the Western Church, Rome was the principal center for dispersal, through *hierarchical diffusion,* to provincial capitals and smaller Roman settlements of Europe. From those nodes and from monasteries established in pagan rural areas, *contagious diffusion* disseminated Christianity throughout the continent. The acceptance of Christianity as the state religion of the empire by the Emperor Constantine in A.D. 313 was also an expression of hierarchical diffusion of great importance in establishing the faith throughout the Roman world. Finally, and much later, *relocation diffusion,* missionary efforts, and in Spanish colonies, forced conversion of Native Americans brought the faith to the New World with European settlers (see Figure 5.19).

Figure 5.21 **Jewish dispersions, A.D. 70–1500.** A revolt against Roman rule in A.D. 66 was followed by the destruction of the Jewish Temple four years later and an imperial decision to Romanize the city of Jerusalem. Judaism spread from the hearth region by *relocation diffusion,* carried by its adherents dispersing from their homeland to Europe, Africa, and eventually in great numbers to the Western Hemisphere. Although Jews established themselves and their religion in new lands, they did not lose their sense of cultural identity and did not seek to attract converts to their faith.

The dissolution of the Roman Empire into a western and an eastern half after the fall of Rome also divided Christianity. The Western Church, based in Rome, was one of the very few stabilizing and civilizing forces uniting western Europe. Its bishops became the civil as well as ecclesiastical authorities over vast areas devoid of other effective government. Parish churches were the focus of rural and urban life, and the cathedrals replaced Roman monuments and temples as the symbols of the social order (Figure 5.23). Everywhere, the Roman Catholic Church and its ecclesiastical hierarchy were dominant.

Secular imperial control endured in the eastern empire, whose capital was Constantinople. Thriving under its protection, the Eastern Church expanded into the Balkans, Eastern Europe, Russia, and the Near East. The fall of the eastern empire to the Turks in the 15th century opened Eastern Europe temporarily to Islam, though the Eastern Orthodox Church (the direct descendant of the Byzantine state church) remains, in its various ethnic branches, a major component of Christianity.

The Protestant Reformation of the 15th and 16th centuries split the church in the west, leaving Roman Catholicism supreme in southern Europe but installing a variety of Protestant denominations and national churches in western and northern Europe. The split was reflected in the subsequent worldwide dispersion of Christianity. Catholic Spain and Portugal colonized Latin America, taking both their languages and the Roman church to that area (see Figure 5.20), as they did to colonial outposts in the Philippines, India, and Africa. Catholic France colonized Quebec in North America. Protestants, many of them fleeing Catholic or repressive Protestant state churches, were primary early settlers of the United States, Canada, Australia, New Zealand, and South Africa.

In Africa and Asia, both Protestant and Catholic missionaries attempted to convert nonbelievers. Both achieved success in sub-Saharan Africa, though traditional religions persist and are common in areas that are shown on Figure 5.19 as predominantly Christian. Neither was particularly successful in China, Japan, or India, where strong ethnic religious cultural systems were less permeable to the diffusion of the Christian faith. Although it still accounts for nearly one-third of the world's population and is territorially the most extensive belief system, Christianity

Figure 5.22 Diffusion paths of Christianity, A.D. 100–1500. Routes and dates are for Christianity as a composite faith. No distinction is made between the Western church and the various subdivisions of the Eastern Orthodox denominations.

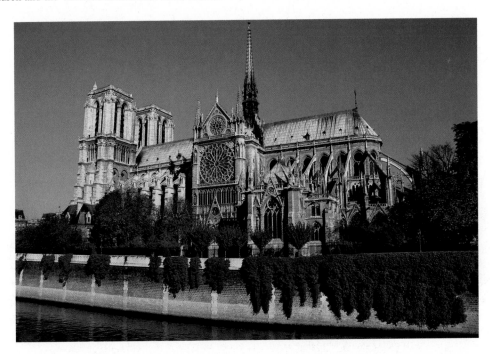

Figure 5.23 The building of Notre Dame Cathedral of Paris, France, begun in 1163, took more than 100 years to complete. Perhaps the best known of the French Gothic churches, it was part of the great period of cathedral construction in Western Europe during the late 12th and the 13th centuries. Between 1170 and 1270, some 80 cathedrals were constructed in France alone. The cathedrals were located in the center of major cities; their plazas were the sites of markets, public meetings, morality plays, and religious ceremonies. They were the focus of public and private life and the symbol not only of the faith, but of the pride and prosperity of the towns and regions that erected them.

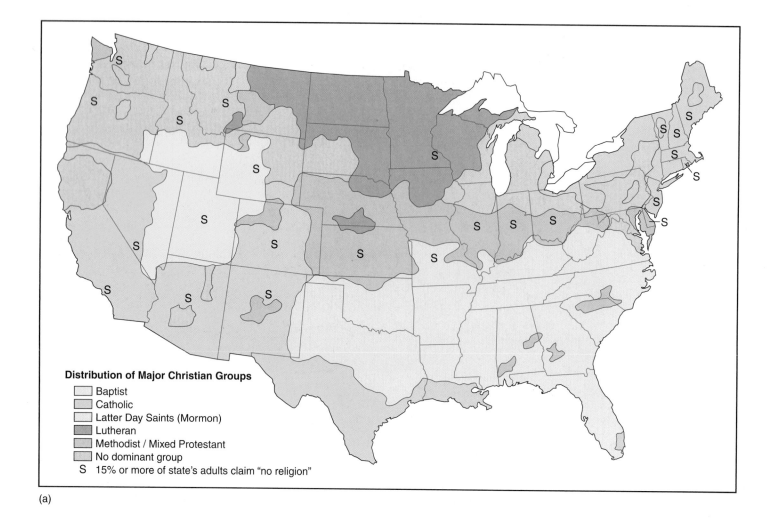

Distribution of Major Christian Groups

- Baptist
- Catholic
- Latter Day Saints (Mormon)
- Lutheran
- Methodist / Mixed Protestant
- No dominant group
- S 15% or more of state's adults claim "no religion"

(a)

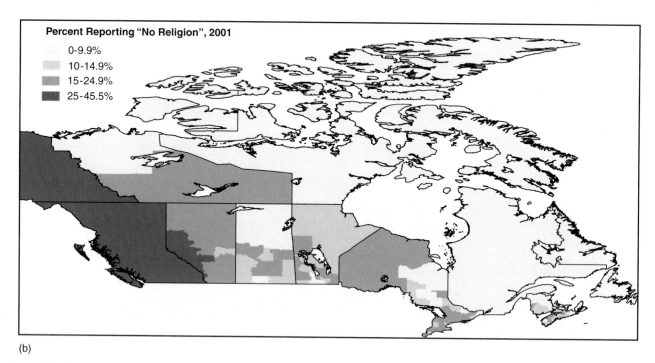

Percent Reporting "No Religion", 2001

- 0-9.9%
- 10-14.9%
- 15-24.9%
- 25-45.5%

(b)

Figure 5.24 (*a*) **Religious affiliation in the conterminous United States.** The greatly generalized areas of religious dominance shown conceal the reality of immense diversity of church affiliations throughout the United States. "Major" simply means that the indicated category had a higher percentage response than any other affiliation; in practically no case was that as much as 50 percent. A sizable number of Americans claim to have "no religion." Secularism (marked by S on the map) is particularly prominent in the Western states, in the industrial Midwest, and in the Northeast. (*b*) **Percentage reporting "No Religious Affiliation" in Canada, 2001.** Persons claiming no religious affiliation are concentrated in western Canada and urban centers.

Sources: (a) Based on data or maps from the 2001 "American Religious Identity Survey" by the Graduate School at City University of New York: religious denomination maps prepared by Ingolf Vogeler of the University of Wisconsin, EauClaire, based on data compiled by the Roper Center for Public Research; and Churches and Church Membership in the United States *(Atlanta, Georgia: Glenmary Research Center, 1992). (b) Based on Statistics Canada (Ottawa, 2001).*

has declined in some regions where it once was strongest. It is no longer numerically important in or near its original hearth. Nor is it any longer dominated by Western adherents. In 1900, 80 percent of all Christians lived in Europe and North America; in 2000, two-thirds of an estimated 2.1 billion total lived elsewhere—in South America, Africa, and Asia.

Regions and Landscapes of Christianity

All of the principal world religions have experienced theological, doctrinal, or political divisions; frequently these have spatial expression. In Christianity, the early split between the Western and Eastern Churches was initially unrelated to dogma but nonetheless resulted in a territorial separation still evident on the world map. The later subdivision of the Western Church into Roman Catholic and Protestant branches gave a more intricate spatial patterning in Western Europe that can be only generally suggested at the scale shown in Figure 5.19. Still more intermixed are the areal segregations and concentrations that have resulted from the denominational subdivisions of Protestantism.

In the United States and Canada, the beliefs and practices of various immigrant groups and the innovations of domestic congregations have created a particularly varied spatial pattern, though intermingling rather than rigid territorial division is the norm (see Figure 5.1). One observer has suggested a pattern of "religious regions" of the country (Figure 5.24) that reflects a larger cultural regionalization of the United States.

Strongly French-, Irish-, and Portuguese-Catholic New England, the Hispanic-Catholic Southwest, and the French-Catholic vicinity of New Orleans (evident in Figure 5.24a) are commonly recognized regional subdivisions of the United States. Each has a cultural identity that includes, but is not limited to, its dominant religion. The Mormon (more properly, Church of Jesus Christ of Latter-Day Saints, or LDS) culture region centered on Utah is a prominent feature. The Baptist presence in the South and that of German and Scandinavian Lutherans in the Upper Midwest (see Figure 5.24a) help determine the boundaries of other distinctive religious regions. The zone of cultural mixing across the center of the country from the Middle Atlantic states to the western LDS region—so evident in the linguistic geography of the United States (see Figure 5.12)—is again apparent on the map of religious affiliation. No single church or denomination dominates, which is also a characteristic of the Far Western zone. The northeastern and northwestern parts of the United States are home to the highest proportion of people claiming no religious identification. In Canada, the three top Christian groups are Roman Catholic, the United Church of Canada, and Anglican, together comprising 60 percent of the country's population. The "No Religion" category ranks second with 16 percent. Muslims comprise about 2 percent, and Hindus, Sikhs, and Buddhist are each about 1 percent.

The mark of Christianity on the cultural landscape has been prominent and enduring. In pre-Reformation Catholic Europe, the parish church formed the center of life for small neighborhoods of every town, and the village church was the centerpiece of every rural community. In York, England, with a population of 11,000 in the 14th century, there were 45 parish churches, one for each 250 inhabitants. In addition, the central cathedral served simultaneously as a glorification of God, a symbol of piety, and the focus of religious and secular life. The Spanish Laws of the Indies (1573) perpetuated that landscape dominance in the New World, decreeing that all Spanish American settlements should have a church or cathedral on a central plaza (Figure 5.25a).

Figure 5.25 In Christian societies, the church assumes a prominent central position in the cultural landscape. (*a*) By royal decree, Spanish-planned settlements in the New World were to focus on a cathedral and a plaza centered within a gridiron street system. (*b*) Individually less imposing than the central cathedral of Catholic areas, the multiple Protestant churches common in small and large U.S. and Canadian towns collectively constitute an important land use, frequently seeking or claiming space in the center of the community. This Protestant church in Minnesota was built by Swedish Lutheran immigrants and is surrounded by a cemetery.

While in Europe and Latin America a single dominant central church was the rule, North American Protestantism placed less importance on the church edifice as a monument and urban symbol. The structures of the principal denominations of colonial New England were, as a rule, clustered in the village center, and that centrality remained a characteristic of small-town America to the present day (Figure 5.25b). Church architecture in North America is highly diverse, ranging from stone or brick revivals of European styles to modern or nondescript styles. In earlier periods, churches were often adjoined by a cemetery, for Christians—in common with Muslims and Jews—practice burial in areas reserved for the dead. In Christian countries in particular, the cemetery—whether connected to the church or separate from it—has traditionally been a significant land use within urban areas. Frequently, the separate cemetery, originally on the outskirts of the community, becomes surrounded by urban growth distorting or blocking the growth of the city.

Islam

Islam—the word means "submission" (to the will of God)—springs from the same Judaic roots as Christianity and embodies similar monotheistic beliefs. Muhammed is revered as the prophet of Allah (God), succeeding and completing the work of earlier prophets of Judaism and Christianity, including Moses, David, and Jesus. The Koran, the holy book of the Muslims, contains not only rules of worship and doctrine, but also instructions on the conduct of human affairs. All Muslims are expected to observe the five pillars of the faith: (1) repeated saying of the basic creed; (2) prayers five times daily at appointed times; (3) a month of daytime fasting during Ramadan; (4) almsgiving; and, (5) if possible, a pilgrimage to Mecca. Two of the five pillars of Islam are explicitly geographical: prayers are done facing Mecca and the pilgrimage to the sacred city of Mecca is among the world's greatest gatherings (Figure 5.26). To pray facing Mecca, the direction known as Qiblah, has traditionally required Muslim scholars to calculate a great circle route. Thus, for example, most North American Muslims pray facing northeast since that is the shortest route to Mecca (try it by stretching a string from North America to Saudi Arabia on a globe).

Islam unites the faithful into a brotherhood that crosses boundaries of race, ethnicity, language, and social status. That law of brotherhood served to unify an Arab world sorely divided by tribes, social ranks, and multiple local deities. Muhammed was a resident of Mecca but fled in A.D. 622 to Medina, where the Prophet proclaimed a constitution and announced the universal mission of the Islamic community. By the time of Muhammed's death in A.D. 632, all of Arabia had joined Islam. The new religion swept quickly by expansion diffusion outward from that source region over most of central Asia and, at the expense of Hinduism, into northern India (Figure 5.27).

The advance westward was particularly rapid and inclusive in North Africa. In Western Europe, 700 years of Muslim rule in

Figure 5.26 Worshipers gathered during *hajj*, the annual pilgrimage to Mecca. The black structure is the Ka'ba, the symbol of God's oneness and of the unity of God and humans. All able-bodied Muslims are expected to make a pilgrimage to Mecca once in their lifetime, if possible. As many as 3 million Muslims converge on Mecca for the *hajj*.

much of Spain were ended by Christian reconquest in 1492. In Eastern Europe, conversions made under an expansionary Ottoman Empire are reflected in Muslim components in Bosnia and Kosovo, regions of former Yugoslavia, in Bulgaria, and in the 70 percent Muslim population of Albania. Later, by *relocation diffusion,* Islam was dispersed into Indonesia, southern Africa, and the Western Hemisphere. Muslims now form the majority population in 39 countries.

Asia has the largest absolute number and Africa the highest proportion of Muslims among its population—more than 42 percent. Through immigration, high birth rates, and conversions, Islam is growing rapidly in Europe and North America. Islam, with an estimated 1.3 billion adherents worldwide, has been a prominent element in recent and current political affairs. Sectarian divisions fueled the 1980–1988 war between Iran and Iraq; Afghan mujahideen—"holy warriors"—found inspiration in their faith to resist Soviet occupation of their country, and Chechens drew strength from Islam in resisting the Russian assaults on their Caucasian homeland during the 1990s and after. Islamic fundamentalism led to the 1979 overthrow of Iran's shah. Muslim separatism is a recurring theme in Philippine affairs, and militant groups seek establishment of religiously rather than secularly based governments in several Muslim states. Extremist Muslim militants carried out the September 11, 2001, World Trade Center attack and other acts of terrorism.

Islam initially united a series of separate tribes and groups, but disagreements over the succession of leadership after the Prophet led to a division between two groups, Sunnis and Shi'ites. Sunnis, the majority (80 percent to 85 percent of Muslims) recognize the first four caliphs (originally, "successor" and later the title of the religious and civil head of the Muslim state) as Muhammed's rightful successors. The Shi'ites reject the legitimacy of the first three and believe that Muslim leadership rightly belonged to the fourth caliph, the Prophet's son-in-law, Ali, and his descendants. Sunnis constitute the majority of Muslims in all countries except Iran, Iraq, Bahrain, and perhaps Yemen.

The mosque—place of worship, community clubhouse, meeting hall, and school—is the focal point of Islamic communal life and the primary imprint of the religion on the cultural landscape. Its principal purpose is to accommodate the Friday prayer service mandatory for all male Muslims. United by the use of Arabic for prayers and readings, many mosques in North America draw worshippers from diverse immigrant groups and multiple native tongues. The mosque is a sacred space with rules pertaining to proper conduct and dress. It is typically a gendered space with certain spaces reserved for men and others for women. Rooms are usually oriented so that worshippers face Mecca. The distinctive mosque architecture found throughout the world of Islam draws upon Roman, Byzantine, and Indian design elements. With its perfectly proportioned, frequently gilded or tiled domes, geometric

Figure 5.27 **Spread and extent of Islam.** Islam predominates in over 35 countries along a band across northern Africa to central Asia, and the northern part of the Indian subcontinent. Still farther east, Indonesia has the largest Muslim population of any country. Islam's greatest development is in Asia, where it is second only to Hinduism, and in Africa, where some observers suggest it may be the leading faith. Current Islamic expansion is particularly rapid in the Southern Hemisphere.

Figure 5.28 The common architectural features of the mosque, with its dome and soaring minaret towers, make it an unmistakable landscape evidence of the presence of Islam in any local culture. The visual dominance and symbolism of minarets has drawn attention to new mosques and provoked controversies about the place of Islam in western societies. Some newer mosques in Europe and North America have forgone the minaret towers to better blend in. The Blue Mosque in Istanbul, Turkey, would not be out of place architecturally in Muslim Malaysia or Indonesia.

artwork, graceful, soaring towers and minarets (from which the faithful are called to prayer), and delicately wrought parapets and cupolas, the carefully tended mosque is frequently the most community's most elaborate and imposing structure (Figure 5.28).

Hinduism

Hinduism is the world's oldest major religion. Though it has no datable founding event or initial prophet, some evidence traces its origin back 4,000 or more years. Hinduism is a polytheistic religion woven into an intricate web of philosophical, social, economic, and artistic elements that comprise a distinctive Indian civilization. Its estimated 850 million to 1 billion adherents are largely confined to India, where it claims 80 percent of the population.

Hinduism derives its name from its cradle area in the valley of the Indus River. From that district of present-day Pakistan, it spread by *contagious diffusion* eastward down the Ganges River and southward throughout the subcontinent and adjacent regions by amalgamating, absorbing, and eventually supplanting earlier native religions and customs (see Figure 5.20). Its practice eventually spread throughout southeastern Asia, into Indonesia, Malaysia, Cambodia, Thailand, Laos, and Vietnam, as well as into neighboring Myanmar (Burma) and Sri Lanka. The largest Hindu temple complex is in Cambodia, not India, and Bali remains a Hindu pocket in dominantly Islamic Indonesia. Hinduism's more recent growing presence in Western Europe and North America reflects a *relocation diffusion* of its adherents.

Hinduism is based on the concepts of reincarnation and passage from one state of existence to another in an unending cycle of birth and death in which all living things are caught. One's position in this life is determined by one's *karma,* or deeds and conduct in previous lives. That conduct dictates the condition and the being—plant, animal, or human—into which a soul is reborn. All creatures are ranked, with humans at the top of the ladder. But humans themselves are ranked, and the social caste into which an individual is born is an indication of that person's spiritual status. The goal of existence is to move up the hierarchy, eventually to be liberated from the cycle of rebirth and death and to achieve salvation and eternal peace through union with the Brahman, the universal soul.

The **caste** (meaning "birth") structure of society is an expression of the eternal transmigration of souls. For the Hindu, the primary aim of this life is to conform to prescribed social and ritual duties and to the rules of conduct for the assigned caste and profession. Those requirements comprise that individual's *dharma*—law and duties. To violate them upsets the balance of society and nature and yields undesirable consequences. Careful observance improves the chance of promotion at the next rebirth. Traditionally, each craft or profession is the property of a particular caste: Brahmins (scholar-priests), Kshatriyas (warrior-landowners), Vaishyas (businessmen, farmers, herdsmen), Sudras (servants and laborers). Dalits, or *untouchables* for whom the most menial and distasteful tasks were reserved, and backwoods tribes—together accounting for around one-fifth of India's population—stand outside the caste system. Caste rules define who you can socialize with, who is an acceptable marriage partner, where you can live, what you may wear, eat, and drink, and how you can earn your livelihood. Conversion of Dalits out of Hinduism to Buddhism, Islam, Christianity, or Sikkhism has been seen as a way to escape the prejudice and discrimination of the caste system. As a secular democracy, religious freedom and protection against caste-based discrimination are written into the Indian constitution. However, well-publicized mass conversions to Buddhism and Christianity have provoked a strong response from Hindu fundamentalists who have successfully fought for legal restrictions on conversions in some Indian states.

The practice of Hinduism is rich with rites and ceremonies, festivals and feasts, processions and ritual gatherings of literally millions of celebrants. Pilgrimages to holy rivers and sacred places are thought to secure deliverance from sin or pollution and to preserve religious worth (Figure 5.29). In what is perhaps the largest periodic gathering of humans in the world, millions of Hindus of all castes, classes, and sects gather about once every 12 years for a ritual washing away of sins in the Ganges River near Allahabad. Worship in the temples and shrines and making offerings to secure merit from the gods are requirements for Hindus. The doctrine of ahimsa—also fundamental in Buddhism—instructs Hindus to refrain from harming any living being.

Temples and shrines are everywhere. Within them, innumerable icons of deities such as Vishnu, Shiva, and Ganesha are enshrined, the objects of veneration, offerings, and daily care. All temples have a circular spire as a reminder that the sky is the real dwelling place of the god who resides only temporarily within the temple (Figure 5.30). The temples, shrines, daily rituals and worship, numerous specially garbed or marked holy men and ascetics, and the ever-present sacred animals mark the cultural landscape of

Figure 5.29 Pilgrims at dawn worship in the Ganges River at Varanasi (Banares), India, one of the seven most sacred Hindu cities and the reputed Earthly capital of Siva, the Hindu god of destruction and regeneration. Hindus believe that to die in Varanasi means release from the cycle of rebirth and permits entrance into heaven.

Hindu societies—a landscape infused with religious symbols and sights that are part of a total cultural experience.

Numerous reform movements have derived from Hinduism over the centuries, some of which have endured to the present day as major religions on a regional or world scale. Jainism, begun in the 6th century B.C. as a revolt against the authority of the early Hindu doctrines, rejects caste distinctions and modifies concepts of karma and transmigration of souls; it counts perhaps 5 million adherents. Combining elements of Hinduism and Islam, *Sikhism* developed in the Punjab area of northwestern India in the late 15th century A.D. Sikhism is an ethnic religion with an estimated 23 million adherents. The great majority of Sikhs live in India, mostly in the Punjab, though substantial numbers have settled in the United Kingdom and Canada.

Buddhism

The largest and most influential of the dissident movements within Hinduism has been **Buddhism,** a universalizing faith founded in the 6th century B.C. in northern India by Siddhartha Gautama, the Buddha (*Enlightened One*). The Buddha's teachings were more a moral philosophy that offered an explanation for evil and human suffering than a formal religion. He viewed the road to enlightenment and salvation to lie in understanding the "four noble truths": existence involves suffering; suffering is the result of desire; pain ceases when desire is destroyed; the destruction of desire comes

through knowledge of correct behavior and correct thoughts. The Buddha's message was open to all castes, raising Buddhism from a philosophy to a universalizing religion.

Contagious diffusion spread the belief system throughout India, where it was made the state religion in the 3rd century B.C. It was carried elsewhere into Asia by missionaries, monks, and merchants. While expanding abroad, Buddhism began to decline at home as early as the 4th century A.D., slowly but irreversibly reabsorbed into a revived Hinduism. By the 8th century, its dominance in northern India was broken by conversions to Islam; by the 15th century, it had essentially disappeared from the Indian subcontinent.

Present-day spatial patterns of Buddhist adherence reflect the schools of thought, or *vehicles,* that were dominant during different periods of dispersion (Figure 5.31). Earliest, most conservative, and closest to the origins of Buddhism was *Theravada* (Vehicle of the Elders) Buddhism, which was implanted in Sri Lanka and Southeast Asia beginning in the 3rd century B.C. Its emphasis is on personal salvation through the four noble truths; it mandates a portion of life to be spent as monk or nun.

Mahayana (Greater Vehicle) was the dominant tradition when Buddhism was accepted into East Asia—China, Korea, and Japan—in the 4th century A.D. and later. Itself subdivided and diversified, Mahayana Buddhism considers the Buddha divine and, along with other deities, a savior for all who are truly

Figure 5.30 **The Hindu temple complex at Khajraho in central India.** The creation of temples and the images that they house has been a principal outlet of Indian artistry for more than 3,000 years. At the village level, the structure may be simple, containing only the windowless central cell housing the divine image, a surmounting spire, and the temple porch or stoop to protect the doorway of the cell. The great temples, of immense size, are ornate extensions of the same basic design.

devout. It emphasizes meditation (contemplative Zen Buddhism is a variant form), does not require service in monasteries, and tends to be more polytheistic and ritualistic than does Theravada Buddhism.

Vajrayana (the Diamond Vehicle) was dominant when the conversion of Tibet and neighboring northern areas began, first in the 7th century and again during the 10th and 11th centuries as a revived Lamaist tradition. That tradition originally stressed self-discipline and conversion through meditation and the study of philosophy, but it later became more formally monastic and ritualistic, elevating the Dalai Lama as the reincarnated Buddha, who became both spiritual and temporal ruler. Before Chinese conquest and the flight of the Dalai Lama in 1959, as many as one out of four or five Tibetan males was a monk whose celibacy helped keep population numbers stable. Tibetan Buddhism was further dispersed, beginning in the 14th century, to Mongolia, northern China, and parts of southern Russia.

Buddhism imprints its presence vividly on the cultural landscape. Buddha images in stylized human form began to appear in the 1st century A.D. and are common in painting and sculpture throughout the Buddhist world. Equally widespread are the three main types of buildings and monuments: the *stupa,* a commemorative shrine; the temple or pagoda enshrining an image or relic of

the Buddha; and the monastery, some of them the size of small cities (Figure 5.32). Common, too, is the *bodhi* (or *bo*) tree, a fig tree of great size and longevity. Buddha is said to have received enlightenment seated under one of them at Bodh Gaya, India, and specimens have been planted and tended as an act of reverence and symbol of the faith throughout Buddhist Asia. Sacred places for Buddhists are largely associated with key events in the life of the Buddha—many of which are in areas that are no longer predominantly Buddhist.

Buddhism has suffered greatly in Asian lands that came under communist control: Inner and Outer Mongolia, Tibet, North Korea, China, and parts of Southeast Asia. Communist governments abolished the traditional rights and privileges of the monasteries. In those states, Buddhist religious buildings were taken over by governments and converted into museums or other secular uses, abandoned, or destroyed. As a consequence, the number of Buddhists is uncertain, with world totals estimated to lie between 225 million and 500 million.

East Asian Ethnic Religions

When Buddhism reached China from the south some 1,500 to 2,000 years ago and was carried to Japan from Korea in the 7th century, it encountered and later amalgamated with already well-established

Figure 5.31 Diffusion paths, times, and "vehicles" of Buddhism.

belief systems. The Far Eastern ethnic religions are **syncretisms** (combinations of different beliefs and practices). In China, the union was with Confucianism and Taoism, themselves becoming intermingled by the time of Buddhism's arrival. In Japan, it was with Shinto, a polytheistic animism and shamanism.

Chinese belief systems address more ethical or philosophical questions than religious ones, having little interest in the hereafter. Confucius (K'ung Fu-tzu), a compiler of traditional wisdom who lived about the same time as the Buddha, emphasized the importance of proper conduct—between ruler and subjects and among family members. The family was extolled as the nucleus of the state, and children's respect for their parents was the loftiest of virtues. There are no places of worship or clergy in **Confucianism,** though its founder believed in a Heaven seen in naturalistic terms, and the Chinese custom of ancestor worship as a mark of gratitude and respect was encouraged. After his death, the custom was expanded to include worship of Confucius himself in temples erected for that purpose. That worship became the official state religion in the 2nd century B.C., and for some 2,000 years—until the start of the 20th century A.D.—Confucianism, with its emphasis on ethics and morality rooted in Chinese traditional wisdom, formed the basis of the belief system of China.

It was joined by, or blended with, **Taoism,** an ideology that according to legend was first taught by Lao-tsu in the 6th century B.C. Its central theme is *Tao,* the Way, a philosophy teaching that eternal happiness lies in total identification with nature and deploring passion, unnecessary invention, unneeded knowledge, and government interference in the simple life of individuals. Beginning in the 1st century A.D., this philosophical naturalism was coupled with a religious Taoism involving deities, spirits, magic, temples, and priests. Buddhism, stripped by Chinese pragmatism of much of its Indian otherworldliness and defining a *nirvana* achievable in this life, was easily accepted as a companion to these traditional Chinese belief systems. Along with Confucianism and Taoism, Buddhism became one of the honored Three Teachings, and to the average person, there was no distinction in meaning or importance between a Confucian temple, Taoist shrine, or Buddhist stupa.

Buddhism also joined and influenced Japanese **Shinto,** the traditional religion of Japan that developed out of nature and ancestor worship. Shinto—the Way of the Gods—is a set of customs and rituals rather than an ethical or moral system. It observes a complex set of deities, including deified emperors, family spirits, and the divinities residing in rivers, trees, certain animals, mountains, and, particularly, the sun and moon.

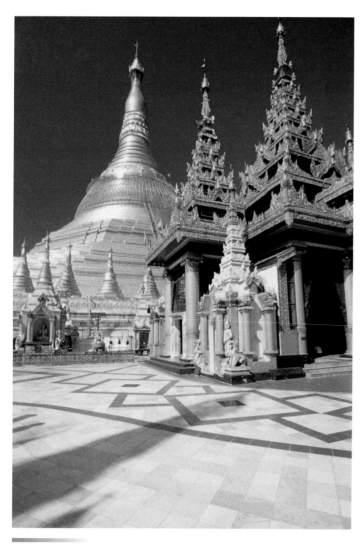

Figure 5.32 The golden stupas of the Swedagon pagoda, Yangon, Myanmar (formerly known as Rangoon, Burma).

Buddhism eventually intertwined with traditional Shinto with Buddhist deities seen as Japanese gods in a different form. More recently, Shinto divested itself of many Buddhist influences and became, under the reign of the Emperor Meiji (1868–1912), the official state religion, emphasizing loyalty to the emperor. The centers of worship are the numerous shrines and temples in which the gods are believed to dwell and which are approached through ceremonial *torii,* or gateway arches (Figure 5.33).

Secularism

One cannot assume that all people within a mapped religious region are adherents of the designated faith, or that membership in a religious community means active participation in its belief system. **Secularism,** a weakening of the influence of religion and an indifference to or rejection of religious belief, is an increasing part of many modern societies. The population of nonreligious persons is most pronounced in the industrialized nations and those now or formerly under communist regimes. In Britain, for example, the state Church of England claims 20 percent of the British population as communicants, but only 2 percent of the adult population attends its Sunday services. While the Church of England's parish churches are an enduring feature of the rural landscape, vacant churches are also a common landscape feature, especially in urban areas. It is not uncommon to see once-grand churches converted to arts facilities, stores, or restaurants, or simply boarded up (Figure 5.34). Two-thirds of the French describe themselves as Catholic, but less than 5 percent regularly go to church. Even in devoutly Roman Catholic South American states, church attendance rates of less than 20 percent in most countries attest

Figure 5.33 Floating torii gate at Itsukushima Shrine on Miyajima Island, Japan.

Figure 5.34 A vacant, boarded-up church in Cardiff, Wales, most recently used for a home and garden store, symbolizes the rise of secularism in Europe.

to the rise of at least informal secularism. Estimates put the world number of the nonreligious at between 800 million and 1.1 billion. In societies undergoing secularization, responsibility for governance, education, health care, and social services is often transferred from religious bodies to nonreligious institutions. In its stronger form, secularism is openly anti-religious and may involve restricting the practice of religion and destroying places of worship. Official governmental policies of religious neutrality (as in the cases of the United States or India, for example) are, of course, distinct from personal secular or nonreligious beliefs.

Change and Diversity in the Geography of Religion

The map of principal world religions is continually changing as religions grow, diffuse, and recede. One of the most dramatic recent changes is the expansion of the universalizing religions of Christianity and Islam in areas of Africa once primarily associated with traditional religions. While traditional African religions have receded from much of the map, traditional religious practices such as fortune-telling or ceremonies honoring ancestral spirits still are widely practiced and are frequently blended with Islam or Christianity. The fault line between expanding Islam and Christianity runs through a number of countries, including Nigeria, Ethiopia, and Tanzania, and has triggered episodic violence. In the former unified Sudan, this religious fault line coincided with ethnic divides, which

together led to the overwhelming vote in 2011 for independence for South Sudan.

While Europe is the continent most closely associated with Christianity, it has witnessed dramatic religious shifts in the past century. The most dramatic changes are the secularization of large portions of European society and the rise of new religions brought by immigrants, primarily Islam and Hinduism. In the 2001 census in the United Kingdom, 72 percent stated that they were Christian, 16 percent reported that they had no religion, 3 percent stated Muslim, and 1 percent stated Hindu. Immigrants, mostly from former colonies in developing regions, have added mosques, temples, and new storefront churches to the landscape.

One striking aspect of the North American religious landscape is the great number of different churches, synagogues, mosques, temples, gurdwaras, and related structures (Figure 5.35). In addition to the formal places of worship of the more established groups, innumerable storefront places of worship—mainly associated with poorer neighborhoods, changing immigrant ethnic communities, and splinter Protestant sects—have become part of the American scene. Another recent feature on the North American religious landscape is the megachurch, defined as a congregation that draws more than 2,000 attendees in a typical weekend. There are an estimated 1,250 megachurches in the United States and Canada. Megachurches, often located in newer suburban areas, feature massive parking lots and architecture more typical of convention centers, sports arenas, or shopping malls (not surprisingly, since many meet in converted buildings once used for those purposes). Also, distinctively (though not exclusively) American

(a)

(b)

(c)

(d)

Figure 5.35 Diverse Religious Landscapes in the United States and Canada. (*a*) A Christian megachurch in the suburbs of Chicago, Illinois. This non-denominational Protestant congregation, Willow Creek Community Church, averages 24,000 weekly attenders at one of its six campuses around the Chicago metropolitan area. The main campus resembles a combination of a shopping mall, convention center, and concert hall. Its location near an interstate highway and its vast parking lots are essential to its success. (*b*) The Thrangu Buddhist monastery on Number 5 Road in the suburb of Richmond, British Columbia, in Canada is built in a traditional Tibetan style. (*c*) Also on Number 5 Road in Richmond is this Islamic center, mosque, and Muslim school. The distinctive minarets are crowned with the traditional crescent moon. (*d*) Next door to the mosque is the Sikh Temple (Gurdwara) and Indian Cultural Centre.

is the proliferation of religious and denominational signage (see Figure 5.1) on city buildings, storefronts, or highway billboards. Compared with more secularized Europe, the religious diversity and vitality of the United States is remarkable. Some scholars attribute this vitality to the lack of an established state religion and to the successive waves of immigrants, most of whom are religious and have found that creating a religious congregation of their own is a way to be American while preserving their ethnic identity.

Summary

Language and religion are basic threads in the web of culture. They are essential elements of cultural identity. A person's speech offers clues as to where they are from, their social status and their education level. In some societies, religion may serve as a similar identifier. Both language and religion are mentifacts, parts of the ideological subsystem of culture; both are transmitters of culture as well as markers. Both have distinctive spatial patterns—reflecting past and present processes of spatial interaction and diffusion—that are basic to the recognition of world culture realms.

Languages may be grouped genetically—by origin and historical development—but the world distribution of language families depends as much on the movement of peoples and histories of conquest and colonization as it does on patterns of linguistic evolution. As different language groups come into contact, pidgin and creole languages may emerge. With increased spatial interaction and global integration, English has become a new lingua franca, prompting efforts to preserve local languages. Toponymy, the study of place names, helps document the historical and cultural geography of a region.

Religion varies in its impact and influence on culture groups. Some societies are dominated in all aspects by their controlling religious belief: Hindu India, for example, or Islamic Iran. Where religious beliefs are strongly held, they can unite a society of adherents and divide nations and peoples holding divergent faiths. Religions may be classified as ethnic religions such as Judaism and Hinduism or universalizing such as Buddhism, Christianity, and Islam. The spatial distribution of religions reflects past and present patterns of migration, conquest, and diffusion, essential dynamics of cultural geography.

While distinct, language and religion are not totally unrelated. Religion can influence the spread of languages to new peoples and areas, as Arabic, the language of the Koran, was spread by conquering armies of Muslims. Religion may conserve as well as disperse language. Yiddish remains the language of worship in Hasidic Jewish communities; many U.S. and Canadian Lutheran churches held services in German, Swedish, or other Scandinavian languages until World War II. Until the 1960s, Latin was the language of liturgy in the Roman Catholic Church and Sanskrit remains the language of the Vedas, sacred in Hinduism. Sacred texts may demand the introduction of an alphabet to nonliterate societies: the Roman alphabet follows Christian missionaries, Arabic script accompanies Islam. The Cyrillic alphabet of Eastern Europe was developed by missionaries. The tie between language and religion is not inevitable. The French imposed their language (but not their religion) on Algeria; Spanish Catholicism (but not the Spanish language) became dominant in the Philippines.

Language and religion are important components of ethnic identities that distinguish and isolate groups from the larger population within which they reside. Our attention turns next, in Chapter 6, to the concept and patterns of ethnicity, a distinctive piece in the mosaic of human culture.

KEY WORDS

animism 148
Buddhism 159
caste 158
Christianity 151
Confucianism 161
creole 139
dialect 135
ethnic religion 148
geographic (regional) dialect 136
Hinduism 158
Islam 156
isogloss 136
Judaism 150

language 126
language family 127
lingua franca 140
linguistic geography 136
monotheism 147
multilingualism 138
official language 141
pidgin 138
polytheism 147
protolanguage 128
religion 146
sacred places 147
secularism 162

shamanism 148
Shinto 161
speech community 134
standard language 134
syncretism 161
Taoism 161
toponyms 144
toponymy 145
tribal (traditional) religion 148
universalizing religion 148
vernacular 135

FOR REVIEW

1. Why might one consider language the most important differentiating element of a culture?

2. In what way can religion affect other cultural traits of a society? In what cultures or societies does religion appear to exert a growing influence? In what cultures does the importance of religion appear to be declining? What might be the broader social or economic consequences of those changes?

3. In what way does the concept of *protolanguage* help us in linguistic classification? What is meant by *language family*? Is *genetic* classification of language an unfailing guide to spatial patterns of languages? Why or why not?

4. What spatial diffusion processes may be seen in the prehistoric and historic spread of languages? What have been the consequences of language spread on world linguistic diversity?

5. In what ways do *isoglosses* and the study of *dialects* help us understand other human geographic patterns?

6. Cite examples that indicate the significance of religion in the internal and foreign relations of nations.

7. How does the classification of religions as *universalizing, ethnic,* or *tribal* help us to understand their patterns of distribution and spatial diffusion?

8. What connection, if any, do you see between language, religion, and intergroup conflict in the contemporary world?

KEY CONCEPTS REVIEW

Language

1. **How are the world's languages classified and distributed?** pp. 126–134.
The 6,900 languages spoken today may be grouped within a limited number of language families that trace their origins to common protolanguages. The present distribution of tongues reflects the current stage of continuing past and recent dispersion of their speakers and their adoption by new users. Languages change through isolation, migration, and the passage of time.

2. **What are standard languages and what kinds of variants can be observed?** pp. 134–142.
All speakers of a given language are members of its speech community, but not all use the language uniformly. The standard language is that form of speech that has received official sanction or acceptance as the "proper" form of grammar and pronunciation. Dialects, regional and social, represent nonstandard or vernacular variants of the common tongue. A pidgin is a created, composite, simple language designed to promote exchange between speakers of different tongues. When evolved into a complex native language of a people, the pidgin has become a creole. Governments may designate one or more official state languages (including, perhaps, a creole such as Swahili).

3. **How does language serve as a cultural identifier and landscape artifact?** pp. 143–146.
Language is a mentifact, a part of the ideological subsystem of culture. It is, therefore, inseparable from group identity and self-awareness. Language may also be divisive, creating rifts within multilingual societies when linguistic minorities seek recognition or separatism. Toponyms (place names) record the perceptions and values of past and present occupants or explorers. Toponymy in tracing that record becomes a valuable tool of historical cultural geography.

Religion

4. **What is the cultural role of religion?** pp. 146–147.
Like language, religion is a basic component of culture, a mentifact that serves as a cultural rallying point. Frequently, religious beliefs and adherence divide and alienate different groups within and among societies. Past and present belief systems of a culture may influence its legal norms, dietary customs, social relations, economic patterns, and landscape imprints.

5. **How are religions classified and distributed?** pp. 147–150.
Distinguishing among universalizing, ethnic, and traditional religions helps understand diffusion processes. The spatial patterns of world religions reflect their origin areas, migrations, conquests, and the converts they have attracted in home and distant areas.

6. **What are the principal world religions and how are they distinguished in patterns of innovation, diffusion, and landscape imprint?** pp. 150–164.
The text briefly traces those differing origins, spreads, and cultural landscape impacts of Judaism, Christianity, Islam, Hinduism, Buddhism, and certain East Asian ethnic religions.

ETHNIC GEOGRAPHY:
Threads of Diversity

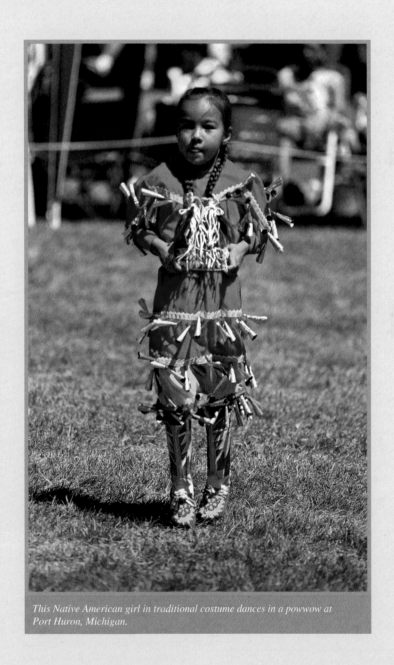

This Native American girl in traditional costume dances in a powwow at Port Huron, Michigan.

Key Concepts

1. Race, ethnicity, ethnic diversity, and the changing immigration streams to multiethnic cities in the United States and Canada, pp. 168–176.

2. Acculturation and the persistence of ethnic clusters and identities in the United States and Canada and elsewhere, pp. 176–189.

3. Urban ethnic diversity and patterns of segregation, pp. 189–199.

4. The landscape impacts of ethnic diversity, pp. 199–200.

*W*e must not forget that these men and women who file through the narrow gates at Ellis Island, hopeful, confused, with bundles of misconceptions as heavy as the great sacks upon their backs—we must not forget that these simple, rough-handed people are the ancestors of our descendants, the fathers and mothers of our children.

So it has been from the beginning. For a century, a swelling human stream has poured across the ocean, fleeing from poverty in Europe to a chance at a new life in America. English, Welsh, Scotch, Irish; German, Swede, Norwegian, Dane; Jew, Italian, Bohemian, Serb; Syrian, Hungarian, Pole, Greek—one race after another has knocked at our doors, been given admittance, has married us and begot our children. We could not have told by looking at them whether they were to be good or bad progenitors, for racially the cabin is not above the steerage, and dirt, like poverty and ignorance, is but skin deep. A few hours, and the stain of travel has left the immigrant's cheek; a few years, and he loses the odor of alien soils; a generation or two, and these outlanders are irrevocably our race, our nation, our stock.[1]

The United States and Canada are cultural composites—as increasingly are most of the countries of the world. North America's peoples include aborigine and immigrant, native-born and new arrival. Had this chapter's introductory passage been written in the 21st century rather than early in the 20th, the list of foreign origins would have been lengthened to include many Latin American, African, and Asian countries as well.

The majority of the world's societies, even those that outwardly seem most homogeneous, house distinctive **ethnic groups,** populations that feel themselves bound together by a common origin and set off from other groups by ties of culture, race, religion, language, or nationality. Ethnic diversity is a near-universal part of human geographic patterns; the current 200 or so independent countries are home to at least 5,000 ethnic groups. The factors driving globalization, such as the growth of transnational corporations, relaxed border restrictions, low-cost travel, and high-speed global communications are all encouraging greater movement and ethnic mixing. In response to labor shortages, European Union (EU) countries increasingly welcome workers from other EU states, as well as African and Asian immigrants and guest workers, effectively making their societies multiethnic. Refugees and job-seekers are found in alien lands throughout both hemispheres (Figure 6.1). Cross-border movements and resettlements in

Southeast Asia and Africa are prominent current events. European colonialism created pluralistic societies in tropical lands through the introduction of both ruling elites and, frequently, nonindigenous laborers. Polyethnic Russia, Afghanistan, China, India, and most African countries have native—rather than immigrant—populations more characterized by racial and cultural diversity than by uniformity. Tricultural Belgium has a nearly split personality in matters political and social. The idea of an ethnically pure nation-state is largely irrelevant.

Like linguistic and religious differences within societies, such population interminglings are masked by the "culture realms" shown in Figure 2.4, but at a larger scale, they are important threads in the cultural-geographic tapestry of our complex world. The multiple movements, diffusions, migrations, and mixings of peoples of different origins are the subject of **ethnic geography.** Its concerns are those of spatial distributions and interactions of ethnic groups, of the cultural characteristics and influences

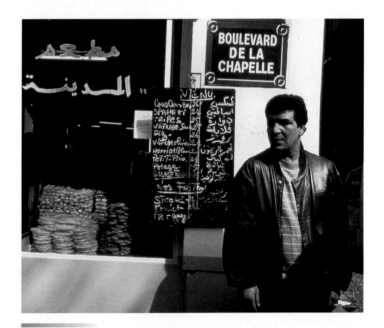

Figure 6.1 "Guest workers"—frequently called by their German name, *Gastarbeiter*—have substantially altered the ethnic mix in formerly unicultural cities of Western Europe. The restaurant shown here is in an Algerian neighborhood of Paris, France. On average, foreigners comprise nearly 10 percent of Western Europe's labor force. They form the majority of the workforce in many Middle Eastern countries; between 60 percent and 90 percent of the workers of the Persian Gulf countries of Bahrain, Kuwait, Oman, Qatar, Saudi Arabia, and the United Arab Emirates are foreigners.

[1]From Walter E. Weyl, "The New Americans," *Harper's Magazine* 129: 615. Copyright 1914 Harper's Magazine Foundation, New York.

underlying them, and of how the built environment reflects the imprint of various ethnic groups.

Culture, we saw in Chapter 2, is the composite of traits making up the way of life of a human group—collective beliefs, symbols, values, forms of behavior, and complexes of such non-material and material traits as social customs, language, religion, food habits, tools, structures, and the like. Culture is learned; it characterizes the group and distinguishes it from all other groups that have collectively created and transmitted to its children still other "ways of life." *Ethnicity,* in contrast, is simply the identifying term assigned to a large group of people who share the traits of a distinctive common culture. It is always based on a clear understanding by members of a group that they are fundamentally different from others who do not share their distinguishing characteristics or cultural heritage.

Ethnicity is not, by itself, a spatial concept. However, ethnic groups are associated with clearly recognized territories—either larger homeland districts or smaller rural or urban enclaves—in which they are primary or exclusive occupants and upon which they have placed distinctive cultural imprints. Since territory and ethnicity are inseparable concepts, ethnicity exhibits important spatial patterns and is an important concern for the human geographer. Further, since ethnicity is often identified with a particular language and/or religion, consideration of ethnicity flows logically from the discussions of language and religion in Chapter 5.

Our examination of ethnic patterns will concentrate on the United States and Canada. Originally, this region was occupied by a multitude of distinctive Native American peoples, each with their own territory, culture, and language. Over time, these populations were overwhelmed and displaced by a wide spectrum of Old World ethnic groups. The United States and Canada provide case studies of how distinctive immigrant culture groups partition urban and rural space and place their claims and imprints on it. The experiences of these countries show the durability of ethnic distinction even under conditions and national myths that emphasize intermixing and homogenization of population as the accepted norm. Examples drawn from other countries and environments will serve to highlight ways in which American-based generalizations may be applied more broadly or in which the North American experience reflects a larger world scene.

Ethnicity and Race

Each year on a weekend in May, New York City celebrates its ethnic diversity and vitality by closing off to all but pedestrian traffic a 1-mile stretch of street to conduct the Ninth Avenue International Food Festival. Along the reserved route from 37th to 57th streets, a million or more New Yorkers come together to sample the foods, view the crafts, and take in the music and dance of the diverse ethnic groups represented among the citizens of the city. As a resident of the largest U.S. metropolis, each of the merchants and artists contributing one of the several hundred separate storefront, stall, or card-table displays of the festival becomes a member of the United States and Canada culture realm. Each, however, preserves a distinctive small-group identity within that larger collective "realm" (Figure 6.2).

The threads of diversity exhibited in the festival are expressions of **ethnicity,** a term derived from the Greek word *ethnos,* meaning a "people" or "nation." Intuitively, we recognize that the literal translation is incomplete. Ethnic groups are composed of individuals who share some prominent cultural traits or characteristics, some evident physical or social identifications setting them apart both from the majority population and from other distinctive minorities among whom they may live. An ethnic identity is recognized by both members of the group and by outsiders. No single trait denotes ethnicity. Group recognition may be based on language, religion, national origin, unique customs, a shared history, or—improperly—an ill-defined concept of race. Common unifying bonds of ethnicity are a shared ancestry and cultural heritage, distinctive traditions, territorial identification, and sense of community. The principal ethnic groups of the United States and Canada are shown in Table 6.2 and Table 6.4, respectively.

Race and ethnicity are frequently equated, but they are actually very different concepts. **Race** is an outdated categorization of humans based on outward physical characteristics such as skin color, hair texture, or eye color or shape. While humans are all one species, there is obvious variation in our physical characteristics. The spread of human beings over the Earth and their occupation of different environments were accompanied by the development of variations in these visible characteristics, as well as internal differences such as blood composition or lactose intolerance. Physical differentiation among human groups is old and can reasonably be dated to the Paleolithic spread and isolation of population groups (occurring 100,000 to about 11,000 years ago). Geographic patterns of distinct combinations of physical traits emerged due to natural selection or adaptation, and genetic drift. **Natural selection** favors the transmission of characteristics that enable humans to adapt to a particular environmental feature, such as climate. Studies have suggested a plausible relationship between solar radiation and skin color, and between temperature and body size. Dark skin indicates the presence of melanin, which protects against the penetration of damaging ultraviolet rays from the sun. Conversely, the production of vitamin D in the body, which is necessary to good health, is linked to the penetration of ultraviolet rays. In high latitudes, where winter days are short and the sun is low in the sky, light skin confers an adaptive advantage by allowing the production of vitamin D. Genetic drift refers to a heritable trait that appears by chance in a group and is accentuated by inbreeding. If two populations are too spatially separated for much interaction to occur (*isolation*), a trait may develop in one but not in the other. Unlike natural selection, genetic drift differentiates populations in nonadaptive ways. Natural selection and genetic drift promote differentiation. Countering them is gene flow via interbreeding, which acts to homogenize neighboring populations. Opportunities for interbreeding, always part of the spread and intermingling of human populations, have accelerated with the growing mobility and migrations of people in the past few centuries.

Racial categorization is a scientifically outdated way of making sense of human variation. Focusing on visible physical characteristics, anthropologists in the 18th and 19th centuries created a variety of racial classification schemes, most of which derived from geographical variations of populations. Some anthropological studies at that time attempted to link physical traits with

Figure 6.2 The annual Ninth Avenue International Fair in New York City became one of the largest of its kind. Similar festivals celebrating America's ethnic diversity are found in cities and small towns across the country.

mental ability in order to construct racial hierarchies that were used to justify slavery, imperialism, immigration restrictions, anti-miscegenation laws, and eugenics. Contemporary biology has rejected racial categorization as a meaningful description of human variation. Skin color does not correspond to genetic closeness between "race" groups. Further, pure races do not exist, and DNA-based evidence shows that there is more variation within the so-called racial groups than there is between the groups.

Living in a society where racial categorization has been widespread, we may be tempted to group humans racially and attribute intellectual ability, athletic prowess, or negative characteristics to particular racial groups. This is problematic for many reasons, the most important being that geneticists have rejected race as a scientific concept; there is only one race—the human race. Second, intellectual ability as measured on standardized tests is mostly a function of socioeconomic status. Finally, the athletic abilities displayed by top athletes are the property of particular individuals, not a group trait, and, like intellectual ability, are strongly influenced by social factors.

Nor does race have meaningful application to any human characteristics that are culturally acquired. That is, race is *not* equivalent to ethnicity or nationality and has no bearing on differences in religion or language. There is no "Irish" or "Hispanic" race, for example. Such groupings are based on culture, not genes. Culture summarizes the way of life of a group of people, and members of the group may adopt it irrespective of their individual genetic heritage. While races do not exist in a scientific, biological sense, race persists as an idea and basis for group identity, and racism— prejudice and discrimination based on racial categories—is very much alive.

If racial categorization was scientifically valid, the categories should be universal. But instead they vary widely from country to country, reflecting the unique history and geography of particular places. In the United Kingdom, the census reserves the Asian category for those of Indian, Pakistani, or Bangladeshi descent, creating a separate category for the Chinese and none for Japanese or Koreans. In Brazil, the census asks respondents to identify as aboriginal or one of four skin colors: white, black, yellow, or brown. As society's understanding of race and ethnicity changes, so do the official census categories. In 2000, the U.S. Census Bureau asked respondents to classify themselves into one of five racial categories and answer a separate question about Hispanic status (which is considered an ethnic category, not a racial category). For the 2010 census, people had their choice of 14 categories. Starting in 2000, respondents were allowed to identify as "Some Other Race" and as more than one race (Table 6.1).

Ethnic Diversity and Separatism

Ethnocentrism is the term describing a tendency to evaluate other cultures against the standards of one's own. It implies the feeling that one's own ethnic group is superior. Ethnocentrism can divide multiethnic societies by establishing rivalries and provoking social and spatial discord and isolation. In addition, it can be a sustaining and identifying emotion, giving familiar values and support to the individual in strange and complex surroundings. The ethnic group maintains familiar cultural institutions and shares traditional food and music. More often than not, it provides the friends, spouses, business opportunities, and political identification of ethnic group members.

Territorial isolation is a strong and supporting trait of ethnic separatism and assists individual groups to retain their identification. In Europe, Asia, and Africa, ethnicity and territorial identity are inseparable. Ethnic minorities are first and foremost associated

Table 6.2

Leading U.S. Ancestries Reported, Census 2000

Ancestry	Number (millions)	Percentage of Total Population
German	42.8	15.2
Irish	30.5	10.8
African American	24.9	8.8
English	24.5	8.7
Mexican	18.4	6.5
Italian	15.6	5.6
Polish	9.0	3.2
French	8.3	3.0
American Indian	7.9	2.8
Scottish	4.9	1.7
Dutch	4.5	1.6
Norwegian	4.5	1.6
Scotch-Irish	4.3	1.5
Swedish	4.0	1.4

Note: More than 20 million persons indicated "United States" or "American" as their ancestry. The tabulation is based on self-identification of respondents, not on objective criteria. Many persons reported multiple ancestries and were tabulated by the Census Bureau under each claim.

Source: Census 2000 special tabulation.

Table 6.1

U.S. Resident Population by Race and Hispanic Origin: April 1, 2010

	Number (millions)	Percent of U.S. Population
Total Population	**308.7**	**100.0**
One race option	299.7	97.1
White	223.6	72.4
Black or African American	38.9	12.6
Asian	14.7	4.8
American Indian and Alaskan Native	2.9	0.9
Native Hawaiian and other Pacific Islander	0.5	0.2
Two or more races	9.0	2.9
Hispanic or Latino (of any race)	50.5	16.3

Note: Race as reported reflects the self-identification of respondents.
Source: U.S. Bureau of the Census.

with *homelands*. This is true of the Welsh, Bretons, and Basques of Western Europe (Figure 12.20); the Slovenes, Croatians, or Bosnians of Eastern Europe (Figure 6.6a); the non-Slavic "nationalities" of Russia; and the immense number of ethnic communities of South and Southeast Asia. These minorities have specific spatial identity even though they may not have political independence.

Where ethnic groups are intermixed and territorial boundaries imprecise—the former Yugoslavia (Figure 6.6a) is an example—or where a single state contains disparate, rival populations—such as in the case of many African and Asian (Figure 6.6b) countries—conflict among groups can be serious if peaceful relations or central governmental control break down. "Ethnic cleansing," a polite term with grisly implications, has motivated brutal civil conflict in parts of the former Soviet Union and Eastern Europe and in several African and southeast Asian countries. The Holocaust slaughter of millions of Jews before and during World War II in Western and Eastern Europe was an extreme case of ethnic extermination, but comparable murderous assaults on racial or ethnic target populations are as old as human history. Such "cleansing" involves, through mass genocide, the violent elimination of a target ethnic group from a particular geographic area to achieve racial or cultural homogeneity and expanded settlement area for the perpetrating state or ethnic group. Its outcome is not only an alteration of the ethnic composition of the region in which the violence takes place, but of the ethnic mix in areas to which displaced victim populations have fled as refugees.

Few true homelands exist within the North American cultural mix. However, the "Chinatown" and "Little Italy" enclaves within North American cities have provided both the spatial refuge and the support systems essential to new arrivals in an alien culture realm. Asian and West Indian immigrants in London and other English cities and foreign guest workers—originally migrant and temporary laborers, usually male—that reside in Continental European communities assume similar spatial separation. While serving a support function, this segregation is as much the consequence of the housing market and of public and private restriction as it is simply of self-selection. In Southeast Asia, with the exception of Thailand, Chinese communities remain aloof from the majority culture not as a stage on the route to assimilation but as a permanent chosen isolation.

By retaining what is familiar of the old in a new land, ethnic enclaves have reduced cultural shock and have paved the way for the gradual process of adaptation that prepares both individuals and groups to operate effectively in the new, larger **host society**—the established, dominant group. The traditional ideal of the United States "melting pot," in which ethnic identity and division would be lost and full amalgamation of all minorities into a blended, composite majority culture would occur, was the expectation voiced in the chapter-opening quotation. For many ethnic groups, however, that ideal has not become a reality.

Recent decades have seen a resurgence of cultural pluralism and an increasing demand for ethnic autonomy not only in North America but also in multiethnic societies around the world (see the feature "Nations of Immigrants"). At least, recognition is sought for ethnicity as a justifiable basis for special treatment in the allocation of political power, the structure of the educational system, the toleration or encouragement of minority linguistic rights, and other evidences of group self-awareness and promotion. In some multiethnic societies, second- and third-generation descendants of immigrants, now seeking "roots" and identity, embrace the ethnicity that their forebears sought to deny. At the same time, **xenophobia**—deep-rooted and unreasonable fears of foreigners on the part of the host society—has led to violence towards outsiders in many multicultural societies.

 ## Vancouver, Canada: Chinatown Versus Ethnoburb

Ethnoburbs differ from traditional ethnic enclaves (such as Chinatowns) due to changes in cities, the global economy, and communications and travel. Whereas ethnic enclaves tend to reflect the lower status of recent immigrants, ethnoburbs are products of globalization, which has led to rising wealth in developing countries and increased flows of people and investment between distant places.

Vancouver's Chinatown dates to the 1880s, when the city was a frontier outpost. Chinese workers, mostly male, were recruited in large numbers to work in the construction of the transcontinental Canadian Pacific Railway. When the railway reached its western terminus at Vancouver in 1885, many Chinese workers settled in Vancouver's Chinatown. While Chinatown was a place where Chinese immigrants lived, worked, and socialized, it was shaped in large part by the racist attitudes of the host society. In 1885, the Canadian government imposed a "head tax" on incoming immigrants that applied to the Chinese, but not to European immigrants. Since Chinese men could not afford the head tax to bring over wives and other relatives, Chinatown was a mostly male, struggling community in its early years. Derogatory cartoons in newspapers, voting restrictions

that forbade the Chinese from participating in elections, mob violence directed against the Chinese, and discriminatory policing were part of the experience of early Chinese immigrants in Vancouver (Figure 6.23). While not required by law to live in segregated areas, the Chinese clustered together for support and defense. Chinese social, cultural, and economic institutions built structures that lent a distinctive appearance to the Chinatown district. After World War II, host society attitudes towards the Chinese softened, and Chinatown came to be viewed as an exotic destination for tourists. The relatively recent addition of a formal Chinese classical garden, distinctive red lampposts, and gateway arches lend a distinctive look to the Chinatown landscape. Nonetheless, Chinatown is located adjacent to Vancouver's poorest, inner-city neighborhood and struggles to escape its marginalized image.

As a result of globalization and increased economic development in East Asia, new, wealthy, entrepreneurial Chinese immigrants began arriving in North American cities in the 1980s. Unlike previous immigrants, these people never formed inner-city enclaves but immediately settled in the suburbs of cities such as Los Angeles, New York, San

Francisco, Toronto, and Vancouver. Chinese immigration was made possible by the elimination of exclusionary immigration laws and encouraged by relaxed regulations for business immigrants. In the years leading up to the British government's transfer of Hong Kong to China in 1997, many Chinese in Hong Kong immigrated to Vancouver. More recently, wealthy Chinese immigrants have immigrated from Taiwan and Mainland China to Vancouver. The suburb of Richmond was one of several popular immigrant destinations and illustrates the differences between ethnoburbs and a traditional Chinatown.

Richmond is home to Vancouver's international airport which features many daily flights to Asia. Immigrants comprise almost 60 percent of the city's 200,000 residents. While the Chinese population is densely clustered in Chinatown, in the ethnoburb of Richmond, the Chinese are spread across a multiethnic suburb among South Asians, Filipinos, Japanese, and whites. Along one street in Richmond, Buddhist temples and monasteries, Chinese Christian churches, a Sikh Gurdwara, Muslim mosque, and Hindu temple sit side by side. While the population at the center of Richmond is 80 percent Chinese and features a collection of

Chinese-themed shopping malls and hotels, it is also home to many non-Chinese businesses, chain stores, and restaurants. While the traditional Chinatown features crowded, high-density housing, Richmond's housing includes many detached, single-family houses alongside modern, mid-rise condominums. Compared to an enclave, the ethnoburb is larger, but with less-defined boundaries. Compared to Chinatown, Richmond's Chinese residents are younger, have higher levels of education, higher incomes, and are deeply connected to the global economy and its flows of people and investment. Unlike traditional Chinatown, the ethnoburb is not the result of discrimination but a voluntary clustering to maximize ethnic social and business contacts in a familiar language and cultural environment.

Immigration Streams

The ethnic diversity found in the United States and Canada today is the product of continuous flows of immigrants representing, at different periods, movements to this continent from nearly all of the cultures and races of the world (Figure 6.3). For the United States, that movement took the form of three distinct immigrant waves, all of which, of course, followed much earlier Amerindian arrivals.

The first wave, lasting from pioneer settlement to about 1870, was made up of two different groups. One comprised white arrivals from western and northern Europe, with Great Britain, Ireland, and Germany best represented. Together, they established a majority society controlled by Protestant Anglo-Saxons and allied groups. The second group of first-wave immigrants was African slaves brought involuntarily to the New World, comprising nearly 20 percent of the U.S. population in 1790. The mass immigration that occurred beginning after the middle of the 19th century began to reduce both the northwest European dominance of American society and the percentage of African Americans within the growing total population.

The wave of social changes that brought about rapid population growth and large-scale immigration diffused outward from the British Isles. That second immigrant wave, from 1870 to 1921, was heavily weighted in favor of eastern and southern Europeans and Scandinavians, who comprised the majority of new arrivals by the end of the 19th century. The second period ended with congressional adoption of a quota system in 1921 regulating both the numbers of individuals who would be accepted and the countries from which they could come. The quota system limited the number of new immigrants from a country to 2 percent of the number that were already present in 1890. The quotas dramatically

Figure 6.3 Although it was not opened until 1892, New York Harbor's Ellis Island—the country's first federal immigration facility—quickly became the symbol of all the migrant streams to the United States. By the time that it was closed in late 1954, it had processed 17 million immigrants. Today, their descendants number over 100 million Americans. A major renovation project was launched in 1984 to restore Ellis Island as a national monument.

Figure 6.9 Ethnic diversity in the Prairie provinces of Canada. In 1991, 69 percent of all Canadians claimed some French or British ancestry. For the Prairie provinces, with their much greater ethnic mixture, only 15 percent declared any British or French descent. Immigrants comprise a larger share of Canadian population than they do of the U.S. population. Early in the 20th century, most newcomers were located in rural western Canada; and by 1921, about half the population of the Prairie provinces was foreign-born. Recent immigrants are mostly from Asia and concentrated in the three largest metropolitan centers of Toronto, Montreal, and Vancouver.

Source: D.G.G. Kerr, A Historical Atlas of Canada, 2nd ed., 1966. Thomas Nelson & Sons Ltd., 1966.

groups settled as collectives. They sometimes acted on the advice and the land descriptions reported by advance agents sent out by the group. In most cases, sizable extents of rural territory received the imprint of a group of immigrants acting in concert. However, later in the century and in the less arable sections of the western United States, the disappearance of land available for homesteading and the changing nature of immigrant flows reduced the incidence of cluster settlement. Impoverished individuals rather than financially solid communities sought American refuge and found it in urban locations. While **cluster migration** created some ethnic concentrations of North America—in the Carolinas, Wisconsin, Kansas, Nebraska, and Oklahoma, for example—others evolved from the cumulative effect of **chain migration**—the assemblage in one area of the relatives, friends, or unconnected compatriots of the first arrivals, attracted both by favorable reports and by familiar presences in specific locales of the New World (see also p. **82**).

Some entire regions of North America—vastly larger than the distinctive ethnic islands—have become associated with larger ethnic or racial aggregations numbering in the thousands or millions. Such **ethnic provinces** include French Canadians in Quebec; African Americans in the southeast United States; Native Americans in Oklahoma, the Southwest, the Northern Plains, and Prairie provinces; and Hispanics in the southern border states

of the United States West (Figure 6.10). The spatial distribution of Native Americans reflects a history of forced relocations onto reservations (Figure 6.11). The identification of distinctive communities with extensive regional units persists, even though ethnicity and race have not been fully reliable bases for dividing North America into regions. Cultural, ethnic, and racial mixing has been too complete to permit U.S. counterparts of Old World ethnic homelands to develop, even in the instance of the now-inappropriate association of African Americans with southern states.

The Black or African American Population

African Americans, involuntary immigrants to the continent, were nearly exclusively confined to rural areas of the South and Southeast prior to the Civil War (Figure 6.12). Even after emancipation, most remained on the land in the South. During the first two-thirds of the 20th century, however, those established patterns of southern rural residence and farm employment underwent profound changes. The decline of subsistence farming and share-cropping, the mechanization of southern agriculture, the demand for factory labor in northern cities starting with World War I (1914–1918), and the general urbanization of the American economy all induced African

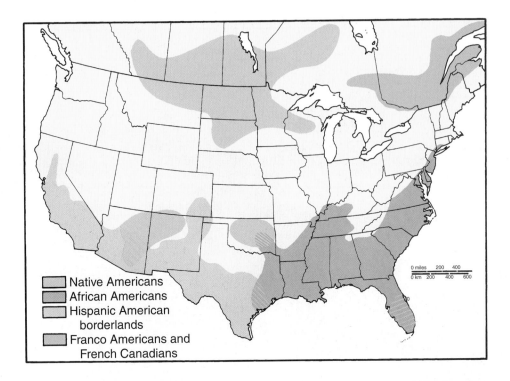

Figure 6.10 Four North American ethnic groups and their provinces. Note how this generalized map differs from the more detailed picture of ethnic distributions shown in Figure 6.8.

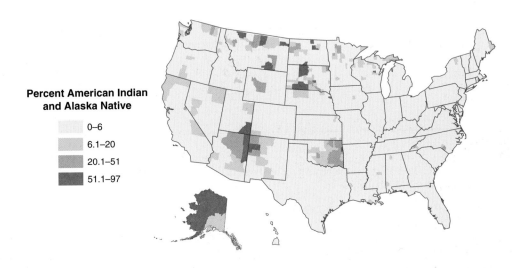

Percent American Indian and Alaska Native

- 0–6
- 6.1–20
- 20.1–51
- 51.1–97

Figure 6.11 American Indian and Alaska Native populations, 2010.

Americans to abandon the South in a "great migration" northward in search of manufacturing jobs and greater social equality.

Created by the U.S. Coast Survey using 1860 Census data, the map shown in Figure 6.12 was perhaps the first choropleth map depicting human geographic data. The map was useful in the Union's war efforts, convincing the public that slavery was the root cause of the war and showing that some sections of the South (such as Appalachia) had few slaves. Note the sharp difference in slave populations between the eastern and western sections of Virginia. That difference led to the secession of West Virginia from Virginia in 1862.

Between 1940 and 1970, more than 5 million African Americans left their homes in the South, in the largest internal ethnic migration ever experienced in the United States. A modest return migration of, particularly, middle-class African Americans that began in the 1970s picked up speed during the 1980s and gave evidence of being a reverse "great migration" in the past decades. That return movement, encouraged by an improving economic and racial environment in the South and by African Americans' enduring strong cultural and family ties, suggests a net inflow to the South of some 3 million African Americans between 1975 and 2010—more than half of the post-1940 out-migration. Prominent

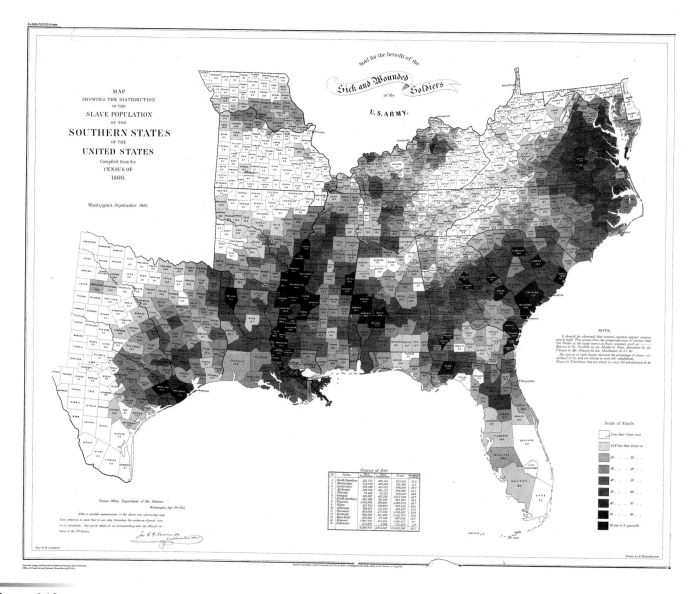

Figure 6.12 **Slave population, 1860.** The map shows the percentage of slaves in the total population, with darker shading indicating areas of high concentration such as South Carolina and the Mississippi Delta.

in that reverse flow are African American professionals leaving such northern strongholds as Chicago, Detroit, and Philadelphia and settling in the suburbs of Atlanta, Charlotte, Dallas, Houston, Miami, and other Sunbelt metropolitan areas.

The growing African American population (about 14 percent of all Americans in 2010) is more urbanized than the general population and yet retains evidence of its rural roots in the former Confederacy states of the South (Figure 6.13). The South is home to 55 percent of the African American population.

Black Americans, like Asian Americans and Hispanics, have had thrust on them an assumed common ethnicity that does not, in fact, exist. Because of prominent physical or linguistic characteristics, quite dissimilar ethnic groups have been categorized by the white, English-speaking majority in ways totally at odds with the realities of their separate national origins or cultural inheritances. Although the U.S. Census Bureau makes some attempt to subdivide Asian ethnic groups—Chinese, Filipino, and Korean, for example—these

are distinctions not necessarily recognized by members of the white majority. But even the Census Bureau, in its summary statistics, has treated "Black" and "Hispanic Origin" as catchall classifications that suggest ethnic uniformities where none necessarily exist.

In the case of African Americans, such categorizing is of decreasing relevance for two reasons. First, immigration has made the black population increasingly heterogeneous. Between 1970 and 2010, the share of foreign-born in the black community rose from just over 1 percent to about 10 percent. The immigrants originated in many countries of the Caribbean and Africa, with the largest percentages coming from Haiti, Jamaica, the Dominican Republic, and Trinidad and Tobago (4 percent); Nigeria was a leading origin of African immigrants. Second, the earlier overwhelmingly rural Southern black community has become subdivided along socioeconomic rather than primarily regional lines, the result of its 20th-century spatial mobility encouraged by northern industrial job opportunities first apparent during World War I and continuing

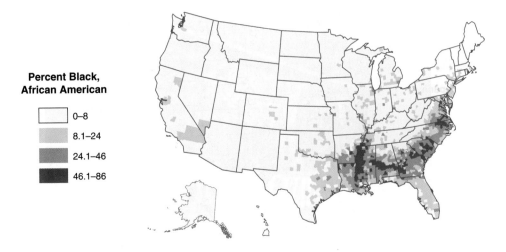

**Percent Black,
African American**

- 0–8
- 8.1–24
- 24.1–46
- 46.1–86

Figure 6.13 **African American population, 2010.** African Americans are particularly significant in the largely rural, relatively low-population states of the Southeast in a pattern reminiscent of their distribution in 1860.

through the 1960s. Government intervention, which mandated and promoted racial equality, further opened the way for the creation of black urban middle and upper income and professional groups. No common native culture united the slaves brought to America; few of their transported traits or traditions could endure their generations of servitude. Now, by long residence and separate experiences, African Americans have become as differentiated as comparably placed ethnics of any other heritage.

Hispanic Concentrations

Similarly, the members of the multiracial, multinational, and multicultural composite population lumped by the Census Bureau into the single category of "Hispanic, Latino, or Spanish origin" are not a homogeneous group. Indeed, it was the Census Bureau, not the

group itself, that created the concept and distinct ethnic category of "Hispanics." Prior to 1980, no such composite group existed.

Hispanic Americans are a diverse group. By commonly used racial categories, they may also be white, black, or Native American; over 50 percent of Hispanic Americans, in fact, report themselves to be white and more than one-third reported "some other race." Individually, they are highly diversified by country and culture of origin. Collectively, they also constitute the most rapidly growing minority component of U.S. residents—accounting for half of the country's population growth between 2000 and 2010, and surpassing African Americans as the largest minority, as Table 6.5 indicates. By 2010, the Hispanic population had grown to 50 million—16 percent of the U.S. population.

Mexican Americans account for about two-thirds of all Hispanic Americans (Table 6.6). Their highest concentrations are

Table 6.5

Actual and Projected U.S. Population Mix: 2000, 2025, and 2050

Population Group (One race options)	Percent of Total		
	2000	2025	2050
Non-Hispanic White	69.1	62.0	52.8
Hispanic or Latino	12.5	18.2	24.5
Black or African American	12.1	12.9	13.2
Asian/Pacific Islander	3.7	6.2	8.9
Native American	0.9	0.8	0.8

Note: Black, Asian, and Native American categories exclude Hispanics, who may be of any race.
Source: U.S. Bureau of the Census, Population Projection Program. Totals do not round to 100 percent.

Table 6.6

Composition of U.S. Hispanic Population, 2010

Hispanic Subgroup	Number (millions)	Percent
Mexican	31.8	63.0
Puerto Rican	4.6	9.2
Cuban	18	3.5
Dominican	1.4	2.8
Central American	4.0	7.9
South American	2.8	5.5
Other Hispanic origin[a]	3.4	6.8
Total Hispanic or Latino	**50.5**	**100**

[a]"Other Hispanics" includes those with origins in Spain or who identify themselves as "Hispanic," "Latino," "Spanish American," and so on.
Source: U.S. Bureau of the Census and Mumford Center, SUNY—Albany.

Among the major racial and ethnic groups in U.S. cities, blacks are the most segregated and Asians the least, The most segregated cities for blacks are industrial cities in the Midwest and Northeast. Collectively, blacks, Hispanics, and Asians lived in more integrated neighborhoods than did whites. Overall, although segregation remains high in America, for blacks, it steadily declined between 1970 and 2010. Of course, each world region and each country has its own patterns of national and urban immigration and immigrant residential patterns. Even when those population movements involve distinctive and contrasting ethnic groups, American models of spatial differentiation may not be applicable.

Foreign migrants to West European cities, for example, frequently do not have the same expectations of permanent residence and eventual amalgamation into the host society as their American counterparts. Many came under labor contracts with no initial legal assurance of permanent residence. Although many now have been joined by their families, they often find citizenship difficult to acquire; in Germany, even German-born children of guest workers are considered aliens. Their residential choices are consequently influenced by difficulties in integration, a high degree of migrant self-identity, restriction to housing units or districts specially provided for them, and the locational pull of chain migration. Culture and religion are important in that regard, as even small, ethnically homogeneous groups, confined perhaps to part of a city block or to a single apartment building, help to maintain the lifestyle and support systems of their home territories.

The Islamic populations from North Africa and Turkey tend to be more tightly grouped and defensive against the surrounding majority culture of western European cities than do African or south and east European Christian migrants. France, with some 5 million Muslim residents, most of them from North Africa, has tended to create bleak, outer suburban ghettoes in which immigrants remain largely isolated from mainstream French life.

Racial and ethnic divisions appear particularly deep and divisive in Britain. A British government report of 2001 claimed that in Britain, whites and ethnic minorities lead separate lives with no social or cultural contact and no sense of belonging to the same nation. Residential segregation in public housing and inner-city areas was compounded by deep social polarization. The nonwhite British population—largely Caribbean and Asian in origin—and the white majority, the report concluded, "operate on the basis of a series of parallel lives . . . that often do not seem to touch at any point," assigning blame for the situation on "communities choosing to live in separation rather than integration" (see the feature "The Caribbean Map in London"). The Home Secretary observed on the basis of the report that many "towns and cities lack any sense of civic identity or shared values." A similar total minority segregation is evident in the Sydney, Australia, suburb of Redfern, which houses an Aboriginal population that rarely ventures out to work or mingle in the surrounding white city and that white Australians avoid and ignore.

Spatial segregation is growing in the developing countries as well. Rapid urbanization in multiethnic India has resulted in cities of extreme social and cultural contrasts. Increasingly, Indian cities feature defined residential colonies segregated by village and caste origins of the immigrants. Chain migration has eased the influx of newcomers to specific new and old city areas; language, custom, religion, and tradition keep them confined. In Mumbai, for example, in Dharavi—considered the world's largest slum—Tamil, not Hindi, is spoken as the main language. Elsewhere, in Bangkok, Thailand, Burmese migrants are largely confined to the slum of Tlong Toey; the population of Hillbrow, a squatter slum in Johannesburg, South Africa, consists largely of Nigerian and French-speaking African immigrants; and the residents of the informal settlements of San José, Costa Rica, generally come from Nicaragua. International and domestic migration throughout ethnically diverse sub-Saharan Africa shows a repetitive pattern of residential segregation: the rural-to-urban population shift has created city neighborhoods defined on tribal and village lines. Worldwide in all continental and national urban contexts, the degree of immigrant segregation is at least in part conditioned by the degree of social distance felt between the newcomer population and the other immigrant and host societies among whom residential space is sought.

Constraints on assimilation and the extent of discrimination and segregation are greater for some minorities than for others. In general, the rate of assimilation of an ethnic minority by the host culture depends on two sets of controls: *external* controls, including attitudes toward the minority held by the charter group and other competing ethnic groups, and *internal* controls of group cohesiveness and defensiveness.

External Controls

When the majority culture or rival minorities perceive an ethnic group as threatening, the group tends to be spatially isolated by external "blocking" tactics designed to confine the rejected minority and to resist its "invasion" of neighborhoods. The more tightly knit the threatened group, the more adamant and overt are its resistance tactics. When confrontation measures (including, perhaps, housing market discrimination, threats, and vandalism) fail, the invasion of charter-group territory by the rejected minority proceeds until a critical percentage of newcomer housing occupancy is reached. That level, the **tipping point,** may precipitate a rapid exodus of the majority population. Invasion, followed by succession, then results in a new spatial pattern of ethnic dominance according to models of urban social geography developed for American cities and examined in Chapter 11.

Racial or ethnic discrimination in urban areas generally expresses itself in the relegation of the most recent, most alien, most rejected minority to the poorest available housing. That confinement has historically been reinforced by the concentration of the newest, least assimilated ethnic minorities at the low end of the job market. Distasteful, menial, low-paying service and factory employment unattractive to the charter group is available to those new arrivals, even when other occupational avenues may be closed. The dockworkers, street cleaners, slaughterhouse employees, and sweatshop garment workers of earlier America had and have their counterparts in other regions. In England, successive waves of West Indians and Commonwealth Asians took the posts of low-pay hotel and restaurant service workers, transit workers, refuse collectors, manual laborers, and the like; Turks in German cities and North Africans in France fill similar low-status employment roles.

The Caribbean Map in London

Although the movement [to England] from the West Indies has been treated as if it were homogeneous, the island identity, particularly among those from the small islands, has remained strong. . . . [I]t is very evident to anyone working in the field that the process of chain migration produced a clustering of particular island or even village groups in their British destination. . . .

The island identities have manifested themselves on the map of London. The island groups can still be picked out in the clusters of settlements in different parts of the city. There is an archipelago of Windward and Leeward islanders north of the Thames; Dominicans and St. Lucians have their core areas in Paddington and Notting Hill; Grenadians are found in the west in Hammersmith and Ealing; Montserratians are concentrated around Stoke Newington, Hackney, and Finsbury Park; Antiguans spill over to the east in Hackney, Waltham Forest, and Newham; south of the river is Jamaica.

That is not to say that Jamaicans are found only south of the river or that the only West Indians in Paddington are from St. Lucia. The mixture is much greater than that. The populations overlap and interdigitate: there are no sharp edges. . . . [Nevertheless, north of the river,] there is a west-east change with clusters of Grenadians in the west giving way to St. Lucians and Dominicans in the inner west, through to Vincentians and Montserratians in the inner north and east and thence to Antiguans in the east.

Source: Ceri Peach, "The Force of West Indian Island Identity in Britain," in *Geography and Ethnic Pluralism*, eds. Colin Clarke, David Ley, and Ceri Peach (London: George Allen & Unwin, 1984).

Historically, in the United States, there was a spatial association between the location of such employment opportunities—the inner-city central business district (CBD) and its margins—and the location of the oldest, most dilapidated, and least desirable housing. Proximity to job opportunity and the availability of cheap housing near the CBD, therefore, combined to concentrate the U.S. immigrant slum near the heart of the 19th-century central city. In the second half of the 20th century, the suburbanization of jobs, the rising skill levels required in the automated offices of the CBD, and the effective isolation of inner-city residents by the absence of public transportation or their inability to pay for private transport maintained the association of the least competitive minorities and the least desirable housing area. But now those locations lack the promise of the entry-level jobs that used to be close at hand.

That U.S. spatial pattern is not universal, however. In Latin American cities, the newest arrivals at the bottom of the economic and employment ladder are most apt to find housing in squatter or slum areas on the outskirts of the urban unit. In French urban agglomerations, the outer fringes frequently have a higher percentage of foreigners than the city itself.

Internal Controls

Although part of the American pattern of urban residential segregation may be explained by the external controls of host-culture resistance and discrimination, the clustering of specific groups into ethnically homogeneous neighborhoods is best understood as the result of internal controls of group defensiveness and conservatism. The self-elected segregation of ethnic groups can be seen to serve four principal functions—defense, support, preservation, and group assertion.

First, it provides *defense,* reducing individual immigrant isolation and exposure by physical association within a limited area. The walled and gated Jewish quarters of medieval European cities have their present-day counterparts in the clearly marked and defined "turfs" of street gang members and the understood exclusive domains of the "black community," "Chinatown," and other ethnic or racial neighborhoods. In British cities, it has been observed that West Indians and Asians fill identical slots in the British economy and reside in the same sorts of areas, but they tend to avoid living in the *same* areas. West Indians avoid Asians; Sikhs isolate themselves from Muslims; Bengalis shun Punjabis. In London, patterns of residential isolation even extend to West Indians of separate island homelands, as the feature "The Caribbean Map in London" makes clear. Their own defined ethnic territory provides members of the group with security from the hostility of antagonistic social groups, a factor also underlying the white flight to "garrison" suburbs.

Second, the ethnic neighborhood provides *support* for its residents in a variety of ways. The area serves as a halfway station between the home country and the alien society. It provides supportive lay and religious ethnic institutions, familiar businesses, job opportunities where language barriers are minimal, and friendship and kinship ties to ease the transition to a new society.

Third, the ethnic neighborhood may provide a *preservation* function, reflecting the ethnic group's positive intent to preserve and promote such essential elements of its cultural heritage as language and religion. The preservation function represents a fear of being totally absorbed into the charter society and a desire to maintain those customs and associations seen to be essential to the conservation of the group. For example, Jewish dietary laws are more easily observed by and exposure to potential marriage partners within the faith is more certain in close-knit communities than when individuals are scattered.

Finally, ethnic spatial concentration can serve as a base for group assertion, a peaceful search for democratic political representation. Voter registration drives and political candidates drawn from ethnic neighborhoods represent concerted efforts to promote group interests at all governmental levels.

Shifting Ethnic Concentrations

Ethnic communities, once established, are not necessarily permanent. For Europeans who came in the 19th and early

20th centuries, and for more recent Hispanic and Asian immigrants, high concentrations were and are encountered in neighborhoods of first settlement (see the feature "Colonies of Immigrants"). Second-generation neighborhoods usually become far more mixed. The older, dominant, urban ethnic groups in places given names like "Little Italy" are now often in the minority, as middle- and upper-middle-class members of the immigrant group move on. That mobility pattern appears to be repeating among Asian and Latino groups, but only, or most clearly, where those groups collectively account for a relatively small share of the total metropolitan area population. Black segregation and black communities, in contrast, appear more pronounced and permanent.

Ethnic clusters initially identified with particular central city areas are frequently or usually displaced by different newcomer groups (Figure 6.20). With recent diversified immigration, older homogeneous ethnic neighborhoods have become highly subdivided and polyethnic. In Los Angeles, for example, the great wave of immigrants from Mexico, Central America, and Asia has begun to push African Americans out of Watts and other well-established black communities, converting them from racially exclusive to multicultural areas. In New York, the borough of Queens, once the stronghold of European ethnic immigrants, has now become home to more than 110 different, mainly non-European nationalities. In Woodside in Queens, Latin Americans and Koreans are prominent among the many replacements of the formerly dominant German and Irish groups. Elsewhere within the city, West Indians now dominate the old Jewish neighborhoods of Flatbush; Poles, Dominicans,

and other Central Americans have succeeded Germans and Jews in Washington Heights. Manhattan's Chinatown has expanded into old Little Italy, and a new Little Italy has emerged in Bensonhurst.

Further, the new ethnic neighborhoods are intermixed in a way that enclaves of the early 20th century never were. The restaurants, bakeries, groceries, specialty shops, and their customers and owners from a score of different countries (and even different continents) are now found within a two- or three-block radius. In the Kenmore Avenue area of East Los Angeles, for example, a half-square-mile (1.3-square-kilometer) area of former Anglo neighborhood now houses over 9,000 people representing Hispanics and Asians of widely varied origins, along with Pacific Islanders, Amerindians, African Americans, and a scattering of native-born whites. Students in the neighborhood school come from 43 countries and speak 23 languages, a localized ethnic intermixture unknown in the communities of single ethnicity so characteristic of earlier stages of immigration to the United States, as the excerpt "Colonies of Immigrants" suggests.

The changing ethnic spatial pattern is not yet clear or certain. Increasing ethnic diversity coupled with continuing immigration flow has, in some instances, expanded rather than reduced patterns of urban group segregation. The tendency for separate ethnic groups to cluster for security, economic, and social reasons cannot be effective if many different, relatively small ethnic groups find themselves in a single city setting. Intermixture is inevitable when individual groups do not achieve the critical mass necessary to establish a true identifiable separate community. But as continuing

Figure 6.20 Landscape evidence of shifting ethnic concentrations. As Jews left North Minneapolis for the suburbs, they were succeeded by African Americans. This former Orthodox synagogue is one of the few reminders of the once vibrant Jewish presence. The building is now used by a nondenominational Protestant Christian congregation and the altered facade mixes carved lions guarding Hebrew scrolls, Stars of David, crosses, and both Jewish and Christian messages.

Colonies of Immigrants

In the following extract from his 1904 book *Poverty,* Robert Hunter conveys a sense of the ethnic diversity found in American cities:

[In American cities] great colonies, foreign in language, customs, habits, and institutions, are separated from each other and from the distinctly American groups on national or racial lines. By crossing the Bowery one leaves behind him the great Jewish colony made up of Russians, Poles, and Roumanians and passes into Italy; to the northeast lies a little Germany; to the southwest a colony of Syrians; to the west lies an Irish community, a settlement of negroes, a remnant of the old native American stock; to the south lie a Chinese and a Greek colony. On Manhattan alone, either on the extreme west side or the extreme east side, there are other colonies of the Irish, the Jews, and the Italians, and, in addition, there is a large colony of Bohemians. In Chicago there are the same foreign poor. To my own knowledge there are four Italian colonies, two Polish, a Bohemian, an Irish, a Jewish, a German, a negro, a Chinese, a Greek, a Scandinavian, and other colonies. So it is also in Boston and many other cities. In New York alone there are more persons of German descent than persons of native descent, and the German element is larger than in any city of Germany except Berlin. There are nearly twice as many Irish as in Dublin, about as many Jews as in Warsaw, and more Italians than in Naples or Venice. . . .

To live in one of these foreign communities is actually to live on foreign soil. The thoughts, feelings, and traditions which belong to the mental life of the colony are often entirely alien to an American. The newspapers, the literature, the ideals, the passions, the things which agitate the community are unknown to us except in fragments. . . .

While there is a great movement of population from all parts of the old world to all parts of the new, the migration to the United States is the largest and the most conspicuous. Literally speaking, millions of foreigners have established colonies in the very hearts of our urban and industrial communities. . . . In recent years the flow of immigrants to the cities, where they are not needed, instead of to those parts of the country where they are needed, has been steadily increasing. Sixty-nine percent of the present immigration avows itself as determined to settle either in the great cities or in certain communities of the four great industrial states, Massachusetts, New York, Pennsylvania, and Illinois. According to their own statements, nearly 60 percent of the Russian and Polish Jews intend to settle in the largest cities. As a matter of fact, those who actually do settle in cities are even more numerous than this percentage indicates. As the class of immigrants, drawn from eastern and southern Europe, Russia, and Asia, come in increasing numbers to the United States, the tendency to settle in cities likewise increases.

Source: Robert Hunter, *Poverty*. (New York: Macmillan, 1904).

immigration and natural increases allow groups to expand in size, they are able to create more distinctive, self-selected ethnic clusters and communities.

Enclaves, Ghettos, and Ethnoburbs

When ethnic residential clusters endure, the clusters may be termed **colonies,** serving essentially as points of entry for members of the particular ethnic group. They persist only to the extent that new arrivals perpetuate the need for them. In American cities, many European ethnic colonies began to lose their vitality and purpose with the reduction of European immigration flows after the 1920s.

When an ethnic cluster does persist because its occupants choose to preserve it, their behavior reflects the internal cohesiveness of the group and its desire to maintain an enduring **ethnic enclave** or neighborhood. When the cluster is perpetuated by external constraints and discriminatory actions, it has come to be termed a **ghetto.** The term *ghetto* was first used in Venice, Italy, in the 16th century to refer to the area of the city where Jews were required to live. In reality, the colony, the enclave, and the ghetto are spatially similar. Growing ethnic groups that maintain voluntary spatial association frequently expand the area of their dominance by outward growth from the core of the city in a radial pattern. That process has long been recognized in Chicago (Figure 6.21) and

has, in that and other cities, typically been extended beyond the central city boundaries into at least the inner fringe of the suburbs.

African Americans have traditionally found strong resistance to their territorial expansion from the Anglo charter group, though white-black urban relations and patterns of black ghetto formation and expansion have differed in different sections of the country. A revealing typology of African American ghettos is outlined in Figure 6.22. In the South, the white majority, with total control of the housing market, was able to assign residential space to blacks in accordance with white, not black, self-interest. In the *early southern* ghetto of such pre–Civil War cities as Charleston and New Orleans, African Americans were assigned small dwellings in alleys and back streets within and bounding the white communities where they worked as (slave) house and garden servants. The *classic southern* ghetto for newly free blacks was composed of specially built, low-quality housing on undesirable land—swampy, perhaps, or near industry or railroads—and was sufficiently far from better-quality white housing to maintain full spatial and social segregation.

In the North, on the other hand, African Americans were open competitors with other claimants for space in a generalized housing market. The *early northern* ghetto represented a "toehold" location in high-density, aged, substandard housing on the margin of the CBD. The *classic northern* ghetto is a more recent expansion of that initial enclave to surround the CBD and to penetrate, through

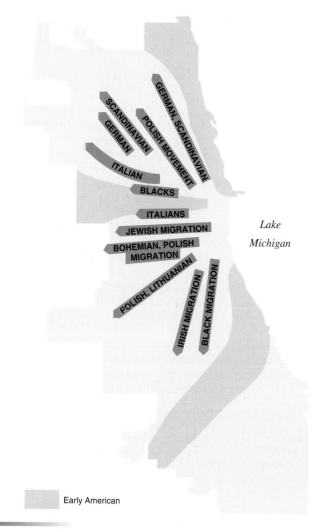

Lake Michigan

Early American

Figure 6.21 **The outward expansion of racial and nationality groups in Chicago.** "Often," Samuel Kincheloe observed in the 1930s, "[minority] groups first settle in a deteriorated area of a city somewhere near its center, then push outward along the main streets." More recently, many—particularly young, innovative, and entrepreneurial—immigrants have avoided traditional first locations in central cities and from their arrival, they have settled in metropolitan area suburbs and outlying cities, where economic opportunity and quality of life is perceived as superior to conditions in the primary inner city.

Source: The American City and its Church *by Samuel Kincheloe. Copyright 1938 by Friendship Press, New York.*

invasion and succession, contiguous zones as far as the numbers, rent-paying ability, and housing discrimination will allow. Finally, in new western and southwestern cities not tightly hemmed in by resistant white neighborhoods or suburbs, the black community may display a linear expansion from the CBD to the suburban fringe.

Increasingly, ethnic communities are found in the outer reaches of major metropolitan areas. In New York City, the outer Queens neighborhood of Elmhurst houses immigrants from 114 different countries and is the city's most ethnically diverse community. In part due to rising affluence among immigrants, "Satellite Chinatowns" are found in Los Angeles's San Gabriel Valley, in San Francisco, and in Vancouver, Canada (Figure 6.23). This has given rise to the *ethnoburb,* a politically independent suburban community with a significant, though not exclusive,

concentration of a single ethnic group (See the feature "Vancouver, Canada: Chinatown Versus Ethnoburb"). Monterey Park, outside Los Angeles, and Richmond, British Columbia, outside Vancouver, are examples of Chinese ethnoburbs. Ethnoburbs differ from traditional, inner-city Chinatowns, which were the product of discrimination and the low socioeconomic status of the Chinese. Ethnoburbs, on the other hand, attract relatively wealthy, well-educated, highly mobile immigrants. Many of the immigrants in ethnoburbs display **transnationalism;** that is, they maintain strong ties with more than one country, often in the form of social and business connections with their homeland. Jet travel and the Internet make it quite possible to run a business on the other side of the Pacific Ocean. While traditional Chinatowns are self-sustaining enclaves filled with small, independent shops, ethnoburbs feature transnational banks, hotels, retail chains, and sellers of luxury goods.

Native-Born Dispersals

Immigration flows to the United States during the last third of the 20th century—unlike those of earlier mass-immigration periods—have begun to affect both the broad regional ethnic makeup of the United States and the internal migration pattern of native-born Americans. The consequence has been dubbed a "demographic balkanization," a spatial fragmentation of the population by race/ethnicity, economic status, and age across extended metropolitan areas and larger regions of the country.

Early 20th-century immigration streams resulted, as we have seen, in temporary ethnic segregation by urban neighborhoods and between central cities and suburbs. Immigration legislation of 1965 dropped the national-origin quotas that had formerly favored European immigrants, replacing that with a more inclusive formula emphasizing family reunification. That change, plus economic and political pressures in many countries of Asia and Latin America, has swelled the influx of poorer, less-skilled Asians and Hispanics. Highly dependent on family members and friends for integration into both the informal and formal American job market, the new arrivals are drawn to primary port-of-entry metropolitan areas by chain migration links. In those areas where immigrants account for most of the present and prospective population growth, the trend is toward increasingly multicultural, younger, and poorer residents, predominantly of Hispanic and Asian origin.

The high degree of areal concentration of recent immigrant groups initiated a selective native-born (particularly white) retreat, not only fleeing the cities for the suburbs but leaving entire metropolitan areas and states. California, with nearly one-quarter of its population foreign-born, saw a departure of one native-born white or black resident for nearly each foreign-born arrival. Individual urban areas echoed California's state experience. The New York, Chicago, Los Angeles, Houston, and Boston metropolitan areas—5 of the top 11 immigrant destinations—lost 9 native residents for every 10 immigrant arrivals. For whites, top destinations were to cities and states away from coastal and southern border immigrant entry points. A visible spatial consequence, then, is an emerging pattern of increasing segregation and isolation by metropolitan areas and regions of the country. Immigrant assimilation may now be more difficult than in the past, and social and political divisions more pronounced and enduring.

EARLY SOUTHERN

Spaces behind master's houses

CLASSIC SOUTHERN

"Other side of the tracks"

"New City"

CBD

Sector growth toward suburbia

EARLY NORTHERN

CBD

Foothold in inner city

CLASSIC NORTHERN

CBD

Compact inner city

Figure 6.22 A typology of black ghettos in the United States.

Source: David T. Herbert and Colin J. Thomas, Urban Geography, *London: David Fulton Publishers, 1987. Redrawn by permission.*

Typical home of Vancouver white workingman.

A warren on Carrall Street infested by 2000 Chinese

(a)

(b)

(c)

Figure 6.23 (*a*) Vancouver newspaper cartoon reflecting racist attitudes towards the Chinese and the supposedly overcrowded and vice-ridden conditions in Chinatown. Note the contrast between the white schoolgirl skipping rope and the Chinese man smoking opium. (*b*) Vancouver's historic Chinatown developed when Chinese railroad workers settled there upon completion of the transcontinental railroad. It features distinctive architecture, ethnic specialty shops, and restaurants. Its population is dense, mostly Chinese, and relatively old. (*c*) Richmond, British Columbia, is an ethnoburb with a large, multiethnic immigrant population. Richmond is a prosperous suburb of Vancouver, and it is filled with expensive, single-family houses, condominiums, international hotels, Chinese-themed shopping malls, and an international airport. Richmond's Chinese make up 44 percent of the city's population, are young, well-educated, and maintain strong social and business ties with Hong Kong, Taiwan, and mainland China.

Figure 6.26 New Glarus, Wisconsin, was settled by Swiss immigrants in the mid-1800s, but over time, it came to look like other small towns in the Midwest. More recently, the town has played up its Swiss heritage to attract tourists.

and Lindsborg, Kansas ("Little Sweden, USA") are good examples. Similarly, urban neighborhoods with identities such as Chinatown, Little Tokyo, Greektown, or Little Italy can attract shoppers and restaurant-goers who seek the novelty or imagined authenticity of an ethnic enclave. New Glarus illustrates the tension between assimilation and preserving for tourists the image of an ethnic place supposedly untouched by assimilation and homogenization (Figure 6.26). The town was settled by Swiss immigrants who, over time, underwent assimilation while still keeping elements of their ethnic heritage. As the rural community struggled economically, it found that by playing up its ethnic heritage through adding chalet-style architecture, ethnic festivals, specialty shops, and museums, it could attract large numbers of tourists from nearby cities. But the town is not Disneyland, and the tourist image of the community can conflict with actually living and working in the town.

Ethnic Regionalism

Patterns of long-established ethnic regionalism are displayed in pronounced contrasts in the built landscape. In areas of intricate mixtures of ethnic homelands—eastern and southeastern Europe, for example—different house types, farmstead layouts, and even the use of color can distinguish for the knowledgeable observer the ethnicity of the local population. The one-story "smoking-room" house of the northern Slavs, with its covered entrance hall and stables all under one roof, marks their areas of settlement south of the Danube River. Blue-painted, one-story, straw-roofed houses indicate Croatian communities. In the Danube Basin, areas of Slovene settlement are distinguished by the Pannonian house of wood and straw-mud. In Spain, the courtyard farmstead marks areas of Moorish influence, just as white stucco houses trimmed with dark green or ochre paint on the shutters indicates Basque settlement.

It is difficult to delineate ethnic regions of the United States that correspond to the distinctive landscapes created by sharply contrasting cultural groups in Europe or other world areas. The reason lies in the mobility of Americans, the degree of acculturation and assimilation of immigrants and their offspring, and the significance of charter cultures and mass communications in shaping ideas, activities, institutions, and material artifacts. What can be attempted is the delimitation of areas in which particular immigrant-group influences have played a recognizable or determinant role in shaping tangible landscapes and intangible regional "character."

Summary

Ethnic diversity is a reality in most countries of the world and is increasing in many of them. Immigration, refugee streams, guest workers, and job seekers all contribute to the mixing of peoples and cultures in an area. The mixing is not complete, however. Ethnicity—affiliation in a group sharing common identifying cultural traits—is fostered by territorial separation or isolation. In much of the world, that separation identifies home territories within which the ethnic group is dominant and with which it is identified. In societies of immigrants—the United States and Canada, for example—such homelands are replaced by ethnic colonies, islands, enclaves, ghettos, and ethnoburbs of self-selected or imposed separation from the larger host society. Cluster migration helped establish such colonies in rural America; chain migration encouraged their development in cities.

The 19th- and early 20th-century American central city displayed pronounced areal segregation as immigrant groups established and clung to protective ethnic neighborhoods while they gradually adjusted to the host culture. A continual population restructuring of urban areas occurred as older groups underwent acculturation, amalgamation, or assimilation, and new groups entered the urban social mix. The durability of ethnic neighborhoods has depended on the degree of social distance separating the minority group from the host culture and on the significance the immigrant group places on long-term maintenance of their own cultural identity. That is, ethnic communities have been the product of both external and internal forces.

In other world regions, similar spatial separation of immigrant groups by racial, cultural, national, tribal, or village origin within the city is common. In Europe, because of the uncertain legal and employment status of many foreign populations and the restricted urban housing market they enter, ethnic enclaves have taken a different form, extent, and level of segregation than has been the case in the United States and Canada.

Ethnicity is one of the threads of diversity in the spatial cultural fabric. Throughout the world, ethnic groups have imprinted their presence on the landscapes in which they have developed or to which they have transported their culture. In house and farm building style, settlement patterns, and religious structures, the beliefs and practices of distinctive groups are reflected in the cultural landscape. Such interweaving of cultural identities and cultural landscapes and their interaction with the homogenizing force of popular culture are the subjects of Chapter 7.

KEY WORDS

acculturation 176	ethnic geography 168	natural selection 169
amalgamation theory 176	ethnic group 168	race 169
assimilation 177	ethnic island 181	residential dissimilarity index 191
chain migration 182	ethnicity 169	segregation 191
charter group 180	ethnic province 182	social distance 190
cluster migration 182	ethnocentrism 171	spatial assimilation 177
colony 195	first effective settlement 180	tipping point 192
culture rebound 199	ghetto 195	transnationalism 196
ethnic enclave 195	host society 172	xenophobia 172

FOR REVIEW

1. How does *ethnocentrism* contribute to preservation of group identity? In what ways might an ethnic group sustain and support new immigrants?

2. What is the difference between race and ethnicity? How are the concepts of *ethnicity* and *culture* related?

3. What have been some of the principal time patterns of immigration flows into the United States? Into Canada?

How are those patterns important to an understanding of present-day social conflicts in either country or both countries?

4. How may *segregation* be measured? Does ethnic segregation exist in the cities of world areas outside North America? If so, does it take different form than in American cities?

5. What forces external to ethnic groups help to create and perpetuate immigrant neighborhoods? What functions beneficial to immigrant groups do ethnic communities provide?

6. How is a ghetto different than an ethnic enclave? How is an ethnoburb different than a traditional ethnic enclave?

KEY CONCEPTS REVIEW

1. **What are the implications and bases of "ethnicity," and how have historic immigration streams shaped multiethnicity in the United States and Canada?** pp. 168–176.

   Ethnicity implies a "people" or "nation," a large group classified according to common religious, linguistic, or other aspects of cultural origin or background, or, often, to racial distinctions. In common with nearly all countries, the United States and Canada are multiethnic. Past and current immigration streams—earlier primarily European, more recently Asian and Latin American—have intricately mixed their populations.

2. **How were the dominant Anglo American culture norms established, and how completely, spatially and socially, are its ethnic minorities integrated?** pp. 176–189.

   The first effective settlers of Anglo America created its English-rooted charter culture to which other, later immigrant groups were expected to conform. Assimilation or acculturation has not been complete, and areal expressions of ethnic differentiation persist in America in the form of ethnic islands, provinces, or regional concentrations. French Canadian, black, Amerindian, Hispanic, Asian American, and other, smaller groups display recognizable areal presences. Among immigrant groups, those concentrations may result from cluster and chain migration.

3. **What patterns of ethnic diversity and segregation exist in the world's urban areas, and how are they created or maintained?** pp. 189–199.

   Ethnic communities, clusters, and neighborhoods are found in cities worldwide. They are a measure of the social distance that separates minority from majority or other minority groups. Segregation measures the degree to which culture groups are not uniformly distributed within the total population. Although different world regions show differing patterns, all urban segregation is based on external restrictions of isolation and discrimination or ethnic group internal separatism controls of defense, mutual support, and cultural preservation. Ethnic colonies, enclaves, ghettos, and ethnoburbs are the spatial result.

4. **What have been some of the cultural landscape consequences of ethnic concentrations in Anglo America and elsewhere?** pp. 199–200.

   Landscape evidence of ethnicity may be subtle or pronounced. Clustered and dispersed rural settlement customs; house and barn types and styles; distinctive, largely urban, "Chinatowns," "Little Havanas," and other cultural communities; and even choices in dwelling-house colors or urban art are landscape imprints of multiethnicity in modern societies.

CULTURAL IDENTITIES AND CULTURAL LANDSCAPES:
Diversity and Uniformity

The Amish, one of the most distinctive folk culture groups in the United States and Canada, pursue traditional farming methods.

Key Concepts

A. Cultural Identities

1. Folk culture characteristics, culture hearths, and culture regions, pp. 204–208.

2. Folk food, drink, and music, pp. 208–211.

3. Popular culture characteristics and diffusion, pp. 211–213.

4. Popular food, drink, and music, pp. 213–217.

5. Reactions against globalized popular culture, pp. 217–218.

6. Vernacular regions, pp. 218–221.

B. Cultural Landscapes

1. Tools for reading landscapes, pp. 218–223.

2. Cultural landscapes: survey systems, houses, landscapes of consumption, and heritage landscapes, pp. 223–237.

A *fter construction workers finish plastering a replica of the Arc de Triomphe and buffing the imitation streets of Hollywood, Paris, and Amsterdam, a giant new shopping theme park here will proclaim itself the world's largest shopping mall. The South China Mall—a jumble of Disneyland and Las Vegas, a shoppers' version of paradise and hell all wrapped in one—will be nearly three times the size of the massive Mall of America in Minnesota. It is part of yet another astonishing new consequence of the quarter-century economic boom here: the great malls of China. Not long ago, shopping in China consisted mostly of lining up to entreat surly clerks to accept cash in exchange for ugly merchandise that did not fit. But now, Chinese have started to embrace America's modern "shop till you drop" ethos and are in the midst of a buy-at-the-mall frenzy.*

Already, four shopping malls in China are larger than the Mall of America. Two, including the South China Mall, are bigger than the West Edmonton Mall in Alberta, which just surrendered its status as the world's largest to an enormous retail center in Beijing. Chinese are swarming into malls, which usually have many levels that rise up rather than out, in the sprawling two-level style typical in much of the United States. Chinese consumers arrive by bus and train, and growing numbers are driving there. On busy days, one mall in the southern city of Guangzhou attracts about 600,000 shoppers.

For sale are a wide range of consumer favorites—cell phones, DVD players, jeans, sofas, and closets that you assemble yourself. There is food from many regions of China and franchises with familiar names—KFC, McDonald's, and IMAX theaters. Stores without Western pedigree sell Gucci and Louis Vuitton goods. While peasants and poor workers may only window-shop, they have joined a regular pilgrimage to the mall that has set builders and developers afire.

Source: David Barboza, "China, New Land of Shoppers, Builds Malls on Gigantic Scale," *New York Times,* May 25, 2005.

The kaleidoscope of culture presents an endlessly changing design, different for every society, world region, and national unit. Ever present in each of its varied patterns, however, are persistent fragments of diversity amidst the spreading color of uniformity. One distinctive element of diversity derives from *folk culture*—the material and nonmaterial aspects of daily life preserved by small, local

groups partially or totally isolated from the mainstream currents of the larger society around them. Additional sources of diverse cultural identities are provided by language, religion, and ethnicity, as we have seen in Chapters 5 and 6. Gender, and norms related to it, add an additional element of cultural diversity. Finally, given time, easy communication, and common interests, globalized *popular* culture may provide a unifying color to the kaleidoscope, reducing differences between formerly distinctive groups, though perhaps not totally eradicating them. In this chapter, we will trace the tensions between diversity and uniformity, particularly in the U.S. and Canadian contexts, where diversified immigration provided the ethnic mix, frontier and rural isolation encouraged folk differentiation, and modern technology produced the leveling of popular culture. Along the way, we shall see the close interconnections between folk and popular culture, as well as reactions against the unifying tendencies of globalized popular culture. For geographers, the world is composed of multiple cultural landscapes bearing the imprint of human culture: values, preferences, activities, social relations, and technologies. Landscape features as varied as land survey systems, houses, shopping malls, and heritage landscapes can all be interpreted to better understand diverse cultural identities and the tensions between diversity and uniformity (Figure 7.1).

Folk Culture

Folk connotes traditional and non-faddish, the characteristic or product of a cohesive, largely self-sufficient group that is isolated from the larger society surrounding it. **Folk culture,** therefore, may be defined as the collective heritage of institutions, customs, skills, dress, stories, music, and way of life of a small, stable, close-knit, usually rural community. Tradition controls folk culture, and resistance to change is strong. The homemade and handmade dominate in tools, food, music, story, and ritual. Buildings are erected without architect or blueprint using locally available building materials. Folk societies, because of their subsistence, self-reliant economies, and limited technologies, are particularly responsive to physical environmental circumstances. Thus, foodstuffs, herbs, and medicinal plants reflect what is naturally available or able to be grown locally, and buildings reflect local climate and available materials.

Folk culture is often understood in opposition to popular or mass culture. It is seen as the unchanging, rural way of life, largely

Figure 7.1 Disney films and merchandise are popular around the world. Part of their popularity may stem from the fact that many of the story lines were adapted from classic folk tales. Disney movies, merchandise, and theme parks symbolize the globalization of popular culture. Starting with Disneyland, which opened in southern California in 1955, Disney has built theme parks in Florida, Paris, Tokyo, Hong Kong, and Shanghai. The Disney parks are themed environments, deliberately created to attract tourists by allowing them to physically enter different times, places, and stories. The success of Disney's Main Street U.S.A. and other themed environments in the Magic Kingdom inspired designers of popular chain stores, chain restaurants, shopping malls, and housing subdivisions to create their own themed environments.

relegated to non-modern, "traditional" peoples untouched by outside influences of mass media and market economies. Where folk culture exists in developed countries like the United States, it is found only among socially or geographically isolated rural groups—for example, the Amish, some Native American communities, or the presumably reclusive mountain folk of Appalachia. The prevailing notion in most of America is that if the artifacts, beliefs, and practices of folk culture are at all relevant to modern society, they serve only as reminders of the past, to be relegated to museums or as curiosities for tourists seeking the quaint and exotic "other." Thus, the relationship between folk and popular culture tends to be portrayed as one of conflict with folk culture doomed to eventual extinction by the forces of modernization and globalization. As we shall see, reality is more complex, with complicated linkages between folk and popular culture.

Although folk cultures are conservative and tend to resist innovations, they are not static. They often demonstrate flexibility and creativity when they encounter new or changing environmental or social circumstances, and they adapt accordingly. Indeed, all cultures were subsistence rural folk cultures until people built cities and developed a class hierarchy in which social and economic stratification began to differentiate the elite from commoners. The popular or mass culture that now so totally dominates modern life is a product of the industrialization and urbanization trends that began in the late 18th and early 19th centuries in Europe and the United States. Recently, globalization of popular culture has affected nearly every inhabited corner of the world. People everywhere tend to discard or alter elements of their folk culture when confronted with the attractions of modernity. Despite the claims of the folk or ethnic tourism trade in its efforts to sell "pristine" traditional cultures as a commodity, few if any groups remain, even in the developing world, that are still totally immersed in folk culture as their dominating way of life.

Yet folk cultural elements persist in all advanced societies. In Japan, traditional culture is tenaciously preserved in a highly industrialized and urbanized society that enthusiastically embraces nearly every fad produced by the Western culture that they have adopted. And the popularity in the United States of folk-themed movies and music (such as *Oh Brother, Where Art Thou?*) and the proliferation of folk music and folk life festivals are evidence that folk culture is far from irrelevant to modern society. Rather, it should be viewed as an underlying foundation for popular culture, intersecting and influencing popular culture.

Folk life in its unaltered form, however, is a cultural whole composed of both tangible and intangible elements. **Material culture** is made of physical, visible things: everything from musical instruments to furniture, tools, and buildings. **Nonmaterial culture,** in contrast, is the intangible part, the mentifacts and sociofacts expressed in oral tradition, folk song and folk story, and customary behavior. Ways of speech, patterns of worship, outlooks, and philosophies are parts of the nonmaterial component passed to following generations by teachings and examples.

Within the United States, true folk societies are rare; the impacts of industrialization, urbanization, and mass communication have been too pervasive for their full retention. The Old Order Amish, with their rejection of electricity, the internal combustion engine, and other "worldly" accoutrements in favor of buggies, hand tools, and traditional dress are one of the least altered—and few—folk societies of the United States (Figure 7.2). Yet the Amish are very adept at dealing with the modern world, often with the assistance of their non-Amish (or "English," in their vernacular) neighbors. For example, they own and operate successful cheese-making and furniture businesses; occasionally ride in, but do not drive, motor vehicles; use their "English" neighbors' telephones; and use propane gas to power their refrigerators instead of the forbidden electrical power grid.

Canada, on the other hand, has more clearly recognizable folk and decorative art traditions. One observer has noted that nearly all of the national folk art traditions of Europe can be found, in one form or another, well preserved and practiced somewhere in Canada. From the earliest arts and crafts of New France to the domestic art forms and folk artifacts of the Scandinavians, Germans, Ukrainians, and others who settled in western Canada in the late 19th and early 20th centuries, folk and ethnic traditions have been adapted to the Canadian context.

and implements, ornaments and toys, cookery and music. The evidence of the homeland was there, but the products became purely indigenous. In the isolated, largely rural American hearth regions, the ethnic culture imported from the Old World was partially transmuted into the folk culture of the New.

Folk Culture Regions of the United States and Canada

When folk **customs**—repeated, characteristic acts, behavioral patterns, artistic traditions, and conventions regulating social life—are shared by a people living in a distinctively area, a *folk culture region* may be recognized. Frontier settlers carrying to new, interior locations the artifacts and traditions of those hearth areas created a small set of indistinctly bounded eastern folk cultural regions (Figure 7.6).

From the small *Mid-Atlantic* region, folk cultural items and influences were dispersed into the North, the Upland South, and the Midwest. Furniture styles, log construction, decorative arts, house and barn types, and distinctive "sweet" cookery were among the European imports converted in the Mid-Atlantic hearth to American folk expressions.

The folk culture of the *Lowland South,* by contrast, derived from English originals and African admixtures. French influences

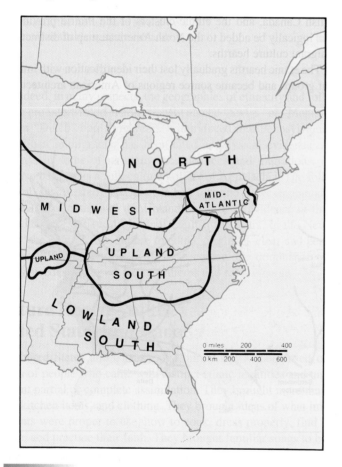

Figure 7.6 Material folk culture regions of the eastern United States.

Source: Redrawn with permission from Henry Glassie, Pattern in the Material Folk Culture of the Eastern United States, *p. 39, copyright © 1968 by the Trustees of the University of Pennsylvania.*

in the Mississippi Delta hearth combined with elements from the highland areas add to the amalgam. Dogtrot and I houses became common; English cuisine was adapted to include black-eyed peas, turnip greens, sweet potatoes, small-bird pies, and syrups from sugarcane and sorghum. African origins influenced the widespread use of the banjo in music.

The *Upland South* showed a mixture of influences carried from the Southern Tidewater hearth and brought south from the Mid-Atlantic folk region along the Appalachian highlands by settlers of German and Scotch-Irish stock. The physical isolation of the Upland South and its Ozark Mountains outlier encouraged the retention of traditional folk culture long after it had been lost in more accessible locations. Log houses and farm structures, rail fences, traditional art and music, and home-crafted quilts and furniture make the Upland South region a prime repository of folk artifacts and customs in the United States.

The *North*—dominated by New England, but including New York State, English Canada, Michigan, and Wisconsin—showed a folk culture of decidedly English origin. The saltbox house and Boston baked beans in stoneware pots are characteristic elements. The New England–British domination is locally modified by French Canadian and central European influences.

The *Midwest*—a conglomerate of inputs from the Upland South, from the North, and, particularly, from the Mid-Atlantic region—is the least distinctive, most intermixed and most Americanized of the cultural regions. Everywhere the interior contains evidences, both rural and urban, of artifacts carried by migrants from the eastern hearths and by newly arriving European immigrants.

Folk Food and Drink Preferences

Food is one of the most important distinguishing elements of cultural groups. Ethnic foods are among the central attractions of the innumerable fairs and "fests" held throughout the United States and Canada. In the case of ethnic foods, what is celebrated is the retention in a new environment of the food preferences, diets, and recipes that had their origin in a distant homeland. Folk food habits, on the other hand, are products of local circumstances; the diet consists of the natural foods derived from hunting, gathering, and fishing or the cultivated foods and domestic animals suited to the local environmental conditions.

Second, most areas of the world have been occupied by a complex mix of peoples migrating in search of food and carrying food habits and preferences with them in their migrations. In the Americas, Australia, New Zealand, and a few other regions of recent colonization, we are aware of these differing *ethnic* origins and the recipes and customs that they imply. In other world regions, ethnic and cultural intermixture is less immediately apparent. In Korea, for example, what outsiders see as a distinctive ethnic cookery best known, perhaps, for *kimch'i*—brined, pickled, and spiced vegetables in endless combinations and uniquely Korean—also incorporates Japanese and Chinese foodstuffs and dishes.

Third, food habits are not just matters of survival but are intimately connected with the totality of *culture*. People eat what is available and also what is, to them, edible. Sheep's brains and eyeballs, boiled insects, animal blood, and pig intestines, which are delicacies in some cultures, may be unclean or disgusting to others. Further, in most societies, food and eating are considered a social experience, not just a personal one, and a specially prepared meal is the true mark of hospitality.

The interconnections between folk, ethnic, and customary food habits are evident in the U.S. diet. Of course, the animals and plants, the basic recipes and flavorings, and the specialized festive dishes of American folk groups have ethnic origins. Many originated abroad and were carried to and preserved in remote New World areas. Many were derived from the diet of the Amerindians and adapted in widely different regional contexts. Turkey, squash, pumpkin, and cranberries are among the foods adapted from Amerindians, as is corn (maize), which appeared over time south of Pennsylvania as Southern grits, Southwestern tortillas, and cornbread. Such classic American dishes as Brunswick stew (a thick stew made with vegetables and two meats, such as squirrel and rabbit or chicken), the clambake, smoked salmon, cornflakes, and beef jerky were originally Indian fare. Gradually, the environmental influences, isolation, and time spans implicit in the concept of folk culture created culinary distinctions among populations recognized as American rather than as ethnic immigrants.

Cookbook categories of New England, Creole, Southern, Chesapeake, Southwestern, and other regional fare may be further refined into cookbooks containing Boston, Pennsylvania Dutch, Charleston, New Orleans, Southern Tidewater, and other more localized recipes. Their diversity is ample proof of the diffusion into national and international popular culture of formerly local folk cultural distinctions. Specific American dishes that have achieved fame and wide acceptance developed locally in response to food availability. New England seafood chowders and baked beans; southern pone, johnnycake, hush puppies, and other corn-based dishes; the wild rice of the Great Lakes states; Louisiana crayfish (crawfish); gumbo; and salmon and shellfish dishes of the Pacific coast are but a few of many examples of folk foods and recipes originally and still characteristic of specific cultural areas but now also—through cookbooks, television cooking shows, and supermarket products—made part of the national food experience.

In the United States, drink also represents a hybrid mixture of ethnic imports and folk adaptations. A colonial taste for rum was based on West Indian and Tidewater sugarcane and molasses. European rootstock was introduced, with mixed results, to develop vineyards in most seaboard settlements; the native scuppernong grape was tried for wine making in the South. Peach, cherry, apple, and other fruit brandies were distilled for home consumption. Whiskey was a barley-based import accompanying the Scots and the Scotch-Irish to America, particularly to the Appalachians. In the New World, the grain base became native corn, and whiskey making became a deeply rooted folk custom integral to the subsistence economy.

Whiskey also had significance in the cash economy. Small farmers of isolated areas far from markets converted part of their corn and rye crops into whiskey to produce a concentrated, low-volume, high-value commodity conveniently transportable by

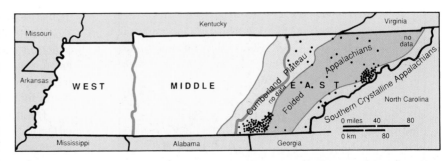

Figure 7.7 In the mid-1950s, official estimates put weekly moonshine production at 24,000 gallons in mountainous eastern Tennessee, at 6,000 gallons in partially hilly middle Tennessee, and at 2,000 gallons in flat western Tennessee. The map shows the approximate number of stills seized each month at that time in East Tennessee. Each dot indicates one still.

Source: Redrawn by permission from Loyal Durand, "Mountain Moonshining in East Tennessee," Geographical Review 46 (New York: American Geographical Society, 1956), 171. Copyright © 1956 American Geographical Society.

horseback over bad roads. Such farmers viewed a federal excise tax imposed in 1791 on the production of distilled spirits as an intolerable burden not shared by those who could sell their grain directly. The tax led first to a short-lived tax revolt, the Whiskey Rebellion of 1794 in western Pennsylvania, and subsequently to a tradition of moonshining—producing untaxed liquor in unlicensed stills. Figure 7.7 suggests the close association between its isolated Appalachian upland environment and illicit whiskey production in East Tennessee in the 1950s.

Folk Music

Folk music in North America is not merely intertwined with popular culture; it is the foundation for American popular music. In turn, American popular music that was derived from folk sources exerts a global influence that since the late 1800s has fostered both popular and folk music genres throughout the rest of the world. And those folk sources continue to serve as inspirations and themes for the commercial music industry, films and film scores, musical theater, concert music, and television. Here again, folk and popular culture intermingle and influence each other.

North American folk music with familiar Old World songs was carried by settlers to the New World. Each group of immigrants established an outpost of a European musical community, making the American folk song, in the words of Alan Lomax, "a museum of musical antiques from many lands." But the imported songs became Americanized, hybridization between musical traditions occurred, and American experience added its own songs of frontier life, of farming, courting, and laboring (see the feature "The American Empire of Song"). Eventually, distinctive American styles of folk music and recognizable folk song cultural regions developed (Figure 7.8).

The *Northern* song area—including the Maritime provinces of Canada, New England, and the Middle Atlantic states—in general featured unaccompanied solo singing in clear, hard tones. Its ballads were close to English originals, and the British connection was continuously renewed by new immigrants, including Scots and Irish. The traditional ballads and popular songs brought by British immigrants provided the largest part of the Anglo Canadian folk song heritage. On both sides of the border, the fiddle was featured at dances, and in the United States, fife-and-drum bands

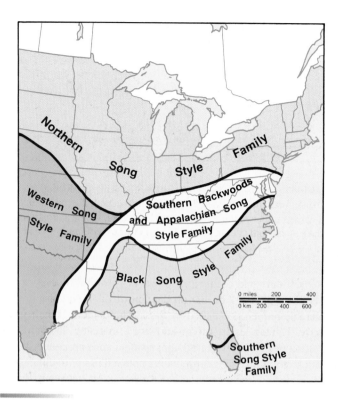

Figure 7.8 Folk song regions of eastern United States. Alan Lomax has indirectly outlined folk culture regions of the eastern United States by defining areas associated with different folk song traditions.

Source: Redrawn "Map depicting folk song regions of the Eastern U.S." by Rafael Palacios, from Folk Songs of North America *by Alan Lomax. Copyright © 1960 by Alan Lomax. Used by permission.*

and nasal solo singing. The music, based on English tradition and modified by Appalachian "hardscrabble" life, developed in isolation in upland and lowland settlement areas. Marked by moral, spiritual, emotional conflict with an undercurrent of haunting melancholy, the backwoods style emerged in the modern period as the major source for the distinctive and popular genre of "country" music.

The northern and southern traditions blended together west of the Mississippi to create the *Western* song area. There, story-telling songs reflected the experiences of the cowboy, riverman, sodbuster, and gold seeker. Natural beauty, personal valor, and feminine purity were recurring themes. Many songs appeared as reworked lumberjack ballads of the North or other modifications from the song traditions of the eastern United States.

Imported songs are more prominent among the traditional folk tunes of Canada than they are in the United States; only about one-quarter of Canadian traditional songs were composed in the New World. Most native Canadian songs—like their U.S. counterparts—reflected the daily lives of ordinary folk. In New-foundland and along the Atlantic coast, those lives were bound up with the sea, and songs of Canadian origin dealt with fishing, seal-ing, and whaling. Particularly in Ontario, it was the lumber camps that inspired and spread folk music. Anglo Canadian songs show a strong Irish character in pattern and tune and traditionally were sung solo and unaccompanied.

The *Black* folk song tradition, growing out of racial and eco-nomic oppression, reflects a union of American folk song, English country dancing, and West African musical patterns. The African American folk song of the rural South or the northern ghetto was basically choral and instrumental in character; hand clapping and foot tapping were used to establish rhythm. A strong beat, a leader-chorus style, and deep-pitched mellow voices were characteristic.

Rounding out the North American scene, there are the river and fur trader songs of the French Canadians and the strong Mexican American musical tradition in the Southwest.

Different folk music traditions metamorphosed and spread in the 20th century as distinctive styles of popular music. Jazz

became common in the early years of the Republic. Remote Cape Breton Island, off the east coast of Canada, remains a refuge of traditional Scottish folk music styles that have mostly disappeared elsewhere.

The *Southern Backwoods and Appalachian* song area, extend-ing westward to East Texas, involved unaccompanied, high-pitched,

The American Empire of Song

The map sings. The chanteys surge along the rocky Atlantic seaboard, across the Great Lakes and round the moon-curve of the Gulf of Mexico. The paddling songs of the French Canadians ring out along the Saint Lawrence and west past the Rockies. Beside them, from Newfoundland, Nova Scotia, and New England, the ballads march towards the West.

Inland from the Sea Islands, slave melo-dies sweep across the whole South, from the Carolinas to Texas. And out on the shadows of the Smoky and Blue Ridge mountains, the old ballads, lonesome love songs, and hoe-downs echo through the upland South into

the hills of Arkansas and Oklahoma. There, in the Ozarks, the Northern and Southern song families swap tunes and make a marriage.

The Texas cowboys roll the little "dough-ies" north to Montana, singing Northern bal-lads with a Southern accent. New roads and steel rails lace the Southern backwoods to the growl and thunder of Negro chants of labor— the axe songs, the hammer songs, and the rail-road songs. These blend with the lonesome hollers of levee-camp mule-skinners to cre-ate the blues, and the blues, America's *cante hondo*, uncoils its subtle, sensual melancholy in the ear of all the states, then all the world.

The blues roll down the Mississippi to New Orleans, where the Creoles mix the musical gumbo of jazz—once a dirty word, but now a symbol of musical freedom for the West. The Creoles add Spanish pepper and French sauce and blue notes to the rowdy tantara of their reconstruction-happy brass bands, stir up the hot music of New Orleans and warm the weary heart of humanity. . . . These are the broad outlines of America's folk-song map.

Source: "Introduction" from *Folk Songs of North America* by Alan Lomax. Copyright © 1960 by Alan Lomax. Used by permission of Doubleday, a division of Random House, Inc.

emerged in New Orleans in the later 19th century as a union of ragtime and the blues, a type of Southern black music based on work songs and spirituals. Urban blues—performed with a raw vocal delivery accompanied by electric guitars, harmonicas, and piano—was a Chicago creation, brought there largely by artists who had migrated from Mississippi. Country music spread from its Southern white ancestral areas with the development of the radio and the phonograph in the 20th century. It became commercialized, electrified, and amplified but retained folk music elements at its core. Bluegrass style, a high-pitched derivative of Scottish bagpipe sound and church congregational singing, is performed unamplified, true to its folk origins. Bluegrass groups often take their name from local places or landscape features, emphasizing the ties of people, performers, and the land. As these examples of musical style and tradition show, the ethnic merges into the folk and the folk blends into the popular—in music and in many other elements of culture.

Popular Culture and National Uniformities

In the early 20th century, rural America was a mosaic of unique regional cultural landscapes. Socially, the cities of the eastern and midwestern parts of the country were a world apart from life on the farm. Brash and booming with the economic success of rampant industrialization, the cities were in constant flux. Building and rebuilding, adding and absorbing immigrants and rural immigrants, increasingly interconnected by telegraph and by passenger and freight railroads, their culture and way of life were far removed from the surrounding agricultural areas.

It was in the countryside that regional cultural differentiation was most clearly seen. Although the flow of young people to the city, responding to the push of farm mechanization and the pull of urban jobs and excitement, was altering traditional social orders, the automobile, electrification, and the lively mass medium of radio had not yet obscured the distinction between urban and rural. The family farm, kinship and community ties, the traditions, ways of life, and artifacts of small town and farm existence still dominated rural life. But those ways and artifacts, and the folk cultural regions they defined, were all eroded and erased with the modernization of North American life and culture.

Regional character is transient. New immigrants, new economic challenges, and new technologies serve as catalysts of rapid change. By World War I and the Roaring Twenties, the automobile, radio, motion pictures, and a national press began to homogenize America. The slowing of the immigrant stream and assimilation of second-generation immigrants blurred some of the most regionally distinctive cultural identifications. Mechanization, mass production, and mass distribution through mail-order catalogs diminished self-sufficiency and household crafts. Popular culture began to replace traditional culture in everyday life for the majority of the population throughout the United States and Canada.

As early as the middle 19th century, women's magazines dictated taste in fashion and household furnishings, at least for urban elites. The Montgomery Ward and Sears Roebuck catalogs appearing in the late 19th century served the same purpose for more ordinary goods, garments, and classes of customers. Popular culture, based on fashions, standards, or fads developed in national centers of influence, diffused across wide areas and diverse social strata. Popular culture promises liberation through exposure to a much broader range of available opportunities—in clothing, foods, tools, recreations, and lifestyles—than the limited choices imposed by custom and isolation.

As we have seen, folk and popular culture are not necessarily opposites, although there certainly are significant differences. Folk or ethnic culture is the domain of distinctive small groups, and above all, tradition. **Popular culture,** in contrast, refers to the general mass of people, mostly urban or suburban, constantly adopting, conforming to, and quickly abandoning ever-changing trends and fads broadcast by the mass media and sold in the market economy. Even so, folk culture often forms the inspiration and backdrop for new popular cultural forms. For example, universally enjoyed popular and spectator sports such as soccer, football, golf, and tennis originated as local and regional folk games, many of them hundreds of years old.

The popular mass culture of the latter part of the 20th century that locked millions of American viewers into sharing the "must see" offerings of variety shows, situation comedies, and evening newscasts on three national television networks had largely passed by the early 21st century. It was replaced by a culture of multiple entertainment and information niches. With hundreds of cable and satellite television channels to choose from, millions of websites, proliferating social-networking Internet sites demanding attention and involvement, the mass-culture era has been transformed into one of fragmented subcultures. Individuals interact electronically with likeminded persons, become their own radio and television programmers, use their iPods, computer, and cell phone as personal media, and forego at least some of the contact with the larger society that is implied by notions of mass popular culture.

Presumably, all mass-produced consumer goods should be equally available to all segments of a society. Our travel experiences, however, have taught us that tastes and styles differ from place to place. Similar "regionalism" can be found throughout the popular culture realm. For example, while most of the world is unfamiliar with the game of cricket, it is remarkably popular in Britain and the countries of its former empire, such as Australia, India, Pakistan, South Africa, and Sri Lanka.

Popular culture uniformity is frequently, though not exclusively, associated with national populations: the American or Canadian way of life distinguished from that of the English, the Japanese, or others. Even these distinctions are eroding as popular culture in many aspects of music, movies, sports (soccer, for example), and fashion becomes internationalized (Figure 7.9). Popular culture becomes dominant with the wide dissemination of common influences and with the mixing of cultures that force both ethnic and folk communities to become part of a larger homogeneous society.

National Uniformities and Globalization

Popular culture exerts a leveling force, reducing but not eliminating locally distinctive lifestyles and material and nonmaterial cultures. Uniformity replaces diversity. Landscapes of popular culture also tend to acquire uniformity through the installation of standardized facilities. Within the United States, for example,

Figure 7.9 Scottish soccer fans. Soccer has become the world's most popular sport. The 2010 FIFA World Cup South Africa™ reached an estimated 3.2 billion people, or nearly half the world's population.

national motel chains announced by identical signs, advertised by repetitious billboards, and featuring uniform facilities and services may comfort travelers with the familiar but also denies them one of the benefits of travel—local variety. Chain gas stations, discount stores, and other enterprises offer familiar standardized products and services wherever one resides or journeys.

Other material and nonmaterial items are subject to the same widespread uniformities. The latest movies are simultaneously released throughout the country; the same children's toys and adults' games are everywhere instantly available to satisfy the generated wants.

Wilbur Zelinsky reported on the speed of diffusion of a manufactured desire:

> In August, 1958, I drove from Santa Monica, California, to Detroit at an average rate of about 400 miles (650 km) per day; and display windows in almost every drugstore and variety store along the way were being hastily stocked with hula hoops just off the delivery trucks from Southern California. A national television program the week before had roused instant cravings. It was an eerie sensation, surfing along a pseudo-innovation wave.[1]

Many of these North American elements of popular culture are oriented toward the automobile, the ubiquitous means of local

and interregional travel. Advertising and distinctive design assures instant recognition as chain outlets cluster along highway retail strips, guaranteeing that whatever regional character still remains, the commercial areas are everywhere the same—*placeless.* Critics perceive that the diffusion of popular culture promotes **placelessness,** the replacement of local identity and variety with a homogeneous and standardized landscape. Increasingly, news reports bring us stories of communities protesting the arrival of a Wal-Mart "big box" store, the multiplication of uniform highway strip malls, and the like. For some people, that uniformity and loss of local control is unacceptable, and individuals and whole communities fight the pervasive influence of popular culture. For these protesters, the modernity of popular culture destroys valuable traditions, unique local identities, and a way of life that is perhaps more in tune with place and the environment. In its defense, popular culture brings a cultural uniformity that is vastly richer in choices than that which was lost.

Those uniformities are transitory. While folk cultures have ingrained traditions that change only slowly and locally, popular culture tends to change rapidly and uniformly over wide expanses. That is, popular culture diffuses rapidly, even instantaneously, in our age of immediate global communication and sharing of ideas through television, radio, and the Internet. Those same media and means assure the widespread quick replacement of old fads with new. The globalization of popular culture is seen in the diffusion of brands and styles of clothing, food and drink, the near-universal display of American movies and television shows, and worldwide acceptance of the cultural norms of urban life and Western business conduct.

The globalization of popular culture is increasingly evident. Imagine this scene: Wearing a Yankees baseball cap, a Hollister shirt, Abercrombie and Fitch jeans, and Nike shoes, a middle-class teenager in Shanghai, China, goes with his friends to see the latest Hollywood release. After the movie, he uses his smart phone to text-message his mother that they plan to eat at a nearby McDonald's. Meanwhile, his sister sits at home, listening to the latest American music on her iPod, uploading pictures to Facebook while playing multiplayer video games with gamers from around the world. The activities of both young people are evidence of the globalization of popular culture that is Western and particularly—though certainly not invariably—American in origin. U.S. movies, television shows, software, music, food, brand names, and fashions are marketed worldwide. They influence the beliefs, tastes, and aspirations of people in virtually every country, though their effect is most pronounced on the young. They, rather than their elders, want to emulate the stars in movies and popular music. They are also the group most apt to use English words and slang in everyday conversation, though the use of English as the worldwide language of communication in economics, technology, and science is an even broader indication of current cultural merging.

Rapid introduction and quickly falling prices of high-tech communication and entertainment devices have had a profound effect on lifestyles wherever personal freedom and Westernized economies, incomes, and cultures prevail. These new communication technologies speed the diffusion of popular culture and expand opportunities for education, recreation, and information. Africa has lagged the rest of the world in telecommunications access because

[1]*The Cultural Geography of the United States.* Rev. ed. (Englewood Cliffs, N.J.: Prentice-Hall, 1992), p. 80, fn 18.

it lacked landline telephone networks in many areas. But with the advent of prepaid mobile phones, Africa has begun to catch up. It would be a mistake to believe that the United States leads in the adoption and development of new communication technologies. Europe leads the United States in the adoption of mobile telephones, and residential broadband Internet service is substantially faster in Japan and South Korea than in the United States.

Popular Food and Drink

Fast-food restaurants—franchised or corporate owned—use a standardized logo, building design, and menu across cultural and political borders (Figure 7.10). With large budgets for advertising and expansion, they are major carriers of the globalization of popular culture. For communities outside the mainstream of popular culture, their arrival is a status symbol. For the traveler, they provide the assurance of a known product, at the cost of insulating the palate from the regionally distinctive. Even food outlets identified with ethnic identities tend to lose their cultural character. Pizza has become American, not Italian (Figure 7.11), just as the franchised

Figure 7.10 Western fast-food chains, classics of standardized popular culture, have gone international—and bilingual—as this KFC outlet in Xian, China, reveals.

Mexican American taco and burrito have escaped their regional and ethnic confines and been carried nationwide and worldwide.

Starting in the 1990s, specialty coffee establishments serving cappuccinos, lattes, and other variants became common features of airports, shopping malls, bookstores, convenience stores, and mobile stands in urban places large and small. Like other globalized products, specialty coffee has a distinct geography and place identity. Drinking coffee connects consumers to the world, offering the sensation of globe-trotting by purchasing beans from Sumatra, Colombia, Kenya, or Ethiopia. The American hearth region for the specialty coffee culture was Seattle, Washington, the original home of Starbucks, the most prominent corporate identity in the trade. Starbucks was established in 1971 in Seattle's Pike Place Market, an eclectic public market and distinctive local landmark, popular with both tourists and locals. Starbucks didn't invent specialty coffee but was inspired by the espresso bars of Milan, Italy. Of course, the Italians didn't invent coffee either—the crop was first domesticated in present-day Ethiopia. Today, Starbucks has 16,000 stores in 48 countries and continues to spread, an expansion diffusion process that is not universally appreciated (Figure 7.12).

The standardization brought about by globalized popular culture, of course, is not complete. Seemingly universal popular icons are always differentially adapted and modified for easy acceptance by different national societies. The term **glocalization** describes this adaptation of globalized products to fit local contexts. Regional food and drink preferences persist. Domino's and Pizza Hut, for example, have a combined total of some 6,000 overseas outlets in over 100 countries, but they do not serve a standard product worldwide. In India, customers likely will order their pizza with spicy chicken sausage or pickled ginger. In Japan, a best seller is pizza topped with potatoes, mayonnaise, and ham or bacon bits. Hong Kong customers prefer their pizza flavoring to be Cajun spices; Thais favor hot spices mixed with lemon grass and lime; and in Australia, the number one topping for pizza is eggs. McDonald's sells the Chicken Maharaja Mac, McVeggie and McCurry Pan in India, kosher Big Macs in Israel, and beer in Germany. Outside the United States, McDonald's advertising emphasizes the use of products from local farms. The store name and logo may be universal, but the product varies to fit local tastes.

In contrast to the standardization of popular food and drink, there has been a movement termed **neolocalism** that emphasizes a return to local or regional food and drink products and a rejection of more homogeneous national and global products. Neolocalism cultivates a distinctive local place identity and can be seen in the popularity of microbrewed beer. Beer was once a local product before refrigeration, interstate highways, national advertising, and industry mergers concentrated production in the hands of two companies, Anheuser Busch and Miller, both located in interior cities with large German immigrant populations, St. Louis and Milwaukee. By contrast, the source or hearth for the microbrewery or craft beer movement in the late 1980s was the West, specifically the Colorado Front Range cities, the San Francisco area, and the coastal cities of Oregon and Washington. The spatial distribution of the approximately 1,500 small-scale microbreweries in the United States, for example, is not uniform across the country but exhibits regional concentrations (Figure 7.13). The names and labels used in microbrewed beers, as well as the decor inside the

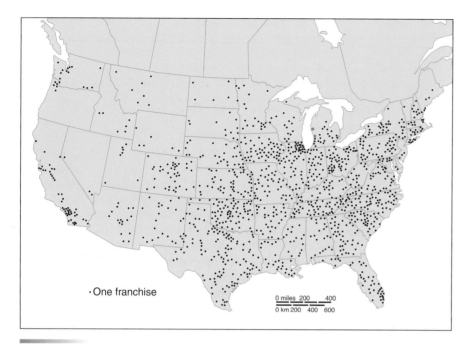

Figure 7.11 The locations of pizza parlors of a single national chain.

Source: Floyd M. Henderson and J. Russel, unpublished drawing.

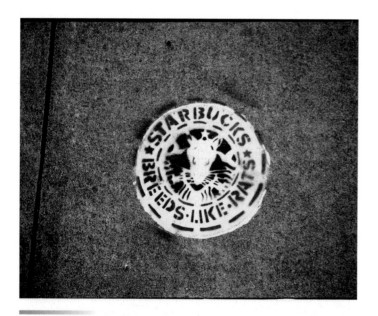

Figure 7.12 Anti-Starbucks graffito on a San Francisco sidewalk contesting the corporate homogenization of the urban landscape.

brew pubs, are often based on local history, landmarks, or distinctive landscapes that create and strengthen the product's place identity (Figure 7.14). For fans, drinking a microbrewed beer is a way of demonstrating one's attachment and loyalty to the local region.

Popular Music and Dance

The music and dance styles of folk and popular culture and high-status and low-status groups intertwine in complex ways. For example, the waltz began as a folk dance in Austria and southern Germany, was refined into an elite style of dance in Vienna, diffused through the cities of Europe and the Americas, and finally sparked a popular culture craze among the rising middle and working classes.

In popular music and dance, geography still matters. Differences in regional tastes and hearth regions for innovation are evident. Music is symbolically expressive of the experiences and emotions of people with particular geographic and group identities. Country music lyrics, for example, contain themes that resonate with the experience of the rural working class. At the local scale, both rap and grunge originated as expressions of the alienation felt by particular segments of the youth population in the Bronx and in Seattle, respectively. And regional musical expressions of culture include Cajun music of south Louisiana, Tejano music of the TexMex borderlands, and the polka of the Upper Midwest. To enter the popular and mass cultural spheres, however, particular regional genres of music must diffuse at the national and global scales and, in turn, be modified to express the collective cultural identities of people occupying different spaces and places. Country music, we saw, was culturally associated with the Upland South. It has long since lost that regional exclusivity, and Nashville has become a product, not a place. By the late 1970s (Figure 7.15), no American with access to radio was denied exposure to slide guitar and melancholy lyrics.

Globalization of popular music with folk culture roots is clearly demonstrated by "world music." It is usually described as music strongly rooted in the folk and/or ethnic traditions of non-Western cultures but often blended with Western music to retain its sense of the exotic and yet be acceptable to Western tastes. Originally used to describe music from Africa and its diaspora in the New World, the term *world music* now more broadly includes the music of folk, ethnic, and minority groups in any culture. Much of world music is hybrid in nature, a fusion of various music genres from different global origins. In that blending process, local musical forms are "deterritorialized" and globalized, taking on transnational and cross-cultural characteristics not tied to a single culture or location. World music, then, not only establishes African, West Indian, or Asian music in Western popular culture but creates new combinations and syncretisms such as Afro-Celtic, a fusion of African rhythms with traditional Celtic folk music, or reggae. World music also broadens the awareness and modifies the purity of such Western ethnic or folk genres as Celtic, zydeco, klezmer, Rom, bluegrass, jazz, and others. Whatever its folk, cultural, or national origin, world music represents a process of transformation of the musically unique and "other" into forms accepted by globalized popular culture.

Although popularly perceived as an authentic Jamaican music form, reggae displayed the hybrid and globalized character of world music even before that separate music category was recognized. Reggae is a fusion of African rhythms, earlier Caribbean music forms such as ska and rock steady, and European melodies

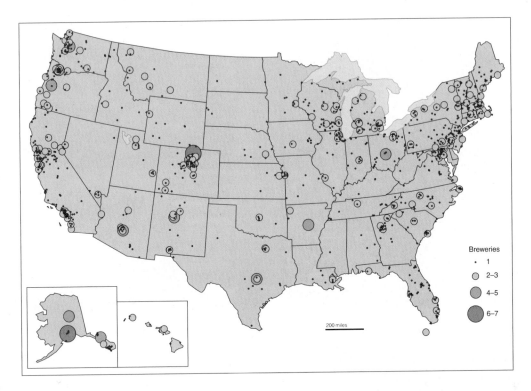

Figure 7.13 **Microbreweries by zip code, 2002.** Heavy concentrations of microbreweries are found in the source regions of the West.

Source: "Microbreweries as Tools of Local Identity," by Steven M. Schnell and Joseph F. Reese from Journal of Cultural Geography, *21, 1 (2003), Figure 1, 50. Reprinted by permission of JCG Press.*

Hip-Hop Undergoes Globalization and Glocalization

Unlike the distant folk background of some world music, the beginnings of hip-hop culture are recent and easily plotted on the map. Hip-hop culture emerged in the Bronx borough of New York City in the 1970s at a time when the South Bronx was undergoing a massive downward spiral. The disruptive Cross-Bronx expressway had been sliced through the neighborhood, the middle class was fleeing to the suburbs, manufacturing jobs were disappearing by the thousands, the city teetered on the edge of bankruptcy, and it had cut back essential services to the South Bronx. Many landlords responded by abandoning their tenement buildings, sometimes setting them afire to collect insurance money. Out of this urban wasteland arose hip-hop culture. DJs at dance clubs and in street parties began stylized talking with a simple four-count beat—which became known as rapping—over a background of funk rock and disco music. Hip-hop culture, which involves rap music, DJs, graffiti, and break dancing, exhibits West African and Jamaican influences and is a contemporary expression of older forms of "talking music," such as spirituals, work songs, talkin' country blues, and the rhythmic sermons of black preachers. From these beginnings, rap developed as underground "protest music," with lyrics voicing the experiences of socially and economically disadvantaged black and Latino youth—alienation, police harassment, drug use, sexual conduct, race relations, and the like. Themes of place, home, and identity abound in rap music, with many songs depicting life in the "hood."

From its hearth in New York City, hip-hop diffused to a second center in Los Angeles (particularly the suburb of Compton) where "gangsta" or "reality" rap developed. Subsequently, hip-hop spread nationally to suburbs and corporate boardrooms, becoming the biggest-selling genre of popular music in America. Other centers of rap music have emerged, such as the South Coast region (including Atlanta, New Orleans, Miami, and Memphis) and a Midwest region (centered on Detroit). Rap music has often been controversial due to lyrics and imagery that frequently celebrate violence, hopelessness, and the oppression of women. For example, among Tibetan immigrant youth, the adoption of hip-hop culture has generated objections because of negative stereotypes and its associations with the black underclass. Hip-hop has also diffused globally and undergone *glocalization*—adaptation to suit local cultures and experiences. In Cuba, popular rap lyrics have protested racial discrimination and inequality that wasn't supposed to exist in Fidel Castro's Cuba. In Mexico, rapper Control Machete has written lyrics that denounce U.S. border controls, while Colombian rap group La Etnia deals with poverty, prostitution, homelessness, and violence in their lyrics. In Germany, community centers became sites for the spread of hip-hop culture among both native and immigrant youth. And from the Americas to South Africa, black youth have used hip-hop as a way to forge a black identity that spans the Atlantic.

Sources: Arlene Tickner, "Aqui en el Ghetto: Hip Hop in Colombia, Cuba, and Mexico," *Latin American Politics and Society,* 50(3):121–146 (2008); Emily Yeh and Kunga Lama, "Hip-hop Gangsta or Most Deserving of Victims? Transnational Migrant Identities and the Paradox of Tibetan Racialization in the USA," *Environment and Planning A,* 2006, 38: 809–829; Marc Perry, "Global Black Self-Fashionings: Hip Hop as Diasporic Space," Identities: *Global Studies in Culture and Power,* 2008, 15: 635–664.

Figure 7.14 Microbrews work to cultivate a regional identity in order to compete with national and international brands. They draw upon their customer's sense of place, often using images of distinctive local landscapes and emphasizing the use of local ingredients.

with pronounced influences from modern American jazz, rhythm blues, and soul. As employed by Rastafarians (members of an African-originated religion associated with the poorer black population of Jamaica), reggae lyrics often address issues of poverty, subordination, oppression, black pride, and pan-Africanism. The globalization of reggae music, however, depended on contracts with the internationalized entertainment industry to package and market the reggae product.

Reggae first diffused to England from Jamaica in the early 1970s, taken up by Jamaicans who migrated there in the 1950s

and 1960s. In Britain, lyrics were modified to express the place-specific immigrant experience of West Indian neighborhoods. Much like the commercialization of rock and roll from its black rhythm and blues roots in America, the mainstreaming of reggae in Britain involved its adoption by white British bands. In that process, reggae as a musical platform of cultural protest was transformed into a cultural commodity that helped reggae reach beyond the Afro-Caribbean community.

The emergence of reggae as a global commodity is identified with Bob Marley's 1972 album *Catch a Fire*. In recording

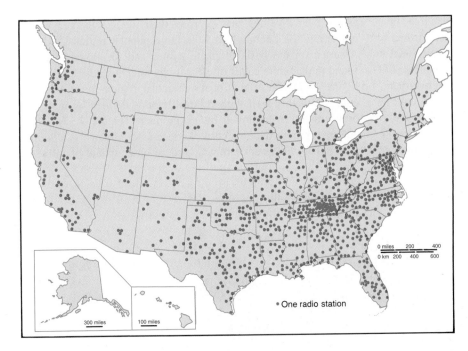

Figure 7.15 Country music radio stations.
Although still most heavily concentrated in the Upland South, radio stations playing only country music had become a national commonplace by the late 1970s.

Source: Redrawn by permission from George O. Carney, "From Down Home to Uptown," Journal of Geography, *76 (Indiana, PA: National Council for Geographic Education, 1977), 107.*

sessions, however, London-based Island Records thought the album's music was too "Jamaican," and an alternative rock album with a strong roots reggae sound was produced. The global was thus fused with the local. To stress the local, however, the record and CD covers purposefully portrayed "dreadlocked revolutionaries" to authenticate their exotic place origins to Western consumers. For a more recent example of the connections between the local and the global in popular music, see the feature "Hip-Hop Undergoes Globalization and Glocalization."

Reactions Against Globalized Popular Culture

As we have seen in the case of popular food, drink, and music, the globalization of popular culture does not erase all regional differences. Globalization of popular culture generates counterreactions. Just as speakers of minority languages have resisted the dominance of English, the globalization of popular culture is resented by many people, rejected by some, and officially opposed or controlled by certain governments. The Canadian government imposes minimum "Canadian content" requirements on television and radio broadcasters, for example, and Iran, Singapore, China, and other states attempt to restrict Western radio and television programming from reaching their people. Governments of many countries—China, Cuba, Iran, Myanmar, North Korea, Saudi Arabia, Syria, Turkmenistan, Uzbekistan, and Vietnam among them—impose pervasive Internet surveillance and censorship and demand that U.S.-based search engines filter content to conform with official restrictions and limitations. Many more countries impose partial censorship on the Internet.

In other instances, religious and cultural conservatives may decry what they see as the imposition of Western values, norms, and excesses through such mass culture industries as advertising, the media, professional sports, and the like. Whether or not movies, music, television programming, or clothing fads accurately reflect the essence of Western culture, critics argue that they force on other societies alien values of materialism, violence, self-indulgence, sexual promiscuity, and defiance of authority and tradition. More basically, perhaps, globalization of popular culture is seen as a form of dominance made possible by Western control of the means of communication and by Western technical, educational, and economic superiority. What may be accepted or sought by the young and better educated in many societies may simultaneously be strongly resisted by those of the same societies more traditional in outlook and belief.

Regional Differences and Culture Regions

Of course, not all expressions of popular culture are spatially or socially uniform. Areal variations do exist in the extent to which particular elements of popular culture are adopted. Spatial patterns in sports, for example, reveal that the games played, the migration paths of their fans and players, and the sports landscape constitutes part of the geographic diversity of the world. For example, Brazil is a hotbed for soccer, the Dominican Republic for baseball, and Canada still dominates the production of hockey players, despite the increasing globalization of these sports. Figure 7.16a, for example, shows that television interest in professional baseball is not universal despite the sport's reputation as "the national pastime." Studies and maps of many regional differences in food and drink preferences, leisure activities, and personal and political tastes such as Figure 7.16 are important to marketers and demonstrate ongoing regional contrasts along with the commonalities of popular culture (see the feature "Lifestyle Segmentation").

Ordinary people have a clear view of space. They are aware of variations from place to place in the mix of phenomena, both physical and cultural. They use and recognize as meaningful such common regional names as Corn Belt, Sunbelt, and "the Coast."

More important, people individually and collectively agree on where they live. They occupy regions that have reality in their minds and that are reflected in regional journals, in regional museums, and in regionally based names employed in businesses, by sports teams, or in advertising slogans. These are **vernacular** or **popular regions;** they have reality as part of folk or popular culture rather than as political impositions or scholarly constructs. Geographers are increasingly recognizing that vernacular regions are significant concepts affecting the way people view space,

assign their loyalties, and interpret their world. One geographer has drawn the boundaries of the large popular regions of North America on the basis of place names and locational identities found in the white pages of central-city telephone directories (see Figure 1.17). The subnational vernacular regions recognized accord reasonably well with cultural regions defined by more rigorous methods employed by geographers (Figure 7.17). These culture regions contain a core of concentrated intensity, a domain where that culture is dominant, and an outer sphere of influence

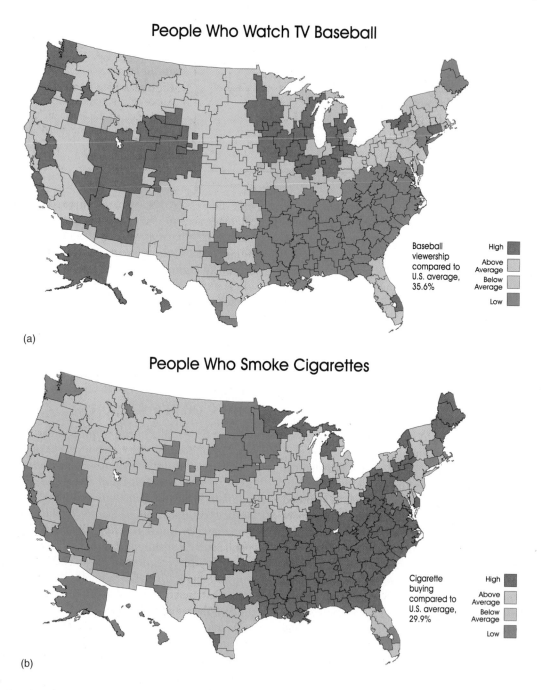

Figure 7.16 Regional variations in expressions of popular culture. (*a*) Part of the regional variation in television viewing of baseball reflects the game's lack of appeal in the African American community and, therefore, its low viewership in the South and in metropolitan centers where, in addition, attendance at games is an alternative to watching TV. (*b*) Even bad habits regionalize. The country's cigarette belt includes many of the rural areas where tobacco is grown.

Source: From Michael J. Weiss, Latitudes and Attitudes: An Atlas of American Tastes, Trends, Politics and Passions, *Boston: Little, Brown and Company, 1994. Used by permission of the author.*

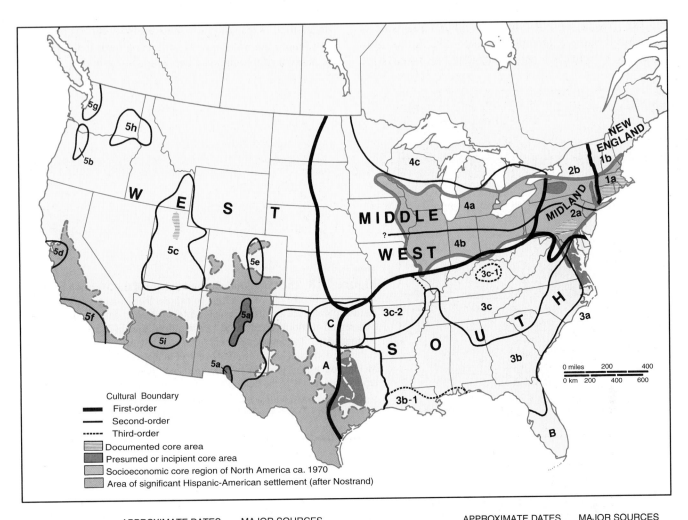

REGION	APPROXIMATE DATES OF SETTLEMENT AND FORMATION	MAJOR SOURCES OF CULTURE (listed in order of importance)
NEW ENGLAND		
1a. Nuclear New England	1620–1750	England
1b. Northern New England	1750–1830	Nuclear New England, England
THE MIDLAND		
2a. Pennsylvania Region	1682–1850	England and Wales, Rhineland, Ulster,19th-Century Europe
2b. New York Region or New England Extended	1624–1830	Great Britain, New England, 19th-Century Europe, Netherlands
THE SOUTH		
3a. Early British Colonial South	1607–1750	England, Africa, British West Indies
3b. Lowland or Deep South	1700–1850	Great Britain, Africa, Midland, Early British Colonial South, aborigines
3b-1. French Louisiana	1700–1760	France, Deep South, Africa, French West Indies
3c. Upland South	1700–1850	Midland, Lowland South, Great Britain
3c-1. The Bluegrass	1770–1800	Upland South, Lowland South
3c-2. The Ozarks	1820–1860	Upland South, Lowland South, Lower Middle West
THE MIDDLE WEST		
4a. Upper Middle West	1800–1880	New England Extended, New England,19th-Century Europe, British Canada
4b. Lower Middle West	1790–1870	Midland, Upland South, New England Extended, 19th-Century Europe
4c. Cutover Area	1850–1900	Upper Middle West, 19th-Century Europe

REGION	APPROXIMATE DATES OF SETTLEMENT AND FORMATION	MAJOR SOURCES OF CULTURE (listed in order of importance)
THE WEST		
5a. Upper Rio Grande Valley	1590–	Mexico, Anglo America, aborigines
5b. Willamette Valley	1830–1900	Northeast U.S.
5c. Mormon Region	1847–1890	Northeast U.S., 19th-Century Europe
5d. Central California	(1775–1848) 1840–	(Mexico) Eastern U.S., 19th Century Europe, Mexico, East Asia
5e. Colorado Piedmont	1860–	Eastern U.S., Mexico
5f. Southern California	(1760–1848) 1880–	(Mexico) Eastern U.S., 19th and 20th-Century Europe, Mormon Region, Mexico, East Asia
5g. Puget Sound	1870–	Eastern U.S., 19th and 20th-Century Europe, East Asia
5h. Inland Empire	1880–	Eastern U.S., 19th and 20th-Century Europe
5i. Central Arizona	1900–	Eastern U.S., Southern California, Mexico
REGIONS OF UNCERTAIN STATUS OR AFFILIATION		
A. Texas	(1690–1836) 1821–	(Mexico) Lowland South, Upland South, Mexico, 19th-Century Central Europe
B. Peninsular Florida	1880–	Northeast U.S., the South, 20th-Century Europe, Antilles
C. Oklahoma	1890–	Upland South, Lowland South, aborigines, Middle West

Figure 7.17 Culture areas of the United States based on multiple lines of evidence.

Source: From Wilbur Zelinsky, The Cultural Geography of the United States, *Rev. ed., 1992, 118–119. Redrawn by permission of Prentice-Hall, Inc., Upper Saddle River, NJ.*

(Figure 7.18). Another, more subjective cultural regionalization of the United States is offered in Figure 7.19. The generalized "consensus" or vernacular regions suggested are based on an understood "sense of place" derived from current population and landscape characteristics, as well as on historical differences that impart distinctive regional behaviors and attitudes.

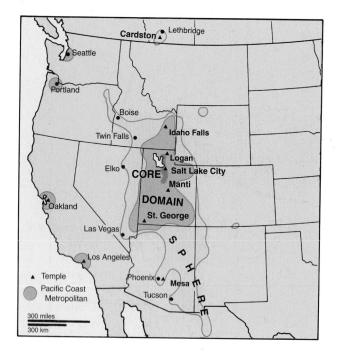

Figure 7.18 **The Core, Domain, and Sphere of the Mormon culture region** as defined by D. W. Meinig. To express the spatial gradation in Mormon cultural dominance and its diffusion, Professor Meinig defined the Salt Lake City *core* region of Mormon culture as "a centralized zone of concentration . . . and homogeneity." The broader concept of *domain* identifies "areas in which the . . . culture is dominant" but less intensive than in the core. The *sphere* of any culture, Meinig suggests, is the zone of outer influence, where only parts of the culture are represented or where the culture's adherents are a minority of the total population.

Source: Redrawn with permission from Annals of the Association of American Geographers, *D. W. Meinig, Vol. 55, 214, Association of American Geographers, 1965.*

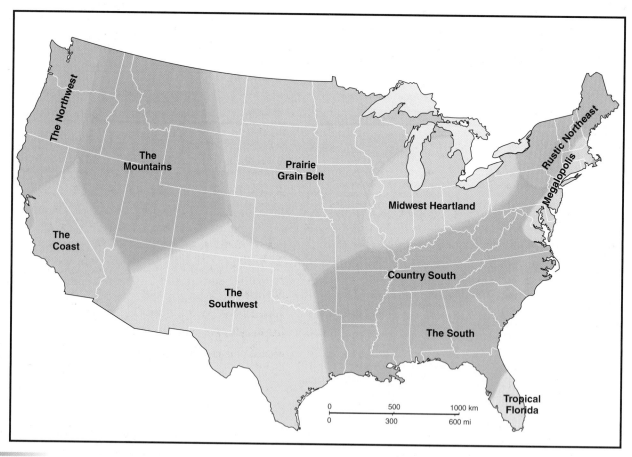

Figure 7.19 **Generalized U.S. culture regions.** "In spite of strong tendencies toward cultural homogenization and place obliteration, . . . regional identities persist," in the view of geographer Larry Ford, who suggests the 11 culture regions shown. Whatever the reasons for that persistence, "the different [culture] regions of the United States continue to have their own personalities and senses of place."

Cultural Landscapes

Folk and popular cultures involve more than food, drink, music, and folklore. Cultures make a distinct impression on the landscape, as they fashion the raw material of the natural landscape into a human habitat. Influential geographer Carl Sauer described it as follows:

> The cultural landscape is fashioned from a natural landscape by a culture group. Culture is the agent, the natural area is the medium, the cultural landscape is the result.[2]

Landscapes are more than pretty scenes: They are all around us, and they tell us a great deal about those who shaped them. The **cultural landscape** is a blended work of nature and culture and offers some of the best evidence of human-environment interactions. American geographer Peirce Lewis wrote,

> "[O]ur human landscape is our unwitting autobiography, reflecting our tastes, our values, our aspirations, and even our fears, in tangible visible form."[3]

In other words, the everyday landscape—farms, gardens, suburbs, cemeteries, trailer parks, shopping malls, and more—offers the savvy observer important insights into a culture's attitudes, priorities, and way of life. While a highway lined with billboards, neon signs, and fast food restaurants is designed to communicate messages to all who pass by, many landscapes are just there. Nonetheless, all landscapes can be "read" and interpreted. For example, a cemetery tells us something about how a culture approaches death, and a derelict trailer park hidden on the "wrong side of the tracks" says something about a society's way of dealing with economic inequality. As students of geography, we develop a vocabulary and basic skills to begin a lifetime of reading the landscape, interpreting its messages, and attempting to understand the culture that produced it.

National and regional cultural identities remain embedded in urban and rural landscapes (Figure 7.20a). Certain landmarks and landscapes take on special significance in the identity, emotions, and politics of a country. In the United States, politicians use the rhetoric of "Main Street" and "Wall Street," referring to places that really exist but are also deeply symbolic and associated with particular vices or virtues (Figure 7.20b). Landmarks come to symbolize a city in the mental imagery of residents and tourists alike. London's Big Ben, Paris's Eiffel Tower, New York's Statue of Liberty, and Sydney's Opera House are just a few examples of symbolic landmarks. Symbolic landscapes and landmarks have great emotional power and are often used in advertising images and political speeches. Not surprisingly then, the targets of the September 11, 2001, terrorist attacks were the World Trade Center and the Pentagon, landscape symbols of economic globalization and U.S. military power. And again, not surprisingly, the 2011 Occupy movement began with the very symbolic occupation of Wall Street by protesters.

Time is an important element in the creation of cultural landscapes. Both urban and rural landscapes, especially those in Europe and Asia, bear the imprint of human reshaping over thousands of years of use. Today's largest cities are often located on the site of ancient settlements. The **sequential occupation** of the landscape by different groups of people almost always leaves behind visible traces, some of which influence future human uses of the land. Ancient paths and roads have often become the busy streets of the contemporary world. The trace of ancient medieval walls remains visible as circular parkways in many European cities. The routes of abandoned railroad lines are often reused for trail networks. Thus, the landscape has been compared to a **palimpsest**—an ancient goatskin or sheepskin document that has been written on over and over again, with the earlier writings scraped away. Just as historians attempt to read the faint traces of earlier writings on a palimpsest, geographers look to the landscape for visible traces of the past (see Figure 7.20c).

Elite landscapes communicate the refined taste and exclusivity of society's most privileged and powerful members. Through imposing architecture, gardens, and gates and the generous use of space, elite landscapes communicate sophistication, power, and status (Figure 7.20d), Vernacular or ordinary landscapes of houses, trailer parks, roadside motels, and fast food restaurants are equally important to the geographer seeking to understand a culture (Figure 7.20e). Derelict landscapes—abandoned buildings, rusting factories, broken windows, overgrown lots—speak to the cultural geographer of change, decay, and a culture's attitude toward progress and the past (Figure 7.20f).

While learning to pay attention to and interpret cultural landscapes is among the pleasures of geography and a source of important insights, we must remember that much remains hidden. Geographer Don Mitchell reminds us of how the landscape works to normalize a particular set of social relationships—relationships that may be unjust or unhealthy. For example, the fertile fields of California's Central Valley communicate a message of prosperity emerging from the harmonious human cultivation of the Earth. Hidden from view, however, are the shacks of exploited migrant workers and the dangerous pesticides, herbicides, and fertilizers that make that productive landscape possible. In the remainder of this chapter, we explore two major elements of the cultural landscape: systems for surveying and dividing land and the houses built in different times and places. We then examine a sampling of different types of landscapes: places of consumption and heritage landscapes.

Land Survey Systems

Flying over North America, one sees a distinct difference between the checkerboard fields of the Midwest, the narrow fields of southern Quebec, and the irregular shaped fields of the Atlantic Seaboard. These differences stem from different land survey systems. In a capitalist system, the division of land into individual holdings is necessary for both agricultural and urban development. The charter group settling an area had to create a system for surveying, dividing, claiming, and allocating land and that system leaves a lasting legacy, shaping the look and feel of both rural and urban landscapes.

---

[2]Carl Sauer, *The Morphology of Landscape*, University of California Publications in Geography Number 22, 1925, 19–53.
[3]Peirce Lewis, "Axioms for Reading the Landscape: Some Guides to the American Scene," in *The Interpretation of Ordinary Landscapes*, D. W. Meinig and F. B. Jackson, eds., Oxford: Oxford University Press 1979, 12.

Figure 7.22 A portion of the Vincennes, Indiana–Illinois, topographic quadrangle (1944) showing evidence of the original French long-lot survey. Note the importance of the Wabash River in both long-lot and Vincennes street-system orientations. This U.S. Geological Survey map was originally published at the fractional scale of 1:62,500.

Source: U.S. Geological Survey map.

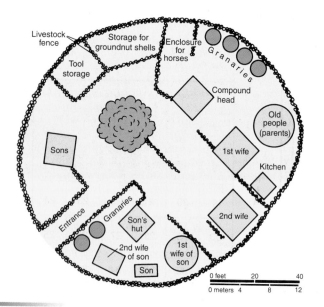

Figure 7.23 The extended family compound of the Bambara of Mali.

Source: Redrawn with permission from Reuben K. Udo, The Human Geography of Tropical Africa *(Ibadan: Heinemann Education Books (Nigeria) Ltd., 1982), 50.*

produce the dispersed pattern of isolated farmsteads that typifies the rural United States and English Canada (Figure 7.24b). It is an arrangement conditioned by the block pattern of land survey, by the homesteading tradition of "proving up" claims through living on them, and the regular pattern of rural roads. The dispersed rural settlement pattern for much of the United States both reflects and reinforces the individualism of U.S. culture.

Other survey systems permitted different culturally rooted settlement choices. The New England village reflected the transplanting of an English tradition. The central village, with its meeting house and its commons area, was surrounded by larger fields subdivided into strips for allocation among the community members. The result was a distinctive pattern of nucleated agricultural villages and fragmented farms. Agricultural villages were found as well in Mormon settlement areas, in the Spanish American Southwest, and as part of the cultural landscapes established by utopian religious communities, such as the Oneida Community of New York; the Rappites's Harmony, Indiana; Fountain Grove, California; and others. On the prairies of Canada, the Mennonites were granted lands not as individuals, but as communities. Their agricultural villages with surrounding communal fields (Figure 7.24c) reflected their religious ideals and re-created in Manitoba the landscape of their European homelands.

The spatial pattern of streets, blocks, and lots exerts a major influence on the feel and social life of urban settlements. Urban street grids may be irregular, rectangular, or contain winding loops and lollipops. Irregular street grids are common in areas of metes-and-bounds surveying, and a rectangular street grid can be easily created in areas of rectangular surveying. The rectangular grid dates back to Greek city planning in the 5th century B.C. and was the norm in North American town plans created before World War II. The best-known rectangular street grid is the 1811 New York City plan with 11 major avenues and 155 perpendicular crosstown streets in Manhattan. Frederick Law Olmsted, the designer of Central Park and many other famous urban parks, created elite, romantic suburbs in the 1800s using winding, picturesque streets and detached single-family houses on large lots. After World War II, middle-class housing developers copied the look of elite suburbs and created the street pattern of loops and lollipops and that typifies most North American suburbs. While often attacked by transportation planners, the winding, dead-end streets of contemporary suburbs reflect the cultural ideal of the house as a quiet, private retreat.

Houses

Houses are among the most important material expressions of a culture and most visible features of the cultural landscape. Nearly a century ago, French geographer Jean Brunhes called houses a "central fact" of human geography. Using Abraham Maslow's hierarchy of human needs as a framework, we can see that houses meet both basic and higher-level human needs. Houses meet physiological needs for shelter, safety needs for the protection of one's person and property, and needs for belonging by placing individuals within a household and a community. At the higher end of the needs hierarchy, houses meet needs for self-esteem by serving as a marker of achievement, and they meet self-actualization and

Figure 7.24 **Contrasting land survey and settlement systems in Canada.** Adjacent areas of Canada demonstrate the effects of different survey systems and cultural heritages on rural settlement patterns. The long-lot survey of Quebec in French Canada (left map) creates a linear village. The regular plots of Ontario in English Canada (center map) display the isolated farmsteads that are characteristic of much of the United States and Canada. The German-speaking Mennonites, a Protestant Christian group, settled in Manitoba in the 1870s. They created an agricultural village that reflected the group's European homeland and strong emphasis on community (right map). Individual farmers were granted strip holdings in the separate fields to be farmed in common with the other villagers. The farmsteads themselves, with elongated rear lots, were aligned along both sides of a single village street in an Old World pattern.

Source: Redrawn by permission from Annals of the Association of American Geographers, *George I. McDermott, Vol. 51, 263, Association of American Geographers, 1961; and from Carl A. Dawson,* Group Settlement: Ethnic Communities in Western Canada, *Vol. 7,* Canada Frontiers of Settlement *(Toronto: Macmillan Company of Canada, 1936), 111.*

self-expression needs through their design, color, and interior and exterior decor.

Vernacular house styles—those built in traditional form but without formal architectural plans or drawings—are of particular interest to cultural geographers. Throughout the world, folk societies established types of housing appropriate to their economic and family needs, available materials and technologies, and local environmental conditions. Thus, folk housing is wonderfully diverse, reflecting ingenious adaptations to local conditions. Industrialization, transportation improvements, and the influences of popular culture have revolutionized styles of house construction so that today, there is more diversity in a given place but fewer differences between places. In some cases, folk housing styles are being revisited as contemporary homebuyers attempt to recover a local sense of place and/or reduce the amount of energy used to heat and cool their houses.

The Mongol or Turkic *yurt* or *ger,* a movable low, rounded shelter made of felt, skin, short poles, and rope, is a housing solution well adapted to the needs and materials of nomadic herdsmen of the Asian grasslands (Figure 7.25a). A similar solution with different materials is reached by the Maasai, another nomadic herding society living on the grasslands of eastern Africa. Their temporary home was traditionally the *manyatta,* an immovable low, rounded hut made of poles, mud, and cow dung that was abandoned as soon as local grazing and water supplies were consumed (Figure 7.25b). As the structures in Figure 7.25 suggest, folk housing solutions in design and materials provide a worldwide mosaic of nearly infinite diversity and ingenuity.

America, like every other world region, had its own indigenous vernacular architecture (Figure 7.26). This was the architecture of Amerindians—the bark houses of the Penobscots, the long houses of the Iroquois, the tipis of the Crow, the mounds of the Mandans, the pueblos of the Zuñi, the hogans of the Navajos, and the plank dwellings of Puget Sound. Despite their elegance and suitability for particular environments, these styles were largely swept away by European settlers. The primary exception is the thick-walled pueblos, which are much more comfortable in desert climates than the wood structures built by some European settlers.

Hearths and Diffusion Streams

Within the United States and Canada, the variety of ethnic and regional origins of immigrants and the differences in environmental conditions led to architectural contrasts between the settlement hearths of the Atlantic Seaboard. The landscapes of structures and settlements creating those contrasts speak to us of their creators' origins, travels, adaptations to new locales, and retention of the customs of other places. The folk cultural heritage is now passing; old farm structures are replaced or collapse with disuse as farming systems change. Old houses are torn down, remodeled, or abandoned, and trendy, contemporary styles replace the evidence of earlier occupants. Preservationists may succeed in retaining and refurbishing some structures but gradually the landscapes—the voices—of the past are lost. Many of those fading voices first took on their North American accents in the culture hearths suggested in Figure 7.5. They are still best heard in the house types

ECONOMIC GEOGRAPHY:
Primary Activities

An abandoned farm house and barn among the vast wheat fields of the Great Plains.

Key Concepts

*T*he crop bloomed luxuriantly that summer of 1846. The disaster of the preceding year seemed over, and the potato, the sole sustenance of some 8 million Irish peasants, would again yield the bounty needed. Yet within a week, wrote Father Mathew, "I beheld one wide waste of putrefying vegetation. The wretched people were seated on the fences of their decaying gardens . . . bewailing bitterly the destruction that had left them foodless." Colonel Gore found that "every field was black," and Father O'Sullivan noted that "the fields . . . appeared blasted, withered, blackened, and . . . sprinkled with vitriol. . . ." The potato was irretrievably gone for a second year; famine and pestilence were inevitable.

Within five years, the settlement geography of the most densely populated country in Europe was forever altered. The United States, Canada, and Great Britain received 2 million Irish immigrants, who provided the cheap labor needed for the canals, railroads, and mines that they were creating in a rush to economic development. New patterns of commodity flows were initiated as American maize for the first time found an Anglo-Irish market—as part of Poor Relief—and then entered a wider European market, which had also suffered general crop failure in that bitter year. Within days, a microscopic organism, the cause of the potato blight, had altered the economic and human geography of two continents.

Although the Irish famine of the 1840s was a regional tragedy, it dramatically demonstrated the intricate interrelations between widely separated peoples and places. It demonstrated the fundamental importance of patterns of economic geography and subsistence. Chapters 8, 9, and 10 explore the dynamic economic innovations that are reworking the landscapes of human activities. Food and raw material production still dominate the economies in some parts of the world, but increasingly, people are engaged in activities that involve the processing of raw materials into finished products and the provision of personal, business, and professional services within an increasingly interconnected world economy. Changing patterns of subsistence, livelihood, exchange, and the pursuit of "development" are the focus of economic geography.

Simply stated, **economic geography** is the study of how people earn their living, how livelihood systems vary from place to place, and how economic activities are spatially interrelated and linked. It applies geography's general concern with spatial variation to the production, exchange, and consumption of goods and services. In reality, of course, we cannot comprehend the totality of the economic pursuits of 7 billion human beings. Instead, economic geographers seek consistencies. They develop generalizations to help understand complex patterns. Studying economic geography reveals the dynamic, interlocking diversity of human activities and the impact of economic activity on all other facets of human life and culture. It reveals the increasing interdependence of differing national and regional economic systems. The potato blight, although it struck one small island, ultimately affected the economies of continents. In like fashion, the exploitation of the natural resources of the United States, the "deindustrialization" of its economy, and the shift to postindustrial service and knowledge activities, are altering the relative wealth of countries, flows of international trade, domestic employment and income patterns, and more (Figure 8.1).

Figure 8.1 This oil tanker is part of a world of increasing economic interdependence. Oil is a global commodity, with its price set by global markets.

The Classification of Economic Activity and Economies

Understanding livelihood patterns is made more difficult by the complex environmental and cultural realities controlling the economic activities of humans. Many production patterns are rooted in the spatially variable circumstances of the *physical environment*. The staple crops of the humid tropics, for example, are not part of the agricultural systems of the mid-latitudes; livestock types that thrive in American feedlots or on Western ranges are not adapted to the Arctic tundra or to the margins of the Saharan desert. The unequal distribution of useful petroleum and mineral deposits make some regions wealthy and others dependent. Forestry and fishing depend on still other natural resources that are unequal in occurrence, type, and value.

Within the bounds of what is environmentally possible, *cultural considerations* may shape economic decisions. For example, culturally based food preferences rather than environmental limitations may dictate the choice of crops or livestock. Corn (maize) is a preferred grain in Africa and the Americas; wheat in North America, Australia, Argentina, southern Europe, and Ukraine; and rice in much of Asia. Pigs are not raised in Muslim areas, where religious belief prohibits pork consumption.

Level of *technological development* of a culture will affect its recognition of resources or its ability to exploit them. **Technology** refers to the totality of tools and methods available to and used by a culture group in producing items essential to its subsistence and comfort. Preindustrial societies have no knowledge of or need for the iron ore, coal, petroleum, or uranium underlying their hunting, gathering, or gardening grounds. *Political decisions* may encourage or discourage—through subsidies, protective tariffs, or production restrictions—patterns of economic activity. And, ultimately, production is controlled by *economic factors* of demand, whether that demand is expressed through a free-market mechanism, government controls, or the consumption requirements of a single family producing for its own needs.

Categories of Activity

One approach to categorize the world's productive work is to view economic activity as ranged along a continuum of both increasing complexity of product or service and increasing distance from the natural environment. Seen from that perspective, three distinctive stages of economic activities may be distinguished: primary, secondary, and tertiary (Figure 8.2).

Primary activities are those that harvest or extract something from the Earth. They are at the beginning of the production cycle, where humans are in closest contact with the resources of the environment. Such activities involve basic food and raw material production. Hunting and gathering, grazing, agriculture, fishing, forestry, and mining and quarrying are examples. **Secondary activities** are those that add value to materials by

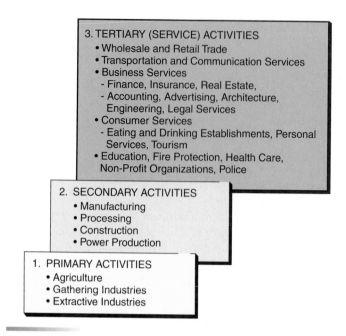

Figure 8.2 The categories of economic activity.

changing their form or combining them into more useful—therefore more valuable—commodities. That processing of raw materials into finished products may range from simple handicraft pottery to the assembly of electronic goods or space vehicles (Figure 8.3). Copper smelting, steel making, metalworking, automobile production, food processing, textile and chemical industries—indeed, the full array of *manufacturing and processing industries*—are included in this phase of the production process. Also included are the production of *energy* and the *construction* industry.

Tertiary or service activities consist of those business and labor specializations that provide *services* to the primary and secondary sectors and *goods* and *services* to businesses and to individuals. The service sector includes wholesale and retail trade, which constitute the vital link between producers and consumers. Business services include accounting, advertising, financial services, insurance, legal services, and real estate. Consumers may use some of these same services, although often from different providers. Examples of consumer service providers include eating and drinking establishments, repair and maintenance providers, and personal service establishments such as hair salons. Education, health care, transportation, and communication services are also included in the tertiary category. Generally, economic development brings a dramatic shift in the distribution of economic activity across the three categories of primary, secondary, and services (Table 8.1). Industrialization leads to an increase in the secondary sector at the expense of agriculture. Further economic development tends to shift the economic structure towards services such that the world's most advanced economies are now largely **postindustrial.** The United States demonstrates this shift, with just 1 percent of its gross domestic product (GDP) derived from

Figure 8.3 These logs entering a paper mill are products of *primary production*. Processing them into paper, boards, plywood, or prefabricated houses is a *secondary activity* that increases their value by altering their form. The products of many secondary industries—sheet steel from steel mills, for example—constitute "raw materials" for other manufacturers.

agriculture and over three-fourths from service activities. Still, primary activities are essential to all human life and are dominant globally on a land area basis.

The term *industry*—in addition to its common meaning as a branch of manufacturing activity—is frequently employed as a substitute, identical in meaning to *activity,* as a designation of these categories of economic enterprise. That is, we can speak of the steel, or automobile, or textile "industry," with all the impressions of factories, mills, raw materials, and products each type of enterprise implies. But with equal logic, we can refer in a more generalized way to the "entertainment" or the "travel" industry or, in the present context, to "primary," "secondary," and "service" industries.

These categories of production and service activities help us see an underlying structure to the nearly infinite variety of things people do to earn a living and to sustain themselves. But by themselves, they tell us little about the organization of the larger economy of which the individual worker or establishment is a part. For that broader organizational understanding, we look to *systems* rather than *components* of economies.

Types of Economic Systems

Broadly viewed, national economies in the early 21st century fall into one of three major types of systems: *subsistence, commercial,* or *planned.* None of these economic systems is "pure." That is, none exists in isolation in an increasingly interdependent world. Each, however, displays certain underlying characteristics based on its distinctive forms of resource management and economic control.

In a **subsistence economy,** goods and services are created for the use of the producers and their kinship groups. Therefore, there is little exchange of goods and only limited need for markets. In the **market (commercial) economies** that have become dominant in nearly all parts of the world, producers or their agents, in theory, freely market their goods and services, the laws of supply and demand determine price and quantity, and market competition is the primary force that shapes production decisions and distributions. In the extreme form of **planned economies** associated with communist societies, producers or their agents disposed of goods and services through government agencies that controlled both

Table 8.1

Stage of Economic Development and the Structure of Economic Activity

Country/Category	Value Added as Percentage of GDP, 2010[1]			
	Agriculture	Mining, Construction, Utilities	Manufacturing	Services
Least Developed				
Central African Republic	56	7	8	29
Mali	37	21	3	39
Newly Industrialized				
Malaysia	10	19	25	46
Thailand	12	11	34	43
Industrial				
Czech Republic	2	15	23	60
South Korea	3	8	28	61
Postindustrial				
Australia	3	19	10	68
United States	1	9	13	77

Source: The World Bank, *World Development Indicators*, 2011.
[1]Some values are from earlier years where 2010 data was missing.

supply and price. The quantities produced and the locational patterns of production were strictly programmed by central planning departments.

With a few exceptions—such as Cuba and North Korea—rigidly planned economies no longer exist in their classical form; they have been modified or dismantled in favor of free market structures or only partially retained in a lesser degree of economic control associated with governmental supervision or ownership of selected sectors of increasingly market-oriented economies. Nevertheless, their landscape evidence lives on in formerly communist societies, such the former Soviet Union and its satellite bloc countries. The physical structures, patterns of production, and imposed regional interdependencies that they created continue to influence the economic decisions of successor societies.

In actuality, few people are members of only one of these systems. A farmer in India may produce rice and vegetables privately for the family's consumption but also save some of the produce to sell. In addition, members of the family may market cloth or other handicrafts they make. With the money derived from those sales, the Indian peasant is able to buy, among other things, clothes for the family, tools, and fuel. Thus, that Indian farmer is a member of at least two systems: subsistence and commercial.

In the United States, government controls on the production of various types of goods and services (such as growing wheat or tobacco, producing alcohol, constructing and operating nuclear power plants, and engaging in licensed personal and professional services) mean that the country does not have a purely market economy. To a limited extent, its citizens participate in a

controlled and planned environment, as well as in a free-market environment. Many African, Asian, and Latin American market economies have been decisively shaped by government or international development and monetary agency policies that encourage the production of export commodities rather than food for domestic markets. Other developing countries promote through import restrictions and currency manipulation the development of their own industrial capacity. Example after example would show that "free" markets depend upon institutions and government controls.

No matter what economic system prevails, transportation is a key variable. No advanced economy can flourish without a well-connected transport network. Subsistence societies—or subsistence areas of developing countries— are characterized by their isolation from regional and world routes (Figure 8.4). That isolation restricts their progression to more advanced forms of economic structure.

Inevitably, spatial patterns of economic activities and systems are subject to change. For example, the commercial economies of Western European countries are being restructured by both increased free market competition and supranational regulation under the World Trade Organization (WTO) and the European Union (EU; see Chapter 12 for more on this topic). Many of the countries of Latin America, Africa, Asia, and the Middle East that traditionally were dominated by subsistence economies are now benefiting from technology transfer and integration into expanding global production and exchange patterns. For example, the phenomenal growth of the Chinese economy is rewriting the map of economic activity and shifting the global balance of economic

Figure 8.4 Patterns of surface transportation and accessibility. Accessibility is a key measure of economic development and of the degree to which a world region can participate in interconnected market activities. Isolated areas of countries with advanced economies suffer a price disadvantage because of high transportation costs. Lack of accessibility in subsistence economic areas slows their modernization and hinders their participation in the world market.

Source: Allen, Paul, Student Atlas of World Geography, *McGraw-Hill. Used with permission.*

power. Economic globalization increases linkages between distant regions and spreads wealth more widely, but also undermines the stability of established production locations. In short, the creative destruction of capitalism produces results that vary widely from place to place.

In the remainder of this chapter, we will center our attention on the primary industries. In Chapter 9, we will consider the secondary and service sectors of the economy.

Primary Activities: Agriculture

Humankind's basic economic concern is producing or securing sufficient food resources to meet daily energy requirements and normal nutritional needs. Those supplies may be acquired directly, through hunting, gathering, farming, or fishing, or indirectly, through performance of other primary, secondary, or service sector endeavors that yield sufficient income to obtain needed daily sustenance. Statistics from the Food and Agriculture Organization (FAO) at the United Nations show that in 2010, 2.6 billion people or 38 percent of the world's population depended on agriculture, hunting, fishing, and forestry for their livelihoods.

Since the 1960s, neo-Malthusians (see Chapter 4) have revived Thomas Robert Malthus's fears that the world's steadily increasing population would exceed food supplies. Instead, although global population has more than doubled since 1950, the total amount of

human food produced worldwide since then has also more than doubled. The FAO has set the minimum daily requirement for caloric intake at 2350 per person. By that measure, annual food supplies are more than sufficient to meet world needs. That is, if total food resources were evenly distributed, everyone would have access to amounts sufficient for adequate daily nourishment. In reality, however, about 850 million people or 13 percent of the world's population are inadequately supplied with food and nutrients. This stark contradiction between sufficient worldwide food supplies and widespread malnutrition reflects, among other reasons, inequalities in national and personal incomes; lack of access to fertile soils, credit, and education; local climatic conditions or catastrophes; and lack of transportation and storage facilities. By mid-century, the increasingly interconnected world population will expand to over 9 billion, and concerns with individual states' food supplies will inevitably remain a persistent international issue. World and regional issues of food security are explored in Chapter 10.

Before there was farming, *hunting* and *gathering* were the universal forms of primary production. These preagricultural pursuits are now practiced by at most a few thousand people worldwide, primarily in isolated and remote pockets within the low latitudes and among the sparse populations of very high latitudes. The interior of New Guinea, rugged areas of interior Southeast Asia, diminishing segments of the Amazon rain forest, and a few districts of tropical Africa and northern Australia still contain such preagricultural people. Much of the Arctic region, of course, is ill suited for any form of food crop production. Hunter-gatherer numbers are few and declining, and wherever they are brought into contact with technologically more advanced cultures, their way of life is eroded or lost.

Agriculture, defined as the growing of crops and the tending of livestock, has replaced hunting and gathering as the most significant of the primary activities. It is spatially the most widespread, found in all world regions where environmental circumstances—including adequate moisture, good growing season length, and productive soils—permit (Figure 8.5). The United Nations (UN) estimates that more than one-third of the world's land area (excluding Greenland and Antarctica) is in some form of agricultural use, including permanent pastureland. Crop farming alone covers some 15 million square kilometers (5.8 million square miles) worldwide, about 10 percent of the Earth's total land area. In many developing economies, at least two-thirds of the labor force is directly involved in farming and herding. In some, such as Bhutan in Asia or Burkina Faso and Burundi in Africa, the figure is more than 90 percent. Overall, however, employment in agriculture is steadily declining in developing economies, echoing but trailing the trend in commercial economies, in which direct employment in agriculture involves only a small fraction of the labor force (Figure 8.6). Globally, in 2010, 40 percent of the world's economically active population worked in agriculture. In the United States, just 2 percent of workers were in agriculture and in the United Kingdom, it was just 1 percent. Indeed, a declining number or proportion of farm workers, along with farm consolidation and increasing

output, are typical in all highly developed commercial agricultural systems. On the other hand, agriculture remains a major component in the economies of many of the world's developing countries, producing for domestic markets and providing a major source of national income through exports (Figure 8.7).

It has been customary to classify agricultural societies on the twin bases of the importance of off-farm sales and the level of mechanization and technological advancement. *Subsistence, traditional* (or *intermediate*), and *advanced* are terms that recognize both aspects. These are recognized stages along a continuum. At one end lies production solely for family sustenance, using rudimentary tools and native plants. At the other is the specialized, highly capitalized, industrialized agriculture for off-farm sale that marks advanced economies. Between these extremes is the middle ground of traditional agriculture, where farm production is in part destined for home consumption and in part oriented toward off-farm sale. Further complicating the contrast between subsistence and advanced agriculture is the rise of organic agriculture and the local foods movement in advanced industrial countries. We will begin our survey of the geography of agriculture by examining the "subsistence" and "advanced" ends of the agricultural continuum.

Subsistence Agriculture

By definition, a *subsistence* economic system involves nearly total self-sufficiency on the part of its members. Production for exchange is minimal, and any exchange is noncommercial; each

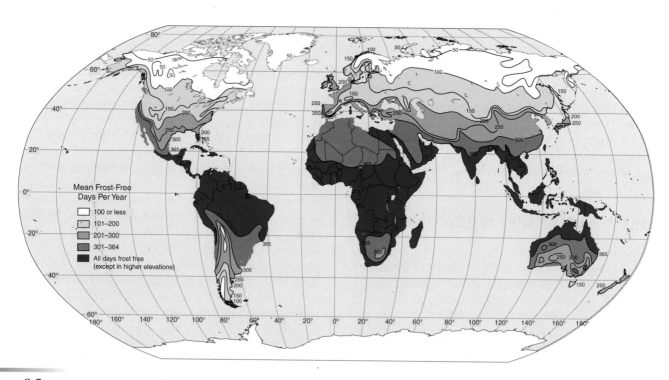

Figure 8.5 Average length of growing season. The number of frost-free days is an important environmental control on agriculture, as is the availability of precipitation sufficient in amount and reliability for crop production. Since agriculture is not usually practicable with less than a 90-day growing season, large parts of Russia and Canada have only limited cropping potential. Except where irrigation water is available, arid regions are similarly outside of the margins of regular crop production.

Source: Courtesy Wayne M. Wendland.

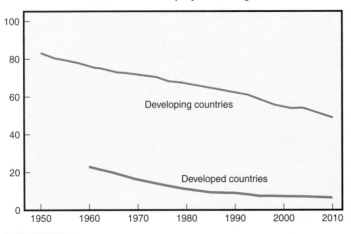

Percent of total employment in agriculture

Figure 8.6 In the developing economies worldwide, the percentage of the labor force in agriculture has been steadily declining—and is projected to decrease to even lower levels. In developed countries, agriculture's share of the labor force typically ranges from only 1 to 4 percent.

Sources: FAO and World Bank.

family or close-knit social group relies on itself for its food and other most essential requirements. Farming for the immediate needs of the family is, even today, the predominant occupation of humankind. In most of Africa, South and East Asia, and much of Latin America, a large percentage of people are primarily concerned with feeding themselves from their own land and livestock.

Two chief types of subsistence agriculture may be recognized: *extensive* and *intensive.* The essential contrast between them is yield per unit of land area and, therefore, the population that can be supported. **Extensive subsistence agriculture** involves large areas of land and minimal labor input per hectare. Both production per land unit and population densities are low. **Intensive subsistence agriculture** involves the cultivation of small landholdings through the expenditure of great amounts of labor per acre. Yields per unit area and population densities are both high (Figure 8.8).

Extensive Subsistence Agriculture

Of the several types of *extensive subsistence* agriculture, two are of particular interest: nomadic herding and shifting cultivation.

Nomadic herding, the wandering yet controlled movement of livestock solely dependent on natural forage, is the most extensive type of land use system (Figure 8.8). That is, it requires the greatest amount of land area per person sustained. Over large portions of semiarid and desert areas of Asia, in certain highland zones, and on the fringes of and within the Sahara, a relatively small number of people graze animals for consumption by the herder group, not for market sale. Sheep, goats, and camels are most common, while cattle, horses, and yaks are locally important. The reindeer of Lapland were formerly part of the same system.

Whatever the animals involved, their common characteristics are hardiness, mobility, and an ability to subsist on sparse forage. The animals provide a variety of products: milk, cheese, blood,

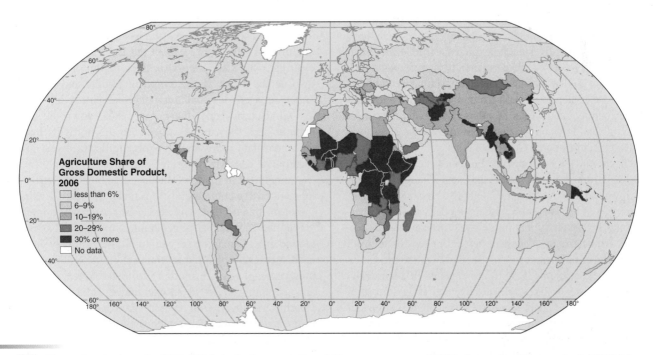

Figure 8.7 Share of agriculture in GDP, 2006. Agriculture contributed 30 percent or more of GDP of more than 29 countries in 2006. Most were small, developing economies with less than US$500 in annual per capita income. Together, they comprise 11 percent of the world's population.

Source: The World Bank, World Development Indicators 2008.

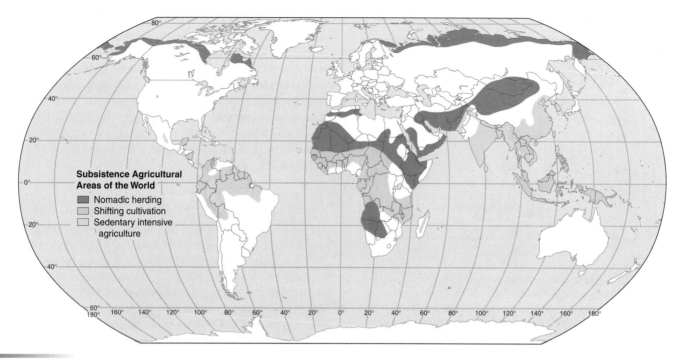

Figure 8.8 **Subsistence agricultural areas of the world.** Nomadic herding, supporting relatively few people, was the age-old way of life in the dry or cold regions of the world. Shifting or swidden agriculture maintains soil fertility by tested traditional practices in tropical wet and wet-and-dry climates. Large parts of Asia support millions of people engaged in sedentary intensive cultivation, with rice and wheat the chief crops.

and meat for food; hair and wool for clothing; skins for clothing and shelter; and excrement for fuel. For the herder, the animals represent primary subsistence, savings, and insurance against an uncertain future. Nomadic movement is tied to sparse and seasonal rainfall or to cold temperatures and to the varying appearance and exhaustion of forage. Extended stays in a given location are neither desirable nor possible. *Transhumance* is a special form of seasonal movement of livestock to exploit specific locally varying pasture conditions. Used by permanently or seasonally sedentary pastoralists and pastoral farmers, transhumance involves either the regular vertical migration from mountain to valley pastures between summer and winter months or horizontal movement between established lowland grazing areas to reach pastures temporarily lush from monsoonal (seasonal) rains.

As an economic system, nomadic herding is declining. Many economic, social, and cultural changes are causing nomadic groups to alter their way of life or to disappear entirely. First and foremost, the nomadic way of life is at odds with the modern world's imperatives of controlled international borders and private land ownership. On the Arctic fringe of Russia, herders under communism were made members of state or collective herding enterprises. In northern Scandinavia, Lapps (Saami) are engaged in commercial more than in subsistence livestock farming and struggle to preserve their culture. In the Sahel region of Africa on the margins of the Sahara, oases formerly controlled by herders have been taken over by farmers, and the great droughts of recent decades have forever altered the formerly nomadic way of life of thousands.

A much differently based and distributed form of extensive subsistence agriculture is found in all the warm, moist, tropical areas of the world. There, many people engage in a kind of nomadic farming. Once put into agricultural use, the soils of those areas rapidly lose many of their nutrients (in hot, wet climates, organic matter rapidly decomposes and heavy rains and groundwater dissolve and *leach* the nutrients from the soil). After several harvests, the soils are depleted and the famer move on. In a sense, the farmers rotate fields rather than crops to maintain soil productivity. This type of **shifting cultivation** has a number of names, the most common of which are *swidden* (an English localism for "burned clearing") and *slash-and-burn*. Each region of its practice has its own name—for example, *milpa* in Middle and South America, *chitemene* in Africa, and *ladang* in Southeast Asia.

Characteristically, the farmers hack down the natural vegetation, burn the cuttings to release the nutrients into the soil, and then plant crops such as corn, millet (a cereal grain), rice, manioc or cassava, yams, or sugarcane (Figure 8.9). Increasingly included in many of the crop combinations are high-value, labor-intensive commercial crops (such as coffee), which provide the cash income that is evidence of the growing integration of all peoples into exchange economies. Initial yields—the first and second crops—may be very high, but they quickly decrease with each successive planting on the same plot. As that occurs, cropping ceases, native vegetation is allowed to reclaim the clearing, and gardening shifts to another newly prepared site. The first clearing will ideally not be used again for crops until, after many years, natural fallowing replenishes its fertility (see the feature "Swidden Agriculture").

Less than 3 percent of the world's people are still predominantly engaged in tropical shifting cultivation on about one-seventh of the world's land area (Figure 8.8). Because the essential characteristic of the system is the intermittent cultivation of the

(a)

(b)

Figure 8.9 Swidden agriculture in Liberia, Africa. First, the vegetation is cut and burned (*a*). Then, the field is planted (*b*). Stumps and trees left in the clearing will remain after the burn.

land, each family requires a total area equivalent to the garden plot in current use, plus all land left fallow for regeneration. Population densities are traditionally low, for much land is needed to support few people. Here as elsewhere, however, population density must be considered a relative term. In actuality, although crude (arithmetic) density is low, people per unit area of *cultivated* land may be high.

Shifting cultivation is one of the oldest and most widely spread agricultural systems of the world. It is found on the islands of Borneo, New Guinea, and Sumatra but is now retained only in small parts of the uplands of Southeast Asia in Vietnam, Thailand, Myanmar, and the Philippines. Nearly the whole of inland Central

and West Africa, Brazil's Amazon basin, and large portions of Central America were engaged in this type of extensive subsistence agriculture.

It may be argued that shifting cultivation is an ingenious, highly efficient cultural adaptation where land is abundant in relation to population. Shifting cultivation generally involves *polyculture,* the production of many different types of crops in a single field. Polyculture reduces vulnerability to pests and diseases and spreads the harvests through the year to provide food security. Polyculture keeps the soil covered by vegetation, reducing the potential for soil erosion. Traditional shifting cultivation has many advantages over commercial agriculture: no chemical fertilizers, herbicides, or pesticides are used and energy is provided by humans or draft animals rather than fossil fuels. Nonetheless, as population densities increase, the system becomes less viable. The basic change, as noted in Chapter 4, is that land is no longer abundant in relation to population in many of the less developed wet, tropical countries. Their growing populations have cleared and settled the forestlands formerly only intermittently used in swidden cultivation. The **Boserup thesis,** proposed by the economist Ester Boserup, is based on the observation that population increases necessitate increased inputs of labor and technology to compensate for reductions in the natural yields of swidden farming. It holds that population growth forces an increased use of technology in farming and—in a reversal of the Malthusian idea that the supply of food is fixed or only slowly expandable—triggers the switch from extensive to intensive subsistence agriculture, which sharply increases food production.

Intensive Subsistence Systems

About 45 percent of the people of the world are engaged in intensive subsistence agriculture, which predominates in the areas shown in Figure 8.8. As a descriptive term, *intensive subsistence* is no longer fully applicable to changing practices in which subsistence and commercial agriculture are increasingly combined. Although families may still be fed primarily with the produce of their individual plots, the exchange of farm commodities within the system is considerable. Production of food for sale in rapidly growing urban markets is increasingly vital for the rural economies of subsistence farming areas and for the sustenance of the growing proportion of national and regional populations no longer themselves engaged in farming. Nevertheless, hundreds of millions of Indians, Chinese, Pakistanis, Bangladeshis, and Indonesians plus further millions in other Asian, African, and Latin American countries remain small-plot, mainly subsistence producers of rice, wheat, corn, millet, or pulses (peas, beans, and other legumes). Most live in monsoon Asia, and we will devote our attention to that area.

Intensive subsistence farmers are concentrated in such major river valleys and deltas as the Ganges and the Chang Jiang (Yangtze) and in smaller valleys close to coasts—level areas with fertile alluvial soils. These warm, moist districts are well suited to the production of rice, a crop that under ideal conditions can provide large amounts of food per unit of land. Rice cultivation requires a great deal of time and attention, for planting rice shoots by hand in standing fresh water is a tedious art (Figure 8.10).

Figure 8.10 Transplanting rice seedlings requires hard manual labor by all members of the family. The newly flooded diked fields, previously plowed and fertilized, will have their water level maintained until the grain is ripe. This photograph was taken in Indonesia. The scene is repeated wherever subsistence wet-rice agriculture is practiced.

In the cooler and drier portions of Asia, wheat is grown intensively, along with millet and, less commonly, upland rice.

Rice is known to have been cultivated in parts of China and India for more than 7,000 years. Today, wet, or lowland, rice is the mainstay of subsistence agriculture and diets of populations from Sri Lanka and India to Taiwan, Japan, and Korea. It is grown on more than 80 percent of the planted area in Bangladesh, Thailand, and Malaysia. Almost exclusively used as a human food, rice provides 25 percent to 80 percent of the calories in the daily diet of some 3 billion Asians, or half the world's population. Its successful cultivation depends on the controlled management of water, relatively easy in humid tropical river valleys with heavy, impermeable, water-retaining soils though more difficult in upland and seasonally dry districts. Throughout Asia, the necessary water management systems have left their distinctive marks on the landscape. Permanently diked fields to contain and control water, levees against unwanted water, and reservoirs, canals, and drainage channels to control its availability and flow are common sights. Terraces to extend level land to valley slopes are occasionally encountered as well (see Figure 4.23).

Intensive subsistence farming is characterized by large inputs of labor per unit of land, by small plots, by the intensive use of fertilizers, mostly animal manure, and by the promise of high yields in good years (see the feature "The Economy of a Chinese Village"). Vegetables and some livestock are part of the agricultural system, and fish may be reared in rice paddies and ponds. Food animals include swine, ducks, and chickens. Religion is a factor as well; since Muslims eat no pork, hogs are absent in their areas of settlement. Hindus generally eat little meat, mainly goat and lamb but not pork or beef. The large number of cattle in India is vital for labor, as a source of milk and cheese, and as producers—through excrement—of fertilizer and fuel.

Urban Subsistence Farming

Not all of the world's subsistence farming is based in rural areas. Urban agriculture is a rapidly growing activity, with some 800 million city farmers worldwide providing, according to a 2007 UN report, 15 to 20 percent of the world's food. Occurring in all regions of the world, developed and underdeveloped, but most prevalent in

Swidden Agriculture

The following account describes shifting cultivation among the Hanunóo people of the Philippines. Nearly identical procedures are followed in all swidden farming regions:

When a garden site of about one-half hectare (a little over one acre) has been selected, the swidden farmer begins to remove unwanted vegetation. The first phase of this process consists of slashing and cutting the undergrowth and smaller trees with bush knives. The principal aim is to cover the entire site with highly inflammable dead vegetation so that the later stage of burning will be most effective. Because of the threat of soil erosion the ground must not be exposed directly to the elements at any time during the cutting stage. During the first months of the agricultural year, activities connected with cutting take priority over all others. It is estimated that the time required ranges from 25 to 100 hours for the average-sized swidden plot.

Once most of the undergrowth has been slashed, chopped to hasten drying, and spread to protect the soil and assure an even burn, the larger trees must be felled or killed by girdling (cutting a complete ring of bark) so that unwanted shade will be removed. The successful felling of a real forest giant is a dangerous activity and requires great skill. Felling in second growth is usually less dangerous and less arduous. Some trees are merely trimmed but not killed or cut, both to reduce the amount of labor and to leave trees to reseed the swidden during the subsequent fallow period.

The crucial and most important single event in the agricultural cycle is swidden burning. The main firing of a swidden is the culmination of many weeks of preparation in spreading and leveling chopped vegetation, preparing firebreaks to prevent flames escaping into the jungle, and allowing time for the drying process. An ideal burn rapidly consumes every bit of litter; in no more than an hour or an hour and a half, only smoldering remains are left.

The Hanunóo, swidden farmers of the Philippines, note the following as the benefits of a good burn: (1) removal of unwanted vegetation, resulting in a cleared swidden; (2) extermination of many animal and some weed pests; (3) preparation of the soil for dibble (any small hand tool or stick to make a hole) planting by making it softer and more friable; (4) provision of an evenly distributed cover of wood ashes, good for young crop plants and protective of newly-planted grain seed. Within the first year of the swidden cycle, an average of between 40 and 50 different types of crop plants have been planted and harvested.

The most critical feature of swidden agriculture is the maintenance of soil fertility and structure. The solution is to pursue a system of rotation of 1 to 3 years in crop and 10 to 20 in woody or bush fallow regeneration. When population pressures mandate a reduction in the length of fallow period, productivity of the region tends to drop as soil fertility is lowered, marginal land is utilized, and environmental degradation occurs. The balance is delicate.

Source: Based on Harold C. Conklin, *Hanunóo Agriculture*, FAO Forestry Development Paper No. 12.

Asia, urban agricultural activities range from small garden plots, to backyard livestock breeding, to fish raised in ponds and streams. Using the garbage dumps of Jakarta, the rooftops of Mexico City, and meager dirt strips along roadways in Kolkata (Calcutta) or Kinshasa, millions of people are feeding their own families and supplying local markets with vegetables, fruit, fish, and even meat—all produced within the cities themselves and all without the expense and spoilage of storage or long-distance transportation.

In all parts of the developing world, urban food production has reduced the incidence of adult and child malnutrition in rapidly expanding cities. City farming is, as well, a significant outlet for underemployed residents. In some cities, as many as one-fifth to two-thirds of all families are engaged in agriculture.

There are both positive and negative environmental consequences of urban agricultural activities. On the plus side, urban farming helps convert waste from a problem to a resource by reducing runoff and erosion from open dumps and by avoiding the costs of wastewater treatment and solid waste disposal. In Khartoum, Sudan, for example, about 25 percent of the city's garbage is consumed by farm animals; in Kolkata, India, city sewage is used to supply some 3,000 hectares (7,400 acres) of lagoons which, in turn, produce some 6,000 tons of fish annually. Nearly everywhere, human and animal wastes, vegetable debris, and table scraps are composted or applied to garden areas, and nearly everywhere, vegetable gardens and interspersed fruit trees, ornamental plants, and flowers enhance the often drab urban scene. Negative consequences include the use of untreated human waste as fertilizers, which exposes both producers and consumers to infectious diseases such as cholera and hepatitis.

Expanding Crop Production

Continuing population pressures on existing resources are a constant spur for ways to increase the available food supply. Two paths to promoting increased food production are apparent: (1) expand the land area under cultivation and (2) increase crop yields from existing farmlands.

The first approach—increasing cropland area—is not a promising strategy. Approximately 70 percent of the world's land area is agriculturally unsuitable, being too cold, too dry, too steep, or totally infertile. Of the remaining 30 percent, most of the area well suited for farming is already under cultivation, and of that area, millions of hectares annually are being lost through soil erosion, salinization, desertification, and the conversion of farmland to urban, industrial, and transportation uses in all developed and developing countries. Only the rain forests of Africa and the Amazon Basin of South America retain sizable areas of potentially farmable land. The soils of those regions, however, are fragile, are low

The Economy of a Chinese Village

The village of Nanching is in subtropical southern China on the Zhu River delta near Guangzhou (Canton). Its traditional subsistence agricultural system was described by a field investigator. The system is still followed in its essentials in other rice-oriented societies.

In this double-crop region, rice was planted in March and August and harvested in late June or July and again in November. March to November was the major farming season. Early in March, the earth was turned with an iron-tipped wooden plow pulled by a water buffalo. The very poor who could not afford a buffalo used a large iron-tipped wooden hoe for the same purpose.

The plowed soil was raked smooth, fertilizer was applied, and water was let into the field, which was then ready for the transplanting of rice seedlings. Seedlings were raised in a seedbed, a tiny patch fenced off on the side or corner of the field. Beginning from the middle of March, the transplanting of seedlings took place. The whole family was on the scene. Each took the seedlings by the bunch, 10 to 15 plants, and pushed them into the soft inundated soil. For the first 30 or 40 days, the emerald green crop demanded little attention except keeping the water at a proper level. But

after this period came the first weeding; the second weeding followed a month later. This was done by hand, and everyone old enough for such work participated. With the second weeding went the job of adding fertilizer. The grain was now allowed to stand to "draw starch" to fill the hull of the kernels. When the kernels had "drawn enough starch," water was let out of the field, and both the soil and the stalks were allowed to dry under the hot sun. Then came the harvest, when all the rice plants were cut off a few inches above the ground with a sickle. Threshing was done on a threshing board. Then the grain and the stalks and leaves were taken home with a carrying pole on the peasant's shoulder. The plant was used as fuel at home.

As soon as the exhausting harvest work was done, no time could be lost before starting the chores of plowing, fertilizing, pumping water into the fields, and transplanting seedlings for the second crop. The slack season of the rice crop was taken up by chores required for the vegetables that demanded continuous attention, since every peasant family devoted a part of the farm to vegetable gardening. In the hot and damp period of late spring and summer, eggplant and several

varieties of squash and beans were grown. The green-leafed vegetables thrived in the cooler and drier period of fall, winter, and early spring. Leeks grew year round.

When one crop of vegetables was harvested, the soil was turned and the clods broken up by a digging hoe and leveled with an iron rake. Fertilizer was applied, and seeds or seedlings of a new crop were planted. Hand weeding was a constant job; watering with the long-handled wooden dipper had to be done an average of three times a day, and in the very hot season when evaporation was rapid, as frequently as six times a day. The soil had to be cultivated with the hoe frequently as the heavy tropical rains packed the earth continuously. Instead of the two applications of fertilizer common with the rice crop, fertilizing was much more frequent for vegetables. Besides the heavy fertilizing of the soil at the beginning of a crop, usually with city garbage, additional fertilizer, usually diluted urine or a mixture of diluted urine and excreta, was given every 10 days or so to most vegetables.

Source: Adapted from C. K. Yang, *A Chinese Village in Early Communist Transition* (Cambridge, Mass.: Massachusetts Institute of Technology, 1959).

in nutrients, have poor water retention, and are easily eroded or destroyed following deforestation.

When population pressures dictate land conversion, serious environmental deterioration may result. Clearing of wet tropical forests in the Philippines, the Amazon Basin, and Indonesia has converted dense woodland to barren desolation within a very few years as soil erosion and nutrient loss have followed forest destruction. In Southeast Asia, some 10 million hectares (25 million acres) of former forestland are now wasteland, covered by useless sawgrass that supplies neither forage, food, nor fuel. By most measures, world food output cannot reasonably be increased by simple expansion of cultivated areas.

Intensification and the Green Revolution

Increased productivity of existing cropland rather than expansion of cultivated area has been the key to agricultural production over the past few decades. Between 1974 and 2004, world total grain production rose nearly 70 percent. Crop output, however, varies considerably from year to year, adversely or favorably affected by weather, insect damage, plant diseases, and other growing season conditions. Overall, despite an additional 2.5 billion people in the

world, grain production per capita today is higher than it was in the 1970s. The vast majority of that production growth was due to increases in yields rather than expansions in cropland. The largest increases were in Asia, primarily China and India, and South America. Two interrelated approaches to those yield increases mark recent farming practices.

First, throughout much of the developing world, production inputs such as water, fertilizer, pesticides, and labor have been increased to expand yields on a relatively constant supply of cultivable land. Irrigated area, for example, nearly doubled between 1960 and 2004. Global consumption of fertilizers has dramatically increased since the 1950s, and inputs of pesticides and herbicides have similarly grown. Traditional practices of leaving land fallow (uncultivated) to renew its fertility have been largely abandoned, and double and triple cropping of land where climate permits has increased in Asia and even in Africa, where marginal land is put to near-continuous use to meet growing food demands.

Many of these intensification practices are part of the second approach, linked to the **Green Revolution**—the shorthand reference to a complex of seed and management innovations adapted to the needs of intensive agriculture and designed to bring larger harvests from a given area of farmland.

Using conventional plant breeding techniques of cross-pollination, American researcher Norman Borlaug developed a dwarf, high-yielding wheat variety at a Mexican research center in the 1940s. Borlaug was later awarded the Nobel Peace Prize, and Mexico soon went from importing half its wheat to being a wheat exporter. Similarly, the International Rice Institute in the Philippines developed dwarf rice strains that yielded many more grains per plant. These high-yielding dwarf varieties respond dramatically to heavy applications of fertilizer, resist plant diseases, and can tolerate much shorter growing seasons than traditional native varieties can. Adopting the new varieties and applying the irrigation, mechanization, fertilization, and pesticide practices they require have created a new "high-input, high-yield" agriculture. Most poor farmers on marginal and rain-fed (nonirrigated) lands, however, have not benefited from the new plant varieties, which require abundant water and chemical inputs.

Expanded food production made possible through the Green Revolution has helped alleviate some of the shortages and famines predicted for subsistence agricultural regions since the early 1960s, saving an estimated one billion people from starvation. According to World Bank calculations, more than 80 percent of people in developing countries now have adequate diets, versus 55 percent in 1950. As Figure 8.11 shows, however, not all world regions share those positive results equally. Although total food production has more than doubled in Africa since 1960, population growth has steadily reduced that continent's per capita food output. Although the *number* of undernourished people globally remains near the 900 million mark because of population growth, total world food supply has increased even faster than population, and the United Nations predicts that it will continue to do so through at least 2030.

A price has been paid for the successes of the Green Revolution. Irrigation, responsible for an important part of increased crop yields, has destroyed large tracts of land; excessive salinity of soils resulting from poor irrigation practices is estimated to have a serious effect on the productivity of 20 million to 30 million hectares (80,000–120,000 square miles) of land around the world, out of a world total of some 270 million hectares of irrigated land. And the huge amount of water required for Green Revolution irrigation has led to serious groundwater depletion, conflict between agricultural and growing urban and industrial water needs in developing countries—many of which are in dry climates—and to worries about scarcity and future wars over water.

And very serious genetic consequences are feared from the loss of traditional and subsistence agriculture. With it is lost the food security that distinctive locally adapted native crop varieties provided and the nutritional diversity and balance that multiple-crop intensive gardening assured. Unlike commercial monoculture farming, subsistence polyculture farming minimized the risk of major crop failures. Many different crops and many different varieties of each crop guaranteed some yield despite adverse weather, disease, or pest problems.

Commercial agriculture, however, aims at profit maximization, not food security. Poor farmers unable to afford the capital investment that the Green Revolution demands have been displaced by a commercial monoculture, one often oriented toward specialty and industrial crops designed for export rather than to food for domestic markets. Traditional rural society has been disrupted, and landless peasants have been added to the urbanizing populations of affected countries. The presumed benefits of the Green Revolution are not available to all subsistence agricultural areas or advantageous to everyone engaged in farming (see the feature "Women and the Green Revolution"). Africa is a case in point (see Figure 8.11). Green Revolution crop improvements have concentrated on wheat, rice, and corn. Of these, only corn is important in Africa, where principal food crops include millet, sorghum,

Index of Per Capita Food Production, 1960–2009

(a)

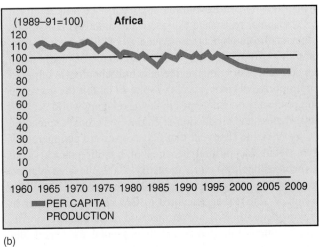

(b)

Figure 8.11 **Trends in per capita food production, 1960–2009.** Globally, per capita production of food increased steadily over the 50-year span shown. The intensification and expansion of farming in Asia resulted in food production outpacing population growth, in contrast to Malthus's predictions. It was a different picture in Africa, where total production of food grew steadily but didn't keep pace with population growth, resulting in less food per person. The food security problem in sub-Saharan Africa continues, with about 30 percent of the population suffering chronic malnutrition.

Source: Data from Food and Agriculture Organization.

cassava, manioc, yams, cowpeas, and peanuts. Belated research efforts directed to African crops, the continent's great range of growing conditions, and its abundance of yield-destroying pests and viruses have denied it the dramatic regionwide increase in food production experienced elsewhere in the developing world. No crop research or genetic modifications can fully compensate for an underlying limitation of African agricultural productivity: 80 percent of the continent's sub-Saharan farmland is severely depleted of the basic nutrients needed to grow crops, a condition that has been steadily worsening since the 1990s.

Some successes have been reported. The most widely cultivated tuber and second most important food staple in sub-Saharan Africa, cassava has been transformed from a low-yielding subsistence hedge against famine to a high-yielding cash crop. Virus-resistant varieties of sweet potatoes and both white and yellow corn and faster-growing bananas are already available (though not yet widespread) and other food and fiber crops are receiving attention from African biotechnology scientists in Kenya, South Africa, and Egypt, with contributions from American and other Western investigators. And in some physically favored areas benefiting in part from foreign investment but particularly reflecting local small farmer enterprise, encouraging pockets of crop specialization and growth in farm productivity, agribusiness creation, and rural income have been emerging. Uganda, for example, enjoys two growing seasons, ample rainfall, rich volcanic soils, and millions of small farmers rapidly expanding production of cash crops, most aimed at export markets in Asia, Europe, and North America.

In many areas that had shown the greatest past successes, Green Revolution gains are falling off. Recent cereal yields in Asia, for example, are growing at only two-thirds of their 1970s rate: the FAO now considers the productivity gains of Green Revolution technologies for Asian rice cultivation to have leveled off. Little prime land and even less water remain to expand farming in many developing countries, and the adverse ecological and social consequences of industrial farming techniques arouse growing resistance. Nor does biotechnology—which many have hailed as a promising new Green Revolution approach—seem likely to fill the gap. Consumer resistance to genetically modified (GM) food crops, fear of the ecological consequences of such modification, the continuing partial rejection of GM foods in the EU market, and the high cost and restrictions on the new biotechnologies imposed by their corporate developers all conspire to inhibit the universal adoption of the new technologies in the developing world.

Nevertheless, the production of engineered crops is spreading rapidly. In 1996, the first year that GM crops were commercially available, about 1.7 million hectares (4.3 million acres) were placed in biotechnology cultivation. By 2009, the area planted to GM crops had increased to 134 million hectares (339 million acres). Initially the acreage devoted to GM crops grew faster in the developed countries. However, because of European concerns about the health of GM foods and the potential for genetically modified crops to cross-pollinate with wild plants, producing "superweeds," GM crop adoption is now proceeding faster in the developing countries. Almost half the global GM crop area in 2009 was located in developing countries, notably Argentina, Brazil, China, India, and South Africa. Globally, the principal GM crops have been GM soybeans, GM corn (including white corn for food

in South Africa), transgenic cotton, and GM canola. Herbicide resistance (Roundup Ready soybeans) and insect resistance (Bt corn and cotton) have been the most important of the genetic crop modifications introduced, as well as the ones responsible for the significant increase in productivity and reduction in costs of the crops involved. Even in those world regions favorable for Green Revolution introductions, its advent has not always improved diets or reduced dependency on imported food. Often, the displacement of native agriculture involves a net loss of domestic food availability. In many instances, through governmental directive, foreign ownership or management, or domestic market realities, the new commercial agriculture is oriented toward food and industrial crops for the export market or toward specialty crop and livestock production for the expanding urban market rather than food production for the rural population.

The genetic diversity of our food supply is now a major concern. The monocultures of the Green Revolution have reduced plant genetic diversity, while globalization has created more uniform diets around the world. Only 150 crops are commercially grown and three grains: rice, wheat, and corn provide 60 percent of the world's calories. The genetic diversity of these crops has dropped dramatically. For example, in Sri Lanka, the number of rice varieties has dropped by 95 percent. "Seed banks" rather than native cultivation have been created to preserve genetic diversity for future plant breeding and as insurance against climate change or catastrophic pest or disease susceptibility of inbred varieties. Much of the world's crop genetic diversity is located in developing countries where crops were first domesticated and where subsistence farmers continue to use diverse varieties (Figure 8.12). However, conserving the world's crop genetic diversity will be a challenge because these places face strong population growth pressures and efforts to commercialize and intensify agriculture.

Commercial Agriculture

Few people or areas still retain the isolation and self-sufficiency that are characteristic of subsistence economies. Nearly all have been touched by a modern world of trade and exchange and have adjusted their traditional economies in response. Modifications of subsistence agricultural systems have inevitably made them more complex by some of the diversity and linkages that mark the advanced economic systems of the more developed world. Farmers in those systems produce not for their own subsistence, but primarily for a market off the farm itself. They are part of integrated exchange economies in which agriculture is but one element in a complex structure that includes mining, manufacturing, processing, and the service activities of the economy. In those economies, farm production responds to market demand, as expressed through price signals, and is related to the consumption requirements of the larger society rather than to the immediate needs of farmers themselves.

Production Controls

Modern agriculture is characterized by *specialization*—by enterprise (farm), by area, and even by country; by *off-farm sale* rather than subsistence production; and by *interdependence* of producers

Women and the Green Revolution

Traditional agricultural labor is often divided by gender, as seen in Figure 8.9 where men prepare the swidden plot and women, often with children on their back, plant the crops. Women farmers grow at least half of the world's food (and up to 80 percent in some African countries). They are responsible for an even larger share of food consumed by their own families: 80 percent in sub-Saharan Africa, 65 percent in Asia, and 45 percent in Latin America and the Caribbean. Further, women comprise between one-third and one-half of all agricultural laborers in developing countries. For example, African women perform about 90 percent of the work of processing food crops and 80 percent of the work of harvesting and marketing.

Women's agricultural dominance in developing states is increasing, as male family members continue to leave for cities in search of paid urban work. In Mozambique, for example, for every 100 men working in agriculture, there are 153 women. In nearly all other sub-Saharan countries, the female component runs between 120 and 150 per 100 men. The departure of men for near or distant cities means, in addition, that women must assume effective management of their families' total farm operations.

Despite their important role, however, women do not share equally with men in the rewards from agriculture, nor benefit from new agricultural technologies. First, most women farmers are involved in subsistence farming and food production for the local market, which yields little cash return. Second, they have far less access than men to credit at bank or government-subsidized rates that would make it possible for them to acquire the Green Revolution technology, such as hybrid seeds and fertilizers. Third, women cannot own land in some cultures and so are excluded from agricultural improvement programs and projects aimed at landowners. For example, many African agricultural development programs are based on the conversion of communal land, to which women have access, to private holdings, from which they are excluded. In Asia, inheritance laws favor male over female heirs, and female-inherited land is managed by husbands.

At the same time, the Green Revolution and its greater commercialization of crops has generally required an increase in labor per hectare, particularly in tasks typically reserved for women, such as weeding, harvesting, and postharvest work. If women are provided no relief from their other daily tasks, the Green Revolution for them may be more burden than blessing. But when mechanization is added to the new farming system, women tend to be losers. Frequently, such predominantly female tasks as harvesting or dehusking and polishing of grain—all traditionally done by hand—are given over to machinery, displacing rather than employing women. Even the application of chemical fertilizers (a "man's task") instead of cow dung ("women's work") has reduced the female role in agricultural development programs. The loss of those traditional female wage jobs means that already poor rural women and their families have insufficient income to improve their diets even in the light of substantial increases in food availability through Green Revolution improvements.

If women are to benefit from the Green Revolution, new cultural norms—or culturally acceptable accommodations within traditional household, gender, and customary legal relations—will be required. These must permit or recognize women's landowning and other legal rights not now clearly theirs, access to credit at favorable rates, and admission on equal footing with males to government assistance programs. The FAO is working to promote gender-based equity in agricultural development.

and buyers linked through markets. Farmers in a free market economy supposedly produce those crops that their estimates of market price and production cost indicate will yield the greatest return. Theoretically, farm products for which demand at a given price increases will command an increased market price. That, in turn, should induce increased production to meet the demand. In some developing countries, that market equilibrium is broken and the farm economy distorted when government policy requires uneconomically low food prices for urban workers. It may also suffer material distortion under governmental programs protecting local producers by inhibiting farm product imports or subsidizing production by guaranteeing prices for selected commodities.

Where free market conditions prevail, however, the crop or the mix of crops and livestock that individual commercial farmers produce is a result of an appraisal of profit possibilities. Farmers must assess and predict prices, evaluate the physical nature of farmland, and factor in the possible weather conditions. The costs of production (seed, fuel, fertilizer, capital equipment, labor, and so on) must be reckoned. A number of unpredictable conditions may thwart farmers' aspirations for profit. Among them are the uncertainties of growing season conditions that follow the original planting decision, the total yield that will be achieved (and therefore the unit cost of production), and the supply and price situation that will exist months or years in the future, when crops are ready for market.

Beginning in the 1950s in the United States, specialist farmers and corporate purchasers developed strategies for minimizing those uncertainties. Processors sought uniformity of product quality and timing of delivery. Vegetable canners—of tomatoes, sweet corn, and the like—required volume delivery of raw products of uniform size, color, and ingredient content on dates that accorded with cannery and labor schedules. And farmers wanted the support of a guaranteed market at an assured price to minimize the uncertainties of their specialization and stabilize the return on their investment.

The solution was contractual arrangements or vertical integration (where production, processing, and sales are all coordinated within one firm) that unite contracted farmer and purchaser-processor. Broiler chickens of specified age and weight, cattle fed to an exact weight, wheat with a minimum protein content, popping corn with prescribed characteristics, potatoes of the kind

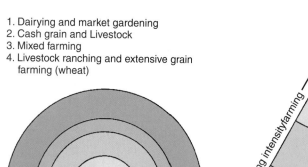

1. Dairying and market gardening
2. Cash grain and Livestock
3. Mixed farming
4. Livestock ranching and extensive grain
   farming (wheat)

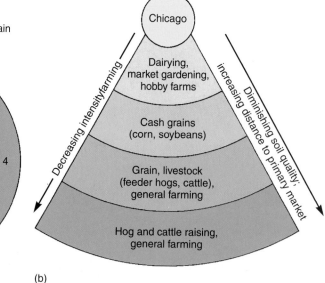

(a)   (b)

Figure 8.14 (*a*) **von Thünen's model.** Recognizing that as distance from the market increases, the value of land decreases, von Thünen developed a descriptive model of intensity of land use that holds up reasonably well in practice. The most intensively produced crops are found on land close to the market; the less intensively produced commodities are located at more distant points. The zones of the diagram represent modern equivalents of the land use sequence von Thünen suggested in the 1820s. As the metropolitan area at the center increases in size, the agricultural specialty areas are displaced outward, but the relative position of each is retained. Compare this diagram with Figure 8.17. (*b*) **A schematic view of the von Thünen zones** in the sector south of Chicago. There, farmland quality decreases southward as the boundary of recent glaciation is passed and hill lands are encountered in southern Illinois. On the margins of the city near the market, dairying competes for space with livestock feeding and suburbanization. Southward into flat, fertile central Illinois, cash grains dominate. In southern Illinois, livestock rearing and fattening and general farming are the rule.

Source: (b) Modified with permission from Bernd Andreae, Farming Development and Space: A World Agricultural Geography, *translated by Howard F. Gregor (Berlin; Hawthorne, N.Y.: Walter de Gruyter and Co., 1981).*

the market (Figure 8.15). Because in this model, transport costs are uniform in all directions away from the center, a concentric zonal pattern of land use called the *von Thünen rings* results.

The von Thünen model may be modified by introducing ideas of differential transport costs (Figure 8.16), variations in topography or soil fertility, or changes in commodity demand and market price. With or without such modifications, von Thünen's analysis helps explain the changing crop patterns and farm sizes evident on the landscape at increasing distance from major cities, particularly in regions dominantly agricultural in economy. Farmland close to markets takes on high value, is used *intensively* for high-value crops, and is subdivided into relatively small units. Land far from markets is used *extensively* and in larger units.

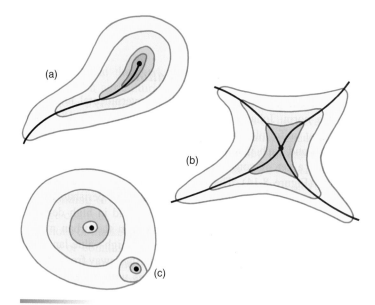

Figure 8.16 **Ring modifications.** Modifications of model assumptions will alter the details but not the underlying pattern of the *von Thünen rings*. For example, a growth in demand, and therefore market price of a commodity, would merely expand its ring of production. An increase in transport costs would shrink the production area, while reductions in freight rates would extend it. (*a*) If transport costs are reduced in one direction, the shape—but not the sequence—of the rings will be affected. (*b*) If several roads are constructed or improved, land use sequences assume a star shape. (*c*) The addition of a smaller outlying market results in the emergence of a set of von Thünen rings that is subordinate to it.

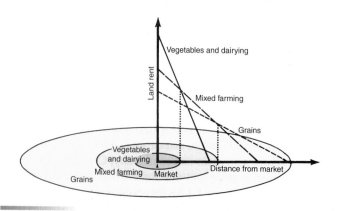

Figure 8.15 **Transport gradients and agricultural zones.**

Historian and geographer William Cronon uses the von Thünen model to help explain the frontier stages during the settlement of the American West. Starting in Chicago, the center of the U.S. agricultural economy, a westward traveler would first encounter a zone of intensively farmed dairies, market gardens, and orchards before reaching the corn and wheat cash grain operations of the Iowa prairie. Farther west, the traveler would reach the open range cattle ranches of the Great Plains, then a zone of trapping, hunting, and Indian trade, and beyond that lay the wilderness. Thus, the settlement of the interior of the continent and the closing of the frontier was intimately connected to the growth of cities and the expansion of urban markets for produce, grain, and cattle. In industrial and postindustrial economies, the basic forces determining land use near cities are often those associated with urban expansion itself. For example, peripheral city growth, hobby farms, you-pick agritourism farms, and the withholding of land from farming in anticipation of future suburban development may locally alter the von Thünen rings. Nonetheless, we can affirm the validity of von Thünen's fundamental insights that the city and countryside are intimately connected and that the distance from the city shapes rural land values and land uses.

Intensive Commercial Agriculture

Following World War II, agriculture in the developed world's market economies turned increasingly to concentrated methods of large-scale production. Machinery, chemicals, irrigation, and dependence on a restricted range of carefully selected and bred plant varieties and animal breeds all were employed in a concerted effort to maximize efficiency and productivity on each unit of farmland.

The goal, of course, was to increase off-farm sales as American agriculture increasingly shifted from an objective of partial self-sufficiency to a total commitment to the commercial, exchange economy. Prior to 1950, most U.S. farms had a significant subsistence orientation; they were "general farms" growing a variety of crops, some for sale and some for feed for farmstead livestock—a milk cow or two, chickens for the pot and for household eggs, and a few hogs and steers, partly for farm slaughter and use. Their extensive kitchen gardens supplied vegetables and fruits for farm family seasonal consumption and home canning. In 1949, the average American farm sold only $4,100 worth of products. By 2007, however, most farms had a full commitment to the market, average off-farm sales rose to more than $135,000, and farm families—like other Americans—shopped at supermarkets for their food needs. With the increases in capital investment and the need for larger farms to maximize return on that investment, many inefficient small farms have been abandoned. Consolidation has reduced the number and enlarged the size of farms still in production. To stay in business, many operations have had to expand by factors of 10 or 100, whether measured in crop acreage of number of livestock. From a high of 6.8 million in 1934, the number of U.S. farms dropped to 5.7 million in 1949 and to 2.2 million by 2007, with many of the smallest units counting as "farms" only because of a generous Department of Agriculture definition.

The reorientation of farm production goals in the United States and in most other highly developed market economies has led to significant changes in regional farm production patterns.

Reflecting the drive for enhanced, more specialized output and the investment of large amounts of capital (for machinery, fertilizers, and specialized buildings, for example), all modern agriculture is "intensive." But the several types of farm specializations differ in how much capital is invested per hectare of farmed land (and, of course, in the specifics of those capital inputs). Those differences underlie generalized distinctions between traditional intensive and extensive commercial agriculture.

The term **intensive commercial agriculture** is now usually understood to refer specifically to the production of crops that give high yields and high market value per unit of land. These include fruits, vegetables, bedding plants for urban gardens, and dairy products, all of which are highly perishable, as well as some "factory farm" production of livestock. Dairy farms and **truck farms** (horticultural or "market garden" farms that produce a wide range of vegetables and fruits) are found near most medium-size and large cities. Since the product is perishable, transport costs increase because of the special handling that is needed, such as the use of refrigerated trucks and custom packaging. Note the distribution of truck and fruit farming in Figure 8.17, which also suggests the importance of climatic conditions in commercial fruit and vegetable growing.

Feed grain and livestock farming involves the growing of grain on a producing farm to be fed to livestock, which constitute the farm's cash product. In Western Europe, three-fourths of cropland is devoted to production for animal consumption; in Denmark, 90 percent of all grains are fed to livestock for conversion not only into meat but also into butter, cheese, and milk. Although livestock-grain farmers work their land intensively, the value of their product per unit of land is usually less than that of the truck farm. Consequently, in North America at least, feed grains and livestock farms are centered in the Midwest, farther from the main markets than are horticultural and dairy farms.

Normally, the profits for marketing livestock (chiefly hogs and beef cattle in the United States) are greater per pound than those for selling corn or other feed, such as alfalfa and clover. As a result, farmers convert their corn into meat on the farm by feeding it to the livestock, efficiently avoiding the cost of buying grain. They may also convert farm grain at local feed mills to the more balanced feed modern livestock rearing requires. Where land is too expensive to be used to grow feed, especially near cities, feed must be shipped to the farm. The grain-livestock belts of the world are close to the great coastal and industrial zone markets. The Corn Belt of the United States and the livestock region of Western Europe are two examples.

In the United States—and commonly in all developed countries—the traditional feed grains and livestock operations of small and family farms have been largely supplanted by very-large-scale concentrated animal feeding operations or "livestock factory farms" involving thousands or tens of thousands of closely quartered animals. From its inception in the 1920s, the intensive, industrialized rearing of livestock, particularly beef and dairy cattle, hogs, and poultry, has grown to dominate meat, dairy, and egg production. To achieve their objective of producing a marketable product in volume at the lowest possible unit cost, operators of livestock factory farms confine animals to pens or cages, treat them with antibiotics and vitamins to maintain health and speed

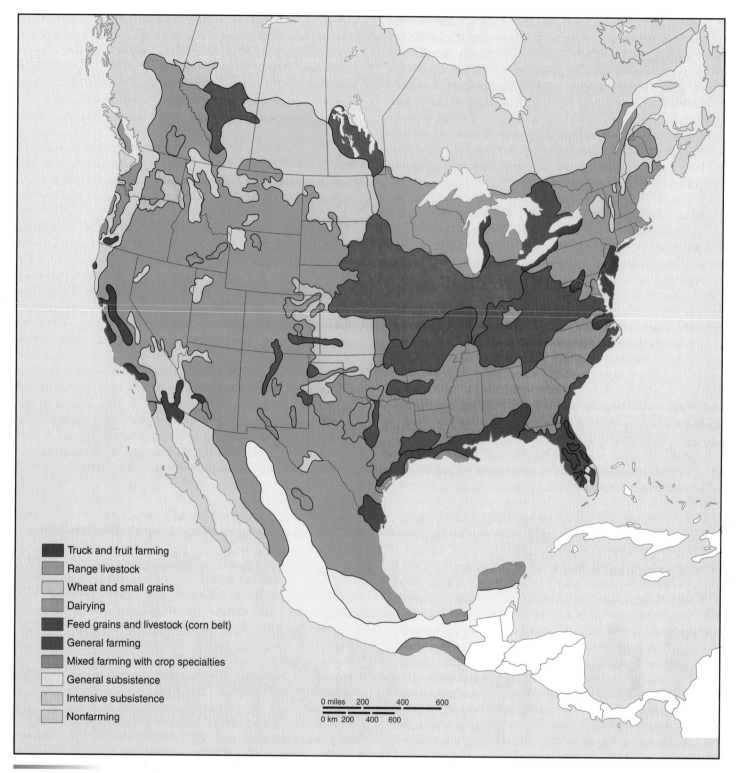

Figure 8.17 **Generalized agricultural regions of North America.**

Sources: U.S. Bureau of Agricultural Economics; Agriculture Canada; and Secretaría de Agricultura y Recursos Hidráulicos, Mexico.

Legend:
- Truck and fruit farming
- Range livestock
- Wheat and small grains
- Dairying
- Feed grains and livestock (corn belt)
- General farming
- Mixed farming with crop specialties
- General subsistence
- Intensive subsistence
- Nonfarming

0 miles 200 400 600
0 km 200 400 600

growth, provide processed feeds that often contain the low-cost animal by-products or crop residue, and deliver them under contract to processors, packers, or their parent company (Figure 8.18). Although serious concerns have been voiced about animal waste management and groundwater, stream, and atmospheric pollution, contract-based concentrated feeding operations now provide almost all supermarket meat and dairy products. The location of this form of intensive commercial farming, however, is often determined not by land value or proximity to market, but by land use restrictions and environmental standards imposed by state and county governments.

Extensive Commercial Agriculture

Farther from the market, on less expensive land, there is less need to use the land intensively. Cheaper land and lower profits per unit of land leads to larger farm units. **Extensive commercial agriculture** is typified by large wheat farms and livestock ranching.

There are, of course, limits to the land use explanations attributable to von Thünen's model. While it is true that farmland values decline westward with increasing distance from the northeastern market of the United States, they show no corresponding increase with increasing proximity to the massive West Coast market region until the specialty agricultural areas of the coastal states themselves are reached. The western states are characterized by extensive agriculture, but as a consequence of environmental, not distance, considerations. Climatic conditions obviously affect the productivity and the potential agricultural use of an area, as do soils and topography. In North America, of course, increasing distance westward from eastern markets happens to be associated with increasing aridity and the beginning of mountainous terrain. In general, rough terrain and dry climates, rather than simple distance from market, underlie the widespread occurrence of extensive agriculture.

Large-scale wheat farming requires sizable capital inputs for planting and harvesting machinery—a large tractor might cost $300,000 and a combine (harvester) $500,000. However, the inputs per unit of land are low; and wheat farms are very large. Nearly half the farms in Saskatchewan, for example, are more than 400 hectares (1,000 acres). The average farm in Kansas is larger than 300 hectares (740 acres), and in North Dakota, more than 525 hectares (1,300 acres). In North America, the spring wheat (planted in spring, harvested in autumn) region includes the Dakotas, eastern Montana, and the southern parts of the Prairie provinces of Canada. The winter wheat (planted in fall, harvested in midsummer) belt centers on Kansas and includes adjacent sections of neighboring states (Figure 8.19). Argentina is the only South American country

(a)

(b)

(c)

Figure 8.18 Industrial poultry and livestock farming. (*a*) Most of the chicken consumed in developed countries comes from factory-style poultry farms such as this. Thousands of broiler chickens are raised together in a single barn for about 45 days before slaughtering. (*b*) On this hog farm in Ohio, thousands of animals are fed and raised indoors in large rectangular barns for the four or five months that it takes them to grow to market weight of 250 pounds. Feces and urine are washed through slots in the floor into pipes and trenches that carry the waste into manure lagoons. The manure is usually applied to fields as a fertilizer. Accidental leaks or spills into nearby waterways can cause devastating fish kills (*c*) Large cattle feedlot operations supply much of the country's beef supply.

Figure 8.19 Contract harvesters follow the ripening wheat northward through the plains of the United States and Canada.

to have comparable large-scale wheat farming. In the Eastern Hemisphere, the system is fully developed only east of the Volga River in northern Kazakhstan and the southern part of western Siberia, and in southeastern and western Australia. Because wheat is an important crop in many agricultural systems—today, wheat ranks first in total production among all the world's grains and accounts for more than 20 percent of the total calories consumed by humans collectively—it is a truly global commodity, bought and sold internationally (Figure 8.20).

Livestock ranching differs significantly from feed grains and livestock farming and, by its commercial orientation, from the nomadism it superficially resembles. A product of the 19th-century

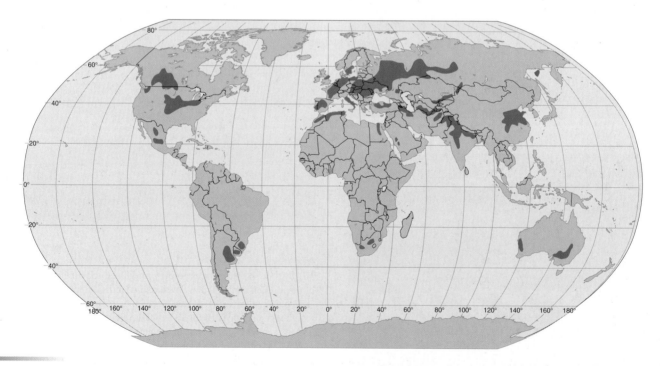

Figure 8.20 **Principal wheat-growing areas.** Only part of the world's wheat production comes from large-scale farming enterprises. In western and southern Europe, eastern and southern Asia, and North Africa, wheat growing is part of general or intensive subsistence farming. Recently, developing country successes with the Green Revolution and subsidized surpluses of the grain in Europe have altered traditional patterns of production and world trade in wheat.

growth of urban markets for beef and wool in Western Europe and the northeastern United States, ranching has been primarily confined to areas of European settlement. It is found in the western United States and adjacent sections of Mexico and Canada (see the range livestock region on Figure 8.17); the grasslands of Argentina, Brazil, Uruguay, and Venezuela; the interior of Australia; the uplands of South Island, New Zealand; and the Karoo and adjacent areas of South Africa (Figure 8.21). All except New Zealand and the humid pampas of South America have semiarid climates. All these areas, even the most remote from markets, were a product of improvements in transportation by land and sea, refrigerated train cars and trucks, and meat-canning technology.

In all of the ranching regions, livestock range has been reduced as crop farming has encroached on their more humid margins, and as feedlots have supplemented traditional grazing. Recently, the growing global demand for beef has been blamed for expanded cattle ranching and extensive destruction of tropical rain forests in Central America and the Amazon Basin, although in recent years, Amazon Basin deforestation has reflected the expansion of soybean farming more than beef production.

In areas of livestock ranching, young cattle or sheep are allowed to graze over thousands of acres. In the United States, when the cattle have gained enough weight so that weight loss in shipping *labor* will not be a problem, they are sent to feed grain livestock farms or *cost* to feedlots near slaughterhouses for accelerated fattening. Because ranching can be an economic activity only where alternative land uses are nonexistent and land quality is low, ranching regions of the world characteristically have low population densities, low capital investment per land unit, and relatively low labor requirements.

Special Crops

Under special circumstances, usually related to unique physical geography, some places far from markets may become intensively developed agricultural areas. Two special cases are Mediterranean agriculture and plantation agriculture (Figure 8.21).

Most of the arable land in the Mediterranean basin itself is planted to grains, and much of the agricultural area is used for grazing. *Mediterranean agriculture* as a specialized farming economy, however, is known for grapes, olives, oranges, figs, vegetables, and similar commodities. These crops need warm temperatures year round and a great deal of sunshine in the summer. The Mediterranean agricultural lands indicated in Figure 8.21 are among the most productive in the world. Farmers benefit from a predictable climate with few storms or severe weather problems. Also, the precipitation pattern of Mediterranean climates—winter rains and dry summers—lends itself to the controlled use of water. Of course, much capital must be spent for the irrigation systems. This is another reason for the intensive use of the land for high-value crops that are, for the most part, destined for export to industrialized countries or areas outside the Mediterranean climatic zone and even, in the case of Southern Hemisphere locations, to markets north of the equator.

Climate is also considered the vital element in the production of what are commonly known as *plantation crops*. **Plantation agriculture** involves the introduction of foreign investment, management, and marketing into an indigenous culture and economy, often employing a nonnative labor force to produce an introduced crop for foreign markets. The plantation itself is an estate whose resident workers produce one or two specialized export crops.

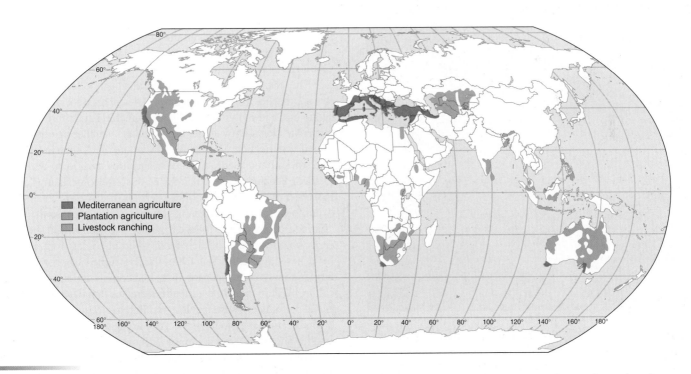

Figure 8.21 Livestock ranching and special crop agriculture. Livestock ranching is primarily a midlatitude enterprise catering to the urban markets of industrialized countries. Mediterranean and plantation agriculture are similarly oriented to the markets provided by advanced economies of Western Europe and North America. Areas of Mediterranean agriculture—all of roughly comparable climatic conditions—specialize in similar commodities, such as grapes, oranges, olives, peaches, and vegetables. The specialized crops of plantation agriculture are influenced by both physical geographic conditions and present or, particularly, former colonial control of the area.

Those crops, although native to the tropics, were frequently foreign to the areas of plantation establishment: African coffee and Asian sugar in the Western Hemisphere and American cacao, tobacco, and rubber in Southeast Asia and Africa are examples (Figure 8.22). Plantation developers from Western countries such as Britain, France, the Netherlands, and the United States became interested in the tropics partly because the climate allowed them to produce agricultural commodities that could not be grown at home. Custom and convenience usually retain the term *plantation* even where native producers of local crops dominate, as they do in cola nut production in Guinea, spice growing in India or Sri Lanka, or sisal production in the Yucatán.

The major plantation crops and the areas where they are produced include tea (India and Sri Lanka), jute (India and Bangladesh), rubber (Malaysia and Indonesia), cacao (Ghana and Nigeria), cane sugar (Cuba and the Caribbean area, Brazil, Mexico, India, and the Philippines), coffee (Brazil and Colombia), and bananas (Central America). As Figure 8.21 suggests, for ease of access to shipping, most plantation crops are cultivated along or near coasts because production for export rather than for local consumption is the rule.

Sustainable Agriculture

The adoption of large-scale, highly industrialized commercial agriculture has increased overall agricultural productivity and benefited successful farmers and agribusinesses. But it has not come without significant costs. The negative effects of industrialized agriculture on the health of rural communities, ecosystems, and food systems have convinced many of the need for a more sustainable mode of agriculture. As farms have grown larger and replaced human labor with machinery, the population involved in farming has dramatically declined. This has led to depopulation of rural areas and struggles to maintain the institutions and basic services necessary for a high quality of life. Industrialized agriculture relies upon heavy inputs of fertilizers, pesticides, and herbicides, each of which has had a negative effect on rural populations, wildlife, surface waterways, and coastal systems that receive agricultural runoff (for more, see Chapter 13). Industrialized agriculture relies on large quantities of fossil fuels to fuel the machinery, manufacture petrochemical-based fertilizers, and distribute the food around the world. Heavy reliance on nonrenewable fossil fuels to produce food is obviously unsustainable over the longer term. Finally, there are serious concerns about the quality of the food supply and its relationship to human health, the obesity epidemic, and diet-related diseases such as cancer and diabetes. Concerns range from the relative lack of fresh fruits and vegetables in the diets of rich countries, the safety of foods with pesticide and hormone residues, to the growth of antibiotic resistance due to the overuse of antibiotics in livestock feed.

The sustainable agriculture movement is a collection of alternative approaches to agriculture that seek to enhance social, ecological, economic, and individual health. Sustainable agriculture advocates emphasize local knowledge, local markets, smaller operations, and farm diversification. Sustainable agriculture relies upon local knowledge of soil and plant conditions, and uses traditional agriculture methods adapted to particular places. Just as neolocalism is evident in the rise of regional microbrew beers (as discussed in Chapter 7), a wider local foods movement is growing in strength (see the feature "Eating Locally on the College Campus"). As consumers show concern about the health of their food, where it comes from, and how far it has traveled to their table, they've turned to organic foods, farmer's markets, urban gardening, and community-supported agriculture. Where industrial agriculture creates monocultures and specialized producers, sustainable agriculture advocates believe in farm diversification and biodiversity. They argue that a region with many smaller producers growing many different crops and raising different livestock is more resilient and creates a healthier local economy and environment. In many ways, sustainable agriculture is a return to methods of agriculture that were widely used prior to World War II, Thus, critics question whether sustainable agriculture will be able to maintain the productivity gains of industrial agriculture and feed the world's growing population.

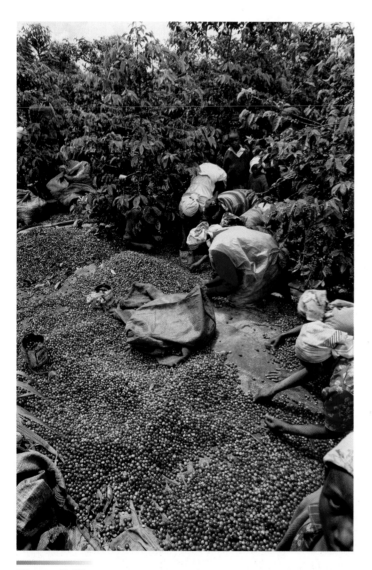

Figure 8.22 Women picking coffee beans on a Kenyan coffee plantation. Coffee is a classic plantation crop, with operations typically established by foreign investors in locations offering a suitable physical environment (climate and soils) and producing an introduced crop for export to distant foreign market. While coffee was first domesticated in Africa, it is grown in many tropical countries, mostly for export to developed countries in the midlatitudes. Note that the women laborers are still responsible for child care even as they work in the fields.

Eating Locally on the College Campus

Stereotypes associate college life with a diet of fast food hamburgers and greasy pizza. However, many college students are starting to pay close attention to their food choices. They are asking where their food comes from and how it affects human health, animal welfare, and the environment. Some are even getting involved in producing their own food. Gustavus Adolphus College in St. Peter, Minnesota, is just one of many colleges and universities where students have succeeded in pressuring the college dining services to offer healthier, locally produced food.

To the west of the Gustavus campus, corn and soybean fields extend into the distance. A couple of generations ago, most Gustavus students came from small Midwest farms. Growing up on farms, the students of the past would have plenty of experience with field work, milking cows, gathering eggs, butchering chickens, gardening, and canning. Back then, farms were diverse general farming operations. In 1940, the typical farm in southern Minnesota grew a variety of crops on about 50 hectares (100 acres) of land and had a few milk cows, chickens for eggs, a couple of pigs, and a large garden for household consumption. Today, a few large farm operations have replaced the numerous small family farms of the past. Grain farmers now plant several thousand hectares of just two crops— corn and soybeans. Other farmers raise thousands of hogs each year, and two nearby industrial dairies house more than 3,000 milk cows each. Cows are milked three times a day while riding a rotating carousel that runs 24 hours a day, 7 days a week and is operated by immigrant Hispanic workers. While the area near Gustavus is among the most productive of agricultural landscapes, almost nothing is for local consumption. Instead, the milk and meat are shipped to distant markets, soybeans are refined for use in industrial processes, and the corn goes to Asian or European markets or to produce ethanol fuel. And no longer does the college get its students from Midwest farms or supply its cafeteria from local farms. Instead, the students come from cities and suburbs, and the cafeteria food is delivered on large refrigerated trucks.

Classes and a campus conference on food inspired several students to ask start asking questions about food supplies, health and environmental sustainability. Two seniors, Cat Weichmann and Eliza Swedenborg, had learned in a geography course how the heavy usage of nitrogen fertilizers on local farms had contaminated local wells with nitrates and contributed to a growing "dead zone" in the Gulf of Mexico. So they decided to develop an organic garden on campus land as their senior project. Their small garden has grown into the Big Hill Farm, an important part of the college's commitment to environmental sustainability. The college supports the farm with land, tillage equipment, and paid summer student internships. A grant paid for a greenhouse, which extends the short Minnesota growing season. The farm and the student dining service have a mutually beneficial relationship. Food waste from the dining service is composted and used as fertilizer and soil amendment on the farm, while the farm produces lettuce, tomatoes, peppers, beans, onions, melons, pumpkins, berries, and much more for the cafeteria. Where possible, the farm uses rare heirloom seed varieties to promote crop diversity. Extra produce is sold to the local food cooperative and at the local farmer's market. Students are now eating healthier, locally grown food, and the college is reducing its impact on the environment. Students who work on the farm learn lifetime skills and describe their labors as both exhausting and deeply rewarding.

Primary Activities: Resource Exploitation

In addition to agriculture, primary economic activities include fishing, forestry, and the mining and quarrying of minerals. These industries involve the direct exploitation of natural resources that are unequally distributed in the environment.

Fishing, forestry, and fur trapping are **gathering industries** based on harvesting the natural bounty of renewable resources that can easily be depleted through overexploitation. Livelihoods based on these resources are areally widespread and involve both subsistence and market-oriented components. Mining and quarrying are **extractive industries,** removing nonrenewable metallic and nonmetallic minerals, including the mineral fuels, from the Earth's crust. They are the initial raw material phase of modern industrial economies.

Resource Terminology

Resources or **natural resources** are the naturally occurring materials that a society perceives to be useful to its economic and material well-being. Their occurrence and spatial distribution are the result of physical processes over which people have little or no direct control. The fact that things exist, however, does not mean that they are resources. To be considered such, a given substance must be *understood* to be a resource—and this is a cultural, not purely a physical, circumstance. Native Americans may have viewed the resource base of Pennsylvania, West Virginia, or Kentucky as composed of forests for shelter and fuel and as the habitat of the game animals (another resource) on which they depended for food. European settlers viewed the forests as the unwanted covering of the resource that *they* perceived to be of value: soil for agriculture. Still later, industrialists appraised the underlying coal deposits, ignored or unrecognized as a resource by earlier occupants, as the item of value for exploitation (Figure 8.23).

Resources may be classified as *renewable* or *nonrenewable*. **Renewable resources** are materials or energy sources that are replenished by natural processes. The sun's energy, wind, water, food crops, soils, forests, fish, and animals are renewable resources. Even renewable resources can be exhausted if exploited to extinction or destruction. Soil can be eroded or its fertility destroyed, and an animal species may be driven to extinction. That is, some resources are renewable only if carefully managed. The **maximum sustainable yield** of a resource is the maximum rate of use that will not impair its ability to be renewed or to maintain the same future productivity. For fishing and forestry, for example, that level is marked by a catch or harvest equal to the net growth of the replacement stock. If that maximum exploitation level is exceeded, the renewable resource becomes a nonrenewable one—an outcome increasingly likely in the case of Atlantic cod and some other food fish species. **Nonrenewable resources** exist in finite amounts or are generated in nature so slowly that for all practical purposes, their supply is finite.

Figure 8.23 Changing perception of natural resources. The original hardwood forest covering these West Virginia hills was removed by settlers who saw greater resource value in the underlying soils. The soils, in their turn, were selectively stripped away for access to the still more valuable coal deposits below. Resources are characterized as a culture perceives them.

Fishing

Although fish and shellfish account for only about 15 percent of all human animal protein consumption, an estimated 1 billion people—primarily in developing countries of eastern and southeastern Asia, Africa, and parts of Latin America—depend on fish as their primary source of protein. Fish are also very important in the diets of most advanced states, both those with and those without major domestic fishing fleets. Although about three-fourths of the world annual fish harvest is consumed by humans, up to one-quarter is processed into fish meal to be fed to livestock or used as fertilizer. Those two quite different markets have increased both the demand for and the annual harvest of fish. Indeed, so rapidly have demand pressures on the world's fish stocks expanded that evidence is unmistakable that at least locally, their *maximum sustainable yield* is being exceeded.

The annual fish supply comes from three sources:

- The *inland catch,* from ponds, lakes, and rivers
- *Fish farming (or aquaculture),* in which fish are produced in a controlled and contained environment
- The *marine catch,* all wild fish harvested in coastal waters or on the high seas

The inland catch supplies a modest fraction of the global fish catch, while fish farming continues to grow, producing nearly 40 percent of the world's fish harvest. While the world's ocean catch is still the most important source of fish, its annual harvest has been stable or declining since the late 1980s (Figure 8.24). Most of the marine catch is made in coastal wetlands, estuaries, and the relatively shallow coastal waters above the *continental shelf*—the gently sloping extension of submerged land bordering most coastlines and reaching seaward for varying distances up to 150 kilometers (about 100 miles) or more. Near shore, shallow embayments and marshes provide spawning grounds, and river waters supply nutrients to an environment highly productive of fish. Increasingly, these areas are also seriously affected by pollution from runoff and ocean dumping, an environmental assault so devastating in some areas that fish and shellfish stocks have been destroyed, with little hope of revival.

Commercial marine fishing is largely concentrated in northern waters, where warm and cold currents join and mix and where such familiar food species as herring, cod, mackerel, haddock, and flounder congregate or "school" on the broad continental shelves and *banks*—extensive elevated portions of the shelf where environmental conditions are most favorable for fish production (Figure 8.25). Two of the most heavily fished regions are the Northeast Pacific and Northwest Atlantic, which together yield about 40 percent of the marine catch total. Tropical fish species tend not to school and, because of their high oil content and unfamiliarity, are less acceptable in the commercial market. They are, however, of great importance for local consumption. Only a very small percentage of total marine catch comes from the open seas that make up more than 90 percent of the world's oceans.

Modern technology and more aggressive fishing fleets from more countries greatly increased annual marine capture in the years after 1950. That technology included use of sonar, radar, helicopters, and satellite communications to locate schools of fish;

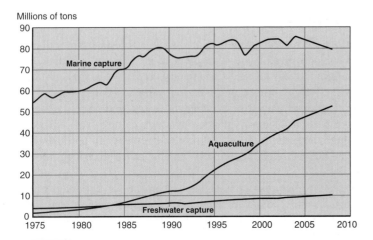

Figure 8.24 **Officially recorded annual fish harvests, 1975–2008.** The marine catch shows evidence of overfishing, while aquaculture continues its rapid growth. The FAO estimates that 20 to 40 million tons per year of unintended marine capture of juvenile or undersized fish and nontarget species are discarded each year.

Source: Food and Agriculture Organization (FAO).

more efficient nets and tackle; and factory trawlers to follow fishing fleets to prepare and freeze the catch. In addition, more nations granted ever-larger subsidies to expand and reward their marine trawler operations. The rapid rate of increase led to inflated projections of the continuing or growing productivity of fisheries and to optimism that the resources of the oceans were inexhaustible.

Quite the opposite has proved to be true, however. In fact, in recent years, the productivity of marine fisheries has declined

because *overfishing* (catches above reproduction rates) and pollution of coastal waters have seriously endangered the supplies of traditional and desirable food species. The decline in marine catch, coupled with the growing world population, has caused a serious drop in the average per capita marine catch. The United Nations reports that all 17 of the world's major oceanic fishing areas are being fished at or beyond capacity; 13 are in decline. The plundering of U.S. and Canadian coastal waters has imperiled a number of the most desirable fish species; in 1993, Canada shut down its cod industry to allow stocks to recover, and U.S. authorities report that 67 North American species are overfished and 61 harvested to capacity.

Overfishing is partly the result of the accepted view that the world's oceans are common property, a resource open to anyone's use with no one responsible for its maintenance, protection, or improvement. The result of this "open seas" principle is but one expression of the so-called **tragedy of the commons**[1]—the economic reality that when a resource is available to all, each user, in the absence of collective controls, thinks he or she is best served by exploiting the resource to the maximum even though this exploitation means its eventual depletion. In 1995, more than 100 countries adopted a treaty—that became legally binding in 2001—to regulate fishing on the open oceans outside territorial waters. Applying to such species as cod, pollock, and tuna—that is, to migratory and high-seas species—the treaty requires fishermen to report the size of their catches to regional organizations that would

---

[1]The *commons* refers to undivided land available for the use of everyone; usually, it meant the open land of a village that all used as pasture. The Boston Common, for instance, originally had this function.

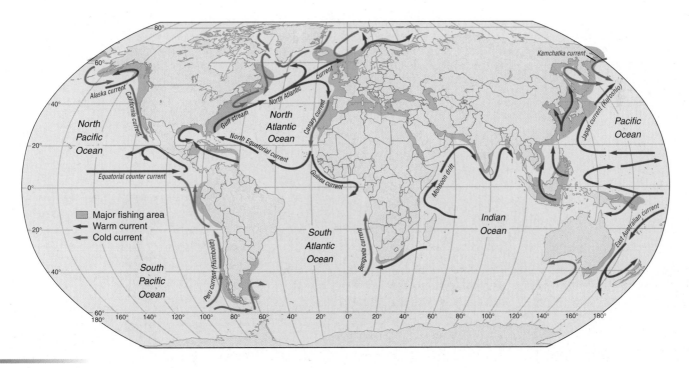

Figure 8.25 **The major commercial marine fisheries of the world.** The waters within 325 kilometers (200 miles) of the United States coastline account for almost one-fifth of the world's annual fish and shellfish harvests. Overfishing, urban development, hydroelectric dams that block access to spawning grounds, and the contamination of bays, estuaries, and wetlands have contributed to the depletion of the fish stocks in those coastal waters.

set quotas and subject vessels to boarding to check for violations. These and other fishing control measures could provide the framework for future sustainability in the fishing industry, although they appear to be too late to save the cod fishery on the Atlantic Coast of Canada. There, the collapse of large fish stocks in the 1990s and the virtual disappearance of cod, haddock, flounder, and hake has induced ecological changes that may prevent the fishery from ever recovering. The collapse of the Atlantic cod fishery caused the loss of 40,000 jobs and immense economic hardship in Canada's Maritime provinces. One approach to increasing the fish supply is through fish farming or **aquaculture,** the breeding of fish in freshwater ponds, lakes, and canals or in fenced-off coastal bays and estuaries or enclosures (Figure 8.26). Aquaculture production has provided about 30 percent of the total fish harvest in recent years; its contribution to the human food supply is even greater than raw production figures suggest. Whereas one-third of the conventional fish catch is used to make fish meal and fish oil, virtually all farmed fish are used as human food. Fish farming has long been practiced in Asia, where fish are a major source of protein, but now takes place on every continent. Marine aquaculture can create serious problems, including water pollution from fish wastes, transfer of disease to wild fish, and genetic damage to wild fish from escaped alien or genetically altered farmed fish. Despite concerns about its potential negative consequences, aquaculture is the fastest-growing sector of the world food economy.

Forestry

Before the rise of agriculture, the world's forests and woodlands probably covered some 45 percent of the Earth's land area, not counting Antarctica and Greenland. They were a sheltered and productive environment for earlier societies that subsisted on gathered fruits, nuts, berries, leaves, roots, and fibers collected from trees and woody plants. Few such cultures still exist, although the gathering of forest products remain an important supplemental activity, particularly among subsistence agricultural societies.

Even after millennia of land clearance for agriculture and, more recently, commercial lumbering, cattle ranching, and fuelwood gathering, forests still cover roughly 30 percent of the world's land area, not counting Greenland and Antarctica. As an industrial raw material source, however, forests are more restricted in area. Although forests of some type reach discontinuously from the equator northward to beyond the Arctic Circle and southward to the tips of the southern continents, *commercial forests* are restricted to two very large global belts. One, nearly continuous, is found in upper-middle latitudes of the Northern Hemisphere; the other is located in the equatorial zones of South and Central America, Central Africa, and Southeast Asia (Figure 8.27). These forest belts differ in the types of trees they contain and in the type of market or use that they serve.

Figure 8.26 Harvesting fish at an aquaculture farm in Thailand. Fish farming is one of the fastest-growing sectors in world food production, with Asian countries supplying the vast majority of the total aquaculture harvest.

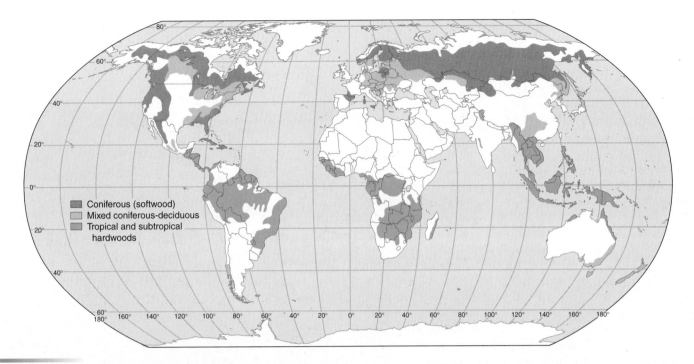

Figure 8.27 Major commercial forest regions. Much of the original forest, particularly in midlatitude regions, has been cut over. Many treed landscapes that remain do not contain commercial stands. Significant portions of the northern forest are not readily accessible and at current prices cannot be considered commercial. Deforestation of tropical hardwood stands involves more clearing for agriculture and firewood than for roundwood production.

The northern coniferous, or softwood, forest is the largest and most continuous stand, extending around the globe from Scandinavia across Siberia to North America, then eastward to the Atlantic and southward along the Pacific Coast. The pine, spruce, fir, and other conifers are used for construction lumber and to produce pulp for paper, rayon, and other cellulose products. On the south side of the northern midlatitude forest region are the deciduous hardwoods: oak, hickory, maple, birch, and the like. These, as well as the trees of the mixed forest lying between the hardwood and softwood belts, have been greatly reduced in areal extent by centuries of agricultural and urban settlement and development. In both Europe and North America, however, their area has been held constant through conservation, protection, and reforestation. They still are commercially important for hardwood applications: furniture, veneers, railroad ties, and the like. The tropical lowland hardwood forests are exploited primarily for fuelwood and charcoal, although an increasing quantity of special-quality woods are cut for export as lumber. In fact, developing countries in the tropics account for most of the world's hardwood log exports (Figure 8.28).

The uses of forests differ significantly between developed and developing countries. In developed countries, trees are primarily cut for various wood product industries, including paper, packaging, personal care products (toilet paper), construction, and furniture. Half of all production of industrial wood is from the United States, Canada, and Russia. Chiefly because of their distance from major industrial wood markets, the developing countries as a group accounted for less than one-quarter of industrial wood production in 2000. The logic of von Thünen's analysis of transportation costs and market accessibility helps explain the pattern. In developing countries, the primary uses of forests are fuelwood and charcoal. Growing populations that depend upon fuelwood and charcoal for energy place pressure on tropical forest stands. For decades, fuelwood gathering was blamed for tropical deforestation. However, recent evidence suggests that fuelwood gathering is not a major source of forest loss and the real problem is forest conversion to agriculture, much of it for the export market. Between 2000 and 2010, the world lost 5.2 million hectares of forestland, half of that in Brazil. Rates of deforestation are highest in Africa, Asia, and South America, while Europe and North America have seen an increase in forested area.

Forests have many noneconomic values, including wildlife habitat, soil conservation, preservation of biological diversity, and carbon storage, which helps slow climate change. Thus, forest loss has serious implications not only economically, but also ecologically.

Mining and Quarrying

Societies at all stages of economic development can and do engage in agriculture, fishing, and forestry. The extractive industries—mining and drilling for nonrenewable mineral wealth—emerged only when technological development and economic necessity turned coal, iron ore, and various minerals into valuable resources. Now those industries provide the raw material and energy for the world's advanced economies. Metals such as iron, copper, and rare earths are the basis for industrial products ranging from automobiles to smart phones. Nonmetallic minerals such as gravel and building stone are widely used in construction, and fossil fuels have provided the energy riches that have made possible the high standards of living in developing countries. The geographic distribution

Figure 8.28 Teak logs for export stacked near Mandalay, Myanmar.

of mineral resources and fossil fuels is highly uneven, and thus, these raw materials are a major part of the international trade connecting the developed and developing countries of the world.

In physically workable and economically usable deposits, minerals constitute only a tiny fraction of the Earth's crust—far less than 1 percent. The Industrial Revolution took place in locations with rich and accessible deposits of the requisite materials such as the coal and iron ore deposits of South Wales and the English Midlands. Economies grew fat by skimming the cream. It has been suggested that should some catastrophe occur to return human cultural levels to a preagricultural state, it would be extremely unlikely that humankind ever again could move along the road of industrialization with the resources available for its use.

Our successes in exploiting mineral resources have been achieved, that is, at the expense of depleting the most easily extractable world reserves and with the penalty of increasing monetary costs as the highest-grade deposits are removed. Costs increase as more advanced and expensive technologies must be applied to extract the desired materials from ever-greater depths in the Earth's crust or from new deposits of lower mineral content. While the Earth's nonrenewable resources are indeed finite, the exact quantity available depends upon both available technology and prices. In fact, as a consequence of advances in exploration

and extraction technologies, known reserves of all fossil fuels and of most commercially important metals are now larger than they were in the middle of the 20th century. *Proved reserves* are those deposits that can be recovered with reasonable certainty, assuming existing economic and operating conditions (Figure 8.29). Proved reserves are not the same as the ultimate crustal limit of a resource. For example, between 1987 and 2010, proved oil reserves increased from 0.91 trillion barrels of oil to 1.38 trillion barrels, despite heavy petroleum consumption—reflecting continued exploration, technological improvements, and price changes. That increasing abundance of at least nonfuel resources is reflected in the steady decrease in raw material prices since the 1950s that has so adversely affected some export-oriented developing world economies.

Metals

Because usable mineral deposits are the result of geological processes, it follows that the larger the country, the more probable it is that such past processes will have occurred within their national territory. And in fact, Russia, Canada, China, the United States, Brazil, and Australia possess abundant and diverse mineral resources. It is also true, however, that many smaller, developing

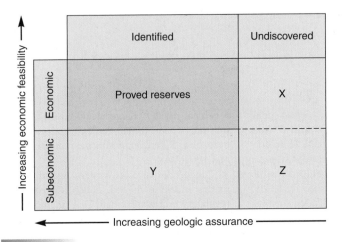

Figure 8.29 The variable definition of reserves. Assume that the large rectangle includes the total world stock of a particular resource. Some deposits of that resource have been discovered and are shown in the left column as "identified." Deposits not yet known are "undiscovered reserves." Deposits that are economically recoverable with current technology are at the top of the diagram. Those below, labeled "subeconomic" reserves, are not attractive for any of several reasons of mineral content, accessibility, cost of extraction, and so on. Only the pink area can be properly referred to as **usable reserves.** These are deposits that have been identified and can be recovered at current prices and with current technology. *X* denotes reserves that would be attractive economically but are not yet discovered; identified but not economically attractive reserves are labeled *Y;* and *Z* represents undiscovered deposits that would not be attractive now even if they were known.

Source: U.S. Geological Survey.

countries are major sources of one or more critical raw materials and therefore become important participants in the growing international trade in minerals.

The production of most metallic minerals, such as copper, lead, and iron ore, is affected by a balance of three forces: the quantity available, the richness of the ore, and the distance to market. A fourth factor, land acquisition and royalty costs, may equal or exceed other considerations in mine development decisions (see the feature "Public Land, Private Profit"). Even if these conditions are favorable, mines may not be developed or even remain operating if supplies from competing sources are more cheaply available in the market. In the 1980s, more than 25 million tons of iron ore-producing capacity was permanently shut down in the United States and Canada. Similar declines occurred in North American copper, nickel, zinc, lead, and molybdenum mining as market prices fell below domestic production costs. Beginning in the early 1990s, as a result of both resource depletion and low cost imports, the United States became a net importer of nonfuel minerals for the first time. Of course, increases in mineral prices may be reflected in opening or reopening mines that, at lower returns, were deemed unprofitable. However, the developed industrial countries of market economies, whatever their former or even present mineral endowment, find themselves at a competitive disadvantage against producers in developing countries with lower-cost labor and state-owned mines with abundant, rich reserves.

When the ore is rich in metallic content (in the case of iron and aluminum ores), it is profitable to ship it directly to the market for refining. Of course, the highest-grade ores tend to be mined first. Consequently, the demand for low-grade ores has been increasing in recent years as richer deposits have been depleted (Figure 8.30). Low-grade ores are often upgraded by various types of separation treatments at the mine site to avoid the cost of transporting waste materials not wanted at the market. Concentration of copper is nearly always mine-oriented (Figure 8.31); refining takes place near areas of consumption. The large amount of waste in copper (98 percent to 99 percent or more of the ore) and in most other industrially significant ores should not be considered the mark of an unattractive deposit. Indeed, the opposite may be true. Because of the cost of extraction or the smallness of the reserves, many higher-content ores are left unexploited in favor of the use of large deposits of even very-low-grade ore. The attraction of the latter is a size of reserve sufficient to justify the long-term commitment of development capital and, simultaneously, to ensure a long-term source of supply.

At one time, high-grade magnetite iron ore was mined and shipped from the Iron Range of northeastern Minnesota. Those deposits are now exhausted. However, immense amounts of capital have been invested in the processing of the virtually unlimited quantities of low-grade iron-bearing rock (taconite) into high-grade iron ore pellets. Naturally, such processing of low-grade deposits takes place at the mine site. Large investments do not guarantee the profitable exploitation of the resource. The metals market is highly volatile. Rapidly and widely fluctuating prices can change profitable mining and refining ventures to losing undertakings very quickly. Marginal gold and silver deposits are opened or closed in response to trends in precious metals prices. Taconite processing in the Lake Superior region nearly ceased as the U.S. steel industry declined, but it has restarted in recent years in response to overseas market demand. In capitalist economies, cost and market controls dominate economic decisions. In planned economies, cost may be a less important consideration than other concerns, such as national development and resource independence.

Figure 8.30 Needed metal content of copper ore for profitable mining. In 1830, 3 percent copper ore in rock was needed to justify its mining; today, rock with 0.5 percent ore content is mined. As the supply of a metal decreases and its price increases, the concentration needed for economic recovery goes down. It also goes down as improved and more cost-effective technologies of rock mining and ore extraction come into play.

Source: Data from the U.S. Bureau of Mines.

Geography and Citizenship

Public Land, Private Profit

When U.S. president Ulysses S. Grant signed the Mining Act of 1872, the presidential and congressional goal was to encourage western settlement and development by allowing any "hard-rock" miners (including prospectors for silver, gold, copper, and other metals) to mine federally owned land without royalty payment. It further permitted mining companies to gain clear title to publicly owned land and all subsurface minerals for no more than $12 a hectare ($5 an acre). Under those liberal provisions, mining firms have bought 1.3 million hectares (3.2 million acres) of federal land since 1872; and each year, they remove some $1.2 billion worth of minerals from government property. In contrast to the royalty-free extraction privileges granted to metal miners, oil, gas, and coal companies pay royalties of as much as 12.5 percent of their gross revenues for exploiting federal lands.

Whatever the merits of the 1872 law in encouraging economic development of lands otherwise unattractive to homesteaders, modern-day mining companies throughout the western states have secured enormous actual and potential profits from the law's generous provisions. In Montana, a company claim to 810 hectares (2000 acres) of land would cost less than $10,000 for an estimated $4 billion worth of platinum and palladium; in California, a gold mining company in 1994 sought title to 93 hectares (230 acres) of federal land containing a potential of $320 million of gold for less than $1,200. Foreign as well as domestic firms may be beneficiaries of the 1872 law. In 1994, a South African firm arranged to buy 411 hectares (1,016 acres) of Nevada land with a prospective $1.1 billion in gold from the government for $5,100. A Canadian firm in 1994 received title to 800 hectares (nearly 2,000 acres) near Elko, Nevada, that cover a likely $10 billion worth of gold—a transfer that Interior Secretary

Bruce Babbitt dubbed "the biggest gold heist since the days of Butch Cassidy." And in 1995, Babbitt conveyed about $1 billion worth of travertine (a mineral used in whitening paper) under 45 hectares (110 acres) of Idaho to a Danish-owned company for $275.

The "gold heist" characterization summarized a growing administration and congressional feeling that what was good in 1872 and today for metal mining companies was not necessarily beneficial to the American public that really owns the land. In part, that feeling results from the fact that mining companies commit environmental sins that require public funding to repair or public tolerance to accept. The mining firms may destroy whole mountains to gain access to low-grade ores and leave toxic mine tailings, surface water contamination, and open-pit scarring of the landscape as they move on or disappear. Projected public cleanup costs of more than 500,000 abandoned mine sites, thousands of miles of damaged or dead streams, and several billion tons of contaminated waste are estimated at a minimum of $35 billion.

A congressional proposal introduced in 1993 would have required mining companies to pay royalties of 8 percent on gross revenues for all hard-rock ores extracted, and prohibited them from outright purchase of federal land. The royalty provision alone would have yielded nearly $100 million annually at 1994 levels of company income. Mining firms claim that imposition of royalties might well destroy the U.S. mining industry. They stress both the high levels of investment that they must make to extract and process frequently low-grade ores and the large number of high-wage jobs they provide as their sufficient contribution to the nation. The Canadian company involved in the Elko site, for example, reports that since it acquired the claims in 1987 from their previous owner, it has expended over $1 billion and also has made donations for town sewer lines and schools and created 1,700 jobs. The American Mining Congress estimates the proposed

8 percent royalty charge would cost 47,000 jobs out of the 140,000 that exist today, and even the U.S. Bureau of Mines assumes a loss of 1,100 jobs.

Public resistance to Western mining activities is taking its toll. State and federal regulatory procedures, many dragging on for a decade or more, have discouraged opening new mines; newly enacted environmental regulations restricting current mining operations (for example, banning the use of cyanide in gold and silver refining) reduce their economic viability. In consequence, both investment and employment in U.S. mining is in a steady decline, eroding the economic base of many Western communities.

Questions to Consider

1. Do you believe that the Mining Act of 1872 should be repealed or amended? If not, what are your reasons for arguing that the law should remain on the books as it is? If so, would you advocate the imposition of royalties on mining company revenues? At what levels, if any, should royalties be assessed? Should hard-rock and energy companies be treated equally for access to public land resources? Why or why not?

2. Would you propose to prohibit outright land sales to mining companies? If not, should sales prices be determined by surface value of the land, or by the estimated (but unrealized) value of mineral deposits that it contains?

3. Do you think that cleanup and other charges now borne by the public are acceptable, given the capital investments and jobs created by mining companies? Do you accept the industry's claim that imposing royalties would destroy American metal mining? Why or why not?

4. Do you favor continued state and federal restrictions on mining operations, even at the cost of jobs and community economies? Why or why not?

Nonmetallic Minerals

From the standpoint of volume and weight of material removed, the extraction of nonmetallic materials is the most important branch of the extractive industries. The minerals mined are usually classified by their end use. Of widest distribution, greatest use,

and least long-distance movement are those used for *construction:* sand and gravel, building stone, and the gypsum and limestone that are the ingredients of cement. Transportation costs play a large role in determining where low-value minerals will be mined. Minerals such as gravel, limestone for cement, and aggregate are found in such abundance that they have value only when they are

Figure 8.31 Copper mine, concentrating mill, and smelter at the Phelps-Dodge mine in Morenci, Arizona. Concentrating mills crush the ore, separating copper-bearing material from the rocky mass containing it. The great volume of waste removed ensures that most concentrating operations are found near the ore bodies. Smelters separate concentrated copper from other, unwanted materials, such as oxygen and sulfur. Because smelting is a "weight-reducing" process, it saves transportation costs to locate it close to the mine as well.

near the site where they are to be used. For example, gravel for road building has value if it is at or near the road-building project, not otherwise. Transporting gravel hundreds of miles is an unprofitable activity (Figure 8.32). For example, while the United States imports 100 percent of its rare earths, it produces 99 percent of its own crushed stone.

The mined *fertilizer* minerals include potash and phosphate, which move in international trade because of their unequal distribution and market value. *Precious* and *semiprecious* stones are also important in the economy of some countries, including the rich diamond deposits of several central African countries and Sri Lanka's gemstones.

Figure 8.32 The Vancouver, British Columbia, municipal gravel quarry and storage yard. Proximity to market is necessary for low-value nonmetallic minerals unable to bear high transportation charges.

Fossil Fuels

The advanced economies have gotten the way they are through their control and use of energy. By using external energy sources, humans can perform tasks beyond the wildest dreams of our human ancestors. This is largely because fossil fuels are incredibly energy-dense. One 42-gallon (166 liter) barrel of oil contains the energy equivalent of 50,000 person-hours of labor. Compare how far $10 of gasoline will take you in an automobile versus how far you could get paying your friends to push that automobile down the road. While slavery made a few rich by harnessing the forced labor of many, fossil fuels can make many "rich" by harnessing fossil fuel energy—at least while prices stay low. Energy consumption goes hand in hand with industrial production and with increases in personal wealth. In general, the greater the level of energy consumption, the higher the gross national income per capita. Further, the application of energy can allow us to transform low-value raw materials into valuable commodities. High-quality iron ore may be depleted, but by massive applications of energy, the iron contained in rocks of very low iron content, such as taconite, can be concentrated for industrial uses.

Because of the close relationship between energy use and economic development, a basic disparity between societies is made clear. Countries that can afford high levels of energy consumption through production or purchase continue to expand their economies and to increase their levels of living. Those without access to energy or those unable to afford it are left behind.

Except for the brief and localized importance of waterpower at the outset of the Industrial Revolution, modern economic advancement has been heavily dependent on the *fossil fuels:* coal, oil, and natural gas. These nonrenewable energy sources represent the capture of the sun's energy by plants and animals in earlier geologic time and its storage in the form of hydrocarbon compounds in sedimentary rocks within the Earth's crust.

Coal was the earliest in importance and is still the most plentiful of the fossil fuels. As the first major industrial energy source, nearby coal deposits were essential to early manufacturing development, as we shall see in Chapter 9. Although coal is a nonrenewable resource, world supplies are so great—on the order of 850 billion tons—that its resource life expectancy is measured in centuries, not in the much shorter time scales cited for oil and natural gas. Worldwide, the most extensive deposits are concentrated in the industrialized middle latitudes of the Northern Hemisphere (Table 8.2). China is the world's largest coal producer, responsible for 48 percent of the world production in 2010. The United States is a distant second, contributing 15 percent of world coal production in 2010.

Table 8.2

Proved Petroleum, Natural Gas, and Coal Reserves, January 1, 2008

	Share of World Total Petroleum (%)	Share of World Total Natural Gas (%)	Share of World Total Coal (%)
North America[a]	5.4	4.5	28.5
Europe	1.0	3.4	9.4
Former Soviet Union	*9.1*	*30.1*	*26.0*
Of which: Russian Federation	5.6	25.2	18.2
Others	3.4	4.9	7.8
Central and South America	17.3	4.4	1.5
Africa	9.5	8.2	3.7
Middle East[b]	54.4	41.3	0.1
Australia	0.3	1.4	8.9
Japan	–.–	–.–	–.–
China	1.1	1.1	13.3
Other Asia Pacific	1.9	5.7	8.6
Total World	100.0	100.0	100.0
Of which OPEC[c]	77.2	NA	NA

[a]Includes Canada, Mexico, United States

[b]Middle East includes the Arabian Peninsula, Iran, Iraq, Israel, Jordan, Lebanon, and Syria.

[c]OPEC: Organization of Petroleum Exporting Countries. Member nations are, by world region:

South America: Venezuela

Middle East: Iran, Iraq, Kuwait, Qatar, Saudi Arabia, and United Arab Emirates (Abu Dhabi, Dubai, Ras-al-Khaimah, and Sharjah)

North Africa: Algeria and Libya

West Africa: Nigeria

Asia Pacific: Indonesia

Source: Data from the BP Amoco *Statistical Review of World Energy,* 2011.

Coal is not a resource of constant quality, varying in *rank* (a measure—from lignite to anthracite—of increasing carbon content and fuel quality) and *grade* (a measure of its waste material content, particularly ash and sulfur). The value of a coal deposit depends on these measures and on its accessibility, which is a function of the thickness, depth, and continuity of the coal seam. Much coal can be mined relatively cheaply by open-pit (surface) techniques, in which huge shovels strip off surface material and remove the exposed coal (see Figure 13.17). Much coal, however, is available only by expensive and more dangerous shaft mining, as in Appalachia, China, and most of Europe. In spite of their generally lower heating value, western U.S. coals are attractive because of their low sulfur content. They do, however, require expensive transportation to market or high-cost transmission lines if they are used to generate electricity for distant consumers (Figure 8.33).

Oil, first extracted commercially in the 1860s in both the United States and Azerbaijan, became a major power source, raw material for the chemical industry, and favorite transportation fuel in the 20th century. It is used as a raw material for a number of important industries, from plastics to fertilizers. However, its supplies are limited, and it is unlikely to retain its present position of importance in the world energy market.

Estimating how much oil (or natural gas) remains in the world and how long it will last is the subject of heated debate. Given the world economy's dependence on petroleum, the stakes are undeniably high. Some experts subscribe to "peak oil theory," which is based on the work of American geologist M. King Hubbert. Hubbert began by showing that the rate of oil pumped from a single well over time followed a symmetrical bell curve, rising, peaking, and finally declining. He also noted that the same bell curve applied to the total production from an entire wellfield or an entire country. By knowing the shape of the rising portion of the curve, one can predict the timing of the peak and the inevitable decline that will follow. Peak oil theorists warn that once the world reaches peak oil production, the inevitable decline in production will cause shortages and skyrocketing prices. Estimates of when the world economy would hit peak oil range from 2010 to 2040, with the forecasts undergoing regular revision. Optimists are encouraged by new horizontal drilling techniques and deep sea drilling that have opened up large new oilfields in North Dakota and the Gulf of Mexico. They also point to a steady drop in the price of solar and other alternative energy sources, which they believe will reduce oil demand long before supply becomes an issue. In a different form of assessment, British Petroleum reported that the world had 1.4 trillion barrels of proven oil reserves at the end of 2010—enough to last for 46 years at the 2010 rate of extraction.

Petroleum is among the most unevenly distributed of the major resources (Table 8.2). A total of 73 percent of proved oil reserves

Figure 8.33 Long-distance transportation to eastern markets adds significantly to the cost of the low-sulfur western coal useful in meeting federal environmental protection standards. To minimize these costs, unit trains carrying only coal engage in a continuous shuttle movement between western strip mines and eastern utility companies.

are concentrated in just seven countries: Saudi Arabia, Venezuela, Iran, Iraq, Kuwait, United Arab Emirates, and the Russian Federation. The underlying role of petroleum in geopolitics and military conflicts over the past 20 years is undeniable. The distribution of petroleum supplies differs markedly from that of the coal deposits on which the urban-industrial markets developed, but the substitution of petroleum for coal did little to alter earlier patterns of manufacturing and population concentration. Because oil is easier and cheaper to transport than coal, it was moved in enormous amounts to the existing centers of consumption via intricate and extensive national and international systems of transportation, a textbook example of spatial interaction, complementarity, and transferability (see Chapter 3, particularly Figure 3.2).

Natural gas has been called the nearly perfect energy resource. It is a highly efficient, versatile fuel that requires little processing, and its emissions do not contribute to urban air pollution or acid precipitation, although they do contain carbon dioxide. Geologists estimate that world recoverable gas reserves are sufficient to last another 60 years at 2010 levels of consumption. New discoveries in the United States, such as the Marcellus Shale formation deep under New York, Ohio, Pennsylvania, and West Virginia, are drawing public attention to the rich possibilities of natural gas extraction, as well as the potential negative effects. *Ultimately recoverable reserves,* those that may be found and recovered at very much higher prices, might last another 200 years.

As we saw for coal and petroleum, reserves of natural gas are very unevenly distributed (Table 8.2). In the case of gas, however, inequalities of supply are not so readily accommodated by massive international movements. Like oil, natural gas flows easily and cheaply by pipeline, but unlike petroleum, it does not move freely in international trade by sea. Transoceanic shipment involves costly terminal equipment for liquefaction and special vessels to contain the liquid under appropriate temperature conditions.

Where the fuel can be moved, even internationally, by pipeline, its consumption has increased dramatically. For the world as a whole, gas consumption has risen to about one quarter of global energy consumption.

Trade in Primary Products

International trade has expanded rapidly since the end of World War II, increasing more than sixfold between 1980 and 2010. Primary commodities—agricultural goods and fuels—made up 30 percent of the total dollar value of those international flows. During much of the first half of the 20th century, the world distribution of supply and demand for those items in general resulted in a colonial pattern of commodity flow: from raw-material producers located within less developed countries to processors, manufacturers, and consumers of the more developed ones (Figure 8.34). The

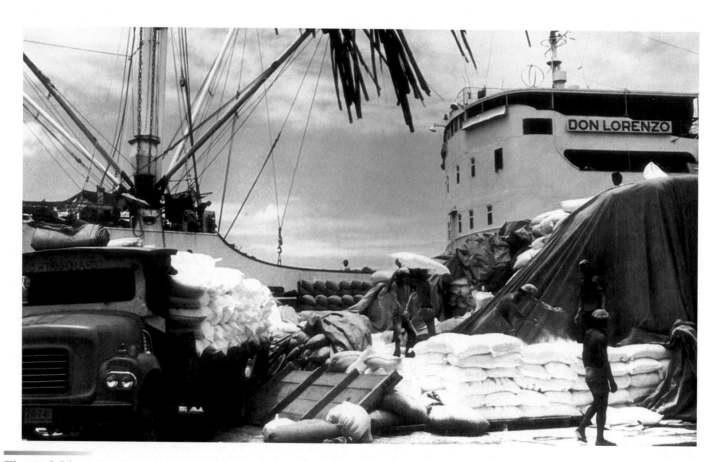

Figure 8.34 Sugar being loaded for export at the port of Cebu in the Philippines. Much of the developing world depends on exports of mineral and agricultural products to the developed economies for the major portion of its income. Fluctuations in market demand and price of some of those commodities can have serious and unexpected consequences.

reverse flow carried manufactured goods from the industrialized states for sale to the developing countries. That two-way trade benefited the developed states by providing access to a continuing supply of industrial raw materials and foods not available domestically, as well as markets for their manufactured goods. While the two-way exchange gave less developed countries some capital to invest in their own development and to purchase imports, they lagged behind in industrialization.

Today, however, world trade flows and export patterns of the emerging economies have changed. Raw materials have greatly decreased, and manufactured goods correspondingly increased in the export flows from developing states. Even with that overall decline in raw material exports, however, trade in unprocessed goods remains dominant in the economic well-being of many of the world's poorest economies. Increasingly, the terms of the traditional trade flows on which they depend have been criticized as unequal and damaging to commodity-exporting countries.

Commodity prices are volatile; they may rise sharply in periods of product shortage or international economic growth. During much of the 1980s and 1990s, however, commodity price movements were downward, to the great detriment of material-exporting economies. Prices for agricultural raw materials, for example, dropped by 30 percent between 1975 and 2000, and those for metals and minerals decreased by almost 40 percent. Such price declines cut deeply into the export earnings of many emerging economies. Of the 141 developing countries, 95 rely on commodities for more than 50 percent of their export earnings and thus are vulnerable to commodity price volatility. Sub-Saharan African countries are particularly dependent on export earnings from a small number of mineral or agricultural commodities. For example, Burundi earned 79 percent of its export income through coffee exports in 2002.

Whatever the current world prices of raw materials may be, raw material exporting states have long expressed resentment as a group at what they perceive as commodity price manipulation by rich countries and corporations to ensure low-cost supplies. Although collusive price-fixing has not been demonstrated, other disadvantages of being a commodity supply region are evident. Technology, for example, has provided industries in advanced countries with a vast array of materials that now substitute for the ores and metals produced by developing states. Glass fibers replace copper wire in telecommunication applications; synthetic rubber replaces natural rubber; carbon fibers are superior in performance and strength to the metals that they replace; and a vast and enlarging array of plastics are the accepted raw materials for commodities

and uses for which natural rivals are not even considered. That is, even as the world industrial economy expands, demands and prices for traditional raw materials remain relatively low.

While prices paid for developing country commodities tend to be low, prices charged for the manufactured goods offered in exchange by the developed countries tend to be high. To capture processing and manufacturing profits for themselves, some developing states have placed restrictions on the export of unprocessed commodities. Malaysia, the Philippines, and Cameroon, for example, have limited the export of logs in favor of increased domestic processing of sawlogs and exports of lumber. Some developing countries have also encouraged domestic manufacturing to reduce imports and to diversify their exports. Frequently, however, such exports meet with tariffs and quotas designed to protect the home markets of the industrialized states.

In 1964, in reaction to the whole range of perceived trade inequities, developing states promoted the establishment of the United Nations Conference on Trade and Development (UNCTAD). Its central constituency—the "Group of 77," which later expanded to 130 developing states—continues to press for a new world economic order based in part on an increase in the prices and values of exports from developing countries, a system of import preferences for their manufactured goods, and a restructuring of international cooperation to stress trade promotion and recognition of the special needs of poor countries. The WTO, established in 1995 (and discussed in detail in Chapter 12) was designed in part to reduce trade barriers and inequities. It has, however, been judged by its detractors as ineffective on issues of importance to developing countries. Chief among the complaints is the continuing failure of the high-income countries to eliminate generous protections for their own agricultural and mineral industries.

In 2001, members of the WTO met in Doha, Qatar, to begin negotiations on opening world markets. Low-income, developing countries argued for the elimination of agricultural subsidies and protectionist policies in the European Union and United States. In turn, the rich economies insisted on significant concessions from poorer countries on trade in both manufactured goods and, particularly, services. The "Doha Round" of trade negotiations continued through 2008, when trade negotiations broke down. Despite the fact that agriculture makes up less than 10 percent of world trade, it has been the roadblock in all global trade talks. The goals of greater fairness and openness in world trade, while maintaining special consideration for the economic development needs of poorer countries, have yet to be achieved to the satisfaction of all parties.

Summary

How different peoples and cultures earn their living and use the diversified resources of the Earth is a fundamental concern in human geography. The economic activities that support us and our society influence our well-being, everyday life, and our perceptions of the world. At the same time, the totality of our culture—technology, religion, customs, and so on—and the circumstances of our natural environment influence the economic choices that we face and the livelihood decisions that we make.

Looking for patterns in the nearly infinite diversity of human economic activity, it is useful to distinguish three types of economic systems: subsistence, commercial, and planned. The first is concerned with production for the immediate consumption of individual producers and family members. In the second, economic decisions ideally respond to impersonal market forces and the profit motive. In the third, at least some nonmonetary social goals, rather than personal ones, influence production decisions. The three system forms are not mutually exclusive; all societies contain some mixture of features of at least two of the three types, and some economies have elements of all three. Recognition of each type's respective features and controls, however, helps us to understand the forces shaping economic decisions and patterns in different cultural and regional settings.

Our search for regularities is advanced by classifying economic activities according to the stages of production and the degree of specialization they represent. We can divide our continuum into primary activities (food and raw material production), secondary production (processing and manufacturing), and tertiary service activities (wholesaling, retail trade, personal service, and business services).

Agriculture is the most extensively practiced of the primary industries. In subsistence economies—whether it takes the form of extensive or intensive, shifting or sedentary production—this industry is responsive to the immediate consumption needs of the producer group and reflective of local environmental conditions. Agriculture in advanced economies involves the application of capital and technology with the goal of increasing productivity and efficiency. Commercialized agriculture increasingly involves large-scale, highly specialized agribusiness operations. Arising in reaction to industrialized agriculture, the sustainable agriculture movement seeks to use local knowledge to improve the health of communities, the food supply, and the environment. Agriculture, fishing, forestry, trapping, and the extractive (mining) industries are closely tied to the uneven distribution of Earth's resources. Their spatial patterns reflect those resource potentials, but they also are influenced by the integration of all societies and economies through the medium of international trade and mutual dependence. The flows of primary products and of manufactured goods suggest the hierarchy of production, marketing, and service activities, which will be the subject of Chapter 9.

KEY WORDS

agriculture 246
aquaculture 268
Boserup thesis 249
commercial economy 243
economic geography 241
extensive agriculture 247
extractive industry 265
gathering industry 265
Green Revolution 252
intensive agriculture 247
market economy 243

maximum sustainable yield 266
natural resource 265
nomadic herding 247
nonrenewable resource 266
planned economy 243
plantation agriculture 263
post industrial 242
primary activity 242
renewable resource 266
resource 265
secondary activity 242

service activity 242
shifting cultivation 248
subsistence economy 243
technology 242
tertiary activity 242
tragedy of the commons 267
truck farm 259
usable reserves 271
von Thünen model 257

FOR REVIEW

1. What are the distinguishing characteristics of the economic systems labeled *subsistence, commercial,* and *planned?* Are they mutually exclusive, or can they coexist within a single political unit?

2. What are the ecological consequences of the different forms of *extensive subsistence* land use? In what world regions are such systems found? What, in your opinion, are the prospects for these land uses and for the way of life they embody?

3. How is *intensive subsistence* agriculture distinguished from *extensive subsistence* cropping? Why,

in your opinion, have such different land use forms developed in separate areas of the warm, moist tropics?

4. Briefly summarize the assumptions and dictates of von Thünen's agricultural model. How might the land use patterns predicted by the model be altered by an increase in the market price of a single crop? A decrease in the transportation costs of one crop, but not of all crops?

5. What is the basic distinction between a *renewable* and a *nonrenewable* resource? Under what circumstances might the distinction between the two be blurred or obliterated?

6. What economic and ecological problems can you cite that do or might affect the viability and productivity of the *gathering industries* of forestry and fishing? What is meant by the *tragedy of the commons?* How is that concept related to the problems that you discerned?

7. Why have fossil fuels been so important in economic development? What are the mineral fuels, and what are the prospects for their continued availability? Which fossil fuels does your country have in abundance and which does it lack? What economic and social consequences might you anticipate if the price of fossil fuels should double?

KEY CONCEPTS REVIEW

1. **How are economic activities and national economies classified?** pp. 242–245.

The innumerable economically productive activities of humans are influenced by regionally varying environmental, cultural, technological, political, and market conditions. Understanding the world's work is simplified by thinking of economic activity as arranged along a continuum of increasing complexity of product or service and increasing distance from nature. Primary industries (activities) harvest or extract something from the Earth. Secondary industries change the form of those harvested items. Tertiary activities render services to consumers or businesses. Those activity stages are carried out within national economies grouped as subsistence, commercial, or planned.

2. **What are the types and prospects of subsistence agriculture?** pp. 245–254.

Subsistence farming—food production primarily or exclusively for the producers' family needs—still remains the predominant occupation of humans on a worldwide basis. Nomadic herding and shifting ("swidden") cultivation are extensive subsistence systems. Intensive subsistence farming involves large inputs of labor and fertilizer on small plots of land. Both rural and urban subsistence efforts are increasingly marked by some production for market; they have also benefited from Green Revolution crop improvements.

3. **What characterizes commercial agriculture, and what are its controls and special forms?** pp. 254–265.

The modern integrated world of exchange and trade increasingly implies farming efforts that reflect broader market requirements, not purely local or family needs. Commercial agriculture is characterized by specialization, off-farm sale, large-scale operations, and interdependence of farmers and buyers linked through complex markets. The von Thünen model of agricultural location suggests that intensive forms of commercial farming—fruits, vegetables, and dairy products—should be located close to markets. More extensive commercial agriculture businesses, including large-scale wheat farms and livestock ranches, are found at more distant locations. Special crops have unique requirements and spatial patterns as in the case of Mediterranean and plantation agriculture.

4. **What are the special characteristics and problems of nonagricultural primary industries?** pp. 265–276.

The "gathering" industries of fishing, forestry, and trapping and the "extractive" industries of mining and quarrying involve the direct exploitation of spatially variable natural resources. Resources are natural materials that humans perceive as necessary and useful. They may be renewable—replenished—by natural processes or nonrenewable once extracted and used. Overexploitation can exceed the maximum sustainable yield of fisheries and forests and eventually destroy the resource. Such nonrenewable minerals and fuels are vital to industrial economies and yet proven reserves are finite.

5. **What is the status and nature of world trade in primary products?** pp. 276–277.

The primary commodities of agricultural goods, fish, forest products, furs, minerals, and fuels account for nearly one-third of the dollar value of international trade. Traditional exchange flows of raw materials from developing states that then imported manufactured goods from advanced economies have changed in recent years. Increasingly, the share of manufactured goods in developing world exports is growing, and dependence on income from raw material sales is dropping. However, material-exporting states argue that current international trade agreements are unfavorable to exporters of agricultural products and other primary commodities.

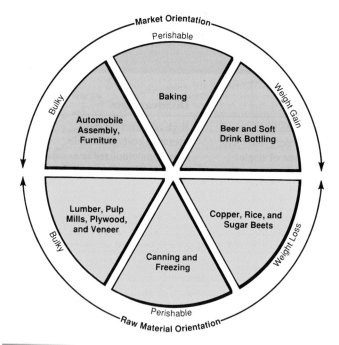

Figure 9.7 **Spatial orientation tendencies.** *Raw material orientation* occurs when there are few alternative material sources, when the material is perishable, or when—in its natural state—it contains a large proportion of impurities or nonmarketable components. *Market orientation* represents the least-cost solution when manufacturing uses commonly available materials that add weight to the finished product, when the manufacturing process produces a commodity bulkier or more expensive to ship than its separate components, or when the perishable nature of the product demands processing close to the market.

Source: Adapted from Interpreting the City: An Urban Geography, *Truman A. Hartshorn. Copyright © 1980 John Wiley & Sons, Inc. Reproduced with permission of John Wiley & Sons, Inc.*

Figure 9.8 **The tapering principle.** The actual costs of transport, including terminal charges and line costs, increase at a decreasing rate as fixed costs are spread over longer hauls. The "tapering" of total cost for the shipping company varies among modes because their mixes of fixed and variable costs are different, as Figure 9.5 diagrams. Note that the actual transport rates charged to customers move in stepwise increments within certain distance ranges.

Industrial Location Theory

In practice, industrial locational decisions are based not on a single factor, but on the interplay of a number of considerations. Implicit in our review has been the understanding that

Figure 9.9 **The short-haul penalty.** Plant locations intermediate between material and market are generally avoided because of the realities of transportation pricing shown here. Two short hauls cost more than a single long haul simply because two sets of fixed costs must be assigned to the interrupted movement.

each type or branch of industry has its own specific set of significant plant siting conditions. Classic industrial location theory was developed in the early 1900s, when the world economy was dominated by railroads, based on heavy industry and goals of national industrial self-sufficiency. Obviously, much has changed in a globalized economy shaped by institutions such as the World Trade Organization (WTO), transnational corporations, environmental protection agencies, and the like. Nevertheless, classic location theory concepts and their spatial implications remain relevant in understanding past and present-day industrial locational decisions.

Least-Cost Theory

The classical model of industrial location theory, the **least-cost theory,** is based on the work of Alfred Weber (1868–1958) and sometimes called **Weberian analysis.** It explains the optimum location of a manufacturing establishment based on minimizing three basic expenses: transport costs, labor costs, and agglomeration costs. **Agglomeration** refers to the clustering of productive activities and people for mutual advantage. Such clustering can produce "agglomeration economies" through shared facilities and services. Diseconomies such as higher rents or wage levels resulting from competition for these resources also may occur.

Weber concluded that transport costs are the major consideration determining location. That is, the optimum location will be found where the costs of transporting raw materials to the factory and finished goods to the market are at their lowest. He noted, however, if variations in labor or agglomeration costs are sufficiently great, a location determined solely on the basis of transportation costs may not in fact be the optimum one.

Weber made five simplifying assumptions:

1. An area is completely uniform physically, politically, culturally, and technologically. This is known as the **uniform,** or **isotropic, plain** assumption.

2. Manufacturing involves a single product to be shipped to a single market in a known location.

3. Inputs involve raw materials from more than one known source location.

components manufactured in Germany, Korea, Taiwan, and Japan, all of which come together in an assembly plant in China.

Through such outsourcing and technology transfers, high-tech activities are spread to newly industrializing countries—from the center to the periphery. This globalization through geographic transfer and diffusion represents an important impact of high-tech activities on world economic geographic patterns. For example, by 2005, China had surpassed the United States in exporting information-technology goods, such as laptop computers, mobile phones, and digital cameras. With rising education levels, countries such as China, India, Singapore, and South Korea are producing large numbers of highly trained scientists and engineers capable of doing much more than assembly work. Thus, computer software companies have begun taking advantage of India's strengths in engineering and computer science, making Bangalore and Hyderabad major world players in software development.

World Manufacturing Patterns and Trends

Growth and change have produced a distinctive world pattern of manufacturing. While Figure 9.20 suggests a large number of industrial concentrations, in fact four regions are commonly recognized as most significant: *Eastern North America, Western and Central Europe, Eastern Europe,* and *Eastern Asia.* Together, the industrial plants within these established regional clusters account for an estimated three-fifths of the world's manufacturing output by volume and value.

Their continuing dominance is by no means assured. The first three—those of North America and Europe—were the beneficiaries of an earlier phase in the development and spread of manufacturing following the Industrial Revolution of the 18th century and lasting until after World War II. The countries within them now are increasingly "postindustrial," and traditional manufacturing and processing are declining in relative importance.

The fourth—the East Asian district—is part of the wider, newer pattern of world industrialization that has emerged in recent years, the result of massive international *cultural convergence* and technology transfers in the latter half of the 20th century and early in the 21st. The older, rigid economic split between the developed and developing worlds has rapidly weakened as the full range of industrial activities from primary metal processing (e.g., the iron and steel industries) through advanced electronic assembly has been established within an ever-expanding list of countries.

Such states as Mexico, Brazil, China, and others of the developing world have created industrial regions of international significance, and the contribution to world manufacturing activity of the smaller newly industrializing countries (NICs) has been growing significantly. The list of NICs includes the four Asian tigers: South Korea, Hong Kong, Singapore, and Taiwan. They each developed by combining a well-educated workforce, infrastructure investments, and policies supporting export-oriented industrialization. Following them came the Asian dragons: Malaysia, Indonesia, and Thailand. The largest of all NICs is China, the world's most populous country, which has seen phenomenal economic growth since the 1970s, passing Japan in 2010 to become the world's second-largest economy after the United States. Latin American NICs include Mexico, Chile, and Brazil.

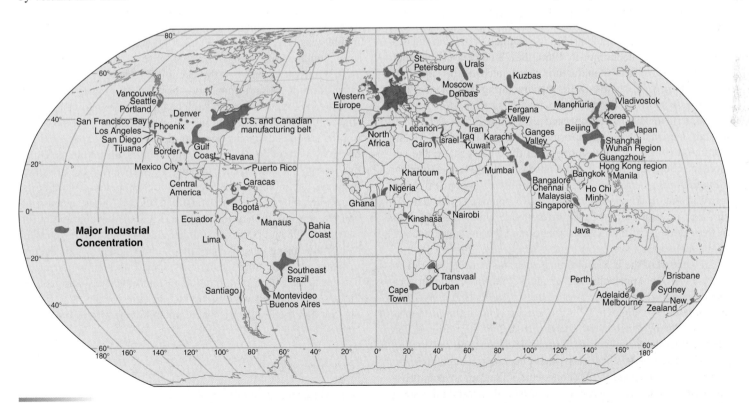

Figure 9.20 World industrial regions. Industrial districts are not as continuous or "solid" as the map suggests. Manufacturing is a relatively minor user of land even in the areas of greatest concentration.

The spreading use of efficient and secure containerized shipment of high-value goods has been a major contributor to the competitive success of NICs. Even economies that until recently were dominated by the primary sector have become important players in world manufacturing. Foreign branch plant investment in low-wage Asian, African, and Latin American states has not only created an industrial infrastructure but also increased their gross national products (GNPs) and per capita incomes sufficiently to permit expanded production for growing domestic—not just export—markets.

Much of that new plant investment and expanded developing country industrial production has concentrated within the great number of *export processing zones* (EPZs) recently created within those countries. An EPZ may be either a delimited geographical area or, frequently, an export-oriented manufacturing enterprise located anywhere within a host country that benefits from special investment incentives. These incentives usually include exemptions from customs duties, preferential treatment from various regulatory and financial regulations, and the provision of high-quality infrastructure—airports, highways, telecommunications, and electric and water facilities—usually provided by the local or national governments. Enterprises operating within or as an EPZ usually enjoy preferential conditions under which they can import equipment, components, and raw materials duty free to produce goods mainly for export. And exports from those zones generally are afforded tariff reductions or duty-free entry into receiving European and North American markets. Because of their obvious production-site advantages, therefore, EPZs are both favored locations for transnational corporation outsourcing and an economic development tool for developing countries competing for TNC investments.

The United States and Canada

The importance of manufacturing in the United States and Canada has been steadily declining. In 1960, the 28 percent of the labor force that engaged in manufacturing generated nearly one-third of the region's wealth. By 2010, manufacturing employment had dropped to just over 10 percent of a much larger labor force.

Manufacturing is concentrated in the urbanized sections of North America, but is not uniformly distributed. Its primary concentration is in the northeastern part of the United States and adjacent sections of southeastern Canada, the *U.S. and Canadian Manufacturing Belt* (Figure 9.21). That district contains the majority of the urban population of the two countries, their densest and best-developed transportation network, the largest number of their manufacturing establishments, and the preponderance of heavy industry.

The heart of the U.S. and Canadian manufacturing belt developed across the Appalachians in the interior of the continent. The Ohio River system and the Great Lakes provided the early—and still important—"highways" of the interior (Figure 9.22), supplemented later by canals and, after the 1850s, by the railroads that tied together the raw materials, the growing cities, and multiplying manufacturing plants. The early heavy metallurgical emphasis—the U.S. Steel plants of the Monongahela Valley are an example—has declined and been succeeded by advanced material processing and fabrication plus high-tech manufacturing, creating a renewed and modernized diversified industrial base.

The Canadian portion of the continent's major manufacturing belt lies close to neighboring U.S. industrial districts. About one-half of Canada's manufacturing labor force is localized in southern Ontario. With Toronto as the hub, the industrial belt extends westward to Windsor, across from Detroit. In the *Southeast,* textiles, tobacco, food processing, wood products, furniture, and a Birmingham-based iron and steel industry became important users of local resources. The textiles and garment industries, concentrated in the Southeast, suffered job losses of about 60 percent from 1999 to 2007, largely due to foreign competition. In the *Gulf Coast–Texas district,* petroleum and natural gas provide wealth, energy, and raw materials for a vast petrochemical industry; sulfur and salt support other branches of chemical production. On the West Coast, three distinctive industrial subregions have emerged. In the *Northwest,* from Vancouver to Portland, orientation to both a regional and a broader Asian-Pacific market is of greater significance than are the primary domestic markets of Canada and the United States. Seattle's aircraft production and the software industry of the Northwest are, by their high-value products, largely unaffected by transport costs to world markets. The *San Francisco Bay district* is home to Silicon Valley and the electronics/computer/high-tech manufacturing that name implies. Food specializations there (wine, for example) for a national market have their counterpart farther south in the *Los Angeles–San Diego corridor,* where fruits and vegetables are grown and packed. More important, however, is diversified production (particularly consumer goods) for the rapidly growing California and western market. North America's fastest growing industrial region lies along the U.S.–Mexican border. Called *la frontera* by its Mexican workers and extending 3,380 kilometers (2,100 miles) from the Pacific Ocean to the Gulf of Mexico, this subregion served us earlier as an example of "outsourcing" and comparative advantage based on its low wages, easy access to U.S. markets, and less stringent environmental regulations.

Deindustrialization—the declining relative share of manufacturing in a nation's economy—has picked up pace in the past two decades. Outsourcing and the new international division have shifted the spatial patterns of industrial production. While the map of production is dynamic, communities are fixed in space and can be devastated by the closure of large manufacturing plants. Cities that lose major employers can enter a downward cycle of falling incomes, declining tax revenues, and higher social services costs. High unemployment, closed factories, closed stores, abandoned houses, and less money for roads and schools become the norm. Between 1998 and 2008, the United States lost about one-fourth of its manufacturing jobs, many of them high-wage jobs. The decline in manufacturing employment was due to a combination of replacing labor with capital (equipment) and overseas competition. Particularly hard hit were the industrial cities of the manufacturing belt and the Southeast, where unemployment rates have been among the highest in the country.

Europe

The Industrial Revolution that began in England in the late 1700s and spread to the continent during the 19th century established Western and Central Europe as the world's premier manufacturing

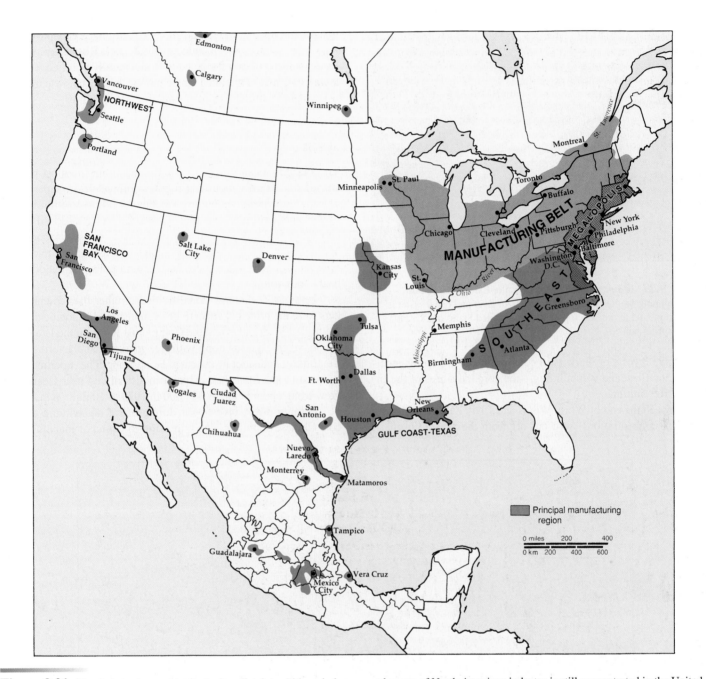

Figure 9.21 North American manufacturing districts. Although the preponderance of North American industry is still concentrated in the United States and Canada, Mexican manufacturing activity is rapidly growing and diversifying—for both expanding domestic and export markets. While Mexico City alone yields nearly half of the country's manufacturing output volume, industrial plants are also localized in the Central Plateau area and along the northern border with the United States, where most *maquiladoras* have been established.

regions and the source areas for the diffusion of industrialization across the globe. Europe accounted for 80 percent of the world's industrial output by 1900, although, of course, its relative position has since eroded, particularly after World War II. Although industry is part of the economic structure of every section and every metropolitan complex of Europe, the majority of manufacturing output is concentrated in a set of distinctive districts stretching from the Midlands of England in the west to the Ural Mountains in the east (Figure 9.23).

Water-powered textile mills in England began the Industrial Revolution, but it was coal that fueled the full industrialization

of Europe. Consequently, coal fields were the sites of new manufacturing districts in England, northern France, Belgium, central Germany, the northern Czech Republic, southern Poland, and eastward to southern Ukraine.

The largest and most important single industrial area of Europe extends from the French-Belgian border to western Germany. Its core is Germany's Ruhr, a compact, highly urbanized industrial concentration of more than 50 major cities housing iron and steel, textiles, automobiles, chemicals, and all the metal-forming and metal-using industries of modern economies. Western Europe is experiencing deindustrialization accompanied

Figure 9.22 Industrial district near Lake Erie in Cleveland, Ohio. Shipping on the Great Lakes and major river and canal systems was instrumental in the development of the United States and Canada manufacturing belt.

by massive layoffs of workers in coal mining, iron mining, steel-making, textiles, and shipbuilding—the core industries of the Industrial Revolution.

Between the end of World War II and 1990, Eastern European industrial concentrations were cut off from the larger European market and instead were controlled by centralized economic plans imposed by the Soviet Union. Since its fall, Russia and Eastern European states have struggled with a generally poorly conceived, technologically antiquated, uneconomic industrial structure that was created without consideration of market realities.

Asia

The Eastern Asian sphere is rapidly becoming the most productive of the world's industrial regions (Figure 9.24). Japan is the world's third-largest economy and has a leading position in electronics and high-tech industries. China, the world's second-largest economy, has built on a rich resource base, massive labor force, and nearly insatiable market demand to industrialize rapidly and now ranks among the top producers of a number of major industrial commodities.

Until 1976, China's domestic needs rather than foreign markets were the principal concern of an industrial development totally controlled by the state and the Communist Party. In the late 1970s, China began experimenting with free-market manufacturing in the Central-South district just north of Hong Kong. The experiment was successful, and Shenzhen, a major industrial city near Guangzhou grew from a population of 300,000 in 1979 to 10 million in 2009.

Foreign direct investment, foreign firm outsourcing to low-cost Chinese suppliers, and relocation to China of manufacturing

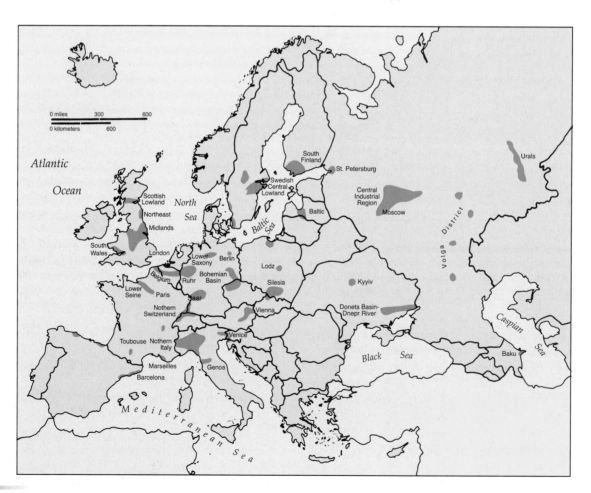

Figure 9.23 The industrial regions of Europe.

Figure 9.24 The industrial districts of Eastern Asia.

and assembly of consumer electronics, clothing, toys, and industrial equipment from other Asian countries propelled China to the forefront as a global industrial powerhouse. Simultaneously, China's economic planners actively shuttered inefficient and uneconomic state-owned enterprises (SOEs) that had been the mandated industrial units of the Communist past. China's admission in 2001 to the WTO (see Chapter 12) further enhanced the competitive position of its export-driven economy.

Tertiary Activities

Primary activities are connected directly to the Earth through gathering, extracting, or growing raw materials. *Secondary* industries, we have seen in this chapter, turn the raw materials of primary industry into useful products through manufacturing or processing. A major and growing segment of both domestic and international economic activity, however, involves *services* rather than the production of commodities. These **tertiary activities** consist of business and labor specialties that provide services to the primary and secondary sectors, to the general community, and to individuals. They provide intangible products ranging from education to haircuts, rather than tangible commodities such as finished goods.

As we have seen, regional and national economies undergo fundamental changes in emphasis in the course of their development. Subsistence societies exclusively dependent on primary industries may progress to secondary stage processing and manufacturing activities. In that progression, the importance of agriculture as an employer of labor or a contributor to national income declines as manufacturing expands. Many parts of the formerly underdeveloped world have made or are making that developmental transition, as we shall review in Chapter 10.

In contrast, many of the economically advanced countries that originally dominated the world manufacturing scene experienced deindustrialization in the late 20th and early 21st centuries. Rising labor costs in advanced economies, space-shrinking technologies for communications and transportation, the growth of transnational corporations, technology transfer to developing countries, and outsourcing of processing or assembly work have produced a new international division of labor. The earlier competitive manufacturing advantages of the developed countries could no longer be maintained and were replaced by a new focus on service activities. Based on the contribution of each sector to their GDPs, it is the advanced economies that have most completely made that transition and are often referred to as "postindustrial" (Table 9.1).

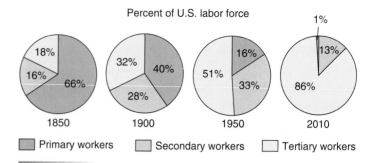

Table 9.1

Contribution of the Service Sector to GDP

Country Group	Percentage of GDP		
	1960	1980	2010
Low-income	32	30	50
Middle-income	47	46	56
High-income	54	59	73
United States	58	63	77
World		55	70

Source: Data from World Bank, World Development Indicators, 2011.

Percent of U.S. labor force

Figure 9.25 **Changing sectoral allocation.** The changing sectoral allocation of the U.S. labor force demonstrates the transition from a largely agricultural to postindustrial status.

Perhaps more than any other major country, the United States has reached postindustrial status. Its primary sector component fell from 66 percent of the labor force in 1850 to 1 percent in 2010, and the service sector rose from 18 percent to 86 percent (Figure 9.25). Virtually all job growth in the past two decades occurred in services. Comparable changes are found in other countries. Today, between 65 percent and 80 percent of jobs in such economies as Japan, Australia, Canada, Israel, and all major Western European countries were also in the services sector.

The significance of tertiary activities to national economies and the contrast between more developed and less developed states are made clear not just by employment but also by the differential contribution of services to the GDPs of states. The relative importance of services displayed in Figure 9.26 shows a marked contrast between advanced and subsistence societies. The greater the service share of an economy, the greater the average incomes and economic complexity of that society. That share has grown over time among most regions, and all national income categories as all economies have shared to some degree in economic growth and integration into the world economy (Table 9.2). Indeed, the expansion of the tertiary sector in modernizing East Asia, South Asia, and the Pacific has exceeded the world average in recent decades as these regions catch up. In Latin America and the Caribbean, for example, services accounted for 64 percent of total output in 2010.

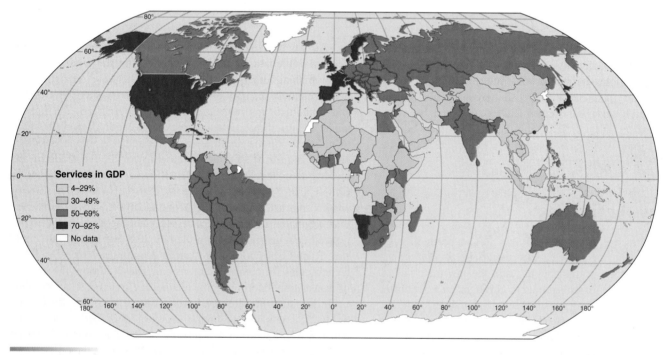

Figure 9.26 Services accounted for 70 percent of global GDP in 2010, up sharply from 55 percent 30 years earlier. As the map documents, the contribution of services to individual national economies varied greatly; Table 9.1 indicates all national income categories shared to some degree in the expansion of service activities.

Source: World Bank, World Development Indicators.

Table 9.2

Shares of World Trade in Commercial Services (Exports, 2006)

Country or Category	% of World
United States	14.4
United Kingdom	8.2
Germany	6.0
France	4.2
Japan	4.2
Spain	3.8
Italy	3.5
China (with Hong Kong)	3.3
High-income states	72.4
Low-income states	4.0
Sub-Saharan Africa	1.3
European Monetary Union	31.5

Sources: Data from World Bank, World Development Indicators, 2008.

Types of Service Activities

Tertiary and *service* are broad, imprecise terms that cover a range of activities, from neighborhood barber to college professor to World Bank president. The category includes both traditional low-order consumer and retail activities and higher-order, knowledge-based professional services performed primarily for other businesses, not for individual consumption. Based on who purchases the services, we distinguish between **consumer services** and **producer services.** Consumer services are performed for individuals and include entertainment, tourism, restaurants, hotels, bars, maintenance services, education, health care, and the vast array of personal services. Producer services are performed for corporations and include finance, insurance, real estate, legal services, accounting, architecture, and engineering consulting services. Wholesale and retail trade are categories of services that link producers and consumers. Transportation and communication services also serve both producers and consumers. In addition, government and nonprofit service providers are important components of the service economy.

Growth in the tertiary sector has numerous explanations. It reflects the development of ever more complex social, economic, and administrative structures, the effects of rising personal incomes and changes in family structure and individual lifestyles. For example, in subsistence economies, families care for their own children, produce and prepare their own food, and build and repair their own houses. In postindustrial societies, people hire child-care workers to care for the children, send their children to formal schools and universities, purchase prepared meals in restaurants, and hire contractors to build and/or repair their houses. Similar needs are met, but with very different employment structures.

As personal incomes rise, a greater proportion of income is spent on services rather than primary products or durable goods. If a person gets a raise, he or she might take a cruise vacation or dine out at restaurants more often, but probably will not add a second washing machine. Growth in the health care industry is driven by both rising incomes and the aging of society that inevitably occurs when a society completes the demographic transition. Growing complexity in the economy translates into the need for higher levels of education and training, as well as more government employees to collect taxes, control borders, alleviate poverty, ensure public safety, plan community development, monitor commerce, protect the environment, and maintain safe workplaces.

Part of the growth in the tertiary component is statistical, rather than functional. We saw in our discussion of manufacturing that "outsourcing" was increasingly used to reduce costs and improve efficiency. In the same way, outsourcing of services formerly provided in-house is also characteristic of current business practice. Cleaning and maintenance of factories, shops, and offices—formerly done by the company itself as part of internal operations—now are subcontracted to specialized service providers. The jobs are still done, perhaps even by the same personnel, but worker status has changed from "secondary" (as employees of a manufacturing plant, for example) to "tertiary" (as employees of a service company).

Locational Interdependence Theory for Services

The locational controls for tertiary enterprises are simpler than those for the manufacturing sector. Service activities are by definition market-oriented. Those dealing with transportation and communication are concerned with the location of people and commodities to be connected or moved; their locational determinants are, therefore, the patterns of population distribution and the spatial structure of production and consumption. Just as Weber offered a classic location theory for manufacturing enterprises, economist Harold Hotelling (1895–1973) used simplifying assumptions to create the locational interdependence model for retail services. In the locational interdependence model, the location decisions of firms are influenced by those of its competitors. Firms choose locations that give them a measure of *spatial monopoly* so that they maximize revenues, rather than minimizing costs as in Weber's model.

Imagine the location decisions of two firms in competition with each other, each selling identical goods to customers evenly spaced along a linear market. The usual example cited is of two ice cream vendors, each selling the same brand at the same price along a stretch of beach with a uniform distribution of people. Beachgoers will purchase the same amount of ice cream (that is, demand is *inelastic*—is not sensitive to a change in the price) and will patronize the store closest to them. Figure 9.27 suggests that the two sellers would eventually cluster at the midpoint of the linear market (the beach) so that each vendor could supply customers at the extremities of the market without yielding locational advantage to the other competitor.

This is a spatial solution that maximizes revenues for sellers but does not minimize costs for customers. The lowest total cost

Figure 9.27 Locational interdependence in retail location. The Hotelling model assumes customers evenly spread in a linear market. An example would be vacationers along a beach. (*a*) The initial *socially optimal* locations that minimize total delivery costs (b) will be vacated in the search for market advantage (*c*), eventually resulting in *competitive equilibrium* at the center of the market. This competitive equilibrium poorly serves customers at the periphery. (*d*). Spatial dispersion may occur if another competitor enters the market or the sellers subdivide the market by agreement.

location would be for each vendor to locate at the midpoint of his or her half of the beach, as shown at the top of Figure 9.27, where the total effort expended by customers walking to the ice cream stands (or cost by sellers delivering the product) is least. To maximize market share, however, one seller might decide to relocate immediately next to the competitor (Figure 9.27b), capturing three-fourths of the market. The logical retaliation would be for the second vendor to jump back over the first to recapture market share. Ultimately, side-by-side location at the center line of the beach is inevitable, and a stable placement is achieved because neither seller can gain any further advantage from moving. But now the average customer has to walk farther to satisfy his or her desire for ice cream than initially; that is, the total cost or delivered price (ice cream purchase plus effort expended) has increased. If a third vendor enters the market, the optimal locations for each vendor change to a more dispersed pattern (Figure 9.27d).

The locational interdependence model offers some simple lessons. First, the locational controls for services depend on the

locations of both customers and competitors and, under one set of conditions, may produce a clustered pattern and under another set, a dispersed pattern. Second, the Hotelling model suggests that a location solution that optimizes revenue for sellers may not be optimal from the point of view of the customers.

Consumer Services

The supply of consumer services must match the spatial distribution of *effective demand*—that is, wants made effective through purchasing power. Retailers, restaurants, and personal service providers are savvy about locating close to their customers and the most successful chains use *geodemographic* analysis to find optimal locations within cities. Prior to the 1960s, shopping for clothes, furniture, or housewares meant a trip downtown, where nearly all the stores were clustered. However, as middle-class residents left central cities for the suburbs, the department stores quickly chased their customers into newly developed suburban shopping malls. The location of retail services is an important topic in urban geography and receives more attention in Chapter 11.

Tourism

Special note should be made of *tourism*—travel undertaken for purposes of recreation rather than business. It has become the most important single tertiary sector activity, and the world's largest industry in jobs and total value generated. On a worldwide basis, travel and tourism in 2010 accounted for some 250 million jobs and about 9 percent of the world's GDP. Domestic tourism leads to spending on transportation, roadside services, lodging, meals, entertainment, theme parks, and national parks. International tourism, on the other hand, generates new income and jobs in developing states as they are "discovered" as tourist destinations, whether for their climate, unspoiled character, or unique culture and cultural landscapes. For half of the world's 50 poorest countries, tourism has become the leading service export sector.

The growth of tourism is part of a broader shift in emphasis from production to consumption that accompanies rising standards of living. Like manufacturing, the tourism industry has experienced a post-Fordist transition away from one-size-fits-all, mass-produced tourist destinations to numerous fragmented consumer niches. Consumers with enough money can choose between cruise vacations, beach vacations, African safaris, ecotourism to "unspoiled" wilderness areas, adventure tourism such as helicopter skiing in the Canadian Rockies or kayaking in Alaska, cultural tourism to exotic places such as Bali or Guatemala, heritage tourism in historic villages and cities, sex tourism, bicycle tours through Europe, wine tourism, gambling, and more (Figure 9.28).

The geographic pattern of tourist destinations is highly uneven. Just imagine the different challenges facing a tourism and convention organization working to promote Iowa versus one working on behalf of Hawaii. The geographic features of the destination matter, but so does the level of tourism infrastructure and proximity to potential customers. Modest hills that would hardly qualify as hills in the mountainous western United States have been turned into downhill ski resorts in the Midwest. The important factors are proximity to major cities, such as Chicago

Figure 9.28 **Tourism** is the world's largest industry and comes in many forms. Ecotourism seeks to empower local communities and preserve wildlife habitat and environmental quality.

or Detroit, and the developer's willingness to add the necessary infrastructure such as snowmaking and lifts. Tourism is an important tool in economic development, but geographers have raised a number of critical questions about the industry. Many of the jobs in the tourism industry are low-skill, low-wage positions such as hotel maids, and the profits often return to developed countries that are the home of the transnational corporations who own and operate the resorts. Tourism can be exploitative, particularly sex tourism. Tourist visits are often highly seasonal and this creates stresses on the destination, both during the on-season and off-season. Tourist destinations, like other expressions of popular culture, can go in and out of style, destabilizing the local economy. Tourism transforms places, often dramatically, and in some cases undermines the original tourist attraction. For example, in the United States, the areas just outside designated wilderness areas have become magnets for new housing, hotels, amusement parks, and other development. Cultural tourism inevitably changes the culture and cultural landscapes on which it is based. In response, ecotourism has emerged as an ethical form of tourism that focuses on education, minimizing environmental impacts, and using locally owned service providers.

Gambling

Gambling is a fast-growing industry that draws large numbers of tourists and in the process remakes places and local economies. In the United States, the gambling industry attracts almost 15 percent of all entertainment or recreation spending and generates more revenue than professional sports, museums, performing arts, fitness centers, golf courses, or amusement parks. The geography of gambling is determined by legal structures, political boundaries, and proximity to consumers. Gambling was once concentrated in a few select locations where it was permitted: Las Vegas, Nevada; Atlantic City, New Jersey; cruise ships (some of which never left shore); Monte Carlo, Monaco; and Macau, the only Chinese territory where gambling is permitted. The dominance of those gambling centers is being challenged by the rise of lotteries and internet gambling. The Indian Gaming Regulatory Act of 1988 allowed Indian reservations to operate casinos, and today there are more than 400 Indian casinos in the United States (Figure 9.29). Indian reservations located near major population centers or interstate highways are major beneficiaries, and have often funneled their substantial profits into improving conditions on the reservation. Reservations in Florida, California, and Connecticut are among the most profitable, although many of the jobs go to outsiders. Unfortunately, reservations in remote locations have usually not benefited from casinos.

Producer Services

Producer services are specialized activities performed for other businesses. They allow producers to realize cost savings by outsourcing specialized tasks when they are needed, without the expense of adding to their own labor force.

One difference between consumer services and producer services is that knowledge and skill-based producer service establishments can be spatially divorced from their clients; they are not tied

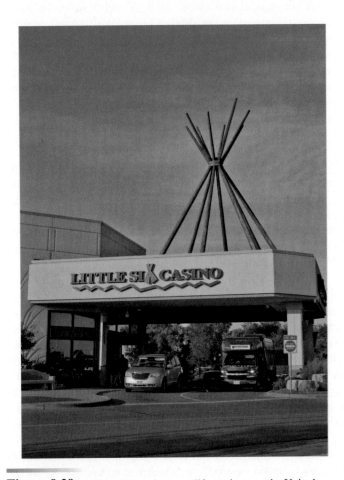

Figure 9.29 **Indian casinos** have proliferated across the United States since the 1988 Indian Gaming Regulatory Act, which recognized the right of tribes to operate casinos as a way of addressing high unemployment and poverty on reservations. Over 400 Indian casinos bring in revenues, which are often invested in education, social services, infrastructure improvements, and natural resource conservation on the reservations. As in all service industries, location is essential, and reservations in or near major metropolitan areas have profited the most.

to resources, affected by the environment, or necessarily localized by market. Of course, when high-level personal, face-to-face contacts are required, service firms will often locate close to their clients, the primary, secondary, or tertiary industries they serve. But the transportability of producer services also means that many of them can be spatially isolated from their client base.

As with other industries, the trade-off between costs and proximity is one of the central tensions when a producer services firm chooses office space. The clients for producer services firms are the major companies, many of which are headquartered in the largest cities, where real estate and labor costs are highest.

Producer services are "knowledge" activities that are highly dependent on communication. The spatial dispersion of some kinds of tasks has been facilitated by innovations in information and communication technologies. Satellite and fiber-optic cables, wireless communications, and the Internet permit the spatial separation of office work into "front-office" and "back-office" tasks. Front-office tasks involve face-to-face interactions with clients where projecting the correct corporate image is imperative. Front-office work requires and can bear the high costs of the most prestigious commercial real estate—in high-quality office buildings with prestigious addresses (Park Avenue, Wall Street) or well-known signature office buildings (Transamerica Tower, Seagram Building). The back office was once literally in the back of the same office building, but now it may be spatially distant from the headquarters of either the service or client firms. Insurance claims, credit card billings, mutual fund and stock market transactions, and consumer help requests are more cost effectively handled in low-rent, low-labor-cost locations—often in suburbs or small towns in rural states—than in the financial districts of major cities. Many suburban back-office operations employ part-time female workers who want to stay close to home because they have primary responsibility for childcare—leading to the label "pink-collar" work. While New York remains the center of the financial sector, the relatively small city of Sioux Falls, South Dakota, has several thousand employees engaged in back-office work for major banks and credit card companies.

Different types of service sector professionals have different locational needs and preferences. Political lobbyists and companies that do consulting work for federal government agencies need to be in Washington, D.C., and often cluster along the famed Capital Beltway. Investment and law firms prefer the most prestigious downtown addresses. Scientific and engineering firms prefer suburban office parks or research campuses. Advertising, architecture, and other design professions often try to project a more relaxed, creative image, frequently choosing old, brick factories or warehouse buildings that have been converted to office space.

The list of services employment is long. Its diversity and familiarity remind us of the complexity of modern life and of how far removed we are from subsistence economies. As societies advance economically, the share of employment and national income generated by the primary, secondary, and tertiary sectors continually changes; the spatial patterns of human activity reflect those changes. The shift is steadily away from production and processing, and toward the trade, personal, and professional services of the tertiary sector. That transition is the essence of the now-familiar term *postindustrial*.

Services in World Trade

Just as service activities have been major engines of national economic growth, so too have they become an increasing factor in international trade flows and economic interdependence. Between 1980 and 2010, services increased from 15 percent of total world trade to 20 percent. Rapid advances and reduced costs in information and communications technology have been central elements in the internationalization of services, as wired and wireless communication and data transmission costs have dropped to negligible levels. Many services considered nontradable, even late in the 1990s, are now actively exchanged at long distance, as the growth of services offshoring clearly shows.

Developing countries have been particular beneficiaries of the new technologies. The increasing tradability of services has expanded the comparative advantage of developing states in labor-intensive service activities, such as data processing. At the same time, they have benefited from increased access to efficient, state-of-the-art equipment and techniques transferred from advanced economies.

That global integration has shifted to higher level economic and professional services. There are clear cost advantages to outsourcing skilled functions such as paralegal and legal services, accountancy, medical analysis and technical services, architectural and engineering design, and research and development. Wired and wireless transmission of data, documents, medical and technical records, charts, and X-rays make distant consumer and producer services immediately and efficiently accessible. Further, many higher-level services are easily subdivided and performable either in sequence or simultaneously in multiple locations. The well-known "follow the sun" practices of software developers who finish a day's tasks only to pass the work to colleagues elsewhere in the world, who then pass it back to them when their workday is over, are now increasingly used by professionals in many other fields. As transnational corporations use computers around the clock for data processing, they can exploit or eliminate time zone differences between home office countries and host countries of their affiliates. Such cross-border intra-firm service transactions are not usually recorded in trade statistics but are part of the growing volume of international services flows. When the practice involves highly educated and talented specialists receiving developing world compensation levels, the cost attractions for developed country companies are irresistible. Increasing volumes of back-office work for Western insurance, finance, accounting, and legal services firms are being performed overseas.

With its large population of well-educated English speakers, India has been particularly successful in attracting outsourced service sector jobs. Customer interaction services ("call centers") formerly based in the United States are now increasingly relocated to India, employing workers trained to use an American nickname and speak in perfect American English (Figure 9.30). Claims processing for life and health insurance firms formerly were concentrated in English-speaking Caribbean states though increasingly such business process outsourcing (BPO) has shifted to India, Eastern Europe, and increasingly to China. In all such cases, the result is accelerated technology transfer in such key areas as information and telecommunications services.

Figure 9.30 Call center in India. With its large number of well-educated, English speakers, India has benefited from the globalization of back-office service sector work. These New Delhi workers are recent university graduates who work night shifts to cater to European and North American customers.

Despite the increasing share of global services trade held by developing countries, world trade—imports plus exports—in services is still overwhelmingly dominated by a very few of the most advanced states (Table 9.3). The country and category contrasts are great, as a comparison of the "high-income" and "low-income" group documents. At a different level, the single small island state of Singapore has a larger share of world services trade than all of sub-Saharan Africa.

The same cost and skill advantages that enhance the growth and territorial expansion of domestic service sector firms also operate internationally. Principal banks of all advanced countries have established foreign branches, and the world's leading banks have become major presences in the primary financial capitals. In turn, a relatively few world cities have emerged as international business and financial centers whose operations and influence are continuous and borderless (Figure 9.31). The world's key cities for banking, securities firms, and stock exchanges are spread across the globe,

Table 9.3

Shares of World Trade in Commercial Services (Exports, 2006)

Country or Category	% of World
United States	14.4
United Kingdom	8.2
Germany	6.0
France	4.2
Japan	4.2
Spain	3.8
Italy	3.5
China (with Hong Kong)	3.3
High-income states	72.4
Low-income states	4.0
Sub-Saharan Africa	1.3
European Monetary Union	31.5

Sources: Data from World Bank, World Development Indicators, 2008.

Figure 9.31 The hierarchy of international financial centers, topped by New York, London, and Tokyo, indicates the tendency of highest-order producer services to concentrate in a few world and national centers.

allowing almost continuous 24-hour per day trading (Figure 9.32). Meanwhile, a host of offshore banking havens have emerged to exploit gaps in regulatory controls and tax laws (Figure 9.33). Accounting firms, advertising agencies, management consulting companies, and similar establishments of primarily North American or European origin have increasingly established their international presence, with main branches located in principal business centers worldwide. Those advanced and specialized service components help swell the dominating role of the United States and European Union in the structure of world trade in services.

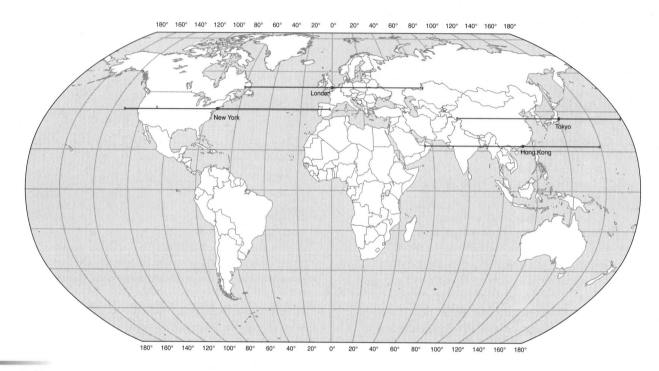

Figure 9.32 **The world's major stock exchanges** are linked by telecommunications and electronic funds transfer systems, creating the potential for 24-hour trading. Based on market capitalization in 2010, New York, London, and Tokyo had the largest exchanges, with Shanghai, Hong Kong, Toronto, São Paulo, Mumbai, Sydney, and Frankfurt filling out the top 10 cities.

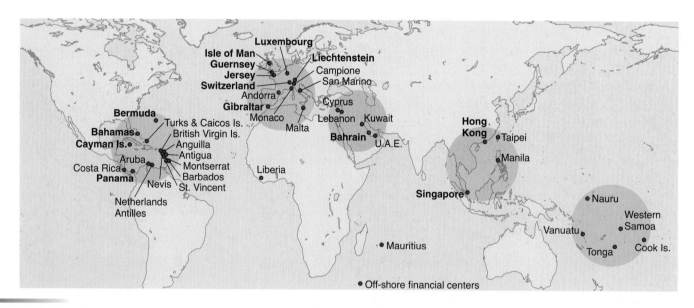

Figure 9.33 **Offshore banking.** Offshore financial centers, mostly in small island countries and micro-states, allow "furtive money" to avoid taxation and regulatory scrutiny. These financial havens have low tax rates and relaxed financial regulations. They are spread around the world to offer proximity to international financial centers and 24-hour trading. International pressure has led most of the tax havens to agree to greater openness and less protective secrecy.

Source: Peter Dicken, Global Shift, *4th ed. New York: Guilford Press, 2003, Figures 13.8 and 13.10.*

Summary

The spatial patterns of the world's manufacturing activities are dynamic and represent the landscape expression of past and recent industrial location decisions. Location theories help us understand how economic behavior motivated by profit responds to variable costs of manufacturing and distribution.

The most important industrial cost components are raw materials, power, labor, market accessibility, and transportation. Weberian analysis, which is most applicable to heavy industry, argues that least-cost locations are strongly or exclusively influenced by transportation charges. Weberian analysis leads us to distinguish between a market orientation for weight increasing and raw materials orientation for weight reducing processes. Profit maximization concepts accept the possibility of multiple satisficing locations within a spatial margin of profitability. Agglomeration economies lead to the growth of industrial clusters through linkages between firms, supporting infrastructure, and a specialized labor force. Location concepts developed to explain industrial distributions under Fordist production constraints have been challenged as new JIT and flexible production systems introduce different locational considerations.

Major industrial districts of the U.S. and Canadian manufacturing belt, Europe, and Eastern Asia contain the vast majority of the world's secondary industrial activity. The most advanced countries, however, are undergoing deindustrialization as newly industrializing countries with lower costs of production compete for markets. The patterns of high-tech industry are highly influenced by agglomeration economies and the location of workers with specialized skills rather than by transportation costs.

In the advanced economies, service activities have become more important as secondary-sector employment and share of gross national income decline. Service activities range from consumer services, such as hair salons, to advanced producer services, such as management and engineering consulting. Markets are a primary consideration in the location of service businesses. Locational interdependence theory suggests that firms situate themselves to assure a degree of market monopoly in response to the location of their competitors. Face-to-face interactions for producer service firms in finance, insurance, law, and accounting take place in prestigious, front-office locations. Routine processing of claims, calls, and bills is done in distant back offices located in lower-cost small cities or overseas. Tourism is the world's largest employer, bringing economic development to diverse locations but creating numerous challenges for host communities.

The nearly empty highway of the Monongahela Valley and the crowded expressways of high-tech and office park corridors are symbols of those changes in North America. As economic activity in North America becomes less concerned with raw materials and freight rates, it becomes freer of the locational constraints of an older industrial society. Increasingly, skills, knowledge, communication, and population concentrations are what attract the growing economic sectors in the most advanced economies. At the same time, much of the less developed world is striving for the transfer of manufacturing technology from developed economies and view industrial growth as the path to future prosperity. Those aspirations for economic development and the geographically uneven patterns of development are topics in Chapter 10.

KEY WORDS

agglomeration 288
agglomeration economies 290
break-of-bulk point 287
brownfield site 294
commodity chains 298
comparative advantage 292
consumer services 305
deindustrialization 300
deglomeration 291
external economies 291
footloose firm 290
Fordism 292
foreign direct investment (FDI) 295
freight rates 286

infrastructure 291
least-cost theory 288
line-haul costs 287
locational interdependence 306
maquiladoras 293
market equilibrium 282
market orientation 285
material orientation 284
multiplier effect 291
new international division of labor (NIDL) 294
offshoring 294
outsourcing 293
producer services 305

satisficing locations 290
secondary activities 283
spatially fixed costs 283
spatially variable costs 283
spatial margin of profitability 289
substitution principle 289
terminal costs 287
tertiary activities 303
transnational corporations 295
ubiquitous industry 285
uniform isotropic plain 288
Weberian analysis 288

FOR REVIEW

1. What are the primary *principles of location* outlined in this chapter? Briefly explain each and note its contribution to a firm's locational search.

2. What is the difference between *fixed* and *variable* costs? Which of the two is of interest in the plant locational decision? What kinds of variable costs are generally reckoned as most important in locational theory?

3. *Raw materials, power, labor, market,* and *transportation* are the "factors of location" usually considered most important in industrial placement decisions. Summarize the role of each, and cite examples of where each could be decisive in a firm's location.

4. What were Weber's controlling assumptions in his theory of plant location? What "distortions" did he recognize that might alter the locational decision?

5. What is deindustrialization, where is it occurring, and what are its effects on communities and workers?

6. How have the concepts or practices of *comparative advantage* and *outsourcing* affected the industrial structure of advanced and developing countries? Which of the "factors of location" is most important in the choice to move production from North America to Mexico or Asia?

7. How are the locational considerations for *high-tech* industries significantly different from those of heavy manufacturing activities? What are the primary factors in the location of high-tech industries in Silicon Valley and other high-tech clusters?

8. What is the difference between "front-office" and "back-office" tasks, and where is each likely to be located?

9. What sorts of challenges does the tourism industry bring to host communities?

10. What are the major centers for finance and stock exchanges? Do you anticipate change in the location of leading financial centers?

KEY CONCEPTS REVIEW

1. **What are the principal elements of locational theory, and how do different classical theories employ them?** pp. 288–290.
   Costs of raw materials, power, labor, market access, and transportation are the assumed controls governing industrial location decisions. They receive different emphases and imply different conclusions in the theories considered here. *Least-cost* (Weber) analysis concludes transport costs are the fundamental consideration; *profit maximization* maintains a firm should locate where profit is maximized by using the substitution principle.

2. **How do agglomeration, JIT, comparative advantage, and TNCs affect location outcomes?** pp. 290–296.
   By sharing infrastructure, agglomerating companies may reduce their individual costs, while JIT supply flows reduce their inventory capital and storage charges.

   Comparative advantage recognizes that different regions or nations have different industrial cost structures. Companies use *outsourcing* to exploit those differences. Transnational corporations distribute their operations based on comparative advantage: manufacturing in countries where production costs are lowest; performing research, accounting, and other service components where economical or convenient; and maintaining headquarters in locations that minimize taxes. Outsourcing and TNC practices get away from the concept of a single optimal location that was the goal of classical location theories.

3. **What influences high-tech activity location, and what is the impact of high-tech growth on established world manufacturing regions?** pp. 296–303.
   Long-established industrial regions in the U.S. and Canadian manufacturing belt and Western, Central, and Eastern Europe developed over time in line with classical location analysis. Eastern Asia, the most recently developed major industrial region, has been influenced by both classical locational pulls, economic development goals of newly industrializing countries and outsourcing in search of lower-cost, reliable labor sources. High-tech industries tend to create regionally specialized agglomerations reflecting proximity to scientific research centers, technically skilled labor pools, venture capital availability, quality of life, and superior transport and communication facilities. Their emergence has altered traditional industrial emphases and distributional patterns.

4. **What are the different types and locational characteristics of service activities,** pp. 304–308, **and how are they reflected in world trade patterns?** pp. 308–311.
   Tertiary industries include all non-goods production activities and provide services to goods producers, the general community, and individuals. Subdivided into consumer services and producer services, the tertiary sector is broad and employs most workers in advanced economies. The location of customers is an important consideration for both consumer and producer services. Front-office and back-office tasks are often spatially distant. The growing world trade in services, made possible by plummeting costs of information transmission, has altered international economic relations and encouraged cultural and functional integration.

ECONOMIC DEVELOPMENT AND CHANGE

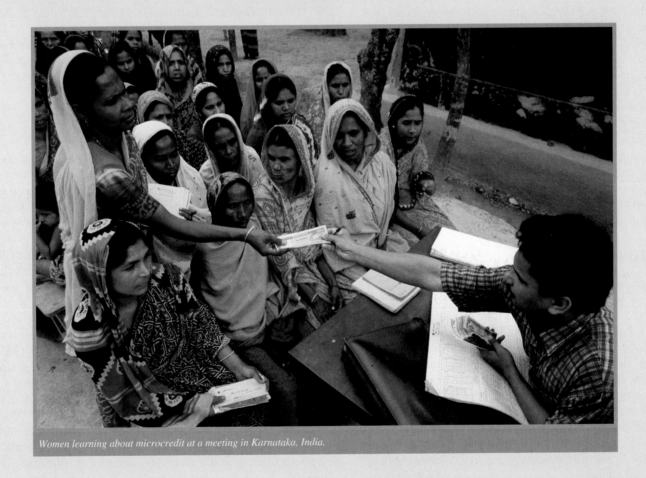

CHAPTER 10

Women learning about microcredit at a meeting in Karnataka, India.

Key Concepts

*I*n January 2010, the world's attention turned for a few days to Haiti, where a 7.0-magnitude earthquake struck near the capital city of Port-au-Prince. The powerful quake shook an estimated 3.5 million of Haiti's 9 million people. The devastation was astounding. As bodies were pulled from the rubble, the estimated death toll climbed to over 220,000, while the true number will probably never be known. After the quake, inadequate food supplies, untreated injuries, and disease outbreaks raised the death toll even higher. With most of the country's infrastructure concentrated in the primate city of Port-au-Prince, the damage to the country's government and systems of transportation and utilities was a major setback. Key structures destroyed or seriously damaged including the presidential palace, national assembly building, national penitentiary, main cathedral, United Nations (UN) headquarters for Haiti, the airport control tower, port docks and cranes, luxury hotels, hospitals, and schools. Approximately 1.5 million Haitians were left homeless as their simple houses collapsed in the quake.

Long after the world's media attention moved on, the presidential palace remained in ruins, and hundreds of thousands of Haitians still lived in dozens of overcrowded tent camps in parks, golf courses, and vacant lots, suffering from poor sanitation, crime, and inadequate food and water supplies. One tent camp, on the lawn of the presidential palace, housed 20,000 people two years after the quake (Figure 10.1). As aid from nongovernmental organizations slowed to a trickle, the internally displaced persons living in the tent camps came to realize that recovery would be a long, hard process, and little additional international assistance would be coming.

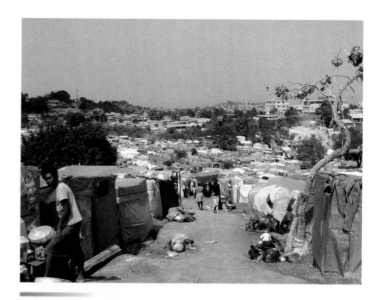

Figure 10.1 One of many tent camps for displaced persons after the January 2010 earthquake in Haiti. This camp was located in the capital city of Port-au-Prince, on Haiti's only golf course. About 1.5 million of Haiti's 9 million people were made homeless by the earthquake. Two years later, hundreds of thousands were still living in tent camps.

An Uneven World

News reports often refer to catastrophes such as the Haitian earthquake as "natural disasters." But the staggering death toll in Haiti would suggest that something more was going on. In recent years, earthquakes of similar strength have hit California, New Zealand, Chile, Indonesia, Japan, and Italy, with far less damage and loss of life. The devastating human consequences of the Haitian earthquake were not due to nature alone. Rather, poverty and the lack of private and public resources, public services, institutions, and social safety nets that we associate with "development" made this natural event much more devastating and the recovery much slower. Haiti is the poorest country in the Western Hemisphere, and like other developing countries, it has undergone a massive migration from rural areas to the crowded city of Port-au-Prince. Haiti's government is burdened by large international indebtedness for loans taken out by previous, corrupt governments, but in the years prior to the earthquake, the country had made substantial progress in stabilizing institutions and renegotiating its international debts. Haitians were aware of their country's earthquake dangers. But in a poor, indebted country where most houses are makeshift slum dwellings and day-to-day survival is a challenge for much of the population, updating and enforcing building codes, creating disaster preparation plans, and earthquake-proofing even key public buildings was not a priority. Partly to blame for the

many deaths were poor construction materials and techniques that could not withstand the forces of earthquakes. Limited financial resources meant little or no government inspection, and builders sometimes succumbed to the temptation to skimp on the amount of cement in their concrete and reduce or leave out altogether the expensive reinforcing steel bars that are necessary to enable buildings to withstand earthquakes. Extreme poverty meant that there was no insurance claim or bank account to fall back upon for many Haitians who lost homes, jobs, and family members.

Any view of the contemporary world quickly shows great—almost unbelievable—contrasts from place to place in levels of economic development and people's material well-being. Such differences are evident in the *artifacts*—energy sources and technologies differing societies use—the kinds of economic activities in which they engage, and in their social organizations—*sociofacts*. The ready distinction we make between the "Gold Coast" and the "slum" indicates that different groups have different access to the wealth, tools, resources, and decision-making power of the global and national societies of which they are a part.

At an international scale, we distinguish between "advanced" or "rich" nations, such as Canada or Switzerland, and "less developed" or "poor" countries, like Bangladesh or Burkina Faso, although neither country may be comfortable with those adjectives. Vast economic differences exist within countries, too. The poverty of drought- and hunger-plagued rural northeastern Brazil stands in sharp contrast to the prosperous, industrialized, urbanized modernity of São Paulo (Figure 10.2). Similarly, in the United States, farmers of the hillsides of Appalachia live in a different economic and cultural reality than Midwestern cash grain farmers.

(a)

(b)

Figure 10.2 (*a*) The modern high-rise office and apartment buildings of prosperous São Paulo, a city that generates over one-third of Brazil's national income, stand a world apart from (*b*) the poverty and peasant housing of northeastern Brazil. The evidence and benefits of "development" are not equally shared by all segments of any country or society.

Dividing the Continuum: Defining Development

Countries display different levels of development. **Development,** in that comparative sense, means simply the extent to which the human and natural resources of an area or country have been brought into full productive use. In common usage, it also suggests urbanization, modernization, and improvement in levels of material production and consumption. For some, it also suggests changes in traditional social, cultural, and political structures to resemble more nearly those displayed in countries and economies deemed "advanced." For others, the concepts of "development" and "underdevelopment" were post–World War II inventions of Western culture. Countries were classified by the degree to which they conformed to Western standards of wealth, well-being, and achievement. Once visualized in this manner, the perceived conditions of underdevelopment could be addressed by international institutions such as the World Bank, International Monetary Fund Bank, and Inter-American Development Bank. While the economic differences between countries are undeniable, some critics challenge development theory, criticizing it as a conscious means of exerting Western influence and control over postcolonial societies.

Whatever the philosophical merits of the two viewpoints, many of the attributes of development under its usual economic definition can be quantified by referring to statistics of national production, per capita income, energy consumption, nutritional levels, labor force characteristics, and the like. Taken together, such variables might calibrate a scale of achievement against which the level of development of a single country may be compared. Such a scale would reveal that countries lie along a continuum from the least advanced in technology or industrialization to the most developed. Geographers (and others) attempt to classify and group countries along the continuum in ways that are useful and informative. The extremes are easy; the middle ground is less clear-cut, and the terminology referring to it is mixed.

We must be careful in choosing the terms that we use to describe these differences, for we are speaking of vast inequalities in economic and political power, access to resources, and chances of survival. In the usage of many governments and nongovernmental organizations, the term *developed* stands in easy contrast to *underdeveloped, less developed,* or the *developing* world. The term *developing* itself was introduced by President Harry S. Truman in 1949 as a replacement for *backward,* the unsatisfactory and unflattering reference then in use. **Underdevelopment,** from a strictly economic point of view, suggests the possibility or desirability of applying additional capital, labor, or technology to the resource base of an area to permit the present population to improve its material well-being.

The catch-all category of *underdeveloped,* however, does not tell us in which countries such efforts at improvement have occurred or been effective. With time, therefore, more refined subdivisions of development have been introduced, including such relative terms as *moderately, less,* or *least developed* countries.[1] Since development is commonly understood to imply industrialization and to be reflected in improvements in national and personal income, the additional terms *newly industrializing countries* (NICs) (which was explored in Chapter 9) and *middle-income countries* have been employed. More recently, *emerging economy* has become a common designation, providing a more positive image than "underdeveloped." The United Nations groups the formerly communist Russia, former USSR republics, and southeast European countries into a category termed *transition economies.* In a corruption of its original meaning, the term *Third World* is still occasionally applied to developing

[1]In 1971, the General Assembly of the United Nations listed 24 "least developed" countries identified by per capita gross domestic product (GDP), share of manufacturing in GDP, and adult literacy. In later years, the criteria were changed to reflect low national income (per capita GDP under $900); weak human assets (a composite index based on health, nutrition, and educational measures); and high economic vulnerability (a composite index based on instability of agricultural production and inadequate diversification of a small economy). In addition, population of a "least developed country" had to be below 75 million. The list of those countries—also recognized as "poorest" countries—has grown over the years. There were 48 countries on the list in 2012: 33 in Africa, 9 in Asia, 5 small island states in Oceania, and Haiti in the Caribbean. Only three countries, Botswana, Cape Verde, and Maldives have "graduated" from the list. See Figure 10.3.

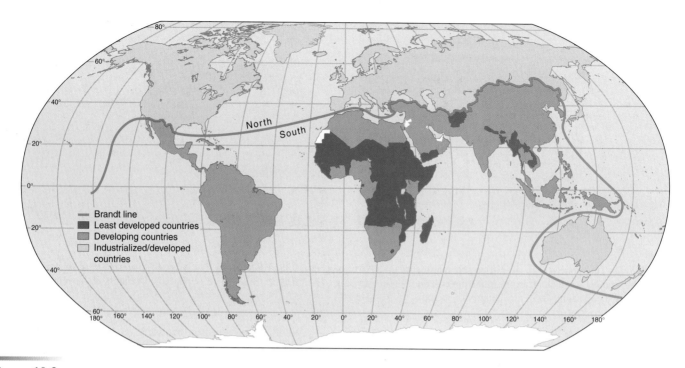

Figure 10.3 Comparative development levels. The "North-South" line of the 1980 *Brandt Report* suggested a simplified world contrast of development and underdevelopment based largely on degree of industrialization and per capita wealth. Following the dissolution of the USSR in 1991, the former Central Asian and trans-Caucasian Soviet republics were added to the "South." In 2004, the United Nations Economic and Social Council and the United Nations Conference on Trade and Development (UNCTAD) expanded to 50 the list of "least developed countries." The inclusive category of "developing countries" ignores recent significant economic and social gains in several Asian and Latin American states, raising them now to "industrialized/developed" status. Some "least developed" states are small island countries not shown at this map scale.

Sources: UNCTAD and United Nations Development Programme.

countries as a group, though when first used, that designation was a purely political reference to nations not formally aligned with a "First World" of industrialized free market (capitalist) nations or a "Second World" of centrally controlled (communist-bloc) economies. In addition, the name *Fourth World* has sometimes been attached to indigenous peoples or other marginalized ethnic groups. Further, some development workers have altered the term *Third World* to *Two-Thirds World* or *Majority World* as a reminder that most of the world's population resides in developing countries.

Because all these terms clearly suggest the possibility of a country progressing from a lower to a higher developmental status, one would expect agreement on which category is applicable to a specific country and when a state has advanced from one category to another. Unfortunately, there is no agreed-upon classification. In common practice, the United Nations considers the United States, Canada, Japan, Australia, New Zealand, and all of Europe to be "developed" and the rest of the world to be "developing." Various international agencies reach different conclusions: for the United Nations, Singapore and South Korea are "developing" or "emerging" economies; for the International Monetary Fund (IMF), they are "advanced economies." On the reasonable basis of per capita wealth (GDP per head), Singapore ("emerging") far surpassed New Zealand ("advanced"), and Hong Kong and South Korea ("developing") exceeded Portugal and Greece ("developed"). And to equate "advanced" with "industrialized" economies, which is commonly done, neglects the fact that these economies are increasingly post-industrial service economies.

In 1980, the contrasting terms *North* and *South* were introduced (by the Independent Commission on International Development Issues, commonly called the Brandt Report[2]) as a broad generalization emphasizing the distinctions between the rich, advanced, developed countries of the Northern Hemisphere (to which Australia and New Zealand are added)—the *North*—and, roughly, the rest of the world—the *South* (Figure 10.3). This split agreed with the UN classification that placed all of Europe and North America, plus Australia, Japan, New Zealand, and the former USSR in a *more developed country* category, with all other states classed as *less developed countries*.

The variety of terms devised—not all of them accurately descriptive or acceptable to the countries that they designate—represent sincere efforts to categorize countries along a continuum of specific or composite measures of economic and social characteristics. In the remainder of this chapter, broad developmental contrasts between countries or regions will conform to the "North-South" and the United Nation's "developed-developing" categorizations. While not ideal, we use the terms *developed* and *developing* because of their common usage in

---

[2]*North-South: A Programme for Survival.* The commission was established in 1977 at the suggestion of the chairman of the World Bank. Under its charge, "global issues arising from economic and social disparities of the world community" were to be studied and "ways of promoting adequate solutions to the problems involved in development" were to be proposed. The former Soviet Union was included within the North at that time; since the breakup of the Soviet Union in 1991, Georgia, Uzbekistan, and other former Soviet republics in Asia have been classified as "less developed" by the United Nations.

reports and statistical databases issued by the United Nations and other organizations. Our primary attention in maps and text, however, will be given to the developing countries of the Third World or "global South."

The terminology of development is usually applied to country units, but it is equally meaningful at the regional and local levels within them, for few countries are uniformly highly developed or totally undeveloped. Many emerging economies contain pockets—frequently the major urban centers—of productivity, wealth, and modernity not shared by the rest of the state. For example, Mexico is a leading NIC, but more than 50 percent of its industrial workers and more than 60 percent of the value of its manufacturing are located in metropolitan Mexico City. Many other parts of the country, and particularly its amerindian population, remain untouched by the development concentrated in the capital city. Similarly, the Mumbai (Bombay) agglomeration, with less than 2 percent of India's population, generates one-sixth of the country's GDP. Even within the most advanced societies, some areas and populations remain outside the mainstream of progress and prosperity enjoyed by the majority.

And finally, we should remember that *development* is a culturally relative term. It is usually interpreted in Western, democratic, market economy terms that presumably can be generalized to apply to all societies. Others insist that it must be seen in light of the cultural and economic aspirations of different peoples, many of whom specifically reject Western cultural and economic standards.

Measures of Development

Discussions of development tend to begin with economic measures because income and national wealth strongly affect the degree to which societies can invest in food supplies, education, sanitation, health services, and other components of individual and group well-being. Indeed, there is a close relationship between economic and social measures of development. While there are exceptions because societies prioritize things differently, in general, the higher the per capita income, the higher the national ranking in such measures as access to safe drinking water, prevalence of sanitation, availability of physicians, and education and literacy levels.

In contrast, the relationship between social-economic and demographic variables is usually inverse. Higher educational or income levels are usually associated with lower infant mortality rates, birth and death rates, and rates of natural increase. However it is measured, the gap between the most and least developed countries in noneconomic characteristics is at least as great as it is in their economies and technologies. Table 10.1 suggests, however, that the Global South as a whole has made progress in reducing its disadvantages in some human well-being measures. By other measures, however, the gap between rich and poor remains or is increasing, and disparities still persist after the three UN "development decades" and a concerted effort by all the world's countries and international development agencies that coincided with the new millennium in 2000 (See the feature "Millennium Development Goals").

 ## Millennium Development Goals

In September 2000, 189 member states of the United Nations adopted the Millennium Declaration to help the world's poorest countries make measured progress toward reducing or eliminating within their borders by 2015 extreme poverty in its many social and economic dimensions. The eight interlinked goals and 18 associated measurement targets that they identified—the Millennium Development Goals (MDGs)—were the outgrowth of a series of international conferences in the 1990s on children, population and development, human rights, women, social development, AIDs, and development financing.

The MDGs are measurable objectives for addressing extreme poverty in its many guises; they aim to do the following:

1. Eradicate extreme hunger and monetary poverty
2. Achieve universal primary education
3. Promote gender equality and empower women
4. Reduce child mortality
5. Improve maternal health
6. Combat HIV/AIDs, malaria, and other diseases
7. Ensure environmental sustainability
8. Create a global partnership for development

The achievement of these goals, according to the founding document, depends on a commitment by developing countries to take primary responsibility for their own development by strengthening their financial management and controls, effectively mobilizing their local resources, and initiating or improving the delivery of basic public services; key actions are to respect human rights and root out corruption. Donor (advanced) countries were charged not only with providing funds adequate to reach the MDGs, but also to ensure that aid-recipient countries create "transparent, credible, and properly costed" national development strategies.

Although significant strides towards achieving many of the goals have been made, progress has not been uniform across the world or the goals. Assessments by the United Nation's Human Development Programme (UNDP) leaders in 2010 found that many regions were on track to meet at least some of the goals. Unmet commitments and inadequate resources have hampered progress, but significant improvements in the well-being of the world's poor have been made. Convinced that development programs are more successful when targeted to specific goals, the MDGs and their target measures remain a focus for individual countries and international agencies.

Table 10.1

The Narrowing North-South Disparity in Human Development, 1960 to 2004

	North		South		Absolute Disparity	
	1960	2004	1960	2004	1960	2004
Life expectancy (years)	69	78	46	62	23	16
Adult literacy (%)	95	97	46	67	49	30
Nutrition (daily calorie supply as % of requirement)	124	141	90	114	34	27
Infant mortality (per 1,000 live births)	37	7	149	62	112	55
Child mortality (under age 5)	46	7	216	90	170	83
Access to safe water (% of population)	100	100	40	78	60	22

Sources: United Nations Development Programme, World Bank, and UNICEF.

Gross National Income (GNI) and Purchasing Power Parity (PPP) per Capita

Two common measures are used to gauge economic activity—gross domestic product (GDP), which was introduced in Chapters 8 and 9, and **gross national income (GNI).** GDP is the total market value of all final goods and services produced annually within the borders of a country. GNI adds to GDP the total foreign income earned by its citizens (GNI was formerly known as *gross national product*, or *GNP*). To make values comparable, we make three adjustments to GNI. First, we convert each country's currency into a single measure, typically U.S. dollars. Second, we divide by the number of people in a country to get GNI per capita. Third, we note that market currency exchange rates fluctuate with business cycles and trading patterns and do not necessarily correspond to prices in a particular country. For example, you may have noticed that prices for most goods are lower in developing countries, and if you have traveled to Scandinavia, you probably noticed that prices are much higher there than in other developed countries. Thus, a **purchasing power parity (PPP)** correction is often applied to GNI to account for price differences. Let's say that a Big Mac costs $4 in the United States and 40 pesos in Mexico. Then, the purchasing power of $1 equals 10 pesos. Of course, the actual PPP calculation uses a bundle of goods rather than just Big Macs.

Even after applying the PPP correction, it still remains difficult to compare personal income figures across national borders. Personal incomes in Sweden are taxed at much higher rates than in the United States. But social welfare programs, higher education, and medicine receive greater central governmental funding in Sweden; the U.S. family must set aside a larger portion of its income for such services. Further, identical incomes will be spent on different amounts and types of goods and services in different countries. Residents of higher latitudes must buy fuel and heavy clothing not necessary in tropical climates.

The World Bank divides the world's countries into low-income, lower-middle, upper-middle, and high-income categories.

As expected, the countries with the highest GNI per capita are those in northwestern Europe, where the Industrial Revolution began, their former midlatitude colonies—United States, Canada, Australia, and New Zealand, and Singapore, a small island city-state that was once a British colony and is now home to prosperous manufacturing and international trading industries (Figure 10.4). In the middle position are found many of the countries of Latin America and of southern and eastern Europe. With the exception of Haiti, the low-income countries are in Africa and Asia. Since the money value of the nontraded goods and services that subsistence farmers provide for themselves and their communities goes unrecorded in the GNI, the differences between countries are less extreme when the PPP correction is used (Figure 10.5).

Like any single development statistic, GNI tells only part of a complex story. While it is still the primary measure used by the World Bank to gauge economic performance, it is under increasing attack as a poor measure of progress and human well-being. GNI simply measures the flow of money through the economy, without regard to purpose, and without regard for the condition of capital stocks that is necessary for productivity. Natural disasters, accidents, illnesses, and divorces trigger additional spending and increase the GNI, without increasing well-being. Similarly, increased spending on security or the military increases GNI, but it is at best a necessary evil and a rather poor indicator of societal health. It is quite possible to increase GNI in the short term while destroying stocks of capital. Like other forms of capital, the condition of the natural environment (natural capital) is not measured in GNI. For example, overfishing the oceans will increase GNI for a few years, but in the long term, it will cause ecological collapse that undermines future productivity in that industry.

Of course, GNI per capita says nothing about the distribution of income within a country; it could be evenly distributed across the population or concentrated in the hands of a few. Nor is per capita GNI a totally realistic summary of developmental status. It overemphasizes the purely monetary circumstances of countries and misses the activities of the **informal economy** that are

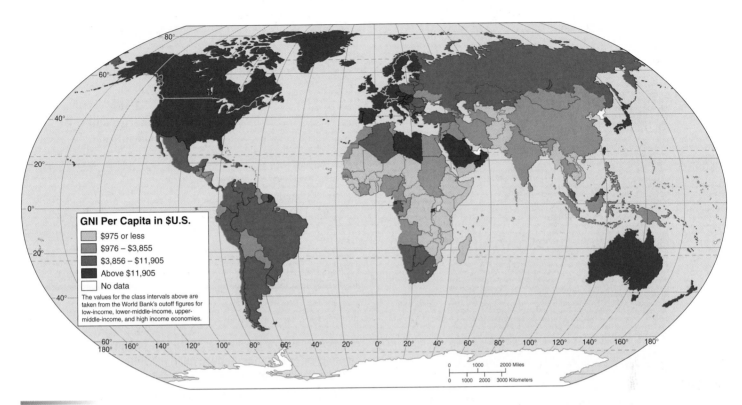

Figure 10.4 **GNI per capita, 2009.** GNI per capita is a frequently employed measure of economic advancement, although high incomes in sparsely populated, oil-rich countries may not have the same meaning in developmental terms as do comparable per capita values in industrially advanced states. The map implies an unrealistic precision. For many states, when uncertain GNI is divided by unreliable population totals, the resulting GNI per capita is at best a rough approximation that varies between reporting agencies. A comparison of this map and Figure 10.8 presents an interesting study in regional contrasts.

Sources: Data from World Bank and Population Reference Bureau.

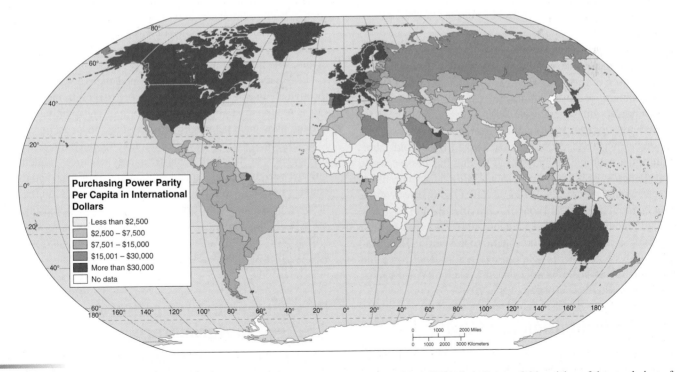

Figure 10.5 **PPP, 2009.** When local currency measures of GNI or GDP are converted into PPPs, there is a twofold revision of the usual view of world economic status. The first result is a sharp increase in developing countries' share of total world output. Second, the abject poverty suggested by per capita GNI or GDP is seen to be much reduced in many developing countries. Compare this map to Figure 10.4 to see how PPP changes our impressions of some countries' economic status.

Sources: Data from World Bank and United Nations.

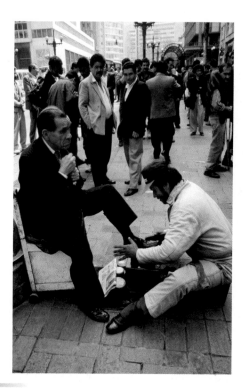

Figure 10.6 **Informal economic** activities include this shoeshine stand in Bogota, Colombia. As commercialization of agriculture reduced employment on farms, many former rural workers found urban work in the informal or shadow economy sector, the source of 40 percent of jobs in Latin American cities. They became errand runners, street vendors, odd-job handymen, open-air dispensers of such personal services as barbering, shoeshining, clothes mending, letter-writing, and the like, as well as unregistered workers in small-scale construction and repair shops.

Table 10.2

Size of the Informal Economy

	Africa	Latin America and Caribbean	Asia
Non-Agricultural Employment	78%	57%	45–85%
Urban Employment	61%	40%	40–60%
New Job Creation	93%	83%	NA

Sources: J. Charmes, *Informal Sector, Poverty and Gender: A Review of Empirical Evidence*, World Bank, 2000, and International Labour Organization, *Women and Men in the Informal Economy: A Statistical Picture*, 2002.

especially important in developing countries. The informal economy is composed of activities, whether self-employment, work in a family business, or for an employer, that are unlicensed, lack formal contracts, and generate earnings that go unreported. Informal activities include traditional subsistence strategies such as raising one's own food, bartering, and unpaid household labor. Other informal activities include home sewing businesses. waste picking, domestic work, sex work, shoeshining, and some forms of street vending (Figure 10.6). Illegal activity is one part of the informal economy. Informal economic activities tend to have low entry requirements for capital, education, and technology and are the major job creators in the poorest parts of the world. The informal economy is a growing proportion of the total labor force and is vital to the livelihoods of many or most workers in Africa, Asia, Latin America, and the Caribbean (Table 10.2).

Energy Consumption per Capita

Per capita energy consumption is another common measure of technological advancement because it loosely correlates with per capita income, degree of industrialization, and use of advanced technology. In fact, the industrialized countries use about 10 times more energy on a per capita basis than developing economies do. The consumption rather than the production of energy is the

concern. Many of the highly developed countries consume large amounts of energy but produce relatively little of it. Japan, for example, must import energy supplies from abroad because its domestic resources are very limited. In contrast, many less developed countries have very high per capita or total energy production figures, but primarily export the resource (petroleum). Libya, Nigeria, and Brunei are cases in point. Most of the less and least developed countries depend on animate energy (human and animal labor) to do work and firewood, crop residues, dung, and peat for cooking fuels (see the feature "The Energy Crisis in Less Developed Countries"). Both rudimentary and some advanced technologies are improving that picture as high-efficiency stoves, solar stoves, waste matter converters, and solar panels become more affordable and diffuse into low-income countries (Figure 10.7).

The advanced countries developed their economic strength through the use of cheap, energy-dense fossil fuels and their application to industrial processes. But energy is cheap only if immense capital investment is made to produce it at a low cost per unit. The less developed nations have been unable to make those necessary investments, or they lack domestic energy resources, widening the gulf between the technological subsystems of the rich and the poor countries of the world. Regardless, the desirability of imitating the developing countries' exorbitant energy use is increasingly suspect. If the developing countries were to do so, it would lead to intensified competition for limited, nonrenewable energy supplies and rising greenhouse gas emissions (see Chapter 13 for more about this topic).

Percentage of the Workforce Engaged in Agriculture

A high percentage of employment in agriculture (Figure 10.8) is almost invariably associated with subsistence agriculture, low per capita gross national income, and low energy consumption—that is, with underdevelopment. Thus, many development programs have focused on commercializing the agriculture sector. The argument is that economic development creates a wider range of

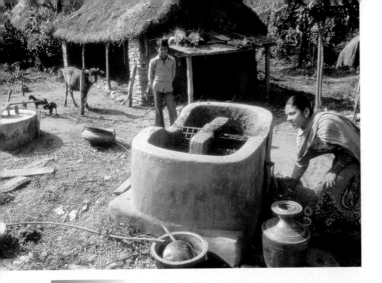

Figure 10.7 A biogas generator in Nepal. Human, animal, and vegetable wastes are significant energy sources in developing economies such as Pakistan, India, Thailand, and China, where such wastes are fermented to produce methane gas (*biogas*) as a fuel for cooking, lighting, and heating. The simple technology involves only a stone fermentation tank (foreground) fed with wastes—straw and other crop residues, manure, human waste, kitchen scraps, and the like. These are left to decompose and ferment; the emitted methane gas passes into a large collection chamber (left background tank) and later is drawn through a tube into the farm kitchen. After the gas is spent, the remaining sludge is pumped out and used for fertilizer in the fields.

occupational choices than those available in a subsistence agricultural society. Mechanization of agriculture increases the productivity of a shrinking farm labor force; surplus rural workers are made available for urban industrial and service employment, and if jobs are found, national and personal prosperity increases. When a labor force is primarily engaged in subsistence agriculture, on the other hand, there is limited capital accumulation or national economic growth. On the other hand, defenders of traditional subsistence agriculture point out that it is often less damaging to the environment, preserves traditional ways of life, and meets the vital food needs of vulnerable poor households.

Food Security and Nutrition

While tragic famines, such as that suffered by Somalia in 2011, generate headlines, long-term chronic undernourishment is a frequent outcome of poverty. Undernourishment has a crippling effect on individual well-being and also creates a major obstacle to community development. Hunger kills more people each year than AIDS, malaria, and tuberculosis combined. Availability of urban employment or access to arable land is far more important in determining national levels of undernourishment than a country's total per capita food production. During the Bangladesh famine of 1974, for example, total food availability per capita was at a long-term peak; starvation, according to World Bank reports, was the result of declines in real wages and employment in the rural sector

The Energy Crisis in Less Developed Countries

"The poor man's energy crisis" is a phrase increasingly applicable to the rising demand for and the decreasing supply of traditional fuels—wood, charcoal, crop residue, and dung—in developing countries. It is a different kind of crisis from that faced by industrialized countries encountering rising prices and diminishing supplies of petroleum and natural gas. The crisis of the less developed societies involves cooking food, basic lighting, and keeping warm, not running central heating and air conditioning systems, powering television displays, or cooling computer data centers.

A 2009 study by the World Health Organization (WHO) found that in developing countries, 28 percent of the population lacked electricity. In the least developed countries, 79 percent of the population lacked electricity, and in sub-Saharan Africa, three-fourths of households lacked electricity. Thus, many people in developing countries live in nighttime darkness and depend on traditional fuels, primarily wood, for cooking. The highest

usage of fuel wood is in the poorest countries, such as Ethiopia and Nepal.

Traditional cooking fuels are typically used in unvented, inefficient stoves. Pollution from indoor cooking on unvented stoves is a major source of disease and premature death, especially among women, who do most of the cooking. Widespread use of traditional fuels has led to deforestation and fuel shortages in the drier areas of Africa, the mountainous districts of Asia, and in the Andean uplands of Latin America. As a result of shortages and deforestation in such widely scattered areas as Nepal and Haiti, families have been forced to change their diets to less nutritious foods that need no cooking. Depletion of forests near villages leads to longer wood gathering trips, taking time away from food- or income-producing activities. Growing populations ensure that the problem of fuel shortages will continue to plague developing countries.

Simple high-efficiency stoves, solar reflector ovens, and backyard fermentation

tanks to convert human and animal waste into methane cooking gas (biodigesters) have improved the quality of life for the rural poor. With more efficient stoves, there is less pollution and less need for distant firewood gathering. Increasingly popular in Africa are small rooftop solar panels that can power a cell-phone charger and several indoor lights. In areas far from electrical or telephone lines, such a system allows children to do homework after dark and allows parents to receive telephone money transfers from family members working in distant cities or countries. In Nepal, miniature hydroelectric systems generate power for basic electric service to remote villages. One challenge of these small-scale innovations is that development agencies are comfortable making large loans for the construction of large power plants or hydroelectric dams costing hundreds of millions of dollars, but they do not have systems in place to make millions of hundred-dollar loans.

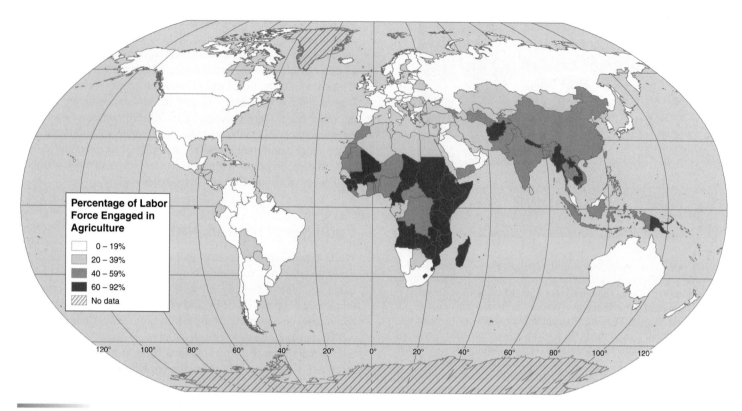

Figure 10.8 **Percentage of labor force engaged in agriculture, 2009.** For the world as a whole, agricultural workers make up about one-third of the total labor force. Highly developed economies usually have relatively low proportions of their labor forces in the agricultural sector, but the contrast between advanced and underdeveloped countries in the agricultural labor force measure is diminishing. Rapid population growth in developing countries has resulted in increased rural landlessness and poverty, causing many to migrate to cities. The resulting reduction in the agricultural labor force percentage is an expression of relocation of poverty and unemployment, not of economic advancement.

Source: World Bank, World Development Indicators, *2011.*

and short-term speculative increases in the price of rice. In India in 2002, huge stockpiles of government-owned wheat rotted in storage while held for sale at prices beyond the reach of malnourished or starving but impoverished citizens.

Nourishment levels, therefore, are as important an indicator of economic development of a country as income. Indeed, no other economic measure of national prosperity or development level can be as meaningful as the availability of food supplies sufficient to meet individual daily energy requirements. Food, as the essential universal necessity, is the ultimate indicator of economic well-being. Thus, a primary goal of development should be **food security**—the provision of sufficient quantities of safe and nutritious food.

Calorie requirements to maintain moderate activity vary according to a person's type of occupation, age, sex, and size, as well as to climate conditions. The Food and Agriculture Organization (FAO) of the United Nations specifies 2,350 calories as the minimum necessary daily consumption level, but that figure has doubtful universal applicability. By way of a benchmark, per capita daily calorie availability in the United States is nearly 3,700. Despite the limitations of the FAO standards, Figure 10.9 uses them to assess the degree of undernourishment of countries' populations.

Like other national indicators, caloric intake figures must be viewed with suspicion; the dietary levels reported by some states

may reflect self-serving estimates or fervent hopes rather than actual food availability. Even if accurate, of course, they report national averages, which may seriously obscure the food deprivation of large segments of a population. But the data in Figure 10.9 support FAO's 2010 estimate that 925 million people (or roughly one in seven worldwide) were undernourished, including 19 million in the developed countries. Rising food prices combined with poverty, rather than crop failures, were the primary cause of the growing numbers of undernourished people. Despite the sobering world statistics, a number of developing countries have succeeded in reducing hunger levels. Most of the improvements have been in East Asia, Southeast Asia, and Latin America. Unfortunately, in the Middle East, South Asia, and sub-Saharan Africa the number of chronically undernourished people has increased. On the basis of those mixed and discouraging trends, it appears that the UN MDG of reducing the number of undernourished people by half by the year 2015 cannot be reached in many countries. Sadly, the tragic reality of inadequate supplies of food energy will persist (Figure 10.10).

Low caloric intake is usually coupled with lack of dietary balance, reflecting an inadequate supply of the carbohydrates, proteins, fats, vitamins, and minerals needed for optimum physical and mental development and maintenance of health. The WHO estimates that more than 2 billion people worldwide suffer from

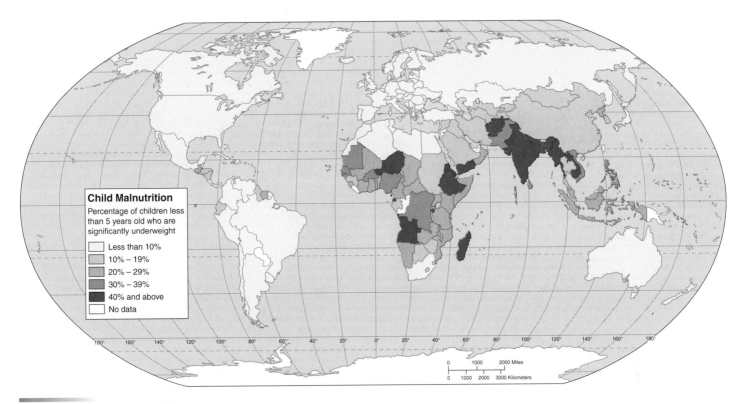

Figure 10.9 **Percentage of children under 5 that are undernourished, 2009.** In 2010, according to the FAO, there were about 925 million undernourished people worldwide facing chronic hunger or starvation, undernutrition, and deficiencies of essential iron, iodine, Vitamin A, and other micronutrients. In contrast, the FAO indicates that all industrialized countries have average daily per capita caloric intake well above physiological requirements and many face an obesity epidemic.

Sources: Data from World Bank, World Development Indicators, *2010.*

Figure 10.10 Malnourished Sudanese children at an aid center. The FAO estimates that in 2010, some 5 million children under 5 years of age died of malnourishment. The occasional and uncertain supplies of food dispensed by foreign aid programs and private charities are not sufficient to assure them of life, health, vigor, or normal development.

some form of micronutrient malnutrition that leads to high infant and child mortality, impaired physical and mental development, and weakened immune responses. Dietary insufficiencies in the first years of life retard later physical and cognitive development and increase vulnerability to infections, creating a cycle of malnutrition and poverty. The problem is most critical in rapidly growing countries that have large proportions of their populations in the young age groups (see Chapter 4). Indeed, undernourishment is damaging and widespread throughout the developing world, where, collectively, one in four children under 5 years is moderately or severely underweight. An estimated 5 million children under the age of 5 die each year due to undernourishment. South Asia shows the highest incidence of childhood nutritional problems measured by standardized weight-for-age and weight-for-height measures. There, of the under-3 age group, 47 percent are moderately or severely underweight, and half the world's undernourished children are found. Malnutrition among young Indians, for example, is one-and-a-half times as high as in sub-Saharan Africa.

Education

A literate, educated labor force is essential to take advantage of advanced technology and to compete for skilled jobs in the global economy. Yet in the poorest societies, half or more of adults are illiterate; for the richest, the figure is 1 percent or less (Figure 10.11). The problem stems in part from a national poverty that denies funds sufficient for teachers, school buildings, books, and other educational necessities. In part, it reflects the lack of a trained pool of teachers and the inability to expand their number rapidly enough to keep up with the ever-increasing size of school-age populations. In African countries worst hit by the

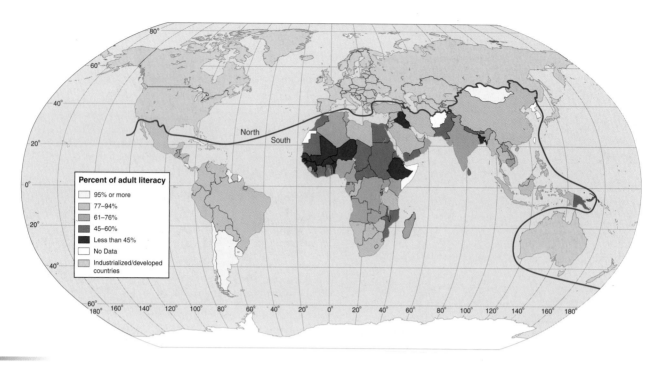

Figure 10.11 **Adult literacy rate, 2009,** as a percentage of the adult population (over 15 years of age) able to read and write short, simple statements relating to their everyday life. With almost no exceptions, adult literacy is 95 percent or more in countries of the North. With only a few exceptions, literacy rates in all countries of the South improved dramatically during past decades. For developing countries as a group, 80 percent of adults were literate in 2003, compared with 64 percent in 1990; for the least developed countries, the improvement was from 45 percent literate at the start of the 1990s to 54 percent literate in 2003.

Source: Data from United Nations Development Programme, Human Development Report 2010.

AIDS epidemic, deaths among existing teachers exceeded the supply of new teachers entering the profession in the late 1990s. For the same number of potential pupils, the richest countries may have 20 to 25 times as many teachers as do the poorest countries. Commitment appears as important as wealth in determining student-teacher ratios; Israel had more teachers per 1,000 students than did the richer Canada or the United Kingdom.

Family poverty makes tuition fees prohibitive and keeps millions of school-age children in full-time work. When Burundi abolished primary school tuition fees in 1999, enrollment increased threefold. The largest numbers of school-age children not enrolled in school are found in sub-Saharan Africa and southern Asia. However, in recent decades, the world's poorest countries have made tremendous improvements in education. Between 1999 and 2008, the percentage of children in school in developing countries grew from 82 percent to 89 percent. Despite recording the most rapid population growth, sub-Saharan Africa increased the percentage in school from 58 percent to 76 percent. The gender gap in education has been closing in recent decades, but it still was pronounced in northern Africa, where 66 percent of out-of-school children in 2010 were girls. Closing the gender gap has important development consequences, as seen in the correlations between levels of female education and birth rates, family size preferences, family nutrition practices, health maintenance, and life expectancies. The urban-rural education gap persists, however, with twice the percentage of children out of school in rural areas compared to urban areas.

Safe Drinking Water and Sanitation

Development implies more than industrial expansion or agricultural improvement. Safe drinking water and toilets, while taken for granted in the North, make profound contributions to human health and quality of life (see Figure 4.18 in Chapter 4). Safe water supplies and sanitation go together, because fecal contamination causes many water-borne diarrheal diseases such as cholera, dysentery, and typhoid fever. The WHO estimates that 1.4 million children die each year due to diarrheal diseases and that about 10 percent of the total global burden of disease is attributable to unsafe water, inadequate sanitation, or poor hygiene. Diarrheal diseases have a disproportionate effect on the very young and contribute to malnutrition and stunted growth. Lack of a nearby improved water supply often forces people, usually women, in developing countries to spend hours every day carrying water for their families.

Worldwide, about 900 million people lacked a dependable sanitary supply of water and 2.6 billion lacked basic sanitation (Figure 10.12). In southern Asia, nearly half the population must rely on open defecation, still a substantial improvement over 1990, when the value was 66 percent. The problems of water and sanitation are most pronounced in urban slums and in rural areas (Figure 10.13). In fact, in all world regions rural areas lag behind urban areas by substantial margins. However, as Table 10.1 notes, disparities in access to safe water are being steadily reduced. Improvements have been registered for access to improved sanitation, although they lag behind safe water improvements.

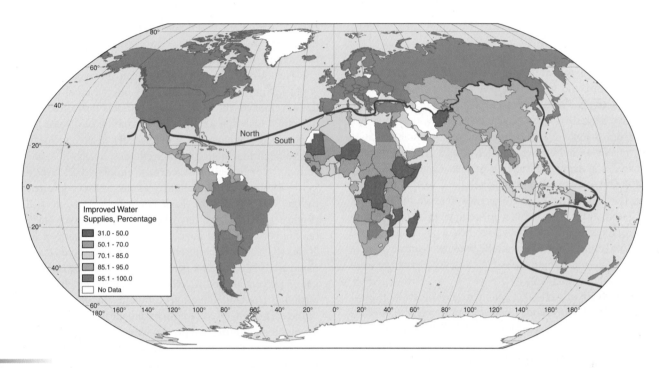

Figure 10.12 **Percentage of population with access to safe drinking water, 2008.** This map shows substantial improvements in the availability of improved drinking water supplies. By the early 21st century, thanks to WHO, United Nations, and World Bank programs and to targeted foreign aid, much of the developing world was approaching the levels of safe water availability formerly found only in industrialized states of the North. Still, rural areas lag behind urban areas.

Source: Population Reference Bureau, 2011.

Figure 10.13 Because they have no access to safe drinking water or sanitary waste disposal, impoverished populations of a developing country's unserved rural districts and urban slums—like this one in Capetown, South Africa—are subject to water-borne and sanitation-related diseases.

Health

Access to medical facilities and personnel is another spatial variable with profound implications for the health and well-being of populations. Within the less developed world, vast numbers of people are effectively denied the services of physicians. The number of persons served by each physician varies widely between countries, from a low of 170 people per physician in Cuba to 50,000 per physician in Nicaragua and Tanzania. The shortage of doctors is a crisis in many sub-Saharan African, Central American, and south Asian countries. In the developing world, there are simply too few trained health professionals to serve the needs of expanding populations. Those few who are in practice tend to congregate in urban areas, or they leave for better pay in developed countries. Rural clinics are few in number and the distance to them so great that many rural populations lack access to even the most rudimentary medical treatment.

The **brain drain** of well-educated medical professionals leaving poor countries to work in developed countries is a major barrier to improving global heath. Developed countries such as the United States simply do not produce enough nurses and general-practice physicians for their needs. Instead, the United States imports about a fourth of its practicing physicians from abroad, mostly from developing countries. A recent study showed more Ethiopian doctors practicing in the Chicago metropolitan area than there are doctors in the entire country of Ethiopia, despite its population of 87 million people.

Health-related contrasts between advanced and developing countries have become matters of international concern and attention. Indeed, three of the eight MDGs deal directly with child mortality, maternal health, and eradication of disease. We saw the importance in Chapter 4 of the transfer of advanced medical and public health technologies: insecticides, antibiotics, and immunization, for example. Most recently, childhood diseases and deaths in developing countries have come under coordinated attack by the WHO under the Task Force for Child Survival program (Figure 10.14). Gains have been impressive, yet stark contrasts remain between most developed and least developed societies. In 2008, 10,000 fewer children under 5 years old died each day compared to 1990. Still, 14 percent of sub-Saharan African children and 7 percent of south Asian children do not live to their fifth birthday. The United Nations estimates that more than 90 percent of the approximately 8.8 million annual infant and child deaths in developing countries are preventable.

Taken at their extremes, advanced and developing countries occupy two distinct worlds of disease and health. One is affluent; its death rates are low, and the chief killers of its mature populations are cancers, heart attacks, and strokes. The other world

Figure 10.14 The WHO is the agency of the United Nations that helps bring modern preventive health care, safe water, and sanitation to the less developed world. WHO workers help to fight certain diseases, advise on nutrition and living conditions, and aid developing countries in strengthening their health services. When the organization launched its immunization program in 1974, only 5 percent of the world's children were immunized against measles, diphtheria, polio, tetanus, whooping cough, and tuberculosis, diseases claiming 7 million young lives annually. Pictured is preventive health care in a Micronesian clinic.

is impoverished and prone to disease. The deadly dangers to its youthful populations are infectious, respiratory, and parasitic diseases made more serious by malnutrition.

As mentioned above, diarrheal diseases are concentrated in areas lacking safe drinking water supplies and sanitation (Figure 10.15a). Unfortunately, resurgence of old diseases and

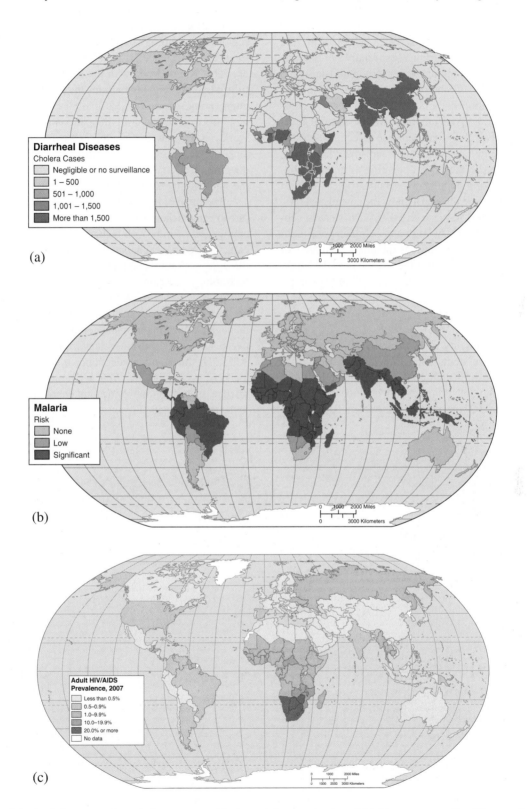

Figure 10.15 (a) Diarrheal diseases such as cholera are spread by bacterial contamination of drinking water supplies. They can be prevented by proper sanitation and improved drinking water systems. (b) Malaria is caused by parasites carried by a type of mosquito that thrives in the warm, moist conditions found in tropical locations. It killed 655,000 people in 2010, mostly African children. Malaria has had a measurable negative effect on the GNI of the most affected African countries. Prevention and control efforts are decreasing rates of infection. (c) In 2010, an estimated 34 million people were living with HIV/AIDS, 23 million in Africa where the disease first emerged.

emergence of new ones may disrupt or reverse the hoped-for transition to better health in many world areas (See the feature "Our Delicate State of Health," p. 110). Almost 10 percent of the world's population now suffers from one or more tropical diseases such as malaria, many of which were formerly thought to be eradicable but now are spreading in drug-resistant forms. Malaria-carrying mosquitoes are mostly found in the tropics, especially sub-Saharan Africa, where that disease is a major barrier to human health and development (Figure 10.15b). Globally there are about 250 million malaria cases and one million malaria deaths each year. According to the WHO, an average African child suffers malarial fever two to five times each year. Solutions combine insecticide-treated mosquito nets, insecticide spraying, and anti-malarial drugs. Another such scourge, tuberculosis, is appearing as a major concern, especially among poorer populations outside tropical regions.

Low-income countries are also hard hit by the spread of AIDS. In 2007, one-third of persons living with HIV/AIDS were in sub-Saharan Africa (Figure 10.15c). The high and rising costs of modern medications place unbearable burdens on strained budgets of developing states. Medicines to control the advance of HIV/AIDS are beyond the reach of most Africans infected with the disease.

Technology

Technology refers to the totality of tools and methods used by a culture group to produce items for subsistence and comfort. We saw in Chapter 2 how in antiquity, there emerged *culture hearths*—centers of technological innovation, new ideas and techniques that diffused from the core region. The ancient hearths (see Figure 2.15) were locales of multiple invention and innovation. Their modern counterparts are the highly urbanized, industrialized advanced nations whose creativity is recorded by patent registrations and product and process introductions.

In all periods, there has existed between hearths and outlying regions a **technology gap,** a contrast in the range and productivity of artifacts introduced at the core and those employed at the periphery. That gap widened with the Industrial Revolution and has continued to grow with innovations in railroads, steelmaking, electrical engineering, chemistry, automobiles, petrochemicals, computers, and information and communications technologies. In the modern world, as we saw in Chapter 2, there is a widespread sharing of technologies, organizational forms, and cultural traits. But not all countries are equally able to draw on advanced technology to create the same products with identical efficiency and quality.

The technology gap matters. Understandably, all countries aspire to expand their resource base, increase its support levels through application of improved technologies, or enter more fully into income-producing exchange relationships with other world regions through economic development. One objective of development is **technology transfer,** the deliberate introduction of technologies and processes that mark the more advanced countries. Of course, not all technology is equally transferable. Computers, information management techniques, and cell phones easily make the move between advanced and emerging economies (Figure 10.16). While Africa lags in landline telephones, it is the world's second-largest market for cell phones. Other technologies, particularly in the life science, materials innovation, and energy sectors, are more specific to the markets, capital resources, and needs of the rich countries and

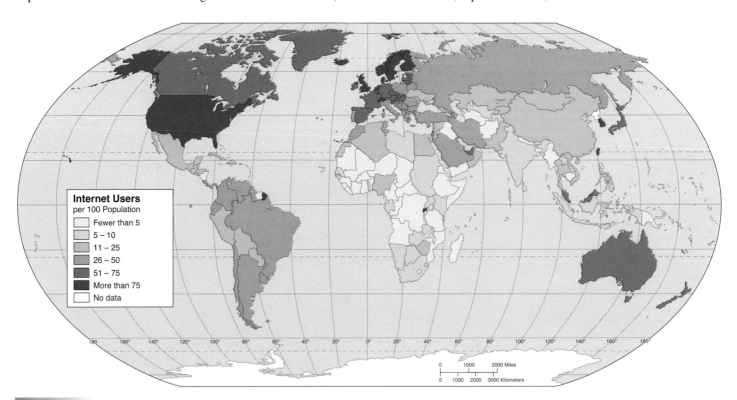

Figure 10.16 **Internet use** has diffused to all corners of the Earth, yet there are still countries where less than 5 percent of the population has used the Internet.

Source: World Bank, World Development Indicators, *2010.*

not adapted to those of the less developed states. Even where transfer is feasible, imported innovations may require domestic markets sufficient to justify their costs, markets that poor countries will not possess at their current national income levels. And the purchase of technology presumes recipient country export earnings sufficient to pay for it, again a condition not met by the poorest states.

Explanations of Development and Underdevelopment

It is one thing to map differences in income or health and to assign countries to categories such as "least developed" or "advanced"; it is quite another to explain the underlying causes and spatial pattern. The widespread disparities in the basic demographic and economic characteristics of countries raises fundamental questions such as why one group of countries is "developed" and another group is "less developed." We observe that the developed countries have high per capita incomes, a small proportion of workers engaged in agriculture, and most of their population living in cities where they enjoy abundant food and high-quality housing, health care, education, and public services. We note that in the least developed countries, incomes are very low, many of their workers are engaged in subsistence agriculture, and the cities are plagued by poor-quality services and slums. We can observe that the developed countries have completed the demographic transition, while the developing countries are in the middle stages of the transition, with higher-than-replacement fertility rates and shorter life expectancies. The statistical differences themselves, however, do not offer a full explanation of development and underdevelopment, nor do they show a clear pathway for countries to follow. Our explanations reflect our theories about how economies and politics work. Explanations are important because they suggest where we should fix blame and what solutions are most likely to work. Some explanations look to physical geography, others to history, and still others to economic or sociological theories.

Physical Geography

The Brandt Report hints at one frequent but simplistic geographic explanation: Development is a characteristic of the rich "North"—the midlatitudes; poverty and underdevelopment are tropical conditions. Proponents of the latitudinal explanation support their conviction not only by reference to such thematic maps as Figures 10.4 and 10.9, but by noting that rich countries—some 35 in number—are mostly in temperate climate zones; the world's poorest states are mostly located in tropical latitudes.

Supporters of simple geographic explanations for inequality point out, for example, that Brazilians of the southeastern temperate highlands have average incomes several times higher than their compatriots of tropical Amazonia. Annual average incomes of Mexicans of the temperate north far exceed those of the southern Yucatán. Australians of the tropical north are poorer than Australians of the temperate south.

Influential economist Jeffrey Sachs argues for the contributing factors of latitude and climate in global economic inequality.

He notes that in 1820, tropical regions had a per capita GNP 70 percent of that of the temperate regions. Economic growth in the temperate regions outpaced the tropics and by 1992, per capita GNP in the tropics was just 25 percent that of the temperate regions. Tropical regions face the major ecological handicaps of low agricultural productivity, challenging soil conditions, and substantially higher incidence of plant, animal, and human disease. Confounding the search for a simple explanation, however, many of the poorer nations of the "South" lie partially or wholly within the midlatitudes or at temperate elevations—Afghanistan, North Korea, and Mongolia are examples—while equatorial Singapore and Malaysia prosper. Location matters, but it is not destiny.

Other simple geographic explanations have some merit, yet are ultimately inconclusive:

1. Resource poverty is cited as a limit to developmental possibilities. Although some developing countries are deficient in raw materials, others are major world suppliers of both industrial minerals and agricultural goods—bauxite, cacao, and coffee, for example. Admittedly, a developing world complaint is that their commodities are underpriced in world markets or are restricted by tariffs and subsidized competitors. Those, however, are matters of marketing, politics, and economics, not of resources. Further, economists have long held that reliance on natural resource wealth and exports by less developed countries undermines their prospects for growth by interfering with their development of manufacturing industries.

2. Overpopulation and overcrowding are frequently discussed as causes of poverty and underdevelopment, but Singapore prospers, with some 7,600 people per square kilometer (19,000 per square mile), while impoverished Mali is nearly empty, with 12 per square kilometer (31 per square mile) (Figure 10.17).

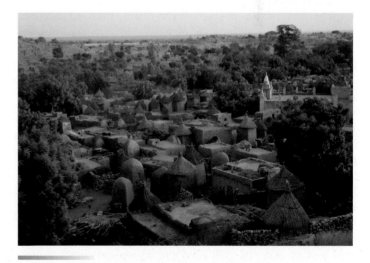

Figure 10.17 Landlocked and subject to severe droughts, Mali is one of the poorest of the least developed countries. Low densities of population are not necessarily related to prosperity, or high densities to poverty. Mali has only 12 people per square kilometer (34 per square mile); Japan has 339 per square kilometer (878 per square mile). In this parched land, Dogon women often spend hours carrying water to their homes. Even in more humid South Africa, rural women on average spend more than three hours each day fetching water, according to a government survey.

3. Landlocked countries have reduced access to global markets and greater costs for transport of goods. For theorists who believe that global trade is the key to development, reduced access to foreign markets is seen as a major impediment. Kazakhstan, Afghanistan, Chad, Niger, Zambia, and Zimbabwe are more than 2,000 kilometers (1,200 miles) from the nearest seacoast. Counterexamples such as Switzerland, which is both poor in resources and landlocked, suggest that these challenges can be overcome with investments in transportation infrastructure.

The Slave Trade and Colonialism

The 500-year history of colonialism played a vital role in shaping the political and economic geography of the contemporary world. Some scholars believe it laid the foundation for the present-day economic differences between countries. It allowed European countries to gain an initial economic advantage by gaining control of territory, natural resources, labor, and markets. Former colonial status is often blamed for underdevelopment because nearly all of the developing countries in the Global South were once colonies. In cases where the colonists largely replaced the original inhabitants—as in Australia, New Zealand, Canada, or the United States—the association of colonial past with present underdevelopment does not hold.

The accusation is arguably valid for countries where—as in sub-Saharan Africa and southern Asia—colonizers left largely intact the indigenous populations but created political structures and physical infrastructures designed for exploitation for mother country profit rather than for balanced economic, social, and political development for the long-term benefit of the colony itself.

The first phase of colonialism dates from Christopher Columbus's first voyage to the New World and peaked just before the American Revolution. Spain and Portugal dominated this phase, which was focused on the Americas and Caribbean islands. The British, Dutch, and French followed in developing their own colonies. The African slave trade played a vital role in this phase of colonialism through the "triangular trade," which sent manufactured goods, liquor, and guns from Europe to Africa, slaves from Africa to the New World, and sugar and tobacco from the New World to Europe. In the early 1800s, the Spanish and Portuguese lost much of their colonial empires to Latin American independence movements. A second phase of colonialism in the late 1800s and early 1900s was dominated by the British and was focused on Africa, Asia, and Oceania. During this period, nearly all the lands in the tropics and subtropics were brought under the control of European powers or the United States (see Figure 12.6). Independence movements in the 20th century, culminating in the independence of Namibia in 1990, brought the colonial era to an end.

One legacy of colonialism is visible in country borders that are often poorly suited to nation-building. African borders were established without regard for the boundaries of ethnic groups. For example, Gambia straddles the Gambia River and is about 10 kilometers (6 miles) wide on each bank of the river and extends 330 kilometers (205 miles) upstream (Figure 10.18). Typically, colonial infrastructure systems were designed to move resources from the interior to coastal ports without developing interconnections or networks to facilitate trade between colonies or develop the interior, Other negative legacies included dependence on the mother country for manufactured goods and authoritarian political institutions that did not transition well after independence.

Modernization Theory

Modernization theory is the most widely accepted understanding of the development process. It dates back to the optimism of the post–World War II era, when the United States began working with European countries and Japan to reconstruct both their war-damaged economies and the global economic order. European countries agreed to begin dismantling their colonial empires and cooperate with the United States, the United Nations, and other non-communist countries in bringing the benefits of science, technology, and industrial progress to the less developed countries of the world. Modernization theory drew upon sociological and economic theories and shaped the original thinking about development in Western countries. Modernization theory begins by arranging all societies on a continuum with "traditional" on one end and "modern" on the other. Development, according to modernization theory, is the logical progression from traditional to modern as societies adopt the characteristics of advanced societies—advanced technology, urbanization, high per capita incomes, high quality of life, a completed demographic transition, individualism, democracy, and capitalism.

Economic historian Walt Rostow (1916–2003) generalized on the "sweep of modern history," theorizing that all developing economies pass through six stages of growth and advancement:

- *Traditional societies* of subsistence agriculture, simple technology, and poorly developed commercial economies are relatively static and limited to low productivity levels.
- *Preconditions for takeoff* are established when an "external intrusion" initiates political and economic change. The nation-state, rather than kinship units, becomes the primary organizing structure for society. Entrepreneurial elites invest in transportation systems and other productive and supportive infrastructure. Economic growth is accepted as a necessity.
- *Takeoff* to sustained growth is the critical developmental stage, lasting perhaps 20 to 30 years, during which rates of investment increase, farmers adopt mechanization and agriculture is commercialized, new industries are established, resources are exploited, and growth becomes the expected norm.
- *The drive to maturity* sees economic output growing faster than population. The country engages in specialization and international trade. Advanced technology is incorporated into all phases of economic activity; diversification carries the economy beyond the industrial emphases first triggering growth, and the economy becomes increasingly self-sufficient.
- *The age of mass consumption* sees consumer goods and services begin to rival heavy industry as leading economic sectors and most of the population achieves consumption levels far above basic needs.

Figure 10.18 The Gambia's borders illustrate a common legacy of colonialism--boundaries designed for the exploitation of natural resources for export markets rather than nation-building. The narrow shape of the country, straddling the Gambia River, inhibits trade and communication between the northern and southern parts of the country.

Source: E. Sheppard, P. Porter, D. Faust, and R. Nagar, A World of Difference: Encountering and Contesting Development, *2d ed., Guilford, 2009.*

- *The postindustrial stage is marked by the rise of services that replace secondary activities* as the principal sector of the economy. Professional and technical skills assume preeminence in the labor force, and information replaces energy as the key productive resource.

Rostow's stages of economic growth turned the experience of western countries into a blueprint for developing countries in Latin America, Asia, and Africa. The 1960s, 1970s, and 1980s were all proclaimed by UN resolutions as "Development Decades," with a belief that foreign assistance, technology transfer from advanced economies, and infrastructure investments would trigger the upward, progressive march of development.

The Core-Periphery Model

In contrast to the optimism of modernization theory, critics point out repeated patterns of **uneven spatial development**. They observed that within developing countries, undergoing modernization there often includes a modern "core" of capitalist production integrated with the global economy alongside a traditional "periphery" with subsistence wages. The **core-periphery model** helps us understand the dualism that exists within many spatial systems such as the urban-rural contrasts commonly seen in infrastructure, health, and education.

The core and periphery are linked parts of a wider system. If for any reason (perhaps a new industrial process or product) one section of a country experiences accelerated economic development, that section becomes increasingly attractive for investors, entrepreneurs, and migrants. Assuming that investment capital is limited, growth in the developing core must come at the expense of the peripheries of the country. Economic growth sets in motion a process of **circular and cumulative causation**. Through the multiplier effect and agglomeration economies (see Chapters 9 and 11), new businesses spur the growth of other businesses. Businesses pay wages to workers, who purchase goods and services such as groceries and housing, supporting the local retail and construction industries. Firms and employees pay taxes, funding public services such as schools, parks, and roads. High-quality public facilities and infrastructure improve business productivity and the quality of life, making it an attractive place for additional businesses to locate, starting the process all over again. Circular and cumulative causation works to polarize development and, according to economist Gunnar Myrdal, leads to a permanent division between prosperous (and dominating) cores and depressed (and exploited) peripheral districts that are milked of surplus labor, raw materials, and profits.

A more optimistic version of this model suggests that within market economies, income disparities tend to be reduced as developmental levels increase. Eventually, it is argued, income convergence will occur as **trickle-down effects,** or **spread effects,** work to diffuse benefits outward from the center in the form of higher prices paid for needed materials or through the dispersion of technology to branch plants or contract suppliers to lower-cost regions of production. The experience of developed countries offers only mixed support for this belief. Nearly all residents of developed countries have access to education, safe drinking water, and other indicators of development. Still, in most developed countries, there remain strong contrasts between wealthy, fast-growing urban cores and prosperous "high-tech" concentrations on the one hand, and depressed, depopulated rural peripheries or declining, deindustrialized "rust belts" on the other.

Dependency Theory

Dependency theory emerged from dissatisfaction with modernization theory and development programs as they were applied to regions such as Latin America. Drawing upon Karl Marx's ideas, dependency theorists extended the core-periphery model to the international scene. They claimed that the development of the advanced core nations depended upon the underdevelopment of the peripheral nations. Unlike modernization theory, which sees poverty as the natural state of affairs, dependency theory argues that development creates underdevelopment. In other words, developing countries were made poor by their interactions with advanced countries, starting with colonialism and the slave trade and continuing in new forms to the present. Dependency theory sees the developing world as effectively held captive by the leading industrial nations. It is drained of wealth and deprived of growth by remaining largely a food and raw material exporter and an importer of manufactured commodities. Developing countries suffer because prices for the primary goods that they export remain low, while the prices for imported manufactured goods continue to rise. Development aid, where proffered, involves a forced economic reliance on donor countries that continues an imposed cycle in which, in a sense, selective industrialization leads not to independent growth, but to further dependent underdevelopment. A condition of **neocolonialism** is said to exist even after legal independence in which economic and even political control is exercised by developed states over the economies and societies of independent countries of the underdeveloped world. This control is said to be exercised through unequal terms of exchange and the power exerted by international bodies such as the WTO and IMF.

Support for dependency theory comes from the growing gap between the world's poorest and richest countries. Dependency theory holds that these differentials are not accidental but the logical result of the ability of developed countries and power elites to exploit other populations and regions to secure for themselves a continuous source of new profits. Today, transnational corporations, the theory contends, tend to dominate through their investments in key areas of developing economies. They introduce technologies and production facilities to further their own corporate goals, not to further the balanced development of the recipient economies. Dependency theory has been criticized for treating developing countries as passive victims and for viewing economic development as a zero-sum game. Critics of dependency theory point out that technological innovations increase economic productivity, creating a larger pie to be shared by all. Another failing of dependency theory is its inability to account for the rising prosperity in newly industrializing countries such as China.

World Systems Theory

World systems theory extends the core-periphery model to the entire capitalist global world economy. On the international scene, core-periphery contrasts are discerned between, particularly, Western Europe, Japan, and the United States as prosperous cores and the least developed countries on the periphery of the global economy. At all spatial scales, core-periphery models assume that in part, the growth and prosperity of core regions come at the expense of exploited peripheral zones. The core controls key high-level functions in the global economy, such as headquarters for transnational corporations, financial centers, and stock exchanges. In contrast with dependency theory, world systems theory acknowledges that countries can shift from a peripheral position to a core position. A semi-periphery of newly industrializing countries, such as South Korea and Brazil, occupies an intermediate position between core countries, such as the United States, and peripheral countries, such as Liberia.

Strategies for Development

Strategies for development have been strongly influenced by modernization theory and Rostow's stages of economic development. From the 1950s through 1970s, the leading model for economic development was the "Big Push" of massive coordinated investments in infrastructure and industry. The stimulus provided by this big push would cause the economy to "take off" through productivity increases, expansion of the consumer base, and the creation of backward- and forward-linked industries. Countries were to focus on industries where they had a *comparative advantage* in order to develop efficient industrial specializations, agglomeration economies, and expanding trade. Because the needed push was too large for the private sector, governments of developing countries were to take the initiative by borrowing large sums of money to finance the necessary investments.

The two major international lending agencies, the IMF and the World Bank, were the outcome of a conference held at Bretton Woods, New Hampshire, near the end of World War II. The IMF is mostly concerned with lending to governments to help stabilize their currencies or to pay for their imports or international debts when their reserves fall short. The World Bank has focused on lending for development, beginning with the restoration of war-devastated countries of Europe, and then shifting its attention to the world's developing countries. For example, from 1960–1975, the World Bank made 135 loans for power plants and 196 loans for roads or railroads in Africa, Asia, Latin America, the Caribbean, and the Middle East.

New Directions in Development

During the 1980s, dissatisfaction with inefficiencies and corruption in government-led development projects led to a different strategy called the "Washington Consensus." The new approach, sometimes called **neoliberal globalization,** was supported by the IMF, World Bank, and U.S. Treasury. It was called *neoliberal* because it revived the liberal faith in the market mechanism and the private sector. Countries were to eliminate tariffs and quotas to promote global free trade, and governments of developing countries were asked to reduce regulations, privatize state-run industries, and remove barriers to foreign firms and foreign investors. Instead of excessive spending on social needs, governments were to balance their budgets carefully and keep taxes low. Neoliberal thinking is reflected in a UN report concluding that "good government," including protection of property rights under a stable political and legal system, should be the top priority in development.

Another approach to development that emerged in the 1980s was a focus on "human capital," a composite of skills, habits, schooling, and knowledge that—more than labor force numbers or capital availability—contributes to successful economic development and sustained growth. Technological progress in recent decades, it is pointed out, has been notably dependent on more educated workforces equipped with high levels of capital investment. The current deep global imbalance in literate and technically trained people has been called the most potent force of divergence in well-being between the rich world and the poor. When developing countries offer incentives to attract foreign direct investment and technology transfer, the imported ideas and technology help create "human capital"—labor and intellectual skills. This creates the potential to develop industrial specializations, export-led development, and rising levels of living, as presumably they did for Taiwan, Singapore, and the other surging Asian economies.

A different sort of foreign assistance comes in the forms of **remittances,** flows of money sent home by workers who have left their homes in developing countries to take jobs in developed countries. Geographic differences in population growth rates and economic opportunities are behind much of the global flow of international migrants. For example, relatively high wages and declining labor forces in Europe versus low wages and rapid population growth in Africa creates strong migration pressures.

Remittances are among the most important flows of money from rich countries to poor countries. In many poor countries, remittances rival foreign direct investment as their largest source of foreign capital. While many transfers go unrecorded, officially recorded remittances were $350 billion in 2011, according to the World Bank. Remittances sent home by migrants from Africa grew by a factor of 4 between 1990 and 2010 to reach $40 billion annually. In most cases, remittances are used to meet basic family needs, such as food, medicine, and school fees, or to allow children to stay in school longer before entering the workforce. They are sometimes used to fund construction of houses for family members or to purchase desired consumer goods that demonstrate the success of the migrant. While not always reaching their potential, remittances offer an important economic development opportunity for poor countries by transferring capital and providing startup funds for businesses ventures.

Development Prospects

Rostow's expectations of an inevitable progression of development have proved illusory. Many developing countries remain locked in one of the first two stages of his model, unable to achieve the takeoff to self-sustained growth despite importing technology and attracting foreign aid investment funds from the more developed world (see the feature "Does Foreign Aid Help?"). Indeed, it has become apparent to many observers that despite the efforts of the world community, the development gap between the most and the least advanced countries may widen rather than narrow over time. A case in point is sub-Saharan Africa; between 1975 and 2000, per capita income declined by almost 1 percent a year, leaving all but a tiny elite significantly poorer at the end of the period. Over the same years, income per head in the industrial market economies grew at a 1.8 percent annual rate. More recently, the picture brightened for the developing world as a whole. On the bright side, newly industrializing countries such as China lead the world in economic growth. Even sub-Saharan Africa posted growth in the 2000–2010 period, growing at an average annual rate of 2.3 percent. For many, faith in the likelihood of growth—even if not in definable "stages of development"—was renewed.

Challenges and Opportunities Facing Developing Countries

In addition to managing population growth and promoting economic development, developing countries often face special challenges. Major challenges facing developing countries include natural hazards, foreign debt, land ownership, and gender inequality. The case of Haiti illustrates several of these challenges. As noted in the chapter's opening vignette, natural disasters are often much more devastating when they strike developing countries. The reconstruction efforts following the 2010 Haitian earthquake demonstrate some of the challenges of providing effective development assistance. After the quake, an outpouring of international sympathy led to promises of $2.5 billion in emergency relief work and $4.5 billion in reconstruction assistance. While debating the aid packages, it was revealed that Haiti was already burdened by immense foreign debts, most of which were forgiven as part of the assistance. Delivery of the promised aid was delayed, and most of the relief and reconstruction work was performed by organizations and companies based in donor countries such as the United States, rather than by Haitian agencies, nongovernmental organizations, or businesses. This method of delivery aid only exacerbated Haiti's position of dependency and missed an opportunity to build the capacities of Haitian agencies and firms. The actual rebuilding of homes and businesses was complicated by issues of land ownership because only about 5 percent of Haiti's land holdings were properly titled and recorded prior to the earthquake. Finally, human rights advocates criticized the reconstruction planning for ignoring gender issues, such as the fact that women living in tent camps for years after the earthquake where highly vulnerable to sexual violence.

Foreign Debt

In the pursuit of development, many developing countries borrowed heavily in the 1960s and 1970s. Money was spent on hydroelectric dams, power plants, ports, and other large, government-directed development projects. Unfortunately, many expensive World Bank–financed development projects were disappointing failures and did not generate sufficient returns to pay back the loans (Figure 10.19). Other borrowed money was spent women than men are wage earners, and Africa, where wage-earning opportunities for women are few.

The present world pattern of gender-related institutional and economic assignments is varied. It is influenced by a country's level of economic development, by the persistence of customary restrictions that some religions and cultures impose on women, and by the specific nature of its economic—particularly agricultural—base. The differential impact of these and other conditions is evident in Figure 10.22. The pattern shows a distinct gender-specific regionalization among the countries of the developing world. Among the Arab or Arab-influenced Muslim areas of western Asia and North Africa, the recorded proportion of the female population that is economically active is low. Religious tradition restricts women's acceptance in economic activities outside the home. The same cultural limitations do not apply in the different rural economic conditions of Muslims in southern and southeastern Asia, where labor force participation by women in Indonesia and Bangladesh, for example, is much higher than it is among Western Muslims.

In Latin America, women have been overcoming cultural restrictions on their employment outside the home, and their active economic participation has been increasing. That participation is occurring almost entirely outside of the agricultural realm, where the high degree of farm labor tenancy as well as custom limits the role of females. Sub-Saharan Africa, highly diverse culturally and economically, is highly dependent on

Empowering Women Financially

The Fourth World Conference on Women, held in Beijing in 1995, called on all governments to formulate strategies, programs, and laws designed to guarantee women their full human rights to equality and development. The conference's final declaration, reinforced at the "Beijing Plus Five" Conference held at the United Nations in 2000, detailed recommended policies in the areas of sexuality and child-bearing, violence against women, discrimination against girls, female inheritance rights, and family protection. Its particular emphasis, however, focused on efforts to "ensure women's equal access to economic resources including land, credit, and markets as a means to further advancement and empowerment of women and girls."

That special economic emphasis was reinforced by the FAO's "Gender and Development Plan (2002–2007)," which aimed at stimulating efforts to enhance gender-based equity in the control of productive resources and providing women with access to credit to enable them to engage as creators and owners of small-scale manufacturing, trade, or service businesses. Still later, the UN General Assembly designated 2005 as the "International Year of Microcredit" to further the same objectives.

Two-thirds of the total amount of work women do is unpaid, but that unpaid work amounts to an $11 trillion addition to the total world economy. The Beijing Plus Five Conference declaration was a recognition that women's economic contribution would be even greater—and of more social and personal benefit—were governments to grant them equal opportunity through financial support to engage as owners in small-scale manufacturing, trade, or service enterprises. In fact, both the model and proof of success in granting women access to credit were already in place.

In 1976, a Bangladeshi economist, Muhammad Yunus, wandered into a poor village and got an idea that has captured international interest and changed accepted beliefs and practices of banking in developing countries. The concept behind the Grameen Bank that he established is simple: If individual borrowers are given access to credit, they will be able to identify and engage in viable income-producing activities, such as pottery making, weaving, sewing, buying and marketing simple consumer goods, and providing transportation and other basic services.

Declaring that "Access to credit should be a human right," Yunus was a pioneer in extending "microcredit" for "microenterprises," with women emerging as the primary borrowers and beneficiaries of Grameen Bank's practice of lending money without collateral and at low rates of interest. Under the original Grameen concept, to be eligible for the average loan of about US$160, women without assets must join or form a "cell" of five unrelated women, of whom only two can borrow at first though all five are responsible for repayment. When the first two begin to repay, two more can borrow, and so on. As a condition of the loan, clients also must agree to increase their savings, observe sound nutritional practices, and educate their children.

By 2005, the bank had made more than 5 million loans in 40,000 villages in Bangladesh alone. More than 90 percent of the borrowers are women, and repayment rates reach above 95 percent. The average household income of Grameen Bank members has risen much faster than that of nonmembers in the same villages, with the landless benefiting most and marginal landowner families following closely. Because of enterprise incomes resulting from the lending program, there has been a sharp reduction in the number of Grameen Bank members living below the poverty line. There has also been a marked shift from low-status agricultural labor to self-employment in simple manufacturing and trading. That shift has encouraged a borrower and lender recognition that larger loans are needed to enable increasingly entrepreneurial women to build small businesses, hire employees, acquire office and manufacturing equipment, and the like. In consequence, some lenders now approve loans of several thousand dollars, although such larger loans are still much in the minority.

Muhammed Yunus was awarded the 2006 Nobel Peace Prize for developing his model of microcredit. His microcredit ideas have spread from their Bangladesh origins to other countries in Asia, Latin America, Eastern Europe, and Africa. Of those poorest clients, the vast majority are women. But the female recipients still represent only a fraction of the women worldwide who have virtually no access to credit—or to the economic, social, educational, and nutritional benefits that come from its availability. It is that globally enormous number of women now effectively denied credit equality that the resolutions of the Fourth World Conference on Women and the FAO and UN General Assembly plans and programs seek to benefit.

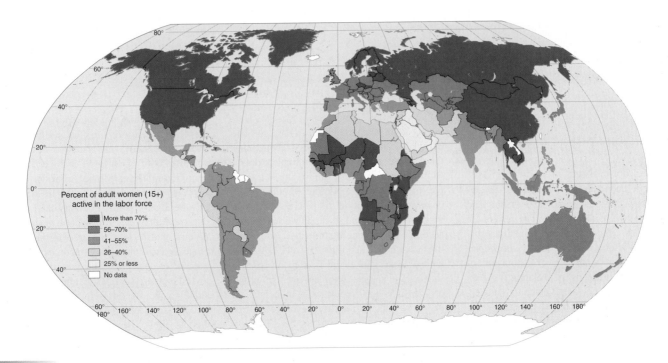

Figure 10.22 Participation of women (ages 15 and above) in the labor force, 2008. Worldwide, 52 percent of women were in the labor force in 2008. Many of the countries with the highest rates of female participation in the labor force were in sub-Saharan Africa. Cultural factors lie behind low rates of female labor force participation in South Asia and the Middle East–North Africa zone.

Source: World Bank, World Development Indicators, *2011.*

female farm labor and market income. The historical role of strongly independent, property-owning females formerly encountered under traditional agricultural and village systems, however, has increasingly been replaced by the subordination of women with the modernization of agricultural techniques and introduction of formal, male-dominated financial and administrative farm-sector institutions.

Alternative Measures of Development and Well-Being

Dissatisfaction with purely economic measures of development has spurred development agencies to seek composite measures that better measure human well-being. Development, it is maintained, goes beyond the purely economic and physical, and personal development may have little or nothing to do with objective statistical measures. The achievement of development must also be seen in terms of individual and collective well-being: a safe environment, freedom from want, opportunity for personal growth and enrichment, and access to goods and services beyond the absolute minimum to sustain life (see the feature "Measuring Happiness"). Health, safety, educational and cultural development, security in old age, political freedom, and similar noneconomic criteria are among the evidence of comparative developmental level that is sought in composite statistics. Also sought is a measure of development that is neither ethnocentric nor colored by political agendas. The values of one culture—for example, in

housing space per person, in educational levels, or in distribution of national income—are not necessarily universally applicable or acceptable, and a true comparative statistic should not imply that they are.

One such ranking that has gained increasing recognition is employed by the UNDP. Its Human Development Index (HDI) combines purchasing power (not just dollar amount of per capita GNI), life expectancy, and education (literacy plus years of schooling) (Figure 10.23). The HDI reflects the program's conviction that the important human aspirations are leading a long and healthy life, receiving adequate education, and having access to assets and income sufficient for a decent quality of life. The weighting of the three input variables lends a further element of subjectivity to the rankings.

The UNDP has also developed a measure of poverty in its Human Poverty Index (HPI). While the HDI measures average *achievement,* the HPI measures *deprivation* in the same three measures of development underlying the HDI. For the poverty index, the benchmarks of concern are probability of not surviving to age 40, exclusion from full social intercourse because of illiteracy, and deprivation of basic needs, as measured by lack of safe water access and percentage of underweight small children. The HPI is discussed in more detail in the feature "What Is Poverty?"

A "gender empowerment measure" (GEM) devised by the UNDP, emphasizes female participation in political, management, professional, and technical positions. The GEM rankings are heavily biased toward measures that technologically advanced, career-oriented, Western cultures consider indicative

Measuring Happiness

Is there a spatial pattern to happiness? And is it related to spatial patterns of development, underdevelopment, high incomes, or poverty? Psychologists have long used surveys of reported well-being to study happiness, and some economists have explored the relationships between economic variables and measures of life satisfaction. The results are fascinating, complicated, and sometimes surprising. Within a country, those with higher incomes tend to report greater happiness, but as standards of living rise, happiness does not necessarily increase. Generally, higher-income countries have higher reported levels of happiness, but the many exceptions suggest that other cultural factors are important

influences. Ruut Veenhoven at Erasmus University in the Netherlands has compiled "The World Database of Happiness," containing the results of surveys of life enjoyment drawn from 155 countries. The following is a sample of top-ranked countries, middle-range countries, and bottom-ranked countries on surveys administered since the year 2000 that asked people to rate their "satisfaction with life as a whole" on a 0 to 10 scale. While the United States ranked fairly high on the life satisfaction survey, with an average rating of 7.0, Canadians report even higher levels of life satisfaction, with an average of 7.6, and Mexicans were even happier. The top five nations for life satisfaction include three

prosperous European countries known for their high quality of life (Iceland, Denmark, and Switzerland), but also two developing countries with much lower incomes than the rest (Colombia and Mexico). Further, Puerto Rico, which was not included in the rankings because it is not a country, had a score that would have put it in second place. Many Asian countries are clustered in the middle range, even though their incomes range by a factor of nearly 10. The countries with the lowest happiness ratings are mostly in Africa, although one, Belarus (a former Soviet republic), has an income level that is much higher than its level of happiness would suggest.

Country	Happiness Score (0–10)	GNI/Capita (US$), 2009
Happiest Countries		
Iceland	8.5	$32,840
Denmark	8.4	$38,780
Colombia	8.1	$8,600
Switzerland	8.1	$47,100
Mexico	8.0	$14,020
Middle-Range Countries		
Philippines	6.3	$3,540
Iran	6.3	$11,470
India	6.0	$3,280
China	5.9	$6,890
South Korea	5.9	$27,240
Least Happy Countries		
Belarus	4.2	$12,740
Chad	4.2	$1,160
Togo	4.1	$850
Zimbabwe	3.3	No Data
Tanzania	3.2	$1,360

Sources: R. Veenhoven, *Average Happiness in 145 Nations 2000–2008*, World Database of Happiness, Rank Report 2009-la, URL: *worlddatabaseofhappiness.eur.ni;* Carol Graham, 2005. "The Economics of Happiness," *World Economics,* 6(3): 41–55.

of gender equality and progress; they do not consider alternate cultural standards or values. As calculated, the GEM shows that gender equality in political, economic, and professional activities is not necessarily related to the level of national wealth or development. According to the measure, some developing countries—South Africa, for example, where women are afforded a large share of legislative seats and political administrative

positions—outperform industrialized Japan. In many countries, women lag behind men in the exercise of economic power and decision making; Northern European countries dominate the top of the GEM rankings—Sweden, Norway, Finland, Denmark, and the Netherlands are the top five countries. While rankings are not available for all countries, the lowest-ranked countries are in western Asia and North Africa.

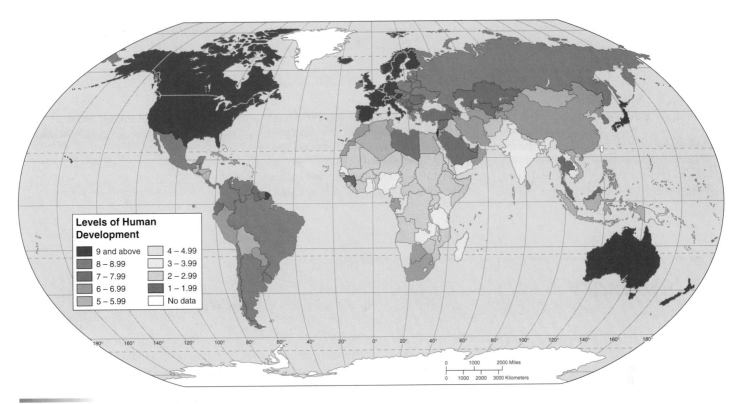

Figure 10.23 **Country rankings according to the HDI, 2009,** of the UNDP. Because this index is intended to measure the absence of deprivation, it discounts incomes higher than needed to achieve an acceptable level of living and therefore is uninformative in comparing the levels of development of the richest countries. The four measures that are used by the UNDP—life expectancy, adult literacy, combined school enrollment ratios, and real (PPP) income—are highly correlated with one another. For that reason, it has been noted, the rankings derived by the HDI differ only slightly from income rankings adjusted for purchasing power parity; the Indian minister for human resources in 2002 objected that the HDI ignored "spiritual happiness" and "intellectual advances." Fifth quintile countries, at the bottom of the HDI, closely match the "least developed" countries recognized by the United Nations and shown on Figure 10.3.

Source: United Nations, Human Development Report, *2009.*

 ## What Is Poverty?

According to the World Bank and the UNDP, of the world's 7.0 billion people (2011), 3.4 billion—some 48 percent—lived on less than $2 per day. At this level, people struggle to meet their basic needs and are vulnerable to a precipitous decline in well-being if they were to experience an illness, natural disaster, crop failure, or economic shock. Although the dollar definition of poverty is applied as if it were a worldwide constant, in reality, poor people define the wealth of people quite differently. One researcher wrote:

> In some ways the "poor" cultures of the Third World are rich psychologically and spiritually, enjoying a contentment and sense of tradition sorely lacking in hectic, ulcer-ridden, depersonalised industrial societies. To many Buddhists, for example, inner peace is more valuable than a high Gross National Product. The highest divorce and suicide rates occur in the First and Second Worlds. If personal happiness were our criterion, the Third World might rank first.[a]

Research on how the poor view poverty suggests that poverty has multiple dimensions, some of which are noneconomic, such as a sense of shame, powerlessness, or insecurity. The poor define poverty not just in monetary terms, but as a lack of education, health, proper housing, physical safety, or decent employment. As a consequence, a multidimensional measure of poverty has been developed by the Oxford Poverty and Human Development Initiative at Oxford University. It measures poverty using a short survey to assess quality of employment, sense of empowerment, feelings of physical safety, shame, and psychological well-being. Survey questions ask, for example, about hazards that respondents might be exposed to while at work, whether they believe that they have control over personal and household decisions, whether they feel respected by others and society, and their degree of satisfaction with life and overall happiness. An overall measure of poverty is created by counting the number of different dimensions in which a poor person feels he or she is deprived.

One key to improving both the economic and social lot of the "poorest of the poor," the

[a]Merriam, A. H., "What Does the 'Third World' Mean?" in J. Norwine and A. Gonzalez, eds., *The Third World: States of Mind and Being.* Boston: Unwin and Hyman, 1988, 15–22.

World Bank and United Nations argue, is to target public spending on their special needs of education and health care and to pursue patterns of investment and economic growth that can productively employ the underused and growing labor force that is so abundant in the least developed countries. These identified socioeconomic needs are important elements in the United Nation's interlocked MDGs. Another needed solution, many argue, is for rich creditor countries and international lending agencies to provide relief from the massive burden of interest and principal repayments owed by the group of 38 or more HIPCs.[b]

---

[b]See the feature "Does Foreign Aid Help?" on p. 335.

Summary

Development is generally understood as a process of change and improvement. It involves the fuller and more productive use of the resources of an area through the application of advanced levels of technology. The result is presumed to be improved conditions of life and human well-being through a fuller integration into and more equal share of the global economy. While this definition of development is widely accepted and has shaped development policies and programs, some critics point out that it reflects a particularly Western conception of progress.

A variety of comparative economic and noneconomic data are available to help identify the relative level of development for individual countries. *Gross national income (GNI)* and *purchasing power parity (PPP) per capita* document the basic core-periphery pattern while making clear the income diversity among the developing countries. A high percentage of a country's *workforce in agriculture* is associated with less developed subsistence economies, with low labor productivity and low levels of national wealth. *Per capita consumption of commercial energy* reveals the immense size of the technology gap between most and least developed states, for energy use may be loosely equated with modern industrial and transportation facilities. While these economic measures are widely used by development agencies, they have serious shortcomings. GNI measures flows of money through the economy but does not measure the condition of capital stocks, the distribution of income, or whether spending contributes to human well-being. Further, using energy consumption as a measure of development neglects the damage done to the natural environment by using "modern" energy sources. Other development measures focus on factors contributing to human development: food security and nutrition, safe drinking water, and sanitation, education, and health.

Modernization theory has dominated thinking about development. Its optimistic forecasts of inevitable progression from traditional to modern society have undergone revision. Many countries appear unable to accumulate the capital, develop the skills, or achieve the technology transfer necessary to carry them along the path to full economic development and prosperity. Without that development, countries score poorly on noneconomic measures such as literacy, safe water, and conditions of health. With it, they can—as the experience of newly industrializing countries demonstrates—experience growing cultural and technological convergence with the most advanced states. The core-periphery model helps us understand how developed and less developed regions can coexist in the same country. Dependency theory argues that development is always spatially uneven, producing underdevelopment in other regions. World systems theory describes the global economy as divided into core, semi-peripheral, and peripheral countries.

Development implies pervasive changes in the organizational and institutional structuring of peoples and space. Urbanization has invariably accompanied economic development, as has a more complete and rigorous political organization of space. We turn our attention in Chapters 11 and 12 to these two important expressions of human geographic variation, beginning first with an examination of city systems and the spatial variations inside urban areas.

KEY WORDS

brain drain 362
circular and cumulative causation 331
core-periphery model 331
dependency theory 332
development 315

food security 322
gender 336
gross national income (GNI) 318
informal economy 318
modernization theory 330

neocolonialism 332
neoliberal globalization 332
purchasing power parity (PPP) 318
remittances 333
spread effect 331

FOR REVIEW

1. What different ways and measures do we have to indicate degrees of development of particular countries or regions? Do you think these measures can be used to place countries or regions into uniform *stages of development?*

2. What kinds of material and nonmaterial economic and noneconomic contrasts can you cite that differentiate more developed from less developed societies?

3. How does the core-periphery model help us understand observed contrasts between developed and developing regions of countries? In what way is *circular and cumulative causation* linked either to the perpetuation or the reduction of those contrasts? How does the concept of *trickle-down effects,* or *spread effects,* explain the equalization of development and incomes on a regional or international scale?

4. What factors of physical geography and history might help explain why some countries are *developed* and others are *underdeveloped?* What are the shortcomings of these explanations?

5. What is modernization theory? What are some of the criticisms of modernization theory made by alternative theories of development?

6. Imagine that you are assigned the task of devising a composite index of national development and well-being. What *kinds* of characteristics would you like to include in your composite index? Why? What specific *measures* of those characteristics would you like to cite?

7. Why did many developing countries experience debt crises, and what significance does it have for their future development?

8. Have both males and females shared equally in the benefits of economic development in its early stages? What regional contrasts within the developing world are evident in the economic roles assigned to women?

KEY CONCEPTS REVIEW

1. **How do we define development?** pp. 314–317.
   Development implies improvement in economic and quality-of-life aspects of a society.

2. **What economic measures mark a country's stage of development?** pp. 317–323.
   GNI and PPP per capita, per capita commercial energy consumption, percentage of labor force in agriculture, and average daily caloric intake are common, accepted measures of development.

3. **What are noneconomic aspects of development, and how are they related to measures of economic growth?** pp. 323–329.
   Education, literacy, safe drinking water, sanitation, and health services are among the many noneconomic indices of development. These noneconomic measures relate directly to human well-being and quality of life. They are correlated with income because higher-income countries can afford to spend more on improvement of quality-of-life conditions.

4. **What different explanations are offered for development and underdevelopment?** pp. 329–332.
   Modernization theory dominates conventional development policies and programs. It sees all societies positioned along a continuum between traditional and modern with modern societies characterized by advanced technology, high standards of living, democratic institutions, and capitalist production. The core-periphery model attempts to explain patterns of uneven spatial development. Dependency theory argues that development in some regions by necessity creates underdevelopment elsewhere. World systems theory posits a system of core, semi-periphery, and periphery countries within the global economy but allows for growth and change in that hierarchy. Rising productivity growth of newly industrializing countries offers some support for modernization theory.

5. **What special challenges face developing countries?** pp. 332–339.
   Natural hazards often have more devastating consequences when they strike poor countries. Foreign indebtedness has crippled the ability of many poor countries to invest in social needs, education and other measures that improve well-being. Debt relief has helped a number of countries. Landlessness is a major cause of poverty in rural areas. Gender inequality hampers the full participation of women in economic and political life. Education and empowerment for women contributes to many positive development outcomes.

6. **What are some alternative ways of measuring development?** pp. 339–342.
   Life expectancy, education, and living standards are the three components of the United Nation's HDI, an improvement over using single measures of development. Gender empowerment indices measure political and economic status of women. International studies of "happiness" suggest that income matters, but as only one of many factors in life satisfaction.

CHAPTER 11

URBAN SYSTEMS AND URBAN STRUCTURES

Hong Kong, China, the world's most densely populated city.

Key Concepts

1. An urbanizing world: the nature of cities, definitions, and locations, pp. 345–353.

2. Systems of cities: the economic base, functions, hierarchies, and networks, pp. 353–360.

3. Inside the city: land uses, social areas, and patterns of change, pp. 360–376.

4. World urban diversity: European and non-Western cities, pp. 376–386.

airo was a world-class city in the 14th century. Situated at the crossroads of Africa, Asia, and Europe, it dominated trade on the Mediterranean Sea. By the early 1300s, it had a population of half a million or more, with 10- to 14-story buildings crowding the city center. A Cairo chronicler of the period recorded the construction of a huge building with shops on the first floors and apartments housing 4,000 people above. One Italian visitor estimated that more people lived on a single Cairo street than in all of Florence. Travelers from all over Europe and Asia made their way to Cairo, and the shipping at its port of Bulaq outdistanced that of Venice and Genoa combined. The city contained more than 12,000 shops, some specializing in luxury goods from all over the world—Siberian sable, chain mail, musical instruments, luxurious cloth, and exotic songbirds. Travelers marveled at the size, density, and variety of Cairo, comparing it favorably with Venice, Paris, and Baghdad.

Today, Cairo (also known as Al-Qahirah) is a vast, sprawling metropolis, plagued by many of the problems common to rapidly urbanizing developing countries where population growth has outpaced economic development. The population of Egypt in 1970 was 35.3 million; it had grown to more than 83 million by 2011 thanks to improved health care in general, a dramatic drop in infant mortality, high total fertility, and longer life expectancies. An estimated 11 million people reside in the Cairo greater metropolitan area. Cairo has a density of more than 32,000 per square kilometer (12,000 per square mile), and the city continues to grow, spreading onto valued farmland and decreasing food production for the country's increasing population.

A steady stream of migrants arrives daily in Cairo, where, they hope, opportunities will be available for a better and brighter life. The city is the symbol of modern Egypt, a place where young people are willing to undergo deprivation for the chance to "make it." But real opportunities continue to be scarce. The poor, of whom there are millions, crowd into row after row of apartment houses, many of them poorly constructed. Tens of thousands more live in rooftop sheds or small boats on the Nile; a half million find shelter living between the tombs in the Northern and Southern Cemeteries—known as the Cities of the Dead—on Cairo's eastern edge. On occasion, buildings collapse; the earthquake of October 12, 1992, measuring 5.9 on the Richter scale, did enormous damage, leveling thousands of structures.

One's first impression when arriving in central Cairo is of opulence, a stark contrast to what lies outside the city center. High-rise apartments, regional headquarters buildings of transnational corporations, and modern hotels stand amid clogged streets, symbols of the new Egypt (Figure 11.1). New suburban developments and exclusive residential communities create enclaves for the wealthy, whose posh apartments are but a short distance from the slums housing a largely unemployed 20 percent of Cairo's population. Like cities nearly everywhere in the developing world, Cairo has experienced explosive growth that finds an increasing proportion of the country's population housed in an urban area without the economy or facilities to support them all. Street congestion and idling traffic generate air pollution comparable to Mexico City, Bangkok and other highly polluted megacities. Both the Nile River and the city's treated drinking water show dangerous levels of lead and cadmium, the unwanted by-products of the local lead smelter.

Cairo is a classic case of the urban explosion in which more than half of the world's population lives in cities. This chapter introduces urban geography, which is divided into two broad categories of approach. The first looks at systems of cities, examining how cities support themselves economically, the functions that they perform in regional, national, and global economies, and how they exist in regular spatial patterns, networks, and hierarchies. Among their many purposes, cities serve as concentrations of people and activities to facilitate social interaction and the efficient exchange of information, goods, and services. Manufacturing, trade, and the exchange of ideas often require concentrations of workers, managers, merchants, and supporting institutions. Cities exist as functional nodes within a broader, hierarchical system of cities. The second approach to urban geography looks inside cities at their internal arrangements. Cities are unique places, with complex patterns of land use and social groups. In this chapter, we begin by examining the nature and evolution of cities, then we look at systems of cities, and finally, we turn our attention to life inside cities in different parts of the world.

An Urbanizing World

In 2008, the world reached a major turning point. As seen on Figure 11.2, after astounding urban growth in the 20th century, the world's urban population surpassed the rural population. Some 442 metropolitan areas had in excess of 1 million people ("million cities") by 2010; in 1900, there were only 12. Expectations are for 547 "million cities" in 2025. As many as 21 metropolises had populations of 10 million or more people in 2010; the United Nations calls them *megacities* (Figure 11.3). In 1900, no city was of that size, and in 1975, there were just 3 (Table 11.1). It follows, of course, that since the world's total population has greatly increased over the centuries, so too would its urban component—from

Figure 11.1 Sprawling Cairo, Egypt. The population growth in the greater metropolitan area—from some 3 million in 1970 to an estimated 11 million today—has been mirrored in most developing countries. The rapid expansion of urban areas and populations brings housing shortages, inadequate transportation and other infrastructure development, unemployment, poverty, and environmental deterioration.

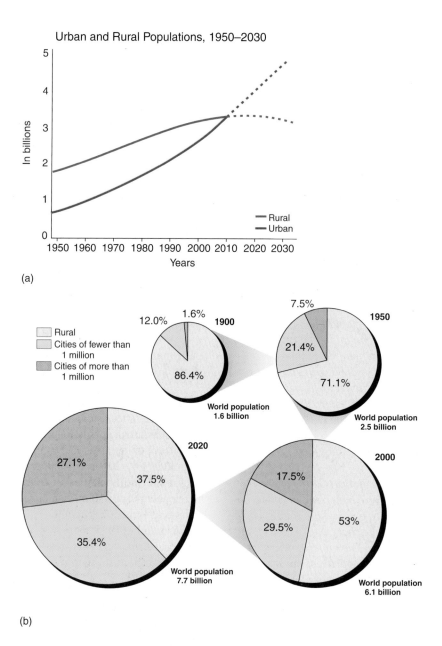

Figure 11.2 **Trends of world urbanization** document the steady decline in rural population proportions throughout the 20th century. *(a)* Since 1950, the growth rate of the rural component has slackened compared to the urban rate; by 2008, world urban numbers overtook the rural.

Source: United Nations, World Urbanization Prospects: The 2009 Revision and 2003 Revision, *Population Reference Bureau, and other sources.*

3 percent in 1800 to more than half today. The urban share of the total has grown everywhere as urbanization has spread to all parts of the globe. Virtually all of the world's population growth in the first half of the 21st century will take place in cities—specifically, the cities of the developing world (Figure 11.4).

The degree of urbanization differs from continent to continent and from region to region (Figure 11.5), but in nearly all countries, the proportion of their population living in cities is rising. The United Nations projects that urban majorities will exist in all regions of the world by 2030 (Table 11.2). While Africa and Asia are the least urbanized continents, cities are growing particularly fast there. While some cities will grow into megacities,

cities with less than 1 million residents will grow faster than the very largest cities.

Industrialization spurred the earlier rapid urbanization in the highly developed regions of Western Europe and North America. In many of the still-developing countries, however, urban expansion is only partly the result of the transition from agricultural to industrial economies. Rather, in many of those areas, people flee impoverished rural districts; by their numbers and high fertility rates, they accelerate city expansion. Even the high-income, highly developed states—with low or negative rates of natural population increase—will experience multicultural expansion as international migrants seek opportunities in their cities. As Ernst

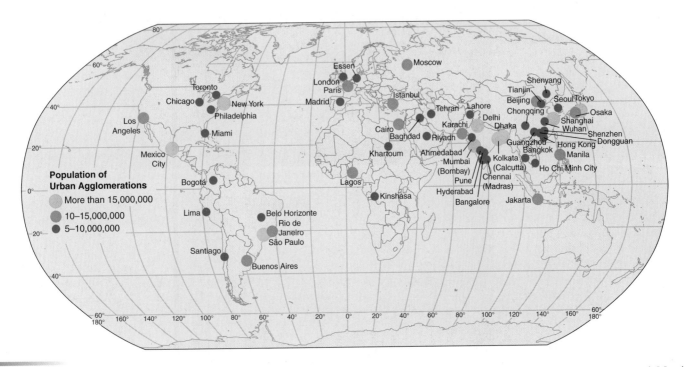

Figure 11.3 **Metropolitan areas of 3 million or more in 2006.** Only metropolitan areas with a population of 5 million or more are named. Massive urbanized districts are no longer limited to the industrialized, developed countries. They are now found on every continent, in all latitudes, as part of most economics and societies. Not all cities in congested areas are shown.

Source: Data from United Nations Population Division.

Ravenstein's studies of migration suggested (see Chapter 3), international migrants—whatever their destination country—tend to settle in large cities. The result everywhere is growing urban cultural diversity, with attendant challenges of social fragmentation, segregation, isolation, and poverty.

Merging Urban Regions

When separate major urban complexes expand along the superior transportation facilities connecting them, they may eventually meet, bind together at their outer margins, and create the extensive urban regions or **conurbations** suggested in Figure 11.3. No longer is there a single city with a single downtown area, set off by open countryside from any other urban unit in its vicinity. Rather, we must now recognize extensive regions of continuous urbanization made up of multiple centers that have come together at their edges.

A major North American example, *Megalopolis* (already encountered in Chapter 9), is a nearly continuous urban string that stretches from north of Boston (southern Maine) to south of Washington, D.C. (southern Virginia). Other North American conurbations shown on Figure 11.6 include the southern Great Lakes region, stretching from north of Milwaukee through Chicago and eastward to Detroit, Cleveland, and Pittsburgh; the Coastal California zone of San Francisco–Los Angeles–San Diego–Tijuana, Mexico; the Canadian "core region" conurbation from Montreal to Windsor, opposite Detroit, Michigan, where it connects with the southern Great Lakes region; the Vancouver–Willamette strip ("Cascadia") in the West; and the Gulf Coast and the Coastal

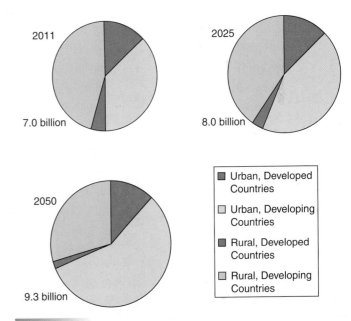

Figure 11.4 **Urban and rural population change** in the developed and developing countries. The United Nations estimates that virtually all future population growth will take place in the cities of the developing countries. Between 2011 and 2050, rural areas in both the developing and developed world will lose population, and urban areas in the developed countries will see only modest population growth.

Source: United Nations, World Urbanization Prospects: The 2011 Revision and 2009 Revision, *Population Reference Bureau, and other sources.*

Table 11.1

World's Largest Urban Areas, 1900–2025 (Population in Millions)

1900		1950		1975		2010		2025	
London, U.K.	6.5	New York	12.3	Tokyo	26.6	Tokyo	36.7	Tokyo	37.1
New York, U.S.	4.2	Tokyo	11.3	New York-Newark	15.9	Delhi, India	22.2	Delhi	28.6
Paris, France	3.3	London	8.4	Mexico City, Mexico	10.7	São Paulo	20.3	Mumbai (Bombay)	25.8
Berlin, Germany	2.7	Paris	6.5	Osaka-Kobe	9.8	Mumbai (Bombay), India	20.0	São Paulo	21.7
Chicago, U.S.	1.7	Moscow	5.4	São Paulo, Brazil	9.6	Mexico City	19.5	Dhaka	20.9
Vienna, Austria	1.7	Buenos Aires, Argentina	5.1	Los Angeles, U.S.	8.9	New York	19.4	Mexico City	20.7
Tokyo, Japan	1.5	Chicago	5.0	Buenos Aires	8.7	Shanghai	16.6	New York	20.6
St. Petersburg, Russia	1.4	Kolkata (Calcutta), India	4.5	Paris	8.6	Kolkata (Calcutta)	15.6	Kolkata (Calcutta)	20.1
Manchester, U.K.	1.4	Shanghai, China	4.3	Kolkata (Calcutta)	7.9	Dhaka, Bangladesh	14.6	Shanghai	20.0
Philadelphia, U.S.	1.4	Osaka-Kobe, Japan	4.1	Moscow	7.6	Karachi, Pakistan	13.1	Karachi	18.7

Sources: United Nations, *World Urbanization Prospects: The 2009 Revision*, and *Four Thousand Years of Urban Growth: An Historical Census*, Tertius Chandler. 1987, St. David's University Press.

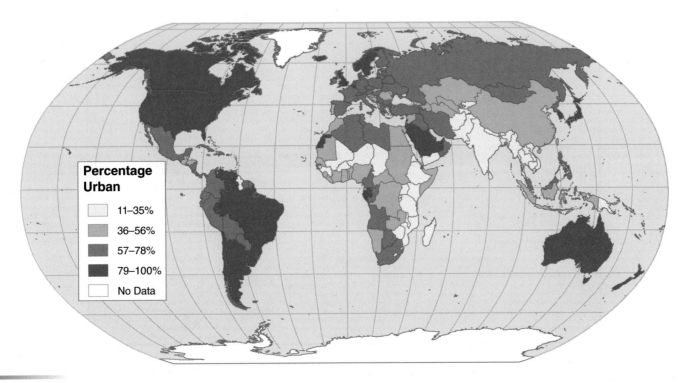

Figure 11.5 Percentage of population classified as urban, 2011. While Africa and South Asia lag behind other world regions in urbanization, they have the highest rates of urban growth.

Source: Population Reference Bureau, 2011.

Table 11.2

Estimated Urban Share of Total Population, Selected Areas: 1950, 2005, and 2030

Region or Country	1950	2005	2030
North America	64	79	87
Latin America and Caribbean	42	76	85
Europe	51	74	78
Russia	45	73	77
Oceania	61	72	71
China	13	37	62
Southeast Asia	15	38	53
Africa	15	36	50
More developed	53	76	81
Less developed	18	42	55
World	29	47	59

Sources: United Nations Population Division and Population Reference Bureau.

Settlement Roots

The major cities of today had humble origins in the simple cluster of dwellings that was the starting point for human settlements everywhere. People are gregarious and cooperative. Even Stone Age hunters and gatherers lived and worked in groups, not as lone individuals or isolated families. All cultures are communal for protection, cooperative effort, sharing of tasks by age and sex, and for more subtle psychological and social reasons. Communal dwelling became the near-universal rule with the advent of sedentary agriculture wherever it developed, and the village became the norm of human society.

In most of the world, rural people still live in nucleated settlements (that is, in villages or hamlets), rather than in dispersed dwellings or isolated farmsteads. Only in North America, parts of northern and western Europe, and in Australia and New Zealand do rural dwellers tend to live apart, with houses and farm buildings located on land that is individually worked. Elsewhere in the world, villages and hamlets were and are the settlement norm, though size and form has varied by region and culture (Figures 11.7 and 11.8).

Rural settlements in developing countries are often expressions of subsistence economic systems in which farming and fishing cultures produce no more than their individual families can consume. When trade does develop between two or more rural settlements, they begin to take on new physical characteristics as their inhabitants engage in additional types of occupations. The villages lose the purely social and residential character of subsistence agricultural settlements and assume urban features. The beginnings of urbanization are seen in the types of buildings that

Florida zones in the Southeast. Outside North America, examples of conurbations are numerous and growing, still primarily in the most industrialized European and East Asian (Japanese) districts, but forming as well in the other world regions where urban clusters and megacities emerged in developing countries that still were primarily rural in residential pattern.

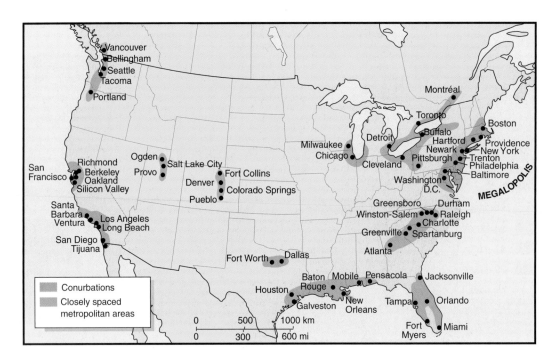

Figure 11.6 **Megalopolis and other North American conurbations.** The northeast U.S. Boston-to-Norfolk urban corridor comprises the original and largest *Megalopolis* and contains the economic, political, and administrative core of the United States. A Canadian counterpart core region anchored by Montreal and Toronto connects with U.S. contributions through Buffalo, New York, and Detroit, Michigan. For some of their extent, conurbations fulfill their classic definition of continuous built-up urban areas. In other portions, they are more statistical than landscape entities, marked by counties that qualify as "urban" or "metropolitan," even though land uses may appear dominantly rural.

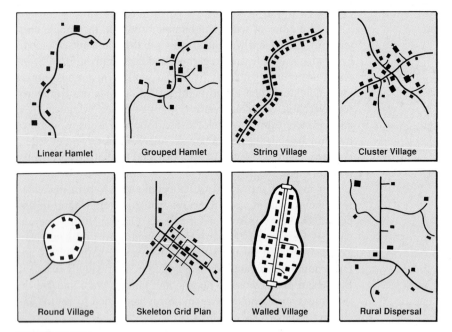

Figure 11.7 **Basic settlement forms.** The smallest organized rural clusters of houses and nonresidential structures are commonly called *hamlets,* and may contain only 10–15 buildings. *Villages* are larger agglomerations, although not as sizable or functionally complex as urban *towns.* The distinction between village and town is usually a statistical definition that varies by country. The rural dispersal settlement pattern is relatively rare, being found mostly in northern and Western Europe, North America, Australia, and New Zealand.

Source: Redrawn from Introducing Cultural Geography, *2d ed., by J. E. Spencer and W. L. Thomas. Copyright © 1978 John Wiley & Sons, Inc. Reproduced with permission of John Wiley & Sons, Inc.*

are erected and in the heightened importance of the main streets and of the roads leading to other settlements. No longer are the settlements self-contained; they become part of a system of towns and cities engaged in urban activities and exchange.

Origins and Evolution of Cities

Cities and civilization are inseparable; indeed, the words *city* and *civilization* have the same Latin root, *civis.* Dating from at least 8,000 years ago, cities originated in—or diffused from—the early culture hearths that first developed sedentary agriculture (see Figure 2.15 in Chapter 2 and Figure 11.9). As centers of cultural, economic, religious, and political life, they are among humanity's greatest achievements. Cities abound with contradictions, simultaneously displaying the extremes of luxury and misery, beauty and squalor. In cities, diverse peoples come together to exchange goods, services, and ideas and yet also stratify by race, ethnicity, and social class.

The earliest cities depended on the creation of agricultural surpluses. Many early cities included farms within their walls, but the main distinction between the city and the countryside stemmed from the nonagricultural work of most urban dwellers.

(a)

(b)

Figure 11.8 Most of the world's rural population lives in small, agricultural villages rather than dispersed farmsteads. (*a*) A compact Zulu village, or kraal, in South Africa. (*b*) Shirakawa village in Japan.

Figure 11.9 Aerial view of Erbil, Iraq. The site of modern Erbil—the ancient Assyrian city of Arabilu—has been continuously inhabited for about 8,000 years. The debris of millennia of urban settlement gradually raised the level of the land surface, producing a mound on which the city sits. The city—one of the oldest in the world—literally was constantly rebuilt at higher elevations on the accumulation of refuse from earlier occupants.

Figure 11.10 By Europe's Middle Ages, the ancient need for city protection remained, but fortifications and defensive structures had assumed elaborate and massive forms that were unknown and unneeded before siege weapons and siege warfare put all cities in jeopardy. The walls of Ávila, Spain, shown here, were built in the 12th century, extending 2,500 meters (8,200 feet) and encircling the entire city at that time; the modern part of Ávila lies outside.

This meant that food had to be provided to the urban population by the **hinterland**—the productive area surrounding a population center. Those in the newly emerging town who were not farmers were free to specialize in other activities—metal working, pottery making, cloth weaving, among others—producing goods for other urbanites and for the farm population on which they depended. Still others became scribes, merchants, priests, and soldiers, providing the services and refining the power structure on which the organized urban and rural society depended.

Social organization and a defined power structure, as reflected in a religious hierarchy and civil administration, were essential in urban development. Ancient cities centered on a temple or palace district housing the priests, the ruler, public storehouses and granaries, public baths, perhaps schools, and certainly a central marketplace. Cities became the seats of local and regional power, exercising control over the rural hinterland and extracting agricultural surplus from it for redistribution in the city. If possible, ancient cities were located in spots easy to defend—often on hilltops—but they were nearly always enclosed within protective walls (Figure 11.10). The massive protective walls of early cities, however, could also limit the expansion of prospering, growing communities. Some cities, like Rome, went through multiple rounds of wall construction, with each new outer wall extending the urban area within which functions could be located and workers housed.

Among those functions and workers were those engaged in long-distance trade, exchanging local goods and materials for raw materials and special products not obtainable locally. Merchants, wholesalers, clerks, scribes, carters, river men and sailors, and those who produced the vessels and supplied the necessary trade support services that came to characterize and dominate the functional base of the city. The importance of city location on navigable waterways, always a key to urban economic success, became ever more important.

In Europe and Asia, from about the 11th to the 18th century, local and distant trade, production of consumer goods by craftsmen organized into protective guilds, and increasing use of water-powered mills for grinding grain, making cloth, and sawing timber moved cities into intricate involvement in nearly modern forms of interregional and international economy. Massive trade fairs, international banking houses, and cooperative leagues of cities were precursors of today's global marketing, stock exchanges, and regional trade alliances (Figure 11.11).

With the Industrial Revolution, another shift in cities took place. Industrialization accelerated the rate of urban growth, initially in Europe and then elsewhere, where European control or influence was extended. Powered by water or steam, the new factories—operated by paid laborers, not by independent guild members—introduced mass production of standardized goods. Industrialization fundamentally changed cities, creating staggering economic and social stratification and, in many early industrial cities, dreadful conditions for the working classes. Cities, once centered on the temple, palace, marketplace, or waterfront wharves, and once surrounded by walls, were changed utterly; they had become places of industrial production centered on factories, canals, and railroads.

As industrialization diffuses around the globe, cities in the newly industrializing countries of Asia or Latin America have witnessed some of the same explosive growth and social polarization that historically accompanied industrialization. Meanwhile, in the more developed countries, the transition to a service economy has caused cities to take on a post-industrial character. Smokestacks have disappeared and former factories, railroad yards, and industrial waterfronts have been redeveloped for parks, housing, and commercial uses. Consumption and service sector activities, rather than heavy industry, dominate the post-industrial city.

The Nature of Cities

Whether ancient or modern, all cities must perform functions—have an economic base—in order to generate the income necessary to support themselves. Second, no city exists in a vacuum; each is part of a larger society and economy with which it has essential relationships. That is, each is a unit in a system of cities and a focus for a surrounding rural area. Third, each urban unit has a more or less orderly internal arrangement of land uses, social groups, and economic functions. Because all urban functions and people cannot be located at a single point, cities themselves must take up space and organize the uses of that space. These arrangements may be partially or completely planned by central authorities or determined by individual decisions and market forces. Finally, all cities, large or small, ancient or modern, have experienced problems of land use, social conflict, and environmental quality. Yet cities, though flawed, remain the capstone of our cultures, the driving force in contemporary societies and economies, and the magnet for people everywhere.

All urban settlements exist for the efficient performance of functions required by the society that creates them. They reflect the saving of time, energy, and money that the agglomeration of people and activities provides. The more accessible the producer to the consumer, the worker to the workplace, the citizen to the town hall, the worshiper to the place of worship, or the lawyer or doctor to the client, the more efficiently they can perform their separate activities. Because interconnection is essential, the transportation system will have an enormous bearing on the total number of services that can be performed and the efficiency with which they can be carried out. The totality of people and urban functions constitutes a distinctive cultural landscape whose similarities and differences from place to place are the subjects for urban geographic analysis.

The Location of Urban Settlements

Urban centers are functionally connected to other cities and to rural areas. In fact, cities exist not only to provide services for themselves, but for others outside of it. The urban center is a consumer of food, a processor of materials, and an accumulator and dispenser of goods and services. But it must depend on outside areas for its essential supplies and as a market for its products and activities.

In order to adequately perform the tasks that support it and to add new functions as demanded by the larger economy, the city must be efficiently located. That efficiency may be marked by centrality to the area that it serves. It may derive from the physical characteristics of its site, or placement may be related

Figure 11.11 The densely built historic medieval section of Florence, Italy, is dominated by the Cathedral Santa Maria del Fiore. Florence prospered in the late Middle Ages as a center for textiles, artisanal craft industries, trade and banking. It reached a population of 95,000 in 1300 before the plague decimated its population. In the 15th century, it was the center for the rediscovery of classical culture and was home to artists such as Sandro Botticelli, Leonardo da Vinci, and Michelangelo.

to the resources, productive regions, and transportation network of the country, so it can effectively perform a wide array of activities.

In discussing urban settlement locations, geographers usually distinguish between site and situation, concepts already introduced in Chapter 1 (see Figures 1.6 and 1.7). You will recall that *site* refers to the exact terrain features associated with the city, as well as—less usefully—to its absolute (globe grid) location. Classifications of cities according to site characteristics have been proposed, recognizing special placement circumstances. These include *break-of-bulk* locations, such as river crossing points where cargoes and people must interrupt a journey; *head-of-navigation* or *bay head* locations, where the limits of water transportation are reached; and *railhead* locations, where a railroad ended. For ancient and medieval cities, security and defense—islands or elevated sites—were considerations in choosing a location for a city. Waterpower sites and later coalfields were the prime city-building locations during the Industrial Revolution, as noted in Chapter 9.

If *site* suggests absolute location, *situation* indicates relative location in relation to the physical and cultural characteristics of surrounding areas. It is important to know what kinds of possibilities and activities exist in the area near a settlement, such as the distribution of raw materials, market areas, agricultural regions, mountains, and the places to which it is connected through rivers, oceans, and transportation systems. The functions and growth potentials of cities are more determined by their situation than their site.

The site or situation that originally gave rise to a city may not remain the essential ingredient for its continued growth and development. Agglomerations originally successful for whatever reason may by their success attract people and activities totally unrelated to the initial localizing forces. By what has been called a process of "circular and cumulative causation" (see Chapter 10), a successful urban unit may acquire new people and functions attracted by the existing markets, labor force, and urban facilities. In the same way, a site that originally favored the success of the new urban unit—on a navigable river or coal field, perhaps—may with the passage of time no longer be important in supporting any or all of its current economic activities.

The Economic Base

We saw that from their ancient beginnings, cities depended on close relationships with their hinterlands. They provided the market where rural produce could be exchanged for the goods produced and the defense or religious functions performed by the city. Such rural service functions remain important. However, not all of the activities carried on within a city are intended to connect that city with the outside world. Some are necessary simply to support the city itself. Understanding the growth or decline of cities hinges on grasping the relationship between the two sectors.

Economic base theory was developed by noticing that the economic well-being of small, remote, resource-dependent towns was proportional to the value of goods they sold to outside markets. Part of the employed population of a city is engaged either in the production of goods or the performance of services for areas and people outside the city itself. They are workers engaged in "export" activities, whose efforts result in money flowing into the community. Collectively, they constitute the **basic sector** of the city's total economic structure. According to economic base theory, the basic sector makes up the **economic base** of the community and is essential to the health of the local economy.

Other workers support themselves by producing goods or services for residents of the city itself. Their efforts, necessary to the well-being and the successful operation of the settlement, do not generate new money but comprise a **nonbasic sector** of its economy. These activities circulate money within the community and are responsible for the internal functioning of the city. They are crucial to the continued operation of its stores, professional offices, city government, local transit, and school systems.

The total economic structure of an urban area equals the sum of its basic and nonbasic activities. In actuality, it is difficult to classify work as belonging exclusively to one sector or the other. It is often assumed that most manufacturing work is basic, although services today are increasingly traded. Some part of most jobs involves financial interaction with residents of other areas. Doctors, for example, may have mainly local patients and thus are members of the nonbasic sector, but the moment they provide a service to someone from outside the community, they bring new money into the city and become part of the basic sector.

Most centers perform many export functions, and the larger the urban unit, the more multifunctional it becomes. Nonetheless, even in cities with a diversified economic base, one export activity or a very small number of activities tends to dominate the structure of the community and to identify its operational purpose within a system of cities. Figure 11.12 indicates the functional specializations of some large U.S. metropolitan areas.

Assuming that it was possible to divide with complete accuracy the employed population of a city into totally separate basic and service (nonbasic) components, a ratio between the two employment groups could be established. This *basic/nonbasic ratio,* shown in Figure 11.13, indicates that as a settlement increases in size, the number of nonbasic personnel grows faster than the number of new basic workers. The graph suggests that service sector jobs, most of which are nonbasic, will be more common in larger cities. In cities with a population of 1 million, the ratio is about two nonbasic workers for every basic worker. This means that adding 10 new basic employees expands the labor force by 30 (10 basic, 20 nonbasic). The resultant increase in total population is equal to the added workers plus their dependents. Thus, a **multiplier effect** exists, in which every new basic sector job creates additional nonbasic jobs. When news media report that a new manufacturing plant will create a certain number of new jobs in addition to those at the plant, they are referring to the multiplier effect. The size of the multiplier effect is determined by the community's basic/nonbasic ratio.

The changing numerical relationships shown in Figure 11.13 are understandable when we consider how settlements add functions and grow in population. A new industry selling services to other communities requires new workers who increase the basic workforce. These new employees in turn demand certain goods and services, such as clothing, food, and medical assistance, which may be provided locally. Those who perform such services must themselves have services available to them. For example, a grocery clerk must also buy groceries. The more nonbasic workers

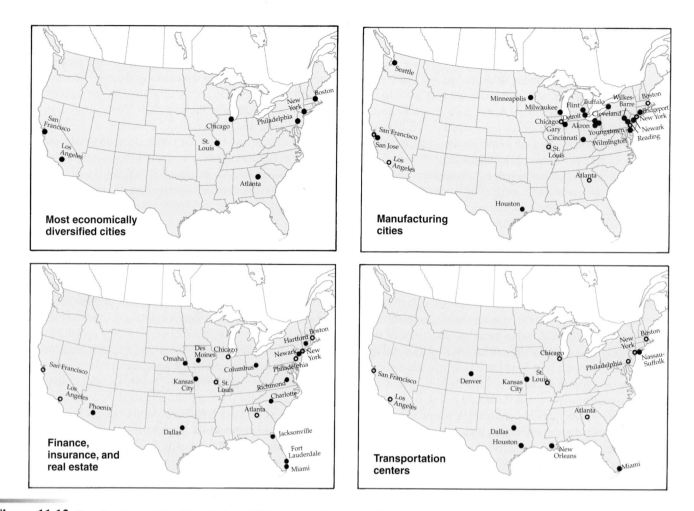

Figure 11.12 Functional specialization of selected U.S. metropolitan areas. Three categories of employment were chosen to show patterns of specialization for some U.S. metropolitan areas. In addition, the category "Most Economically Diversified" includes representative examples of cities with a generally balanced employment distribution. Because their "balance" implies performance of a variety of functions, the diversified cities are included as open circles on the other specialization maps. Note that the most diversified urban areas tend to be the largest.

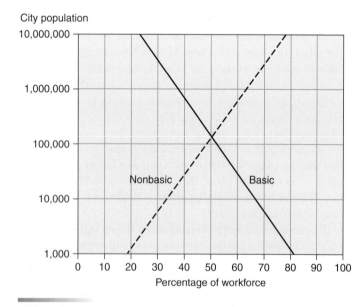

Figure 11.13 A generalized representation of the proportion of the workforce engaged in basic and nonbasic activities. As settlements become larger, a greater proportion of the workforce is employed in nonbasic activities. Larger centers are, therefore, more self-contained.

a city has, the more nonbasic workers are needed to support them. The reason that the size of the city influences the basic/nonbasic ratio is because money circulates more efficiently in large cities. In a town too small to support a clothing store, grocery store, or hospital, worker paychecks will be spent purchasing those goods and services from other communities, with no increase in the small town's nonbasic employment. On the other hand, large cities are more self-sufficient and can meet more of their needs internally, so that each new basic job generates additional nonbasic jobs.

The growth of cities may be self-generating—circular and cumulative as industries that specialize in the production of material objects for export, like automobiles and paper products, bring money into a community and set off chain reactions of additional economic activity, much of it involving *service* activities. In recent years, service industries have developed to the point where new service activities serve older ones. In addition to the spending by firms and their workers, the property taxes that they pay support public services such as schools, parks, and transportation systems. These public investments make the city an attractive place to live and do business, in turn attracting more new firms and residents.

In much the same way as settlements grow in size and complexity, so do they decline. When the demand for the goods and services produced by a city falls, less money comes into the community, and both the basic and nonbasic components are affected. Cities that experience deindustrialization often undergo a spiral of decline, losing additional nonbasic jobs and having less money to pay for local public services. There is, however, a resistance to decline that delays its impact. That is, settlements can grow rapidly as migrants respond quickly to the need for more workers, but under conditions of decline, those that have developed roots in the community are hesitant to leave or may be financially unable to move to another locale.

The Functions of Cities

Urban-based economic activities account for more than 50 percent of the gross national product (GNP) in all countries and up to 80 percent or more in the more urbanized states. Modern cities take on multiple functions. These include manufacturing, retailing, wholesaling, transportation, public administration, housing cultural and educational institutions and, of course, the housing of their own citizens. Most cities, however, specialize in, or are dominated by, only one or a very few of the full range of economic activities. Only a relative few very large members of a national system of cities are importantly multifunctional and truly diversified.

No matter what their size, cities exist for the efficient performance of necessary functions. Those functions reflect cities' roles as transportation nodes and central places. The spatial pattern of *transportation centers* is that of alignment along seacoasts, rivers, canals, or railways. Transportation routes form the orienting axes along which cities developed and on which at least their initial functional success depended (Figure 11.14). *Special-function cities* are those engaged in mining or manufacturing, and they must be located where the raw materials occur, or agglomeration economies are present. Special-function cities show a pattern of urban clustering—as the mining and manufacturing cities of the Ruhr district of Germany, the Midlands of England, or the Donets Basin in Ukraine, for example.

Beginning with the Industrial Revolution of the 18th century, manufacturing industries were a major impetus for urban growth. The handicraft production of goods was, of course, always a part of the functional base of even the earliest urban units. Only with the rise of mass production, however, did industry become a primary basic urban function, producing wealth and, through the *multiplier effect,* expanding the numbers of basic and nonbasic workers through the export of manufactured goods throughout the larger economy.

All settlements serve as a central location for the provision of goods and services for a surrounding tributary area. For many, including mining or major manufacturing centers, service to tributary areas is only a very minor part of their economic base. Some settlements, however, have that rural service and trade function as their dominant role, and these make up the third simplified category of cities: *central places.*

Cities as Central Places

Central places are nodes for the distribution of economic goods and services to surrounding nonurban populations. For as long as

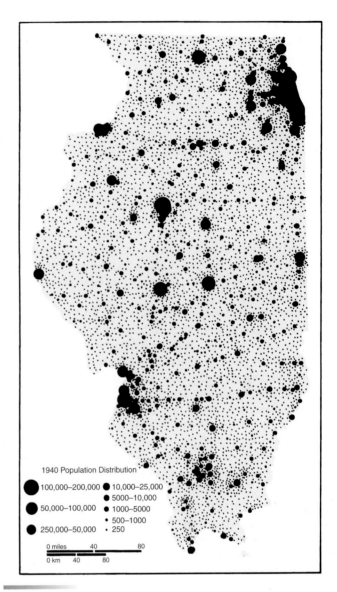

Figure 11.14 Urban alignments in Illinois. Railroads preceded settlement in much of the U.S. and Canadian continental interior, and urban centers were developed—frequently by the railroad companies themselves—as collecting and distributing points expected to grow as the farm populations increased. Located at constant 8- to 10-kilometer (5- to 6-mile) intervals in Illinois, the rail towns were the focal points of an expanding commercial agriculture. The linearity of the town pattern in 1940, at the peak of railroad influence, unmistakably marks the rail routes. Also evident are such special-function clusterings as the Chicago and St. Louis metropolitan districts and the mining towns of southern Illinois. In addition to the linear and cluster patterns, the smallest towns show the uniform distribution characteristic of central places.

cities have existed, they have served as marketplaces, not only for their own residents, but also for the population beyond the city limits. Small cities provide a range of goods and services that suffice for most everyday needs. But specialized, "higher-order" expensive or unique commodities and skilled specialized services can be found only in the largest cities. To serve the rural populations, central places show size and spacing regularities unrelated to the patterns of alignment and clustering characteristic of transportation and special-function cities. In many locations around the world, central places display a regular distribution. Towns of about the same size, performing similar functions, tend to be uniformly spaced (Figure 11.14).

The geographer Walter Christaller developed **central place theory** to explain those observed settlement size and spacing regularities (see the feature "Central Place Theory"). He observed a pattern of interdependent small, medium, and larger towns that together could provide the goods and services needed by a dispersed rural population. Small towns, Christaller postulated, would serve as marketplaces for frequently required "low-order" commodities and services, while expensive "high-order" luxury goods would be available only in larger communities that were central to a number of surrounding small towns. That is, people would have to travel only short distances for low order items, such as gasoline, convenience groceries, or haircuts, and longer distances for expensive and infrequently demanded goods and services, such as art museums, professional sports, luxury automobiles, or specialized medical treatments.

Christaller's explanation and description of the urban size and spacing regularities he observed have been shown to be generally applicable in widely differing regions of the world. When varying incomes, cultures, physical landscapes, and transportation systems are taken into consideration, his theory holds up rather well. It is particularly applicable, of course, to agricultural areas with a uniform distribution of consumers and purchasing power. If we combine a Christaller-type approach with the ideas of industrial location that help us understand the cluster patterns of special-function cities (see Chapter 9) and the alignments of transportation-based cities, we have a fairly good understanding of the distribution of most towns and cities. Central place theory is less relevant, of course, to arid regions such as the southwestern United States, where the lack of water prevented a uniform rural settlement and urban growth is much more concentrated.

The interdependence of small, medium, and large cities can also be seen in their influence on each other. A small city may influence a local region of some 1,000+ square kilometers (400 square miles) if, for example, its newspaper is delivered to that district. Beyond that area, another city may be the dominant influence. **Urban influence zones** are the areas outside a city that are still affected by it. As the distance away from a community increases, its influence on the surrounding countryside decreases (recall the idea of distance decay that was discussed in Chapter 3). The sphere of influence of an urban unit is usually proportional to its size.

For example, a large city located 100 kilometers (62 miles) away from a small city may influence that and other smaller communities through its banking services, TV stations, professional sports teams, and large shopping malls. There is an overlapping hierarchical arrangement, and the influence of the largest cities is felt over the widest areas, a "market area" dominance that is basic to central place theory.

Intricate relationships and hierarchies are common. Consider Grand Forks, North Dakota, which for local market purposes dominates the rural area immediately surrounding it. However, Grand Forks is influenced by political decisions made in the state capital, Bismarck. For a variety of cultural, commercial, and banking activities, Grand Forks is influenced by Minneapolis. As a center of wheat production, Grand Forks and Minneapolis are subordinate to the grain market in Chicago. Of course, the pervasive agricultural and other political controls exerted from Washington, D.C., on Grand Forks, Minneapolis, and Chicago indicate the size and complexity of urban zones of influence.

Systems of Cities

The systems of cities approach to urban geography considers the functions that cities perform in regional, national, or international economies, their relationships with the surrounding rural land and other cities, and how they are arranged in spatial patterns, networks, and hierarchies.

The Urban Hierarchy

Perhaps the most effective way to recognize how systems of cities are organized is to consider the **urban hierarchy,** a ranking of cities based on their size and functional complexity. One can measure the numbers and kinds of functions that each city or metropolitan area provides. The hierarchy is, then, like a pyramid; a few large and complex cities are at the top and many smaller, simpler ones are at the bottom. There are always more smaller cities than larger ones.

When a spatial dimension is added to the hierarchy as in Figure 11.15, it becomes clear that an areal system of metropolitan

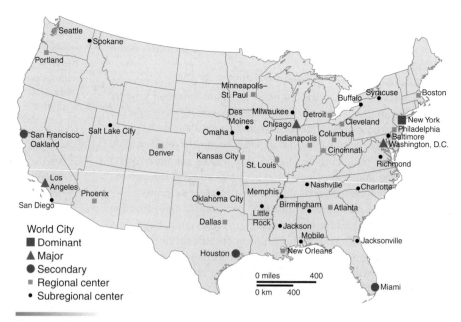

Figure 11.15 A functional hierarchy of U.S. metropolitan areas. Only the major metropolitan areas are shown. The hierarchy includes smaller urban districts (not shown) that depend on or serve the larger centers.

Source: Redrawn from P. L. Knox, ed., The United States: A Contemporary Human Geography. *Harlow, United Kingdom. Longman, 1988, Fig. 5.5, p. 144.*

Central Place Theory

In 1933, the German geographer **Walter Christaller** attempted to explain the size and spacing regularities he observed for towns in Southern Germany. In doing so, he developed a framework called *central place theory,* which provided the descriptive understandings that he sought. Christaller did recognize that his explanatory theory would best describe an idealized and somewhat artificial situation with the following characteristics:

1. Towns that provide the surrounding rural agricultural population with such fundamental goods as groceries and clothing would develop on a uniform plain, with no topographic barriers, channelization of traffic, or variations in farm productivity.

2. The rural population would be dispersed in an even pattern across that plain.

3. The characteristics of the people would be uniform; that is, they would possess similar tastes, demands, and incomes.

4. Each kind of product or service available to the dispersed population would have its own *threshold,* or minimum number of consumers needed to support its supply. Because such goods as sports cars or fur coats are either expensive or not in great demand, they would have a high threshold, while a fewer number of customers within smaller tributary areas would be sufficient to support a small grocery store.

5. Consumers would purchase goods and services from the nearest opportunity (store or supplier).

When all of Christaller's assumptions are considered simultaneously, they yield the following results:

1. Since each customer patronizes the nearest center offering the needed goods, the agricultural plain is automatically divided into noncompeting market areas—*complementary regions*—where each individual town (and its merchants) has a sales monopoly.

2. Those market areas will take the form of a series of hexagons that cover the entire plain, as shown in the diagram. There will be a central place at the center of each of the hexagonal market areas.

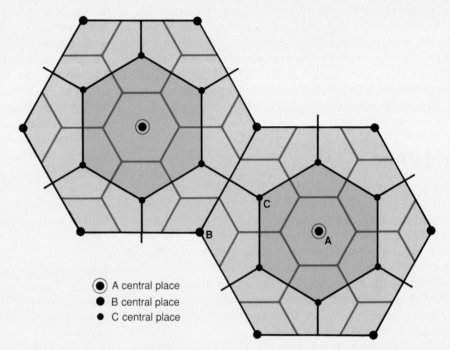

A central place

B central place

C central place

Complementary regions and the pattern of central places. *The two (A) central places are the largest on this diagram of one of Christaller's models. The (B) central places offer fewer goods and services for sale and serve only the areas of the intermediate-sized hexagons. The many (C) central places, which are considerably smaller and more closely spaced, serve still smaller market areas. The goods offered in the (C) places are also offered in the (B) and (A) places, but the latter offer considerably more and more specialized goods. Notice that places of the same size are equally spaced.*

Source: Arthur Getis and Judith Getis, "Christaller's Central Place Theory." Journal of Geography, 1966. Used with permission of the National Council for Geographic Education.

3. The size of the market area of a central place will be proportional to the number of goods and services offered from that place and the largest central places (with the largest market areas) will supply all the goods and services the consumers in that area demand and can afford.

4. As the diagram indicates, the central place pattern shows a "nesting" of complementary regions in which part or all of multiple lower-order service areas are contained within the market area of a higher-order center.

In addition, Christaller reached two important conclusions. First, towns at the same size (functional level) in the central place system will be evenly spaced, and larger towns (higher-order places) will be farther apart than smaller ones. This means that many more small than large towns will exist. In the diagram, the ratio of the number of small towns to towns of the next larger size is 3 to 1. This distinct, steplike series of towns in discrete classes differentiated by both size and function is called a *hierarchy of central places.*

Second, the system of towns is interdependent. If one central place were eliminated, the entire system would have to readjust. Consumers need a variety of products and services, each of which has a different minimum number of customers required to support it. The towns containing many goods and services become regional retailing centers, while the smaller central places serve just the people in their immediate vicinity. The higher the threshold of a desired product, the farther, on average, the consumer must travel to purchase it.

centers, large cities, small cities, and towns exists. Goods, services, communications, and people flow up and down the hierarchy. The few high-level metropolitan areas provide specialized functions for large regions, while the smaller cities serve smaller districts. The separate centers interact with the areas around them, but since cities of the same level provide roughly the same services, those of the same size tend not to serve each other unless they provide some very specialized activity, such as housing the political capital of a region or a major hospital or university. Thus, the settlements of a given level in the hierarchy are not independent but interrelated with communities of other levels in that hierarchy. Together, all centers at all levels in the hierarchy constitute an urban system.

World Cities

Standing at the top of national systems of cities are a relatively few places that may be called **world cities** (or global cities). These large urban centers are command and control points for the global economy. When manufacturing dominated the economy, much of what an individual company did—production, management, sales, accounting, etc.—took place in a single city, often in the same building. Now, the globalized economy and transnational corporations (TNCs) have scattered those functions and jobs across the world. But all those activities must be coordinated somewhere, and that place is the world city.

London, New York, and Tokyo, the world's three largest cities in 1950, are generally recognized as the three most dominant world cities today. They are no longer the world's three most populous cities, but they contain the highest number of producer services offices and TNC headquarters, and they dominate commerce in their respective parts of the world. Each is directly linked to a number of other primary- and secondary-level world cities. All are bound together in complex networks that control the organization and management of the global system of finance, production, and trade. Figure 11.16 shows the links between the dominant centers and some of the major and secondary world cities, which include Paris, Hong Kong, Singapore, Milan, Toronto, Chicago, and Los Angeles. These cities are all interconnected by advanced communication systems between governments, major corporations, stock and futures exchanges, securities and commodity markets, major banks, and international organizations.

World cities are home to society's most powerful and elite members, and thus they are centers for arts, culture, and the consumption of luxury goods. Some critics suggest that the forces of economic globalization that create world cities also increase inequality. Certainly, the incredible wealth generated in world cities leads to high costs for housing, creating affordability problems for lower-wage service workers.

Rank-Size and Primacy

In addition to considering city systems on a global scale, urban geographers also inquire about the organization of city systems within regions or countries. The observation that there are many more small than large cities within an urban system ("the larger the fewer") is itself a statement about expected city hierarchies. In some countries, especially those with complex economies and

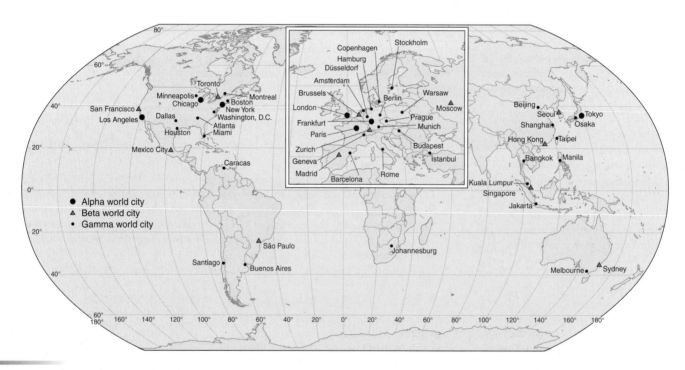

Figure 11.16 A classification of world (or global) cities based on international business services of advertising, accounting, banking, and law. These cities are bound together in complex networks, all interconnected by the flow of financial and economic information. A classification based on a different set of economic activities would yield a slightly different list but a similar hierarchy.

Source: Adapted from P. J. Taylor, D. R. F. Walker, and J. V. Beverstock, "Firms and Their Global Service Networks," In S. Sassen, ed. (2002), Global Networks, Linked Cities, New York: Routledge, pp. 93–115.

a long urban history, the city size hierarchy is summarized by the **rank-size rule.** It tells us that the *n*th largest city of a national system of cities will be 1/*n* the size of the largest city. That is, the second-largest settlement will be 1/2 the size of the largest, the 10th biggest will be 1/10 the size of the first-ranked city, and so on. Although no national city system exactly meets the predictions of the rank-size rule, that of Russia, Canada, and the United States closely approximate it.

Rank-size ordering is less applicable to countries with developing economies or where the city system is dominated by a **primate city,** one that is far more than twice the size of the second-ranked city. In fact, there may be no obvious "second city" at all, for a characteristic of a primate city hierarchy is one very large city, few or no intermediate-sized cities, and many subordinate smaller settlements. For example, Seoul (at 9.8 million in 2010) contains about 20 percent of the total population of South Korea, and Luanda, Angola, and Bangkok, Thailand, are each home to about 40 percent of their country's urban population.

The capital cities of many developing countries display that kind of overwhelming primacy. In part, their primate city pattern is a heritage of their colonial past, when economic development, colonial administration, and transportation and trade activities were concentrated at a single point (Figure 11.17); Nairobi (Kenya), Dakar (Senegal), and many other African capital cities are examples.

In other instances—Egypt (Cairo) or Mexico (Mexico City), for example—development and population growth have tended to concentrate disproportionately in a capital city whose very size attracts further development and growth. Many European countries, such as Austria, the United Kingdom, and France, also show a primate structure due to the historic concentration of economic and political power in a capital city that was the administrative and trade center of a larger colonial empire.

Figure 11.17 **Primate city evolution.** At first colonial contact (*a*) settlements are coastal and unconnected with each other. Joining a newly productive hinterland by European-built railroads to a new colonial port (*b*) begins to create a pattern of core-periphery relations and to focus European administration, trade, and settlement at the port. Mineral discoveries and another rail line in a neighboring colony across the river (*c*) mark the beginnings of a new set of core-periphery relationships and of a new multifunctional colonial capital nearby but unconnected by land with its neighbor. With the passage of time and further transport and economic development, two newly independent nations (*d*) display *primate city* structures in which further economic and population growth flows to the single dominating centers of countries lacking balanced regional transport networks, resource development, and urban structures. Both populations and new functions continue to seek locations in the primate city where their prospects for success are greatest.

Source: Adapted from E. S. Simpson, The Developing World: An Introduction *(Harlow, Essex, England: Longman Group UK Limited, 1987).*

Network Cities

The history of urban growth includes episodes of intense competition between cities, often over dominance of transportation networks. In recent years, a new kind of urban spatial pattern, the network city, has begun to appear as nearby cities work together. A **network city** evolves when two or more previously independent cities with potentially complementary functions develop high-speed transportation corridors and communications infrastructure to facilitate cooperation.

For example, since the reunion of Hong Kong and China proper in 1997, an infrastructure of highway and rail lines and communications improvements has been developed to help integrate Hong Kong with Guangzhou, the huge, rapidly growing industrial and economic hub on the mainland. In Japan, three distinctive, nearby cities—Kyoto, Osaka, and Kobe—are joining together to compete with the Tokyo region as a major center of commerce. Kyoto, with its temples and artistic treasures, is the cultural capital of Japan; Osaka is a primary commercial and industrial center; and Kobe is a leading port. Their complementary functional strengths are reinforced by high-speed rail transport connecting the cities and by a new airport (Kansai) designed to serve the entire region.

In Europe, the major cities of Amsterdam, Rotterdam, and The Hague, together with intermediate cities such as Delft, Utrecht, and Zaanstad, are connected by high-speed rail lines and a major airport. Each of these cities has special functions not duplicated in the others, and planners have no intention of developing competition between them. This region—called the Randstad—is second only to London in its popularity for international head many urban geographers and planners are arguing for a return to the transit-oriented pattern of urban growth for reasons of energy conservation and environmental sustainability.

Models of Urban Form

We all have mental maps that help us summarize and make sense of the diverse places we've experienced in large cities. The meanings we associate with terms such as *inner-city* or *West End* reflect the content of those mental maps. Simple, graphic models of urban growth and land use patterns began to appear during the 1920s and 1930s. Those models generalized the varied urban universe and helped explain some regularities in city growth and structure. More recently, urban geographers have begun to offer models that address the newer patterns of the decentralized automobile city.

The common starting point of the early models is the distinctive CBD found in every older central city. The core of the CBD displays the intensive land use development already discussed: the major shopping concentration, tall office buildings, and streets crowded by pedestrians. Framing the core is a fringe area of warehousing, transportation terminals, and light industries. Just beyond the fringe, residential land uses begin.

The **concentric zone model** (Figure 11.24a) was developed by University of Chicago sociologists to explain the structuring of U.S. cities, specifically ethnically diverse, mass transit–based cities like Chicago in the 1920s. It describes the urban community as a set of nested rings of mostly residential uses at increasing distances in all directions from the CBD fringe. The first, a zone of transition, is characterized by change and deterioration and contains warehouses and factories mixed in with high-density, low-income slums, rooming houses, and perhaps ethnic ghettoes. Moving outward, the next ring is a zone of workers' homes, usually smaller, older homes on small lots. The third zone houses better residences, single-family homes or higher-rent apartments for those able to exercise choice in housing location and afford the longer journey to CBD employment. Finally, just beginning to emerge when this model was proposed, was an outer zone of low-density suburban development.

The concentric zone model is dynamic. Each type of land use and each residential group tends to move outward into the next outer zone as the city matures and expands. That movement was seen as part of a ceaseless process of invasion and succession that yielded a restructured land use pattern and population segregation by income level. The least attractive housing is in the inner-city zone of transition where smelly factories are interspersed with aging, crowded apartments. As one travels outward, the housing is progressively newer and more spacious, and the social and economic status of the residents rises accordingly.

The **sector model** (Figure 11.24b) was devised in the 1930s by the land economist Homer Hoyt, who mapped housing values in major U.S. cities. The sector model posits that high-rent residential areas are dominant in city expansion. The high-rent sector is typically established in areas of natural amenities such as lakeshore, large parks, or prominent ridges or hills. The high-rent

(a) Concentric Zone Model

(b) Sector Model

(c) Multiple-Nuclei Model

1 Central business district
2 Wholesale, light manufacturing
3 Low-class residential
4 Medium-class residential
5 High-class residential
6 Heavy manufacturing
7 Outlying business district
8 Residential suburb
9 Industrial

Figure 11.24 Three classic models of the internal structure of cities.

Source: Redrawn from "The Nature of Cities" by C.D. Harris and E.L. Ullman, in Vol. 242 of The Annals of the American Academy of Political and Social Science. *Copyright © 1945 The American Academy of Political and Social Science, Philadelphia. Used by permission of the publisher and authors.*

sector grows outward from the city center along major transportation routes such as streetcar and elevated railroad lines or suburban commuter routes. Low-income populations occupy districts adjacent to the areas of industry and associated heavy transportation corridors, such as freight railroad lines. Middle-income housing fills in between the low-income and high-income districts.

The sector model is also dynamic, marked by a *filtering-down* process as older areas are left behind by the outward movement of their original higher-income inhabitants, with the lower-income populations moving into the recently vacated areas. The expansion of the city is radial, shaped by radial transportation systems. The social status of inner-ring neighborhoods extends outward into the suburbs. The accordance of the sector model with the actual pattern observed in Dallas-Fort Worth, Texas is suggested in Figure 11.25.

The basic assumption of the concentric circle and sector models—that urban growth and development proceeded outward from a single central core—was countered by the **multiple-nuclei model** (Figure 11.24c) proposed by geographers Chauncy Harris and Edward Ullman. In their view, large cities developed outward from several nodes of growth, not just one. Certain activities have specific locational requirements: the retail district needs accessibility; a port function needs a waterfront site; heavy industry requires level land adjacent to railroads. Peripheral expansion of the separate centers eventually leads to coalescence and the meeting of incompatible land uses along the lines of juncture. The urban land use pattern, therefore, is not regularly structured from a single center in a sequence of circles or a series of sectors but based on separately expanding clusters of contrasting activities.

Although there have been many social, economic, and technological changes since these three models were developed, the patterns that they explained remain as vestiges and controls on the current landscape of older central cities. North American cities prior to 1945 resembled the concentric zone or sector models with a clearly defined and dominant CBD, but both new and expanding older cities grew more sprawling and complex in the automobile era following World War II. The multiple-nuclei model gives a better insight into the urban structure of the more recent past, but should be supplemented by newer visualizations of contemporary metropolitan complexes or "galactic cities."

The **peripheral model** (Figure 11.26) take into account the major changes in urban form that have taken place since World War II, especially the suburbanization of what were once central city functions. The peripheral model focuses on the peripheral belt that lies within the metropolitan area, but outside the central city itself.

In these models, circumferential highways and expressways outside the central city make large tracts of land available for development in the low-density sprawl characteristic of individual rather than mass-transit movement of people. Residences are segregated by price level into relatively homogenous suburban clusters, and individual nodes in the peripheral belt are centers for employment or services: shopping malls, industrial parks, distribution and warehouse concentrations, office parks, airport-associated clusters containing hotels, meeting facilities, car rental agencies, and the like.

Much of the life of the residents of the periphery takes place outside the central city, as they shop for food, clothing, and services in the shopping malls, seek recreation in country clubs and entertainment complexes, and find employment in outlying industrial or office parks. While residents of the periphery may feel no need to travel to the old CBD with its problems of congestion, expensive parking, and homeless people, the periphery, however, remains a functional part of the metropolitan complex. Job markets are regional and the office parks and shopping malls of the periphery rely on low-wage service sector workers who often travel from the urban core where they find affordable housing. The urban core also retains an important cultural role, housing key institutions such as art museums, performance halls, universities, and stadiums.

The models of urban form just discussed aid our understanding of urban structure and development, but it must be stressed that a model is not a map, and that many cities contain elements and characteristics of more than a single model.

Dallas/Fort Worth

Income per Capita
by Census tract, 2000
— Less than $6,600

— $20,000

— $35,000

— $100,000
... and greater

Figure 11.25 Incomes in Dallas–Fort Worth, Texas, 2000. The high-income sector extending over 20 miles north from downtown Dallas (east side of map) illustrates the applicability of the sector model. The inner rings of low-income residents are consistent with the concentric ring model.

Source: Cartography by Bill Rankin, data from the U.S. Census Bureau.

Social Areas of Cities

Vestiges of the ring and sectoral features depicted in the early models of U.S. cities are evident in the observed social segregation within urban areas. The larger and more economically and socially complex the city, the stronger the tendency for residents to sort themselves into groups based on *social status, family status,* and *ethnicity.* In a large metropolitan region with a diversified population, this territorial behavior may be a defense against the unknown or the unwanted, a desire to be among similar kinds of people, a response to income constraints, or a result of social and institutional barriers. Most people feel more at ease when they are near those with whom they can easily identify. In traditional societies, these groups are the families and tribes. In modern society, people tend to group according to

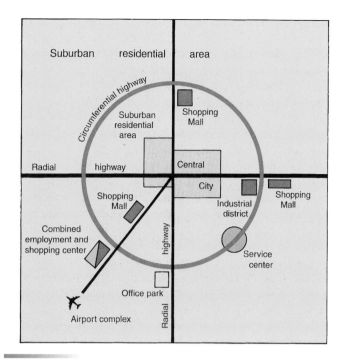

Figure 11.26 Metropolitan peripheral model. The galactic city's multiple downtowns and special function nodes and corridors are linked by the metropolitan expressway systems in this conceptualization proposed by Chauncy Harris.

Source: Reprinted with permission from Urban Geography, *Vol. 18, No. 1, pp. 15–35.*

income or occupation (social status), stages in the life cycle (family status), and language or race (ethnic characteristics); see the feature "Birds of a Feather" in Chapter 7.

Many of these social area groupings are fostered by the size and the value of available housing. Land developers, especially in cities, produce homes of similar quality and type in specific areas. Of course, as time elapses, there is a change in the condition and quality of that housing. Land uses may change and new groups may replace previous tenants, leading to the evolution of new neighborhoods with different social characteristics.

Social Status

The social status of an individual or a family is determined by income, education, occupation, and home value, although it may be measured differently in different cultures. In the United States, high income, a college education, a professional or managerial position, and high-value housing confer high status. High-value housing can mean an expensive rental apartment, a spacious loft in a former warehouse, or a large suburban house with extensive grounds. A good housing indicator of social status is persons per room or floor area per person. A low number of persons per room tends to indicate high status. Low status characterizes people with low income and lower levels of education, living in low-value housing.

Patterns of social status agree with the sector model. In most cities, people of similar status are grouped in sectors that fan out from the innermost urban residential areas (Figure 11.27). If the number of people within a given social group increases, they tend

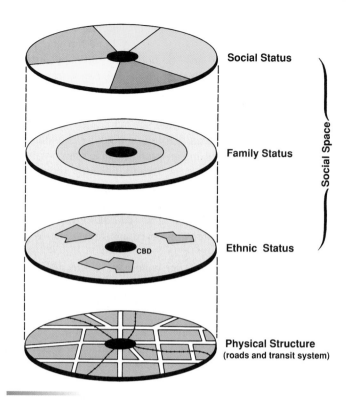

Figure 11.27 The social geography of American and Canadian cities.

Source: Redrawn with permission from Robert A. Murdie, Factorial Ecology of Metropolitan Toronto. Research Paper 116. Department of Geography Research Series, University of Chicago, 1969.

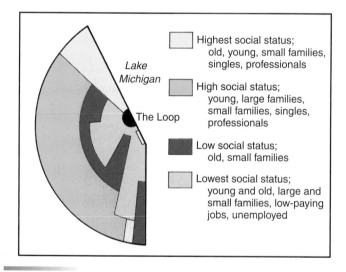

Figure 11.28 A diagrammatic representation of the major social areas of the Chicago region. The CBD of Chicago is known as the "Loop."

Source: Redrawn with permission from Phillip Rees, "The Factorial Ecology of Metropolitan Chicago," M. A. thesis, University of Chicago, 1968.

to move away from the central city along an arterial connecting them with the old neighborhood. Major transport routes leading to the city center are the usual migration routes out from the core. Chicago's elite Gold Coast along Lake Michigan and its low-income Southside neighborhoods display the extremes of social status (Figure 11.28).

Today, social status divisions are often perpetuated by political boundaries between separate municipalities or school districts. Communities on either side of the divide may differ greatly in income. Many residential developments are also income-segregated because their houses are of similar value. To preserve the upscale nature of a development and protect land values, self-governing community associations may be formed to enact and enforce land use restrictions (see the feature "The Gated Community"). Pervasive and detailed, these restrictions may specify such things as the size, construction, and color of exterior walls and fences, the size and permitted uses of rear and side yards, and the design of outside lights and mailboxes. Some go so far as to tell residents what ages they must be, what pets they may keep, where they may park their boats or recreational vehicles, and what landscaping and lawn ornaments are allowed.

Family Status

As the distance from the city center increases, the average age of the adults declines, the size of their family increases, or both. Within a particular sector, singles, young professionals without children, and older people whose children have left home (empty-nesters), tend to live close to the city center. In contrast, young families seeking space for child rearing and good schools live farther from the city center. Those without children at home may covet the accessibility of the cultural and business life of the urban core. The arrangement that emerges is a set of concentric circles divided according to family status, as Figure 11.27 suggests.

Ethnicity

For some groups, ethnicity is a more important factor in residential location than social or family status. Areas of a single ethnic group appear in the social geography of cities as separate clusters or nuclei, reminiscent of the multiple-nuclei concept of urban structure. For some ethnic groups, cultural segregation is both sought and vigorously defended, even in the face of pressures for neighborhood change exerted by potential competitors for housing space, as we saw in Chapter 6. The durability of "Little Italys" and "Chinatowns" and of Polish, Greek, Armenian, Korean, and other ethnic enclaves in many U.S. cities is evidence of the persistence of self-maintained segregation. As each ethnic group assimilates, however, a growing share of its members live outside the enclave.

Certain ethnic or racial groups, especially African Americans, have had segregation forced on them. Sometimes this occurs through housing discrimination or real estate agents who "steer" people of certain racial and ethnic groups into neighborhoods that the agents think are appropriate. Every city in the United States has one or more African American areas that may be considered cities within a city, with their own self-contained social geographies of social status, income, and housing quality. Social and economic barriers to movement outside the area have always been high, as they also have been for Hispanics and other non-English-speaking minorities.

As whites and Asians increase their household incomes, they tend to move to neighborhoods that match their economic standing. Due to persistent residential segregation, as Census data document, blacks with similar income growth are less able to move to integrated neighborhood settings. Although segregation has moderated somewhat, at the start of the 21st century, the average African American city resident lived in a census tract that was more than 75 percent minority and three-fifths black. Figure 6.19 in Chapter 6 illustrates the concentration of whites, blacks, Hispanics, and other ethnic groups in Chicago. Elsewhere, black segregation varies by region. Black-white separation is highest in metropolitan areas in the Northeast and Midwest in cities such as Milwaukee; greatest integration is found in the metropolitan south and west and, notably, in military towns like Norfolk, Virginia, and San Diego.

All three factors in the social geography of cities have undergone widespread change in recent years. The diversity of household types has proliferated. Two-parent families with children living at home make up less than one-fourth of all U.S. households. Today, the suburbs house large numbers of singles and childless couples. Areas near the CBD have become popular for young professionals, some of whom have no plans to have children. Lesbian and gay couples and families often choose to live in urban centers, but increasing numbers are choosing suburbs as well. With more women in the workforce than ever before, and as a result of multiple-earner families, residential site selection has become a more complex undertaking. The heavy losses of manufacturing jobs and the rise of the service sector with its extremes of high-paying jobs (finance, insurance, and law, for example) and low-paying jobs have led to greater extremes of wealth and poverty and fewer middle-income neighborhoods. Immigration continues to diversify cities, but many immigrant groups now head directly to the suburbs. The city structure is constantly changing, reflecting changes in family and employment makeup.

Institutional Controls

Over the past century, and particularly since World War II, institutional controls have strongly influenced the land use arrangements and growth patterns of most U.S. cities. Indeed, the governments—local and national—of most Western urbanized societies have instituted myriad laws to control all aspects of urban life, with particular emphasis on the ways in which individual property can be developed and used. In the United States, emphasis has been on land use planning, subdivision control and zoning ordinances, and building, health, and safety codes. All have been designed to assure an orderly pattern of urban development, and all are based on broad applications of the police powers of municipalities to ensure public health, safety, and well-being, even when private property rights are infringed.

These nonmarket controls on land use are designed to minimize incompatibilities (residences adjacent to heavy industry, for example), set aside appropriate locations for public uses (the transportation system, waste disposal facilities, government buildings, parks, and so on), and private uses (colleges, shopping centers, housing, and so on) needed for a balanced, orderly community. In theory, such careful planning should prevent the emergence of slums, so often the result of undesirable adjacent uses, and should stabilize neighborhoods by reducing market-induced pressures for land use change.

However, zoning ordinances and land use planning have frequently been criticized as being unresponsive to contemporary

Figure 11.46 The Cyber Gateway Building in Hyderabad's Hitec City. The complex houses firms like the multinational software companies Microsoft, IBM, and Toshiba, as well as Indian companies like Wipro, which provides information technology services and product design. Hitec City also houses professional schools in business and information technology.

Summary

The city is the essential focus of activity for every society that advances beyond the subsistence level. Although they are among the oldest marks of civilization, only in the past decade have cities become the home of the majority of the world's people. Virtually all population growth worldwide in the first decades of the 21st century will be captured by cities in the developing world.

All settlements growing beyond their village origins take on functions uniting them to the countryside and to a larger system of settlements. As they grow, they become functionally complex. Their economic structure, composed of both *basic* and *nonbasic* activities, may become diverse. Basic activities represent the functions performed for the larger economy and urban system; nonbasic activities satisfy the needs of the urban residents themselves. Functional classifications distinguish the economic roles of urban centers, while simple classification of them as transportation and special-function cities or as central places helps define and explain their role within the broader system of cities.

Systems of cities are reflected in the urban hierarchy and in part described by the rank-size rule, primacy, and central place theory. When a city is far larger than all others in its country, it is termed a *primate city*. Many countries display this dominating city pattern, but there are only a few *world cities* dominating the global economy.

Repetitive physical and social patterns are found inside North American cities. At the core, the central business district (CBD), localized originally by mass-transit line convergence, has the highest land values and accessibility. Outside the CBD, lower-order commercial centers are also transport-route-oriented. Low-density residential uses occupy less valuable and less accessible land. These patterns inspired geographers to summarize early 20th-century urban form by the concentric zone, sector, and multiple-nuclei models. Automobile-based expansion brought more recent recognition of metropolitan peripheral models. The period following World War II brought massive changes in urban organization, with the decline and regeneration of the central city accompanied by the rise and expansion of suburbs. Urban social patterns have been influenced by the tendency for urban dwellers to sort themselves spatially by family status, social status, and ethnicity. In Western countries, these patterns are also influenced by governmental controls that help determine land uses.

Urbanization is a global phenomenon, and North American models of city systems, land use, and social area patterns differ substantially from cities in the rest of the world, reflecting diverse heritages and economic structures. Western European cities differ from those in Eastern Europe, where land uses reflect earlier communist principles of city structure. Explosive growth in developing-world cities is rendering them unable to provide all their residents with employment, housing, safe water, sanitation, and other minimally essential services and facilities.

KEY WORDS

basic sector 353
brownfields 372
central business district (CBD) 362
central city 360
central place 355
central place theory 356
Christaller, Walter 357
city 360
concentric zone model 364
conurbation 347
economic base 353

edge city 370
gated community 368
gentrification 376
hinterland 351
Latin American city model 385
metropolitan area 360
multiple-nuclei model 365
multiplier effect 353
network city 359
nonbasic (service) sector 353
peak land value intersection 362

peripheral model 365
primate city 359
rank-size rule 359
sector model 364
suburb 360
town 360
urban hierarchy 356
urban influence zone 356
urbanized area 360
world city 358

FOR REVIEW

1. Consider the city or town in which you live, attend school, or with which you are most familiar. In a brief paragraph, discuss that community's *site* and *situation*. Point out the connection, if any, between its site and situation and the basic functions that it originally performed or now performs.

2. Describe the *multiplier effect* as it relates to the population growth of urban units.

3. Is there a hierarchy of retailing activities in the community with which you are most familiar? Of how many and of what kinds of levels is that hierarchy composed? What localizing forces affect the distributional pattern of retailing within that community?

4. Briefly describe the urban land use patterns predicted by the *concentric circle*, the *sector,* and the *multiple-nuclei* models of urban development. Which one, if any, best corresponds to the growth and land use pattern of the community most familiar to you?

5. In what ways do *social status, family status,* and *ethnicity* affect the residential choices of households? What distributional patterns are associated with each factor? Does the social geography of your community conform to the predicted pattern?

6. How has suburbanization damaged the economic base and the financial stability of the U.S. central city?

7. In what ways does the Canadian city differ from the pattern of its U.S. counterpart?

8. Why are metropolitan areas in developing countries expected to grow larger than many Western metropolises by 2020?

9. What are *primate cities?* Why are primate cities so prevalent in the developing world? Why are they so overburdened in populations and functions? What might be some disadvantages of a primate city distribution?

10. How does the Latin American city model differ from models of urban structure developed in the United States?

KEY CONCEPTS REVIEW

1. **What common features define the origin, nature, and locations of cities?** pp. 350–353.
Cities arose 4,000–6,000 years ago as distinctive evidence of the growing cultural and economic complexity of early civilizations. Distinct from the farm villages of subsistence economies, true cities provided an increasing range of functions—religious, military, trade, production, etc.—for their developing societies. Their functions

and importance were affected by the sites and situations chosen for them. The massive recent increase in number and size of cities worldwide reflects the universality of economic development and total population growth in the latter 20th century.

2. **How are cities structured economically and how are systems of cities organized?** pp. 353–360.
The economic base of a city—the functions it performs—is divided

between basic and nonbasic (or service) activities. Through a multiplier effect, adding basic workers increases both the number of service workers and the total population of a city. The amount of growth reflects the base ratio characteristic of the city. Cities may be hierarchically ranked by their size and functional complexity. Rank-size, primate, and central place hierarchies are commonly cited but distinctly different.

3. **How are cities structured internally and how do people distribute themselves within them?** pp. 360–376.

Cities are themselves distinctive land use and cultural area landscapes. In the United States, older cities show repetitive land use patterns that are largely determined by land value and accessibility considerations. Classical land use models include the concentric circle, sector, and multiple nuclei patterns. Distinct social area arrangements have been equated with those land use models. Newer cities and growing metropolitan areas have created different land use and social area structures with suburbs, edge cities, and galactic metropolises as recognized urban landscape features.

4. **Are there world regional and cultural differences in the land use and population patterns of major cities?** pp. 376–386.

Cities are regional and cultural variables; their internal land use and social area patterns reflect the differing historical, technological, political, and cultural conditions under which they developed. We are most familiar with the U.S. city, but we can easily recognize differences between it and Western European, Eastern European, and developing-world cities, themselves of great regional, physical, and cultural complexity.

Specks and Spoils

The UNCLOS gives to owners of islands claims over immense areas of the surrounding sea and, of course, to the fisheries and mineral resources in and under them. Tiny specks of land formerly too insignificant in size or distant in location to arouse the emotions of any nation now are avidly sought and fervently claimed. Remote Rockall, a British islet far west of Scotland, was used by Britain in 1976 to justify extending its fishing rights claim farther into the North Atlantic than otherwise was possible. Argentina nearly went to war with Chile in 1978 over three islands at the tip of South America at the Atlantic end of the Beagle Channel. Chile had lodged its claim of ownership hoping to gain access to known South Atlantic fish resources and hoped-for petroleum deposits. In 1982, Argentina seized the Falkland Islands from Britain, ostensibly to reclaim the Islas Malvinas (their Spanish name) as national territory, but with an underlying economic motive as well. British forces retook the islands and subsequently used sovereignty over them to claim a sea area three times as large as Britain. Japan has encased a disappearing islet in concrete to maintain territorial claims endangered through erosion of the speck of land supporting them.

The Paracel and Spratly Islands, straddling trade routes in the South China Sea, have attracted more attention and claimants than most island groups, thanks to presumed large reserves of oil and gas in their vicinities. The Japanese seized the Paracels from China during World War II and at the end of that war surrendered them to Nationalist Chinese forces that soon retreated to Taiwan. South Vietnam took them over until 1974, when they were forcibly ejected by the mainland Chinese. In 1979, a united Vietnam reasserted its claims, basing them on 17th- and 18th-century maps. China countered with reference to 3rd-century explorations by its geographers and maintained its control.

The location of the Paracels to the north, near China, in the South China Sea places them in a different and less difficult status than that of the Spratlys, whose nearest neighbors are the Philippines and Malaysia. Mere dots in the sea, the largest of the Spratlys is about 100 acres—no more than one-eighth the size of New York's Central Park. But under the UNCLOS, possession of the island group would confer rights to the resources (oil, it is hoped) that could be found beneath about 400,000 square kilometers (150,000 square miles) of sea. That lure has made rivals of six governments and posed the possibility of conflict. Until early in 1988, Vietnam, the Philippines, Malaysia, Taiwan, and tiny Brunei had all maintained in peaceful coexistence garrisons on separate islets in the Spratly group. Then China landed troops on islands near the Vietnamese holdings, sank two Vietnamese naval ships, and accused Vietnam of seizing "Chinese" territory on the pretext of searching for their missing sailors. Although China agreed in 1992 that ownership disputes in the Spratlys should be resolved without violence, it also passed a law the following year repeating its claims to all the islands and its determination to defend them. In early 1995, China occupied "Mischief Reef," close to—and already claimed by—the Philippines, but in late 2002, it agreed with other Southeast Asian countries to avoid future disputes over the islands.

Assertions of past discovery, previous or present occupation, proximity, and simple wishful thinking have all served as the basis for the proliferating claims to seas and seabeds. The world's oceans, once open and freely accessible, are increasingly being closed by the lure of specks of land and the spoils of wealth that they command.

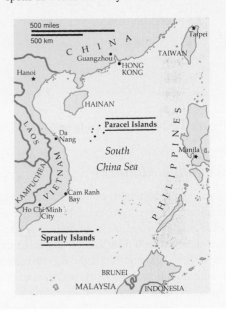

but with affiliated relationships with the United Nations and operating under its auspices. Among them are the FAO, the International Bank for Reconstruction and Development (World Bank), the International Labor Organization (ILO), UNICEF, the WHO, and—of growing economic importance—the WTO.

The WTO, which came into existence at the start of 1995, has become one of the most significant of the global expressions of supranational economic control. It is charged with enforcing the global trade accords that grew out of years of international negotiations under the terms of the General Agreement on Tariffs and Trade (GATT). The basic principle behind the WTO is that the member countries (153 as of August 2009, with additional states preparing for membership or seeking admission) should work to cut tariffs, dismantle nontariff barriers to trade, liberalize trade in services, and treat all other countries uniformly in matters of trade. Any preference granted to one should be available to all.

Increasingly, however, regional rather than global trade agreements are being struck, and free trade areas are proliferating. Only a few WTO members are not already part of some other regional trade association. Such areal associations, some argue, make world trade less free by scrapping tariffs on trade among member states but retaining them separately or as a group on exchanges with nonmembers.

Regional Alliances

In addition to their membership in such international agencies, countries have shown themselves willing to relinquish some of their independence to participate in smaller multinational systems. These groupings can be economic, military, or political, and many have been formed since 1945. Cooperation in the economic sphere seems to come more easily to states than does military and political collaboration.

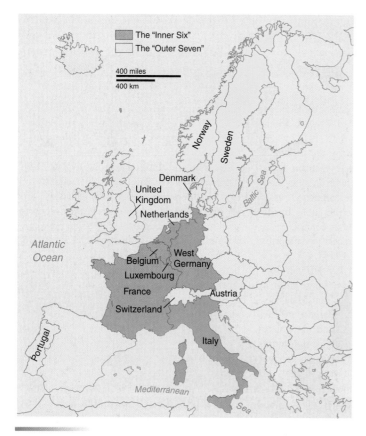

Figure 12.24 The original Inner Six and Outer Seven of Europe.

Economic Alliances

Among the oldest, most powerful, and far-reaching of the regional economic alliances are those that have evolved in Europe, particularly the European Union and its several forerunners. Shortly after the end of World War II, the Benelux countries (Belgium, the Netherlands, and Luxembourg) formed an economic union to create a common set of tariffs and to eliminate import licenses and quotas. Formed at about the same time were the Organization for European Cooperation (1948), which coordinated the distribution and use of Marshall Plan funds, and the European Coal and Steel Community (1952), which integrated the development of that industry in the member countries. A few years later, in 1957, the *European Economic Community (EEC),* or *Common Market,* was created, composed at first of only six states: France, Italy, West Germany, and the Benelux countries.

To counteract these Inner Six, as they were called, other countries in 1960 formed the European Free Trade Association (EFTA). Known as the Outer Seven, they were the United Kingdom, Norway, Denmark, Sweden, Switzerland, Austria, and Portugal (Figure 12.24). Between 1973 and 1986, three members (the United Kingdom, Denmark, and Portugal) left EFTA for membership in the Common Market and were replaced by Iceland and Finland.

The **European Union (EU)** grew out of the Common Market. It added new members slowly at first, as Greece, Spain, and Portugal joined during the 1980s; Austria, Finland, and Sweden joined in 1995. As it gathered momentum, more

countries were admitted to the European Union during the early 2000s, including the island states of Malta and Cyprus and 10 former Soviet bloc nations from Estonia in the north to Bulgaria and Slovenia in the South (Figure 12.25). These additions brought the number of member nations to 27, increased the total population of the European Union to some half-billion people, and expanded its economy to rival that of the United States. The European Union is now the world's largest and richest bloc of nation-states.

Over the years, members of the European Union have taken many steps to integrate their economies and coordinate their policies in such areas as transportation, agriculture, and fisheries. A council of ministers, a commission, a European parliament, and a court of justice give the European Union supranational institutions with effective ability to make and enforce laws. By January 1, 1993, the European Union had abolished most remnant barriers to free trade and the free movement of capital and people among its members, creating a single European market. In another step toward economic and monetary union, the European Union's single currency, the *euro,* replaced separate national currencies in 1999. And all applicant members in 2002 added 80,000 pages of EU law to their own legal systems.

We have traced this European development history, not because the full history of the EU is important to remember, but simply to illustrate the fluid process by which regional alliances are made. Countries come together in an association, some drop out, and others join. New treaties are made, and new coalitions emerge. Indeed, a number of such regional economic and trade associations have been added to the world supranational map. None are as encompassing in power and purpose as the European Union, but all represent a concession of national independence to achieve broader regional goals.

NAFTA, launched in 1994, links Canada, Mexico, and the United States in an economic community aimed at lowering or removing trade and movement restrictions among the countries. It is perhaps the best known to North American students. The Americas as a whole, however, have other similar associations with comparable trade enhancement objectives, though frequently they—in common with other world regional alliances—have social, political, and cultural interests also in mind. The Caribbean Community and Common Market (CARICOM), for example, was established in 1974 to further cooperation among its members in economic, health, cultural, and foreign policy arenas. Mercosur, the Southern Cone Community Market, which unites Brazil, Argentina, Uruguay, and Paraguay in the proposed creation of a customs union to eliminate levies on goods moving among them, is a South American example.

A similar interest in promoting economic, social, and cultural cooperation and development among its members underpins the Association of Southeast Asian Nations (ASEAN), formed in 1967. A similar, but much less wealthy African example is the Economic Community of West African States (ECOWAS). The Asia Pacific Economic Cooperation (APEC) forum includes China, Japan, Australia, Canada, and the United States among its 18 members and has a grand plan for "free trade in the Pacific" by 2020. More restricted bilateral and regional preferential trade arrangements have also proliferated, numbering more than 250 by

Figure 12.25 The 27 members of the European Union. The admission of Romania and Bulgaria on January 1, 2007, marked the end of EU expansion, according to the European Commission, until "further institutional reform" increased its absorption capacity. The European Union earlier stipulated that in order to join, a country must have stable institutions guaranteeing democracy, the rule of law, human rights, and protection of minorities; a functioning market economy; and the ability to accept the obligations of membership, including the aims of political, economic, and monetary union.

Finally, it does not seem to matter whether countries are alike or distinctly different in their economies, as far as joining economic unions is concerned. There are examples of both. If the countries are dissimilar, they may complement each other. This was one basis for the European Common Market. Dairy products and furniture from Denmark are sold in France, freeing that country to specialize in the production of machinery and clothing. On the other hand, countries that produce the same raw materials hope that by joining together in an economic alliance, they might be able to enhance their control of markets and prices for their products. The Organization of Petroleum Exporting Countries (OPEC), mentioned in Chapter 8, is a case in point. Other attempts to form commodity cartels and price agreements between producing and consuming nations include the International Tin Agreement, the International Coffee Agreement, and others.

Military and Political Alliances

Countries form alliances for other than economic reasons. Strategic, political, and cultural considerations may also foster cooperation. The League of Arab States, for example, was established in 1945 primarily to promote social, political, military, and foreign policy cooperation among its 22 members. In the Western Hemisphere, the Organization of American States (OAS), founded in 1948, concerns itself largely with social, cultural, human rights, and security matters affecting the hemisphere. A similar concern with peace and security underlay the Organization of African Unity (OAU), formed in 1963 by 32 African countries and, by 2001, expanded to 53 members and renamed the African Union.

Military alliances are based on the principle that unity assures strength. Such pacts usually provide for mutual assistance in the case of aggression. Once again, action breeds reaction when such an association is created. The formation of NATO, a defensive alliance of many European countries and the United States, was countered by the establishment of the Warsaw Treaty Organization, which joined the USSR and its satellite countries of Eastern Europe. Both pacts allowed the member states to base armed forces in one another's territories, a relinquishment of a certain degree of sovereignty uncommon in the past.

Military alliances depend on the perceived common interests and political goodwill of the countries involved. As political realities change, so do the strategic alliances. NATO was created to defend Western Europe and North America against the Soviet military threat. When the dissolution of the USSR and the Warsaw Pact removed that threat, the purpose of the NATO alliance became less clear. Since the 1990s, however, the organization has added seven members and has taken on a greater role in peacekeeping activities (Figure 12.27).

2006, up from only 50 in 1990, with another 60 or so under negotiation. They create a maze of rules, tariffs, and commodity agreements that result in trade restrictions and preferences contrary to the free trade intent of the WTO.

Three further points about regional international alliances are worth noting. The first is that the formation of a coalition in one area often stimulates the creation of another alliance by countries left out of the first. Thus, the union of the Inner Six gave rise to the treaty among the Outer Seven. Similarly, a counterpart of the Common Market was the Council of Mutual Economic Assistance (CMEA), also known as Comecon, which linked the former communist countries of Eastern Europe and the USSR through trade agreements.

Second, the new supranational unions tend to be composed of contiguous states (Figure 12.26). This was not the case with the recently dissolved empires, which included far-flung territories. Contiguity facilitates the movement of people and goods. Communication and transportation are simpler and more effective among adjoining countries than among those far removed from one another, and common cultural, linguistic, historical, and political traits and interests are more to be expected in spatially proximate countries.

(a)

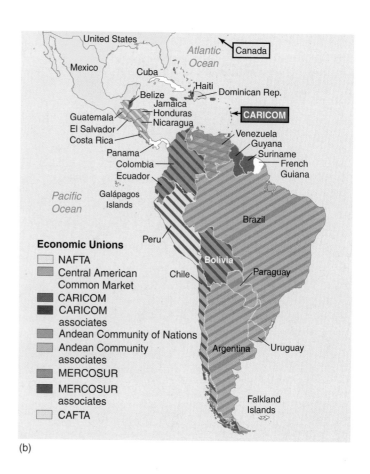

Economic Unions

- NAFTA
- Central American Common Market
- CARICOM
- CARICOM associates
- Andean Community of Nations
- Andean Community associates
- MERCOSUR
- MERCOSUR associates
- CAFTA

(b)

Figure 12.26 (*a*) **NAFTA** is intended to unite Canada, the United States, and Mexico in a regional free trade zone. Under the terms of the treaty, tariffs on all agricultural products and thousands of other goods were to be eliminated by the end of 1999. In addition, all three countries are to ease restrictions on the movement of business executives and professionals. If fully implemented, the treaty will create one of the world's richest and largest trading blocs. (*b*) **Western Hemisphere economic unions** in 2009. In addition to these subregional alliances, President George H. W. Bush in 1990 proposed a "free trade area of the Americas" to stretch from Alaska to Cape Horn.

All international alliances recognize communities of interest. In economic and military associations, common objectives are clearly seen and described, and joint actions are agreed on with respect to the achievement of those objectives. More generalized mutual concerns or appeals to historical interest may be the basis for primarily *political alliances.* Such associations tend to be rather loose, not requiring their members to yield much power to the union. Examples are the Commonwealth of Nations (formerly the British Commonwealth), composed of many former British colonies and dominions, and the OAS, both of which offer economic as well as political benefits.

There are many examples of abortive political unions that have foundered precisely because the individual countries could not agree on questions of policy and were unwilling to subordinate individual interests to make the union succeed. The United Arab Republic, the Central African Federation, the Federation of Malaysia and Singapore, and the Federation of the West Indies fall within this category.

Although many such political associations have failed, observers of the world scene speculate about the possibility that "superstates" will emerge from one or more of the economic or political alliances that now exist. For example, will a "United States of Europe," under a single government, be the logical outcome of the successes of the European Union? No one knows, but so long as the individual state continues to be regarded as the highest form of political and social organization, and as the body in which sovereignty rests, such total unification is unlikely.

Local and Regional Political Organization

The most profound contrasts in cultures tend to occur between, rather than within, states, one reason political geographers traditionally have been primarily interested in country units. The emphasis on the state, however, should not obscure the fact that it is at the local level that most of us find our most intimate and immediate contact with government and its influence on the administration of our affairs. In the United States, for example, an individual is subject to the decisions and regulations made by the school board, the municipality, the county, the state, and, perhaps, a host of special-purpose districts (water, fire, sewer, etc.)—all in addition to the laws and regulations issued by the federal familiar to most of us. We should remember, however, North American structures of municipal governments, minor civil divisions, and special-purpose districts have counterparts in other regions of the world.

The Geography of Representation: The Districting Problem

There are more than 85,000 local governmental units in the United States. Slightly more than half of these administrative regions are municipalities, townships, and counties. The remainder are school districts, water-control districts, airport authorities, sanitary districts, and other special-purpose bodies. Around each of these districts, boundaries have been drawn. Although the number of districts does not change greatly from year to year, many boundary lines are redrawn in any single year. When the size or shape of a district is based on population numbers or distribution, such *redistricting* is made necessary by shifts in population, as areas gain or lose people. Alternatively, or in addition, the number of representatives allotted to each district may be modified, a process known as *reapportionment*.

For example, every 10 years following the U.S. Census, updated figures are used to reapportion the 435 seats in the House of Representatives among the 50 states. Redrawing the congressional districts to reflect population changes is required by the Constitution, the intention being to make sure that each legislator in the House represents roughly the same number of people. Since 1964, Canadian provinces and territories have entrusted redistricting for federal offices to independent electoral boundaries commissions. Although a few states in the United States also have independent, nonpartisan boards or commissions draw district boundaries, most rely on state legislatures for the task (with the consequent control of redistricting by whichever party is currently in power in that state). Across the United States, decennial census data are also used to redraw the boundaries of legislative districts within each state, as well as those for local offices, such as city councils and county boards.

Analyzing how the shape and location of voting district boundaries influences election outcomes is one aspect of **electoral geography,** which also addresses the spatial patterns yielded by election results and their relationship to the socioeconomic characteristics of voters. In a democracy, it might be assumed that

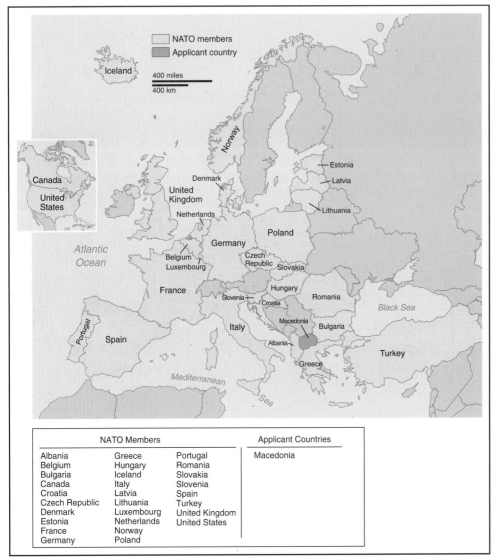

NATO Members

NATO Members			Applicant Countries
Albania	Greece	Portugal	Macedonia
Belgium	Hungary	Romania	
Bulgaria	Iceland	Slovakia	
Canada	Italy	Slovenia	
Croatia	Latvia	Spain	
Czech Republic	Lithuania	Turkey	
Denmark	Luxembourg	United Kingdom	
Estonia	Netherlands	United States	
France	Norway		
Germany	Poland		

Figure 12.27 The NATO military alliance in 2011 had 28 members. Countries that have recently joined the alliance include Estonia, Latvia, Lithuania, Slovakia, Romania, Bulgaria, and Slovenia in 2004 and Albania and Croatia in 2009. Proponents of expansion argue that NATO is necessary in order to create a zone of stability and security throughout Europe. Opponents contend that enlargement is a divisive move that will cast a shadow over the future of relations with Russia, which is opposed to expansion so close to its borders.

government and its agencies. Among other things, local political entities determine where children go to school, the minimum-size lot on which a person can build a house, and where one may legally park a car. Adjacent states of the United States may be characterized by sharply differing personal and business tax rates; differing controls on the sale of firearms, alcohol, and tobacco; variant administrative systems for public services; and different levels of expenditures for them (Figure 12.28).

All of these governmental entities are *spatial systems.* Because they operate within defined geographic areas and because they make behavior-governing decisions, they are topics of interest to political geographers. In the concluding sections of this chapter, we examine two aspects of political organization at the local and regional level. Our emphasis will be on the U.S. and Canadian scene simply because their local political geography is

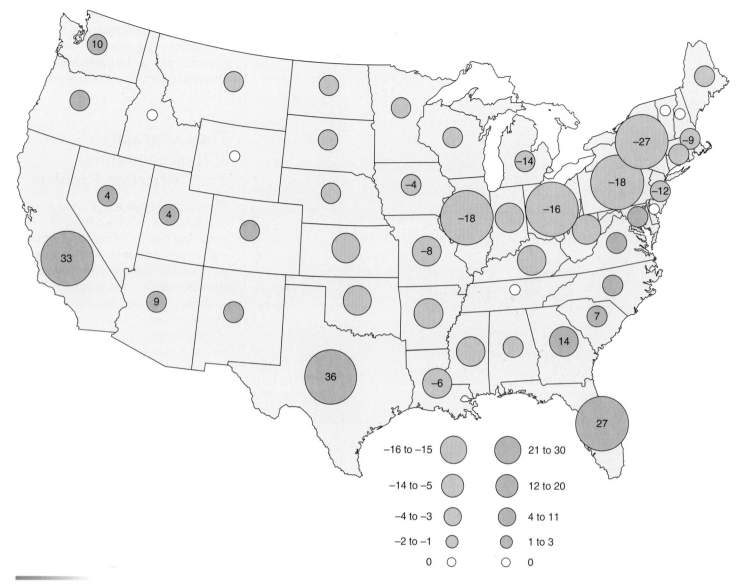

Figure 12.28 **Geographic shifts in congressional apportionment between 1930 and 2010** illustrate dramatic population movements to the South and West. Seats in the U.S. House of Representatives are reapportioned after each census with the goal of achieving an equitable distribution based on population while maintaining at least one member for each state. Since 1930, New York has lost 18 seats and Pennsylvania 16, while California has gained 33, Florida gained 22, and Texas gained 15. After the 2010 census, 12 seats were shifted. Alaska and Hawaii are not shown because they were not states in 1930.

Source: Office of the Clerk, U.S. House of Representatives.

electoral districts should contain roughly equal numbers of voters, that they should be reasonably compact, and that the final proportion of elected representatives of a particular political party or ideology should roughly correspond to the proportion of voters who vote for candidates of that party or ideology. But in fact, these proportions can be quite discrepant because the way in which district boundary lines are drawn can maximize, minimize, or effectively nullify the representational power of a group of voters.

Gerrymandering is the practice of drawing the boundaries of electoral districts so as to give particular candidates or classes of candidates an electoral advantage beyond the share of the electorate that supports them (Figure 12.29). This practice may advantage particular classes of candidates in a way that most people

would find undemocratic; examples include *partisan, incumbent,* and *discriminatory racial* gerrymandering. Alternatively, it may advantage classes of candidates in a way that attempts to right historical injustices and achieve greater fairness in the electoral system; the classic example of this is *affirmative racial* gerrymandering (see the feature "Geography and Citizenship"). Whether in the service of ends that are just or unjust, several characteristic strategies have been employed over the years to achieve gerrymandered districts. Gov. Elbridge Gerry (Figure 12.29) designed districts to concentrate his Federalist opponents in just a few districts, diluting their power outside those few districts, a technique known as *packing*. Electoral districts in Mississippi were once drawn intentionally to make sure black voters were never in the majority

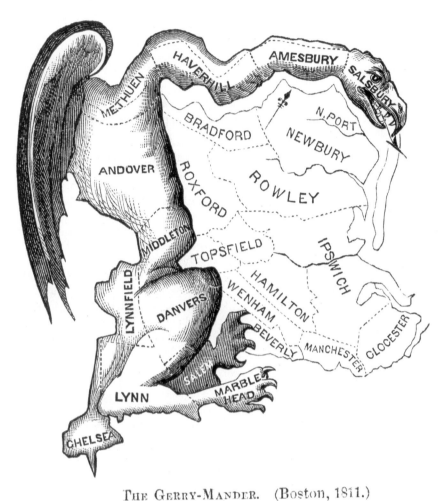

THE GERRY-MANDER. (Boston, 1811.)

Figure 12.29 The original gerrymander. The term *gerrymander* originated in 1811 from the shape of an electoral district formed in Massachusetts while Elbridge Gerry was governor. When an artist added certain animal features, the district resembled a salamander and quickly came to be called a gerrymander.

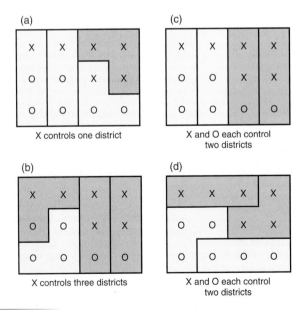

Figure 12.30 Alternative districting strategies. *Xs* and *Os* might represent Republicans and Democrats, urban and rural voters, blacks and whites, or any other distinctive groups.

in any district, even though a large proportion of the voters in the state were black. Distributing and diluting classes of voters in this way is known as *cracking*.

Let's look at a concrete, if hypothetical, example (Figure 12.30). Assume that *X* and *O* represent two groups with an equal number of voters, but different policy or candidate preferences. Although there are equal numbers of *X*s and *O*s, the way that electoral districts are drawn can dramatically affect voting results. In Figure 12.30a, the *X*s are concentrated in one district but diluted in the other three, and will probably elect only one representative of the four. The power of the *X*s is maximized in Figure 12.30b, where they are the majority in three of the four districts but completely absent from the fourth. The voters are evenly divided in Figure 12.30c, where the *X*s are the majority in two districts and the minority in the other two. Finally, the *X*s completely control two districts and the *O*s completely control the other two in Figure 12.30d. This pattern might result from both groups agreeing to design electoral districts so that incumbent candidates have "safe seats." Such incumbent gerrymandering offers little chance for electoral change.

Figure 12.30 depicts a hypothetical district, compact in shape with an even population distribution and only two groups competing for representation. In actuality, voting districts are often oddly shaped because of such factors as the city limits, current population distribution, and transportation routes—as well as past gerrymandering. Further, in any large area, many groups vie for power. Each electoral interest group promotes its version of fairness in the way boundaries are delimited. Minority interests, for example, seek representation in proportion to their numbers so that they will be able to elect representatives who are concerned about and responsive to their needs (see the feature "Voting Rights and Race").

In practice, gerrymandering is not always and automatically successful. First, a districting arrangement that appears to be unfair may be appealed to the courts. Further, voters are not unthinking party loyalists; key issues may cut across party lines, scandal may erode support for a candidate, or personal charm increase votes unexpectedly; and the amount of candidate financing or number of campaign workers may determine election outcomes if compelling issues are absent.

The Fragmentation of Political Power

Boundary drawing at any electoral level is never easy, particularly when political groups want to maximize their representation and minimize that of opposition groups. Furthermore, the boundaries that we may want for one set of districts may *not* be those that we want for another. For example, sewage districts must take natural drainage features into account, whereas police districts may be based on the distribution of the population or the number of miles of street to be patrolled, and school attendance zones must consider the numbers of school-aged children and the capacities of individual schools.

Geography and Citizenship

Voting Rights and Race

Irregularly shaped Congressional voting districts were created by several state legislatures after the 1990 census to make minority representation in Congress more closely resemble minority presence in the state's voting-age population. Most were devised to contain a majority of black voters, but this *affirmative racial* gerrymandering was in a few cases used to accommodate Hispanic majorities. States that intentionally created *majority-minority districts* after the 1990 census included Florida, Georgia, Illinois, Louisiana, North Carolina, Texas, and Virginia. All represented a deliberate attempt to balance voting rights and race; all were specifically intended to comply with the federal Voting Rights Act of 1965, which provides that members of racial minorities shall not have "less opportunity than other members of the electorate . . . to elect representatives of their choice."

Because at least some of the newly created districts had very contorted boundaries, on appeal by opponents, they have been ruled unconstitutional by the Supreme Court and have been redrawn. The state legislatures' attempts at fairness and adherence to congressional mandate contained in the Voting Rights Act were held not to meet other standards, such as rough equality of district population size, reasonably compact shape, and avoidance of disenfranchisement of any class of voters. The conflicts reflected the uncertainty of exactly what were the appropriate controlling requirements in voting district creation.

In North Carolina, for example, although 24 percent of the 1990 population of that state was black, past districting had divided black voters among a number of districts (a practice known as *discriminatory racial* gerrymandering), with the result that blacks had not elected a single congressional representative from that state in the 20th century. In 1991, the Justice Department ordered North Carolina to redistrict so that at least two districts would contain black majorities. Because of the way the black population was distributed, the only way to form black-majority districts was to string together cities, towns, and rural areas in very elongated, sinuous belts. The two newly created districts had slim (53 percent) black majorities.

The redistricting in North Carolina and other states had immediate effects. Black membership in the House of Representatives increased from 26 in 1990 to 39 in 1992; blacks constituted nearly 9 percent of the House, as opposed to 12 percent in the total population. Within a year, those electoral gains were threatened as lawsuits challenging the redistricting were filed in a number of states. The chief contention of the plaintiffs was that the irregular shapes of the districts amounted to reverse discrimination against whites.

In June 1993, a sharply divided Supreme Court ruled in *Shaw v. Reno* that North Carolina's 12th Congressional District might violate the constitutional rights of white voters and ordered a district court to review the case. The 5–4 ruling gave evidence that the country had not yet reached agreement on how to comply with the Voting Rights Act. It raised a central question: Should a state maximize the rights of racial minorities or not take racial status into consideration? A divided Court provided answers in 1995, 1996, and 1997 rulings that rejected congressional redistricting maps for Georgia, Texas, and North Carolina on the grounds that "race cannot be the predominant factor" in drawing election district boundaries.

The difficulty in interpreting and complying with the Act is illustrated by the fact that although the Supreme Court in 1996 ruled North Carolina's 12th Congressional District unconstitutional, federal courts in 1998 and 1999 rejected alternate district designs. In *Easley v. Cromartie* (2001), the Court approved both a redrawn 12th District and the use of race as a redistricting consideration, so long as it was not the "dominant and controlling" one. Some research suggests that race-based redistricting results in more polarized politics, with some districts more solidly liberal and others more solidly conservative. Results of elections since some majority-minority districts were dismantled by the courts suggest that minorities can win even if their group is not in the majority in a district. While the use of geographic information systems (GISs) in redistricting has increased the speed and power with which officials can evaluate alternative districting schemes, it cannot resolve what are fundamentally ethical issues regarding race, democracy, and electoral geography.

Questions to Consider

1. Do you believe that race should be a consideration in the electoral process? Why or why not? If so, should voting districts be drawn to increase the likelihood that representatives of racial or ethnic minorities will win elections? If not, how can one be certain that the voting power of minorities will not be unacceptably diluted?

2. With which of the following arguments in *Shaw v. Reno* do you agree? Why?

   ". . . Racial gerrymandering, even for remedial purposes, may balkanize us into competing racial factions; it threatens to carry us further from the goal of a political system in which race no longer matters." (Justice Sandra Day O'Connor)

   ". . . Legislators will have to take race into account in order to avoid dilution of minority voting strength." (Justice David Souter).

3. One of the candidates in North Carolina's 12th Congressional District said, "I love the district because I can drive down I-85 with both car doors open and hit every person in the district." Given a good transportation and communication network, how important is it that voting districts be compact?

4. Critics of affirmative racial gerrymandering contend that blacks have been and can continue to be elected in white-majority districts and, further, that white politicians can and do adequately represent the needs of all voters in their districts, including blacks. Do you agree? Why or why not?

5. Given partisanship and the desire of incumbent legislators to protect their own seats, is there an inherent conflict in having legislators draw district boundaries? Defend your answer.

6. After the 1990 census, more than 130 suits were filed in 40 states challenging either the states' overall redistricting plans or individual districts. The result was that, in many cases, courts determined final district boundaries. Does it seem democratic for a judge elected in one district to draw up a redistricting plan for an entire state? Defend your answer.

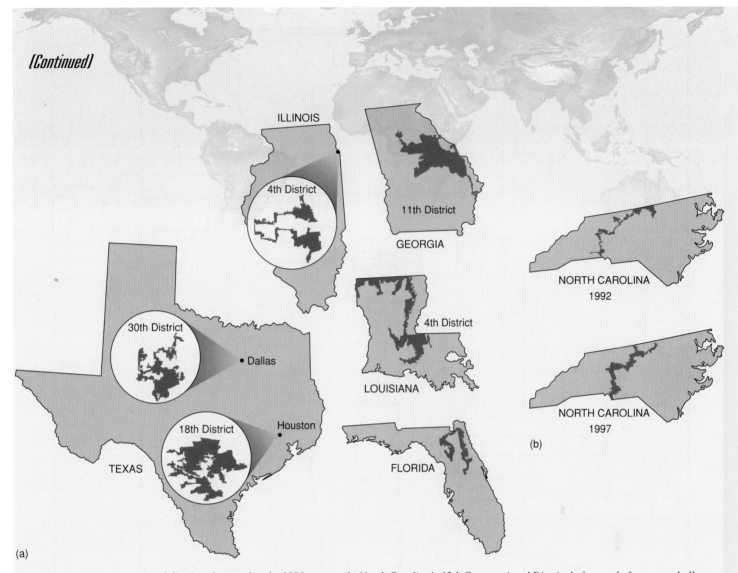

ILLINOIS

4th District

GEORGIA

11th District

TEXAS

30th District

• Dallas

18th District

Houston •

LOUISIANA

4th District

FLORIDA

NORTH CAROLINA
1992

NORTH CAROLINA
1997

(b)

(a)

Majority-minority congressional districts drawn after the 1990 census. (b) North Carolina's 12th Congressional District before and after court challenges.

As these examples suggest, the United States is subdivided into great numbers of political administrative units whose areas of control are spatially limited. The 50 states are partitioned into more than 3,000 counties ("parishes" in Louisiana), most of which are further subdivided into townships, each with a still lower level of governing power. This political fragmentation is further increased by the existence of nearly 88,000 special-purpose districts whose boundaries rarely coincide with the standard major and minor civil divisions of the country or even with each other (Figure 12.31). Each district represents a form of political allocation of territory to achieve a specific aim of local need or legislative intent.

Canada, a federation of 10 provinces and 3 territories, has a similar pattern of political subdivision. Each of the provinces contains minor civil divisions—municipalities—under provincial control, and all (cities, towns, villages, and rural municipalities) are governed by elected councils. Ontario and Quebec also have counties that group smaller municipal units for certain purposes. In general, municipalities are responsible for police and fire protection, local jails, roads and hospitals, water supply and sanitation, and schools, duties that are discharged either by elected agencies or appointed commissions.

The existence of such a great number of districts in urban areas may cause inefficiency in public services and hinder the orderly use of space. *Zoning ordinances,* for example, control the uses to which land may be put. They are determined by each municipality and are a clear example of the effect of political decisions on the division and development of space. Unfortunately, in large urban areas, the efforts of one community may be hindered by the practices of neighboring communities. Thus, land zoned for an industrial park or shopping mall in one city may abut land zoned for single-family residences in an adjoining municipality. Each community pursues its own interests, which may not coincide with those of its neighbors or the larger region.

Figure 12.31 **Political fragmentation in Champaign County, Illinois.** The map shows a few of the independent administrative agencies with separate jurisdictions, responsibilities, and taxing powers in a portion of a single Illinois county. Among other such agencies forming the fragmented political landscape are Champaign County itself, a forest preserve district, a public health district, a mental health district, the county housing authority, and a community college district.

Inefficiency and duplication of effort characterize not just zoning, but many of the services provided by local governments. The efforts of one community to reduce or stop air and water pollution may be, and often are, counteracted by the rules and practices of other towns in the region, although state and national environmental protection standards are now reducing such potential conflicts. Social as well as physical problems spread beyond city boundaries. Thus, nearby suburban communities are affected when a central city lacks the resources to maintain high-quality schools or to attack social ills. The provision of health care facilities, electricity and water, transportation, and recreational space affects the whole

region and, many professionals think, should be under the control of a single consolidated metropolitan government.

The growth in the number and size of metropolitan areas has increased awareness of their administrative and jurisdictional problems. Too much governmental fragmentation and too little local control are both seen as metropolitan problems demanding attention and solution. The one concern is that multiple jurisdictions prevent the pooling of resources to address metropolitan-wide needs. The other is that local community needs and interests are subordinated to addressing the social and economic problems of a core city for which outlying communities feel little affinity or concern.

Summary

The sovereign state is the dominant entity in the political subdivision of the world. It constitutes an expression of cultural separation and identity as pervasive as that inherent in language, religion, or ethnicity. A product of 18th-century political philosophy, the idea of the state was diffused globally by colonizing European powers. In most instances, the colonial boundaries they established have been retained by newly independent countries as their international boundaries.

The greatly varying spatial characteristics of states contribute to national strength and stability. Size, shape, and relative location influence countries' economies and international roles, while national cores and capitals are the heartlands of states. Boundaries, the legally defined borders that determine a state's size and shape, also determine the limits of its sovereignty. They may or may not reflect preexisting cultural landscapes, and in any given case, may or may not prove to be viable. Whatever their nature, boundaries conflicts are at the root of many international disputes. Maritime boundary claims, particularly as reflected in the UNCLOS, add a new dimension to traditional claims of territorial sovereignty.

State cohesiveness is promoted by a number of centripetal forces. Among these are national symbols, a variety of institutions, and confidence in the aims, organization, and administration of government. Also helping to foster political and economic integration are transportation and communication connections. Destabilizing centrifugal forces, particularly ethnically based separatist movements, threaten the cohesion and stability of many states.

Although the state remains central to the partitioning of the world, a broadening array of political entities affects people individually and collectively. Recent decades have seen a significant increase in supranationalism in the form of a number and variety of global and regional alliances to which states have surrendered some sovereign powers. At the other end of the spectrum, expanding North American urban areas and governmental responsibilities raise questions of fairness in districting procedures and of effectiveness when political power is fragmented.

KEY WORDS

antecedent boundary 401
artificial boundary 401
autonomous nationalism 407
centrifugal force 403
centripetal force 403
compact state 397
consequent (ethnographic) boundary 401
core area 398
devolution 407
electoral geography 417
elongated state 397
enclave 397
ethnic cleansing 408
European Union (EU) 414
exclave 397

exclusive economic zone (EEZ) 412
fragmented state 397
functional dispute 403
geometric boundary 401
geopolitics 390
gerrymandering 418
irredentism 402
nation 391
nationalism 403
nation-state 392
natural boundary 401
perforated state 397
physical boundary 401
political geography 390
positional dispute 402

prorupt state 397
regionalism 407
relic boundary 401
resource dispute 403
separatism 407
state 391
subnationalism 406
subsequent boundary 401
superimposed boundary 401
supranationalism 410
territorial dispute 402
terrorism 408
United Nations Convention on the
    Law of the Sea (UNCLOS) 411

FOR REVIEW

1. What are the differences between a *state,* a *nation,* and a *nation-state?* Why is a colony not a state? How can one account for the rapid increase in the number of states since World War II?

2. What attributes differentiate states from one another? How do a country's size and shape affect its power and stability? How can a piece of land be both an *enclave* and an *exclave?*

3. How can boundaries be classified? How do they create opportunities for conflict? Describe and give examples of three types of border disputes.

Figure 13.2 **Average temperatures in (a) January and (b) July.** The rotation of the Earth around the sun, along with the tilt of the Earth's axis, cause more direct solar energy to fall on the Northern Hemisphere in June and on the Southern Hemisphere in January. Note how over water, the temperatures decrease evenly with increased distance from the equator. The effect of land/water contrasts can be seen in the more dramatic temperature differences between January and July at continental locations in the midlatitudes compared to coastal locations.

Plants and animals are adapted to particular climate conditions. Thus, the biosphere is divided into separate groups of biological communities called **biomes,** which are established by the pattern of global climates. In fact, the original classification of global climates was based on observations of plant communities, not temperature and precipitation records, many of which did not exist at that time. In essence, plant communities served as weather stations, recording climate conditions by the ability of different species to survive. We know the Earth's biomes by such descriptive names as *desert, grassland,* or *steppe* or as the *tropical rain forest* and *northern coniferous forest* that was discussed in Chapter 8. Biomes, in turn, contain smaller, more specialized **ecosystems:** self-contained, self-regulating, and interacting communities adapted to local combinations of climate, topography, soil, and drainage conditions.

The structure of the ecosphere is not eternal and unchanging. On the contrary, alteration is the constant rule of the physical environment and would be so even in the absence of humans and their distorting impacts. Natural climatic change, year-to-year variations in weather conditions, fires, windstorms, floods, diseases, or the unexplained rise and fall of predator and prey populations all call for new environmental configurations and

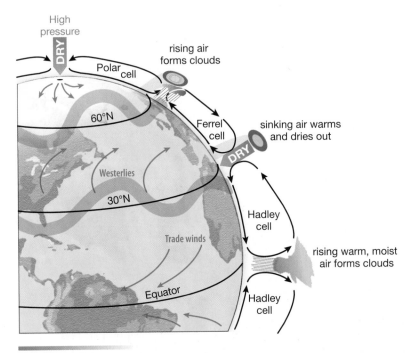

Figure 13.3 Uneven heating of the Earth's surface creates persistent air circulation patterns that move air, moisture, and energy around the Earth. One of those circulation patterns, the Hadley cell, creates wet climates near the tropics and deserts at about 30 degrees north and south.

forever prevent the establishment of a single, constant "balance of nature."

Remember that we began to track cultural geographic patterns from the end of the last continental glaciation, some 11,000 to 12,000 years ago. Our starting point, then, was a time of environmental change when humans were too few in number and primitive in technology to have had any impact on the larger structure of the ecosphere. Their numbers increased and their technologies became vastly more sophisticated and intrusive with the passage of time, but for nearly all of the period of cultural development to modern times, human impact on the world environment was absorbed and accommodated by it with no more than local distress. The rhythm and the regularity of larger global systems proceeded largely unaffected by people.

Impacts on the Atmosphere

Ecosystems have long felt the destructive hand of humans and the cultural landscapes they made. Chapter 2 explored the results of human abuse of the local environment in the Chaco Canyon and Easter Island deforestations. Forest removal, overgrazing, and ill-considered agriculture turned lush hillsides of the Mediterranean Basin into sterile and impoverished landscapes by the end of the Roman Empire. At a global scale, however, human impact was minimal. But slowly, unnoticed

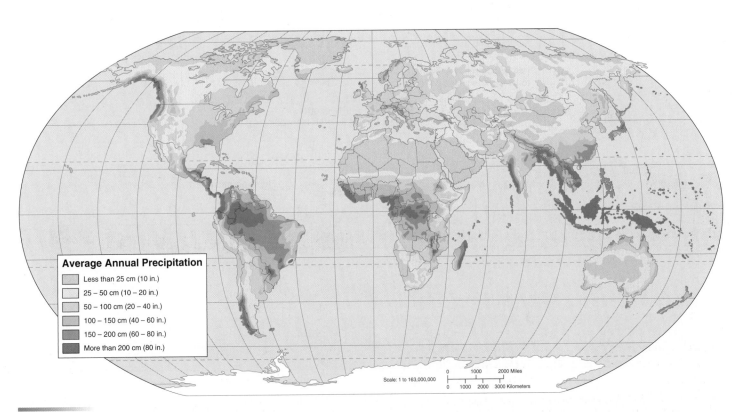

Figure 13.4 Average annual precipitation. Regional contrasts of precipitation clearly demonstrate the truism that natural phenomena are unequally distributed over the surface of the Earth. Global wind patterns create areas of high rainfall in equatorial and tropical areas of Central and South America, Africa, and South and Southeast Asia. A band of deserts is found at about 30 degrees from the equator. Proximity to large water bodies, and position with respect to prevailing winds and mountain ranges also contribute to the patterns of annual precipitation.

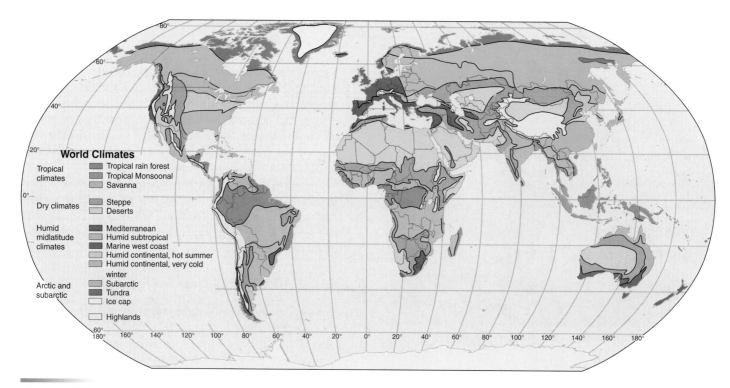

Figure 13.5 **Climates of the world.** Complex interrelationships of latitude, land and water contrasts, ocean currents, topography, and wind circulation create this generalized global pattern of climates.

Figure 13.6 **The hydrologic cycle.** Water may change form and composition, but under natural environmental circumstances, it is marvelously purified in the recycling process and is again made available with appropriate properties and purity to the ecosystems of the Earth. The sun provides energy for the evaporation of fresh and ocean water. The water is held as vapor until the air becomes supersaturated. Atmospheric moisture is returned to the Earth's surface as solid or liquid precipitation to complete the cycle. Precipitation is not uniformly distributed, and moisture is not necessarily returned to areas in the same quantity as it has evaporated from them. The continents receive more water than they lose; the excess returns to the seas as surface water or groundwater. A global water balance, however, is always maintained.

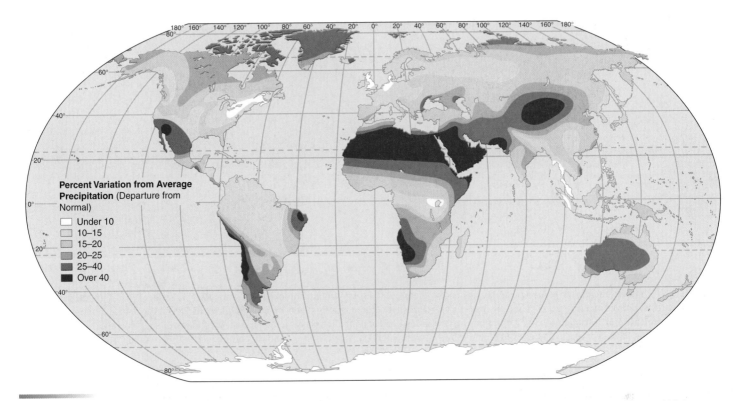

Figure 13.7 **The pattern of precipitation variability.** Note that steppe and desert climate regions have both low total precipitation and high variability. In general, the dryer the climate, the greater the variability. This creates vulnerability to shortages when humans develop agriculture or cities in these regions. Short-run variability in climatic conditions is the rule of nature and occurs independent of any human influence.

at first, human activity began to have a global impact, carrying the consequences of human abuse of the ecosphere far beyond the local scene. Air pollution was at first local, in the form of household air pollution and negative health effects from indoor cooking over open fires. However, the Industrial Revolution in the 18th century and continued increase in the use of fossil fuel energy sources has changed the scale of impacts on the atmosphere. At the metropolitan scale, urban air pollution episodes have rendered the air unsafe in many cities, at the continental scale, acid precipitation is carried across international borders, and at the global scale, destruction of the ozone layer and climate change threaten the entire planet.

Air Pollution and Acid Precipitation

Every day, thousands of tons of pollutants are discharged into the air by natural events and human actions. Air is polluted when it contains substances in sufficient amounts to have a harmful effect. Truly clean air has never existed, for atmospheric pollution can and does result in nature from ash from volcanic eruptions, marsh gases, smoke from naturally occurring forest fires, and windblown dust. Normally, these pollutants are of low volume, are widely dispersed in the atmosphere, and have no significant long-term effect on human health or ecosystems.

Far more damaging are the substances discharged into the atmosphere by human actions. These pollutants come primarily from burning fossil fuels—coal, oil, and natural gas—in power plants, factories, furnaces, and vehicles, and from fires deliberately set to clear forests and grasslands for agricultural expansion or shifting cultivation clearing and burning. In 1952, smoke from coal-burning

factories and home fireplaces combined with fog to cause a four-day smog episode in London that blackened the skies in daytime and killed an estimated 4,000 people. By the 1950s, air pollution in Los Angeles from car exhausts and other sources stung people's eyes and noses and caused rubber tires to deteriorate rapidly (Figure 13.8). Since then, in London, Los Angeles, and other cities in the developed world, environmental regulations and pollution control technologies have dramatically cleared the air (although Los Angeles still does not meet some air quality standards).

Today, air pollution is a global problem; areas far from the polluting source may be adversely affected as atmospheric circulation moves pollutants freely without regard to political boundaries. Just as manufacturing activity has shifted to newly industrializing countries, so too has the world's worst air pollution. For example, current full-color satellite cameras regularly reveal a nearly continuous, 2-mile-thick blanket of soot, organic compounds, dust, ash, and other air debris stretching across much of India, Bangladesh, and Southeast Asia, reaching northward to the industrial heart of China. The pollution shroud in and around India, researchers find, reduces sunlight enough to cut rice yields across much of the country. The World Health Organization (WHO) reports that of India's 23 cities of more than 1 million people, not one meets the organization's air pollution standards. In southern China and Southeast Asia, as many as 2 million people die annually from respiratory diseases caused by human-induced pollution that drifts across the Pacific to the Western Hemisphere and beyond.

In addition to the very serious human health consequences of air pollution, the interaction of pollutants with each other or with natural substances such as water vapor may create secondary pollutants.

(a)

(b)

Figure 13.8 **Photochemical smog.** (*a*) a clear day in Los Angeles, and (b) a day when photochemical smog sharply reduces visibility, damages vegetation, and stings eyes and noses. When the air over the city remains stagnant, sunlight acts on automobile exhausts and industrial pollutants to create photochemical smog. Strict air quality regulations and pollution control technologies have reduced the frequency of such episodes. Peak levels of photochemical smog have dropped to a quarter of their 1955 levels, although Los Angeles is still not in compliance with federal air quality standards.

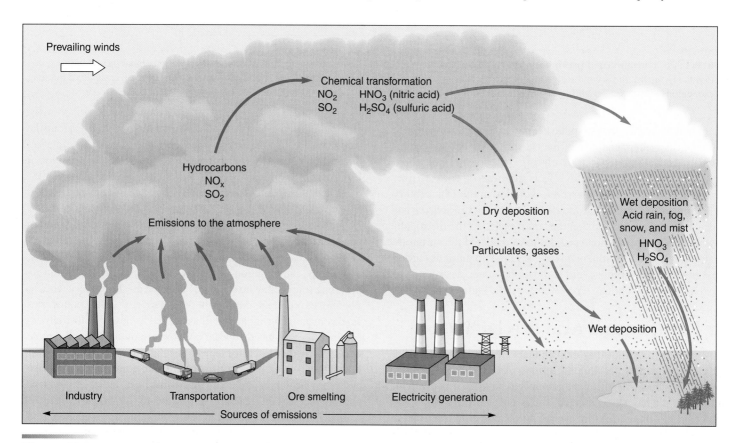

Figure 13.9 **The formation of acid precipitation.** Sulfur dioxide and nitrogen oxides produced by the combustion of fossil fuels are transformed into sulfate and nitrate particles; when the particles react with water vapor, they form sulfuric and nitric acids. Often carried long distances on prevailing winds, the acids are deposited on the surface in the form of fog, rain, snow, or particles.

Among these secondary pollutants is the acid precipitation that occurs when sulfur and nitrogen compounds in emissions from automobiles, coal-fired power plants, and industrial sources produce sulfuric acid and nitric acid in clouds (Figure 13.9). Acid precipitation is often carried long distances by prevailing winds to places where it is highly damaging to trees, lakes, and even structures.

Unexpectedly, acid precipitation is a condition in part traceable to actions taken in developed countries to alleviate the smoke and chemicals that poured into the skies from the chimneys of their power plants, mills, and factories. The clean air programs demanded by environmentalists usually incorporated prohibitions against the discharge of atmospheric pollutants damaging to areas near the

Figure 13.10 Dilution is not the solution to pollution. Before concern about acid rain became widespread, the U.S. Clean Air Act of 1970 set standards for ground-level air quality that could be met most easily by building tall smokestacks high enough to discharge pollutants into the upper atmosphere. Stacks 300 meters (1,000 feet) and higher became common at utility plants and factories, far exceeding the earlier norm of 60–90 meters (200–300 feet). What helped cleanse one area of pollution greatly increased damage elsewhere. The farther and higher the noxious emissions go, the longer they have to combine with other atmospheric components and moisture to form acids. Thus, the taller stacks directly aggravated the acid precipitation problem. Recognizing this, the Environmental Protection Agency (EPA) in 1985 issued rules discouraging the use of tall smokestacks to dilute and disperse emissions.

discharge point. The response was to raise smokestacks to such a height that pollutants were diluted and dispersed far from their origin by higher-elevation winds (Figure 13.10).

But when power plants, smelters, and factories were fitted with tall smokestacks to free local areas from pollution, the sulfur dioxide and nitrogen oxides in the smoke were pumped high into the atmosphere instead of being deposited locally. There, they combined with water and other chemicals and turned into sulfuric and nitric acid that was carried to distant areas. They were joined in their impact by other sources of acid gases. Such as motor vehicle exhausts.

Once the pollutants are airborne, winds can carry them thousands of kilometers, depositing them far from their source. In North America, most of the prevailing winds are westerlies (see Figure 13.3), meaning that much of the acid precipitation that falls on the eastern seaboard and eastern Canada originated in the central and upper Midwest. Similarly, airborne pollutants from the United Kingdom, France, and Germany cause acidification problems in Scandinavia (Figure 13.11).

When acids from all sources are washed out of the air by rain, snow, or fog, the result is **acid precipitation.** Acidity levels are described by the *pH factor,* the measure of acidity/alkalinity on a scale of 0 to 14. The pH of normal rainfall is 5.6, slightly acidic, but acid rainfalls with a pH of 2.4—approximately the acidity of vinegar and lemon juice—have been recorded. Primarily occurring in industrialized nations, acid precipitation has become a serious problem in many parts of Europe, North America, and East Asia. It expresses itself in several forms, though the most visible are its corrosive

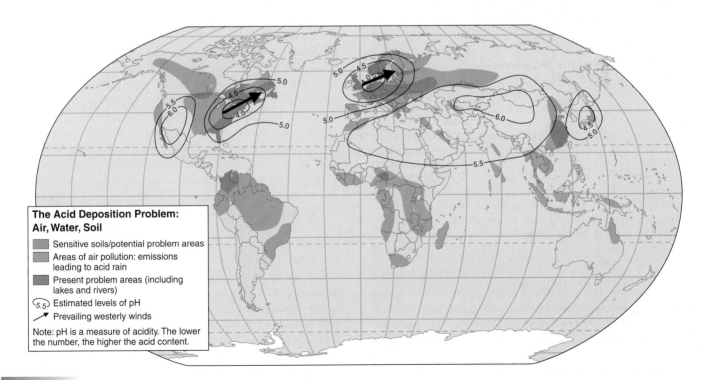

Figure 13.11 Acid precipitation: areas of origin and impacts. Prevailing winds can deposit acid precipitation far from its area of origin and across international boundaries. Prevailing westerly winds carry acid precipitation east from the Ohio and Tennessee River valleys and from the industrial districts of Western Europe toward Scandinavia where it harms vegetation, lakes, and buildings. It is estimated that 90 percent of the sulfuric acid and 80 percent of the nitric acid falling on Norway is from outside the country. Compare this map with the centers of industrial production in Figure 9.20.

Source: Adapted from Student Atlas of World Geography, *4th ed. John Allen, Map 55, p. 70. McGraw-Hill/Dushkin, 2005.*

(a)

(b)

Figure 13.12 **Effects of acid precipitation.** *(a)* The destructive effect of acid rain is evident on this limestone statuary at the cathedral in Reims, France. *(b)* The Germans call it *Waldsterben*—forest death— a term used to summarize the destruction of trees by a combination of acid precipitation, ozone, and heavy metals. It first strikes at higher elevations where natural stresses are greatest and acidic clouds most prevalent, but it slowly moves downslope until entire forests are gone. Here, at Mount Mitchell in North Carolina, *Waldsterben* is thought to result from pollution traveling eastward from the Ohio and Tennessee valleys. Forests throughout the Appalachian Mountains from Georgia northward into Canada display evidence of similar pollution-related damage as do forests in the Front Range of Colorado, the San Gabriel Mountains near Los Angeles, and Europe.

effects on marble and limestone sculptures and buildings and on metals such as iron and bronze and in the destruction of forests (Figure 13.12). Trees at higher elevations are particularly susceptible, with widespread forest loss clearly apparent on the hillsides and mountain tops of New England, Scandinavia, and Germany, where acid precipitation had apparently degraded much of that country's famous forests by the early 1990s.

Damage to lakes, fish, and soils is less immediately evident, but more widespread and equally serious. Acid precipitation has been linked to the disappearance of fish in thousands of streams and lakes in New England, Canada, and Scandinavia, and to a

decline in fish populations elsewhere. It leaches toxic constituents (such as aluminum) from the soil and kills soil microorganisms that break down organic matter and recycle nutrients through the ecosystem. Acid precipitation has decreased in Europe and North America due to international agreements brokered by the United Nations, strict air emission standards, and deindustrialization— the closure of heavy industrial plants such as steel mills that were once major sources of emissions. The changing geography of industrial production suggests that the geographic patterns of acid precipitation will be shifting toward Asia.

The Trouble with Ozone

The potential destruction of the Earth's ozone layer offers another example of the global nature of air pollution. However, it is also a success story of international cooperation and using science and technology to improve the environment. **Ozone** is a reactive molecule consisting of three oxygen atoms rather than the two of normal oxygen. Ozone can lead to confusion because high in the atmosphere, it offers essential protection against the sun's rays, but when it is near the surface, it is one of the main components in photochemical smog and highly damaging to plants and animals. Sunlight produces it from standard oxygen, and a continuous but thin layer of ozone accumulates at upper levels in the atmosphere. There, it is essential to all life forms because it blocks the cancer-causing ultraviolet (UV) light that damages DNA, the molecule of heredity and cell control.

In the summer of 1986, scientists for the first time verified that a "hole" had formed in the ozone layer over Antarctica. In fact, the ozone was not entirely absent, but it had been reduced from earlier recorded levels by some 40 percent. As a result, Antarctic life—particularly the microscopic ocean plants (phytoplankton) at the base of the food chain—that had lived more or less in UV darkness was suddenly getting a trillionfold (1 followed by 12 zeros) increase above the natural rate of UV receipt. The ozone hole typically occurs over Antarctica during late August through early October and breaks up in mid-November.

Scientists attribute the ozone decline to pollution from human-made chemicals, particularly *chlorofluorocarbons (CFCs)* used as coolants, cleansing agents, propellants for aerosols, and in insulating foams. In a chain reaction of oxygen destruction, each of the chlorine atoms released can destroy upwards of 10,000 ozone molecules. Ozone reduction is a continuing and spreading atmospheric problem. A similar ozone hole about the size of Greenland opens in the Arctic, too, and the ozone shield over the midlatitudes has dropped significantly since 1978.

Why should the hole in the ozone layer have appeared first so prominently over Antarctica? In most parts of the world, horizontal winds tend to keep chemicals in the air well mixed. But circulation patterns are such that the freezing whirlpool of air over the south polar continent in winter is not penetrated by air currents from warmer regions of the Earth. In the absence of sunlight and atmospheric mixing, the CFCs work to destroy the ozone. During the Southern Hemisphere summer, sunlight works to replenish it. In either hemisphere, ozone depletion has identical adverse effects. Among other things, greater exposure to UV radiation increases the incidence of skin cancer and, by suppressing bodily defense mechanisms, increases risk from a variety of infectious diseases. Many crop plants are sensitive to UV radiation, and the very existence of the microscopic plankton at the base of the marine food chain is threatened by it.

Production and use of CFCs has been phased out under the Montreal Protocol, a 1987 international agreement made effective in 1992. The developing countries were given a grace period before they began their phaseout schedule for ending use of CFCs. Industries involved in the production or use of CFCs initially resisted the agreement but have since responded by finding substitute chemicals. The Montreal Protocol is an encouraging example of the ability of international agreements to address a global environmental problem successfully. Because of those restrictions, ozone depletion has been slowed or even stopped.

Recent oscillations in the extent of the ozone hole suggest its peak may have been reached by 2003 to 2006, although that expectation has been tempered by evidence that despite the Montreal Protocol, ozone-depleting chemicals are still leaking into the atmosphere from old appliance discharges in North America.

As a result, the earlier predicted date by which the hole should be mended has been postponed from 2050 to perhaps 2075.

Global Climate Change

Scientists agree that humans have significantly altered the chemical composition of the atmosphere since the advent of the Industrial Revolution in the 1700s. Human activities have increased the concentrations of three greenhouse gases—carbon dioxide, methane, and nitrous oxide, intensifying the natural **greenhouse effect,** leading to **global climate change.** The greenhouse effect is caused by a group of atmospheric gases that partially capture the heat energy radiated from the Earth back toward space. Without the greenhouse effect, the Earth would be substantially colder and its temperatures would fluctuate wildly. What is of concern today is that human activities have significantly increased the concentrations of greenhouse gases, intensifying the greenhouse effect and causing anthropogenic (human-caused) climate change (Figure 13.13). Humankind's massive assault on the atmosphere

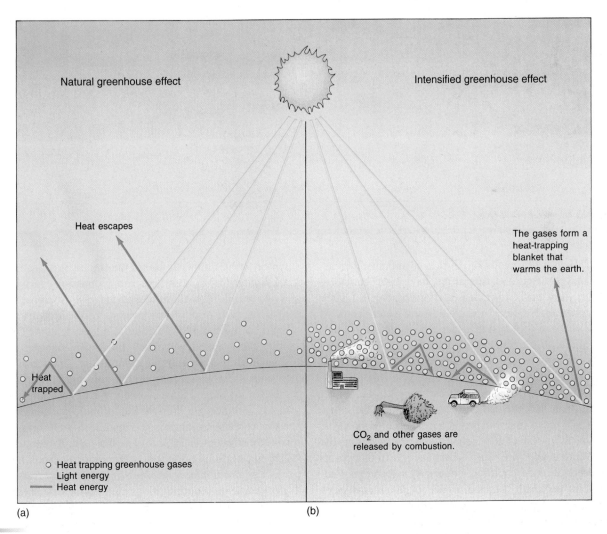

Figure 13.13 Intensified greenhouse effect. When the level of carbon dioxide (CO_2) in the air is low, as in (*a*), incoming solar radiation strikes the Earth's surface, heating it up, and the Earth radiates the energy back into space as heat. Some of the heat energy is captured by naturally occurring greenhouse gases, thereby heating the atmosphere. The intensified greenhouse effect depicted in (*b*) is the result of the more than 7 billion tons of CO_2 that the burning of fossil fuels adds to the atmosphere each year.

Table 13.1

Carbon Dioxide Emissions from Energy Consumption

	Total Emissions (Millions of Metric Tons/Year)				Per Capita Emissions (Metric Tons/Year)
	1980	**2009**	**Change (%)**	**Rank, 2009**	**2009**
China	1,448	7,707	432%	1	5.8
United States	4,777	5,425	14%	2	17.7
India	291	1,591	446%	3	1.4
Russia	N/A	1,557	N/A	4	11.1
Japan	947	1,098	16%	5	8.6
Germany	1,056	766	−28%	6	9.3
Canada	457	541	18%	7	16.2
Iran	117	529	352%	8	7.0
Korea, South	132	528	301%	9	10.9
United Kingdom	614	520	−15%	10	8.4
South Africa	235	451	92%	11	9.2
Mexico	240	444	85%	12	4.0
Saudi Arabia	177	438	148%	13	17.3
Brazil	186	425	129%	14	2.1
Australia	199	418	110%	15	19.6
United Arab Emirates	30	193	543%	26	40.3
Sweden	82	51	−38%	59	5.6
Ghana	2	8	300%	104	0.3
Costa Rica	2	7	201%	113	1.5
WORLD	18,434	30,313	64%		4.5

Source: U.S. Energy Information Administration, 2012.

began with the Industrial Revolution. First, coal and then increasing amounts of petroleum and natural gas have been burned to power industry, heat and cool cities, and drive vehicles. Their burning has turned fuels into carbon dioxide and water vapor. At the same time, the world's forest lands have been cleared for timber and agriculture. With more carbon dioxide in the atmosphere and fewer trees to capture the carbon and produce oxygen, carbon dioxide levels have risen steadily.

The role of trees in managing the carbon cycle is simple: Probably more than half the carbon dioxide put into the atmosphere by burning fossil fuels is absorbed by the Earth's oceans, plants, and soil. The rest of the carbon dioxide remains in the atmosphere where it traps the Earth's heat energy. In theory, atmospheric carbon dioxide could be reduced by expanding plant carbon reservoirs, or "sinks," on land. Under actual circumstances of expanded combustion of fuels and reduction of forest cover, atmospheric carbon dioxide levels have increased from about 280 parts per million (ppm) at the start of the Industrial Revolution to 392 ppm in 2011.

Yearly carbon emissions from energy consumption totaled 18 billion metric tons in 1980, but reached more than 30 billion tons in 2009. China has passed the United States as the single largest emitter (Table 13.1). Per capita emissions vary widely across world regions, mostly reflecting the vast differences in standards of living. For example, an average resident of the United States emits as much carbon dioxide as 52 residents of Ghana. On the other hand, Japan and many European countries achieve high standards of living with much lower per capita carbon emissions. Sweden's per capita carbon emissions are less than one-third of those of the United States, largely due to government and individual commitments to lifestyle and technology changes that promote environmental sustainability (Figure 13.14). Of course, one problem with the statistics in Table 13.1 is that they do not account for the carbon emissions associated with exported or imported products.

Carbon dioxide gets most of the media coverage, but other greenhouse gas concentrations are also increasing (Figure 13.15). Methane levels have increased largely due to agricultural expansion to feed a growing world population. Methane is formed by decomposition processes and is emitted from the intestinal tracts of livestock and from flooded rice paddies. Nitrous oxide emissions are a byproduct of increased fertilizer use, again a consequence of agricultural expansion and intensification.

Figure 13.14 Technologies for reducing greenhouse gas emissions are part of the solution as suggested by the IPAT equation. Many European countries maintain high standards of living with per capita carbon emissions half or one-third that of U.S. residents. Denmark is a world leader in wind energy, generating about 20 percent of its electricity with renewable wind power, mostly in offshore turbine installations. The Beddington Zero Energy Development (BedZed) is one of many examples of an eco-community. At BedZed in South London, passive solar heating, solar panels to generate electricity, a car-sharing club, and rooftop gardens allow residents to reduce significantly or even eliminate their emissions of greenhouse gases.

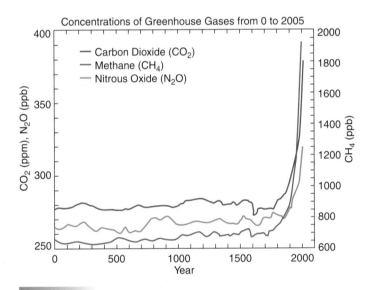

Figure 13.15 Trends in greenhouse gases are upward, and this trend is believed to be due to human activities.

Source: Intergovernmental Panel on Climate Change, Climate Change 2007. The Physical Science Basis, Figure 6-4, 2007.

Warming of the climate system during the 20th and early 21st centuries was unequivocal. The global average temperature increased 0.76°C from the 1850–1899 period to 2001–2005, with an increased rate of warming occurring in the past 50 years (Figure 13.16). The global mean temperature evidence is supported by shrinking glaciers and ice caps, rising sea levels, rising ocean temperatures, and satellite and weather balloon measurements of temperatures above the Earth's surface. The pattern of high and increasing average global temperatures has continued into the present when nearly every year has been among the warmest ever recorded.

The most complete assessment of global climate change is done by the United Nations Intergovernmental Panel on Climate Change (IPCC). The panel, a group of more than 2,000 scientists from around the world that is affiliated with the United Nations and the World Meteorological Organization, was established in 1988 to assess the science of climate change, determine the impact of any changes on the environment and society, and formulate strategies to respond. In 2007, the IPCC issued a "best estimate" global temperature increase of 1.8° to 4°C (3.2° to 7.2°F) over the 21st century. The effects of such an increase on world climates would be profound.

While past climates have fluctuated substantially apart from human influence, the IPPC's 2007 report was at least 90 percent certain that human emissions of greenhouse gases rather than natural variations are responsible for warming the Earth's surface. A 2006 review of available evidence by the federal Climate Change Science Program reached the same conclusion: that there is "clear evidence" of climate change caused by human activities and that trends over the last 50 years "cannot be explained by natural processes alone." Pinpointing the blame, the IPPC reported it was 99 percent sure that humankind's reliance on fossil fuels—coal, fuel oil, and natural gas—was the culprit in global warming.

Climatologists agree on certain of its general consequences in addition to—and the result of—increasing temperatures:

- Arctic summer sea ice is likely to disappear in the second half of the century.
- Sea levels will rise by 28 to 43 cm (11 to 17 in.) by 2100, with an additional 10 to 20 cm (4 to 8 in.) possible if recent accelerated melting of polar ice continues.
- Islands and coastal areas—including densely settled river deltas such as in Bangladesh—will be inundated, affecting the livelihoods and existence of millions.

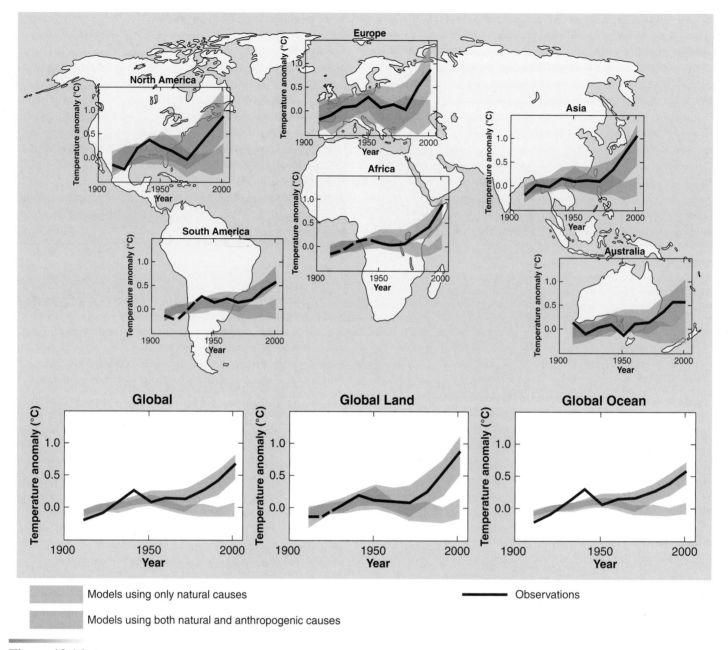

Figure 13.16 Changes in global and continental temperatures. Climate models using only natural causes cannot account for the observed temperature increases experienced on every continent since the second half of the 20th century. Only by incorporating human influences can the models agree with the observed warming. The thickness of the blue and pink bands shows the range of results in different computer simulations using different models.

- There will be spreading droughts in southern Europe, the Middle East, sub-Saharan Africa, the American Southwest, and Mexico.

- Many world regions facing the greatest risk or certainty of adverse environmental change are among the world's poorest; damage and misery will not be evenly shared.

- Many parts of the world will see an increase in the number of heat waves and an increase in the intensity of tropical storms.

- If climate change proceeds as the IPPC projects, there will be mass extinctions of perhaps one-fourth of the world's species within 100 years.

The onset of these and other human-induced environmental changes is clearly evident. For example, from 1979 to 2011, the coverage of Arctic sea ice in winter decreased at a rate of 3.5 percent per decade. Melting sea ice itself would have no effect on sea levels; however, the already significant melting of the Greenland ice sheet and accelerating retreat of mountain glaciers throughout the world is adding to ocean volumes. Already, sea levels that rose between 15 and 20 centimeters (6–9 inches) in the 20th century are causing serious coastal erosion and inundation, and even a conceivable 1-meter (3-foot) rise would be enough to cover the Maldives and other low-lying island countries. The homes of between 50 and 100 million people would be inundated, a fifth of Egypt's arable land in the Nile Delta would be flooded, and the impact on the people of the Bangladesh chars would be catastrophic.

One of the major impacts of global climate change will be on water resources. Warmer temperatures will increase evaporation, precipitation, and the demand for water, intensifying the movement of water through the hydrologic cycle. The prolonged crippling early 21st century droughts in Australia and the American Southwest emphasize the likelihood of the predicted desert advances. In all drought-prone areas of the world, aridity has become more intense and enduring since the 1970s. Earlier IPCC assessments warned that much of the continental interiors of middle latitudes would receive less precipitation than they do now and suffer at least periodic drought, if not absolute aridity. More frequent droughts are likely in the U.S. Corn and Wheat Belts, drastically reducing agricultural productivity and altering world patterns of food supply and trade. Higher temperatures and less snowpack would translate into significantly reduced flows of such western rivers as the Colorado, cutting back the water supply of major southwestern cities and irrigated farming districts. In other world areas, torrential rains and consequent destructive floods of the early 21st century are predicted to increase in severity and frequency. And in many regions, winters no longer get cold enough to kill off a variety of insect pests and diseases formerly kept at lower latitudes and elevations.

Not all the projected impacts of climate change are negative. The IPPC also observed that climate shifts could benefit some regions. It projected more rainfall and longer growing seasons in high latitudes, for example; Canada, Scandinavia, and Siberia will have improved agricultural prospects. In North America, crop patterns could shift northward, making the northern Great Lakes states and Canada the favored agricultural heartland climatically, though without the rich soils of the Corn Belt. On average, some climatologists conclude, established middle and upper-middle latitude farm districts would be net beneficiaries of global warming through longer growing seasons and faster crop growth resulting from extra atmospheric carbon. Skeptics, however, remind us that a scientific rule of thumb is that a 1°C (1.8°F) rise in temperature above the optimum reduces grain yields by 10 percent. Long-term studies clearly document the ratio of temperature rise to yield decline for rice, the staple food for most of the world's expanding population. Greater summer warmth, that is, might reduce, not increase farm productivity.

Because of the effects of decreasing snow and ice cover, higher latitudes will warm faster than equatorial regions. In recent decades, average temperatures in the Arctic have increased almost twice as fast as they have in the rest of the world. Among the consequences of that northward shift of warmth is an already observed 80- to 100-kilometer (50- to 60-mile) poleward shift of the ranges of many animal and bird species. Shifts in structure and distribution of ecosystems and biomes will be inevitable. Arctic seaways will become more open, finally realizing the long-sought and economical Northwest Passage through the northern seas, although the economy and culture of the Inuit will be irreversibly altered at the same time.

Of course, global climate change would have the most severe impact on developing countries that are highly dependent on natural, unmanaged environments for their economic support. Agriculture, hunting and gathering, forestry, and coastal fishing are likely to be more vulnerable than many secondary and tertiary economic activities. Tropical states would be most vulnerable as increased heat and higher evaporation rates would greatly stress wheat, maize, rice, and soybean crops. Global climate change would at the very least disrupt existing patterns of economy, productivity, and population-supporting potential. Certainly, the patterns of climates and biomes developed since the last glaciation would be drastically altered. At the worst, severe and pervasive changes could result in a total restructuring of the present cultural landscapes and human-environmental relationships. Nothing, from population distributions to the relative strength of countries, would ever be quite the same again. Such dire predictions were the background for major international conferences and treaty proposals on global climate change (see the feature "From Kyoto to Durban: Global Climate Change Treaties").

Impacts on Land Cover

The human population growth, agricultural advances, industrialization, and urbanization detailed in the preceding chapters required a massive transformation of the face of the Earth. Humans have always managed to leave their mark on the landscapes that they occupy. The search for minerals, for example, has altered whole landscapes, beginning with the pockmarks and pits marking Neolithic diggings into chalk cliffs to obtain flints or early Bronze Age excavations for tin and culminating with modern open-pit and strip-mining operations that create massive new landforms of depressions and rubble (Figure 13.17). Ancient irrigation systems still visible on the landscape document both the engineering skills and the environmental alterations of early hydraulic civilizations

Figure 13.17 About 400 square kilometers (some 150 square miles) of land surface in the United States are lost each year to the strip mining of coal and other minerals; far more is chewed up worldwide. On flat or rolling terrain, strip mining leaves a landscape of parallel ridges and trenches, the result of stripping away the unwanted surface material. That material—*overburden*—taken from one trench to reach the underlying mineral is placed in an adjacent one, leaving the wavelike terrain shown here. Besides altering the topography, strip mining interrupts surface and subsurface drainage patterns, destroys vegetation, and places sterile and frequently highly acidic subsoil and rock on top of the new ground surface. Current law not always successfully requires stripped areas to be returned to their original contours.

From Kyoto to Durban: Global Climate Change Treaties

Our understanding of global climate change depends upon the cooperative work of scientists from around the world. The IPCC, a group of scientists who review and assess the latest scientific, technical, and socio-economic data on climate change and impacts, is a model of international cooperation on scientific issues of climate change. The IPCC doesn't do the actual research; rather, it reviews thousands of published scientific papers and reports. Working groups within the IPCC take on different tasks such as reviewing the scientific data, assessing vulnerability to climate change, or developing strategies for combatting climate change. The IPCC issued its first assessment report in 1990 and in 2007 released its fourth assessment report.

In 1994, the United Nations established a Framework Convention on Climate Change (UNFCCC) that set up arrangements for sharing data on climate, developing national plans for controlling greenhouse gas emissions, and for adapting to climate change. Three years later in Kyoto, Japan, 191 countries signed and ratified a protocol for combatting global climate change. The Kyoto Protocol called for stabilization of greenhouse gases at levels that would not harm the climate system. The agreement assigned different levels of responsibility to countries based on their level of economic development. Arguing that the developed countries had contributed the largest share to the historic increase in greenhouse gases and were the major emitters, the Kyoto Protocol required more of them. The developed countries committed to reducing their greenhouse gas emissions to below 1990 levels by the year 2012. Developing countries were allowed to increase their emissions to meet social and economic needs, but were given financial supports to encourage emission cuts. The United States signed the protocol, but it remains the only signatory that never ratified the treaty. The United States argued that emission cuts would be damaging to its economy and would not address the growing emissions from developing countries such as China. In 2011, Canada withdrew from the Kyoto Protocol, citing similar reasons. Meanwhile, countries in the European Union have made significant progress in honoring their Kyoto commitments.

World leaders met again in Copenhagen (2009), Cancún, Mexico (2010), and Durban, South Africa (2011). Little progress was made at Copenhagen or Cancún. Negotiations were tense as world leaders debated the trade-offs between economic development and environmental sustainability. The major complicating factor was the highly uneven geographic distributions of both responsibility and vulnerability. As indicated in Table 13.1, the carbon dioxide emissions of a typical American equal those of 50 sub-Saharan Africans. On the other hand, many of the places most vulnerable to climate change, such as the low-lying deltas of Bangladesh and the Sahel of Africa, are in the developing world. Meanwhile, some high-latitude regions, mostly in developed countries, will benefit from a longer growing season in a warmer climate. The Durban meeting ended with a marathon 60-hour negotiation session in which all the developed and developing countries, including China and the United States, agreed to legally binding restrictions on greenhouse gas emissions. The actual amount of those emission cuts was not resolved at Durban. Rather, governments committed to having a new climate agreement ready to be signed by 2015 and to go into effect after 2020.

in the Near East, North Africa, and elsewhere. The raised fields built by the Mayas of the Yucatán are still traceable 1,000 years after they were abandoned, and aerial photography reveals the sites of villages and patterns of fields of medieval England. Large sections of the midlatitudes best suited to agriculture have been nearly completely transformed.

Status as a developed core country seems to entail the partial or nearly complete transformation of the land cover (Figure 13.18). The places least transformed by humans are those too cold, too dry, too high, or in the least developed regions of the world economy. Vast portions of the Earth's surface have been modified, whole ecosystems destroyed, and global biomes altered or eliminated. North American and European native forests have largely vanished; the grasslands of the interior United States, Canada, and Ukraine have been converted to farmland. Marshes and wetlands have been drained, dams built, and major water impoundments created. Steppe lands have become deserts; deserts have blossomed under irrigation.

Tropical Deforestation

Forests, we saw in Chapter 8, still cover some 30 percent of the Earth's land surface, though the forest biomes have suffered mightily as human pressures on them have increased. Forest clearing accompanied the development of agriculture and spread of people throughout Europe, Central Asia, the Middle East, and India. European colonization had much the same impact on the temperate forests of eastern North America and Australasia. In most midlatitude developed countries, although original forest cover is largely gone, replanting and reversion of cropland to timber has tended to replenish woodlands at about their rate of cutting.

Now it is the tropical rain forest biome that is feeling the pressure of growing populations, the need for more agricultural land, and expanded demand for fuel and commercial wood. These disappearing forests—covering no more than 6 percent of the planet's land surface—extend across parts of Asia, Africa, and Latin America, and are the world's most diverse and least understood biome.

Tropical forest removal raises three principal global concerns and a host of local ones. First, on a worldwide basis, all forests play a major role in maintaining the oxygen and carbon balance of the Earth. This is particularly true of tropical forests because of their total area and volume. Humans and their industries consume oxygen; vegetation replenishes it through photosynthesis and the release of oxygen back into the atmosphere as a by-product. At the same time, plants extract carbon dioxide from the atmosphere, regulating the levels of this important greenhouse gas. Each year, each hectare (2.47 acres) of Amazon rain forest absorbs a ton of carbon dioxide. When the tropical rain forest is cleared, not only

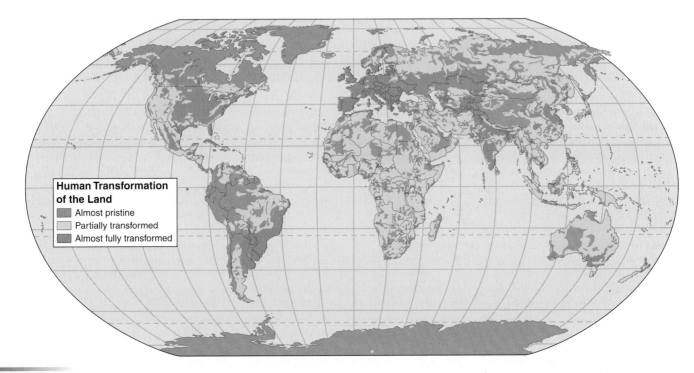

Figure 13.18 **Human transformation of the land.** Humans have altered much of the Earth's surface in some way. The "almost pristine" areas, covered with original vegetation, tend to be too high, dry, cold, or otherwise unsuitable for human habitation in large numbers. They generally have very low population densities. "Partially transformed" describes areas of secondary vegetation, grown after removal of the original cover. Most are used for agriculture or livestock grazing. "Almost fully transformed" areas are those of permanent and intensive agriculture and urban settlement.

Human Transformation of the Land
- Almost pristine
- Partially transformed
- Almost fully transformed

is its role as a carbon sink lost but the act of destruction itself through decomposition or burning releases as carbon dioxide the vast quantities of carbon the forest had stored.

A second global concern is also climate related. Forest destruction changes surface and air temperatures, moisture content, and reflectivity It is calculated that cutting the forests of South America on a wide scale could raise regional temperatures from 3°C to 5°C (5.5° to 9°F), which in turn would extend the dry season and greatly disrupt not only regional but global climates.

In some ways, the most serious long-term global consequence of the eradication of tropical rain forests will be the loss of a major part of the biological diversity of the planet. Of the estimated 5–10 million plant and animal species believed to exist on Earth, a minimum of 40 percent to 50 percent—and possibly 70 percent or more—are native to the tropical rain forest biome. Many of the plants have become important world staple food crops: rice, millet, cassava, yam, taro, banana, coconut, pineapple, and sugarcane, to name but a few well-known ones. Unknown additional potential food species remain as yet unexploited. Reports from Indonesia suggest that in that country's forests alone, some 4,000 plant species have proved useful to native peoples as foodstuffs of one sort or another, though less than one-tenth have come into wide use. The rain forests are, in addition, the world's main storehouse of drug-yielding plants and insects, including thousands with proven or prospective anticancer properties and many widely used as sources of antibiotics, antivirals, analgesics, tranquilizers, diuretics, and laxatives, among a host of other items. The loss of the zoological and botanical storehouse that the rain forests represent would deprive humans of untold potential benefits that might never be realized.

On a more local basis, tropical forests play for their inhabitants and neighbors the same role taken by forests everywhere. They protect watersheds and regulate water flow. After forest cutting, unregulated flow accentuates the problems of high and low water variations, increases the severity of valley flooding, and makes more serious and prolonged the impact of low water flow on irrigation agriculture, navigation, and urban and rural water supply. Accelerated **soil erosion**—the process of removal of soil particles from the ecosystem, usually by wind or running water—quickly removes the always thin, infertile tropical forest soils from deforested areas. Lands cleared for agriculture almost immediately become unsuitable for that use partially because of soil loss. The surface material removed is transported and deposited downstream, changing valley contours, extending the area subject to flooding, and filling irrigation and drainage channels; or it may be deposited in the reservoirs behind the increasing number of major dams on rivers within the tropical rain forests or rising there (see the feature "Dam Trouble in the Developing World").

Desertification

With no intent to destroy or alter the environment, humans are also negatively affecting the arid and semiarid regions of the world. The process is called **desertification,** the expansion or intensification of areas of degraded or destroyed soil and vegetation cover. While the Earth Summit of 1992 defined desertification broadly as "land degradation in arid, semiarid, and dry subhumid areas, resulting from climatic variations and human activities," the process is often blamed on increasing human pressures exerted through

Dam Trouble in the Developing World

By the 1970s, the construction of large dams in the developed countries such as the United States had slowed to a trickle, as the best sites had already been dammed and environmental groups protested the loss of wild rivers. Thus, the focus of dam building shifted to the developing countries. The developing countries have a sizable percentage of the world's undeveloped power potential. The lure of that power and its promise for economic development and national prestige have proved nearly irresistible. China is now the world's leader in large dams and its immense Three Gorges Dam on the Yangtze River is the world's largest hydropower project. China's engineering companies and banks are also actively involved in building large dams in many other developing countries, primarily in Africa and Southeast Asia. The dams (and their reservoirs) often carry a heavy ecological price, and the clearing and development of the areas that they are meant to serve often ensure a shortened life of the dam projects themselves.

The creation of Lake Brokopondo in Suriname in 1964 marked the first large reservoir in a rain forest locale. Without being cleared of their potentially valuable timber, 1,480 square kilometers (570 square miles) of dense tropical forest disappeared underwater. As the trees decomposed, producing hydrogen sulfide, an intolerable stench polluted the atmosphere for scores of miles downwind. For more than two years, employees at the dam wore gas masks at work. Decomposition of vegetation produced acids that corroded the dam's cooling system, leading to costly continuing repairs and upkeep. Identical problems have occurred at the Tucuruí dam and reservoir in Brazil, started in 1984 and covering 2,850 sq. km (1,100 square miles) of uncleared rain forest.

Water hyacinth spreads rapidly in tropical impoundments, its growth hastened by the rich nutrients released by tree decomposition. Within a year of the reservoir's completion, a 130-square-kilometer (50-square-mile) blanket of the weed was afloat on Lake Brokopondo, and after another year, almost half the reservoir was covered. Another 440 square kilometers (170 square miles) were claimed by a floating fern, *Ceratopteris*. Identical problems plague most rain forest hydropower projects.

The expense, the disruption of the lives of valley residents whose homes are to be

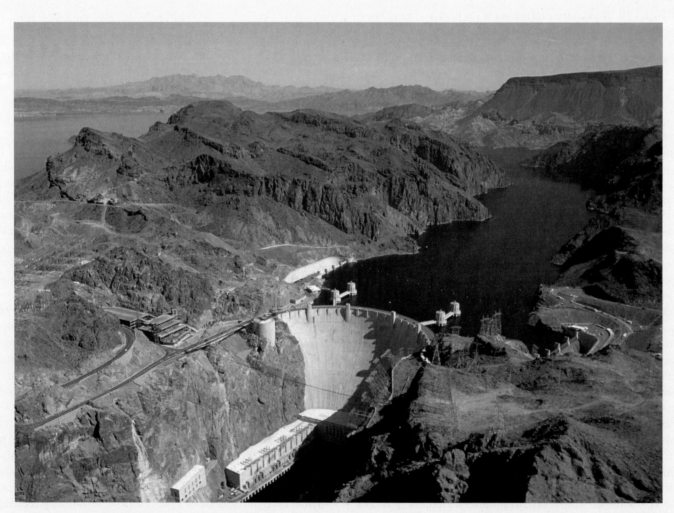

Hoover Dam on the Colorado River, completed in 1935, created a model for the construction of large, hydroelectric dams.

(continued)

flooded, and the environmental damage of dam projects in the rain forest all may be in vain. Deforestation of river banks and clearing of vegetation for permanent agriculture usually results in accelerated erosion, rapid sedimentation of reservoirs, and drastic reduction of electrical generating capacity. The Ambuklao Reservoir in the Philippines, built with an expected payback period of 60 years, now appears certain to silt up in half that time. The Anchicaya Reservoir in Colombia lost 25 percent of its storage capacity only 2 years after it was completed and was almost totally filled with silt within 10 years. The Peligre Dam in Haiti was completed in 1956, with a life expectancy of at least 50 years; siltation reduced its usefulness by some 15 years. El Cajón Dam in Honduras, Arenal in Costa Rica, Chixoy in Guatemala, and many others—all built to last decades or even centuries—have, because of premature siltation, failed to repay their costs or fulfill their promise. The price of deforestation in wet tropics is high indeed.

overgrazing, deforestation for fuel wood, clearing of original vegetation for cultivation, and burning.

Certainly much past periodic desertification of vast areas has been induced by nature rather than by humans. Over the past 10,000 years, for example, several prolonged and severe droughts far more damaging than the "Dust Bowl" period of the 1930s converted vast stretches of the Great Plains from Texas and New Mexico to Nebraska and South Dakota into seas of windblown sand dunes like those of the Sahara. Such conditions were seen most recently in the 18th and 19th centuries, before the region was heavily settled, but after many explorers and travelers noted—as did one in 1796 in present-day Nebraska—"a great desert of drifting sand, without trees, soil, rock, water, or animals of any kind." Today, those same areas in the Great Plains are covered only thinly by vegetation and could revert to shifting desert—as they almost did in the 1930s— with a prolonged drought of the type that might accompany global climate change.

Whether natural or anthropogenic, every year desertification makes 12 million hectares (46,000 square miles) useless for cultivation. Regardless of its causes, it begins in the same fashion: the disruption or removal of the native cover of grasses and shrubs through farming or overgrazing. If the disruption is severe enough, the original vegetation cannot reestablish itself and the exposed soil is made susceptible to erosion during the brief, heavy rains that dominate precipitation patterns in semiarid regions. Water runs off the land surface instead of seeping in, carrying soil particles with it and leaving behind an *erosion pavement*. When the water is lost through surface flow rather than seepage downward, the water table is lowered. Eventually, even deep-rooted bushes are unable to reach groundwater, and all natural vegetation is lost. The process is accentuated when too many grazing animals pack the dirt down with their hooves, blocking the passage of air and water through the soil. When both plant cover and soil moisture are lost, desertification has occurred.

Worldwide, desertification affects about 1 billion people in 110 countries and about 1.2 billion hectares of land—about the size of China and India combined. According to the United Nations—which declared 2006 the "International Year of Deserts and Desertification" to address their problems and solutions— between one-quarter and one-third of the planet's land surface now qualifies as degraded semidesert. Africa is most at risk; the United Nations has estimated that 40 percent of that continent's nondesert land is in danger of human-induced desertification. But nearly a fifth of Latin America's lands and a third of Asia's are similarly endangered. China's Environmental Protection Agency reports, for example, that the country lost 94,000 square kilometers (36,000 square miles)—an area the size of Indiana—to desert from the 1950s to early in the 21st century and each year has an additional 3,900 square kilometers (1,500 square miles) buried by sand.

In countries where desertification is particularly extensive and severe (Algeria, Ethiopia, Iraq, Jordan, Lebanon, Mali, and Niger) per capita food production declined by nearly half between 1950 and 2000, while in the Sahel as a whole, population expanded fourfold between 1930 and 2005, with continuing growth predicted. The resulting threat of starvation spurs populations of the affected areas to increase their farming and livestock pressures on the denuded land, further contributing to their desertification. It has been suggested that Mali may be the first country in the world rendered uninhabitable by environmental destruction. Many of its more than 11 million inhabitants begin their day by shoveling their doorways clear of the night's accumulation of sand (Figure 13.19). The United Nations has identified desertification as a major barrier to poverty elimination in arid regions and has established programs to fight desertification (Figure 13.20).

Soil Erosion

Desertification is but one expression of land deterioration. Over much of the Earth's surface, the thin layer of topsoil upon which life depends is only a few inches deep, usually less than 30 centimeters (1 foot). Below it, the lithosphere is nearly as lifeless as the surface of the moon. **Soil** is a complex mixture of rock particles, inorganic mineral matter, organic material, living organisms, air, and water. Under natural conditions, soil is constantly being formed by the physical and chemical decomposition of rock material and by the decay of organic matter. It is simultaneously being eroded, for soil erosion is as natural a process as soil formation and occurs even when land is totally covered by forests or grass. Under most natural conditions, however, the rate of soil formation equals or exceeds the rate of soil erosion, so soil depth and fertility tend to increase with time.

When land is cleared and planted to crops or when the vegetative cover is broken by overgrazing, deforestation, or other

Figure 13.19 Desertification, affecting about 1 billion people in 110 countries, is the advance of the margins of the world's deserts into their bordering dry lands. In this scene, windblown dust engulfs a scrub forest in a drought-stricken area of Mali, near Timbuktu. This region is part of the Sahel of Africa where desertification is accelerated by both climate fluctuations and human pressures on the land. The Sahara has expanded significantly on its margins over the past century. On an annual basis, the desert margins fluctuate, and some scientists prefer to speak of an "ebb and flow" of the Sahara margins and land degradation rather than permanent conversion to desert.

Figure 13.20 Fighting desertification in Nigeria with a nursery support by the United Nations International Fund for Agricultural Development.

disturbances, the process of erosion inevitably accelerates. When its rate exceeds that of soil formation, the life-sustaining veneer of topsoil becomes thinner and eventually disappears, leaving behind only sterile subsoil or barren rock. At that point the renewable soil resource has been converted through human impact into a nonrenewable and dissipated asset. Carried to the extreme of bare rock hillsides or wind-denuded plains, erosion spells the total end of agricultural use of the land. Throughout history, such extreme human-induced destruction has occurred and been observed with dismay.

Any massive destruction of the soil resource could spell the end of the civilization it had supported. For the most part, however, farmers—even those in difficult climatic and topographic circumstances—devised ingenious ways to preserve and even improve the soil resource on which their lives and livelihoods depended. Particularly when farming was carried on outside of fertile, level valley lands, farmers' practices were routinely based on some combination of crop rotation, fallowing, and terracing.

Rotation involves the planting of two or more crops simultaneously or successively on the same area to preserve fertility or to provide a plant cover to protect the soil. **Fallowing** leaves a field idle (uncropped) for one year or more to achieve one of two outcomes. In semiarid areas, the purpose is to accumulate soil moisture from one year to apply to the next year's crop; in tropical wet regions, as we saw in Chapter 8, the purpose is to renew soil fertility of the swidden plot. **Terracing** replaces steep slopes with a series of narrow-layered, level fields, providing cropland where little or none existed previously. In addition, because water moving rapidly down-slope has great erosive power, breaking the speed of flow by terracing reduces the amount of soil lost. Field trials in Nigeria indicate that cultivation on a 1 percent slope (a drop of 1 foot in elevation over 100 feet of horizontal distance) results in soil loss at or below the rate of soil formation; farming there on a 15 percent slope would totally strip a field of its soil cover in only 10 years.

Pressures on farmlands have increased with population growth and the intensification of agriculture. Farming has been forced higher up on steeper slopes, more forest land has been converted to cultivation, grazing and crops have been pushed farther and more intensively into semiarid areas, and existing fields have had to be worked more intensively and less carefully. Many traditional agricultural systems and areas that were ecologically stable and secure as recently as 1950, when world population stood at 2.5 billion and subsistence agriculture was the rule, are disintegrating under the pressures of 7 billion people and an integrated global economy.

The evidence of that deterioration is found in all parts of the world (Figure 13.21). The International Food Policy Research Institute reports that each year some 10 million hectares (25 million acres) of cropland worldwide are abandoned because of soil erosion and diminished production caused by erosion. Nearly 40 percent of the world's agricultural land is seriously degraded, though the percentages differ by region. Almost 75 percent of cropland in Central America shows serious degradation, as does 11 percent in Asia. In Africa, some 500 million hectares (1.2 billion acres) have been affected by soil erosion since the mid-1950s, including as much as 65 percent of agricultural land, a major factor limiting food production in that continent to, at most, an inadequate 2 percent annual increase.

Soil deterioration expresses itself in two ways: through decreasing yields of cultivated fields themselves and in increased stream sediment loads and downstream deposition of silt. In Guatemala, for example, some 40 percent of the productive capacity of the land has been lost through erosion, and several areas of the country have been abandoned because agriculture has become economically impracticable; the figure is 50 percent in El Salvador. In Turkey, a reported 75 percent of the land is affected,

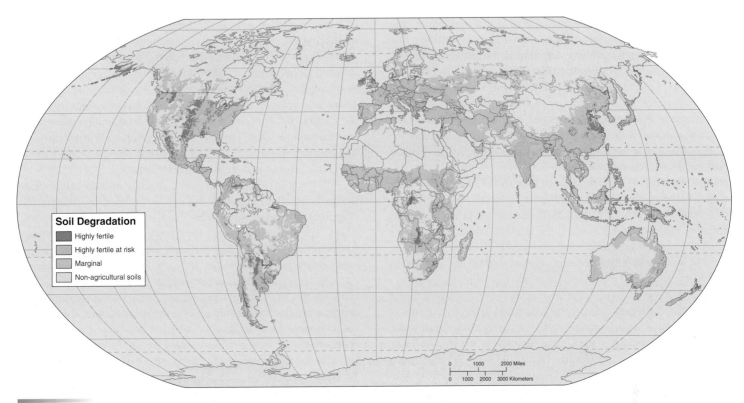

Figure 13.21 The world pattern of soil degradation concern. Between 1945 and 2000, nearly 2 billion hectares (almost 5 billion acres) of the world's 8.7 billion hectares (21.5 billion acres) of cropland, pastures, and forests used in agriculture—an area as large as Russia and India combined—were added to the existing total of degraded soils. Globally, about 18 percent of forest area, 21 percent of pastures, and 37 percent of cropland have undergone moderate to severe degradation. Water erosion accounted for 56 percent of that recorded deterioration, wind erosion for 28 percent, chemical deterioration (salinization and nutrient loss) for 12 percent, and physical degradation (e.g., compaction and waterlogging) for 4 percent.

Map: John L. Allen, Student Atlas of World Geography, *7th edition, McGraw-Hill, p. 124. Data: World Resources Institute and International Soil Reference and Information Center.*

and 54 percent is severely or very severely eroded. Haiti has no high-value soil left at all. A full one-quarter of India's total land area has been significantly eroded: some 13 million hectares (32 million acres) by wind and nearly 74 million hectares (183 million acres) by water. Between 1960 and 2000, China lost more than 15 percent of its total arable land to erosion, desertification, or conversion to nonagricultural use; some 700,000 hectares (1.7 million acres) of cultivated land annually are taken by construction. Its Huang River is the most sediment-laden of any waterway on Earth; in its middle course it is about 50 percent silt by weight, just under the point of liquid mud.

Off-farm erosion evidence is provided by silt loads carried by streams and rivers and by the downstream deposition that results. In the United States, about 3 billion tons of sediment are washed into waterways each year; off-site damage in the form of reduced reservoir capacity, fish kills, dredging costs, and the like, is estimated at over $6 billion annually. The world's rivers deliver about 24 billion tons of sediment to the oceans each year, while additional billions of tons settle along stream valleys or are deposited in reservoirs (see the feature "Dam Trouble in the Developing World").

Agricultural soil depletion through erosion—and through salt accumulation and desertification—has been called "the quiet crisis." It continues inexorably and unfolds gradually, without the abrupt attention attracted by an earthquake or volcanic explosion. Unfortunately, silent or not, productive soil loss is a crisis of growing importance and immediacy, not just in the countries of its occurrence but—because of international markets and relief programs—throughout the world.

Impacts on Water Resources

Water is essential to all life on Earth. Our bodies are about 60 percent water and about 70 percent of the Earth's surface is covered by water. The supply of water is essentially constant, but highly uneven in its distribution. Careful management of water resources, often for irrigation, has been essential to many early human civilizations such as those of Egypt, Mesopotamia, the Indus Valley, and Meso-America (see Figure 2.15). Ancient civilizations that failed to properly manage water resources such as the Anasazi of the American Southwest were subject to collapse (see the feature "Chaco Canyon Desolation" in Chapter 2). Today, managing water resources is critical because rising human populations and increased agricultural, urban, and industrial development have stressed water resources in many regions.

Water Availability

The problem is not with the global amount of water, but with its distribution, its availability, and its quality. The vast majority of water on Earth (96.5 percent) is saltwater found in oceans, seas, and bays, and most freshwater is in ice caps and glaciers. Only about 1 percent of all water is available as liquid fresh water, and most of that is beneath the surface in groundwater **aquifers** that may be difficult and expensive to pump to the surface. Even so, enough rain and snow fall on the continents each year to cover the Earth's total land area with 83 centimeters (33 inches) of water. Observations about global supplies of fresh water ignore the ever-present geographic reality: things are not uniformly distributed over the surface of the Earth. Populations are rising in many regions where water supplies are limited. For example, the Middle East and North Africa are home to 6.3 percent of the world's population but contain only 1.4 percent of the world's renewable fresh water. Arizona, Nevada, and Utah were the three fastest-growing U.S. states between 2000 and 2010 and are all in arid/semiarid climates. Compounding matters, the demand for water by natural processes of evaporation and transpiration varies spatially as well. In hot, dry subtropical deserts annual evaporation may equal 250 centimeters (100 inches) of water per year or more.

For thousands of years, human cultures have responded to the uneven distribution of water in both time and space by constructing small dams and diversion canals for irrigation. During the height of the Depression, the United States built the Hoover Dam (1931–1936) and Grand Coulee Dam (1933–1942); they were bold engineering feats that raised dams to unprecedented heights and impounded enormous volumes of water. These dams generate large quantities of low-cost, renewable, hydroelectric power for cities and industry, and their reservoirs provide a reliable supply of water for cities and agriculture. Perhaps more significantly, these dams established a model for economic development of arid regions based on large water engineering projects. That model has diffused globally, promoted by international aid agencies and seen as prestigious symbols of development by developing countries. There are many economic, social, and environmental costs of large dams, but they are still being built in developing countries (see the feature "Dam Trouble in the Developing World" earlier in this chapter). Today, the flow in more than half the world's major rivers has been altered significantly by dams.

Within the hydrologic cycle, surface runoff takes place within basins or watersheds that are determined by topography; ridgelines divide the waters flowing toward different streams and rivers. Thus, river basins are the primary areal unit to use when studying water. We can then calculate and compare the quantity of renewable water available per person within different river basins. Areas of high water stress are defined as those with less than 1,000 cubic meters of water per person per year. Of course, not all of this water is needed for human consumption. Rather, it is needed for producing food, sanitation, industry, and other essential uses. As of 1995, 1.7 billion persons lived in highly stressed river basins and that population is conservatively estimated to increase to 3.5 billion persons by 2025 (Figure 13.22).

In North America, two large river basins with potential water stress are the Colorado and the Rio Grande, both in the Southwest and both reduced to a trickle at times by diversions

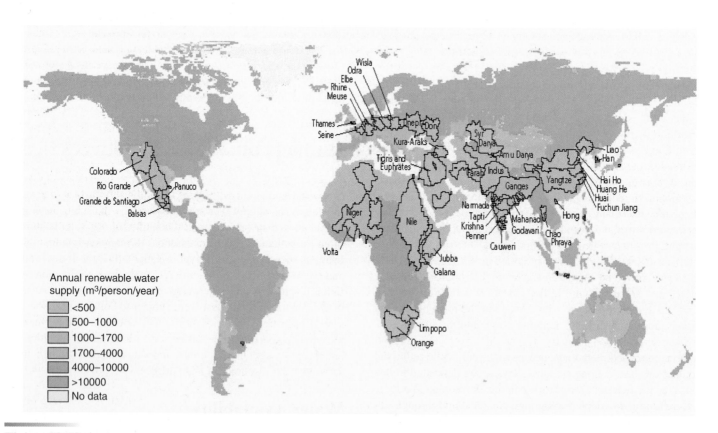

Figure 13.22 **Renewable water supplies per person in 2025.** This conservative analysis by river basins shows much of the world experiencing water stress, defined as areas with less than 1,700 cubic meters per person per year. Highly stressed river basins are those with less than 1,000 cubic meters of water per person per year. The Rio Grande basis is predicted to be highly stressed and the Colorado River basin stressed.

Source: World Resources Institute, 2007.

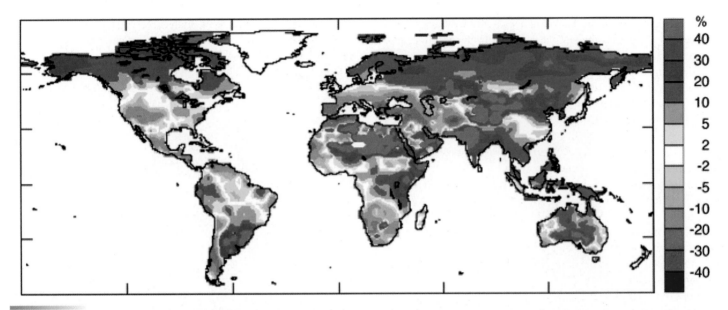

Figure 13.23 **Predicted change in annual runoff** by the mid-21st century compared to 1900–1970. This map from the IPCC report is based on 12 global climate model simulations using middle-range assumptions about greenhouse gas emissions. A substantial reduction in water availability is predicted for a number of already dry regions such as the American Southwest, Mexico, southern Africa, southern Europe, northern Africa, and the Middle East.

Source: Intergovernmental Panel on Climate Change, 2007. Climate Change 2007: Working Group II: Impacts, Adaptation, and Vulnerability, *Figure 3.4.*

for agriculture and cities. Complicating management of the limited water supplies of the Colorado and the Rio Grande is the fact that they are international rivers shared by the United States and Mexico. International treaties govern the obligations of each country with respect to quantity and quality of the river's waters. **Transboundary river basins**—basins straddling two or more countries—cover an estimated 40 percent of the Earth's land area and contain more than 60 percent of the world's population.

Water conflict is a distinct possibility when a substance so essential to life is shared by more than one country. Notable transboundary rivers with potential conflicts include the Indus, Jordan, Nile, and Tigris-Euphrates. The Indus has its source in India but provides irrigation water essential to Pakistan's food supply. Despite a series of wars between India and Pakistan, the two countries continue to observe a negotiated treaty regarding the waters of the Indus. The Jordan River basin takes in parts of Israel, Jordan, Lebanon, the Palestinian Territories, and Syria and has major issues related to scarcity and international security. In fact, the amount of renewable water available per person is below recommended minimums in Israel, Jordan, and Palestine. The Nile River drains 10 countries in Africa and is subject to colonial-era treaties that some believe favor Egypt over the upstream countries such as Ethiopia. The Tigris-Euphrates was among the birthplaces of civilization and today is shared by Turkey, Syria, and Iraq, each with their own water development objectives. Yet, despite the very real possibility of water wars, international cooperation has been more common than hostilities.

The climate system and hydrosphere are intimately connected. Climate change is likely to alter the hydrologic cycle, increasing both the demand for water and annual precipitation in many areas. Climate models forecast altered patterns of water availability with increased dryness in many areas already subject to water scarcity (Figure 13.23). Of particular concern is the American Southwest

and Indus Basin, where growing populations will need to adapt to declining water supplies. In both regions, declining snowpack in the mountains will lead to decreased river flow in the dry season.

Water supplies and energy supplies are intimately connected. If energy supplies were unlimited, so too would be water supplies. The ocean offers almost unlimited water supplies but making that water drinkable requires expensive, energy-intensive desalination. The world's largest desalination plants are in the Middle East, where water is scarce and energy supplies are abundant. Wastewater reclamation, also quite expensive, is the treatment of sewage so that it can be reused for irrigation or as a drinking water source. For cities in desert regions, their own sewage is often the last remaining untapped water resource. Australia, Israel, Singapore, Florida, and Southern California are leaders in the use of reclaimed water. Use of reclaimed sewage for drinking water was used in the space program and is now growing in acceptance for city supplies. Water reclamation for drinking water uses ultrafiltration technologies and reinjection into aquifers to address health concerns.

Water Use and Abuse

Water supplies and food supplies are intimately connected. Irrigation uses about three-fourths of all water used by humans and a higher percentage in the least developed countries. Irrigation agriculture produces some 40 percent of the world's total harvest and 60 percent of its grain from about 17 percent of its cropland. The productivity gains of the Green Revolution depended on an expansion of irrigation, as will future increases in the food supply. In dry climates, rivers and lakes have shrunk or even disappeared due to irrigation demands. The Aral Sea in Kazakhstan and Uzbekistan was once the world's fourth-largest lake by area before irrigation diversions caused it to shrink by 90 percent

(a)

(b)

Figure 13.24 **Aral Sea decline.** (a) This map from 1975 shows the original extent of the sea when it was the fourth-largest inland sea in the world. (b) In this satellite image from 2005, the Aral Sea has shrunk due to diversions of water for irrigated agriculture. Water levels have declined by 18 meters (59 feet), causing the lake to split into two parts. Fishing, port, and resort towns are now 80 kilometers (49.6 miles) or farther from the water. The remaining flow into the sea is contaminated by agricultural runoff, yielding a toxic, salty brine. Dust storms whip up particulates and toxic chemicals from the dry lake bed. Restoration work is being done on the Little Aral Sea in the north in Kazakhstan.

Source: EROS Data Center, United States Geological Survey.

(Figure 13.24). Groundwater can be used unsustainably if it is pumped faster than it is replenished by natural infiltration. In the United States, a major concern is the dropping groundwater levels in the Ogallala Aquifer, which provides irrigation water for agriculture in eight Great Plains states.

When humans introduce wastes into the biosphere in kinds and amounts that the natural system cannot neutralize or recycle, the result is **environmental pollution.** In the case of water, pollution exists when water composition has been so modified by the presence of one or more substances that either it cannot be used for a specific purpose or it is less suitable for that use than it was

in its natural state. In both developed and developing countries, human pressures on freshwater supplies are now serious and pervasive concerns (see the feature "A World of Water Woes").

Water pollution can come in a variety of forms. Human wastes often contain infectious agents that cause waterborne diseases such as cholera, dysentery, and typhoid fever. Waterborne diseases kill an estimated 1.5 million persons each year, largely due to lack of sanitation, sewage treatment, and/or access to safe drinking water supplies. An estimated 1.2 billion people around the world lack safe drinking water supplies. Thus, one of the United Nations' Millennium Development Goals (MDGs) is to

A World of Water Woes

Water covers almost three-quarters of the surface of the globe, yet *scarcity* is the word increasingly used to describe water-related concerns in both the developed and developing world. Globally, fresh water is abundant. Each year, an average of over 7,000 cubic meters (some 250,000 cubic feet) per person enters rivers and underground reserves. But rainfall does not always occur when or

where it is needed. Already, 80 countries with 40 percent of the world's population have serious water shortages that threaten to cripple agriculture and industry; 22 of them have renewable water resources of less than 1,000 cubic meters (35,000 cubic feet) per person—a level generally understood to mean that water scarcity is a severe constraint on the economy and public health. Another

18 countries have less than 2,000 cubic meters per capita on average, a dangerously low figure in years of rainfall shortage. Most of the water-short countries are in the Middle East, North Africa, and sub-Saharan Africa, the regions where populations (and consumption demands) are growing fastest. By 2025, two-thirds of the world's people are likely to be living in areas of acute water stress.

(continued)

In several major crop-producing regions, water use exceeds sustainable levels, threatening future food supplies. The largest underground water reserve in the United States, stretching from west Texas northward into South Dakota, is drying up, partially depleted by more than 150,000 wells pumping water for irrigation, city supply, and industry. In parts of Texas, Oklahoma, and Kansas, the underground water table has dropped by more than 30 meters (100 feet). In some areas, the wells no longer yield enough to permit irrigation, and farmed land is decreasing; in others, water levels have fallen so far that it is uneconomical to pump it to the surface for any use.

In many agricultural districts of northern China, west and south India, and Mexico, water scarcity limits agriculture even though national supplies are adequate. In Uzbekistan and adjacent sections of Central Asia and Kazakhstan, virtually the entire flow of the area's two primary rivers—the Amu Darya and the Syr Darya—is used for often wasteful irrigation, with little left to maintain the Aral Sea or supply growing urban populations. In Poland, the draining of bogs that formerly stored rainfall, combined with unimaginable pollution of streams and groundwater, has created a water shortage as great as that of any Middle Eastern desert country. And salinity now seriously affects productivity— or prohibits farming completely—on nearly 10 percent of the world's irrigated lands.

Water scarcity is often a regionwide concern. More than 200 river systems draining over half the Earth's land surface are shared by two or more countries. Egypt draws on the Nile for 86 percent of its domestic consumption, but virtually all that water originates in eight upstream countries. Turkey, Iraq, and Syria have frequently been in dispute over the management of the Tigris and Euphrates rivers, and the downstream states fear the effect on them of Turkish impoundments and diversions. Mexico is angered at the U.S. depletion of the Colorado River before it reaches the international border.

Many coastal communities face saltwater intrusions into their drinking water supplies as they draw down their underlying freshwater aquifers, while both coastal and inland cities dependent on groundwater may be seriously depleting their underground supplies. In China, 110 mostly large cities face acute water shortages; for at least 50 of them, the problem is groundwater levels dropping on average 1 to 2 meters (3 to 6 feet) each year. In Mexico City, groundwater is pumped at rates 40 percent faster than natural recharge; the city has responded to those withdrawals by sinking 30 feet during the 20th century. Millions of citizens of major cities throughout the world have had their water rationed as underground and surface supplies are used beyond recharge or storage capacity.

cut in half the proportion of the population without access to safe drinking water and basic sanitation. The world regions that lag behind are sub-Saharan Africa and southern Asia, although all world regions are making substantial progress (Figure 13.25). The expansion of cities places additional burdens of sewage discharges on rivers, bays, and estuaries. However, it is easier to provide sewage treatment and safe drinking water when populations are clustered as in urban areas. Sanitation improvements and sewage treatment have been major components of modernization and the demographic transition, but currently lag in rural areas of the developing world.

Agriculture is the leading cause of poor water quality in the rivers of most countries. Large confined animal feeding operations and fertilizer additions to fields have contributed to rising agricultural productivity. However, both practices lead to excessive nutrients in runoff that create coastal **dead zones** (Figure 13.26). These "dead" zones have little or no oxygen because they are choked with decaying algae that grew on the nutrient rich runoff from agricultural lands. The largest dead zones are found where rivers draining rich agricultural regions discharge to coastal bays or estuaries, such as the mouth of the Mississippi River in the Gulf of Mexico (Figure 13.27).

Wastes

Humans have always managed to leave their mark on the landscapes that they occupy. Among the most enduring of landscape evidences of human occupancy is the garbage produced and discarded by every society. Prehistoric dwelling sites are located and analyzed by their *middens,* the refuse piles containing the kitchen wastes, broken tools, and other debris of human settlement. We have learned much about Roman and medieval European urban life by examination of the refuse mounds that grew as man-made hills in their vicinities. In the Near East, whole cities gradually rose on the mounds of debris accumulating under them (see Figure 11.9).

Modern cultures differ from their predecessors by the volume and character of their wastes, not by their habits of discard. Generally, the greater the society's population and standard of living, the greater the quantity of its garbage. Developed countries are increasingly discovering that their material wealth and technological advancements are submerging them in a volume and variety of wastes—solid and liquid, harmless and toxic—that threaten both their environments and their established ways of life.

Solid Wastes

Americans produce rubbish, garbage, and other municipal waste at a rate of about 2 kilograms (4.5 pounds) per person per day. As populations grow, incomes rise, and consumption patterns change, the volume of disposable materials continues to expand. Relatively little residue is created in subsistence societies that move food from garden to table, and wastes from table to farm animals or compost heaps. The problem comes with urban dwellers who purchase packaged foods, favor plastic wrappings and containers for every commodity, and seek (and can afford) an ever-broadening array of manufactured goods, both consumer durables

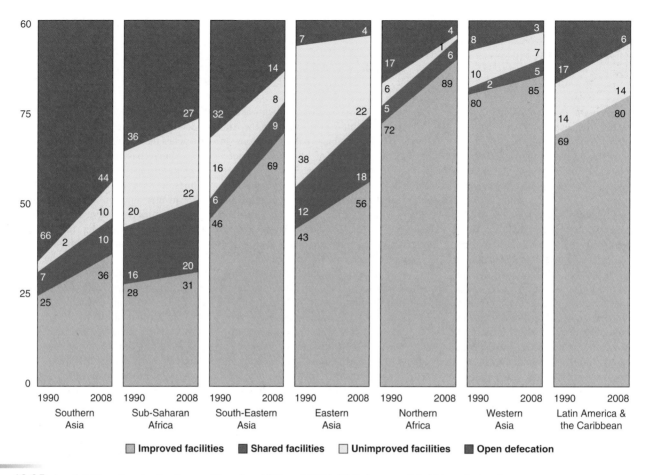

Figure 13.25 **Availability of sanitation by world region, 1990 and 2008.** While improved facilities (flush toilets and sewage disposal systems) are the norm in developed countries, only 52 percent of people in developing regions have access to this level of sanitation. The United Nations MDGs call for cutting in half the proportion without improved sanitation. Substantial progress on sanitation was made between 1990 and 2008, promising major benefits for human health.

Figure 13.26 This slum in Mumbai, India, sits atop a drainage channel and lacks access to clean water and sanitation. Waterborne diseases, mostly stemming from water supplies contaminated with human wastes, are estimated to cause 1.5 million deaths a year.

such as refrigerators and automobiles and many designed for single use and quick disposal.

The fastest growing category of waste is electronic waste (or e-waste), thanks to the rapid innovation in information and communications technologies. Products are often designed to be cheaper to replace than repair. New models of cell phones, computers, televisions, digital cameras, iPods, and iPads create massive quantities of obsolete electronics. They are added to the growing pile of fax machines, computer printers, VCRs, and cathode ray tube televisions and computer monitors. E-waste differs from other consumer waste in that it contains toxic metals such as arsenic, cadmium, lead, and mercury. In most locations, disposal of e-waste in municipal trash is forbidden, although still widely practiced.

The first priorities for solid waste management should be, in order, waste reduction, reuse, and recycling. Beyond that the remaining options for solid wastes are generally landfills or incineration. Landfills are an improvement

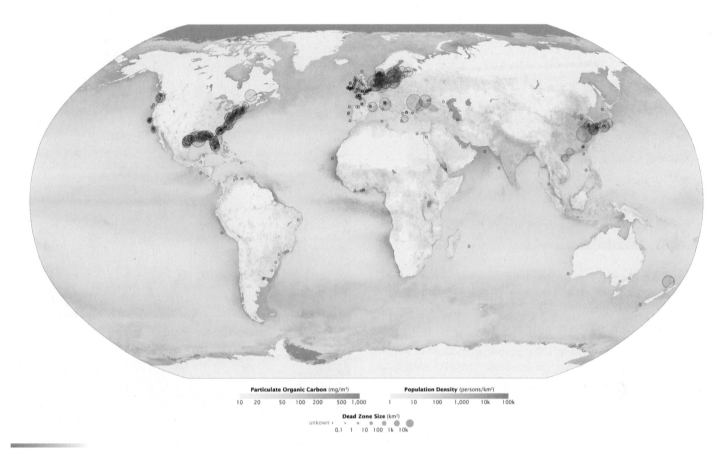

Figure 13.27 **Coastal dead zones** are places so low in dissolved oxygen that most marine life cannot survive. Nutrients in sewage and agricultural runoff are the most common culprit. Note the prevalence of dead zones where populations are highest in the developed countries.

over the unregulated, open dumps they replaced and receive the bulk of solid wastes in most countries. The solid wastes are compacted inside a lined cell and covered with soil at the end of each day. Still, groundwater contamination due to water infiltration through the waste is a major technical challenge to address. Beyond technical details, an increasing problem is where to locate a landfill since most communities will protest, expressing **Not in My Backyard (NIMBY)** sentiments.

Over the years, of course, many filled dumps have posed problems for the cities that gave rise to them. New York City, for example, for years placed all of its daily 14,000 tons of residential waste into the world's largest dump, Fresh Kills on Staten Island. Opened in 1947 as a three-year "temporary" 500-acre facility, it became a malodorous 1,214 hectares (3,000 acres) of decomposing garbage rising 15 stories above the former ground level. Generating 140,000 cubic meters (5 million cubic feet) of methane gas annually and illegally exuding contaminated water, Fresh Kills—finally closed in 2001 at a cost of more than $1 billion—symbolized the rising tide of waste engulfing cities and endangering the environment.

Incineration recovers some of the energy in waste by burning it to produce steam or electricity. Incinerators produce air pollution, including highly toxic metals and organic compounds such as dioxin,[1] so pollution control equipment is required. As with

landfills, proposing a location for a solid waste incinerator often leads to community resistance.

For coastal communities around the world the ocean has long been the preferred sink for not only municipal garbage, but for (frequently untreated) sewage, industrial waste, and all the detritus of an advanced urban society. Along the Atlantic coast of North America from Massachusetts to Chesapeake Bay, reports of dead dolphins, raw sewage, tar balls, used syringes, vials of contaminated blood and hospital waste, diapers, plastic products in unimagined amounts and varieties, and other foul refuse has kept swimmers from the beach, closed coastal shellfisheries, and elicited health warnings against entering the water (Figure 13.28).

Whether the solution to solid waste disposal is sought by land, by fire, or by sea, humanity's rising tide of refuse threatens to overwhelm the environments that must deal with it. The problems that continue to surface remind us that the Earth's environmental systems are interrelated, so that all too often, our solutions simply move the problem from the land to the sea or air or groundwater. The problem is present, growing, and increasingly costly to manage. Solutions are still to be found, a constant reminder for the future of the threatening impact of the environments of culture upon those of nature.

Toxic Wastes

The problems of municipal and household solid-waste management are daunting; those of treatment and disposal of hazardous chemical or radioactive wastes from industry seem overwhelming.

---

[1]Any of several types of hydrocarbon compounds that are extremely toxic, persistent in the environment, and biologically magnified in the food chain. Dioxin is often formed during incineration of waste matter.

Figure 13.28 Warning signs and beaches littered with sewage, garbage, and medical debris are among the increasingly common and distressing evidences of ocean dumping of wastes.

Hazardous wastes are substances that pose an immediate or long-term risk to human health or the environment. The EPA has classified more than 400 substances as hazardous, and currently about 10 percent of industrial waste materials are so categorized.

Prior to the introduction of strict regulations governing the transportation and disposal of hazardous wastes in the 1970s, hazardous wastes were often dumped or buried in pits or lagoons, leading to groundwater contamination. Today, they are disposed of in highly regulated incinerators or lined landfills designed to prevent the release of contaminants to the environment.

Radioactive Wastes

Every facility that either uses or produces radioactive materials generates at least *low-level waste,* material whose radioactivity will decay to safe levels in 100 years or less. Nuclear power plants, industries that manufacture radiopharmaceuticals, smoke alarms, and other consumer goods, and research establishments, universities, and hospitals also produce low-level radioactive waste materials.

High-level waste can remain radioactive for 10,000 years and more; plutonium stays dangerously radioactive for 240,000 years. It consists primarily of spent fuel assemblies of nuclear power reactors—termed "civilian waste"—and such "military waste" as the by-products of nuclear weapons manufacture. The volume of civilian waste accumulates rapidly because approximately one-third of a reactor's rods need to be disposed of every year.

"Spent fuel" is a misleading term: the assemblies are removed from commercial reactors not because their radiation is spent, but because they have become too radioactive for further use. The assemblies will remain radioactively "hot" for thousands of years. By 2009, 63,000 metric tons of accumulated nuclear waste (spent fuel) was in storage in the containment pools or above ground in dry casks at America's 103 commercial nuclear power reactors, awaiting a more permanent solution (Figure 13.29). Stored spent fuel rods were among the most serious concerns and sources of radiation releases when the Fukushima nuclear power plant in Japan was hit by an earthquake and tsunami in 2011. Spent fuel is not

(a)

(b)

Figure 13.29 Spent nuclear fuel from nuclear power plants continues to generate heat and emit radiation long after it is removed from the reactor. *(a)* Initially after it is removed, spent fuel is stored in water-filled pools equipped with continuously circulating water baths to keep it from overheating. Spent fuel remains in the cooling water a year or longer before it can be transferred to *(b)* aboveground dry casks stored at the nuclear reactor site. The lack of a permanent disposal solution in the United States means spent fuel continues to accumulate at nuclear power plants. Stored spent nuclear fuel was one of the causes of radiation releases at the Fukushima nuclear plant in Japan when an earthquake and tsunami knocked out power to the water pumping systems.

contained as well as the fuel rods inside reactors, so they must be constantly covered in cool water to prevent overheating.

The U.S. Department of Energy spent two decades developing plans for a centralized nuclear waste depository inside Yucca Mountain in the desert 90 miles from Las Vegas, Nevada. The plan was to encase the radioactive waste in extremely strong glass inside steel canisters beneath 300 meters (1,000 feet) of volcanic rock. Local opponents to the plan pointed out the potential for accidents in shipment or earthquakes in the area and succeeded in having the project scrapped. No alternative, permanent disposal

Geography and Citizenship

Environmental Justice

In Houston, a city of some 2 million people, about 25 percent of the population is African American. Yet, when researchers examined the placement of garbage facilities in the city, they found that 11 of 13 solid waste disposal facilities owned by the city were in mostly black areas and all five of the city's garbage incinerators were in black and Hispanic neighborhoods. Thus, when the city proposed establishing a new dump in a primarily black neighborhood in 1979, near houses and a high school, local residents protested and brought the waste management company to court, charging it with racial discrimination in the selection of the landfill site. The court decided in favor of the company, and the landfill was built.

In 1982, a few states away, in Warren County, North Carolina, the rural, mostly African American residents were shocked to learn that the state was proposing their county as the site of a hazardous waste landfill for disposing of polychlorinated biphenyls (PCBs). Their protests resulted in more than 500 arrests, and the effort to block the landfill failed. The Warren County activists were the first to use the term "environmental racism."

Environmental racism refers to any policy or practice that differentially affects or harms individuals, groups, or communities because of their race or color. The harm may be intentional or unintentional. *Environmental justice* is the fair treatment and meaningful involvement of all people regardless of race, color, national origin, or income with respect to the development, implementation, and enforcement of environmental laws, regulations, and policies. No group of people should bear a disproportionate share of negative environmental consequences. In many cases, environmental racism and injustice result from long-established and unexamined structural inequality: those who have a reduced political voice compared to the dominant groups in society live in the worst environments because authorities and companies have faced little opposition in placing hazardous facilities, such as landfills, in their vicinity.

The problem is not confined to the United States. In most countries, poorer people and minorities tend to live in areas that are disproportionately exposed to polluting industries, waste disposal facilities, toxic soils, and polluted air and water, in. In Kagiso township, southwest of Johannesburg, South Africa, poor African residents live near a gold mine. In the past, when the gold was extracted from the ore, the waste product was pumped into a waste pile a distance from the residential area. However, the pile was eventually expanded to the extent that it now lies less than 27.4 meters (30 yards)—or less than half the length of a typical city block—from some of the houses. The drying waste produces dust that is high in alpha quartz particles, or silica, which cause silicosis. The inhalation of silica causes lung disease characterized by shortness of breath, fever, and cyanosis, and it also leaves its victims susceptible to tuberculosis. The condition is irreversible. The township is dominated by "informal" housing, which has few city services, is overcrowded, and has poor sanitation; it includes areas that were set aside for black Africans during apartheid.

The United States has taken some steps to rectify the wrongs of environmental injustice. Following the Warren County, North Carolina, protests, President Bill Clinton signed an executive order that made environmental justice a national priority and directed all federal agencies to develop policies to reduce environmental inequity, in 1992, the EPA established an Office of Environmental

Poverty and Environmental Risk *The distribution of household income and facilities that release toxic materials in Santa Clara County, California. Black lines represent census tracts. (Source: Data from M.R. Meusar and A. Szosz "Environmental Inequality in Silicon Valley." www. mapcnjzin .com/EI/index.hmi.)*

Equity (now called the Office of Environmental Justice). The agency, however, has had an uneven record since its founding. Organizations outside the government continue to call attention to disturbing conditions often using a geographic information systems (GIS) to identify inequalities.

Consider Louisiana's Chemical Corridor, or Cancer Alley, a 130-kilometer (80-mile) stretch of the Mississippi River that is home to a chemical plant every half mile and a predominantly poor, African American population. While community groups protested a proposed new polyvinyl chloride (PVC) plant, the state government gave the owners tax exemptions. The EPA delayed the new plant's permit until the state addressed the citizens' environmental justice concerns. In the end, the owners bowed to community opposition and built the new plant 48 kilometers (30 miles) upstream, which may represent a Pyrrhic victory because the plant will still contaminate the air and water nearby.

Environmental injustice has its origins both in neglect and overt discrimination.

There are many instances of intentional placement of environmentally hazardous plants and waste sites in areas already home to minorities and the poor. Government attempts to address the issue of environmental injustice have had an uneven track record. A body of case law regarding environmental justice in the United States has not developed yet, and some scholars contend that, because the issue falls between civil rights law and environmental law, development will continue only slowly.

Questions to Consider

1. Environmentally hazardous institutions—landfills, chemical plants, factories—have to be placed somewhere. How should communities and governments make decisions about the relative merits of different sites? Should the activism of local populations affect government decisions?

2. How would you or your college or university react if a company wanted to site a new landfill for toxic wastes nearby?

3. Where are landfills, polluting industries, and other environmental hazards located in your hometown or where you attend school? Are low-income residents and minorities exposed to greater-than-average amounts of pollution and thus bearing greater health risks than the rest of the population?

Adapted from: Getis and Getis, *Introduction to Geography*, 12th ed., McGraw-Hill, 2008, 326–327.

---

method has been devised. Much low-level radioactive waste has been placed in tanks and buried in the ground at 13 sites operated by the U.S. Department of Energy and three sites run by private firms. Millions of cubic feet of high-level military waste are temporarily stored in underground tanks at four sites: Hanford, Washington; Savannah River, South Carolina; Idaho Falls, Idaho; and West Valley, New York. Several of these storage areas have experienced leaks, with seepage of waste into the surrounding soil and groundwater. Nuclear power plants continue to store spent fuel on site.

Exporting Wastes

The problem with throwing away wastes is that on Earth, there is no true "away." The Earth's atmosphere, hydrosphere, lithosphere, and biosphere are all interrelated, and every place is somebody's backyard. Almost everywhere that governments or industries have proposed to build landfills, hazardous waste incinerators, or nuclear waste repositories, communities and NIMBY movements have arisen in opposition. As a consequence, unwanted facilities such as these tend to be located in places where there is the least community resistance and least political power, often low-income, minority communities (See the feature "Geography and Citizenship: Environmental Justice").

In a leaked 1991 memorandum, World Bank chief economist Larry Summers shared his opinion that it made perfect economic sense to encourage the movement of dirty industries to poor countries. He argued that residents of less developed countries were less likely to be concerned about the environment, and if they suffered negative health effects from pollution, the economic cost would be lower because their wages were so much lower. He wrote, "I think the economic logic behind dumping a load of toxic waste in the lowest-wage country is impeccable, and we should face up to that."[2]

Regulations, community resistance, and steeply rising costs of disposal of hazardous wastes in the developed countries

encouraged producers of those unwanted commodities to seek alternate areas for their disposal. Transboundary shipments of dangerous wastes became an increasingly attractive option for producers, continuing the globalization of the world economy. In total, such cross-border movement amounted to tens of thousands of shipments annually by the early 1990s, with destinations including debt-ridden Eastern European countries and impoverished developing ones outside of Europe that were willing to trade a hole in the ground for hard currency. It was a trade, however, that increasingly aroused the ire and resistance of destination countries and, ultimately, elicited international agreements among both generating and receiving countries to cease the practice.

The Organization of African Unity (OAU) adopted a 1988 resolution condemning the dumping of all foreign wastes on that continent. Under the sponsorship of the United Nations, 117 countries adopted a treaty—the Basel Convention on the Control of Transboundary Movements of Hazardous Wastes—aimed at regulating the international trade in wastes. That regulation was to be achieved by requiring exporters to obtain consent from receiving countries before shipping waste and by requiring both exporter and importer countries to ensure that the waste would be disposed of in an environmentally sound manner. The Basel Convention came into force in 1992, but the United States has not yet ratified it.

The European Union only allows its members to export hazardous wastes to developed countries which are assumed to have satisfactory treatment capabilities. However, the lack of global ratification of the Basel Convention means that export of hazardous wastes to developing countries continues.

The line between reusable products and wastes is often fuzzy and depends on local standards of living and costs of labor. Thus, obsolete manufactured goods and recyclable materials are often shipped from high-income countries to low-income developing countries for the labor-intensive and potentially dangerous tasks of sorting, disassembly, and recycling. An estimated 80 percent of e-waste collected in the United States for recycling is exported to areas such as China, India, Pakistan, Nigeria, and Mexico. Reports warn of environmental pollution and accidental toxic exposures due to the unregulated recycling of e-waste in low-income countries.

---

[2]Quoted from David Harvey, *Justice, Nature, and the Geography of Difference*, 366, 2006.

Future Prospects and Perspectives

Not surprisingly, the realities of the human impacts upon the environment that we have looked at in this chapter bring us directly back to ideas first presented in Chapter 2, at the start of our examination of culture and the development of human geographic patterns on the surface of the Earth. Humans, in their increasing numbers, growing technical sophistication, rising standards of living, and expanding global reach, have transformed the Earth's landscapes since the end of the last glaciation. Humans have adopted a domineering role in the human-environment relationship, all too often forgetting that they depend upon the environment for their very existence.

That dominance reflected itself in the growing divergence of human societies as they separated themselves from common hunting-gathering origins. In creating their differing cultural solutions to common concerns of sustenance and growth, societies altered the environments they occupied. Diverse systems of exploitation of the environment were developed in and diffused from distinctive culture hearths. They were modified by the ever-expanding numbers of people occupying Earth areas of differing carrying capacities and available resources. Gradually developing patterns of spatial interaction and exchange did not halt the creation of distinctive regional subsystems of culture or assure common methods of utilization of unequally distributed Earth resources or environments. Sharp contrasts in levels of economic development and well-being emerged and persisted even as cultural convergence through shared technology began increasingly to unite societies throughout the world.

Each culture placed its imprint on the environment it occupied. In many cases—Chaco Canyon and Easter Island were our earlier examples—that imprint was ultimately destructive of the resources and local environments upon which the cultures developed and depended. To satisfy their felt needs, humans have learned to manipulate their environment. The greater those needs and the larger the populations with both needs and technical skills to satisfy them, the greater is the manipulation of the natural landscape. Paralleling the global reach of the world economy, the human impact on the environment has shifted scales from the local or regional to the continental and global scales. Increasingly, the most pressing environmental issues are those that cross international boundaries, such as depletion of the ozone layer, acid precipitation, global climate change, managing transboundary river basins, and transboundary shipment of wastes. This final chapter, detailing a few of the damaging pressures placed upon the environment by today's economies and cultures, is not meant as a litany of despair. Rather, it is a reminder of the potentially destructive ecological dominance of humans alongside examples of humans learning to work together to reduce their impacts. The world's diverse religions, belief systems, and cultures can each offer resources to guide human behavior in ways that are more respectful of the Earth. The scientific and technological advances that lie behind many of our environmental problems can also be used to monitor and restore the environment.

Against the background of our now fuller understanding of human geographic patterns and interactions, this chapter is also meant to remind us yet again of the often repeated truism that everything is connected to everything else; we can never do just *one* thing. The ecological crises described in this chapter show how intimately our created environment is joined to the physical landscape we all share. There is growing awareness of those connections, of the adverse human impacts upon the natural world, and of the unity of all cultural and physical landscapes. Climate change, air and water pollution, soil loss and desertification, toxic wastes, and a host of other environmental problems are all matters of contemporary public debate and international compacts, and treaties. Acceptance of the interconnectedness and indivisibility of cultural and natural environments—the human creation and the physical endowment—is now more the rule than the exception.

Summary

Cultural landscapes may buffer but cannot isolate societies from the physical environments that they occupy. All human activities, from the simplest forms of agriculture to modern industry, have an impact upon the biosphere. Cumulatively, in both developed and developing countries, that impact is now evident in the form of serious and threatening environmental deterioration. As humans have increased in number and affluence, and expanded their use of fossil fuel energy sources, their impact on the Earth has shifted from local to regional, continental, and global scales.

The Earth's environmental systems of atmosphere, hydrosphere, lithosphere, and biosphere are intricately interlinked. Tropical deforestation alters the hydrologic cycle and impacts the climate system. Most threateningly, climate change will have significant effects on all the other environmental systems, altering the availability of water for agriculture and cities and changing the frequency and intensity of floods and droughts. Climate change will lead to rising sea levels and changing geographical limits for the Earth's biomes, allowing some species to expand their range and threatening others with extinction.

The atmosphere unites us all, and its global problems of rising greenhouse gases, ozone depletion, and particulate pollution endanger us all. Desertification, soil erosion, and tropical deforestation may appear to be local or regional problems, but they have worldwide implications of both environmental degradation and reduced population-supporting capacity. Freshwater supplies are deteriorating in quality and decreasing in sufficiency through contamination and competition. Finally, the inevitable end product of human use of the Earth—the garbage and hazardous wastes of civilization—are beginning to overwhelm both sites and technologies of disposal.

We do not end our study of human geography on a note of despondency, however. We end with the conviction that the fuller knowledge that we now have of the spatial patterns and structures of human cultural, economic, and political activities will aid in our understanding of the myriad ways in which human societies are bound to the physical landscapes that they occupy—and which they have so substantially modified.

KEY WORDS

acid precipitation 433
aquifer 446
biome 428
dead zones 449
desertification 441
ecosphere 427
ecosystem 428
environment 426

environmental justice 454
environmental pollution 448
fallowing 444
global climate change 435
greenhouse effect 435
hazardous waste 452
hydrologic cycle 427
IPAT equation 426

Not In My Backyard (NIMBY) 451
ozone 434
rotation 444
soil 443
soil erosion 441
sustainable development 426
terracing 444
transboundary river basins 447

FOR REVIEW

1. What are the components in the IPAT equation? How does the study of human geography inform our understanding of environmental problems?

2. Were there any evidences of human impact upon the natural environment prior to the Industrial Revolution? If so, can you provide examples? If not, can you explain why not?

3. What lines of reasoning and evidence suggest that human activity is altering global climates? What kind of alteration has occurred or is expected to occur? Which places on Earth are most vulnerable to climate change?

4. What is *desertification?* What types of areas are particularly susceptible to desertification? What kinds of land uses are associated with it? How

easily can its effects be overcome or reversed?

5. What agricultural techniques have been traditionally employed to reduce or halt soil erosion? Since these are known techniques that have been practiced throughout the world, why is there a current problem of soil erosion anywhere?

6. What effects has the increasing use of fossil fuels over the past 250 years had on the environment? What is *acid precipitation,* and where is it a problem? What factors affect the type and degree of air pollution found at a place?

7. Describe the chief sources of water pollution of which you are aware. How has the supply of fresh water been affected by pollution and human use? When water is used, is it forever lost to the environment? If so, where

does it go? If not, why should there be water shortages now in regions of formerly ample supply?

8. What is a transboundary river basin? Which transboundary river basins are most likely to become sites of international water conflicts?

9. Since waste disposal is a technical problem, why should there be any concern with waste disposal in modern advanced economies? Why is there a growing international trade in wastes and recyclable products?

10. What are some examples of success stories of humans working to reduce environmental impacts?

11. Suggest ways in which your study of human geography has increased your understanding of the relationship between culture and nature.

KEY CONCEPTS REVIEW

1. **What are contributing causes and resulting concerns of urban air pollution, acid precipitation, ozone depletion, and global climate change?** pp. 430–440.
Environmental impact depends on the size of the population, standards of living, and the technologies a culture uses. Combustion of various fuels is the primary source of air

pollution problems. Historic urban smog episodes were due to home heating with coal (London) and vehicle exhausts (Los Angeles). Pollution control regulations and technologies have helped clean the air, although many places have a long ways to go. Building taller smokestacks at factories and coal-fired power plants changed the scale of air

pollution from local to regional or even continental. Acid precipitation is carried by prevailing winds across international boundaries, corroding stone and metals, destroying forests, and acidifying some lakes and soils. Upper-air ozone depletion, with serious effect on plant and animal life, is due to use of particular chemicals which are now subject to international bans. Rising concentrations of greenhouse gases due to fossil fuel combustion and deforestation are responsible for rising global temperatures. Global climate change is of great concern because the climate, sea levels, water availability, and the biosphere are intimately interrelated.

2. **What human actions have contributed to tropical deforestation, desertification, and soil erosion? What are the consequences?** pp. 440–446.
Current rapid destruction of tropical forests reflects human intentions to expand farming and grazing areas and harvest tropical wood. Their depletion endangers or destroys the world's richest, most diversified plant and animal biome and adversely affects local, regional, and world patterns of temperature and rainfall. Their loss also diminishes a vital "carbon sink" needed to absorb excess carbon dioxide. Desertification—the expansion of areas of destroyed soil and plant cover in dry climates—results from both natural climatic fluctuations and human pressures from plowing, woody plant removal, or livestock overgrazing. Those same human actions and pressures can accelerate the normal erosional loss of soil beyond natural soil regeneration potential. Such loss reduces total and per capita area of food production, diminishing the human carrying capacity of the land.

3. **How are emerging water resources problems related to human numbers and impacts?** pp. 446–450.
The hydrologic cycle assures water will be continuously regenerated for further use. But growing demand for irrigation, industrial use, and individual and urban consumption means increasing lack of balance between natural water supplies and consumption demands. Pollution of those supplies by human actions further reduces water availability and utility. A significant portion of the world's land area lies within transboundary river basins. Proper management of these vital water resources requires international cooperation.

4. **How are societies addressing the problems of solid and toxic waste disposal?** pp. 451–456.
Increasingly, all societies are becoming more dependent on advanced manufacturing and packaging of industrial, commercial, and consumer products. The easy recycling of waste materials found in subsistence cultures is no longer possible, and humans are presented with increasing needs for sites and facilities to safely dispose of solid wastes. Sanitary landfills and incineration are employed to handle nontoxic wastes. The former demands scarce and expensive land near cities or costly export to distant locations; the latter is often opposed because of unsafe emissions and ash residue. Disposal of toxic and hazardous wastes including radioactive wastes, products of modern societies and technologies, poses problems that have yet to be solved satisfactorily and safely.

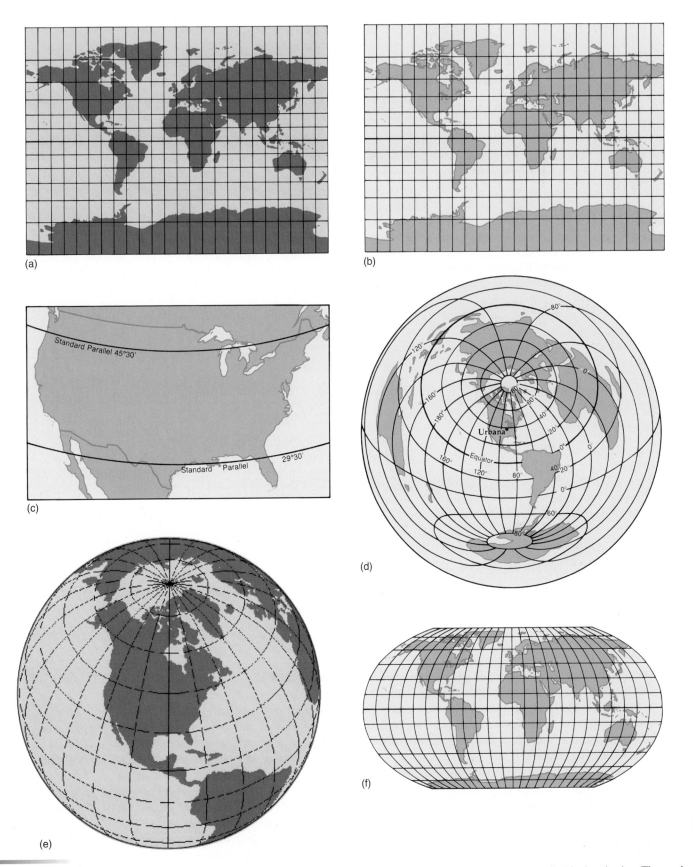

Figure A.9 Some sample members of the principal projection families. (*a*) The equirectangular projection is a simple cylindrical projection. The version shown here was created by setting the x-value equal to the longitude and the y-value equal to the latitude. (*b*) The Miller cylindrical projection is also mathematically derived. (*c*) The Albers equal-area conic projection, used for many official U.S. maps, has two standard parallels: 29 1/2° and 45 1/2° . (*d*) A planar, or azimuthal, equidistant projection centered on Urbana, Illinois. (*e*) The perspective projection is a planar projection that simulates the view from space. (*f*) The Robinson projection of the oval family; neither conformal nor equivalent, it was designed as a visually satisfactory world map.

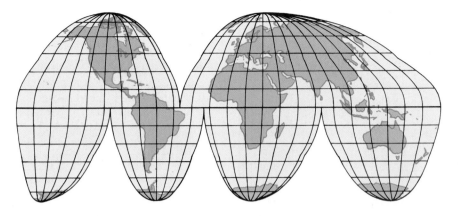

Figure A.10 Goode's interrupted homolosine grafts an upper latitude homolographic (Mollweide) onto a sinusoidal projection at about 40° North and South. To improve shapes, each continent is placed on the middle of a lobe approximately centered on its own central meridian. The projection can also interrupt continents to display the ocean areas intact.

Figure A.11 **The Fuller dymaxion projection.** The equilateral triangles can be folded into a solid approximating the globe.

nearly unlimited. R. Buckminster Fuller, an architect and designer of the geodesic dome, produced the Fuller dymaxion projection (Figure A.11). It consists of 20 equilateral triangles, which can be hinged along different boundaries to show interesting earth relationships. The projection minimizes distortion of the sizes and shapes of the world's landmasses.

Map properties to be retained, size and shape of areas to be displayed, and overall map design to be achieved may influence the cartographer's choices in reproducing the globe grid on the flat map. Special effects and properties may also be achieved geometrically by adjusting the aspect of the projection. **Aspect** simply means the positional relationship between the globe and the developable surface on which it is visually projected. Although the fundamental distortion pattern of a given projection system will

remain constant, shifting the point or line of tangency will materially alter the appearance of the graticule and of the geographical features shown on the map.

Although an infinite number of aspects are possible for any of the geometric projections, three classes of aspects are most common. Named according to the relation of the axis of the globe to the cylinder, cone, or plane projection surface, the three classes are usually called *equatorial, polar,* and *oblique.* In the equatorial, the axis of the globe parallels the orientation of the plane, cylinder, or cone; a parallel, usually the central equator, is the line of tangency. In the polar aspect, the axis of the globe is perpendicular to the orientation of the developable surface. In the oblique aspect, the axis of the globe makes an oblique angle with the orientation of the developable surface, and a complex arrangement of the graticule results.

A Cautionary Reminder

Mapmakers must be conscious of the properties of the projections they use, selecting the one that best suits their purposes. It is not possible to transform the globe into a flat map without distortion. But cartographers have d   evised hundreds of possible mathematical and geometrical projections in various modifications and aspects to display to their best advantage the variety of earth features and relationships they wish to emphasize. Some projections are highly specialized and properly restricted to a single limited purpose; others achieve a more general acceptability and utility.

If the map shows only a small area, the choice of a projection is less critical because distortion due to projection decreases as map scale increases (i.e., as the earth surface area shown decreases)—virtually any can be used. The choice becomes more important when the area to be shown extends over a considerable longitude and latitude; then the selection of a projection clearly depends on the purpose of the map. As we have seen, Mercator or gnomonic projections are useful for navigation. Unfortunately, the Mercator projection grossly exaggerates the area of high latitude features, giving a misleading impression when used for books or wall maps. If numerical data are being mapped, the relative sizes of the areal units (countries, states, counties, and so forth)should be correct, and equivalence is the sought-after map property. Conformality and equal distance may be required in other instances.

While selection of an appropriate projection is the task of the cartographer, understanding the consequences of that choice and recognizing and allowing for the distortions inevitable in all flat maps are the responsibility of the map reader. When skillfully designed maps are read by knowledgeable users, they clearly and accurately convey important spatial information and earth relationships.

KEY WORDS

aspect 466
azimuthal projection 463
conformal projection 462
conic projection 464
cylindrical projection 463
developable surface 460

equal-area (equivalent) projection 460
equidistant 462
equirectangular projection 464
geometrical (perspective) projection 460
gnomonic projection 460
great circle 462

mathematical projection 460
Mercator projection 463
orthographic projection 460
perspective projection 464
planar (azimuthal) projection 464
stereographic projection 460

Appendix B

2011 WORLD POPULATION DATA

	Population Mid-2011 (millions)	Births per 1,000 Population	Deaths per 1,000 Population	Natural Increase Rate, %	Net Migration Rate, per 1,000	Projected Population (millions), Mid-2050	Projected Population Change, 2011-2050, %	Infant Mortality Rate[a]	Total Fertility Rate[b]	Percent of Population Ages < 15	Percent of Population Ages 65+	Life Expectancy at Birth (Years)	Percent Urban	Population Density, Person per Square km	% of Population with Improved Water Supply, 2008	GNI PPP per Capita ($US), 2009	Percent of Population Below $US2/Day PPP, 2009
WORLD	**6,987**	**20**	**8**	**1.2**	**—**	**9,587**	**37%**	**44**	**2.5**	**27**	**8**	**70**	**51**	**51**	**87**	**10,240**	**48**
MORE DEVELOPED	1,242	11	10	0.2	2	1,333	7%	5	1.7	16	16	78	75	27	99	32,470	—
LESS DEVELOPED	5,745	22	8	1.4	-1	8,254	44%	48	2.6	29	6	68	46	69	84	5,440	51
LESS DEVELOPED (Excl. China)	4,400	25	8	1.7	-1	6942	58%	52	3	33	5	66	44	60	82	5,000	56
LEAST DEVELOPED	861	35	11	2.4	-1	1,826	112%	76	4.5	41	3	59	28	41	61	1,220	77
AFRICA	**1,051**	**36**	**12**	**2.4**	**-1**	**2,300**	**119%**	**74**	**4.7**	**41**	**4**	**58**	**39**	**35**	**65**	**2,720**	**63**
SUB-SAHARAN AFRICA	**883**	**38**	**13**	**2.6**	**-1**	**2,069**	**134%**	**80**	**5.2**	**43**	**3**	**55**	**37**	**36**	**60**	**2,000**	**72**
NORTHERN AFRICA	**213**	**25**	**6**	**1.8**	**-1**	**323**	**52%**	**33**	**2.9**	**31**	**5**	**71**	**51**	**25**	**84**	**5,540**	**18**
Algeria	36.0	19	5	1.5	-1	46.5	29%	22	2.3	27	5	73	67	15	83	8,110	24
Egypt	82.6	25	5	2.0	-1	123.5	50%	23	2.9	31	5	73	43	83	99	5,680	19
Libya	6.4	22	4	1.8	-8	8.8	38%	14	2.5	31	4	75	78	4	—	16,400	—
Morocco	32.3	19	6	1.3	-3	39.2	21%	30	2.2	28	6	72	56	72	81	4,400	14
South Sudan[c]	8.1	30	8	2.2	—	15.4	90%	102	3.9	44	4	62	17	13	55	—	—
Sudan, Republic of[d]	36.5	34	9	2.4	—	75.6	107%	49	4.6	39	4	61	46	19	57	—	—
Tunisia	10.7	18	6	1.2	0	12.6	18%	18	2.1	24	7	75	68	65	94	7,810	13
Western Sahara[e]	0.5	32	9	2.3	8	1.2	140%	60	4.3	39	4	61	82	2	—	—	—
WESTERN AFRICA	**313**	**40**	**14**	**2.6**	**-1**	**792**	**153%**	**85**	**5.5**	**43**	**3**	**54**	**45**	**51**	**64**	**1,690**	**75**
Benin	9.1	40	11	2.9	0	21.7	138%	78	5.4	44	3	56	43	81	75	1,510	75
Burkina Faso	17.0	43	12	3.1	-1	46.7	175%	73	5.8	45	2	56	24	62	78	1,170	81
Cape Verde	0.5	22	5	1.7	-5	0.6	20%	19	2.5	32	6	74	62	123	84	3,530	40
Côte d'Ivoire	22.6	37	13	2.3	-1	45.6	102%	97	4.9	41	4	52	51	70	81	1,640	46
Gambia	1.8	39	9	3.0	-1	4.0	122%	68	5	44	2	59	59	157	92	1,330	57
Ghana	25.0	31	8	2.3	0	49.1	96%	45	4.1	38	4	64	52	105	82	1,530	54
Guinea	10.2	39	13	2.7	-1	23.0	125%	86	5.3	43	3	54	28	42	69	940	70

	Population Mid-2011 (millions)	Births per 1,000 Population	Deaths per 1,000 Population	Natural Increase Rate, %	Net Migration Rate, per 1,000	Projected Population (millions), Mid-2050	Projected Population Change, 2011-2050, %	Infant Mortality Rate[a]	Total Fertility Rate[b]	Percent of Population Ages < 15	Percent of Population Ages 65+	Life Expectancy at Birth (Years)	Percent Urban	Population Density, Person per Square km	% of Population with Improved Water Supply, 2008	GNI PPP per Capita ($US), 2009	Percent of Population Below $US2/Day PPP, 2009
Guinea-Bissau	1.6	39	16	2.3	-1	3.3	106%	103	5.1	41	3	48	30	45	61	1,060	78
Liberia	4.1	43	12	3.1	-1	10.8	163%	78	5.8	43	3	57	47	37	64	290	95
Mali	15.4	45	15	3.1	-5	35.2	129%	116	6.4	48	3	52	33	12	56	1,190	77
Mauritania	3.5	33	9	2.4	-1	7.1	103%	71	4.4	40	3	59	42	3	49	1,940	44
Niger	16.1	48	12	3.6	0	55.4	244%	88	7	49	2	55	17	13	49	680	76
Nigeria	162.3	41	16	2.5	0	433.2	167%	89	5.7	43	3	52	51	176	59	2,070	84
Senegal	12.8	36	9	2.8	-2	28.6	123%	51	4.7	44	2	59	43	65	69	1,810	60
Sierra Leone	5.4	37	15	2.2	0	13.6	152%	89	5	42	4	53	39	75	49	790	76
Togo	5.8	36	8	2.8	0	14.3	147%	55	4.7	42	4	62	37	103	58	850	69
EASTERN AFRICA	**336**	**39**	**11**	**2.8**	**-1**	**826**	**146%**	**69**	**5.3**	**44**	**3**	**56**	**22**	**53**	**54**	**1,080**	**75**
Burundi	10.2	42	10	3.2	5	27.1	166%	66	6.4	46	3	57	11	367	72	390	94
Comoros	0.8	36	8	2.8	-3	1.7	113%	65	4.8	43	3	61	28	337	95	1,180	65
Djibouti	0.9	29	10	1.9	0	1.6	78%	76	3.7	35	3	58	76	39	87	2,480	41
Eritrea	5.9	34	8	2.6	0	11.4	93%	43	4.7	43	4	62	22	51	61	580	—
Ethiopia	87.1	37	10	2.7	-1	173.8	100%	77	5.3	44	3	56	17	79	38	930	78
Kenya	41.6	37	10	2.7	0	96.9	133%	59	4.7	42	3	57	18	72	58	1,570	40
Madagascar	21.3	35	6	2.8	0	53.6	152%	42	4.6	43	3	67	31	36	42	990	90
Malawi	15.9	42	15	2.7	0	37.4	135%	84	5.7	45	3	54	14	134	80	780	91
Mauritius	1.3	12	7	0.5	0	1.6	23%	12.5	1.5	22	7	73	42	630	99	13,270	—
Mayotte	0.2	33	3	3.0	0	0.5	150%	6	4.2	46	2	77	50	563	—	—	—
Mozambique	23.1	41	14	2.8	-4	59.3	157%	86	5.6	45	3	52	31	29	44	880	82
Reunion	0.9	17	6	1.1	0	1.1	22%	6	2.3	25	8	78	94	341	—	—	—
Rwanda	10.9	33	12	2.1	0	23.1	112%	50	4.6	42	3	55	19	415	65	1,130	90
Seychelles	0.1	18	8	1.0	0	0.1	0%	11.5	2.4	23	8	73	56	194	—	16,790	1
Somalia	9.9	43	15	2.8	-12	22.6	128%	107	6.4	45	2	51	38	16	31	—	—
Tanzania	46.2	40	11	2.9	-1	138.3	199%	51	5.4	45	3	57	27	49	54	1,360	88
Uganda	34.5	46	12	3.4	-1	105.6	206%	74	6.4	48	3	54	15	143	68	1,190	65
Zambia	13.5	46	15	3.1	-1	45.0	233%	84	6.3	46	3	49	36	18	61	1,280	82
Zimbabwe	12.1	34	15	1.9	0	25.2	108%	57	4.1	44	4	46	29	31	80	—	—
MIDDLE AFRICA	**131**	**43**	**16**	**2.7**	**0**	**291**	**122%**	**106**	**5.7**	**45**	**3**	**50**	**44**	**20**	**54**	**1,760**	**70**
Angola	19.6	43	15	2.8	1	48.0	145%	102	5.7	47	3	50	59	16	51	5,190	70
Cameroon	20.1	37	15	2.2	0	43.7	117%	91	4.8	41	4	51	59	42	75	2,190	31
Central African Republic	5.0	37	15	2.1	0	10.3	106%	102	4.7	41	4	50	39	8	67	750	82
Chad	11.5	45	16	2.9	-2	27.3	137%	125	6	45	3	50	28	9	50	1,160	83
Congo	4.1	36	11	2.5	-1	8.8	115%	68	4.7	40	4	58	63	12	72	3,040	74
Congo, Dem. Rep.	67.8	45	17	2.8	0	148.5	119%	111	6.1	46	3	49	36	29	47	300	80
Equatorial Guinea	0.7	37	15	2.3	5	1.7	143%	95	5.3	39	3	51	40	26	—	19,330	—
Gabon	1.5	27	9	1.8	1	2.8	87%	45	3.4	35	4	63	86	6	87	12,450	20
Sao Tome and Principe	0.2	34	7	2.7	-9	0.3	50%	45	4.6	44	3	62	63	187	89	1,850	57

Glossary

Terms in italics identify related glossary items.

A

absolute direction Direction with respect to global location references, such as cardinal directions or macroscopic features.

absolute distance (*syn:* geodesic distance) The physical separation between two places measured on a standard unit of length (e.g., miles or kilometers).

absolute location (*syn:* mathematical location) The position of a feature or place expressed in spatial coordinates of a grid system designed for locational purposes. In geography, the most common reference system is the *globe grid* or *graticule* of *parallels of latitude* north or south of the *equator* and of *meridians of longitude* east or west of a *prime meridian.* Absolute globe locations are cited in degrees, which are often subdivided for greater precision into minutes and seconds, or tenths and hundredths of degrees, of latitude and longitude north or south and east or west of the equatorial and prime meridian base lines.

accessibility The relative ease with which a destination may be reached from other locations; the relative opportunity for *spatial interaction.* May be measured in spatial, social, or economic terms.

acculturation Cultural modification or change that results when one *culture* group or individual adopts traits of a dominant or *host society;* cultural development or change through "borrowing."

acid precipitation *Precipitation* that is unusually acidic; created when oxides of sulfur and nitrogen change chemically as they dissolve in water vapor in the *atmosphere* and return to earth as acidic rain, snow, or fog.

activity space The area within which people move freely on their typical rounds of regular activity (not unusual exceptions).

administrative region Geographic *region* created by law, treaty, or regulation; includes political regions such as countries and states, and internal regions such as school and voting districts

agglomeration The spatial grouping of people or activities for mutual benefit; in *economic geography,* the concentration of productive enterprises for collective or cooperative use of *infrastructure* and sharing of labor resources and market access.

agglomeration economy (*syn:* external economy) The savings to an individual enterprise derived from locational association with a cluster of other similar economic activities, such as other factories or retail stores.

agricultural density The number of rural residents per unit of agriculturally productive land; a variant of *physiological density* that excludes urban population.

agriculture The science and practice of farming, including the cultivation of the soil and the rearing of livestock.

amalgamation theory In *ethnic geography,* the concept that multiethnic societies become a merger of the *culture traits* of their member groups.

animism A belief that natural objects may be the abode of dead people, spirits, or gods who occasionally give the objects the appearance of life.

antecedent boundary A *boundary* line established before the area in question is well populated.

aquaculture Farming of cultivated fish and shellfish under controlled conditions, in contrast to the harvesting of wild fish and shellfish.

aquifer A porous, water-bearing layer of rock, sand, or gravel below ground level.

arithmetic density See *crude density.*

artifact A material manifestation of *culture,* including tools, housing, systems of land use, clothing, and the like. An element in the *technological subsystem* of culture.

artificial boundary See *geometric boundary.*

aspect In *map projections,* the positional relationship between the globe and the *developable surface* on which it is visually projected: the polar aspect is tangent at the pole; the equatorial aspect is tangent at the equator; the oblique aspect is tangent anywhere else.

assimilation A process by which a minority population reduces or loses completely its identifying cultural characteristics and blends into the *host society.* One component is *spatial assimilation.*

atmosphere The air or mixture of gases surrounding the earth.

attitude Belief and feeling about places, people, or events.

autonomous nationalism Movement by a dissident minority intent on achieving partial or total independence of territory it occupies from the *state* within which it lies.

awareness space Locations or places about which an individual has knowledge even without visiting all of them; includes *activity space* and additional areas newly encountered or about which one acquires information.

azimuthal projection See *planar projection.*

B

barrier A *geographic feature* that impedes spatial interaction, either by blocking it totally, slowing it down, or redirecting it. Barriers may be physical, socio-cultural, or psychological.

basic sector Those products or services of an *urban* economy that are exported outside the city itself, earning income for the community.

behavior Coordinated and goal-directed action by people or institutions.

behavioral approach A way of doing *human geography* that focuses on a disaggregate (individual) level of analysis, appreciating the role of *cognition* and emotion in determining human actions.

bilingualism Describing a society's use of two *official languages.*

biomass The total dry weight of all living organisms within a unit area; plant and animal matter that can in any way be used as a source of energy.

biome A major ecological community, including plants and animals, occupying an extensive earth area.

biosphere (*syn:* ecosphere)

birth rate See *crude birth rate.*

Boserup thesis The view that population growth independently forces a conversion from extensive to intensive *subsistence* agriculture.

brain drain The loss of a developing country's most educated citizens as they emigrate in search of better educational and career opportunities in developed countries.

break-of-bulk point A location where goods are transferred from one type of carrier to another (e.g., from barge to railroad).

brownfield A former industrial or commercial site that is under-used, vacant, or abandoned where there is the potential for environmental contamination.

Buddhism A *universalizing religion,* primarily of eastern and central Asia, based on teachings of Siddhartha Gautama, the Buddha, that suffering is inherent in all life but can be relieved by mental and moral self-purification.

built environment That part of the *physical landscape* that represents *material culture;* the buildings, roads, bridges, and similar structures large and small of the *cultural landscape.*

C

carrying capacity The maximum population numbers that an area can support on a continuing basis without experiencing unacceptable deterioration; for humans, the numbers supportable by an area's known and used resources—usually agricultural ones.

cartogram A *thematic map* that shows the values of a quantitative variable for each region by shrinking or expanding the sizes of the regions to correspond with the variable's value.

cartography The art and science of maps and mapping.

caste One of the hereditary social classes in *Hinduism* that determines one's occupation and position in society.

central business district (CBD) The nucleus or "downtown" of a city, where retail stores, offices, and cultural activities are concentrated, mass transit systems converge, and land values and building densities are high.

central city That part of the *metropolitan area* contained within the boundaries of the main city around which suburbs have developed.

central place An *urban* or other settlement node whose primary function is to provide goods and services to the consuming population of its *hinterland, complementary region,* or trade area.

central place theory A deductive theory formulated by Walter *Christaller* (1893–1969) to explain the size and distribution of settlements through reference to competitive supply of goods and services to dispersed rural populations.

centrifugal force 1: In *urban geography,* economic and social forces pushing households and businesses outward from central and inner-city locations. 2: In *political geography,* forces of disruption and dissolution threatening the unity of a *state.*

centripetal force 1: In *urban geography,* economic and social forces attracting establishments or activities to central and inner-city locations. 2: In *political geography,* forces tending to bind together the citizens of a state, thus promoting its unity.

chain migration The process by which *migration* movements from a common home area to a specific destination are sustained by links of friendship or kinship between first movers and later followers.

channelized migration The tendency for *migration* to flow between areas that are socially and economically allied by past migration patterns, by economic and trade connections, or by some other affinity.

charter group In plural societies, the early arriving ethnic group that created the *first effective settlement* and established the recognized cultural norms to which other, later groups are expected to conform.

choropleth map A *thematic map* that shows the values of a quantitative variable for each region by shading or coloring the regions to correspond with the variable's value.

Christaller Walter Christaller (1893–1969), German geographer credited with developing *central place theory* (1933).

Christianity A *monotheistic, universalizing religion* based on the teachings of Jesus Christ and of the Bible as sacred scripture.

circular and cumulative causation A process through which tendencies for economic growth are self-reinforcing; an expression of the *multiplier effect,* it tends to favor major cities and *core* regions over less-advantaged *peripheral* regions.

city A multifunctional nucleated settlement with a *central business district* and both residential and nonresidential land uses.

climate A summary of weather conditions in a place or region over a period of time.

cluster migration A pattern of movement and settlement resulting from the collective action of a distinctive social or *ethnic group.*

cognition Knowledge and beliefs about something, and the thinking and memory processes that create and modify them; it varies somewhat across individual people and cultural groups; *perception* is sometimes used broadly as a synonym for cognition.

cognitive map See *mental map.*

cohort A population group unified by a specific common characteristic, such as age, and subsequently treated as a statistical unit for data analysis.

colony In *ethnic geography,* an urban ethnic area serving as point of entry and temporary *acculturation* zone for a specific immigrant group.

commercial economy A system of production of goods and services for exchange in competitive markets where price and availability are determined by supply and demand forces.

commodity chain The set of activities involved in the production of a single good or service. A commodity chain encompasses the relationships between buyers and suppliers and the flows of materials, finance, and knowledge.

compact state A *state* whose territory is nearly circular.

comparative advantage The principle that an area produces the items for which it has the greatest ratio of advantage or the least ratio of disadvantage in comparison to other areas, assuming free trade exists.

complementarity The actual or potential relationship of two places or regions that each produce different goods or services for which the other has an effective demand, resulting in an exchange between the locales.

concentration In *spatial distributions,* the clustering of a phenomenon around a central location.

concentric zone model A model describing urban land uses as a series of circular belts or rings around a core *central business district,* each ring housing a distinct type of land use. It also describes a common urban residence pattern corresponding to different family life stages (family status).

conformal projection A *map projection* that retains correct shapes of small areas; lines of *latitude* and *longitude* cross at right angles and *scale* (**1**) is the same in all directions at any point on the map.

Confucianism A Chinese *value system* and *ethnic religion* emphasizing ethics, social morality, tradition, and ancestor worship.

conic projection A *map projection* employing a cone placed over the globe as the presumed *developable surface.*

connectivity The directness of routes linking pairs of places; an indication of the degree of internal connection in a transport *network.* More generally, all of the tangible and intangible means of connection and communication between places.

consequent boundary (*syn:* ethnographic boundary) A *boundary* line that coincides with some cultural divide, such as religion or language.

consumer service A portion of the services (tertiary) sector of the economy involved in providing services to individuals and households. Examples include hair salons and retailers.

contagious diffusion A pattern of *diffusion* in which cultural innovations spread to closer places before they spread to further places (it reflects distance decay). Contagious expansion diffusion typically results from direct contact between actual and potential adopters of the *innovation,* in a manner analogous to the spread of contagious diseases.

conurbation A continuous, extended *urban* area formed by the growing together of several formerly separate, expanding cities. Called Consolidated Metropolitan Area by the U.S. Census.

core area 1: In *economic geography,* a "core region," the national or world districts of concentrated economic power, wealth, innovation, and advanced technology. 2: In *political geography,* the heartland or nucleus of a *state,* containing its most developed area, greatest wealth, densest populations, and clearest national identity.

core-periphery model A model of the spatial structure of an economic system in which underdeveloped or declining peripheral areas are defined with respect to their dependence on a dominating developed *core region.*

counter migration (*syn:* return migration) The return of migrants to the regions from which they earlier emigrated.

creole A *language* developed from a *pidgin* to become the native tongue of a society.

critical distance The distance beyond which cost, effort, and/or means play a determining role in the willingness of people to travel.

crude birth rate (CBR) The ratio of the number of live births during one year to the total population, usually at the midpoint of the same year, expressed as the number of births per year per 1000 population.

crude death rate (CDR) (*syn:* mortality rate) The ratio of the number of deaths during one year to the total population, usually at the midpoint of the same year, expressed as the number of deaths per year per 1000 population .

crude density (*syn:* arithmetic density) The number of people per unit area of land.

cultural autonomy The view that cultures can develop any particular set of cultural traits independent of their environmental circumstances, a view opposite of *environmental determinism.*

cultural convergence The tendency for *cultures* to become more alike as they increasingly share *technology* and organizational structures in a modern world united by improved transportation and communication.

cultural divergence The likelihood or tendency for *cultures* to become increasingly dissimilar with the passage of time.

cultural ecology The study of the interactions between societies and the natural *environments* they occupy.

cultural integration The interconnectedness of all aspects of a *culture:* no part can be altered without creating an impact on other components of the culture.

cultural landscape The *natural landscape* as modified by human activities and bearing the imprint of a *culture* group or society; the *built environment.*

cultural system A generalization suggesting shared, identifying traits uniting two or more *culture complexes.*

culture 1: A society's collective beliefs, symbols, values, forms of behavior, and social organizations, together with its tools, structures, and artifacts created according to the group's conditions of life; transmitted as a heritage to succeeding generations and undergoing adoptions, modifications, and changes in the process. 2: A collective term for a group displaying uniform cultural characteristics.

culture complex A related set of *culture traits* descriptive of one aspect of a society's behavior or activity. Culture complexes may be as basic as those associated with food preparation, serving, and consumption, or as involved as those associated with religious beliefs or business practices.

culture hearth A nuclear area within which an advanced and distinctive set of *culture traits,* ideas, and *technologies* develops and from which there is *diffusion* of those

characteristics and the *cultural landscape* features they imply.

culture realm A collective of *culture regions* sharing related culture systems; a major world area having sufficient distinctiveness to be perceived as set apart from other realms in terms of cultural characteristics and complexes.

culture rebound The readoption by later generations of *culture traits* and identities associated with immigrant forebears or ancestral homelands.

culture region A *thematic* or *functional region* within which common cultural characteristics prevail. It may be based on single *culture traits,* on *culture complexes,* or on political, social, or economic integration.

culture trait A single distinguishing feature of regular occurrence within a *culture,* such as the use of chopsticks or the observance of a particular caste system. A single element of learned behavior.

custom The body of traditional practices, usages, and conventions that regulate social life; an expression of *culture.*

cylindrical projection A *map projection* employing a cylinder wrapped around the globe as the presumed *developable surface.*

D

dead zone Coastal zone, often near the mouth of major rivers, where waters are very low in oxygen and subject to major die-offs of marine life. Coastal dead zones are generally caused by *environmental pollution* from fertilizers and manure in agricultural runoff, as well as urban sewage.

death rate See *crude death rate.*

deforestation The clearing of land through total removal of forest cover.

deglomeration The process of deconcentration; the location of industrial or other activities away from established *agglomerations* in response to growing costs of congestion, competition, and regulation.

deindustrialization The cumulative and sustained decline of manufacturing activities in a regional or national economy, involving the loss of both firms and jobs.

demographic equation A mathematical expression that summarizes the contribution of different demographic processes to the population change of a given area during a specified time period. $P_2 = P_1 + B_{1-2} - D_{1-2} + IM_{1-2} - OM_{1-2}$, where P_2 is population at time 2; P_1 is population at beginning date; B_{1-2} is the number of births between times 1 and 2; D_{1-2} is the number of deaths during that period; IM_{1-2} is the number of in-migrants and OM_{1-2} the number of out-migrants between times 1 and 2.

demographic momentum See *population momentum.*

demographic transition A model of the effect of economic development on population growth, originally expressed in terms of four stages but now including a final fifth stage.

demography The scientific study of population, with particular emphasis upon quantitative aspects of births and deaths.

density The quantity of some feature (people, buildings, animals, traffic, etc.) per unit area or size.

dependency ratio The number of dependents, old or young, that each 100 persons in the economically productive years must on average support.

dependency theory A theory that attempts to explain patterns and processes of economic development by extending the *core-periphery model* to the international scene, arguing that the development of the advanced core nations has depended upon the underdevelopment of the peripheral nations. Dependency theory argues that developing countries were made poor by their interactions with the advanced countries, starting with colonialism and the slave trade and continuing in new forms to the present.

desertification Extension of desert-like landscapes as a result of overgrazing, destruction of the forests, or other human-induced changes, usually in semiarid regions.

developable surface *Map projection* surface (including the plane, cone, or cylinder) that can be made flat without further distorting the earth surface it depicts, beyond the distortion arising from projecting onto that surface as it is wrapped around the earth.

development The process of growth, expansion, or realization of potential; bringing regional resources into full productive use.

devolution The transfer of certain powers from the *state* central government to separate political subdivisions within the state's territory.

dialect A *language* variant marked by vocabulary, grammar, or pronunciation differences from other variants of the same common language. When those variations are spatial or regional, they are called *geographic dialects;* when they are indicative of socioeconomic or educational levels, they are called *social dialects.*

diffusion The spread or movement of a phenomenon over space and through time.

The dispersion of a *culture trait,* such as a new idea or practice, from an origin area (e.g., *language,* plant *domestication,* new industrial *technology*).

dispersion In *spatial distributions,* a statement of the amount of spread of a phenomenon over area or around a central location. Dispersion in this sense represents a continuum from clustered, concentrated, or agglomerated (at one end) to dispersed or scattered (at the other).

distance decay The declining intensity of any *spatial interaction* with increasing distance from its point of origin.

domestication The successful transformation of plant or animal species from a wild state to a condition of dependency on human management, usually with distinct physical change from wild forebears.

doubling time The time period required for a population to double in size.

E

ecology The scientific study of the interrelationships among living plants and animals, and the organic and inorganic matter and energy that make up their environments.

economic base The manufacturing and service activities performed by the *basic sector* of a city's labor force; functions of a city performed to satisfy demands external to the city itself and, in that performance, earning income to support the urban population.

economic geography The branch of *systematic geography* concerned with how people support themselves, with the spatial patterns of production, distribution, and consumption of goods and services, and with the areal variation of economic activities over the surface of the earth.

ecosphere The region of air, water, solid earth, and living organisms where life is found. The ecosphere includes the *atmosphere,* the *hydrosphere* of surface and subsurface waters, the *lithosphere* of the upper reaches of the earth's crust, the *biosphere* of living organisms.

ecosystem A population of organisms existing together in a small, relatively homogeneous area (pond, forest, small island), together with the energy, air, water, soil, and chemicals upon which it depends.

ecumene That part of the earth's surface physically suitable for permanent human settlement; the permanently inhabited areas of the earth.

edge city Distinct sizable nodal concentration of retail and office space of lower than

central city densities and situated on the outer fringes of older metropolitan areas; usually localized near major highway intersections.

Ehrlich Paul Ehrlich (1932-), population biologist and author of the influential *neo-Malthusian* book, *The Population Bomb (1968).*

electoral geography The study of the geographical elements of the organization and results of elections.

elongated state A *state* whose territory is long and narrow.

enclave A small bit of foreign territory lying within a *state* but not under its jurisdiction.

environment Surroundings; the totality of things that in any way may affect a person or other living organism, including both biophysical and sociocultural conditions.

environmental determinism The view that the physical *environment,* particularly *climate,* controls human action, molds human behavior, and conditions cultural development.

environmental justice The notion that all people, regardless of race, ethnicity, or income, should live in a safe environment and be equally protected from environmental hazards and pollution.

environmental perception Attitudes and beliefs about places, regions, landscapes, and environments. They may be based on little or no direct experience, and may not correspond closely with objective reality.

environmental pollution See *pollution.*

equal-area (equivalent) projection A *map projection* with the property that a unit area drawn anywhere on the map always represents the same area on the earth's surface.

equator An imaginary east-west line (*parallel of latitude*) that encircles the globe halfway between the North and South Poles.

equidistant The property of *map projections* showing true distances in all directions only from the center of the projection; all other distances are incorrect.

erosion The wearing away and removal of rock and soil particles from exposed surfaces by agents such as moving water, wind, or ice.

ethnic enclave A small area occupied by a distinctive minority *culture.*

ethnic geography The study of spatial distributions and interactions of *ethnic groups* and of the cultural characteristics on which they are based.

ethnic group People who share common identity as members of a distinctive group, based on common national origin or heritage, *religion, language,* ideology, or *race.*

ethnic island A small rural area settled by a single, distinctive *ethnic group* that placed its imprint on the landscape.

ethnic province A large territory, urban and rural, dominated by or closely associated with a single *ethnic group.*

ethnic religion A *religion* identified with a particular *ethnic group* and largely exclusive to it. Such a religion does not seek converts (does not proselytize).

ethnicity Ethnic quality; affiliation with a group whose racial, cultural, religious, or linguistic characteristics or national origins distinguish it from a larger population within which it is found.

ethnic separatism Desired *regional autonomy* expressed by a culturally distinctive group within a larger, politically dominant *culture.*

ethnocentrism Evaluating other ethnic groups based exclusively on the perspective of one's own *ethnic group.*

European Union (EU) An economic association established in 1957 by a number of Western European countries to promote free trade among members; often called the Common Market. It currently has almost 30 member countries.

exclave A portion of a *state* that is separated from the main territory and surrounded by another country.

exclusive economic zone (EEZ) As established in the *United Nations Convention on the Law of the Sea,* a zone of exploitation extending 200 nautical miles (370 km) seaward from a coastal state that has exclusive mineral and fishing rights over it.

expansion diffusion The spread of ideas, behaviors, or other culture traits from one place to another through direct or indirect contact and exchange of information; the diffusion increases the number of people or cultural groups practicing the trait while leaving the trait intact or intensified in its area of origin.

extensive commercial agriculture A crop or livestock system in a commercial economy characterized by low inputs of labor and capital, and low value, per unit area of land. Range herding and consumption grain are important examples.

extensive subsistence agriculture A crop or livestock system in a subsistence economy characterized by low inputs of labor and capital, and low value, per unit area of land. Nomadic herding and swidden agriculture are important examples.

extractive industry *Primary activity* involving the mining and quarrying of *nonrenewable* metallic and nonmetallic mineral resources.

F

fallowing The practice of allowing plowed or cultivated land to remain (rest) uncropped or only partially cropped for one or more growing seasons.

field *Geographic feature* thought of as a continuously varying surface that completely covers the space of the landscape it occupies without overlapping other fields of the same type. Examples include average precipitation or landform elevation.

first effective settlement The influence that the characteristics of an early dominant settlement group exert on the later *social* and *cultural geography* of an area.

First Law of Geography (*syn:* distance decay) "Everything is related to everything else, but near things are more related than distant things"; attributed to the American geographer Waldo Tobler (1930–).

folk culture The body of institutions, customs, dress, *artifacts,* collective wisdoms, and traditions of a homogeneous, isolated, largely self-sufficient, and relatively static social group. Unlike *popular culture,* folk culture varies greatly over space but not much over time.

food security Refers to the situation wherein every person has access to safe and nutritious food of sufficient quantity for an active and healthy lifestyle.

footloose A descriptive term applied to manufacturing activities for which the cost of transporting material or product is not important in determining location of production; an industry or firm showing neither *market* nor *material orientation.*

forced migration When people are compelled by someone or some event to relocate their residence.

Fordism The manufacturing economy and system derived from assembly-line mass production and the mass consumption of standardized goods. Named after Henry Ford, who innovated many of its production techniques.

fragmented state A *state* whose territory contains isolated parts, separated and discontinuous.

freight rate The charge levied by a transporter for the loading, moving, and unloading of goods; includes *line-haul costs* and *terminal costs.*

friction of distance A measure of the retarding or restricting effect of distance on *spatial interaction.* Generally, the greater the distance, the greater the "friction" and the less the interaction, or the greater the cost of achieving the interaction.

functional dispute (*syn:* boundary dispute) In *political geography,* a disagreement between neighboring *states* over policies to be applied to their common border; often induced by differing customs regulations, movement of nomadic groups, or illegal immigration or emigration.

functional region (*syn:* nodal region) Geographic *region* emerging from patterns of interaction over space and time that connect places.

G

gated community A restricted access subdivision or neighborhood, often surrounded by a barrier, with entry permitted only for residents and their guests; usually totally planned in land use and design, with "residents only" limitations on public streets and parks.

gathering industry *Primary activity* involving the *subsistence* or *commercial* harvesting of *renewable* natural resources of land or water. Primitive gathering involves local collection of food and other materials of nature, both plant and animal; commercial gathering usually implies forestry and fishing industries.

gender In the cultural sense, a reference to socially created—not biologically based—distinctions between femininity and masculinity.

gentrification The movement into the inner portions of American cities of middle- and upper-income people who replace low-income populations, rehabilitate the structures they occupied, and change the social character of neighborhoods.

geodemographic analysis A form of marketing analysis that uses GIS to infer demographic and lifestyle characteristics of potential consumers according to their residential location.

geographic dialect (*syn:* regional dialect) See *dialect.*

geographic feature Natural or cultural entity on the landscapes of the earth's surface, e.g., mountain, river, forest, cornfield, city, country.

geographic information system (GIS) Integrated computer software and hardware for storing, processing, analyzing, and displaying data specifically referenced to locations on the surface of the earth.

geometrical projection (*syn:* perspective projection; visual projection) A *map projection* theoretically created by tracing the *graticule* shadow projected on a *developable surface* from a light source placed relative to a transparent globe.

geopolitics Study of how spatial relations among *regions* influence their current and past political activities and relations.

gerrymandering To redraw electoral voting district boundaries in such a way as to give particular candidates or classes of candidates an electoral advantage beyond the share of the electorate that supports them. Different varieties of gerrymandering may be seen as motivated by nondemocratic objectives or attempts to implement social justice.

ghetto A forced or voluntarily segregated residential area housing a racial, ethnic, or religious minority.

GIS See *geographic information system.*

global climate change Change in the earth's climate system, whether natural or caused by humans.

globalization A reference to the increasing interconnection of all parts of the world as the full range of social, cultural, political, and economic processes becomes international in scale and effect. One result of *space-time compression.*

globe A spherical physical model of the earth.

glocalization The adaptation of globalized products to local tastes and contexts.

GNI See *gross national income.*

gnomonic projection A *geometrical projection* produced with the light source at the center of the earth.

graphic scale A visual expression of cartographic *scale* in a map legend, consisting of a graduated line showing how much distance on the map represents a particular distance on the earth surface.

graticule (*syn:* globe grid) The network of *meridians of longitude* and *parallels of latitude* that make up a coordinate reference system on the globe.

gravity model A mathematical prediction of the interaction between two places as a function of their size (or other measure of attractiveness to interaction) and some measure of the distance separating them.

great circle Line formed by the intersection with the earth's surface of a plane passing through the center of the earth; definition of a straight line on the surface of a sphere, an arc of a great circle is the shortest distance between two points on the earth's surface.

Green Revolution A series of agricultural technology transfers during the 1940s-70s from the U.S. to subtropical areas of undeveloped and developing countries, accomplished through the introduction of very high-yielding hybrid grain crops, particularly wheat, maize, and rice; increased irrigation infrastructure; synthetic

fertilizers and pesticides; and new forms of agricultural management. It has been estimated to have saved the lives of over a billion people from starvation but has been heavily criticized as well.

greenhouse effect Heating of the earth's surface as shortwave solar energy passes through the *atmosphere,* which is transparent to it but opaque to reradiated long-wave terrestrial energy; also, increasing the opacity of the atmosphere through addition of increased amounts of carbon dioxide and other gases that trap heat.

gross domestic income (GDI) See *gross domestic income.*

gross national income (GNI) The total value of goods and services produced per year at home or abroad by domestically-owned interests within a country; formerly called "gross national product."

H

hazardous waste Discarded solid, liquid, or gaseous material that poses a substantial threat to human health or to the *environment* when improperly disposed of or stored.

heritage landscape Landscape strongly associated with the history of a particular cultural group.

hierarchical diffusion A pattern of *diffusion* in which cultural *innovations* spread by "jumping" between places of more importance (such as larger cities) before they spread to places of less importance; reverse hierarchical diffusion from less important to more important places occurs less often.

hierarchy of central places The step-like series of *urban* units in classes differentiated by both size and function.

Hinduism An ancient and now dominant *value system* and *religion* of India, closely identified with Indian *culture* but without central creed, single doctrine, or religious organization. Dharma (customary duty and divine law) and *caste* are uniting elements.

hinterland The rural market area or region served by an *urban* center.

host society The established and dominant society within which immigrant groups seek accommodation.

human geography One of the two major divisions (the other is *physical geography*) of *systematic geography;* the spatial analysis of human populations, their *cultures,* their activities and behaviors, and their interrelationships with the physical landscapes they occupy.

hunter-gatherer/hunting-gathering An economic and social system based primarily

or exclusively on the hunting of wild animals and the gathering of food, fiber, and other materials from uncultivated plants, insects, eggs, and so on.

hydrologic cycle The natural system by which water is continuously circulated through earth systems by evaporation, condensation, and *precipitation.*

hydrosphere All water at or near the earth's surface that is not chemically bound in rocks, including the oceans, surface waters, *groundwater,* and water held in the *atmosphere.* It also includes frozen water, although this is sometimes distinguished as the *cryosphere.*

I

ideological subsystem The complex of ideas, beliefs, knowledge, and means of their communication that characterize a *culture,* along with the *technological* and *sociological subsystems.*

independent invention (*syn:* parallel invention) *Innovations* developed in two or more unconnected locations by individuals or groups acting independently. See also *multilinear evolution.*

Industrial Revolution The term applied to the rapid economic and social changes in manufacturing that followed the introduction of mechanized production to the textile industry of England in the last quarter of the 18th century, and subsequently to other economic activities and places around the globe since then.

infant mortality rate A refinement of the *death rate* to specify the ratio of deaths of infants age 1 year or less per 1000 live births.

informal economy That part of a national economy that involves productive labor not subject to formal systems of control or payment, such as taxation; economic activity or individual enterprise operating without official recognition or measured by official statistics. It ranges from "under the table" employment to buying and selling on the "black market."

infrastructure The basic structure of services, installations, and facilities needed to support industrial, agricultural, and other economic activity, including transportation and communication, along with water, power, and other utilities.

innovation Introduction of new *culture traits,* whether ideas, practices, or material objects.

insolation The solar radiation received at the earth's surface (from *intercepted solar radiation*).

intensive commercial agriculture A crop or livestock system in a commercial economy characterized by high inputs of labor and/ or capital, and high value, per unit area of land. *Truck farming* is an important example.

intensive subsistence agriculture A crop or livestock system in a subsistence economy characterized by high inputs of labor and/ or capital, and high value, per unit area of land. Consumption rice is an important example.

intervening opportunity The concept that closer opportunities will materially reduce the attractiveness of interaction with more distant—even slightly better—alternatives; a closer alternative source of supply between a demand point and the original source of supply.

IPAT equation An equation relating the environmental impact of a society to the key factors of population, affluence, and technology.

irredentism The policy of a *state* wishing to incorporate within itself territory inhabited by people who have ethnic or linguistic links with the people of the state but that lies within a neighboring state.

Islam A *monotheistic, universalizing* religion that includes belief in Allah as the sole deity and in Mohammed as his prophet completing the work of earlier prophets of *Judaism* and *Christianity*.

isogloss A mapped boundary line marking the limits of a particular linguistic feature.

isoline A map line connecting points of equal value on some variable, such as elevation, precipitation, or travel time.

isotropic plain See *uniform plain*.

J

J-curve A curve shaped like the letter J, depicting exponential or geometric population growth (e.g., 1, 2, 4, 8, 16…).

Judaism A *monotheistic, ethnic religion* first developed among the Hebrew people of the ancient Near East; its determining conditions include descent from Israel (Jacob), the Torah (law and scripture), and tradition.

L

landlocked Describing a *state* that lacks a sea coast.

language The system of words, their pronunciation, and methods of combination used and mutually understood by a community of individuals.

language family A group of *languages* thought to have descended from a single, common ancestral tongue.

Latin American model A description of land uses in Latin American cities. The model combines wedge-shaped sectors and concentric rings emanating from a central business district. The wealthy live along a well-served commercial spine and the poorest residents live in peripheral squatter settlements.

latitude Angular distance of a location north or south of the *equator,* measured in degrees, minutes, and seconds. Grid lines marking latitude are called *parallels.* The equator is 0°; the North Pole is 90°N; the South Pole is 90°S.

law of retail gravitation Any *gravity model* of shopping behavior, such as *Reilly's Breaking-Point Law* or the *potential model* when applied to multiple stores or shopping centers.

least-cost theory (*syn:* Weberian analysis) The view that the optimum location of a manufacturing establishment is at the place where the costs of transporting raw materials and finished products, as well as labor, and the advantages of *agglomeration* or *deglomeration* are most favorable.

line-haul cost (*syn:* over-the-road cost) A cost involved in the actual physical movement of goods (or passengers); cost of haulage (including equipment and route costs), excluding *terminal costs.*

lingua franca Any of various auxiliary *languages* used as common tongues among people of an area where several languages are spoken; literally, "Frankish language."

linguistic geography (*syn:* dialect geography; dialectology) The study of the spatial distribution of languages, including the study of language groups and families, dialects, creoles and pidgins, and so on.

link A transportation or communication connection or route within a *network.*

lithosphere The earth's solid crust and mantle.

locational interdependence The circumstance under which the locational decision of a particular firm is influenced by the locations chosen by competitors. For example, retail businesses often choose their location in order to attract customers away from competing retail businesses.

longitude Angular distance of a location east or west of a designated *prime meridian*, measured in degrees, minutes, and seconds. Grid lines marking longitude are called *meridians*. Distances are measured from 0° at the *prime meridian* to 180° both east and west, with 180°E and W being the same line. For much of its extent, the 180°

meridian also serves as the *International Date Line.*

long-lot system A survey system that divides land into long, narrow strips extending back from a river or road, found in areas settled by French colonists.

M

Malthus Thomas R. Malthus (1766–1843). English economist, demographer, and cleric who suggested that unless self-control, war, or natural disaster checks population, it will inevitably increase faster than will the food supplies needed to sustain it. This view is known as Malthusianism. See also *neo-Malthusianism.*

map projection A systematic method of transferring the *globe grid* system from the earth's curved surface to the flat surface of a map. Projection automatically incurs error, but an attempt is usually made to preserve one or more (though never all) of the characteristics of the spherical surface: equal area, correct distance, true direction, proper shape.

map scale (*syn:* cartographic scale) See *scale*.

maquiladora Foreign-owned manufacturing plant located in Mexico for the low cost assembly of clothing, electronics, automobiles, and other export products.

mariculture Production and harvesting of fish and shellfish in fenced confinement areas along coasts and in estuaries.

market economy An economic system in which most goods and services are privately produced and distributed for monetary exchange; an economy characterized by free market exchange (freely varying prices and production systems) with no or only minimum state intervention.

market equilibrium The theoretically stable point of intersection of demand and supply curves of a given commodity; at equilibrium the market is cleared of the commodity.

market orientation The tendency of an economic activity to locate close to its market; a reflection of large and variable costs of transporting finished products.

Marx Karl Marx (1818–1883), German philosopher, economist, and social theorist who decried the inequalities produced by capitalism and advocated revolutionary change in order to bring about a communist system.

material culture The tangible, physical items produced and used by members of a specific *culture* group and reflective of their traditions, lifestyles, and technologies.

material orientation The tendency of an economic activity to locate near or at its source of raw material; this is experienced when the costs of transporting materials are highly variable spatially and/or represent a significant share of total costs.

mathematical projection The systematic rendering of the *globe grid* on a *developable surface* to achieve *graticule* characteristics not obtainable by visual means of *geometrical projection.*

maximum sustainable yield The maximum rate at which a *renewable resource* can be exploited without impairing its ability to be renewed or replenished.

Mediterranean agriculture An agricultural system based upon the mild, moist winters; hot, sunny summers; and rough terrain of the Mediterranean basin. It involves cereals as winter crops, summer tree and vine crops (olives, figs, dates, citrus and other tree fruits, and grapes), and grazing animals (sheep and goats).

mental map (*syn:* cognitive map) By analogy to a cartographic map, the set of mental representations people hold in their mind that expresses their beliefs and knowledge about the layout of the environment at different scales, whether neighborhoods, cities, regions, countries, or the entire world. The representations are subjective and influenced by personal feelings, and may be quite incomplete and distorted as compared to the actual layouts.

mentifact A central element of a *culture* expressing its values and beliefs, including *language, religion, folklore,* artistic traditions, and the like. An element in the *ideological subsystem* of culture.

Mercator projection A true *conformal cylindrical projection* first published in 1569; because straight lines drawn on this projection are lines of constant compass direction (*rhumb lines*), it is especially useful for navigation.

meridian A north-south line of *longitude* indicating distance east or west of the *prime meridian* running through Greenwich, England.

metes-and-bounds A system of property description and surveying using natural features (streams, rocks, trees, etc.) to trace and define the boundaries of individual parcels.

metropolitan area In the United States, a large functionally integrated settlement area comprising one or more whole county units and usually containing several *urbanized areas;* discontinuously built up, it operates as a coherent economic whole.

migration The permanent (or relatively permanent) relocation of an individual or group to a new place of residence.

migration field The area from which a given city or region draws the majority of its in-migrants.

mobility General term for all types of human movement through space and time, including *temporary travel* and *migration.*

model An idealized representation, abstraction, or simulation of reality. It is designed to simplify real-world complexity and eliminate extraneous phenomena in order to isolate for detailed study causal factors and interrelationships of *spatial systems.*

modernization theory An influential theory that attempts to explain patterns and processes of economic development. It sees societies arranged on a continuum between traditional and modern with modernization occurring as a society adopts advanced technologies and market mechanisms and experiences industrialization, urbanization, and rising prosperity.

monolingualism A society's or country's use of only one *language* for all purposes of communication.

monotheism The belief that there is but a single God.

mortality rate (*syn:* death rate) See *crude death rate.*

movement bias Any aggregate control on or regularity of movement of people, commodities, or communication. Included are *distance bias, direction bias,* and *network bias.*

multilinear evolution A concept of independent but parallel cultural development advanced by the anthropologist Julian Steward (1902–1972) to explain cultural similarities among widely separated peoples existing in similar environments but who could not have benefited from shared experiences, borrowed ideas, or diffused technologies. See *independent invention.*

multilingualism The common use of two or more *languages* in a society or country.

multiple-nuclei model The postulate that large cities develop by peripheral spread not from one *central business district* but from several nodes of growth, each of specialized use. The separately expanding use districts eventually coalesce at their margins. It also describes a common urban residence pattern corresponding to different ethnic groups (ethnic status).

multiplier effect The direct, indirect, and induced consequences of change in an activity. **1:** In industrial *agglomerations,* the cumulative processes by which a given change (such as a new plant opening) sets in motion a sequence of further industrial employment and *infrastructure* growth.

2: In *urban geography,* the expected addition of *nonbasic* workers and dependents to a city's total employment and population that accompanies new *basic sector* employment.

N

nation A culturally distinctive group who self-identity as a separate group, may or may not occupy a territorial homeland, and are bound together by a sense of unity arising from shared *ethnicity,* beliefs, and *customs.*

nationalism A sense of unity binding the people of a *state* together; devotion to the interests of a particular country, an identification with the state and an acceptance of its goals.

nation-state A *state* whose territory is identical to that occupied by a single particular *ethnic group* or *nation.*

natural boundary (*syn:* physical boundary) A *boundary* line based on recognizable physiographic features, such as mountains or rivers.

natural hazard A process or event in the natural environment that has consequences harmful to humans.

natural landscape The physical *environment* unaffected by human activities. The duration and near totality of human occupation of the earth's surface assures that little or no "natural landscape" strictly defined remains intact. Opposed to *cultural landscape.*

natural resource A feature or material in the environment that a population perceives to be necessary and useful to its maintenance and well-being.

neocolonialism A disparaging reference to economic and political policies by which major developed countries are seen to retain or extend influence over the economies of less developed countries and peoples. A continuing expression of dependency theory.

neolocalism A social movement advocating a return to local products, locally owned businesses, and locally controlled institutions in reaction against mass popular culture and globalization.

neo-Malthusianism The advocacy of population control programs to preserve and improve general national prosperity and well-being, and avoid the catastrophic consequences of overpopulation.

net migration The difference between in-migration and out-migration of an area.

network The areal pattern of sets of places (*nodes*) and the routes (*links*) connecting them, along which movement or communication can take place.

network bias The view that the pattern of *links* in a *network* will affect the likelihood of flows between specific *nodes*.

network city One of two or more nearby cities, potentially or actually complementary in function, that cooperate by developing transportation links and communications infrastructure joining them.

new international division of labor (NIDL) A spatial rearrangement of production in which developing countries capture more of the world's manufacturing activity while developed countries shift to services.

NIMBY (Not-In-My-Backyard) Protests from local residents that often appear when companies or public agencies try to select a location for a waste treatment facility or other potentially polluting facility.

node An origin, destination, or intersection place in a communication or transportation *network*.

nomadic herding Migratory but controlled movement of livestock solely dependent on natural forage. A type of *extensive subsistence agriculture*.

nonbasic sector Those economic activities of an urban area that supply the resident population with goods and services, have no "export" implication, and do not bring in wealth from outside the city.

nonecumene (*syn:* anecumene). That portion of the earth's surface that is uninhabited by people or only temporarily or intermittently inhabited. See also *ecumene*.

nonmaterial culture The oral traditions, songs, and stories of a *culture* group along with its beliefs and customary behaviors.

nonrenewable resource A *natural resource* that is not replenished or replaced by natural processes or is used at a rate that exceeds its replacement rate.

O

object *Geographic feature* thought of as a discrete bounded entity separated from other entities by space that can be conceived of as empty. Examples include mountain peaks or roads.

official language A governmentally designated *language* of instruction, of government, of the courts, and other official public and private communication.

offshoring The relocation of business processes and services to a lower-cost foreign location; the offshore *outsourcing* of, particularly, white-collar technical, professional, and clerical services.

orthographic projection A *geometrical projection* that results from placing the light source at infinity.

outsourcing 1: Producing abroad parts or products for domestic use or sale; 2: Subcontracting production or services rather than performing those activities "in house."

overpopulation A judgment that the resources of an area are insufficient to sustain adequately its present population numbers.

ozone A gas molecule consisting of three atoms of oxygen (O_3) formed when diatomic oxygen (O_2) is exposed to *ultraviolet radiation*. In the upper *atmosphere* it forms a normally continuous, thin layer that blocks ultraviolet light; in the lower atmosphere it constitutes a damaging component of *photochemical smog*.

P

palimpsest Originally a reused leather document with visible traces of previous writing. In cultural geography, the landscape may be viewed as a palimpsest containing evidence of previous cultures and previous land uses.

parallel invention See *independent invention*.

parallel An east-west line of *latitude* indicating distance north or south of the equator.

partial displacement migration *Migrations* wherein migrants move to a new residence nearby, with a new activity spaces that overlap some with their former home ranges.

pattern The design or spatial arrangement of phenomena on the earth surface.

peak land value intersection The most accessible and costly parcel of land in the *central business district* and, therefore, in the entire *urbanized area*.

perceptual region (*syn:* cognitive region) Geographic *region* created informally to reflect the subjective beliefs and feelings of individuals or cultural groups (in the latter case, they are also known as *vernacular regions*).

perforated state A *state* whose territory is interrupted ("perforated") by a separate, independent state totally contained within its borders.

peripheral model A depiction of the contemporary metropolitan area emphasizing patterns of suburban location and functions.

periphery/peripheral The outer regions or boundaries of an area. See also *core-periphery model*.

personal communication field An area defined by the distribution of an individual's

short-range informal communications. The size and shape of the field are defined by work, recreation, school, and other regular contacts and are affected by age, sex, employment, and other personal characteristics.

personal space An invisible, usually irregular area around a person into which he or she does not willingly admit others. The sense (and extent) of personal space is a situational and cultural variable.

physical boundary See *natural boundary*.

physical geography One of two major divisions (the other is *human geography*) of *systematic geography;* the study of the structures, processes, distributions, and change through time of the natural biophysical phenomena of the earth's surface that are significant to human life.

physiological density The number of persons per unit area of arable (cultivable) land.

pidgin An auxiliary *language* derived, with reduced vocabulary and simplified structure, from combinations of other languages. Not a native tongue, it is a cultural syncretism used for limited communication among people with different languages, such as in situations of trade.

place A particular geographic location with its unique biophysical, cultural, and social characteristics.

place perception Beliefs and attitudes people have about particular places, regions, or landscapes.

place stereotype A simplified belief or set of beliefs about a place that often reflect actual characteristics of the place somewhat inaccurately.

place utility 1: In human movement and *migration* studies, a measure of an individual's perceived satisfaction or approval of a place in its social, economic, or environmental attributes. 2: In *economic geography,* the value imparted to goods or services by *tertiary* activities that provide things needed in specific markets.

placelessness The loss of locally distinctive characteristics and identity and replacement by standardized landscapes.

planar projection (*syn:* azimuthal projection) A *map projection* employing a plane as the presumed *developable surface*.

planned economy A system of production of goods and services, usually consumed or distributed by a governmental agency, in quantities, at prices, and in locations determined, at least in part, by governmental programs.

plantation agriculture A large agricultural holding, frequently foreign owned, devoted to the production of a single export crop.

political geography A branch of *human geography* concerned with the spatial analysis of political phenomena.

polytheism Belief in or worship of more than one god.

popular culture The constantly changing mix of material and nonmaterial *culture traits* available through mass production and the mass media to an urbanized, heterogeneous, nontraditional society. Unlike *folk culture,* popular culture varies quickly over time but not much over space.

popular region See *vernacular region.*

population density A measurement of the numbers of persons per unit area of land within predetermined limits, usually political or census boundaries. See also *physiological density.*

population geography A division of *human geography* concerned with spatial variations in distribution, composition, growth, and movements of population.

population momentum (*syn:* demographic momentum) The tendency for population growth to continue despite rapid changes to fertility rates (such as due to stringent family planning programs) because of a relatively high concentration of people in the childbearing years.

population projection A prediction of a population's future size, age, and sex composition based on the application of stated assumptions to current data.

population pyramid A bar graph in pyramid form showing the age and sex composition of a population, usually a national one.

positional dispute (*syn:* boundary dispute) In *political geography,* disagreement about the actual location of a *boundary.*

possibilism The philosophical viewpoint that the physical *environment* offers human beings a set of opportunities from which (within limits) people may choose according to their cultural needs and technological awareness. The emphasis is on a freedom of choice and action not allowed under *environmental determinism,* while still recognizing the influence of the environment on culture.

post-industrial A stage of economic development in which service activities become relatively more important than goods production; professional and technical employment supersedes employment in agriculture and manufacturing; and level of living is defined by the quality of services and amenities rather than by the quantity of goods available.

potential model A measurement of the total interaction opportunities available under *gravity model* assumptions to a center in a multicenter system.

primary activity A part of the economy involved in making *natural resources* available for use or further processing; included are mining, *agriculture,* forestry, and fishing and hunting.

primate city When a country's leading city is disproportionately larger and functionally more complex than any other city; a city dominating an urban hierarchy composed of a base of small towns and an absence of intermediate-sized cities. Contrary to the *rank-size rule,* primate cities are considerably larger than twice the size of the second largest city in a country or region.

prime meridian An imaginary line passing through the Royal Observatory at Greenwich, England (now a suburb of London), serving by international agreement as the 08 line of *longitude.*

producer service A service sector activity performed for other businesses such as accounting, advertising, engineering consulting, and public relations.

projection See *map projection.*

prorupt state A *state* of basically *compact* form but with one or more narrow extensions of territory.

protolanguage An assumed, reconstructed, or recorded ancestral *language.*

Public Land Survey System (PLSS) A *rectangular survey* system adopted in the Land Ordinance of 1785 and used to divide land over much of the United States from Ohio to the West Coast. The PLSS creates a checkerboard township and range pattern, dividing land into square townships six miles on a side. Townships are further subdivided into 36 sections of land with each section one mile on a side.

pull factor Characteristic of a locale that acts as an attractive force, drawing migrants from other regions.

purchasing power parity (PPP) A measurement of a country's wealth that takes account of what money actually buys in the country, relative to the cost of living.

push factor Unfavorable characteristic of a locale that contributes to the dissatisfaction of its residents and impel their emigration.

R

rank-size rule An observed regularity in the city-size distribution of some countries. In a rank-size hierarchy, the population of any given town will be inversely proportional to its rank in the hierarchy; that is, the nth-ranked city will be $1/n$ the size of the largest city.

rate The frequency of an event's occurrence during a specified time period.

rate of natural increase *Birth rate* minus the *death rate,* suggesting the annual rate of population growth without considering *net migration.*

reapportionment The process and outcome of a reallocation of electoral seats to defined territories, such as congressional seats to states of the United States.

rectangular survey A survey system that superimposes a rectangular grid upon the land rather than using natural features to describe and divide land.

redistricting The drawing of new electoral district boundary lines in response to changing patterns of population or changing legal requirements.

reference map A general-purpose map that attempts to show *geographic features* such as roads and landforms accurately and in detail.

refugee *Forced* or *reluctant* migrant, usually at the international scale, fleeing difficult or dangerous environmental, military, economic, or political conditions.

region (*syn:* geographic region) Any earth area with distinctive and unifying physical or cultural characteristics that set it off and make it substantially different from surrounding areas. Regions and their boundaries are devices of areal generalization, intellectual concepts rather than just visible landscape entities.

regional concept The view that physical and cultural phenomena on the surface of the earth are rationally arranged by complex, diverse, but comprehensible interrelated spatial processes.

regional geography The study of the natural and cultural characteristics of geographic *regions;* the study of areal differentiation.

regionalism In *political geography,* group— frequently ethnic group—identification with a particular region of a *state* rather than with the state as a whole.

Reilly's Breaking-Point Law A *law of retail gravitation* proposed by William J. Reilly that finds the breaking point or boundary line of the market area *functional regions* around two cities' trade areas. It predicts that consumers will make shopping trips to the city within the market area in which they live.

relative direction Direction with respect to personal or cultural ideas rather than objective systems such as cardinal directions or landmarks.

relative distance A transformation of *absolute distance* into such relative measures as time or monetary costs. Such measures yield different explanations of human spatial behavior than do linear distances alone.

Distances between places are constant by absolute terms, but relative distances may vary with improvements in transportation or communication technology or with different perceptions of space.

relative location The position of a place or activity in relation to other places or activities (see *situation*). Relative location implies spatial relationships and usually suggests the relative advantages or disadvantages of a location with respect to all competing locations.

relic boundary A former *boundary* line that is still discernible and marked by some *cultural landscape* feature, such as a fence.

religion A personal or institutionalized system of worship and of faith in the sacred and divine.

relocation diffusion The transport of ideas, behaviors, or articles from one place to another through the *migration* of those possessing the feature transported.

reluctant relocation When people relocate their residence (migrate) somewhat involuntarily.

remittance Money sent by international migrants back to family members in their home country.

remote sensing Any of several techniques of obtaining images of an area or object without having the sensor in direct physical contact with it, as by aerial photography or satellite sensors.

renewable resource A *natural resource* that is potentially inexhaustible either because it is constantly (as solar radiation) or periodically (as *biomass*) replenished as long as its use does not exceed its *maximum sustainable yield*.

replacement level (*syn:* replacement fertility rate) The number of children per woman that will supply just enough births to replace parents and compensate for early deaths, keeping the population size of an area constant, with no allowance for *migration* effects; depending on the rate of survival into the reproductive years, calculated at between 2.1 and 2.5 children per woman.

representative fraction The *scale* of a map expressed as a ratio of a unit of distance on the map to distance measured in the same unit on the ground, e.g., 1:250,000 means that one inch on the map represents 250 thousand inches on the earth surface.

residential dissimilarity index A measure of how segregated a group is from other groups.

resource See *natural resource*.

resource dispute In *political geography,* disagreement over the control or use of shared resources, such as boundary rivers or jointly claimed fishing grounds.

return migration See *counter migration.*

rhumb line A directional line that crosses each successive *meridian* at a constant angle; a rhumb line accurately shows a constant compass direction. All straight lines are rhumb lines on the *Mercator projection* map.

rotation The agricultural practice of planting two or more crops simultaneously or successively on the same area to preserve fertility or to provide a plant cover to protect the soil.

S

sacred place Location with special significance to a religious group, and often attracting pilgrimages or worship rituals. Sacred places are often natural features or religious structures directly connected with a deity or associated with significant events in the history of a particular religion.

satisficing location A less-than-ideal best location, but one providing an acceptable level of utility or satisfaction.

scale 1: In cartography, the ratio between the size of area on a map and the actual size of that same area on the earth's surface. **2:** In more general terms, scale refers to the size of the area studied or over which some phenomenon exists, from local to global.

S-curve The horizontal bending, or leveling, of an exponential or J-*curve* of population growth.

secondary activity Part of the economy involved in the processing of raw materials derived from *primary activities* and in altering or combining materials to produce commodities of enhanced utility and value; included are manufacturing, construction, and power generation.

sector model A description of urban land uses as wedge-shaped sectors radiating outward from the *central business district* along transportation corridors. The radial access routes attract particular uses to certain sectors, with high-status residential uses occupying the most desirable wedges. Thus, it also describes a common urban residence pattern corresponding to different levels of socioeconomic status (social status).

secularism A rejection of or indifference to *religion* and religious practice.

segregation A measure of the degree to which members of a minority group are not uniformly distributed among the total population.

separatism See *ethnic separatism.*

service sector See *tertiary activities.*

sequential occupation The use and modification of the cultural landscape

by successive cultural groups, reflecting differing cultural values, technologies, and social relations.

shamanism A set of beliefs and practices in some *tribal religions* based on belief in a hidden world of gods, ancestral spirits, and demons responsive only to a shaman or interceding priest.

shifting cultivation (*syn:* slash-and-burn agriculture; swidden agriculture) Crop production on tropical forest clearings kept in cultivation until their quickly declining fertility is lost. Cleared plots are then abandoned and new sites are prepared. A type of *extensive subsistence agriculture.*

Shinto The *polytheistic, ethnic religion* of Japan that includes reverence of deities of natural forces and veneration of the emperor as descendent of the sun-goddess.

Simon Julian Simon (1932–1998), American economist who rejected *neo-Malthusian* arguments, instead arguing that population growth generates economic growth and innovation.

site A concept of *absolute location*, describes a place by reference to characteristics at the location of the place itself, such as local landforms, climate, ethnicity of residents, and other physical or cultural characteristics.

situation A concept of *relative location*, describes a place by reference to characteristics that derive from the place's location relative to other places or the larger regional or *spatial system* of which it is a part. Situation implies spatial interconnection and interdependence.

slash-and-burn cultivation See *shifting cultivation.*

social dialect See *dialect.*

social distance A measure of the perceived degree of social separation between individuals, *ethnic groups,* neighborhoods, or other groupings; the voluntary or enforced *segregation* of two or more distinct social groups for most activities.

sociofact A rule, custom, or institution that links individuals and groups as part of a *culture,* including family structure and political, educational, and religious institutions. An element in the *sociological subsystem* of culture.

sociological subsystem The totality of expected and accepted patterns of interpersonal relations and social rituals that characterize a *culture*, along with the *ideological* and *technological subsystems.*

soil The complex mixture of loose material including minerals, organic and inorganic compounds, living organisms, air, and water found at the earth's surface and capable of supporting plant life.

soil erosion See *erosion.*

space As used by geographers, it does not refer to outer space but to areal extent on the earth's surface, in and around which all humans exist and their activity occurs.

space-time compression/ convergence Expressions of the extent to which improvements in transportation and communication have reduced the *friction of distance* and permitted, for example, the very rapid *diffusion* of ideas across space. *Globalization* depends in part on space-time compression.

space-time path A diagram of the line through space and time which describes where we are at any given time, how long we spend there, and how fast we move between locations; they are usually described at the scale of single days but may be monthly, yearly, or lifetime paths. Space-time paths must fit within space-time prisms.

space-time prism A diagram of the volume of space and the length of time within which our activities are confined by constraints of our bodily needs (eating, resting), our daily responsibilities, and the means of mobility at our command.

spatial assimilation A part of the assimilation process in which a minority population leaves its segregated enclaves and becomes widely distributed through a territory.

spatial association When the spatial arrangements of two distributions of features correspond or covary with each other in some way.

spatial diffusion See *diffusion.*

spatial distribution The arrangement of things on the earth's surface; the descriptive elements of spatial distribution are *density, dispersion,* and *pattern.*

spatial interaction The movement (e.g., of people, goods, information) between different places; an indication of contact and interdependence between different geographic locations or areas.

spatial margin of profitability The set of points delimiting the area within which an economic activity can be profitably carried out.

spatial search The process by which individuals evaluate the alternative locations to which they might move.

spatial system The arrangement and integrated operation of phenomena produced by or responding to spatial processes on the earth's surface.

spatially fixed cost An input cost in manufacturing that remains constant wherever production is located; locational decisions are not influenced much by such costs.

spatially variable cost An input cost in manufacturing that changes significantly from place to place in its amount and its relative share of total costs; locational decisions are influenced considerably by such costs.

speech community A group of people having common characteristic patterns of vocabulary, word arrangement, and pronunciation.

spread effect (*syn:* trickle-down effect) The diffusion outward of the benefits of economic growth and prosperity from the power center or *core area* to poorer districts and people.

standard language A *language* substantially uniform with respect to spelling, grammar, pronunciation, and vocabulary and representing the approved community norm of the tongue.

standard line Line of contact between a projection surface and the globe; locations covered by the line are transformed from the sphere to the plane surface without distortion.

state (*syn:* country) An independent political unit occupying a defined, permanently populated territory and internationally recognized as having full sovereign control over its internal and foreign affairs.

step (stepwise) migration A *migration* in which an eventual long-distance relocation is undertaken in stages as, for example, from farm to village to small town to city. See also *hierarchical migration.*

stereographic projection A *geometrical projection* that results from placing the light source at the *antipode.*

subnationalism The feeling that one owes primary allegiance to a traditional group or nation rather than to the state.

subsequent boundary A *boundary* line that is established after the area in question has been settled and that reflects the cultural characteristics of the bounded area.

subsistence agriculture Any of several agricultural economies in which crops are grown or livestock are raised nearly exclusively for local or family consumption.

subsistence economy An economic system of relatively simple technology in which people produce most or all of the goods to satisfy their own and their family's needs; little or no exchange occurs outside of the family or social group.

substitution principle In industry, the tendency to substitute one factor of production for another in order to achieve optimum plant location.

suburb A functionally specialized segment of a large *urban* complex located outside the boundaries of the *central city;* usually, a relatively homogeneous residential community, separately incorporated and administered.

superimposed boundary A *boundary* line placed over and ignoring an existing cultural pattern.

supranationalism Term applied to associations created by three or more states for their mutual benefit and achievement of shared objectives.

sustainable development A concept popularized by the World Commission on Environment and Development's Bruntland Report (1987) calling for development that meets the needs of the present without endangering the ability of future generations to meet their needs; the concept of sustainable development seeks to balance the desire for economic growth with the recognition of environmental limits to growth.

syncretism The development of a new form of *culture trait* by the fusion of two or more distinct parental traits.

systematic geography An approach to geographic study that selects a particular aspect of the physical or cultural *environment* for detailed study of its areal differentiation and interrelationships. Branches of systematic geography are labeled according to the topic studied (e.g., recreational geography) or the related science with which the branch is associated (e.g., *economic geography*).

T

Taoism (*syn:* Daoism) A Chinese *value system* and *ethnic religion* emphasizing conformity to Tao (Way), the creative reality ordering the universe.

tapering principle The diminution or tapering of costs of transportation with increasing distance from the point of origin of the shipment because of the averaging of *fixed costs* over a greater number of miles of travel.

technological subsystem The complex of material objects together with the techniques of their use by means of which people carry out their productive activities and that characterize a *culture*, along with the *ideological* and *sociological subsystems.*

technology The integrated system of knowledge, skills, tools, and methods developed within or used by a *culture* to successfully carry out purposeful and productive tasks.

technology gap The contrast between the *technology* available in developed *core regions* and that present in *peripheral areas* of *underdevelopment.*

technology transfer The *diffusion* to or acquisition by one *culture* or *region* of the *technology* possessed by another, usually more developed, society.

temporary travel Short-term *mobility*, such as journeys to stores, workplaces, school, entertainment locales, or vacation destinations, in which people intend to return home at the end of the day or soon thereafter.

terminal cost (*syn:* fixed cost of transportation) A cost incurred, and charged, for loading and unloading freight at origin and destination points and for the paperwork involved; cost charged each shipment for terminal facility use and unrelated to distance of movement or *line-haul cost.*

terracing The practice of planting crops on steep slopes that have been converted into a series of horizontal step-like level plots (terraces).

territorial dispute (*syn:* boundary dispute; functional dispute) In *political geography,* disagreement between *states* over the control of surface area, including the locations of boundaries.

territoriality An individual or group attempt to identify and establish control over a defined territory considered partially or wholly an exclusive domain; the behavior associated with the defense of the home territory.

terrorism Systematic open and covert action employing the inducement of fear and terror as a means of political coercion.

tertiary activity (syn: service sector) A part of the economy that fulfills the exchange function, that provides market availability of commodities, and that brings together consumers and providers of services; included are wholesale and retail trade, associated transportation and government services, and personal and professional services of all kinds.

thematic map (*syn:* statistical map) A specific-purpose map that shows the distribution of one or a few themes or variables, such as unemployment rates by county.

thematic region (sometimes *formal region*) Geographic *region* based on the pattern of one or more objectively measurable themes or properties, such as soil types or linguistic dialects.

themed landscape Built environments designed to suggest or simulate a distinctive place, created to attract visitors by allowing them to fantasize about being in different times, places, and events. Disneyland and Las Vegas are two of the most famous examples, but more modest examples can be found in many shopping malls, chain restaurants, housing subdivisions, and the like.

Third World Originally (1950s) designating countries uncommitted to either the "First World" Western capitalist bloc or the "Second World" Eastern communist bloc; subsequently, a term applied to countries considered in a state of *underdevelopment* in economic and social terms.

threshold In *economic geography* and *central place theory,* the minimum market area or population needed to support the supply of a product or service.

time geography The study of temporal and spatial properties of human activity, particularly temporary travel.

tipping point The degree of neighborhood racial or ethnic mixing that induces the former majority group to move out rapidly.

toponym A place or geographic feature name.

toponymy The place names of a region or, especially, the study of place names.

total displacement migration *Migrations* wherein migrants move far enough so their new activity spaces do not overlap at all with their former home ranges.

total fertility rate (TFR) The average number of children that would be born to each woman during her childbearing years if she bore children at the current year's rate for women of that age.

town A nucleated settlement that contains a *central business district* but that is small and less functionally complex than a *city.*

tragedy of the commons The observation that in the absence of collective control over the use of a resource available to all, it is to the advantage of all users to maximize their separate shares even though their collective pressures may diminish total yield or destroy the resource altogether.

transboundary river basin Drains land from two or more countries, thus requiring international cooperation over the management of water resources.

transferability Acceptable costs of a spatial exchange; the cost of moving a commodity relative to the ability of the commodity to bear that cost.

transnational corporation (TNC) A large business organization operating in at least two separate national economies; a form of *multinational corporation.*

transnationalism The practice of immigrants maintaining close social or economic ties to their country of origin through frequent travel or communications.

tribal religion (*syn:* traditional religion) An *ethnic religion* specific to a small, localized, preindustrial culture group.

trickle-down effect See *spread effect.*

truck farming (*syn:* horticultural farming; market gardening) The intensive production of fruits and vegetables for market rather than for processing or canning.

U

ubiquitous industry A *market-oriented* industry whose establishments are distributed in direct proportion to the distribution of population.

underdevelopment A level of economic and social achievement below what could be reached—given the natural and human resources of an area—were necessary capital and technology available.

uneven spatial development The uneven spatial pattern observed in standards of living and levels of economic development.

uniform (*syn:* isotropic) **plain** A hypothetical portion of the earth's surface assumed to be an unbounded, uniformly flat plain with uniform and unvarying distribution of population, purchasing power, transport costs, accessibility, and the like. Commonly assumed as a simplification in geographic models of spatial interaction and economic activity.

unitary state A *state* in which the central government dictates the degree of local or *regional autonomy* and the nature of local governmental units; a country with few cultural conflicts and with a strong sense of national identity.

United Nations Convention on the Law of the Sea (UNCLOS) A code of maritime law approved by the United Nations in 1982 that authorizes, among other provisions, territorial waters extending 12 nautical miles (22 km) from shore and 200-nautical-mile-wide (370-km-wide) *exclusive economic zones.*

universalizing religion A *religion* that claims global truth and applicability, regardless of ethnicity or culture group, and seeks the conversion of all humankind via proselytizing.

urban geography The geographical study of cities; the branch of *human geography* concerned with the spatial aspects of (1) the locations, functional structures, size hierarchies, and intercity relationships of national or regional systems of cities, and (2) the *site,* evolution, *economic base,* internal land use, and social geographic patterns of individual cities.

urban hierarchy A ranking of cities based on their size and functional complexity.

urban influence zone An area outside of a *city* that is nevertheless affected by the city.

urbanization Transformation of a population from rural to *urban* status; the process of city formation and expansion.

urbanized area A continuously built-up *urban* landscape defined by building and population densities with no reference to the political boundaries of the city; it may contain a *central city* and many contiguous towns, *suburbs,* and unincorporated areas.

usable reserves Mineral deposits that have been identified and can be recovered at current prices and with current technology.

V

vernacular 1: The nonstandard indigenous *language* or *dialect* of a locality. 2: Of or related to indigenous arts and architecture, such as a *vernacular house.* 3: Of or related to the perceptions and understandings of the general population, such as a *vernacular region.*

vernacular house An indigenous style of building constructed of native materials to traditional plan, without formal drawings.

vernacular region A *perceptual region* defined informally by inhabitants of a cultural group, usually with a popularly given or accepted nickname.

voluntary migration When people relocate their residence by free choice, without being forced or compelled.

von Thünen model Model developed by Johann Heinrich von Thünen (1783–1850), German economist and landowner, to explain the forces that control the prices of agricultural commodities and how those variable prices affect spatial patterns of agricultural land utilization.

W

Weberian analysis See *least-cost theory.*

world city One of a small number of interconnected, internationally dominant centers (e.g., New York, London, Tokyo) that together control the global systems of finance and commerce.

X

xenophobia A hatred or fear of that which is foreign, often directed at immigrant minority groups.

Z

zero population growth (ZPG) A term suggesting a population in equilibrium, fully stable in numbers with births (plus immigration) equaling deaths (plus emigration).

Credits

Chapter One

Opener 1: © Thinkstock/Masterfile RF; 1.1: © Karl Weatherly/Corbis; 1.10: © Doug Sherman/Geofile RF; 1.11: © NASA; 1.12a: © Historical Museum of Southern Florida; 1.12b: © South Florida Water Management District; 1.18: © Brand X Pictures/PunchStock RF; 1.22: © U.S. Geological Survey

Chapter Two

Opener: © Roger De La Harpe/Gallo Images/Corbis; 2.1a: © McGraw-Hill Companies, Inc./Lissa Harrison, photographer; 2.1b: © Tim McCabe, U.S. Dept. of Agriculture National Resource Conservation Service.; 2.2a: © Walter Gans/The Image Works; 2.2b: © 1997 IMS Communications Ltd./Capstone Design. All Rights Reserved; 2.3: © The McGraw-Hill Companies, Inc./Barry Barker, photographer; 2.5: © Jeremy/Woodhouse/Getty RF; 2.6: © DLILLC/Corbis RF; p. 39: © Jon Malinowski/Human Landscape Studio; 2.7: © Brand X Pictures/PunchStock RF; 2.11: © Aubrey Land/Valan Photos; 2.14a: © Galen Rowell/Corbis; 2.14b: © Bojan Brecelj/Corbis; 2.16: © 1998 IMS Communications Ltd./Capstone Design. All Rights Reserved; 2.17a: © The McGraw-Hill Companies/Barry Barker, photographer; 2.17b: Scott Bauer/USDA Agriculture Research Services; 2.18a: © Cary Wolinsky/Stock Boston; 2.18b: © Somos Photography/Veer RF; 2.18c: © John Eastcott/Momatiuk/The Image Works; 2.18d: © PhotoDisc/Getty RF; 2.19a: © Vol. 94/Corbis RF; 2.19b: © Rob Melnychuk/Getty RF; 2.19c: © Vol. 145/Corbis RF; 2.24: © Geoffrey Hiller/eStock Photography; 2.25: Jon C. Malinowski/Human Landscape Studio

Chapter Three

Opener: © Goodshot/PunchStock RF; 3.1: © Mark Bjelland; 3.8a: McGraw-Hill Higher Education, Inc.; 3.8b: © Daniel Montello; 3.20: © Bettmann/Corbis; 3.21: © Jocelyn Augustino/FEMA; 3.22: © Vanderlei Almeida/AFP/Getty; 3.26: © AP Photo/Ron Haviv; 3.28: © AP Photo/Dennis Poroy; 3.33: © Arthur Getis

Chapter Four

Opener: © Goodshoot/Fotosearch RF; 4.2: © PhotoDisc/Getty RF; p. 98: © Alasdair Drysdale; 4.17: © Topham/The Image Works; 4.18: Lynn Betts, USDA, Natural Resources Conservation Center; 4.23: © Glen Allison/Getty RF; 4.24: © U.S. Fish and Wildlife Service, Alaska; 4.26: © The McGraw-Hill Companies/Barry Barker, photographer; 4.28: © Carl Purcell; 4.30: © Nathan Benn/Corbis

Chapter Five

Opener: © Jenny Matthews/Panos Pictures; 5.1: Courtesy Susan Reisenweaver; 5.8: © Mark Antman/The Image Works; 5.15: © Mark Bjelland; 5.18: © The McGraw-Hill Companies, Inc./photographer Mike Camille; 5.23: © Corbis RF; 5.25b: © Mark Bjelland; 5.26: © Topham/The Observer/The Image Works; 5.28: © Getty RF; 5.29: © Porterfield/Chickering/Photo Researchers; 5.30: © Fred Bruemmer/Valan Photos; 5.32: © MedioImages/Getty RF; 5.33: © Geostock/Getty RF; 5.34 and 5.35 a–d: © Mark Bjelland

Chapter Six

Opener: © Dennis MacDonald/Alamy RF; 6.1: © Philippe Gontier/The Image Works; 6.2: © J. Messerschmidt/BCI/Photoshot; 6.3: © Comstock RF; 6.5: © Mark Bjelland; 6.7: © Chromosohm Media/The Image Works; 6.12: Library of Congress, Geography and Map Division (g3861ecw0013200) © Historic, Inc.; 6.16: © Stephanie Maze/Corbis; 6.17: © Perry Mastrovito/Creatas/PictureQuest RF; 6.20, 6.23b&c: © Mark Bjelland; 6.24: © Martha Cooper/Peter Arnold/Alamy; 6.25: © Tony Freeman/Photo Edit; 6.26: © Sue Moen suepics.com

Chapter Seven

Opener: © Corbis RF; 7.1: © Ilene MacDonald/Alamy RF; 7.2a: © Courtesy of Jean Fellmann; 7.3: © Susan Reisenweaver; 7.4: © Farrell Grehan/Photo Researchers; 7.9: © 1997 IMS Communications Ltd./Capstone Design. All Rights Reserved.; 7.10: Jon C. Malinowski/Human Landscape Studio; 7.12: © Jerry Fellmann; 7.14a: Courtesy of Uinta Brewing Company; 7.14b: © Weeping Radish Farm Brewery, Grandy, NC; 7.14c: Courtesy of Ruby Mountain Brewing Company; 7.20 (tl): Author's Image/PunchStock RF; 7.20 (ml), (bl): © Mark Bjelland; 7.20 (tr): Comstock/PunchStock RF; 7.20 (mr): © Michael Dwyer/Stock Boston; 7.20 (br): Copyleft Elvin Wyly; 7.25a: © Ira Kirschenbaum/Stock Boston; 7.25b: © Pam Hickman/Valan Photos; 7.25c: © Courtesy of Professor Colin E. Thorn; 7.25d: © Steven Rothfeld/Getty; 7.25e: © Photofrenetic/Alamy RF; 7.35f: © Corbis RF; 7.27: Courtesy of Professor John A. Jakle; 7.28: Jon C. Malinowski/Human Landscape Studio; 7.29a: Courtesy of Professor John A. Jakle; 7.29b: © Susan Reisenweaver; 7.29c & 7.31a: Courtesy of Professor John A. Jakle; 7.31b & 7.32: © Susan Reisenweaver; 7.33: © Sharon Wildman; 7.34a: © Jerry Fellmann; 7.35: © Mark Bjelland; 7.36: © Robert Moline; 7.37a–c, 7.38, 7.39a–c: © Mark Bjelland; 7.40: © Corbis RF; 7.41: © Syracuse Newspapers/David Lassman/The Image Works; 7.42: © Joseph Nettis/Stock Boston; 7.43: © Goodshoot/PunchStock RF; 7.44: Image from the Metropolitan Design Center, College of Design, University of Minnesota. © Regents of the University of Minnesota. All rights reserved. Used with permission. (www.dcl.umn.edu); 7.45: © Digital Vision/PunchStock RF

Chapter Eight

Opener: © Design Pics/Kelly Redinger RF; 8.1: © Getty RF; 8.3: © Corbis RF; 8.9a: © David Meisner; 8.9b: © David Meisner; 8.10: © Lindsay Hebberd/Corbis; 8.13: © Bill Gillette/Stock Boston; 8.18a: © Digital Vision/PunchStock RF; 8.18b: © Keith Meyers/New York Times Pictures; 8.18c: © Cathryn Dowd; 8.19: © Corbis RF; 8.22: © Christopher Pillitz/The Image Bank/Getty; p. 265: © Michelle Palm; 8.23: © Corbis RF; 8.28: © Larry Tackett Productions; 8.31: © McGraw-Hill Companies, Inc./photographer Stephen Reynolds; 8.32: © Thomas Kitchin/Valan Photos; 8.33: © Medioimages/Superstock RF; 8.34: © United Nations/DPI Photo; 8.26: © Cameramann International

Chapter Nine

Opener: © Getty RF; 9.1: © Mark Bjelland; 9.6: © Digital Vision/Getty RF; 9.13: © Cameramann International; 9.14: © Sharon Stewart; 9.15: © Mark Bjelland; 9.16a&b: © Mark Henley/Panos Pictures; 9.16c: © Cancan Chu/Getty; 9.16d: © Caroline Penn/Panos Pictures; 9.16e: © Reuters/Corbis; 9.18: © David McNew/Getty; 9.19: © STR/AFP/Getty; 9.22: Copyleft Elvin Wyly; 9.28: © Brand X Pictures/SuperStock RF; 9.29: © Mark Bjelland; 9.30: © Sondeep Shankar/Bloomberg/Getty

Chapter Ten

Opener: © John Van Hasselt/Sygma/Corbis; 10.1: © Anna Versluis; 10.2a: © Cameramann International; 10.2b: © Jason Clay/Anthro Photo File; 10.6: © Flat Earth Images RF; 10.7: © Sean Sprague/Panos Pictures; 10.10: © AP Photo/Brennan Linsley; 10.13: © Louise Grubb/The Image Works; 10.14: © David Hiser/Stone/Getty; 10.17: © Gail Shore/Cultural Jambalaya; 10.19: © Sharon A. Jones, University of Portland, Shiley School of Engineering; 10.20: © Design Pics/Bildenburch RF; 10.21: © Liba Taylor/Corbis

Chapter Eleven

Opener: © Corbis RF; 11.1 © Scott Gilchrist/ Masterfile; 11.8a: © William E. Ferguson; 11.8b: © Akira Kaede/Getty RF; 11.9: © J. Baylor Roberts/ National Geographic Image Collection; 11.10: ©Pixtal/age Fotostock RF; 11.11: © Pixtal/age fotostock RF; 11.18a: © TongRo Image Stock/ Alamy RF; 11.18b & 11.20: © Mark Bjelland; p. 369: © Ilene MacDonald/Alamy RF; 11.32: © Kevin Bauman; 11.33 (left & right) & p. 375: © Bettmann/Corbis; 11.35: Photo by Lynn Betts, USDA Natural Resources Conservation Service; 11.36a&b, p. 378: © Mark Bjelland; 11.37: © David Grossman/The Image Works; 11.38: © Stockbyte/Getty RF; p. 380: © Amanda Clement/ Getty RF; 11.39: © Eastcott/Momatuik/The Image Works; 11.40: © alasdair Drysdale RF; 11.41a: © Julia Waterlow/Corbis; 11.41b: © Jose Fuste Raga/Corbis; 11.42: © Adalberto Rios Lanz/Sexto Sol/Getty RF; 11.43: © Mark Henley/Panos Pictures; 11.44: © Paul Almay/Corbis; 11.46: © Mehdi Chebil/Alamy

Chapter Twelve

Opener: © Peter Adams/Getty RF; 12.1: Courtesy of the Pilgrim Society, Plymouth, MA; 12.2: © Joseph Sohm/Visions of America/Corbis RF; 12.11: © Chris Groenhout; 12.13a: © D. Falconer/ PhotoLink/Getty RF; 12.13b: © Corbis RF; 12.14: © 1997 IMS Communications Ltd./Capstone Design. All rights reserved/RF; 12.17b: © John Nelson/San Diego Union Tribune/ZUMA; 12.18: McGraw-Hill Higher Education, Inc./Jill Braaten, photographer; 12.20b: © AP Photo/Aranberri; 12.21: © AFP/Getty

Chapter Thirteen

Opener: © AP Images/Rajesh Nirgude; 13.8a: © Gregory Mancuso/Stock Boston; 13.8b: © Robert Landau/Corbis; 13.10: © Brand X Pictures/ PunchStock RF; 13.12a: © William E. Ferguson; 13.12b: © Susan Reisenweaver; 13.14a: © Mark Bjelland; 13.14b: © BioRegional; 13.17: © Jim Richardson/Corbis; 13.19: © Lissa Harrison; 13.20: © David Rose/Panos Pictures; 13.24 a&b: EROS Data Center USGS; 13.26: © The McGraw-Hill Companies/Barry Barker, photographer; 13.28: © Roger A. Clark/Photo Researchers; 13.29a: © Getty RF; 13.29b: Courtesy Office of Civilian Waste Management. Department of Energy; p. 455: Photo by Lynn Betts, USDA Natural Resources Conservation Service

INDEX

A

locational interdependence theory, 305–306
locational triangle, 289
location maps, 22
log cabins, 229
logarithms, 55
Lomax, Alan, 209, 210
longitude, 7, 22–23
long-lot survey system, 223
Lowland South folk culture region, 208
low-level waste, 452
Luxembourg, 414

M

Maasai, 35–36, 225, 226
Madagascar, 40
Mahayana, 159–160
Majority World, 316
Makuei, Chief, 126
malaria, 110, 327, 328
Malaysia
    agriculture, 250, 264
    political geography, 400, 413
    religion, 158
    trade, 277, 295
    urban systems, 384, 385
Mali, 224, 329, 443
malls, shopping, 234–235, 236
malnutrition, 102, 321–323
malquiladoras, 293, 295
Malta, 414
Malthus, Thomas Robert, 119–121
Mandarin language, 126–127, 134–135, 136, 140
manufactured goods, 276–277
manufacturing, 242, 283
    city functions and, 355
    clothing and textile industry, 295
    high-tech, 297–299
    industrial location theory, 288–290
    locational decisions, 283–286, 290–294
    transnational corporations, 295–296
    transportation and location, 286–288
    world patterns and trends, 299–303
manyatta, 225, 226
Maori, 39
MapQuest, 25
maps, 19–25
    mental, 28, 29
    systems and models and, 28, 30
map scales, 11, 19–22
Marielitos, 186
marine catch, 266
maritime boundaries, 411
market economy, 243–244, 282–283, 285, 288. *See also* economic geography
market mechanisms, 282
market orientation, 285
Marx, Karl, 120, 332
mass communication, 72–73
mass culture, 211
master-planned communities, 368
material culture, 205, 234–235, 236
material orientation, 284
maternal mortality rates, 100–102

mathematical location, 7
maximum sustainable yield, 266
Maya, 48
Mayflower Compact, 390
Mecca, 156
media, 72–73, 212. *See also* communication
Mediterranean agriculture, 263
megachurches, 163, 164
megacities, 345–347
megalopolis, 347, 350
Meinig, D. W., 220
melting pot, 176
membership functions, uniform and non-uniform, 18
mental maps, 28, 29
mentifacts, 49, 51, 54, 198, 206. *See also* language; religion
MERCOSUR (Southern Cone Community Market), 89, 414
meridians, 22–23
Mesoamerica, 48
Mesoamerican language, 132
Mesolithic period, 42, 43
Mesopotamia, 47, 48, 56
metals, 270–271
metes-and-bounds system, 223
methane, 436
metropolitan areas, 360–361
metropolitanization, 370
metropolitan statistical area, 361. *See also* urban systems
Mexican Americans, 185–187
Mexico
    agriculture, 263, 264
    charter cultures, 180–181
    clothing and textile industry, 295
    cultural landscape, 12
    early culture hearths, 48
    foreign aid, 334
    garbage and toxic waste, 454
    landlessness, 336
    manufacturing trends, 299
    migration and, 82, 83, 84–85, 88
    NAFTA, 293
    political geography, 414
    urban systems, 359, 383
    water supply and quality, 449
microbreweries, 213–214, 215, 216
microdistricts, 380
microlending, 338
Mid-Atlantic folk culture region, 208
middens, 449
Middle Atlantic culture hearths, 227–230
Middle East
    agriculture development, 45, 46
    deforestation, 440
    early culture hearths, 47
    economy, 244
    food insecurity, 322
    fossil fuels, 274
    political geography, 408
    population issues, 121
    urban systems, 381
    water supply and quality, 446, 448–449
Middle English, 133
middle-income countries, 315
Middle Stone Age, 42, 43
Midwest folk culture region, 208

Mien, 198
migration
    controls on, 81–89
    demographic equation, 111–113
    ethnic geography, 173–176, 186
    illegal, 80, 82, 83
    impact of, 111, 113
    "laws of," 86–87
    overview, 67, 78
    patterns of, 78–79
    political geography, 395
    types of, 79–81
migration fields, 85, 86
militant fundamentalism, 57, 149, 157
military alliances, 415–416
military systems, 50, 405
Millennium Declaration, 317
Millennium Development Goals, 101, 317, 384
milpa, 248
minerals, 265, 269–276
mining, 265, 269–276
ministates, 396
Minneapolis, 67, 72
minorities. *See* ethnic geography
Mississippi cultural landscape, 230
Mitchell, Don, 221
mobility, 67, 67, 193–194, 196, 197
models, maps as, 28, 30
moderately developed countries, 315
modernity, 205
modernization theory, 330–331
Moldova, 180
Mongols, 178
Monmonier, Mark, 26
monolingualism, 142
monotheism, 147
Montreal Protocol, 435
more developed countries, defined, 316
Mormon Church, 154, 155, 220
Moros, 407
mortality rates, 100–102, 107–113
mortgage lending, 369–370
motherhood, risks of, 101
motor trucks, 286, 287
movement biases, 65–66
Mozambique, 381
multiculturalism, 178, 403
multilinear evolution, 48–49
multilingualism, 138, 141–142
multinational corporations, 90, 168, 295–296, 390, 410
multinational state, 392
multiple-nuclei model, urban systems, 364, 365
multiplier effect, 291, 353, 355
music, 209–210, 214–217,
Muslims, 97, 121, 146, 147, 156–158, 250, 338
Myanmar (Burma), 158, 217, 249, 400
Myrdal, Gunnar, 331
mythology, 49

N

NAFTA (North American Free Trade Agreement), 293, 414
Namibia, 330
Napier, John, 55

national census, 118–119
national housing styles, 231–232
nationalism, 180, 395, 403–404, 406
national uniformity, 211–213
nation building, 393, 395
nations
    authority of, 405–409
    cohesion, 403–405
    cooperation among, 410–416
    evolution of, 392–395
    geographic considerations, 395–400
    overview, 391–392
nation-states, 391–392
Native American languages, 132
Native Americans, 39, 80, 178–180, 183, 205, 207, 225, 226, 227, 307. *See also* folk culture
native-born dispersal, 196, 197
NATO (North Atlantic Treaty Organization), 415, 417
natural boundaries, 401
natural catastrophes, 48, 80, 314
natural gas, 276
natural hazards, 75–77
natural landscape, 11–12
natural resources, 11–12, 119–121, 252–254, 265–276, 282–283, 284, 329
natural systems
    acid precipitation, 431–434
    air pollution, 431–434
    climates, biomes and change, 427–429, 430
    cultural impacts on, 429, 431
    dams, 442–443
    desertification, 441–443
    global climate change, 435–439
    land use, 439–445
    ozone, 434–435
    prospects and perspectives, 455
    soil erosion, 443–445
    solid wastes, 449–451
    toxic wastes, 451–454
    tropical deforestation, 440–443
    wastes, 449–454
    water supply and quality, 445–449
navigation websites, 25
Near East, 44, 45, 47, 121, 140, 368
NeDené languages, 132
neocolonialism, 332
neoliberal globalization, 332–333
Neolithic period, 45–46
neolocalism, 213
neo-Malthusianism, 120–121
Nepal, 256, 321, 336
Netherlands, 414
networks, 66
network cities, 359
networks, 14
New Guinea, 141, 249
new international division of labor (NIDL), 294
newly industrialized countries (NICs), 121, 299, 315
New Orleans, 9
New Stone Age, 45
New World culture hearths, 47–49
New York, 170, 224, 377
New World, 330
New Zealand, 39, 121, 263, 318, 330
Newton, Isaac, 55, 64

NGOs (nongovernmental organizations), 395, 410
Nicaragua, 186, 326, 382
NICs (newly industrialized countries), 299, 316
Niger, 443
Nigeria, 141, 180, 264, 320, 383, 385, 400, 454
nodal regions, 18, 20
nodes, 66
nomadic farming, 248–249
nomadic herding, 247–248
nonbasic sector, economic, 353
nonecumene, 115, 116
nongovernmental organizations (NGOs), 395, 410
nonmaterial culture, 205
nonmetallic minerals, 272–273
nonrenewable resources, 266
non-uniform membership regions, 18
North Africa, 121
North America, 132, 135–138, 163–165, 260, 269, 274, 301, 347, 349, 440. See also Canada; United States
North America Free Trade Agreement (NAFTA), 89, 293, 410
North Atlantic Treaty Organization (NATO), 415, 417
North folk culture region, 208
North Korea, 217, 244
North Pole, 22
North-South line, 316–317, 318–320, 329
Northern culture hearths, 227, 228
Northern Ireland, 146, 149
Northern song era, 209–210
Norway, 340, 414
Not in My Backyard (NIMBY), 451
Notre Dame, 152
nuclear waste, 452, 454
nutrition, 321

O

objects, 7
occupational groups, 82
oceans, 12, 26, 411–412, 413, 449, 451
off-farm sale, 254–255
Office of Environmental Justice, 453
official language, 141–142, 143
offshoring, 294, 308–310
oil, 274, 275, 431
Old Stone Age, 40, 42
Old World culture hearths, 47–49
Olmec, 48
Olmstead, Frederick Law, 224
OPEC (Organization of Petroleum Exporting Countries), 415
opportunities, mobility and, 69
optimum point of production, 289
oral traditions, 205
organic foods, 264–265
Organization for European Cooperation, 414
Organization of African Unity (OAU), 415, 454
Organization of American States (OAS), 415
Ottoman Empire, 157

outsourcing, 294, 299, 305, 308–310, 395
overburden, 439
overpopulation, 116–118, 329
over-the-road costs, 287
Oxford English, 135
ozone, 434–435

P

packing, 418
Pahlavi, Mohammed Reza, 54
Pakistan
  energy consumption, 321
  foreign aid, 334
  garbage and toxic waste, 454
  language, 144
  political geography, 401, 402, 404
  religion, 147
  United States immigration, 187
  urban systems, 383, 385
Paleo-Asiatic languages, 128
Paleolithic age, 40, 41, 52
Palestinians, 407, 408
palimpsest, 221, 222
Paracel Islands, 413
Paraguay, 414
parallel invention, 55
parallels, 22–23
partisan gerrymandering, 418
part-nation state, 392
patriotism. See nationalism
pattern, 16–17
peak land value intersection, 362
per capita income, 342
perceptual regions, 18, 20
perforated state, 397
peripheral model, urban systems, 365, 366
personal communication field, 73
personal space, 67, 68
Peru, 336
pesticides, 252–254
petroleum, 275–276, 320
pH factor, 433
Philippines
  agriculture, 249, 251, 256, 264
  economic geography, 277
  environmental geography, 443
  language, 141
  political geography, 407, 413
  religion, 146, 152, 157
  trade, 277
philosophy, 49
photochemical smog, 432
physical attributes, 11–12
physical boundaries, 401
physical environment, 242
physical geography, 4, 8, 329–330
physical gravity, law of, 64
physicians, 326
physiological density, 15, 116
pidgin language, 138–140
pipelines, 286
place
  attributes of, 12–13
  defined, 6–7
  interrelations between, 13–14
  names for, 145–146
  similarity and regions, 17–19

structured content of, 14–17
placelessness, 6, 212
place perception, 74
place stereotype, 6
place utility, 81
planned cities, 380, 385
planned economy, 243–244, 271
plantation crops, 263–264
plants, domestication of, 43–44
Pleistocene overkill, 39
political asylum, 175
political geography, 5
  barrier to diffusion, 57
  economic activity and, 242
  fragmentation of power, 419–422
  geographic considerations, 395–400
  industrial location and, 290
  local and regional organization, 416–422
  modern state, evolution of, 392–395
  overview, 390
  regional alliances, 413–416
  states, boundaries, 400–403
  states, challenges to, 395, 405–409
  states, cohesion, 403–405
  states, cooperation among, 410–416
  states, nations, and nation-states, 391–392
  states, spatial characteristics of, 395–400
  supranationalism, 410
  United Nations, 410–413
pollution, 431–434, 448, 449–454
Polynesians, 39
polytheism, 147
popular culture, 90, 211
  food and drink, 213–214
  globalization and, 211–213, 217
  music and dance, 214–217
  reactions against, 217
popular regions, 218, 220
population density, 15–16, 24, 363
population explosion, 111, 121–122
population geography. See also migration; urban systems
  aging, 122
  birth rates, 96–97
  data and projections, 118–119
  death rates, 100–102
  defined, 94
  demographic equation, 111–113
  demographic transition model, 107–111
  fertility rates, 97–99
  immigration and, 113, 173–176
  implosions, 121–122
  IPAT equation, 426
  momentum, 122
  natural increase and doubling time, 105–107
  overpopulation, 116–118, 329
  population controls, 119–121
  population data, 118
  population density, 11, 78, 115–118, 372
  population growth, 78, 94–96
  population implosion, 121–122
  population projections, 118–119
  population prospects, 121–122
  population pyramids, 102–104
  relocation, 111–113

urbanization, 107, 108, 110, 112
  world population distribution, 113–115
population maps, 23, 24, 25
Population Reference Bureau, 94, 118
Portugal, 152, 330, 368, 414
Portuguese, 139
positional disputes, 402
possibilism, 37
postindustrial status, 242–243, 303–304, 308, 331
potential model, interaction, 65
potential support ratio (PSR), 122
poverty. See also development, economic
  demographic transition model, 110–111
  economic development and, 339–341
  environmental justice and, 453–454
  feminization of, 373, 384
  health and, 326–327
  migration and, 78, 80
  Millennium Development Goals, 317
  nutrition and, 321–323
power supplies, manufacturing, 284–285
precipitation, 429, 431–434
preconditions for takeoff, development, 330
predictions, defined, 118
pregnancy, risks of, 101
price, 282–283
primary activities, economic, 242. See also mining; quarries
primary production, 243
primary products, trade in, 276–277
primate city, 359, 399
prime meridian, 23
private property, 46
processing industries, 242
producer services, 305, 307–308
production, 289, 291–292, 299–303. See also manufacturing
production controls, agriculture, 254–255
profit-maximization, 282–283, 289
projection, defined, 21, 118
projections, map, 21–22
pronatalist, 119, 121
property, private, 46
proportional area symbols, 23
prorupt states, 397
protectorates, 391
Protestant Reformation, 152
Protestants, 146, 149
proto-Germanic language, 128, 133
proto-Indo-European language, 128
protolanguage, 128
Ptolemy, 4
public housing projects, 372, 373
Public Land Survey System (PLSS), 223
public policy
  Cairo plan, 112
  environmental justice, 453–454
  foreign aid, 332–333, 333–335
  homeless, 374
  illegal migration, 84
  industry location, 290

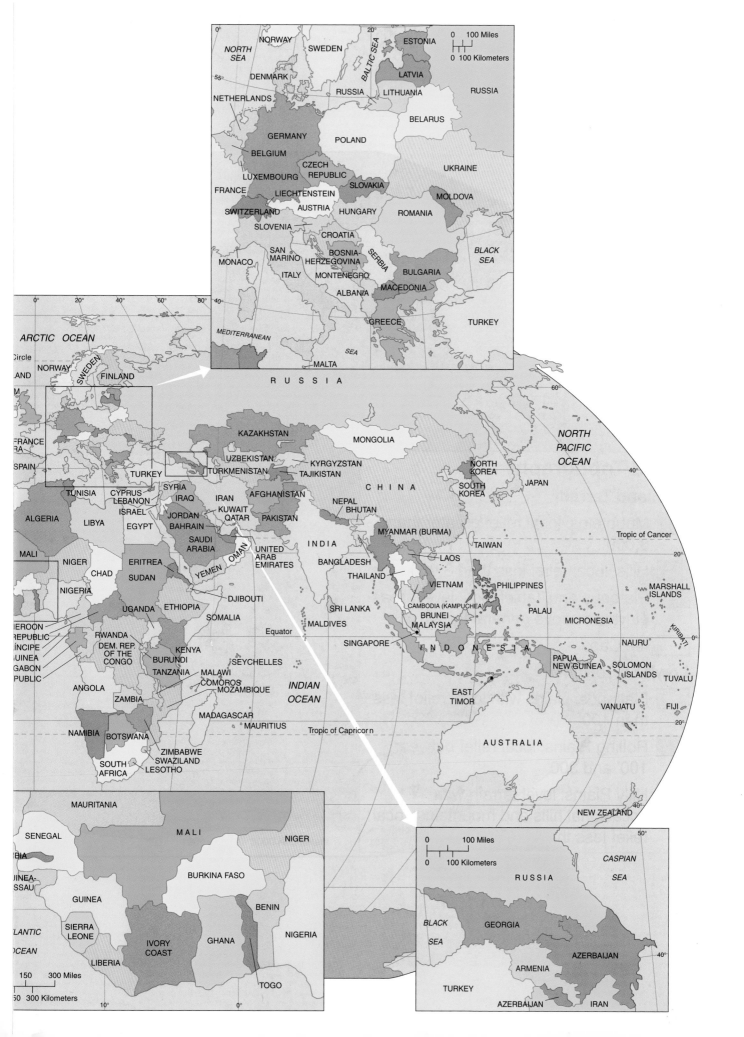